THE NAVAJO VERB

THE NAVAJO VERB

A GRAMMAR FOR STUDENTS AND SCHOLARS

Leonard M. Faltz

UNIVERSITY OF NEW MEXICO PRESS
ALBUQUERQUE

Library of Congress Cataloging-in-Publication Data
Faltz, Leonard M., 1940–
The Navajo verb: a grammar for students and scholars / Leonard Faltz.
p.   cm.
Includes bibliographical references and index.
ISBN 0-8263-1901-7 (hardcover).—ISBN 0-8263-1902-5 (pbk.)
1. Navajo language—Verb.
2. Navajo language—Grammar.
I. Title.
PM2007.F35   1998
497'.2—dc21
98-18326
CIP

For Maureen

CONTENTS

Preface   x
Chapter 1   Background   1
Chapter 2   Introduction to the Verb   6
Chapter 3   The Modes, Stem-sets, and Other Preliminaries   14
Chapter 4   Getting Started with the Imperfective Mode   20
Chapter 5   Fourth Person Subjects and Plural Subjects   32
Chapter 6   Classifiers, and Introduction toTransitive Verbs   40
Chapter 7   Prefixless Verbs, and More about Subject Prefixes   52
Chapter 8   Introduction to the Perfective, More about Verb Bases,
            and the s-P Conjugation   63
Chapter 9   The y-P Conjugation: Zero and Barred-1 Classifiers   81
Chapter 10 The y-P Conjugation: Plain-1 and d Classifiers   97
Chapter 11 Object Prefixes for Transitive Verbs   107
Chapter 12 Unspec Object and 4 Person Object Prefixes; Lexical Objects   121
Chapter 13 Voiced Fricative Verb Stems   136
Chapter 14 The Future Mode   147
Chapter 15 The Inner Prefix **d** and Outer Objects   158
Chapter 16 Some Irregular Verbs   183
Chapter 17 Introduction to Motion Verbs, "go", and Verb Themes   194
Chapter 18 More about Motion Verbs, and the n-I and n-P Conjugations   215
Chapter 19 More Outer Prefixes and More Motion   235
Chapter 20 The Long-Vowel Conjugations   255
Chapter 21 Those Pesky **n**'s, and the Conjunct High Tone   283
Chapter 22 "More" and "Back"   312
Chapter 23 The Iterative, Usitative, and Optative Modes   326
Chapter 24 The Seriative   340
Chapter 25 The Progressive Mode   362
Chapter 26 The Reflexive, Reciprocal, and Passive   369
Chapter 27 Some Final Topics   383
            The s-I Conjugation   383
            Conjugation Combinations   384
            Pre-stem Vowel Harmony   386
            Conjunct Prefixes   388
            Stem-sets   391
            Pre-stem Syllable Effects   397
            Disjunct Prefixes   398
            Verb Bases and Verb Themes   401
            Vocabulary Principles   403
Appendix   407
            Part A: The Rules   407

CONTENTS

Rules involving general structure   407

Rules involving subject prefixes and classifiers   408

Rules involving conjunct prefixes   409

Rules involving disjunct prefixes   413

Part B: Subject Prefixes   416

Imperfective mode   416

Perfective mode   417

Future mode   420

Optative mode   420

Progressive mode   421

Part C: Vocabulary Principles   422

Bibliography   425

Verb Base Index   427

English Verb Index   439

Verb Theme Index   444

Index   445

THE NAVAJO VERB

PREFACE

Sometime during the spring semester of 1991 a linguist friend of mine, knowing that I'd been working on the Navajo language for several years, asked me to describe the system of the Navajo verb to him. I spent perhaps twenty minutes talking to him and writing out some forms on the blackboard. Afterwards, I realized that the way I was approaching the Navajo verb was different in significant ways from what could be found in the standard sources, so I thought it would be worthwhile to write up what I had described orally to my friend. I first produced a sketch of about forty pages, which then subsequently grew into larger and larger texts. Years passed, and the result is this book.

It may seem odd to write an entire book about one part of speech in one language. However, there are two related facts about Navajo verbs which makes this not only a reasonable enterprise, but, I believe, a very useful one. First, as any linguist will tell you, the inflection of Navajo verbs gives the appearance of great complexity . And second, the Navajo verb includes within it systems which allow the expression of a great many nuances of meaning, so much so that it is often said that a single verb in Navajo is much like an entire sentence. This richness alone makes the Navajo verb system a worthy subject for a study, but it also leads to problems: students wanting to learn to speak Navajo or scholars wanting information about the grammatical system of the language are often so daunted by the profusion of forms (and the fact that different verbs often exhibit very different forms) that they become discouraged. Textbooks of the language are not much help: they deal with the verbs by providing paradigm charts while shying away from describing the grammatical system of the verb in an adequate way. To be sure, this system is well covered in the currently available scholarly materials, but these materials have proven difficult to use for linguistically untrained readers. A scholarly study of a grammatically complex system tends to present the entire system as a unit, which means that when reading such studies it is sometimes hard to know which parts of the system are primary or fundamental rather than secondary or elaborative, or how structures at different levels interact. My intent in this book was to present the material in such a way that the overall structure of the system emerges naturally as the book progresses, so that the reader always has a clear notion of how the parts of the system fit together. It seemed to me that a study organized incrementally this way, starting with the most fundamental parts of the system and gradually adding on the more complex parts, would be of great use to anyone working seriously with the Navajo language. My hope is that this book will succeed in introducing many people to the beautifully expressive verb system of the Navajo language.

Being guided by the desire to create a work that would make it as easy as possible, given the complexity of the material, for the reader to come to understand the grammar of Navajo verbs, I found that certain innovations would smooth the way. For example, it is reasonable to use a template to describe the positioning of prefixes in the verb. However, rather than defining a global template that would correctly position every possible prefix in every possible situation, I felt it would be more effective to define a much reduced template that would position the major prefix types and which would suffice for the simpler verbs. The more complicated positionings (for example, the positioning of the future mode marker **d** or of the iterative mode marker **ná**) can then be described relative to the

x

positions in the simpler template. My belief was that, not only would doing this make it easier for the reader to learn to find his/her way among the parts of the verb, but that this was also a better representation of what a native Navajo speaker actually learned when learning to speak his/her language. This approach also clarifies certain structural properties of the verb system, such as the movements undergone in some circumstances by prefixes like the unspecified object prefix, the fourth person subject prefix, the reflexive disjunct prefix, or the seriative. If a reader familiar with the classical Athabaskan literature feels, on looking at the initial chapters, that the template presented is an oversimplification, all s/he needs to do is read the book through to the end; in doing so, s/he will have found all the facts concerning prefix positions eventually presented in the text.

Another innovation concerns the treatment of subject marking. Very early on (even while I was talking at that blackboard back in 1991) I realized that the mode inflections would be more lucidly described by taking an approach familiar from European languages, namely, by defining sets of different subject prefixes for different modes. Thus, the reader will find no "mode markers" in this book - rather, the combinations of the classical mode markers with the classical subject prefixes are themselves viewed as the synchronic subject prefixes which differ, therefore, not only from mode to mode but also from conjugation type to conjugation type. The effect on the reader is, hopefully, that the subject marking systems for the various modes become much easier to learn to recognize and to produce. Certain formal properties of the inflectional system also emerge in a natural way. We see clearly that the mode of a Navajo verb is signalled by a combination of the stem and the shape of the subject prefix. Subject marking and object marking are revealed to be very different: not only are they marked by prefixes in different positions, but subject marking depends on the mode while object marking is the same for all modes. More abstract relationships also become clearer; for example, if we regard the classifier as representing a general conjugation class (much like the three conjugation classes of Spanish verbs), then the dependence between perfective mode subject prefixes and the classifier can be seen as an instance of the kind of familiar relation exemplified by the dependence of imperfect subject suffixes on conjugation class in Spanish, or the dependence of future subject suffixes on conjugation class in Latin and Irish.

Because of the richness of the Navajo verb system, it would be meaningless to attempt a study of it without dealing in a significant way with the structure of the verb lexicon. Here, the innovations were expositional rather than analytic. I have more or less followed the analysis which underlies the material in Young, Morgan, and Midgette 1992 (henceforth YMM 92), but the structure of this analysis is presented here in (I hope) very gentle stages. For example, the reader is shielded from the fact that there exist related stem-sets until Chapter 11, giving him/her time to master the most important parts of the inflectional system; even in Chapter 11 the sudden appearance of two related stem-sets is presented only as a curiosity, to be taken up somewhat more seriously in Chapter 15 and then further elaborated on later on. However, given the fact that the full range of derivational processes shades off from grammar into lexicon, I did not feel it was appropriate (or even possible) to try to study every derivational pattern; rather, it seemed best to work through a number of these carefully as examples and then use them as the basis for more general discussions. The reader who makes it through the entire book will be well prepared to deal with those derivational processes that are not specifically covered.

I have found it impossible to avoid using phonological rules; these, however, are presented in what I hope is a user-friendly way. The reader who is a phonologist may notice certain points of view; for example, I have tried to skirt issues of rule ordering, although in some cases such issues were unavoidable (and I did use a general principle of "movement-before-form" that seemed intuitive.) Working out these rules led to occasional discoveries. For example, I hadn't seen the "sandwiched y rule" described anywhere before, nor had I seen an explicit statement of the regularity that the prefixes **na** and **ná** do not reduce to **ni** or **ní** when followed by an object prefix. The special role played by the syllable that immediately precedes the verb stem syllable (called the *pre-stem syllable* in the book), something that has been noticed recently by scholars, is clearly revealed in the presentation here.

In writing this book, I was mindful of the fact that the reference materials found in YMM 92 and also in Young and Morgan 1987 (henceforth YM 87; collectively, I refer to these two books as "YM") will remain the most useful near-complete sources of information on the Navajo language for decades to come. For this reason, I have mostly conformed to the terminology found in those works. However, in a few instances I found it convenient either to alter the terminology or to invent new terms. Whenever this is done the text explains the difference in usage so that the reader will know what to expect when s/he turns to YM for further study. In general, I have included hints to help the reader match up what s/he finds here with what is found in YM.

In the book, I have tried somewhat to stick to relatively common verbs as examples. But this was not always possible, since at certain points in the exposition it was necessary to study examples that demonstrate particular combinations of structure, and some of these combinations are found only with less common verbs. Also, some very common verbs could not be considered until a large amount of the material was laid out.

In the text some attempt is made to point out what kinds of variation the reader is likely to encounter. However, the descriptions of variation are certainly incomplete, especially in the context of the more complex constructions. The reader should always be on the lookout for alternate forms. The variety of Navajo presented in this book is based on a combination of my field notes together with published material (scholarly works and textbooks as well as works written in Navajo.) But because of the huge number of verb forms, it was impossible to check all of them with native speakers; when in doubt I have simply taken the forms given in YM as standard. I believe that all of the Navajo in this book is correct at least for some speakers, but it should be kept in mind that, like all languages, Navajo exhibits variation based on factors such as geography, age of speakers, and individual preference. If the reader is unsure about any form in this book, native speakers should be consulted.

At several points in the text I have included hints on how particular elements can be recognized when they occur in verbs. Such hints make it easier both to produce an analysis of any particular verb and to recognize and understand new, unfamiliar verbs (a common experience for nonnative speakers.)

Officially, the book does not presuppose any prior knowledge of Navajo. However, although a brief presentation of the spelling system and the sounds of the language is given in Chapter 1, it would probably be best if the reader were already somewhat familiar with the Navajo writing system and with Navajo sounds. Also, in the earlier chapters, when phrases and sentences are given as examples, there is a brief explanation of the words found in those examples in addition to the verbs that are being analyzed. But in the later chapters it is assumed that the reader has either picked up some Navajo vocabulary, or else will avail himself/herself of the dictionary part of YM 87 (words that are not verbs are easy to look up alphabetically.)

The mode of presentation of material changes somewhat throughout the book. In the earlier sections, there is a fair amount of detailed explanation of analysis procedures and also some repetition of examples. But as the book progresses the reader is assumed to have absorbed more and more of the analytical processes so that more and more of the elementary details can be left out for him/her to fill in. In the final chapters material is presented quite succinctly, with fewer examples and without detailed discussions. A reader who has carefully worked through the earlier sections of the book should have no trouble understanding the more abbreviated presentations of the later sections.

Let me suggest a number of uses for this book.

First of all, although this book should probably not be the primary text in an elementary course in the Navajo language, it would be a useful adjunct text in such a course. As mentioned earlier, existing Navajo language texts do not explain the verb system of the language. Many students become confused when faced with a bewildering variety of verb forms for which little or no explanation is given - this book will help dispel their bewilderment. Used this way, I would suggest starting to work with this book perhaps three weeks into the first semester. At the slow pace of a beginning course, the entire book could probably not be covered in two semesters - perhaps covering all of Chapters 1-19, most of Chapters 20 and 21 (leave out the section in Chapter 20 on the combinations of 'a with the unspecified object prefix, and leave out the section in Chapter 21 on the yn inner prefix), all of Chapter 22, and the iterative mode from Chapter 23, would consitute a suitable chunk of material that is doable in the 30 weeks of two semesters. Since Chapters 1-3 are introductory, they could be covered very quickly, which would mean that well over a week could be devoted to each of the remaining chapters.

A second way to use this book would be as a primary text for a university level course in the Structure of Navajo. This is not to say that the only grammar needed to understand Navajo is verb grammar - obviously, the other parts of speech, as well as phrase and sentence structure and questions of usage need to be addressed. However, generally speaking, these other aspects of Navajo grammar are relatively straightforward and can be easily explained and illustrated by an instructor with minimal expenditure of preparation. This book provides a way of structuring the part of such a course that will take up most of the time, namely, the study of the verb. In such a course the entire book should be covered, possibly even in one semester if the level of the students permits it.

Incidentally, throughout the book there are study questions, mostly with the answers given right there in the text. An instructor using this book as a text will find it (mostly) easy to create additional exercises that students can practice with. The one thing to keep in mind is that any verb that is part of an exercise should not contain any grammatical feature or process that has not yet been studied. This is not a trivial matter since the verb system is very rich and it is sometimes hard to avoid certain structures. In order to insure that a particular verb is appropriate as the basis of an exercise for a particular part of the course, an instructor should, ideally, be familiar with the contents of the entire book, even if the whole book won't be covered in the course.

But apart from being used as a text in a course, this book will, I hope, serve as a practical entry way into the Navajo verb system for people who need to acquire a serious knowledge of that system. Linguists, psycholinguists, anthropologists, and especially educators are among those who would benefit from the knowledge which this book attempts to convey. Because of the rising concern that the Navajo language might be in danger of dying out, the preparation of bilingual educational materials has become all the more crucial. I believe that the effectiveness of such materials is greatly increased when they are structured in a way that respects the grammatical systems of the two languages involved. My hope is that this book will contribute to the preservation of the Navajo language by providing educators with knowledge that will help them design more effective bilingual materials.

A book such as this one would be completely impossible without the prior hard work of many persons. The Navajo language has been the object of intense study for over a century, and the results of that body of work provided the foundation for the study here. I have also been inspired by the Navajo language textbooks currently available. These books, an excellent first attack on a very difficult problem, provided a number of important hints on how to approach this material, particularly at the beginning stages.

Of all the people who have worked on the Navajo language, one person deserves special mention. The analysis presented in this book would have been an inconceivable task were it not for the lifetime work of Professor Robert W. Young. That body of work, an achievement of immense depth and breadth, was the basis on which the study in this book builds. There is no way I can properly express the debt I owe to his work.

It is now my happy duty to thank the many people who have helped me personally in the preparation of this work. I apologize to any that I may have inadvertently omitted.

First, I would like to thank the following persons, speakers of the Navajo language, for their willingness to share their knowledge of their beautiful language and for their encouragement in support of my efforts to study it: Arlene Arviso, Elroy Bahe, Lucy Benally, Daniel Nez Martin, Alyse Neundorf, Evangeline Parsons, and MaryAnn Willie.

Next, I am grateful for the help of the following colleagues for their suggestions, criticisms, encouragement, coffee, and all manner of useful assistance: Glenn Ayres, Emmon Bach, Dawn Bates, Soonja Choi, Willem DeReuse, Ted Fernald, Michael Gottfried, Ken Hale, Eloise Jelinek, Michael Krauss, Jeff Leer, Sally Midgette, Bill Pagliuca, Keren Rice, Matt Rispoli, Leslie Saxon, Maureen Schmid, Clay Slate, Carlota Smith, Peggy Speas, Dick Stanley, Detlef Stark, Elly Van Gelderen, Wendy Wilkins, Garth Wilson, and Robert Young.

Finally, I am greatly indebted to Elizabeth Hadas, David Holtby and Emmy Ezzell of the University of New Mexico Press and to Wayne Woodland here at ASU for the crucial roles they played in helping this book to see the light of day.

Tempe, Arizona
September 8, 1997

THE NAVAJO VERB

CHAPTER 1

BACKGROUND

In any language, the words called *verbs* play a key role in building sentences. Verbs are words that tell what kind of event, action, or situation is being talked about. Different languages build their verbs in different ways. In this book we are going to study how the Navajo language builds its verbs.

As we said, in any language, a verb gives information about an action, event, or situation. But verbs in different languages often give different kinds of information. Any verb in any language tells what kind of action or situation is involved, but in many languages, a verb can give more information than this. For example, in Navajo, the verb can often provide information that answers questions like: Who did the action? Who is the action done to? Did the action already happen, or is it happening now, or will it happen in the future? Is the action a simple event or is it a series of events? Was the action completed?

To see an example of how Navajo and English verbs have different kinds of information in them, let's look at an example. Here is a sentence in English:

(1)   I kissed Sally.

In this sentence, the verb is the word **kissed**. This word tells us that the sentence is about an event of a certain sort, an event in which somebody touched somebody in a certain way, the way that we call kissing. This word also tells us that the event already happened (we know this because of the **ed** at the end of the word **kissed**.) But the English verb **kissed** doesn't give us any more information.

Now, look at the following Navajo sentence:

(2)   Sally nánéts'ǫ́ǫz.

The meaning of this sentence is similar to the meaning of the English sentence in (1). Sentence (2) has in it the name **Sally**, and, besides this name, it contains the Navajo verb **nánéts'ǫ́ǫz**.

Now, the Navajo verb **nánéts'ǫ́ǫz** gives us more information than the English verb **kissed**. First of all, like **kissed**, the word **nánéts'ǫ́ǫz** tells us that the sentence is about an event in which somebody kissed somebody, and it also tells us that this event already happened. But, in addition, it tells us that the person who did the kissing is the person that would be called **I** or **me** in English. In English, this information is conveyed by adding in a separate word, namely the word **I**, at the beginning of sentence (1). But in Navajo, we don't have to use a separate word to indicate this, since the information is already in the verb.

But this is not all. The English word **kissed** doesn't give any information about how the kissing was

1

done. For example, did I give Sally one peck, or did I give her a series of kisses? If someone is speaking English and says sentence (1), the person who hears the sentence cannot answer this question. However, if someone is speaking Navajo and says sentence (2), the person who hears this sentence can answer it: the verb **nánéts'ǫ́ǫ́z** tells us that there was a repetitive series of kisses, not just one. This last piece of information is missing from the English sentence entirely. The English sentence (1) could mean that I kissed Sally repeatedly, or it could mean that I kissed her exactly once. The Navajo sentence in (2) is more precise, because the verb includes in it the meaning of repeated action. Of course, we could express this extra information in English too, by saying something like "I gave Sally a bunch of kisses", but we have to add all sorts of words to the sentence to do it. In English, there is no way to change the form of the verb **kissed** to express this additional information. But in Navajo, the verb all by itself can express this information.

Because a Navajo verb might contain a lot of information like this (and sometimes more!), the structure of the Navajo verb sometimes gets to be complicated. In order to learn how all this works in the Navajo language, we will study the verb bit by bit, looking first at easier verbs and building up our knowledge one step at a time. At the end of the entire study, you should be able to understand how any Navajo verb, with any meaning, is constructed.

As you become more and more familiar with the structure of the Navajo verb, and of the Navajo language as a whole, you are probably going to want to use some of the reference materials that have been published for Navajo. The books that will be most useful to you are Young and Morgan 1987 and Young, Morgan, and Midgette 1992. It is best to have both of these books. If we need to refer to these books, we'll use the abbreviation "YM 87" to refer to the first one and "YMM 92" to refer to the second one. We'll also use the abbreviation "YM" to refer to the two books together. The bibliography at the back lists a number of other books that you might find useful.

In general, the terminology that we will use in our study here will be the same as the terminology found in YM, but in a few places we will find it convenient to use some terms that are not found in those books. Whenever we do this, we'll note the differences so that you'll know that you won't find a certain term if you look the material up in YM. We will also use the same spelling of Navajo as found in YM, in most cases. However, like all languages, Navajo is spoken slightly differently in different places, and individual Navajo speakers sometimes differ a little in the way they say things. Also, if you look at books and articles written in Navajo, you will see that there is sometimes some variation in the way some words are spelled. We will sometimes call attention to these variations and differences, but we will not be able to discuss all of them, so don't be surprised if you know someone who speaks Navajo using forms that are occasionally slightly different from the forms found in these lessons.

If you already know how Navajo is written and pronounced, you can skip the rest of this chapter and go on to Chapter 2. But if you are unsure about the way the letters and the diacritics are used to write Navajo, here is a brief explanation that you might want to read through before starting the next chapter.

First, the vowels.

There are four vowel qualities, represented by the letters **a**, **e**, **i**, and **o**. Roughly, **a** is pronounced like the "o" in "hot", or like the "a" in "dark" (but without the "r"); **e** is pronounced like the "e" in "bed"; **i** is pronounced like the "i" in "bit", and **o** is pronounced like the "o" in "fort" (but without the "r"), or like the "oa" in "coat".

Vowels can be long or short. Long vowels are written double, and short vowels are written single. So, for example, in the word **azee'** ("medicine"), the first syllable, written **a**, has a short vowel in it, while the second syllable, written **zee'**, has a long vowel. Long vowels are pronounced more or less with the same quality as short vowels, except that they're held longer. However, long **ii** is pronounced somewhat like the "ee" of "meet".

Vowels of different qualities can be combined to form what are called diphthongs. For example, in the word **deiłbéézh** ("they are boiling it"), the first syllable has the diphthong **ei** in it. This is pronounced by starting out with an "e" sound and changing it to an "i" sound.

We sometimes need to know if a syllable has a short vowel or not. If we see a syllable with a diphthong in it, we will automatically assume that that syllable does not have a short vowel. In order for a syllable to have a short vowel, it must be written so that no more than one vowel letter is in that syllable.

Be careful! Diphthongs involve vowels of different qualities that are really pronounced together. For example, in the word **haiilgizh** ("we cut it out"), the letters **aii** in the first syllable are all run together, so we have a diphthong (note that when we write this word, we just put the letters **a**, **i**, and **i** next to each other.) However, in the word **mą'ii** ("coyote"), we don't have a diphthong: the first vowel **ą** is separated from the second vowel by a consonant, namely, the consonant which is written the same way as an apostrophe, like this: **'**. The word **mą'ii** has two syllables. The first syllable has a short vowel in it, namely **ą**, and the second syllable has a long vowel in it, namely **ii**. These vowels are not run together. When we write this word, we write in the symbol that represents the consonant that separates the two syllables, and this consonant is written **'**. (That hook under the "a" in **ą** indicates that the vowel is nasal. We'll say something about that in a moment.)

While we're talking about the symbol **'**, let's recall that this consonant is sometimes called the *glottal stop*. There is something we should remember about this consonant. It happens that in the Navajo language as it is actually pronounced, no word can begin with a vowel. Now, sometimes we see a word written down where the first letter of the word is a vowel, like the word for medicine: **azee'**. However, this word is really pronounced as though it had been written like this: **'azee'**. That is, the word really starts with a glottal stop. Some printed materials actually write **'azee'**, although nowadays it's probably more common to leave out the glottal stop symbol at the beginnings of words and just write **azee'**. However, it would be wrong to leave out the glottal stop symbol anywhere else in a word. For example, if we wrote the word for coyote as **maii**, we'd be making a mistake, because this way of writing it would suggest that the **a** and the **ii** were run together. But this is not the way this word is pronounced! Similarly, it would be a mistake to write the word for medicine as **azee**, since this would suggest that when you say this word, there is no glottal stop at the end. But there actually is a glottal stop at the end of the Navajo word for medicine, so we have to write it **azee'**.

Getting back to vowels, let's remember that vowels can be pronounced with a high tone (higher pitch) or with a low tone (lower pitch). When a vowel is pronounced with a high tone, we put an accent mark over it, as in the second syllable of the word **diné** ("person", or "Navajo"), and when a vowel is pronounced with a low tone, we don't put anything special near the vowel, as in the first syllable of the word **diné**.

Also, vowels are sometimes nasal, that is, pronounced through the nose. When this happens, we put a hook under the vowel as we see in the word **adą́ą́dą́ą́'** ("yesterday"), where the vowels in the second and third syllables are nasal. (The first vowel in the word for "coyote", **mą'ii**, is also nasal.)

This is pretty much what we need to remember about the vowels, so, on to the consonants!

The consonants are a bit more complicated, and we will need to learn certain things about them at various stages in our study. What we are going to do here is simply list the consonants that are found in the Navajo language and say one or two simple things about the way they are pronounced. Later on, though, we'll classify consonants into several different types, and we'll see how these different types of consonants fit into the way Navajo verbs are structured.

Here are the Navajo consonants, with a very approximate statement telling how each one is pronounced:

b	a little like "b" in English
ch	like "ch" in the English word "church"
d	a little like "d" in English
dl	a little like "dl" in the English word "saddle", but faster
dz	like Navajo "d" followed very quickly by a "z"
g	a little like "g" in the English word "give"
gh	(not like any English sound - see below)
h	a little like "h" in English (see below)
j	a little like "j" in the English word "jay"
k	like "k" in English, but with heavier breathing
l	a little like "l" in English
ł	(not like any English sound - see below)
m	like "m" in English
n	like "n" in English
s	like "s" in the English word "see"

sh	like "sh" in the English word "shoe"
t	like "t" in English, but with heavier breathing
tł	like "t" followed very quickly by Navajo "ł"
ts	like "ts" in English "cats"
w	like "w" in English
x	same as Navajo "h"
y	like "y" in English
z	like "z" in English
zh	like the "s" in the English word "vision"

In Navajo, when the letter "h" is at the beginning of a syllable, it is usually pronounced heavier than the English "h". At the end of a syllable, Navajo "h" is pronounced about like an English "h", or even a little lighter.

The sound written "gh" in Navajo is like the Navajo "h", except that in addition to the breathiness there is what is called *voicing*, which means that the vocal cords are making the humming noise that they make when you sing.

The sound written "ł" in Navajo is pronounced by putting your mouth and tongue in the same position as though you were making an "l", but then pushing the air out through your mouth without any voicing of the vocal cords. (When you make a regular "l" sound, you do voice your vocal cords.)

The letter "x" is used in Navajo instead of "h" if the previous written letter in the word is "s" or "h". This way, we won't get confused by "h"s next to each other, or think that there's an "sh" in the word. An example is **tódilchxoshí** "soda pop". We write it this way instead of **tódilchhoshí**, to avoid the two "h"s next to each other, which would confuse the reader. Another example is the word **tsxį́įłgo** "hurry up!", where we write "x" instead of "h" so that the reader doesn't think there is an "sh" sound in this word.

In addition to the consonants shown above, Navajo has five *glottalized* consonants. These are written like this:

ch', k', t', tł', ts'

Each of these is pronounced as though you were pronouncing the regular consonant and then almost immediately following it with a glottal stop (the consonant and the glottal stop are practically pronounced together.)

CHAPTER 2

INTRODUCTION TO THE VERB

In this chapter and the next, we will learn about some general facts having to do with verbs in Navajo. We need to do this before we get to really look at actual forms of Navajo verbs, because these general facts will give us perspective and help us to see what it is that we will need to study. In this chapter, we will learn about inflection and about transitivity.

Let's start by looking at English. Here are three sentences:

(1)   Bill is playing in the schoolyard.
        Bill plays every day.
        Bill played in the game yesterday.

Each of these sentences has a verb in it. In the first sentence, the verb is **playing**, in the second sentence, the verb is **plays**, and in the third sentence, the verb is **played**. If we examine the meanings of these words, and compare the meaning of each word with the form of that word (by the "form" of the word we just mean the way the word is written or pronounced), we find something interesting. The meanings of these three verbs all have something in common: all of these verbs tell us that the sentence is about the same kind of activity, namely, the activity of playing. The forms of these three verbs also have something in common: all of these verbs have inside them a part that consists of the four letters **play**. However, going back to meaning, although the three verbs name the same kind of activity, the three verbs differ in that one form (**playing**) has to do with the action happening right now, the second form (**plays**) has to do with the action happening habitually, and the third form (**played**) has to do with the action having happened in the past. In terms of form, these verbs are different in the way they end: in the first word, there is a piece written **ing** that goes at the end, in the second word, there is an **s** stuck on, and in the third word, we see **ed** at the end of the word.

So how can we describe these English verbs? We can say this: there is a part of these words which looks like this: **play**, and this part tells us the kind of action or event that is involved. We'll call this part of the verb the *verb stem*. Then, in addition to the verb stem, there are pieces that are added on to the end that give us other information, such as when the action takes place. These pieces are called *suffixes* (a *suffix* is just a piece that is tacked on after a stem). Actually, we should call them *inflectional suffixes*, where the word *inflectional* means that the information they give us is not about the kind of action or event, but rather about something else, in this case, about the time of the action.

Now, what we want to do is make a careful, thorough analysis, not of English verbs, but of Navajo verbs. We saw in Chapter 1 that in Navajo the verb can be very complicated. In fact, Navajo verbs are quite a bit more complicated than English verbs, because there is more information packed into the Navajo verb. But the general idea is not very different. A Navajo verb will consist of a stem, and there will be extra pieces added to this stem.

But first of all, in Navajo, we don't have suffixes. Instead, we have *prefixes*, that is, pieces that are tacked on the front of the stem (instead of the back of the stem.) So, we can start our study by saying this: a Navajo verb consists of a verb stem and some prefixes.

Note: With very few exceptions (involving irregular verbs), every Navajo verb has at least one prefix. Very many Navajo verbs have more than one prefix, so we should be prepared to see a bunch of prefixes lined up in front of the verb stem.

Another note: Most Navajo verb stems consist of exactly one syllable. Since Navajo verbs have prefixes rather than suffixes, it's usually easy to pick out the verb stem if you're looking at a verb: it's simply the last syllable in the verb. Also, all Navajo verb stems begin with a consonant.

(A few Navajo verb stems that are build on the basis of nouns have more than one syllable. You may occasionally run into a verb with a stem like that.)

So, English verbs and Navajo verbs are different because English adds suffixes to the verb stem, whereas Navajo adds prefixes.

But, Navajo is different in another way. To see what is involved, let's look at this idea of playing. If someone wants to say "Bill is playing" in Navajo, he or she would say:

(2)   Bill naané.

If he or she wanted to say "I'm playing", it would be:

(3)   Naashné.

If he or she wanted to say "The two of you are playing", it would be:

(4)   Naohné.

(Some of you might say: **naahné**.) Now, in all these words, the stem is the part at the end that looks like this: **-né**. (We put that hyphen in front of it to remind us that the stem cannot stand alone. A stem has to have prefixes in order to make a word.) But if we ask: what part of these words means "play", it would be wrong to say: the verb stem **-né**. The reason is this: the verb stem is not the only part of the verb that is always there when you build a Navajo verb that means "play": the verb also has to start with the prefix **na-**. In other words, if somebody wants to use a Navajo verb that talks about playing, the speaker has to do more than put together a verb with the verb stem **-né**. The speaker also has to be sure and use the prefix **na-** as well.

Here's how we can think of this. Whenever we are looking at an actual word which happens to be a verb, part of this word tells us the kind of action or event or situation that is involved, whereas the rest of the word tells us other things, such as when does the action happen, or who performs the action. What we need to think about is: which part of the word tells us what kind of action or event is involved, and which part tells us the rest of the information. In English, generally speaking, the verb stem tells us the kind of action, and the suffixes provide the rest of the information. But in Navajo, in many cases, the kind of action is indicated not just by the verb stem, but by the verb stem together with one or more prefixes. Additional prefixes provide the rest of the information.

It will be handy to have some terms to refer to the different parts of a verb according to the kind of information they provide. The part of a verb that tells us what kind of action is involved will be called the *verb base*. So, for the words in (2), (3), and (4) above, which talk about playing, the verb base consists of the verb stem **-né** together with the prefix **na-**. Another way to say this is to say that the Navajo equivalent of the English verb stem **play** is the combination of the verb stem **-né** with the prefix **na-**. This combination is the Navajo verb base whose meaning is the same (more or less) as the meaning of the English verb stem **play**.

Now, in addition to the verb stem and the prefixes that are part of the verb base, there are usually other prefixes in a Navajo verb that give other information, such as the part of the word in (3) spelled **-sh-**, which indicates that the playing is being done by the speaker of the sentence (the person called "I" in English.) These prefixes will be called *inflectional prefixes*. If we need to refer to the first kind of prefix, the prefixes that are part of the verb base, we will use the term *lexical prefixes*.

("Lexical" means "having to do with a lexicon". The word "lexicon" is just a fancy word for "dictionary". The idea is this: suppose we had an English-Navajo dictionary. If we look up the English word **play**, this dictionary had better tell us not only that the Navajo verbs that have the meaning of this English verb are built with the verb stem **-né**; it had better tell us that the prefix **na-**is needed, too.)

So, for the Navajo verb base that means "play", we will say that this verb base consists of the verb stem **-né** together with the lexical prefix **na-**. And the Navajo verb **naashné** (which means "I'm playing") consists of the verb stem **-né** (which is part of the verb base), the lexical prefix **na-** (which is also part of the verb base), and the inflectional prefix **-sh-** (which tells us who's doing the playing.)

Well, so far, it looks as though a Navajo verb base is something that consists of a verb stem and a lexical prefix. But be careful: there are some Navajo verb bases that don't have any lexical prefixes: in such cases, the verb base consists of the stem only. Also, there are some Navajo verb bases that have more than one lexical prefix. We'll see lots of examples of these possibilities later on as we go along.

Now, to understand the verb better, we need to think more carefully about the kind of information that the inflectional prefixes tell us. To get started, we are going to look at two particular kinds of information. These are:

Who is involved in the action?

and

When does the action occur?

In the rest of this chapter, we'll look at the idea that there is information in the verb about who is involved in the action. We'll leave the matter of when the action occurs to Chapter 3.

In Navajo, we will divide all the verbs into two groups, which will be called the *intransitive verbs* and the *transitive verbs*. The first group, the group called the intransitive verbs, will be those verbs where the action is something that involves only one person, or only one group of people that are all doing more or less the same thing. An example of an intransitive verb is the verb that means "play". In sentence (2), for example, the person named "Bill" is the only one doing the playing. In sentence (3), the speaker (the person called "I" in English) is the only one doing the action. In sentence (4), there is a group of (probably) two people doing the action, but they're each doing more or less the same thing, that is, each one of them is playing.

The second group of verbs, the group called the transitive verbs, consists of verbs where the action involves two roles. One role, taken by one person or thing or group of people, involves one kind of relationship to the action, and the second role, taken by another person or thing or group of people, involves a really different relationship to the action. An example of a transitive verb is "eat". Look at the following sentence:

(5)   Sally bilasáana ła' yiyą́.

which means "Sally is eating an apple". Here, there are two participants to the event of eating. There's Sally, who's doing the eating, and there's the apple (**bilasáana**), which is getting eaten. Note that this is different from the case of the two people who are playing in sentence (4). In sentence (4), the two people are doing more or less the same thing: they're both playing. But the two participants in (5) (Sally and the apple) are involved in the event in very different ways: Sally is doing the eating, and the apple is getting eaten. This difference between the way that Sally is involved and the way that the apple is involved is what makes "eat" a transitive verb.

Incidentally, in sentence (5), the fact that we are talking about eating is indicated by the verb **yiyą́**. This is one of the forms of the Navajo verb that means "eat".

(What about the word **ła'** in sentence (5)? Roughly, it means "a", and it goes with the word that means "apple". Look this word up in YM 87.)

2 INTRODUCTION TO THE VERB

We need some terminology. If we have an intransitive verb, the person doing the action is called the *subject* of the verb. If we have a transitive verb, the one doing the action is still called the *subject*, and the one that the action is done to is called the *object*. So, in (2), Bill is the subject, in (3), the speaker ("I") is the subject, and in (4), two people, including the person spoken to, is the subject. In (5), Sally is the subject, and the apple is the object.

Now, if we go back to sentences (2), (3), and (4), we see that the form of a Navajo verb changes to tell us who is doing the action, that is, to tell us who the subject is. In (3), the subject is definitely the person who is speaking (the person called "I" in English.) In (4), the subject is a group of two people, at least one of whom is the person that the speaker is talking to. In (2), we know at least that the subject is not the speaker and also not the person being spoken to. Thus, we can say that a Navajo verb will have a prefix inside it which tells us about the subject. Such a prefix will be called a *subject prefix*. In (3), that prefix is the part that goes -sh-, and in (4), that prefix is the part that goes -oh-. (In (2), the situation is a little different - we'll learn all about this in Chapter 4.)

Well, these examples show that at least an intransitive Navajo verb has a subject prefix. If we looked at a few examples of transitive verbs, we'd see that transitive Navajo verbs also have subject prefixes. But transitive Navajo verbs also have object prefixes as well, that is, prefixes that tell us about the person or thing that the action is being done to. Before we look at more and more complicated verbs to see how this works, let's stop a moment.

We've seen that a Navajo verb will have a verb stem, possibly one or more lexical prefixes, definitely a subject prefix, possibly an object prefix, and maybe even more complicated things. With all that, we might wonder how all these prefixes are put together. The main thing to keep in mind is that the prefixes have to come in a certain order in order for the verb to be a real Navajo word. At this point, we can make a diagram showing how a Navajo verb is constructed. Here is such a diagram:

(6)   outer + plural + object + inner + subject + cl + stem
        prefixes   prefix   prefixes   prefix

We'd better explain some of this.

The piece labelled "outer prefixes" refers to lexical prefixes that some verb bases have. We saw that the Navajo verb base that means "play", for example, has a lexical prefix **na-**. When we build any Navajo verb that means "play", this prefix will be placed into the "outer prefixes" position in (6). Note again: some verb bases have no lexical prefixes at all, which means that the position labelled "outer prefixes" will be empty. There are also some verb bases where there is more than one outer prefix.

The piece labelled "plural" is a specific prefix (pronounced **da**) which is usually inserted into the verb if the subject (or sometimes the object) involves three or more persons or things. This piece is simply left out if there is no such plural subject or object. In the verbs in (2), (3), (4), and (5), this **da** is not there, since there are no pluralities. We'll study this prefix in Chapter 5.

Note: the plural element **da** is usually called the *distributive plural* in the reference works, and from now on we'll call it that too.

The piece labelled "object prefix" in (6) is the prefix that tells us about the object of a transitive verb. If the verb is intransitive, we simply leave this piece out.

The piece labelled "inner prefixes" in (6) can contain certain very special lexical prefixes. Many verb bases, including the verb base that means "play", do not have any inner lexical prefixes, so this position is simply empty for those verbs. However, many important verbs do have inner prefixes, and we'll have to study them. We'll start to study inner prefixes in Chapter 15.

The piece labelled "subject prefix" in (6) is the prefix that tells us about the subject of the verb.

The piece labelled "cl" in (6) is something called a *classifier*. We'll explain this in Chapter 6. Some verbs don't have a classifier. In fact, the verbs in (2), (3), (4), and (5) don't have classifiers.

We will use the term *inflectional prefixes* to refer to the subject prefixes, the object prefixes, and the distributive plural prefix. So, besides the verb stem, a Navajo verb may have inflectional prefixes of three kinds (subject, object, and distributive plural). In addition, it might have lexical prefixes (which are part of the verb base for that verb), and a classifier (which is a special kind of thing; the classifier will also turn out to be a part of the verb base.)

An important thing to note about (6) is that lexical prefixes can come in two different places in a Navajo verb. They can either come at the beginning, before any other prefixes (in which case we call them "outer prefixes") or they can come sandwiched in between the object and the subject prefixes (in which case we call them "inner prefixes".) Any particular lexical prefix has to be placed in just one of these two positions (there isn't a choice!)

Important: the terms "outer prefix" and "inner prefix" are not found in YM. Because the prefix systems of a Navajo verb are so important, we should say something about the terminology used in YM. This will also prepare us for studying the actual forms of Navajo verbs.

To discuss this, go back to the word in example (3). There is something about this word that you might be wondering about: if the outer prefix is **na-**, and the subject prefix is **-sh-**, how come there's a long **aa** vowel in the word **naashné**? The reason is this: when prefixes are put together to form whole words, certain adjustments are sometimes made to the pronunciation of the prefixes. These adjustments don't just happen in weird ways - they obey rules. One of the important things we'll be studying will be the rules that control these little changes in the prefixes. In Chapter 4, for example, we'll learn why the prefix **na-** becomes **naa-** in the word **naashné**.

Now, here's the issue: when we study the rules that tell us how to adjust the prefixes in a verb, we find that the prefixes come in two kinds, where each kind obeys its own special set of rules. All the prefixes that go in the slot called "outer prefixes" in (6), together with the distributive prefix (the prefix that goes in the slot called "plural" in (6)), follow one set of rules. On the other hand, the object prefixes together with the inner prefixes follow a different set of rules. (The subject prefix and the classifier are very special - they have their own rules, as we'll see.) Since the outer prefixes and the distributive plural have the same rules, it is convenient to have a term that covers them both. YM uses the term "disjunct prefix" for these two kinds of prefixes. Similarly, since the object prefixes and the inner prefixes have the same rules, but a different bunch of rules than the disjunct prefixes, it is convenient to have a term that covers these two kinds of prefixes. YM uses the term "conjunct prefix" for them.

To summarize, we have the following new terms for different kinds of prefixes:

(7)

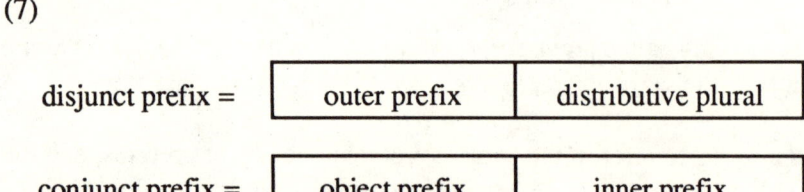

| disjunct prefix = | outer prefix | distributive plural |
| conjunct prefix = | object prefix | inner prefix |

As we said earlier, verb bases might have different combinations of lexical prefixes. A particular verb base might have one or more outer prefixes, so these lexical prefixes would all be disjunct. Another particular verb base might have no outer prefixes at all, which means that it would have no disjunct lexical prefixes. A particular verb base might have one (or occasionally, more than one) inner prefixes (these would all be conjunct prefixes), while another verb base might have no inner prefixes. Some verb bases have no lexical prefixes at all, disjunct or conjunct. Forms of such verbs consist only of the stem, the classifier (if there is one), and whatever inflectional prefixes are needed. Other verb bases might have many lexical prefixes. It would be easy to give an example of a verb base that has both disjunct and conjunct lexical prefixes (we'll see examples later on in our study.) But for now, the most important thing to remember is this: if a verb base has lexical prefixes, these prefixes will appear in all forms of that verb.

(You might be wondering: since lexical prefixes can be outer or inner, and since outer prefixes are called "disjunct" and inner prefixes are called "conjunct", why don't we drop the terms "outer" and "inner" and simply call those prefixes "disjunct lexical prefixes" and "conjunct lexical prefixes"? In fact, YM actually do something like this - we said that they don't use the terms "outer" and "inner". As we learn more about the way Navajo verbs are structured it will become clearer why we'd rather have the terms "outer" and "inner".)

We said earlier that the lexical prefix **na-** which is part of the verb base that means "play" is an outer (disjunct) prefix. How do we know this? We'll see in Chapter 5.... But for now, it might be fun to diagram the way the word **naashné** "I'm playing" is constructed. We can make a diagram like this:

(8) outer   subject   verb
     prefix   prefix   stem

       na   -   sh   -   né

Why is the "plural" prefix missing? Answer: the subject of this verb is not plural. Why is the "object" prefix missing? Answer: this verb is intransitive, so it will never have an object. Why is there no inner prefix? Answer: the Navajo verb base that means "play" doesn't happen to have an inner prefix. Why is the prefix called "cl" missing? Answer: the Navajo verb base that means "play" doesn't have a classifier. And why does the actual word **naashné** have a long **aa** in it? Answer: There is a rule that applies to disjunct prefixes that lengthens the **a** of **na-** in certain cases (we'll learn about this rule in Chapter 4.)

As we progress through our studies, we'll be learning about all sorts of facts like these about the structure of the Navajo verb. You may wonder how people figured out all these facts. It happens that the Navajo language has been studied intensively for over a century. The way we will analyze Navajo verbs in this book is the result of the work of many people. If you are curious about how the analysis of Navajo verbs developed, you might want to check the books and articles listed in the bibliographies in YM 87 and YMM 92. The earliest book listed there is dated 1852 - and since then, there have been many studies published. A few studies that were published too recently to be included in those bibliographies can be found in the books listed in the Bibliography at the back of this book.

We are now almost ready to begin looking carefully at our first verb. But before we do that, let's take a brief survey of the second kind of inflectional information, the kind having to do with when the action takes place. We'll do this in the next chapter.

CHAPTER 3

THE MODES,
STEM-SETS,
AND OTHER PRELIMINARIES

In the previous chapter, we learned that Navajo verbs contain inflectional prefixes that indicate who performs the action and, for transitive verbs, who or what the action is performed on. In this chapter, we want to introduce ourselves to how the notion of time is shown in the Navajo verb.

If you've studied a language like Spanish, you know that in languages like that the form of a verb tells something about when the action of the verb happens. Some of the verb forms are used when the action is happening in the present - these forms taken together are called the *present tense* of the verb. Other groups of verb forms are used when the action happens at other times, so that there might be a *past tense* (a group of verb forms that indicate that the action is in the past), a *future tense* (a group of verb forms that indicate that the action is in the future), and so forth.

Now, Navajo works in much the same way: there are different groups of forms that are used when the action takes place at different times. Since the uses of these groups of verb forms in Navajo is a little different than the uses of the tenses of languages like Spanish, the standard reference works on the Navajo language do not call these groups of forms "tenses"; rather, they are called *modes*. We will also call them modes here, but they're really almost the same kind of thing as tenses in a language like Spanish.

Navajo verbs have up to seven modes (quite a few Navajo verbs have fewer than seven modes - we'll discuss this matter as we go along.) These modes have the following names: Imperfective, Perfective, Future, Iterative, Usitative, Optative, and Progressive. For convenience, we will often abbreviate the names of these modes using one- or two-letter abbreviations, as follows:

(1)   Imperfective: I
        Perfective: P
        Future: F
        Iterative: R
        Usitative: U
        Optative: O
        Progressive: Pg

In our study here, we are concentrating on learning the forms and the meanings of Navajo verbs. We are not focussing on the usages of the various categories. On the other hand, it might be good to give a brief, approximate indication of how each of these modes is used, just to provide a framework for thinking about them. If you already speak Navajo, you already know when to use each of the modes. If you do not speak Navajo, you'll need to refine your understanding of when to use which mode, which you can do by reading more in the standard reference works, by asking Navajo speakers which forms they prefer in certain circumstances, by paying attention to how the modes are used in texts, and by listening to speakers to hear how they use the modes in their conversations.

Below are statements of the usages of the modes. In these statements, we sometimes distinguish an "independent" use of the mode from a "dependent" use of the mode. Here's what we mean by these terms. A mode is used independently if it is the mode of the main verb of a sentence, where the time of the action is understood without having to refer to the time of any other verb in the sentence. A mode is used dependently if it is the mode of a verb in a dependent structure; for example, a verb that has the special suffix **-go** (which means, very approximately, "when" or "as" or "while") is an example of a verb being used dependently. When a verb mode is used dependently, the time of the action is usually understood to be with reference to the time of some other verb in the sentence. This other time is called the *reference time*.

(If you speak Navajo, or if you have been studying it for some time, you may have noticed that even if a verb is used as the main verb in a sentence, the time of the action can sometimes be dependent on some other time that has been set up in the context of the discourse. This makes it harder to give an exact statement of the usages of the modes.)

The following descriptions of usages are just for your general orientation. They are not complete, but they give an idea of how each mode is used. You should read them through to orient yourself with respect to the usages of the modes, but don't bother memorizing them.

Imperfective (I-mode): Independently, this mode signals ongoing action in the present, or sometimes in the immediate future. Dependently, this mode tends to mean that the action occurs at the same time as a reference time. This mode can be used with past and future markers (the words **nít'éé'** and **dooleeł**, which are placed after the verb) to signify ongoing action in the past or future.

Perfective (P-mode): Independently, this mode signals a completed event in the past. Dependently, it tends to mean that the event was completed before a reference time.

Future (F-mode): Independently, this mode signals an event in the future. Dependently, it tends to mean that the event is later than a reference time.

Iterative (R-mode) and Usitative (U-mode): These convey generic actions, that is, actions that tend to happen over and over again in a habitual way. The difference between the two modes is subtle, with the usitative perhaps emphasizing the notion of a customary or habitual occurrence, while the iterative emphasizes the idea that the occurrences are repetitive. In general, it would appear that the iterative is used more commonly than the usitative when there is a choice.

Optative (O-mode): Most commonly, this mode is used in certain dependent structures whose meaning involves a notion of desire.

Progressive (Pg-mode): Many Navajo verbs do not have a progressive mode. For some of those verbs that do have this mode, the progressive is used instead of the imperfective to indicate ongoing action in the present. For other verbs, the progressive is used only to emphasize the idea that the ongoing action is being viewed as a process that is on its way to completion.

There is a class of words in Navajo that appear to be inflected more or less like verbs, except that they have only one mode. These will be called *neuter verbs*. In terms of meaning, neuter verbs often (but not always) correspond to English adjectives. In terms of form, some neuter verbs are inflected in what appears to be the imperfective mode, although these neuter imperfectives often have forms that are different from the usual I mode patterns in certain ways. Other neuter verbs are inflected in the perfective only.

When we study a verb, we will sometimes find it useful to list all the forms of that verb for a particular mode. When we do this, we say that we are *conjugating* the verb in that mode. We'll use the word *conjugation* to mean the pattern of forms that that verb exhibits when we list the forms of that verb in some mode.

In terms of the actual inflected forms, the I and P modes are the most complicated. Each exhibits more than one conjugation pattern, and there are a number of adjustments where lexical prefixes change their form slightly; these will require our attention. We will study these modes step by step, slowly building up a picture of the full range of verb forms in these modes. The forms for the other modes are considerably simpler, and will require less detailed study for their complete understanding.

Now, here's a question we might want to ask at this point: Exactly how does a verb indicate what its mode is? In other words, if we are looking at a verb (or if we hear someone say a verb), how do we know which mode the verb is in? Or, turning the question around, if we want to build a verb that is in a certain mode, how do we make sure that the verb ends up in that mode and not in another one?

The answer to this question has two parts. There are two things that are done simultaneously that determine the mode of a verb.

Firstly, each mode has its own set of subject prefixes. We saw in the last chapter that in any verb, there is a place for a prefix that indicates who does the action. Well, different modes use different sets of subject prefixes to indicate this. (But note: the object prefixes are the same for all the modes.)

Secondly, the mode is (usually) shown by the form of the verb stem. That is, there is actually a slightly different form of the verb stem that is used for each mode.

We can illustrate this using the verb base that means "play" (these forms also illustrate some other things that we will have to study later on in our lessons.) If we want to say "I am playing", we'll use the I mode, and the form will look like this:

(2)   naashné.

If we want to say "I played", we'll use the P mode, and the form will look like this:

(3)   niséne'.

If we want to say "I'll play", we'll use the F mode, and the form will look like this:

(4)   nideeshneeł.

Let's stop with these three modes, and see what we've got.

Each of the verbs in (2), (3), and (4) are built more or less the same way. First, there is a lexical prefix (it happens that it's a disjunct (outer) prefix) starting with an "n". Right now, we're going to say that the prefix is exactly **na-**, but we will need to say more (later on), since in (2) it looks as though the prefix has the form **naa-**, while in (3) and (4) it looks as though this prefix is really **ni-**. After this prefix, there is another prefix, which is the one that tells us that the subject is the person called "I" in English. Finally, there is the verb stem.

Looking at the verb stem first, we see that **-né** is found in (2). Now, the verb in (2) is in the I mode, and when we study the I mode more, we'll see that any verb in the I mode that means "play" always has **-né** as the stem. Since this particular form of the stem tells us that we're in the I mode, we'll say that -né is the *imperfective stem* (or *I mode stem*) for the verb base that means "play".

Next, look at the verb stem in (3). We see that it is **-ne'**, slightly different from the verb stem **-né** found in (2). Now, the verb in (3) is in the P mode, and we'll learn later that any verb in the P mode that means "play" has **-ne'** as its stem. Therefore, we'll say that **-ne'** is the *perfective stem* (or *P mode stem*) for this verb base.

Similarly, the stem **-neeł** that we find in (4) is the stem for any verb form that means "play" when the mode is F, so **-neeł** will be called the *future stem* (or *F mode stem*) for this verb base.

The other modes will also have particular stems for them. Here is the complete set of stems used in the verb base that means "play":

(5) I: **né**
    P: **ne'**
    F: **neeł**
    R: **neeh**
    O: **ne'**

You may have noticed that there are only five modes shown here. What happened to the two other modes? Well, for any verb, the usitative (U) mode takes the same stem as the iterative (R) mode. And, for any verb that has a progressive (Pg) mode, the progressive takes the same stem as the future (F) mode. So, a complete set of stems will always have five members. But note: the stems for the five different modes might not always be different. In (5), for example, the P mode stem and the O mode stem are the same.

A set of stems, one for each mode, such as the set listed in (5), will be called a *stem-set*. Whenever you learn a Navajo verb, you need to know the entire stem-set for that verb in order to be able to create the forms for all of the modes. Incidentally, this means that our notion of verb base has to be changed. Back in Chapter 2, we said that a verb base consists of a stem possibly together with some lexical prefixes. But what we should say instead is that a verb base consists, not of a stem, but of a stem-set, possibly with some lexical prefixes. For example, the Navajo verb base that means "play" consists of the stem-set shown in (5), together with the lexical prefix **na-**.

Let's now look at the subject prefixes in the verbs in (2), (3), and (4). In (2), we see that the subject prefix is **-sh-**, and when we study the I mode, we'll learn that this is the prefix used in the I mode that means that the subject is "first person singular". ("First person singular" just means the same as: the person called "I" or "me" in English.) In (3), the subject prefix is **-sé-**, and when we study the P mode, we'll learn that this is the prefix used in the P mode for a first person singular subject. (There is a complication in the P mode that we're not mentioning now: sometimes a different subject prefix is used. We'll study this in Chapter 8.) In (4), the subject prefix **-deesh-** is the first person singular prefix for the F mode. Obviously, in order to learn all the forms for Navajo verbs, we'll need to study the subject prefixes for each mode in turn. This is exactly what we'll do.

The fact that the modes in (2), (3), and (4) are different are really indicated by the difference in the subject prefixes and the difference in the verb stems. However, you may wonder, the lexical prefix is also different: it's **naa-** in (2) and **ni-** in (3) and (4). Does that have anything to do with the mode? Well, it happens that it doesn't. We'll see in Chapters 4 and 5 that in the I mode alone, the prefix is sometimes **naa-**, sometimes **ni-**, and sometimes **na-**. What's going on is that this prefix is changing form for reasons that have to do with pronunciation: we will say that there are *phonological rules* (meaning, rules that have to do with pronunciation) that change the prefix from one form to another. Starting in Chapter 4, and continuing for quite a few later chapters, we'll learn what these rules are. But these rules are automatic; that is, they don't have to do with the information that is contained in the verb. They only have to do with getting the pronunciation correct - you don't choose which form of the prefix to use, you simply follow the rules in order to get the right form of the verb. This is different from the modes: you do choose a mode, and if you choose a different mode, you get a word that means something different.

So, to summarize what we know about Navajo verbs so far: in any one mode, the verb will be inflected to show the subject, and, if the verb is transitive, it will be inflected to show the object as well. The stem used will be chosen from the stem-set for the verb base - the stem you choose will be the one that corresponds to the mode you want. The subject prefix you choose will correspond to who did the action, but the set of prefixes you choose from will depend on what mode you want, since each mode has its own set of subject prefixes. (But note: object prefixes are the same for all modes.) Any lexical prefixes will be put into their correct positions. You may have to apply some phonological rules in order to make some small adjustments to the pronunciation of some of the pieces to insure that the final word is correct.

With this, we are (finally!) ready to look more seriously at the forms of a real verb.

CHAPTER 4

GETTING STARTED WITH THE IMPERFECTIVE MODE

In this chapter, we are going to look at the whole imperfective mode of a Navajo verb. This will enable us to learn the basics of how verbs are built in Navajo.

To keep things simple, we'll take an intransitive verb. This way, we won't have to bother with prefixes that refer to the object. In fact, let's take as an example the verb base that means "play". From Chapters 2 and 3, we know that any imperfective form of this verb has the verb stem **-né**, as well as the lexical prefix **na-**.

Now, we know that inside the verb there has to be a prefix that tells who the subject is. Our first question is: what are the possible subjects that a Navajo verb can have?

We can begin answering this question by looking at the following diagram:

(1)

	sg	dpl
1	a	b
2	c	d
3	e	

Whenever we talk about subject prefixes, or whenever we list forms of a verb arranged according to subject, we'll use a diagram like this, with the letters "a", "b", etc. replaced by the prefixes or the forms that we are interested in. (In (1), the letters "a", "b", etc. are only there to mark the positions in the diagram.)

Here's what this diagram means. The column labelled "sg" is for *singular subjects*, that is, subjects consisting of one person or one thing. The column labelled "dpl" is for *duoplural subjects*. Duoplural subjects are subjects that are most often groups of two people or two things.

(You might ask: what if the subject is a group of three or more persons? Such a subject is not in the chart! We'll learn how such subjects are represented in the verb when we get to Chapter 5.)

The rows refer to *person*. The row labelled "1" is *first person*, which means that the speaker of the sentence is involved. The position labelled "a", which is in the first person row and the singular column, corresponds to the subject "I" in English. The position labelled "b", which is in the first person row and the duoplural column, corresponds to the subject "we" in English, except that in

Navajo, the duoplural would almost always be used only if there are exactly two people involved. (So, a first person duoplural subject means, usually, that the speaker, together with one other person, does the action.)

The row labelled "2" is *second person*, which means that the person being spoken to is involved. The position labelled "c", which is in the second person row and the singular column, corresponds to the subject "you" in English, except that in Navajo, this subject form is used when the "you" is just one person (rather than two or a group), that is, when only one person is being addressed by the speaker. The position labelled "d", which is in the second person row and the duoplural column, corresponds to the subject "you" in English when two people are being addressed.

The row labelled "3" is *third person*, which means that the subject is neither the speaker nor the person or persons spoken to. Note that there is only one third person position shown in the chart, the position labelled "e". The reason for this is that, in Navajo, there is never any difference between third person singular and third person duoplural - the same prefix is always used for both. The position "e" corresponds to English subjects like "he", "she", "it" or "they" (where "they" is a group of two.)

In Chapter 3, we learned that each Navajo mode has a set of subject prefixes. What are the subject prefixes for the I mode? Here they are:

(2)

	sg	dpl
1	sh	iid
2	ni	oh
3	zero	

These prefixes are very important, and should be memorized!

Note: the 3 person prefix is shown as "zero". What this means is: there is no prefix that you actually use. If the subject is 3 person, you simply leave out the subject prefix.

Another note: these subject prefixes should really be called the subject prefixes for the *regular* I mode. You may remember that in Chapter 3 we warned you that the I mode and the P mode are more complicated than the other modes. One of the complications is that sometimes another set of subject prefixes is used for the I mode. But the set in (2) is the most common one, so we'll start with it.

We can now build I mode forms for the verb base meaning "play". To see how to do this, first look at the chart in item (6) of Chapter 2. (Note: In the future, we'll abbreviate this by saying: look at the chart in Chapter 2(6).) If we look at that chart, we see that any imperfective form of this verb will have to be built like this:

(3) outer   subject   verb
     prefix   prefix   stem

     na -   (whatever) - né

There are some mysteries here.

First of all, why is **na** listed as an outer (disjunct) prefix rather than an inner (conjunct) prefix? This will become clear in Chapter 5 - for now, let's just take it as true.

Second, what happened to the piece called "cl" (the classifier) in Chapter 2(6)? The answer is, for the verb base that means "play", the classifier is simply missing. We need to talk about these classifiers, but we'll postpone that to Chapter 6.

Third, what happened to the piece called "plural" in Chapter 2(6)? The answer is, in this chapter, we are only looking at forms where the subject is either singular or "strictly" duoplural (that is, where the subject might be a group of two persons.) The piece called "plural" (which, as we said, we're really going to call the "distributive plural") is only present when the subject involves a group of three or more persons, so here we simply leave it out. We'll study the distributive plural in Chapter 5.

Fourth, what happened to the piece called "object prefix" in Chapter 2(6)? The answer is, the verb base that means "play" is intransitive, so there is never an object. The object prefix is simply left out.

(With all these pieces left out, do you see why we cannot tell just yet whether **na-** is an outer (disjunct) lexical prefix or an inner (conjunct) lexical prefix?)

Now, using the diagram in (3) and the prefixes in (2), we can try to build five imperfective mode forms of the Navajo verb "play". The real forms of this verb turn out to be the following:

(4)   sg   dpl

1   naashné   neii'né
2   naniné   naohné
3   naané

Whoops: more mysteries! To understand what's happening here, it will be helpful to focus our attention separately on different places inside the verb.

To start with, one of the weird things about the forms in (4) is that the prefix **na-** has a number of different shapes. The way to understand this is to recall that in Chapter 3 we talked about the idea that there are automatic rules, sometimes called *phonological rules*, that tell us how certain things are pronounced in certain circumstances. What we have here is a situation where the pronunciation of **na-** is changed in some of the forms in (4) because of the action of particular rules. Rather than studying many, many cases in order to come up with exactly the right rules, let's just go ahead and write down rules in a form that will be useful to us throughout our entire study. Here is our first one:

Rule Disj-1: Whenever a disjunct prefix is followed by a consonant, and the next syllable in the verb is the verb-stem syllable, make the following changes:

(a)   If the disjunct prefix ends in a short, low-tone **a**, lengthen it to **aa**.

(b)   .... (other cases)

Let's take a look at this rule carefully.

First of all, the rule is numbered "Disj-1". What this means is, this is our first rule about disjunct prefixes. We are studying what happens at different places in the verb separately, and right now we're looking at something that has to do with disjunct prefixes. We're going to have a group of rules that tell us about disjunct prefixes, and these will all be numbered like this: Disj-(number). But, we'll also have a different group of rules that tell us about conjunct prefixes, and also other sets of rules that tell us about other places in the verb. All in all, we'll have four sets of rules, and the rules in each set will be numbered separately. The rules in each set will be collected in Part A of the Appendix, so you can refer to any rule there whenever it is mentioned somewhere in the lessons.

For review: What is a disjunct prefix? Answer: It's either an outer prefix, or else it's the distributive plural prefix (the prefix that goes in the slot called "plural" in Chapter 2(6).) We'll learn about the distributive plural prefix in Chapter 5.

Next, notice how the rule is stated. There are a number of conditions. In fact, there are four conditions. First, you have to have a disjunct prefix; second, the prefix has to be followed by a consonant; third, the next syllable in the verb has to be the verb-stem syllable; and fourth, the prefix has to end in a short, low-tone **a**. What the rule says is this: If all of these four conditions are satisfied, then go ahead and do something (in the case of this rule, what you do is lengthen the **a** in the prefix to **aa**.) But if any of these conditions are not satisfied, the rule is simply ignored - it's just not applied.

Finally, notice that the conditions are separated out into two groups inside the rule. The part about the disjunct prefix being followed by a consonant, and the part about the next syllable being the verb-stem syllable, are put together at the beginning of the rule. Then, there is a separate clause, labelled (a), that talks about the prefix ending in a short, low-tone **a**. The reason we do this is that the conditions that are placed first (the ones at the beginning of the rule) are general conditions that are going to cause many disjunct prefixes to undergo some changes. But the specific changes depend on the actual sounds in the prefix. We'll list these in separate clauses. Here, we've only given the first one, but if you look up this rule in the Appendix, you'll see that there are other clauses listed that tell what happens when a disjunct prefix has other sounds in it. (Advice: don't look this rule up in the Appendix just yet - we're going to rewrite it slightly in just a little bit.)

Now, let's see what Rule Disj-1 tells us about the forms in (4).

First of all, the 1sg form is built like this:

(5)   outer   subject   verb
       prefix   prefix   stem

       na   -   sh   -   né

Make sure you understand where these pieces come from. The outer prefix **na** and the verb stem **né** are part of the verb base that means "play". The particular stem **né** is chosen because we want to form a verb in the I mode (see the stem-set in Chapter 3(5) - remember, this means look for the item numbered (5) in Chapter 3.) The subject prefix **sh** comes from the chart in (2) - it's just the 1sg subject prefix for the regular I mode.

Now, when we look at Rule Disj-1, we ask ourselves: Is there a disjunct prefix here? Yes! The outer prefix **na** is a disjunct prefix. Next: Is this prefix followed by a consonant? Yes! It's followed by **sh**, which is a consonant. Is the next syllable in the verb the verb-stem syllable? Yes! The next syllable is **(sh)né**, which is the syllable that has the verb stem **né** in it. Does the disjunct prefix here end in a short, low-tone **a**? Yes! The prefix **na** ends this way. The answers to all the questions posed by Rule Disj-1 (part (a)) are yes, so the rule tells us to lengthen the vowel of **na** and make the prefix **naa** instead. This gives us **naashné** as the form that means "I am playing". This is exactly the 1sg I mode form of "play" shown in (4).

(To make sure you understand the business about the next syllable being the verb-stem syllable: how do we tell whether this is so or not? We start at the disjunct prefix, we read to the right, and we stop at the first vowel that we come to. If that vowel is inside the verb stem, then the next syllable is the verb-stem syllable. In the case of **na-sh-né**, when we move to the right of the **na**, the next vowel we come to is the **é** which is inside the verb stem **né**. So the next syllable really is the verb-stem syllable.)

Let's try this with the 2sg I mode form of this verb, for comparison. This form, which means "you (singular) are playing", is built like this:

(6)   outer   subject   verb
       prefix   prefix   stem

       na   -   ni   -   né

Looking at Rule Disj-1, we ask: Is there a disjunct prefix here? Yes: the outer prefix **na**. Is this prefix followed by a consonant? Yes: it's followed by the **n** of **ni** (**ni** is the 2sg I mode subject prefix, which we can find in the chart in (2) above.) Is the next syllable the verb-stem syllable? No! The next syllable is **ni**, which is the subject prefix. (If we read to the right following the prefix **na**, the first vowel we come to is the **i** of **ni**. This vowel is not inside the verb stem, which is **né**.) So the rule doesn't apply (even though **na** ends in a short, low-tone **a**), and we just have **naniné** as the form that means "you (singular) are playing".

What happens if we try this with the 3 I mode form of the verb? This form is build like this:

(7)   outer   subject   verb
       prefix   prefix   stem

       na   -   né

Recall that in the I mode, the 3 subject prefix is "zero", that is, there actually isn't any prefix. Looking at rule Disj-1, we see that we do have a disjunct prefix (the outer prefix **na**), this prefix is followed by a consonant (the **n** of **né**), the next syllable is the verb-stem syllable (the syllable **né**), and the prefix does end in a short, low-tone **a**, so the rule changes **na** to **naa**. This gives us the correct form **naané**, meaning "he's playing", or "she's playing", or "they (two) are playing".

If we look at the 1dpl and 2dpl forms, something different happens. As far as Rule Disj-1 is concerned, the difference is that the disjunct prefix **na** is not followed by a consonant. We can see this by looking at the way that these forms are built:

(8)   outer   subject   verb
       prefix   prefix   stem

       na   - $\left\{ \begin{array}{c} \text{iid} \\ \text{oh} \end{array} \right\}$ -   né

In the 1dpl form, **na** is followed by the vowel **ii**, and in the 2dpl form, **na** is followed by the vowel **o**. So, for both of these forms, Rule Disj-1 doesn't apply. This is fine, since neither of these forms have **naa** in them. However, the 1dp form doesn't have **na** in it either. There must be another rule that has to do with vowels coming together. Here it is:

<u>Rule Disj-2</u>: If a disjunct prefix is followed by a vowel, the following adjustments are made:

(a)   If **a** is followed by **i** or **ii**, then the whole thing becomes **ei** or **eii**, except if the **a** is preceded by **g**, **gh**, **h**, **k**, or **k'**, in which case nothing happens. If the **a** is high tone (that is, **á**), then the new combination is **éi** or **éii**.

(b)   .... (other cases)

Note that the form of this rule is similar to the form of Rule Disj-1. First, we have the general conditions (there's a disjunct prefix, and it's followed by a vowel), and then we have a list of cases that tell what happens depending on the specific situation. Again, we've only listed one case (it's actually more than we need for now), but if you look up Rule Disj-2 in the Appendix, you'll see other cases.

How does this rule work? Well, if we review the way that the 1sg, 2sg, and 3 I mode forms of "play" were built (see (5), (6), and (7)), we see that for these forms the disjunct prefix **na** isn't followed by another vowel, so Rule Disj-2 doesn't apply. But for the 1dpl form, we do have this situation: the prefix **na** is followed by the **ii** of the subject prefix **iid**. So, Rule Disj-2 does apply in this case, changing the combination **aii** to **eii**, and the verb form is **neii...** instead of **naii...**. (There is something going on with the **d** of **iid** which we'll discuss in a moment.)

In the case of the 2dpl form, Rule Disj-1 doesn't apply (because the prefix **na** is not followed by a consonant). However, **na** is followed by a vowel, so we have to take a look at Rule Disj-2. But clause (a) of Rule Disj-2 doesn't apply, since we don't have an **a** followed by an **i** or **ii**. Assuming that none of the missing clauses of Rule Disj-2 apply either, we just get the form **naohné** "you (two) are playing" directly.

But there is something to be said about the 2dpl form. You may have noticed that some people who speak Navajo don't say **naohné** when they want to say "you (two) are playing", but rather they say **naahné** (if you speak Navajo yourself, you might say **naahné** instead of **naohné**.) This seems to have to do with geography: generally speaking, people from the Western parts of Navajoland say **naohné**, and people from the Eastern parts say **naahné**. If we want to create the form **naahné**, we need to put another clause into Rule Disj-2 that says: if **a** is followed by **o**, the combination becomes **aa**. We won't officially put this clause in, since not all speakers of Navajo have this form, but you should keep it in mind. In printed materials, you may run into either the form **naohné** or the form **naahné**, so be prepared to recognize both of them. This variation will be the same for all verbs where a disjunct prefix ending in **a** meets the 2dpl subject prefix **oh**, so you should be ready for it.

The two rules we've given create the different forms of the prefix **na** correctly, at least as we've seen these forms so far. You might want to keep in mind the particular conditions that are involved in these two rules. There are quite a few cases in Navajo where a particular disjunct prefix has different forms. Very often, the circumstances in which the different forms are used are the same as the circumstances in which the different forms of **na** are used. The general circumstances that are most important are the ones that we gave at the beginnings of Rules Disj-1 and Disj-2. For example, a particularly important condition that affects disjunct prefixes is the one that says: if the next syllable is the verb-stem syllable, the prefix might have a slightly different form. A good habit to get into, when looking at disjunct prefixes, is to notice whether the syllable that directly follows that prefix is the verb-stem syllable or not. If you do this, you will find it easy to make sense out of a lot of the way prefixes change from one verb form to another. In fact, this condition is so important that it will be handy to have a special technical term that we can use when we run into this situation. To explain this new term, let's go back to the diagrams in (5) and (7).

What we said about the prefix **na** in (5) and in (7) was that the syllable which follows this prefix was the verb-stem syllable. Here's another way of thinking of it. The prefix **na** itself consists of a syllable. In (5) and in (7), this syllable immediately precedes the verb-stem syllable (that is, it precedes the verb stem syllable, but there isn't any other syllable in between it and the verb-stem.) Let's use the term *pre-stem syllable* to mean the syllable that immediately precedes the verb-stem syllable, in any verb or verb structure. So, we can say that in (5) and (7), the prefix **na** is the pre-stem syllable. But in (6), **na** is not the pre-stem syllable, since it's separated from the verb stem by the subject prefix **ni**. In (6), the pre-stem syllable is this subject prefix **ni**. Note: in any verb, exactly one syllable is the pre-stem syllable (it's whichever syllable immediately precedes the verb-stem syllable.) We'll learn later that, with very few exceptions, every Navajo verb has a pre-stem syllable.

If we use our new term, we can rewrite Rule Disj-1 like this:

Rule Disj-1: Whenever the last syllable of a disjunct prefix is the pre-stem syllable and the disjunct prefix is followed by a consonant, make the following changes:

(a)   If the disjunct prefix ends in a short, low-tone **a**, lengthen it to **aa**.

(b)   .... (other cases)

The reason we said that the last syllable of the prefix has to be the pre-stem syllable is that there are disjunct prefixes that have more than one syllable in them. We'll occasionally run into prefixes like that.

This rewritten form of Rule Disj-1 is the basis of the version of this rule that you'll find in the Appendix. If you want to see other ways that disjunct prefixes change, look this rule up in the Appendix.

The condition at the beginning of Rule Disj-2 is also important. This might be a good time to let you into a secret: all disjunct prefixes end in vowels! This means that whenever a disjunct prefix satisfies the general condition of Rule Disj-2, the vowel at the end of the prefix will be followed immediately by another vowel. This situation (two vowels coming together) sometimes leads to changes in the vowels. These changes are exactly what are listed in the clauses of Rule Disj-2. Keeping this

27

possibility in mind will help you learn a lot about the forms of many real Navajo verbs.

Let's summarize the important conditions that affect a disjunct prefix.

First, if a disjunct prefix (which we said always ends in a vowel) is followed by another vowel, then check Rule Disj-2 to see how the vowels coming together need to be adjusted (if they do.)

Second, if a disjunct prefix is followed by a consonant, check if the next syllable is the verb-stem syllable; that is, check if the last syllable of the disjunct prefix is the pre-stem syllable. If it is, then check Rule Disj-1 to see if the form of the disjunct prefix has to be adjusted.

Question: What happens if a disjunct prefix is followed by a consonant and the next syllable is not the verb-stem syllable? Well, usually, nothing happens! That is, no rules apply, and no adjustments are made. (However, we'll see that there are a few "irregular" disjunct prefixes where a change is sometimes made. We'll learn these individually as we go on.) Go back and review our discussion of the form built in (6) above to see an example of this situation.

Review question: why didn't Rule Disj-1 change the form of **na** in (6)? Answer: **na** is not the pre-stem syllable in this form. Another review question: since the subject prefix **ni** in (6) is the pre-stem syllable in this form, why doesn't Rule Disj-1 change it's form? Answer: **ni** is not a disjunct prefix, and Rule Disj-1 only changes the forms of disjunct prefix. Remember: subject prefixes aren't disjunct prefixes, and they also aren't conjunct prefixes (see the chart in Chapter 2(7) to remind yourself which prefixes are disjunct prefixes and which ones are conjunct prefixes.)

One final thing to keep in mind about Rules Disj-1 and Disj-2 is that neither of these rules have anything specific to do with the I mode. These rules are general rules involving disjunct prefixes. They apply whenever the conditions given in the rules are fulfilled, no matter what the mode is. We happened to have learned about them in our study of the regular I mode, but we'll see these (and other rules like them) applying over and over again in lots of different forms in various other modes.

There is one more point we have to deal with in order to explain the forms in (4), namely: what happened to the **d** of **iid**? We should note first of all that this is a different place in the verb than the disjunct prefixes. This **d** is located where the subject prefix meets the verb stem. We are going to have a special group of rules that deal specifically with things that happen where the subject prefix meets either the verb stem or the classifier, or where the classifier meets the verb stem. We will number these rules separately from the Disj rules. These rules will be numbered by calling them "Rule Subj-(number)".

For the **d** of **iid,** here is the rule we need, but when you read it you will see that we have to explain what this rule really means:

<u>Rule Subj-1</u>: Whenever the **d** at the end of a 1dpl subject prefix is immediately followed by the first consonant of the verb stem, then that **d** causes d-effect on the first consonant of the verb stem. (The **d** itself disappears.)

First of all, this rule talks about the **d** at the end of a 1dpl subject prefix. In the regular I mode, as we've seen it so far, the 1dpl prefix does in fact end in a **d**. But it happens that in Navajo all the 1dpl subject prefixes (that is, the 1dpl prefixes for all of the conjugations of all the modes) end in **d**. (And, actually, these are the only subject prefixes that end in **d**.) So, Rule Subj-1 is really about 1dpl subject prefixes in general.

Next, Rule Subj-1 only applies if the **d** at the end of the subject prefix is <u>immediately</u> followed by the verb stem. Why shouldn't it be immediately followed by the verb stem? Well, when we come to study the classifiers in Chapter 6, we'll see that we might have a situation where the **d** is separated from the verb stem by a classifier. If this happens, then Rule Subj-1 doesn't apply. In the case of the verb base meaning "play", there is no classifier, so the **d** is immediately followed by the verb stem.

Now, the real issue is: what does it mean to say that the **d** "causes d-effect"? This is an abbreviated way of talking about a process in which a consonant is changed into another consonant. The term *d-effect* is used here, and in the standard reference works, to mean a particular process that changes some consonants into others. What we need to learn is what this change actually is for any consonant in the Navajo language.

There are several ways we can learn d-effect. One would be to memorize for each consonant what happens to it when d-effect applies. This is not a particularly good idea, but just in case you feel like doing it, here is a list of the consonants of Navajo, together with the consonant that it turns into when d-effect applies to it:

(9)

	before d-effect	after d-effect

before d-effect	after d-effect
z	dz
zh	j
gh	g

before d-effect	after d-effect
w	g or 'w
y	g or 'y

before d-effect	after d-effect
m	'm
n	'n

before d-effect	after d-effect
l	dl (usually)

before d-effect	after d-effect
'	t'

before d-effect	after d-effect
b	b
ch	ch
ch'	ch'
d	d
dl	dl
dz	dz
g	g
j	j
k	k
k'	k'
t	t
t'	t'
tł	tł
tł'	tł'
ts	ts
ts'	ts'

You may have noticed several things about this table.

First of all, not all Navajo consonants have been listed in the left-hand column. For example, the consonants **s**, **sh**, **h**, and **ł** were left out. The reason that these consonants were left out is that it so happens that these consonants can never be in a position to have d-effect apply to them (the reason for this will become clearer much later; for now, just think of it as a strange fact.)

Second, the consonants were not arranged alphabetically. Rather, they were put into groups. If you look carefully, you'll see that d-effect works in a similar way for all the consonants that are in any one group. The last group is the biggest. It consists of consonants for which d-effect has no effect at all. You might notice that there is something similar about the consonants in the last group: they all involve making a noise by releasing a sudden puff of air.

Third, the consonants **w** and **y** have two possible outcomes. What's happening here is that sometimes **w** and **y** behave as though they were "versions of" **gh** and become **g** under d-effect. But sometimes they behave as though they were in the same group as **m** and **n**, and become **'w** and **'y** under d-effect. What this means for us is that whenever a verb stem begins with a **w** or a **y**, we'll simply have to memorize, for that verb stem, what happens to that **w** or **y** under d-effect. (But for some verb stems there will be hints that will tell us how the **w** or the **y** behaves.)

Fourth, the consonant **l** is shown as usually becoming **dl**. There are a few irregularities concerning this consonant, however. For example, there is a verb stem-set whose meaning has to do with ropelike things. The stems in this set all begin with **l**, and, for these stems, d-effect changes the **l** to **ly** instead of to **dl**. Irregularities like this will simply have to be learned for the particular verbs involved.

Finally, let's note that the glottal stop **'** has its own special behavior under d-effect: it turns into **t'**.

The best way to learn (9) is probably to study the groups of consonants as groups rather than trying to memorize the individual consonants. After you look at a lot of verbs, you'll probably end up learning all of (9) anyway. While you're studying, you can always remember that the chart in (9) showing d-effect is here in Chapter 4, and you can refer to it.

In the case of our verb base meaning "play", we can now fully understand the form that means "We (two) are playing". The verb is built as in (8), Rule Disj-2 applies to change **naii...** into **neii...**, and Rule Subj-1 tells us that the **d** of **iid** causes d-effect to apply to the **n** at the beginning of the verb stem **né**, turning it into **'n**, as we can see in the chart in (9). This gives us the actually 1dpl I mode form: **neii'né**.

With this, we've finished our first encounter with a real Navajo verb. It may seem to you that we've had to do a lot of complicated thinking in order to figure out only five words. However, the thinking we've been doing is very general: very many thousands of words are built using these rules together with a few (!) more that we'll be learning in the chapters to follow.

CHAPTER 5

FOURTH PERSON SUBJECTS
AND PLURAL SUBJECTS

In Chapter 4, we became acquainted with the basic I mode forms of the verb base that means "play". However, there are a number of other important I mode forms of this verb (and of all verbs) that we haven't yet seen. In this chapter we will learn about two important prefixes that are used to form these other I mode forms.

If you speak Navajo, you may have noticed that there is an alternate form of the verb that can be used when speaking about the action performed by somebody other than the speaker or hearer. This is a form that has a **j** sound in it. In YM, these forms are called 3a ("alternate third person" forms), but we will call them 4 (*fourth person* forms) here. We cannot give a complete description of when the fourth person is used, but roughly we can say that it has uses such as: indicating an unspecified or indefinite subject (a little like "one", or sometimes "they", in English); a polite way of referring to somebody who is present in the conversation; a way of keeping one third person entity separate from another when telling a story.

(Incidentally, like the 3 person, the 4 person forms of Navajo verbs are the same for singular and for duoplural. Remember that the duoplural is used mostly for groups of two.)

In any case, we want to begin this chapter by learning how to build verbs where the subject is specified as 4 person. Again, to get started, we'll restrict our attention to the regular I mode, and to intransitive verbs; in fact, we'll use our old friend "play" as an example.

Now, in dealing with the 4 person, we run into a complication that is typical of languages in general: the structure of the language is set up so that pieces that have different kinds of meaning go in certain particular places, and then the language goes ahead and puts pieces with certain meanings into the wrong places! In the case of the 4 person, we have the following situation: we learned that there is a position inside the Navajo verb, just in front of the verb stem (really, just in front of the classifier), for a prefix that indicates what the subject is. However, the prefix that indicates that the subject is 4 person does not go into this position! In fact, the prefixes shown in Chapter 4(2) are the only prefixes (in the regular I mode) that can appear as subject prefixes. The way we show that the subject of a verb is 4 person is by adding in a prefix into the <u>object</u> prefix position! As you may have guessed from above, this prefix is simply the consonant **j**.

But, if **j** is placed into the object prefix position, what do we put into the "real" subject prefix position? The answer is: whenever we put **j** into the object prefix position, we put a 3 person subject prefix into the subject prefix position. The actual subject prefix that we use will depend on the mode and the conjugation pattern, but the 4 person **j** prefix is the same for all modes.

So, to summarize: if we want to indicate that the subject is 4 person, we put **j** into the object position, and in addition to this, we use the 3 person subject prefix, which we put into its normal position. For the regular I mode, we've seen that the 3 person subject prefix is actually zero, but for other modes it won't be zero. In those cases, whatever the 3 person subject prefix is, it has to be there along with the special **j** in the object prefix position, if you want to indicate that the subject is 4 person.

Okay, let's try to build the verb form that means "one is playing", using a 4 subject with the verb base that means "play". We get this:

(1)
outer prefix	object prefix	subject prefix	verb stem
na	j	(zero)	né

But when we look at the actual word, we see that we need to learn about a few more rules, because the actual word turns out to be:

(2)   nijiné

There are two separate processes that are at work here. One of them is described by the following rule:

Rule Conj-1: If a conjunct prefix (ending in a consonant) is followed directly by a consonant, insert the vowel **i** between the consonant at the end of the conjunct prefix and the consonant that follows it.

This is the first rule that we've seen from a new collection of rules, namely, rules that apply to conjunct prefixes. We are going to number all the rules in this group like this: "Rule Conj-(number)".

Why are we calling this a rule about conjunct prefixes? Well, first of all, recall that in Chapter 2 we used the term *conjunct prefix* to mean any prefix which is either an inner prefix or else an object prefix. The 4 person **j** that we're studying here appears in the object prefix position. While its meaning does not involve an object, the fact that it comes in the object prefix position means that it acts like an object prefix. In other words, rules that apply to conjunct prefixes are going to apply to this **j**.

But does the process described in Rule Conj-1 really apply to any conjunct prefix, or does it only apply to 4 person **j**? We'll see as we go along that this rule is actually very general - it does apply to all conjunct prefixes (except for a few special exceptions (there are always some of those!) that we'll study individually.)

Incidentally, in the statement of Rule Conj-1, the phrase "ending in a consonant" was put in parentheses. The reason for that is that it turns out that all conjunct prefixes end in consonants! In fact, many of them consist just of one consonant, like the prefix **j** that we're learning about here. This is a difference between conjunct and disjunct prefixes: conjunct prefixes end in consonants, and (as we learned near the end of Chapter 4) disjunct prefixes end in vowels.

(But wait! Maybe the prefix that means 4 person isn't **j**, maybe it's **ji**? Well, you could analyze it that way, and if you did, you wouldn't need a rule like Rule Conj-1. But, if you did this, you'd need other rules for other circumstances that would get rid of the **i** in those cases. We think it turns out to be easier to talk about it the way we're doing, where conjunct prefixes all end in consonants, and Rule Conj-1 puts that **i** in, but if you find it easier to think about it the other way, go ahead!)

If we look at the structure in (1), we see that Rule Conj-1 will insert an **i** after the **j** and before the **n** of the verb-stem **né**. So this rule is responsible for creating the second **i** in the word **nijiné**. But there is still another process at work in this word, namely the process that changed the disjunct prefix **na** into **ni**. This is <u>not</u> a general process about disjunct prefixes, because it only happens with the prefixes **na** and **ná**. (We haven't seen the prefix **ná** yet, and we won't for quite a while, but the same change happens with **ná** as with **na**, so we'll include **ná** in our discussion here.) We'll give a special rule that applies only to these prefixes, but we'll number the rule as a disjunct prefix rule, since the **na** or **ná** prefixes are outer prefixes, and therefore disjunct prefixes:

<u>Rule Disj-3</u>: The syllable **na** becomes **ni**, and the syllable **ná** becomes **ní**, if it is immediately followed by:

(a)   the **j** which indicates 4 person.

(b)   (other cases)

If you look this rule up in the Appendix, you will see that what we have written above is only part of the rule: part (a) is just one circumstance among a whole group of circumstances that we'll learn about when the change from **na** or **ná** to **ni** or **ní** occurs.

A good thing to do now is to review the discussion in Chapter 4 about conditions that apply to disjunct prefixes. Then look up Rule Disj-3 in the Appendix, and also look at Rule Disj-2. You'll notice that the circumstances that make Rule Disj-3 apply all involve the syllable **na** or **ná** being followed by a consonant. This means that for Rule Disj-3 to apply, Rule Disj-2 could not have applied (since the next sound is not a vowel.) Something that might not be as clear is that if Rule Disj-3 applies, then Rule Disj-1 could not have applied either. The reason for this is that all of the elements listed in Rule Disj-3 that cause the rule to work when they follow **na** or **ná** are elements that are going to end up having syllables of their own, so the next syllable is not the verb-stem syllable. (For example: if the next element is the **j** that indicates 4 person, we know that Rule Conj-1 will come along and insert an **i** after this **j**. This means that the next syllable will be **ji**. This isn't the verb-stem syllable - the verb stem is further on down the line.) So, Rule Disj-3 applies only in the circumstance that, according to Chapter 4, we normally do not apply any rule! What we have here is a kind of exception or irregularity: the prefixes **na** and **ná** are irregular, because they sometimes change their form even when a normal disjunct prefix would not change its form.

How does this rule work? Well, in the case of the word in (2), we have **na** followed by the **j** which indicates 4 person, so condition (a) is fulfilled, and the rule changes **na** to **ni**.

You might want to compare this with the 2sg person subject form of this verb that we studied in Chapter 4 (see Chapter 4(6).) In that word, **na** is not followed by the **j** that indicates 4 person. Does this mean that Rule Disj-3 doesn't apply? No! Why not? Because we haven't learned all of the circumstances that when Rule Disj-3 applies! Now, if you check the statement of Rule Disj-3 in the Appendix, you can probably figure out that this rule doesn't apply here, because none of the circumstances seem to involve the **na** or **ná** being followed directly by the **ni** that indicates a 2sg subject. But this situation is not very good: it's as though we have to jump ahead through the whole book in order to figure out whether or not to apply this rule. However, it's not as bad as it seems, because we're going to follow the following principle: whenever we learn about something that makes Rule Disj-3 apply, we'll say so! That is, we'll put it into Rule Disj-3. If we need to see if Rule Disj-3 applies in some particular case, and that case is not yet listed in Rule Disj-3, then that means that the rule does not apply. At this point, we only have seen one case that makes Rule Disj-3 apply, and that's the case where **na** or **ná** is followed by the **j** that indicates 4 person.

By the way, you may have noticed that in order to figure out why Rule Disj-1 doesn't apply when Rule Disj-3 applies, we had to look at the word as it's actually spelled and pronounced. For example, in the case of the word in (2) (which is diagrammed in (1)), we needed to know that the **j** started the syllable **ji**, which was not the verb-stem syllable. If we looked at the diagram in (1), and if we didn't happen to know about Rule Conj-1, we wouldn't find this syllable! In general, when we need to check the conditions for some rule in order to see whether to apply the rule or not, we will look at the actual spelling or pronunciation of the word to see if those conditions are satisfied, rather than looking at a diagram of how the word was built.

(Review question: what is the pre-stem syllable in the word in (2)? Answer: **ji**.)

Before moving on to the next topic of this chapter, here is something you might want to know about. In a word like **nijiné**, some people pronounce the first syllable practically without any vowel, as though they were saying **njiné**. In fact, you'll sometimes see this word spelled this way. We won't give another rule that produces this spelling, but you might want to keep in mind that this other spelling is sometimes used. This works the other way too: if you ever see a Navajo word written with an **n** followed directly by a consonant, you can always spell it **ni** instead. In our studies here, we'll use the **ni** spelling throughout, but keep in mind that the spelling with the **i** left out is pretty common in print.

The second new prefix we want to learn about in this chapter is the prefix that we've already mentioned back in Chapter 2, the prefix called the "distributive plural", which has the shape **da**. The basic use of this prefix is easy to state. If the subject of the verb is a group of three or more persons or things, then the **da** prefix is put into the verb in addition to the appropriate duoplural subject prefix. So, for example, if we want to say "we're playing", where "we" means a group of three or more (including the speaker), we'll use the 1dpl I mode subject prefix **iid**, but we'll also put the distributive plural **da** prefix into the verb. Remember, though, that this plural prefix has its own special position in the verb - see the chart in Chapter 2(6).

Oh, by the way: the distributive plural prefix is the same for all modes: in any mode, if the subject is a group of three or more persons or things, the same **da** prefix is put into the verb.

Again working with the verb base that means "play", we see that any distributive plural I mode form of this verb will be built like this:

(3) outer   distributive   subject   verb
      prefix   plural   prefix   stem

        na   -   da   -   (whatever) - né

where the "whatever" will be one of the duoplural subject prefixes (which, for the regular I mode, is going to end up being **iid**, **oh**, or zero.)

And, while we're thinking of it, if the subject is 4 person, the distributive plural form will be built like this:

(4) outer   distributive object subject verb
      prefix   plural   prefix prefix   stem

        na   -   da   -   j   - (zero) - né

Before looking at the actual forms, we've got to reveal a secret: in order to get the right forms with **da** in them, we'll already need to expand Rule Disj-3. What we need to do is add a second circumstance that makes this rule apply:

Add to Rule Disj-3: (...the **na** or **ná** is immediately followed by :)

(b)   the distributive plural prefix **da**.

The idea of this addition is that the change of **na** to **ni** (and of **ná** to **ní**) happens if it is followed either by the **j** (in object position) that means 4 person subject or by the distributive plural prefix **da**.

With this addition, we've learned all the rules we need. If we apply these rules correctly, the forms will come out exactly right. You might want to try this without looking at the forms given below. Here is one thing to remember: we mentioned in Chapter 2 that the distributive plural prefix **da** is a disjunct prefix. This means that all the rules that we've studied that can apply to disjunct prefixes can apply to **da** (if the conditions for the rule are satisfied, of course!) Don't forget to take this into consideration when you try to form verbs with **da**.

What are the actual forms? Here they are:

(5)	1	nideii'né	("we're playing")	(three
	2	nidaohné	("you're playing")	or
	3	nidaané	("they're playing")	more
	4	nidajiné	("they're playing")	people)

You should make sure you understand how each of these words is built. Rule Disj-3 applies to all of them to change **na** to **ni** (the **na** is followed directly by the distributive plural prefix **da**.) Rule Disj-2 applies to create the vowel **eii** in the distributive 1dpl form exactly the same way that it applied in the case of the non-distributive 1dpl form in Chapter 4. Rule Disj-1 applies only to the 3 person form (can you see why?) Rule Conj-1 supplies the **i** vowel that follows the **j** in the 4 form. Rule Subj-1 applies d-effect to the first consonant of the verb stem in the 1dpl form.

We have now worked out the complete I mode of the verb base that means "play". Here is a chart showing all the I mode forms of this verb. You should study the way this chart is laid out, because as we study more verbs and more modes, we will lay out the forms in the same way.

(6)	sg	dpl	distr dpl
1	naashné	neii'né	nideii'né
2	naniné	naohné	nidaohné
3	naané		nidaané
4	nijiné		nidajiné

Incidentally, we can now answer the question: "How do we know that the lexical prefix **na-** found in the verb base meaning "play" is an outer (disjunct) prefix, and not an inner (conjunct) prefix?"

The best answer has to do with position. If you go back to Chapter 2 and look at the diagram in Chapter 2(6), you'll see that an outer prefix precedes the distributive plural, whereas an inner prefix appears in between the distributive plural and the verb stem. This means that, if you already know Navajo, you can tell if a lexical prefix is outer or inner by building a verb form that has the distributive plural **da** in it and seeing where the prefix goes. If you do that and you find that the prefix goes in the position shown by the arrows in the following diagram:

⇓

..... **da**   (other stuff) verb-stem

⇑

then the prefix is outer. But if the prefix goes in the position shown here:

⇓

da .....   verb-stem

⇑

then the prefix is inner.

(If you don't know Navajo, then you just have to learn whether a prefix is outer or inner, and make sure that it, and all other prefixes, are put into the right place.)

In the case of "play", the forms in (5) and (6) show that the **na-** prefix is outer, since this prefix comes in front of **da**. (Of course, part of the trick is to recognize that the **ni-** that you see in the forms in (5) and (6) is the same prefix as the **na-** or **naa-** in other forms of this verb!)

Another way to tell the difference also involves order. If you've got a verb form with a 4 person subject, an outer prefix will precede the **j** but an inner prefix will follow the **j**, since the **j** is placed into the object prefix position. The 4 person forms that we've seen in this chapter all show the **na-** prefix (changed into **ni-** by Rule Disj-3) appearing in front of the **j**, so again we see that we have an outer prefix.

Finally, we repeat that disjunct prefixes end in vowels and conjunct prefixes end in consonants, so if we're looking at an analytical diagram of some sort that shows the prefixes in a verb base or a verb form, we can tell the difference between outer (disjunct) and inner (conjunct) prefixes by the way they end.

Another kind of thinking that you should start getting used to has to do with "unpacking" verbs that you find in print or that you hear being used. Suppose you're looking at an actual Navajo verb and you're trying to understand it. It will help a lot if you can recognize the pieces inside it. So, suppose you see a **da** somewhere to the left of the verb stem - is that **da** necessarily the distributive plural prefix? Well, it turns out that there are some other prefixes that sometimes show up as **da**, but most of the time, the **da** you'll see is the distributive plural prefix. Also, don't forget that you may see **de** instead, but only if it is followed by **i** or **ii**. This too will usually turn out to be the distributive plural. However, if you see a **d** followed by something other than **a** or **e**, for example **di** or **dii**, or if you see **de** but there isn't any **i** or **ii** after it, then this won't be the distributive plural prefix. (We'll learn later what this is.)

Or, suppose you see a **j** somewhere in a Navajo verb to the left of the verb stem. Is that **j** the 4 person prefix? Again, it turns out that there are some other prefixes that involve a **j** sound, but most of the time, a **j** you see will be the 4 person prefix.

CHAPTER 6

CLASSIFIERS,
AND INTRODUCTION TO TRANSITIVE VERBS

In the previous chapters, we have occasionally mentioned a mysterious piece, called a classifier, that occurs in some Navajo verbs. (You might want to look at the diagram in Chapter 2(6) to see where this piece goes.) In this chapter, we want to study these classifiers. We will need to learn a few rules that will give us the correct forms of all verbs that have classifiers in them.

In doing this study, we will find it convenient to allow ourselves to use some transitive verbs as examples. In order to do this, we will have to examine at least some cases of how object prefixes work. For now, we will only consider the case where the object of a transitive verb is third person; the full set of objects will be studied in Chapters 11 and 12.

In this chapter, we will be looking at the regular I mode conjugation of a number of verbs. But the facts that we will be studying will actually be more general: they will apply to any conjugation of any mode. We will formulate our rules in a general way, so that they apply correctly to any verb form in Navajo.

Here is an idea that may help as we go along. The regular I mode subject prefixes that we listed in Chapter 4(2) are, in some sense, the "basic" subject prefixes. The subject prefixes of other conjugations and other modes often seem to have the regular I mode subject prefixes inside of them. For this reason, the phonological adjustments that we'll be learning in this chapter, using regular I mode forms as examples, arc adjustments that we'll see happening over and over again in all sorts of conjugation patterns in all the modes of the Navajo language.

Now, what exactly is a classifier?

If you've studied a language like Spanish, you might remember that Spanish verbs come in three conjugations, which differ from one another according to the vowel that the suffixes start with. The Navajo classifiers are really conjugation patterns like this, with the difference that it isn't a vowel that's involved, it's a consonant. Also, Navajo has four conjugation classes, which we'll describe by saying that there are four possible classifiers.

In Chapters 4 and 5 we saw the regular I mode conjugation of the verb base that means "play". We said that for this verb base there was no classifier (that is, the position for the classifier, shown in the diagram in Chapter 2(6), was empty.) Many Navajo verbs are like "play" - they don't have any piece in the classifier position. Rather than saying that these verb bases don't have a classifier, we're going to say that they have a *zero classifier*. The zero classifier case corresponds to one of the conjugation classes for Navajo. The other three conjugation classes will correspond to three classifiers, called the *barred-l classifier*, the *plain-l classifier*, and the *d classifier*. What we have to do is examine what each of these classifiers actually is.

Let's look first at the d classifier case. To say that a verb base has a d classifier is going to mean that d-effect has applied to the first consonant of the verb stem. We could imagine that the position labelled "cl" in Chapter 2(6) is occupied by a **d**, and that this **d** then has the effect of causing the first consonant of the verb stem to undergo d-effect. Now, what does this do to the actual forms of such a verb? Well, the first consonant of the verb stem will have to be one of the consonants shown in the right hand column of Chapter 4(9). But are there any other ways in which a d classifier verb differs from a zero classifier verb? No! We don't need any special new rules. The only thing we should say is that the **d** of the 1dpl prefix **iid** will simply disappear, since Rule Subj-1 says that this **d** causes d-effect on the first consonant of the verb stem, and, if you check the chart in Chapter 4(9), you'll see that d-effect doesn't change any consonant that has resulted if d-effect has already been applied.

But wait! The combinations **'w, 'y, 'm** and **'n** that are in the right hand column of Chapter 4(9) aren't anywhere in the left column of that chart, so what does d effect do to them? The answer is still: nothing. In other words, when the 1dpl prefix **iid** precedes any one of these combinations, the **d** of **iid** still just disappears.

As an example of a verb base with a d classifier, let's look at the verb base that means "crawl around". In the I mode, the stem is **-'na'** . If we want, we can say that the stem is really **-na'**, that there was a **d** in the classifier position, and that this d classifier caused d-effect to apply to the first consonant in this stem, changing the **n** into **'n**. In other words, we could imagine that I mode forms of this verb are built like this:

(1)   (other prefixes)   cl   verb stem

     (whatever)   -   d   -   na'
                 \   /   (d-effect)
             'na'

Now, this verb base also has an outer prefix, which happens to be the same **na-** prefix that we saw in the "play" verb base. So, if we want to build, for example, an I mode form of this verb that doesn't happen to have the distributive plural prefix, and where the subject is not 4 person, we'll build the verb like this:

(2)   outer   subject   verb
    prefix   prefix   stem

    na   -   (whatever) - 'na'

In (2), "whatever" will be any of the five prefixes listed in Chapter 4(2). In diagram (2), we've assumed that the process shown in (1) has already happened: the d classifier has already caused d-effect on the first consonant of the verb stem.

If the subject is 4 person, we'll build the verb this way:

(3)   outer   object   subject   verb
      prefix   prefix   prefix   stem

      na -   j   -   'na'

Question: why isn't there anything in the subject prefix position in (3)? Answer: because, when the **j** prefix is used (in the object position) to indicate a 4 person subject, the subject prefix position has to be filled with the 3 person subject prefix. In the regular I mode, the 3 person subject prefix is zero.

If we want to build distributive plural forms of this verb, we'll do this, if the subject is not 4 person:

(4)   outer   distributive   subject   verb
      prefix   plural   prefix   stem

      na   -   da - (whatever) - 'na'

In (4), "whatever" is any of the three duoplural subject prefixes in the chart in Chapter 4(2).

Finally, if we want a distributive plural, 4 person subject verb form, we'll build it like this:

(5)   outer   distributive   object subject   verb
      prefix   plural   prefix prefix   stem

      na - da - j   -   'na'

If we apply the rules that we've learned, we'll automatically get the correct forms. In fact, if you look at the structures in (2), (3), (4), and (5), you'll see that if we build forms with this verb base, we get the same structures as we got in Chapters 4 and 5 when we built forms using the "play" verb base: the only thing that is different is the verb stem. You might want to try writing down all the I mode forms of this verb base right now, before you read ahead. But if you want to see the actual forms, here they are:

(6)	sg	dpl	distr dpl
1	naash'na'	neii'na'	nideii'na'
2	nani'na'	naoh'na'	nidaoh'na'
3	naa'na'		nidaa'na'
4	niji'na'		nidaji'na'

You should compare these forms with the forms for "play" in Chapter 5(6). You will see that the verb forms shown here in (6) are exactly parallel to the verb forms of "play" - only the verb stem is different. The rules we've already learned will apply in exactly the same way for this verb base as they did for the "play" verb base in Chapters 4 and 5. (And, we can see that the **d** of the 1dpl subject prefix **iid** has just disappeared in front of **'n** in the forms **neii'na'** and **nideii'na'** in (6).)

Since the forms in (6) are built exactly the same way as the I mode forms for a verb base with a zero classifier, we might ask the question: does it make any sense to say that there is such a thing as a d classifier at all? That is, if there is no difference between the conjugation of a zero classifier verb and the conjugation of a d classifier verb, why talk about d classifiers? The answer is: if we were only looking at conjugations in the I mode, then it would indeed make no sense to talk about d classifiers. We will see, however, that in the P mode, there is an important difference between the way zero classifier verbs and d classifier verbs are conjugated. Still, we should keep in mind that if we are only looking at the I mode forms of a verb (or actually, any mode other than the P mode), then we cannot tell whether that verb has a zero classifier or a d classifier, at least if the verb stem syllable begins with the sort of consonant that can result from d-effect. In the case of the verb "play", we know that the classifier is really zero, since the d-effect cannot produce the consonant **n** which begins the verb-stem syllable **né** (a plain **n** is not found anywhere in the right hand column of Chapter 4(9).) In the case of "crawl around", we can guess that we might have a d classifier, since the verb stem syllable begins with the combination **'n**, which really seems like two consonants and which therefore suggests that a d classifier has operated on an ordinary **n**. However, suppose we run into an I mode form like **naakai**, which means "they are going around". The verb stem begins with the consonant **k**, which is one of those consonants that isn't changed by d-effect (see Chapter 4(9).) Is this a zero classifier verb, or is this a d classifier verb, where the d classifier applied d-effect to a **k**, which remained **k**? If we stay in the I mode, we have no way of telling! As it happens, this particular verb is really a d classifier verb, but this is something that we will only be able to tell by looking at the P mode forms for it.

We can now move on to our study of the remaining two classifiers, which, as you may remember, we called the barred-l classifier and the plain-l classifier.

The general idea is this: just as we could say that the d classifier conjugation results from an actual **d** in the cl position in the verb (where this **d** then causes d-effect), we can say that the barred-l classifier conjugation results from a barred l, that is, **ł**, which is actually present in the verb in the cl position. And similarly, the plain-l classifier conjugation results from a plain l, that is, just **l**, in the cl position. We will now look at some examples of verb forms with these classifiers. We'll see that in order to understand these forms, we will have to learn a few new phonological rules.

As an example of a verb with a barred-l classifier, we're going to take the verb base that means "cut it out" (that is, "remove it by cutting"). Now, this verb is transitive, so we will also have to deal with object prefixes. However, to keep things simple for now, we'll only look at the case that the object is 3 person. The way that Navajo verbs indicate 3 person objects is pretty easy, but there's one little twist. The twist is, it depends on what the subject is. If the subject is 1 person, 2 person, or 4 person, then a 3 person object is indicated by *zero*, that is, there is actually no object prefix in the verb at all. However, if the subject is 3 person (that is, "real" 3 person, not 4 person), then an object prefix is indeed required in the verb to indicate a 3 person object. This object prefix is simply the consonant **y**. Let us formulate this as a rule. This rule is different from any of the rules that we've seen so far, because it talks about the way the structure of a verb is built. Let's put it into a fourth group of rules, a group that we will call *structure rules*. We'll number these rules like this: "Rule Str-(number)". The rule we need here is:

Rule Str-1: If the subject of a transitive verb is 1, 2, or 4 person, then a 3 person object is represented by zero. If the subject of a transitive verb is 3 person, then a 3 person object is represented by the object prefix **y**.

(If you look this rule up in the Appendix, you will see that we have only given part of the rule here. This part is enough for now, but we will amend this rule several times in later chapters to include some other facts.)

The effect of this is that if we compare the conjugation of an intransitive verb with the conjugation of a transitive verb, where the forms of the transitive verb involve a 3 person object, then the conjugations will look the same, except for when the subject is 3 person. For those forms, the transitive verbs will have a **y** in them in the object position which the intransitive forms won't have.

Well, we cannot tell a lie. There are some purely phonological adjustments that involve this **y** that sometimes have to be made, so you might not actually see the letter **y**. What you might see just as often, or maybe even more often, is an **i**. The reason is that a phonological rule might come along and do something like change the **y** into an **i**. We can describe the most common situation when this happens by writing a new rule for conjunct prefixes:

Rule Conj-2: If a conjunct prefix **y** is followed directly by a consonant and preceded by the vowel at the end of a disjunct prefix, then change the **y** to an **i**.

We have written this rule so that it talks about a "conjunct prefix **y**" rather than the 3 person object prefix. Why? Because later on we'll run into other conjunct prefixes that just consist of a **y**, and these other prefixes also turn into **i**'s under the same circumstances as the 3 person object prefix.

44

One way of thinking about what this rule does is to say that if a vowel to the left of the **y** squeezes the **y** against a consonant on its right, the **y** changes into an **i** under the pressure. We'll see this rule at work as soon as we look at the Navajo verb base that means "cut it out" (remember, we're looking at this verb base because it has a barred-l classifier.)

But wait: what about Rule Conj-1? If we apply that rule first, then the **y** won't be followed by a consonant any more, and Rule Conj-2 won't apply. This would mess everything up! To prevent this from happening, we'll put a little note into Rule Conj-1 that says if the conjunct prefix is just **y**, we should ignore Rule Conj-1 and go to Rule Conj-2 instead. That way we'll do the right thing.

Now let's get back to the verb base that means "cut it out". In the I mode, the verb stem for this verb base is **-géésh**. This verb base also has an outer prefix, which is **ha-**. As we just said, this verb base has a barred-l classifier, which means that we are going to analyze it as though there were a ł right in front of the verb stem. The actual I mode forms of this verb, assuming a 3 person object, are these:

(7)	sg	dpl	distr dpl
1	haashgéésh	haiilgéésh	hadeiilgéésh
2	haniłgéésh	haołgéésh	hadaołgéésh
3		haiłgéésh	hadeiłgéésh
4		hajiłgéésh	hadajiłgéésh

First, before we examine what's going on with the classifier, let's look at the part of these words that have to do with the other prefixes. Most of what's happening here is the same as what we've already seen with other verbs. Rule Disj-1 applies to lengthen the vowel of **ha-** to **haa-** in the 1sg form. Rule Disj-2 applies to the distributive 1dpl form to create the diphthong **eii**, but in the nondistributive 1dpl form we get **aii** (because of the **h** that precedes this combination - you might want to reread Rule Disj-2 to remind yourself that the consonants **g**, **gh**, **h**, **k**, and **k'** prevent the change from **aii** to **eii**.) Rule Conj-1 inserts an **i** right after the **j** in the 4 person forms.

The 3 person forms are new to us, because this verb is transitive, so the 3 person subject requires the 3 person object prefix **y**. The nondistributive 3 person form is built this way:

(8)	outer prefix	object prefix	subject prefix	cl	verb stem
	ha -	y -	(zero) -	ł -	géésh

The new Rule Conj-2 that we just learned applies to this structure, since the 3 person **y** is followed directly by a consonant (in this case, the classifier **ł**) and preceded by the vowel **a** (from the disjunct prefix **ha**.) What the rule does is change the **y** to an **i**, which gives us directly the correct form **haiłgéésh**.

(Why didn't Rule Disj-1 apply to this word? Because the condition that the syllable **ha-** has to be the pre-stem syllable, that is, that the syllable immediately following the syllable **ha-** is the verb-stem syllable, is a condition that has to be true of the actual word as it's pronounced and spelled. Rule Conj-2 insures that the syllable following **ha-** is not the verb-stem syllable. In fact, there ends up being no syllable "ha" at all - the actual first syllable of the word is **hai**. (Another way to say it is that **ha** is now followed by a vowel, namely **i**.)

Let's compare this to the distributive 3 person form, which is built this way:

(9) outer   distributive object   subject   cl   verb
     prefix   plural   prefix   prefix   stem

     ha - da - y - (zero) - ł - géésh

In this form, none of our rules do anything to change **ha** into anything else. Since the object prefix **y** is preceded by a vowel (the **a** of **da**) and followed by a consonant (the classifier **ł**), Rule Conj-2 applies, changing the **y** to an **i**, which would give us "hadaiłgéésh". But now, Rule Disj-2 applies (since the **a** of the disjunct prefix **da** is followed by the vowel **i**). It changes the **ai** into **ei**, giving us the actual form: **hadeiłgéésh**.

(Why didn't **ai** change into **ei** in the form **haiłgéésh** (built in (8))? Because the **h** that precedes the **ai** in this word prevents the change from happening.)

Now, for these 3 person forms, we've just seen that we get exactly the right results with our rules if we assume that there is actually an **ł** in the verb in the position marked "cl" in Chapter 2(6). But what about the other forms?

First, what about the forms where the subject is 4 person? The nondistributive form is build like this:

(10) outer   object   subject   cl   verb
      prefix   prefix   prefix   stem

      ha - j - (zero) - ł - géésh

(Recall that the 4 person prefix **j** is put into the verb in the object prefix position. Also, since the subject is 4 person, Rule Str-1 says that the 3 person object is represented by zero, that is, there is no special extra prefix put in for the real object.) You should try all our rules so far and convince yourself that only Rule Conj-1 actually does anything here, inserting an **i** after the **j** and creating the correct form **hajiłgéésh**. The distributive plural 4 person form is equally straightforward, and requires no new rules or explanation.

Next, what about the form with a 2sg subject? This form is built like this:

(11) outer   subject   cl   verb
      prefix   prefix   stem

      ha - ni - ł - géésh

(Why isn't there an object prefix in this form? Answer: since the subject is 2 person, Rule Str-1 says that a 3 person object is represented by zero.) Check through our rules so far, and you'll see that no rules change anything here, so the actual word is **haniłgéésh**.

Now, we've seen that the 3 person, 4 person, and 2sg person forms can be built correctly if we just assume that the position marked "cl" in Chapter 2(6) is filled with a ł and if we use the rules that we've already learned. But if we look at the remaining forms in (7), we see that there are some other things happening that we have to study.

The issue is this: if we go back and look at the I mode subject prefixes in Chapter 4(2), three of them, namely 1sg **sh**, 1dpl **iid**, and 2dpl **oh**, end in consonants. When one of these prefixes is used, and if the classifier is ł, we end up with a situation where there are three consonants in a row. The first consonant is the consonant at the end of the subject prefix. The second one is the classifier ł. Finally, the third one is the first consonant of the verb stem (recall that Navajo verb stems always begin with consonants.) In general, Navajo phonology tries to avoid having three consonants in a row, so we can expect something to happen in these cases. But rather than give some rules right now, what we'll do instead is move on to an example of a plain-l classifier verb. The reason we're doing this is that some of the same kinds of things happen with plain-l classifier verbs as with barred-l classifier verbs. We'll find that it's easier if we come up with an answer that deals with both together.

As an example of a verb base that has a plain-l classifier, we'll take the verb base that means "work". In the I mode, the stem of this verb base is **-nish**. In addition to this stem, this verb base also has the outer prefix **na-** that we're now familiar with. This verb is intransitive, so the 3 person subject forms have no special object prefixes in them. The I mode forms of this verb base are:

(12)   sg   dpl   distr dpl

1   naashnish   neiilnish   nideiilnish
2   nanilnish   naołnish   nidaołnish
3   naalnish   nidaalnish
4   nijilnish   nidajilnish

If we look carefully at these forms, we see, first of all, that the **na-** prefix behaves exactly the same in this verb base as it did in the verb bases that mean "play" and "crawl around" that we've already studied. Also, if we look at the 3 person, 4 person, and 2sg person forms, we see that we get exactly the right form if we just assume that there is a plain l in the "cl" position of the verb. For example, the distributive 3 form is built this way:

(13)　outer　distributive　subject　cl　verb
　　　　　prefix　plural　　　prefix　　　stem

　　　　　na　-　da　-　(zero) - l - nish

Rule Disj-1 lengthens the vowel of the distributive plural prefix (since the **da** is followed by a consonant, namely the classifier **l**, and the next syllable is the verb stem syllable so **da** is the pre-stem syllable), and Rule Disj-3 changes **na-** to **ni-** (since the **na** is directly followed by the distributive plural prefix.) No other rules apply, and we end up with the correct form, which is **nidaalnish**.

So again, it's those forms where the subject prefix ends in a consonant that we have to say something about. We will handle each of the three cases where the subject prefix ends in a consonant with a separate rule. First, let's deal with 1sg subjects.

Rule Subj-2: The barred-l classifier (that is, the ł in the "cl" position) and the plain-l classifier (that is, the **l** in the "cl" position) disappear when sandwiched in between any subject prefix that ends in **sh** or **s** and the first consonant of the verb stem.

We can think of Rule Subj-2 as the "sandwich rule". Note that the barred-l and the plain-l classifiers work the same with respect to this rule: they both drop out when sandwiched in between a subject prefix that ends in **sh** or **s** and the verb stem. The 1sg forms in (7) and (12) can now be derived correctly. For example, the 1sg form in (7) is built like this:

(14)　outer　subject　cl　verb
　　　　　prefix　prefix　　　stem

　　　　　ha　-　sh　-　ł　-　géésh

(Why isn't there an object prefix in this verb to represent the 3 person object? Answer: Rule Str-1 says that if the subject is 1 person, then a 3 person object is represented by zero.) Rule Subj-2 (the sandwich rule) applies, removing the ł from this form (and Rule Disj-1 also applies to the outer (disjunct) prefix in this word), giving the correct final result: **haashgéésh**.

Note the way that Rule Subj-2 is formulated. It will apply not only to all cases of regular I mode forms with 1sg subjects, but also to any verb form in any mode where there is any subject prefix that ends in **sh** or **s**. Whenever a barred-l or plain-l classifier is sandwiched in between such a subject prefix and the verb stem, the classifier will drop out. Right now, the only subject prefix like this that we know about is the 1sg I mode subject prefix **sh**, but we will learn about others later on. Every time we meet a new prefix that could trigger Rule Subj-2, we'll mention this fact.

If we think about the effect of this sandwich rule, it seems that if we are looking at an I mode form with 1sg subject, we cannot tell just by looking at the word what the classifier is! (Except, of course, that in some cases we can rule out the d classifier, if the stem-initial consonant cannot be the result of d-effect.) For example, if we just saw the word **naashnish**, meaning "I'm working", we would have no way of knowing that the verb base meaning "work" has a plain-1 classifier. To actually see the classifier, we'd need to look at another form of the verb, where the classifier wouldn't be sandwiched in between noisy consonants, such as, for example the 2sg form **nanilnish**, where we clearly see the plain l in front of the verb stem.

Let's move on now to the verb forms that have the 1dpl subject prefix. The rule we need is this:

Rule Subj-3: The **d** at the end of any 1dpl subject prefix disappears when immediately followed by a plain-l classifier. It also disappears when immediately followed by a barred-l classifier, except that in this case, the barred-l, that is, the **ł**, changes to a plain **l**.

Note, first, that Rule Subj-1, which we learned in Chapter 4, does not apply to the case of a barred-l or plain-l classifier, since these classifiers separate the d of **iid** from the first consonant of the verb stem. In these cases, we use Rule Subj-3 instead. This rule gets rid of the d of **iid**, and changes ł to l. The effect of this change is that the end result of Rule Subj-3, as far as the classifier is concerned, is the same: there'll be a plain l in front of the verb stem. We see this in the 1dpl forms **haiilgéésh** and **neiilnish**: Both verbs have a plain l in front of the verb stem. This means that if we see a plain l in front of a verb stem in a 1dpl form, we know that the classifier is ł or l, but we cannot tell which one. To tell the difference, we'd have to look at some other form of the same verb base.

The last consonant-final subject prefix we have to look at is the 2dpl prefix. The rule we need is:

Rule Subj-4: If a 2dpl subject prefix ends in **h**, this **h** disappears when immediately followed by the barred-l classifier (**ł**). It also disappears when immediately followed by the plain-l classifier (**l**), but the **l** changes into a **ł** in this case.

Again, the end result of Rule Subj-4 is the same whether we start out with a barred-l or a plain-l classifier: the **h** of **oh** disappears, and there's a ł in front of the verb stem. We see this in the 2dpl forms **haołgéésh** and **naołnish**: for both verbs, the h of **oh** has dropped out, and there's a ł in front of the verb stem. This means that if we are looking at a 2dpl verb form and we see ł in front of the verb stem, we know that the classifier is barred-l or plain-l, but we cannot tell which one. To tell which one, we'd have to look at some other form of the same verb base.

(Also: don't forget that some people, especially from the eastern part of Navajoland, pronounce these words **haałgéésh** and **naałnish** (we talked about this a little in Chapter 4.) You may see these spellings in print as well.)

Rules Subj-1, Subj-2, Subj-3, and Subj-4 are all the rules we need for all forms of the subject prefix and the classifier for all conjugations of all modes in Navajo, with the exception of a few details. We will study these details in Chapter 7 and Chapter 13.

Before finishing this chapter, we should say something about the concept "verb base". You may have noticed that this concept has changed again! Originally, we said that a Navajo verb base consisted of a verb stem possibly with one or more lexical prefixes. Then, in Chapter 3, we learned that stems actually come in stem-sets, where different forms of the stem are used for different modes. So, we realized that a verb base has to consist of a stem-set (one stem per mode), together with any lexical prefixes. But now, in this chapter, we've been talking about classifiers, and although we didn't say it out loud, you may have noticed that any particular verb base has one particular classifier (one of the four possible ones.) Also, some verb bases are transitive and some are intransitive, and we have to say which one. So, a verb base really consists of four things: (1) a stem-set; (2) a classifier; (3) possibly a lexical prefix, or several lexical prefixes; and (4) the transitivity (that is, a statement about whether the verb base is transitive or intransitive.) For example, to give the verb base that means "play", we have to say four things. First, the stem-set is the one we saw in Chapter 3(5). Second, the classifier is zero. Third, there is an outer prefix **na-**. And fourth, this verb base is intransitive. We can put all this information together in the form of a chart, like this:

(15)

Stem-set	Classifier: zero
I: **né**	
P: **ne'**	Lexical prefixes: **na** (outer)
F: **neeł**	
R: **neeh**	Transitivity: intransitive
O: **ne'**	

It is convenient to present all the information about a verb base in this way, so from now on, we will give new verb bases using charts like this. For practice, let's write up the verb base that means "cut it out" in this format. We get:

(16)

Stem-set	Classifier: zero
I: **géésh**	
P: **gizh**	Lexical prefixes: **ha** (outer)
F: **gish**	
R: **gish**	Transitivity: transitive
O: **géésh**	

(This chart shows the complete stem-set for this verb base, but, of course, we've only been looking at I mode forms so far.)

This might be a convenient place to say something about the choice of classifier. In contemporary Navajo, each verb base has one particular classifier, and the classifier that it has is something that you simply have to learn as part of the verb base. Historically, it may be the case that the classifiers had particular meanings. As a kind of left-over of this, there is a very rough correlation between the classifier of a verb base and whether that verb base is transitive or intransitive. Approximately, verb bases with barred-l classifiers tend to be transitive, and verb bases with plain-l and d classifiers tend to be intransitive. Zero classifiers are found with transitive as well as intransitive verb bases.

Let's finish this chapter by saying something about our rules. As we continue with our studies, there are going to be more and more rules. Now, to figure our the correct form of any verb, we need to see which rules apply, and then we need to apply them. This seems to mean that we'll have to sit and figure out for each rule whether that rule applies or not. If we have a lot of rules, this could be a pretty big job!

One way we are making it easier on ourselves is by dividing the rules into groups. For example, we have a group of rules that have to do with disjunct prefixes. Now, suppose we are looking at a verb that doesn't have any disjunct prefixes. We'll simply ignore all the rules about disjunct prefixes (the rules numbered Disj-(number)) - they certainly couldn't apply. This will save us a lot of time. Similarly, if we are working with a form where there are no conjunct prefixes, we can ignore all the rules numbered Conj-(number). However, we'll always have to look at the Subj (subject) and the Str (structure) rules, since every verb form has a subject, and since the structure rules are general and apply to all forms, potentially. But if we learn to think about the conditions of these rules, we'll be able to tell very quickly whether they apply or not, and our analysis will actually go quite quickly.

CHAPTER 7

PREFIXLESS VERBS,
AND MORE ABOUT SUBJECT PREFIXES

Let's stop a moment and take stock of where we have come. We have learned how to conjugate Navajo verbs in the regular I mode, for any of the four classifiers, at least in the case of certain verb bases that have one outer prefix and no inner prefixes. (We can conjugate intransitive verbs this way, and also transitive verbs, provided that the object is 3 person.) To expand our knowledge we need to: (a) learn how verbs are conjugated in other modes; (b) learn about other kinds of verb bases (besides those that have an outer prefix and no inner prefix); (c) learn about objects of transitive verbs that are not 3 person; and (d) learn about any other phonological adjustments that are found in Navajo verbs but that we have not yet seen.

In this chapter, we are going to do some of task (b) and some of task (d). As far as task (b) is concerned, we will look at verb bases that have no lexical prefixes at all. And as to task (d), we will look at a few new phonological adjustments that affect subject prefixes.

First, suppose we try to create the I mode forms for a verb base that has no lexical prefixes at all. For example, the verb base that means "cry" has no lexical prefixes. Using the format for writing up verb bases that we introduced at the end of Chapter 6, we can represent this verb base as follows:

(1)

Stem-set		Classifier: zero
I:	**cha**	
P:	**cha**	Lexical prefixes: (none)
F:	**chah**	
R:	**chah**	Transitivity: intransitive
O:	**cha**	

Let's look for a moment at the simplest I mode forms of this verb base, the ones that have neither the distributive plural nor the 4 person prefix. These forms will be built this way:

(2) subject   verb
        prefix   stem

    (whatever) - cha

where the subject prefix (the "whatever" in (2) is chosen from the chart in Chapter 4(2). We won't have any problem if the subject we choose is 2sg, which has the prefix **ni**. In this case, the verb form just comes out as **nicha**, which is what we'd expect. But with the four other subject prefixes, we have to deal with some issues.

First of all, if we want to use either the 1sg or the 3 subject prefix, we'd build the verb form this way:

(3)   subject   verb
        prefix   stem

$$\left\{ \begin{array}{c} \text{sh} \\ \text{(zero)} \end{array} \right\} - \quad \text{cha}$$

In either case, the result would be a verb where the first syllable of the verb is the verb stem syllable. (Note that the 1sg prefix **sh** doesn't have a vowel in it, so it doesn't contribute a syllable.) Now, except for a very few irregular forms, no Navajo verb form is allowed to have its first syllable be the verb stem syllable. So what happens when we try to build a word with the structures in (3)? Here's a rule that takes care of exactly this situation:

<u>Rule Str-2</u>: If a verb form has no syllable preceding the verb-stem syllable (either from the subject prefix or from any other prefix), then put in the prefix **yi**. (This prefix is sometimes called the *peg element* in the literature.) Note that this prefix has <u>no meaning</u>: it is simply put in so that the verb-stem syllable has a syllable preceding it.

We can call this rule the "peg rule", since it inserts the peg element into some verbs.

One way to think of the peg rule is as follows: except for a very few irregular forms, every Navajo verb has to have a pre-stem syllable. If the verb structure doesn't provide one, then the peg rule comes in and inserts the peg element. The peg element is then the pre-stem syllable.

How does the peg rule work? In the case of the 1sg and 3 subject I mode forms of "cry", the peg rule gives us the words **yishcha** for "I'm crying" and **yicha** for "he/she's crying" (don't forget that the 3 person I mode subject prefix is zero, so the peg element is the only prefix in the verb form that means "he/she's crying".)

Let's move on now to the 1dpl and 2dpl subject prefixes. If we want to use these prefixes with the verb base that means "cry", we run into a different problem. To see what happens, let's look at the structure we'd be building:

(4)   subject   verb
        prefix   stem

$\begin{Bmatrix} \text{iid} \\ \text{oh} \end{Bmatrix}$ -   cha

Now, for these forms, we don't have to worry about syllables, since the subject prefix furnishes a syllable that precedes the verb stem. However, something else is going to bother us here. You may remember from our brief introduction in Chapter 1 that no Navajo word begins with a vowel. But the 1dpl and 2dpl prefixes begin with vowels! If we formed the words directly as shown in (4), without any further adjustment, we'd end up with words beginning with vowels....

But be careful: When we say that a word cannot begin with a vowel, we are talking about pronunciation, not spelling! There are many Navajo words that are spelled starting with a vowel, like the word for "medicine": **azee'**. But these words actually are pronounced starting with the consonant that is usually spelled ' (the glottal stop). Now, we could write the prefix **iid** or the prefix **oh** in front of a verb stem, and come out with something that looks like a legal Navajo word. But if we did this, we would have done something else without knowing it: we would have put a glottal stop at the beginning of the word! This might not seem like much, but it turns out that glottal stops in Navajo are very important. In fact, we'll see later (in Chapters 11 and 12) that there is an object prefix which is just a glottal stop! If we put in a glottal stop this way in a verb, it would be tantamount to adding in an extra prefix that might change the meaning, or create an impossible meaning. So, we really are faced with a problem when we want to begin a Navajo verb with the 1dpl or 2dpl I mode subject prefixes. The way the problem is handled is as follows:

Rule Str-3: If a verb form is stranded with an initial vowel, prefix **y** to the verb if the vowel is **i** or **ii**, and prefix **w** to the verb if the vowel is **o** or **oo**.

With this rule (and also Rule Subj-1), the form meaning "We (two) are crying" comes out **yiicha**, and the form meaning "you (two) are crying" comes out **wohcha**. These are the correct forms.

Incidentally, you may notice from time to time that there is often more than one way to describe what's going on in a verb. For example, the peg rule (Rule Str-2) tells us to prefix **yi** when we need a pre-stem syllable. But there are at least two other ways that we could have described what's going on. Firstly, we could have said that if we need that extra syllable, put in the special conjunct prefix **y**. Rule Conj-1 would then come along and put the **i** in. Or, secondly, we could have said that if we need that extra syllable, put in the prefix **i**. Rule Str-3 would then put a **y** in front of this **i**. Either of these other ways of describing the situation would have given the same result. It really doesn't matter how we say it. The thing that we need to learn, really, is that if there isn't a syllable in front of the verb-stem syllable, there's going to end up being a **yi** sitting there.

As it happens, the peg rule is going to have to be improved slightly. Our statement above is correct for the I mode, but we'll see later on that some special things happen in certain other modes. If you're curious, you can find a fuller statement of this rule in the Appendix.

Here is the complete I mode chart for "cry". You should make sure that you understand how these forms were made. The 4 person forms and the distributive plural forms are all completely normal. They follow the rules just as we've learned them in the previous chapters.

(5)

	sg	dpl	distr dpl
1	yishcha	yiicha	deiicha
2	nicha	wohcha	daohcha
3		yicha	daacha
4		jicha	dajicha

The verb base meaning "cry" is intransitive. It will be interesting to compare the forms in (5) with the forms for a transitive verb base that doesn't have any lexical prefixes. One example of such a verb base is "boil it". Here it is:

(6)

Stem-set		Classifier: barred-l
I:	**béézh**	
P:	**béézh**	Lexical prefixes: (none)
F:	**bish**	
R:	**bish**	Transitivity: transitive
O:	**béézh**	

As in Chapter 6, we're only going to look at the forms of this verb where the object is 3 person. With this restriction, here is the complete I mode for this verb:

(7)

	sg	dpl	distr dpl
1	yishbéézh	yiilbéézh	deiilbéézh
2	niłbéézh	wołbéézh	daołbéézh
3		yiłbéézh	deiłbéézh
4		jiłbéézh	dajiłbéézh

Now, these forms are different from the forms in (6) for two reasons. The first reason is that the "boil it" verb base has the barred-l classifier, which means that Rule Subj 2, Rule Subj-3, and Rule Subj-4, which we studied in Chapter 6, affect the way the subject prefixes appear. You should compare the forms in (7) above with the forms in Chapter 6(7), and see that at least the subject prefixes here look the same as the subject prefixes in that other verb. For example, in the 1sg form **yishbéézh**, the **ł** classifier disappears, because it's sandwiched in between the 1sg subject prefix **sh** and the first consonant of the verb stem, which is **b** (Rule Subj-2.) In the forms that have the 1dpl prefix, which are **yiilbééézh** and **deiilbééézh**, the **ł** classifier has changed to **l**, and the **d** of **iid** has disappeared (Rule Subj-3.) In the forms that have the 2dpl prefix, which are **wołbéézh** and **daołbéézh**, the **h** of the prefix has disappeared (Rule Subj-4.) (Incidentally, the **y** at the beginning or **yiilbééézh** and the **w** at the beginning of **wołbéézh** are the result of Rule Str-3, which we just learned.)

However, besides this, this "boil it" verb base is transitive, whereas the "cry" base was intransitive. To see what this means, let's compare some forms.

First of all, look at these two forms:

(8)   yishcha   "I'm crying"
        yishbéézh "I'm boiling it"

In both of these forms, the initial syllable **yi** is the peg element. Why? Well, in the case of "cry", we've already seen how this works: the subject prefix is just **sh**, and there is no other prefix, so we need to provide a pre-stem syllable to precede the verb stem. Rule Str-2 (the peg rule) comes along and inserts the peg. In the case of "boil it", we have to say one more thing. Since the verb is transitive and the object is 3 person, we have to represent the object somehow. However, Rule Str-1 tells us that the object is represented by zero, since the subject is 1 person. Thus, the form that means "I'm boiling it" also consists only of the subject prefix **sh** and the verb stem. Therefore, just like "I'm crying", it too needs a pre-stem syllable. The peg rule comes along and provides it with the peg **yi**. So both verbs in (8) are built in the same way; in fact, they're both built like this:

(9)   subject   cl   verb
        prefix   stem

        sh   -   ⎰ (zero) - cha ⎱
                   ⎱   ł   - béézh ⎰

Now, let's compare the following two forms:

(10)   yicha   "He/she's crying"
        yiłbéézh "He/she's boiling it"

In this case, the **yi**'s at the beginning are different. The **yi** at the beginning of **yicha** is the peg, supplied by the peg rule. But the **yi** at the beginning of **yiłbéézh** is the 3 object prefix (required by Rule Str-1, since the subject is now 3 also), to which Rule Conj-1 has added the vowel **i**. This is a little tricky: the two words in (10) have the same syllable at the beginning (they both start with **yi**), but their structure is different. We can think of it in terms of meaning: the **y** at the beginning of

56

yicha doesn't have any meaning; it's just there to make the word come out right. But the **y** at the beginning of **yiłbéézh** does have a meaning: it signals that the object (the thing that's getting boiled) is 3 person.

The difference between the two words in (10) shows up when the distributive plural prefix is added. Look at the following:

(11)   daacha   "They are crying"
         deiłbéézh   "They are boiling it"

In the word **daacha**, the peg rule doesn't apply, since the distributive plural prefix provides a syllable that precedes the verb stem. This word is built like this:

(12)   distributive   subject   verb
            plural   prefix   stem

        da   -   (zero) - cha

No peg is needed for this form. (Rule Disj-1 lengthened the **a** of **da** to **aa**, of course.) However, the word that means "They are boiling it" has an object prefix in it:

(13)   distributive   object   subject   cl   verb
            plural   prefix   prefix   stem

        da   -   y - (zero) - ł - béézh

This object prefix was put in there by Rule Str-1. (Rule Conj-2 applied to change the **y** in (13) to an **i**, and then Rule Disj-2 changed **dai**... to **dei**...)

Thus, the two words in (11) are not built the same, and they are not pronounced the same either. The difference between the way that the two words in (11) are built is parallel to the difference between the way the two words in (10) are built. However, it happens that when we apply all our rules, the two words in (10) come out looking as though they had the same structure.

(Can you diagram the way the two words in (10) are built? Here are the diagrams. The word **yicha** is built this way:

(14)   subject   verb
          prefix   stem

        (zero) - cha

Note that this word needs a peg.

The word **yiłbéézh** is built this way:

(15)　object　subject　cl　verb
　　　　prefix　prefix　　　stem

　　　　y　-　(zero)　-　ł　-　béézh

This word does not need a peg.)

Before moving on, here is something that has to do with pronunciation.

The distributive 3 person form of "boil it" was shown above as **deiłbéézh**. However, some speakers, when they are speaking slowly and carefully, seem to say **dayiłbéézh**. Can you see where this form comes from? This is exactly the form that we'd get if Rule Conj-2 didn't exist! Why? Well, if that rule didn't exist, Rule Conj-1 would put in an **i** right after that **y** in (13). This would give **dayi**.... At this point, neither Rule Disj-1 nor Rule Disj-2 would apply, so the word would end up being **dayiłbéézh**. If we want, we can say that Rule Conj-2 is part of "fast-speech Navajo", or perhaps "colloquial Navajo", for those speakers. You should keep in mind, however, that most of the time, the distributive 3 person form of transitive verbs with 3 person object is actually spelled **dei**... in printed materials, so let's keep Rule Conj-2.

(By the way, the same story can be told about the word **haiłgéésh**, which we diagrammed in Chapter 6(8). You might see this word spelled **hayiłgéésh**, for example, which is what we'd get if Rule Conj-2 didn't exist.)

This takes care of those adjustments that we needed to study that have to do with verb bases without lexical prefixes. As we learn about other modes, we will occasionally add to our story of prefixless verbs. But now, let's finish off this chapter by studying two phonological adjustments that affect subject prefixes. These adjustments are really of a different sort than the kind of thing we saw in Chapter 6, but they occur often enough that we should become acquainted with them at this time. The first adjustment has to do with tone. Here is the rule that we need:

Rule Subj-5: If the pre-stem syllable has a short vowel in it, then it acquires a high tone if the syllable immediately preceding it has a high tone on the vowel that it ends with.

(We've numbered this rule as though it applied only to subject prefixes. Actually, it also can change the tone of a conjunct prefix. But that's okay: since every verb form has a subject prefix, we'll always check to see if this rule applies.)

As an example of this, let's look at the verb base that means "speak". Here it is:

(16)

Stem-set		
I: **ti'**	Classifier: barred-l	
P: **ti'**		
F: **tih**	Lexical prefixes: **yá** (outer)	
R: **tih**		
O: **ti'**	Transitivity: intransitive	

Note that the outer prefix **yá** ends in a high tone vowel. This prefix will cause Rule Subj-5 to apply in certain cases. Can you tell which forms are involved?

Well, here are the I mode forms for this verb:

(17)	sg	dpl	distr dpl
1	yáshti'	yéiilti'	yádeiilti'
2	yáníłti'	yáołti'	yádaołti'
3	yáłti'		yádaałti'
4	yájíłti'		yádajiłti'

There are several things to note about these forms.

First, since the classifier is barred-l, Rules Subj-2, Subj-3, and Subj-4 apply in the usual way, just as they did for the "boil it" verb.

Second, this verb is intransitive, so we do not find any 3 person object **y** prefix in the 3 person subject forms.

Third, Rule Subj-5 applies to put a high tone on the **ni** syllable of **yáníłti'** and the **ji** syllable of **yájíłti'**.

Question: Why didn't Rule Subj-5 put a high tone on the **aa** of **yádaałti'**? (Answer: Rule Subj-5 only puts a high tone on short vowels. Note that in order to see that Rule Subj-5 should not apply here, we have to look at the way the word is actually pronounced and spelled. The basic distributive plural prefix is **da**, which does indeed have a short vowel. But in this word, the prefix ends up spelled and pronounced as **daa**, with a long vowel, because of Rule Disj-1.)

Question: Why didn't Rule Subj-5 put a high tone on the **da** syllable of **yádajiłti'**? (Answer: Rule Subj-5 only puts a high tone on the pre-stem syllable. The syllable **da** in this word is followed by the syllable **ji**, which is not the verb stem, so **da** is not the pre-stem syllable. In this word, **ji** is the pre-stem syllable, and it has a short vowel, but it doesn't acquire a high tone since the syllable immediately preceding it doesn't have a high tone.)

Question: Why didn't Rule Disj-1 lengthen the vowel of **yá** in the 1sg and nondistributive 3 forms (**yáshti'** and **yáłti'**)? (Answer: Rule Disj-1 doesn't lengthen a high-tone **á**.)

Question: Why didn't Rule Subj-5 put a high tone on the **o** of **yáołti'**? (Answer: the **o** of **yáołti'** isn't a separate syllable. The **o** forms a diphthong with the **á** of **yá**.)

In connection with the word **yáołti'**, let's note that speakers who say **naahné** instead of **naohné** for "you (two) are playing" tend to say **yáłti'** instead of **yáołti'** for "you (two) are speaking". The high tone on **yá** prevents the vowel here from starting a diphthong just as it prevents the lengthening of a vowel by Rule Disj-1. For such speakers, we'd really need to add a clause to Rule Disj-2 that says that when **á** is followed by **o**, the whole thing just becomes **á**. But we won't actually add this in, since not everybody speaks this way. Still, you should be aware that forms like **yáłti'** (with the meaning "you (two) are speaking") may be found (in written as well as in spoken Navajo.)

The last phonological adjustment that we'll study in this chapter is sometimes called "sibilant-assimilation". A sibilant is a consonant that involves a hissing sound, and assimilation is the process by which one sound becomes similar to another. The actual rule is as follows:

Rule Subj-6: This rule has two parts (really: two directions.) First: if the verb stem contains one or more of the consonants **s**, **z**, **dz**, **ts**, or **ts'**, then any **sh** or **zh** that occurs in a subject prefix is replaced by **s** or **z** respectively. And second: if the verb stem contains one or more of the consonants **sh**, **zh**, **j**, **ch**, or **ch'**, then any **s** or **z** that occurs in a subject prefix is replaced by **sh** or **zh** respectively.

Now, so far, the only subject prefix that we've learned about that contains one of the sounds **s**, **sh**, **z**, or **zh**, is the 1sg regular I mode subject prefix, which is **sh**. What Rule Subj-6 does is change this prefix to **s** if the verb stem has one or more of the following consonants in it: **s**, **z**, **dz**, **ts**, or **ts'**. Later on we'll learn about other subject prefixes which are affected by this rule. We'll also learn that object prefixes can optionally be affected by this rule.

(If you compare the two lists of consonants that you have to look for in the verb stem to see if this rule applies, you might notice that the consonants pair off this way:

(18)   s   sh
       z   zh
       dz   j
       ts   ch
       ts'   ch'

where the consonants in the column on the left are pronounced with the tongue pointing towards a spot just behind the upper teeth, while the consonants in the column on the right are pronounced with the tongue curled further back.)

To illustrate Rule Subj-6, let's look at the verb base that means "think". This verb base will also illustrate the operation of Rule Subj-5, and it will require us to make an addition to Rule Disj-1 and two additions to Rule Disj-2 (so we're really learning five new phonological adjustments in this chapter!) Here is the verb base:

(19)

Stem-set	Classifier: zero
I: **kees**	
P: **kééz**	Lexical prefixes: **nitsí** (outer)
F: **kos**	
R: **kos**	Transitivity: intransitive
O: **kees**	

Let's start by giving the additions to the disjunct rules that we mentioned we'd need.

First of all, note that the lexical prefix in (19) ends in a short, high-tone í. Under the conditions of Rule Disj-1, this vowel undergoes a change, so let's add the following clause to Rule Disj-1:

(Add to Rule Disj-1): (assuming the general conditions of Rule Disj-1),

(b) If the disjunct prefix ends in a short, high-tone í, change this vowel to short, high-tone é.

The two additions to Rule Disj-2 also have to do with an í at the end of disjunct prefixes. Here they are:

(Add to Rule Disj-2): (assuming the general conditions of Rule Disj-2),

(b) If í is followed by ii, then the whole thing becomes íi.

(c) If í is followed by o, then the whole thing becomes ó.

We are now ready to look at the I mode forms of the "think" verb base. The I mode verb stem for this verb is **kees**, which has the sound s in it. According to Rule Subj-6 (the sibilant-assimilation rule), the 1sg subject prefix will be s instead of sh. Since the 1sg subject prefix is the only inflectional prefix that we find in the I mode forms that has an sh or a zh in it, this is the only prefix that Rule Subj-6 changes. However, Rule Subj-5 will also apply in some of the forms, because of the high tone on the second syllable of the prefix **nitsí**. Also, our addition to Rule Disj-1 (clause (b) of that rule)

61

will apply in some forms to change **nitsí** to **nitsé,** and our additions to Rule Disj-2 (clauses (b) and (c)) will apply in some cases as well. Can you create the forms? Here they are:

(20)   sg   dpl   distr dpl

	sg	dpl	distr dpl
1	nitséskees	nitsíikees	nitsídeiikees
2	nitsíníkees	nitsóhkees	nitsídaohkees
3		nitsékees	nitsídaakees
4		nitsíjíkees	nitsídajikees

Note that the 1sg subject prefix is **s,** not **sh,** in **nitséskees** (it's the **s** right in front of the **k.**) Rule Subj-5 put the high tone on **ni** in **nitsíníkees,** and on **ji** in **nitsíjíkees** (this is exactly the same action that we saw in connection with the verb base that means "speak" - look at the forms in (17).) Clause (b) of Rule Disj-1 changes **nitsí** to **nitsé** in the forms **nitséskees** and **nitsékees,** where the syllable that follows **nitsí** is the verb stem syllable. Clause (b) of Rule Disj-2 applies in the case of the form **nitsíikees,** and clause (c) of that rule applies in the case of the form **nitsóhkees,** where **nitsí** is followed by **iid** and **oh,** so that the **í** of **nitsí** is followed directly by either the **ii** of **iid** or the **o** of **oh.**

Let's end this chapter with another interesting detail about pronunciation. The 4 person forms are shown in (20) as **nitsíjíkees** and **nitsídajikees.** But some people say **nitsídzíkees** and **nitsídadzikees.** Can you see what is happening? For these people, Rule Subj-6 applies not only to subject prefixes, but to object prefixes as well. And not only that: for these people, this rule applies not only to prefixes that have **s** or **sh** in them, but also to prefixes that have **j** in them. The 4 person "subject" prefix **j** (which is put in the object prefix position, remember?) can become **dz** whenever the verb stem has consonants from the left hand column of (18) in it. Since the verb stem has an **s** in it, the 4 person prefix becomes **dz** in this verb, for some speakers.

CHAPTER 8

INTRODUCTION TO THE PERFECTIVE, MORE ABOUT VERB BASES, AND THE S-P CONJUGATION

At this point in our study, we are going to start learning about the perfective mode. This does not mean that we have finished learning everything there is to learn about the imperfective mode. However, we will find it easier to expand our knowledge of the imperfective later, after we've seen some of the other modes. By starting the perfective mode now, we will get a better and wider view of Navajo verb conjugation.

The perfective mode is the hardest mode in Navajo. We will have to learn about a number of complicated things that we haven't had to deal with yet. The good news is that once we've mastered the perfective, then the rest of the system is very easy.

The first complication that we have to deal with in connection with the perfective is that the subject prefixes for the perfective conjugation depend on the classifier. What does this mean? Well, in the case of the imperfective, we could give the subject prefixes for the regular I mode conjugation in one chart (see Chapter 4(2).) This will not be possible in the case of the perfective mode. Instead, we're going to need at least two charts. The reason is that verb bases that have the zero or the barred-l classifier use one set of subject prefixes in the perfective, while verb bases that have the plain-l or the d classifier use another set.

However, we cannot write out charts of the subject prefixes yet, because there is a second complication that we have to deal with. This is the fact that there are two different regular P mode conjugations! We are going to name these two conjugations the y-P and the s-P conjugations (YM calls these the "yi-perfectives" and the "si-perfectives".) For each of these conjugations, there is one set of subject prefixes that is used by verb bases with zero or barred-l classifiers, and another set of subject prefixes used by verb bases with plain-l or d classifiers. In other words, we really need four charts of subject prefixes when studying the perfective (as compared with the one chart that we used when studying the imperfective), corresponding to the following four cases:

y-P conjugation, zero and barred-l classifiers

y-P conjugation, plain-l and d classifiers

s-P conjugation, zero and barred-l classifiers

s-P conjugation, plain-l and d classifiers

(If you've been looking at YM or other materials on Navajo grammar, you may have noticed that those materials mention perfective conjugations other than the y-P and the s-P conjugations. In fact, there are two additional P mode conjugations that we will need to study. These correspond to two additional I mode conjugations that we also have not yet learned. We will study these other I mode and P mode conjugations in Chapter 18 and Chapter 20.)

(And before you get too comfortable: it will turn out that the subject prefix charts for the y-P conjugations will have to be broken up even more. Don't worry.)

Before getting to the actual P mode conjugations, there is something we should mention. If there are two regular P mode conjugations rather than one, when is each one used? The answer is, for almost all verb bases, any particular verb base uses exactly one of the P mode conjugation patterns for its P mode forms. But which one? The most general answer to this question is: we cannot tell by means of any rule. We have to memorize, for each verb base, which P mode conjugation it uses. This means that our concept of "verb base" has to be changed (again!) In addition to learning (a) the stem-set, (b) the classifier, (c) the lexical prefixes, if any, and (d) the transitivity of a verb base, we also have to learn which P mode conjugation it uses!

For example, in the previous chapters, we have given what we thought were complete verb bases in connection with some of our examples. But now we see that those verb bases lacked a piece of information: the P mode conjugation they used. For example, Chapter 6(15) presents the verb base that means "play". The stem-set, classifier, lexical prefixes, and transitivity are given. However, we should add a fifth statement, telling which P mode conjugation is used. For this verb base, the correct P-mode conjugation is the s-P conjugation, so we should add something like:

(1)   Perfective: s-P

to the material in Chapter 6(15).

Similarly, the verb base in Chapter 6(16) is incomplete in the same way. This verb base, which means "cut it out", takes the y-P conjugation, so a statement like:

(2)   Perfective: y-P

should be added to the material in Chapter 6(16).

In Chapter 7, more new verb bases were presented. What perfective conjugations do they take? Well, the verb base that means "cry" takes the y-P conjugation, so (2) should be added to Chapter 7(1); the verb base that means "boil it" takes the s-P conjugation, so (1) should be added to Chapter 7(6); the verb base that means "speak" takes the y-P conjugation, so (2) should be added to Chapter 7(16); and finally, the verb base that means "think" takes the s-P conjugation, so (1) should be added to Chapter 7(19).

64

It looks like our verb bases are beginning to get fairly big. Learning a single verb base seems to require memorizing quite a bit of material. However, if we start looking at many verbs, we'll begin to see some patterns emerging which will make it easier to learn lots of verb bases. We are not yet in a position to study all of these patterns, but this is a good time to point out a few of them, so that we can realize that the task is not quite as bad as it might look.

First of all, for each verb base, there is the stem-set. In principle, we have to be prepared to memorize five stems for each verb base, and remember which stem goes with which mode. However, there are certain patterns to these which show up again and again. If we keep these in mind, it will make the job easier.

For example, if you look at the verb bases that mean "cry", "boil it", and "speak", you'll see that, for these verbs, there are only two different forms of the stem: one form is used for the F and R modes, and one form is used for the other modes. This is one pattern that occurs with moderate frequency. A quick look at the other verb bases will show that there are plenty of stem-sets where this easy situation is not the case; but at least for some verbs, the stem-set won't be hard to learn.

A question you might be wondering about: can we find rules that tell us how the different forms of any stem-set are related to each other (so we wouldn't have to memorize the different forms for the different modes if we already knew one of the forms)? In general, the answer is no. But there are a number of regularities. We will mention these as we go along. If Navajo is not your language already (so that you have to learn everything from scratch), you might want to learn only the I, P, and F mode stems to start with. It turns out that, if you know these stems for a stem-set, it is almost always possible to figure out what the R mode stem is, and it is usually easy to guess what the O mode stem is (we'll discuss this in Chapter 23 when we study the R and O modes.)

As far as the I, P, and F modes go, you more or less have to memorize these. Actually, if you've learned the I and P modes, there are certain patterns that occur often enough that make it easy to add on the F mode. For example, the I mode stem of "cry" ends in a vowel, and the I mode stem of "speak" ends in a glottal stop. Note that the F mode stem of both of these verbs ends in **h**. This change happens with some frequency: for a reasonable number of stem-sets, if the I mode stem ends in a vowel or in ', the F mode stem will end in **h**.

Here's another pattern that you might want to keep in mind. Compare the vowel in the I mode stem with the vowel in the F mode stem for the verb bases that mean "cut it out", "boil it", and "think". Note that the I mode stems in these stem-sets have a long vowel (actually, **ee** or **éé** for these verbs), whereas the F mode stems have a short vowel (**i** for two of these verbs, and **o** for one of them.) This change of length is common: if the I mode stem has a long vowel, the F mode stem will often have a short vowel.

Finally, there is something to learn from the stem-set in the verb base that means "play". If you compare the I mode stem with the F mode stem, you'll see that the F mode stem has a ł tacked on.

This is also common: reasonably often, the F mode stem of a stem-set ends in an ł that has been either added to the I mode stem or else has replaced another consonant that was at the end of the I mode stem.

Incidentally, you may have noticed a conflict: if the I mode stem ends in a vowel, one of our patterns says that the F mode stem adds on an **h**, whereas another of our patterns says that the F mode stem adds on an ł. Which one happens? We cannot tell in advance. We simply have to memorize for each stem-set what actually happens. However, it is a great help to our memory to keep in mind that most of the time, one of only two specific things are likely to happen!

If we're just thinking about the I and P mode stems, it's harder to come up with patterns that relate the forms of the stems. We'll mention one later on; for now, the best thing is simply to decide that you'll have to memorize these.

Memorizing the stem-set is probably the heaviest memorization task in learning a verb base. The other parts of the verb base are easier, partly because there are fewer possibilities, and partly because there are patterns that involve them as well.

In the case of the classifier, any verb base has one of only four possible classifiers. Learning which classifier is used is made slightly easier by the comment at the end of Chapter 6, where we related the classifier to the transitivity. If the classifier is barred-l, the verb base is very likely to be transitive - we can see examples of this in the verbs that mean "cut it out" and "boil it", which are transitive verb stems that have barred-l classifiers. If the classifier is plain-l or d, the verb is very likely to be intransitive. We have not given full verb bases that illustrate this, but if you go back and look at the I mode forms of the verbs that means "crawl around" and "work" (in Chapter 6), you'll see that "crawl around" has a d classifier and "work" has a plain-l classifier, and both of these verbs are intransitive. However, in the case of the zero classifier, we really cannot say anything about the transitivity. The verb bases meaning "cry", "play", and "think" all have the zero classifier, and they all happen to be intransitive. However, we'll see that there are transitive verb bases with zero classifiers as well. And, unfortunately, there are exceptions. We have already seen one: the verb that means "speak" is intransitive, even though it has a barred-l classifier.

If you want to go in the other direction (that is, from the transitivity to the classifier), the thing to remember is this: if the verb is transitive, it probably will have either the barred-l or the zero classifier. If the verb is intransitive, it probably won't have the barred-l classifier, but it can have any one of the other three. (But, again, there are exceptions, like "speak".)

Incidentally, the transitivity of a verb base is not something that you actually have to memorize. Usually, you can tell just from the meaning of the verb whether it's transitive or intransitive. For example, "cry" is an activity that one person can do all by himself/herself (so "cry" is intransitive), whereas "boil" is typically something that a person does to a liquid (so "boil" is transitive.) However, we've decided to put the transitivity in as an explicit part of the verb base, since transitivity is important for Navajo verb conjugations. (Why is it important? Because if a verb is transitive, we have to think about what goes into the object pronoun position - remember the 3 person object pronoun **y** that we learned about in Chapter 6? You might want to review Rule Str-1.)

What about lexical prefixes? Well, for some verb bases, we'll simply have to memorize that a certain prefix is used. However, for other verb bases, there again tend to be patterns. In particular, certain prefixes have certain kinds of meanings associated with them. We can give one example of this with the verb bases that we've seen.

If we look at the verbs that mean "play", "crawl around", and "work", we see that they all have the outer prefix **na-**. Now, there is a kind of abstract meaning associated with this prefix. Maybe you don't quite see what "play", "crawl around", and "work" have in common. However, these three activities do have something in common: they are all activities that can go on for any length of time, and that can stop at any time. For example, if you're playing, you can keep on playing for any (reasonable!) length of time. Also, if you're playing, you can stop playing whenever you want, and it is still true that you have played. Compare this to an activity such as "cut it out". If you're cutting out a picture from a magazine, you can't just keep cutting it out: after a while, you've cut out the whole picture, and then you have to stop, because there's no more to do. Also, if you're in the middle of cutting out a picture from a magazine and you stop (let's say you were interrupted), then it isn't true that you've cut out the picture (yet) - you only started to cut it out.

For convenience, we can give names to these two kinds of activities. Activities like "play" (and "crawl around", and "work"), which can go on or stop at any time, are called *atelic* activities. Activities like "cut it out" (and "boil it"), which involve an inherent finishing point, are called *telic* activities.

Now, there are many Navajo verb bases that have the outer prefix **na-** where the meaning of the verb base is an atelic activity. We can say, therefore, that this **na-** prefix means that the activity is atelic. If we keep this in mind, it will help us remember the **na-** prefix for those verb bases that have it.

But be careful: not every atelic verb base has the prefix **na-**. For example, "cry" is an atelic activity, but there is no lexical prefix in the "cry" verb base. So, we cannot give a rule about this. All we can say is that there is a pattern: for a fair number of verb bases that have atelic activities as their meanings, we'll see the **na-** prefix.

Some other outer prefixes have meanings associated with them. For example, the prefix **ha-** found in the verb base that means "cut it out" means, by itelf, something like "up and out". We can expect to find this prefix as part of other verb bases that involve a meaning where something moves up and out. But then there are prefixes like **nitsí-** which don't seem to have special meanings of their own - this prefix simply goes together with the stem-set shown in Chapter 7(19) to form the base that means "think".

Now, at the beginning of this chapter, we learned that there are two regular P mode conjugations. Are there any patterns which will help us learn which verb bases use the y-P and which verb bases use the s-P? It happens that there are, and we can learn about one of them right now.

The pattern we can learn now has to do with outer prefixes. The idea is this: certain outer prefixes require certain P mode conjugation choices. An example: we've been talking about the outer prefix **na-**, meaning that the action is atelic. It happens that this prefix requires the verb base to use the s-P conjugation. This means that we don't actually have to memorize, for example, that the verb base meaning "play" is conjugated with the s-P conjugation in the P mode: since this verb base has the atelic **na-** prefix, we know that it uses the s-P. Similarly, we can predict that the verb bases that mean "crawl around" and "work" will be conjugated using the s-P conjugation, since these verbs also have the atelic **na-** prefix.

Another example is the **ha-** prefix that means "up and out". This prefix requires the y-P conjugation. Knowing this, we don't have to memorize that "cut it out" is conjugated in the y-P - we know it already!

(Warning: there is a different outer prefix **na-** (which has a different meaning from the atelic **na-**) which requires the y-P conjugation! There is also a different **ha-**, with a different meaning from the one we've seen, which takes the s-P conjugation! Do not worry about this - when you've learned a lot of verb bases, it'll all get sorted out.)

If a verb base has no lexical prefixes, or if there is a lexical prefix that isn't like **na-** or **ha-**, we simply will have to memorize which P conjugation is used. Later on, though, we will learn more about other patterns that involve the choice of P mode conjugation.

Well, having gone through all that, let's treat ourselves to some actual verb forms! Since we've been spending so much time on preliminaries, let's learn the s-P conjugation in the rest of this chapter (it's the easier of the two P-mode conjugations.) We'll leave the y-P conjugation for Chapters 9 and 10.

As we mentioned earlier, there will be two sets of subject prefixes for the s-P conjugation, one to be used with zero and barred-l classifiers, and the other to be used with plain-l and d classifiers. Let's start with the prefixes for the zero and barred-l classifiers:

(3)   s-P subject prefixes, zero/barred-l classifiers:

	sg	dpl
1	sé	siid
2	síní	soo
3	z or s	

The 3 person subject prefix is shown as "**z** or **s**". The choice is simple: if the classifier is zero, use **z**, whereas if the classifier is barred-l, use **s**. And here's something to keep in mind: if the classifier is indeed barred-l (so you're using **s**), the sandwich rule (Rule Subj-2) is going to apply. We'll see this happening in a little while.

Note on pronunciation: Some people pronounce the 1sg s-P subject prefix as **sá** rather than **sé**. (People who use this pronunciation sometimes also pronounce words like **nitsékees** as **nitsákees**. In fact, some people pronounce the **é** vowel very often as **á**. The circumstances when this is done need to be studied further.)

To help remember these prefixes, it might be instructive to compare them with the regular I mode prefixes. If you do this, a number of interesting patterns emerge.

Let's look first at the 1dpl zero/barred-l s-P prefix **siid**. It looks as though this prefix can be broken up into two parts. The first part is the **s**, which maybe tells us that we're in the s-P conjugation of the P mode. And the second part is **iid**, which is the same as the regular I mode subject prefix for 1dpl.

Now, can we play the same game with the other s-P prefixes? Not exactly. We can almost do this with the 2sg prefix **síní**. If we say that this is just an **s** followed by the I mode 2sg prefix **ni**, we can get the **i** after the **s** by applying Rule Conj-1 (assuming that the **s** is a conjunct prefix, which it certainly would seem to be, since it consists just of one consonant). What we cannot explain, and what we simply have to remember, is the high tone on the two syllables of this prefix (perhaps the high tone on the **ni** syllable of **síní** can be blamed on Rule Subj-5, assuming that we already know somehow that the **sí** syllable of **síní** has a high tone....)

What about the 3 person zero/barred-l s-P prefix? If we say that we take an **s** and follow it with the I mode 3 person prefix, which is zero, we'd get just **s**, which is correct for the barred-l classifier case. But for the zero classifier case, we'd have to make up some sort of rule that changes this **s** into a **z**.

Well, for three of the five prefixes in (4), we can almost say that the prefix consists of an **s** followed by the corresponding I mode prefix. But for the remaining two prefixes, namely, the 1sg and the 2dpl, we really cannot say that. If we assume that the **s** at the beginning of the 1sg prefix **sé** is the **s** that tells us we're in the s-P conjugation, then there is really no sign in this prefix of anything resembling the I mode 1sg prefix **sh**. (Also, there's that short, high-tone vowel **é**. Where did it come from?) Similarly, although the 1dpl zero/barred-l s-P prefix **soo** has the vowel **oo** in it, which is like the **o** of the I mode 2dpl prefix **oh** (but why is it long?), there is no sign of the **h** in the s-P prefix.

Well, thinking about the prefixes in (3) this way might help you to remember them, and then again, it might not help you at all. Perhaps the simplest thing is just to memorize the chart in (3). However, for future learning, here is something that you might really want to keep in mind: for all of the P mode conjugations, if the classifier is zero or barred-l, the subject prefix for 1sg has nothing in it that corresponds to the **sh** of the I mode prefix, and the subject prefix for 2dpl has nothing in it that corresponds to the **h** of the I mode prefix. But for the plain-1 and d classifiers, the P mode prefixes for 1sg and 2dpl subjects do have parts in them that correspond to the **sh** and the **h** in these I mode prefixes!

At any rate, let's illustrate the actual s-P forms of some verbs. If we look at the verb base for "play" which is given in Chapter 6(15), we see that this verb base has the zero classifier and takes the s-P conjugation (of course, we don't have to memorize that this verb base uses the s-P, since this verb has the atelic outer prefix **na-** in it.) Look at the stem-set for "play" and find the correct verb stem for the P mode, and then look at the prefixes in (3). Can you build the forms? You will need to apply a few of the rules that we've already learned....

Well, here is the P mode conjugation for this verb:

(4)	sg	dpl	distr dpl
1	niséne'	nisii'ne'	nidasii'ne'
2	nisíníne'	nisoone'	nidasoone'
3	naazne'		nidaazne'
4	nijizne'		nidajizne'

If you examine this chart carefully, you'll see that we need to add something to Rule Disj-3, which is the rule that tells us when **na** becomes **ni**. The issue is that, in addition to the cases specified in (a) and (b) of that rule (as we learned it back in Chapter 5), this change also happens when the **na** is followed by most of the s-P subject prefixes. We can add a new part to Rule Disj-3 that tells us exactly what is going on:

(Add to Rule Disj-3): (...the **na** or **ná** is immediately followed by:)

(c) an s-P subject prefix other than the 3 person prefixes **z** or **s**.

(If you look up Rule Disj-3 in the Appendix, you'll see that we'll need to put in even more additions later on.)

You might be wondering why the 3 person s-P subject prefix is an exception. There is a reason for this. Back in Chapter 5 we mentioned that Rule Disj-3 never applies if either Rule Disj-1 or Rule Disj-2 could apply. This means, for example, that Rule Disj-3 is never going to apply if the **na** or **ná** is the pre-stem syllable. Now, if you look at the s-P subject prefixes in (3), you'll see that the prefixes for the 1 and 2 persons all have their own syllable. This means that if, say, **na** is right in front of such a prefix, the syllable that follows the **na** is the syllable that belongs to the subject prefix, so **na** isn't the pre-stem syllable and Rule Disj-1 couldn't apply. But the 3 person prefixes are just single consonants. If **na** is followed by the 3 person prefix **z** or **s**, then the next syllable is the verb stem syllable, which means that **na** is the pre-stem syllable and Rule Disj-1 can apply (and, in fact, it does apply - notice the long **aa** in the word **naazne'**.) This is why Rule Disj-3 can't apply in this case. In our statement of Rule Disj-3, we'll list exactly the cases where the rule applies, but in the Appendix we've added on some general statements about syllables that are handy to remember, such as: if the **na** or **ná** is the pres-stem syllable, then Rule Disj-3 will definitely not apply.

Important reminder: Subject prefixes are not conjunct prefixes! Why are we mentioning this? Because we want to remember that Rule Conj-1 does not insert a vowel after the s-P subject prefixes **z** and **s**!

Okay. How does all this work? Well, look for example at the 1sg s-P form of "play". This form is built this way:

(5) outer   subject   verb
     prefix   prefix   stem

     na   -   sé   -   ne'

Where did the subject prefix **sé** come from? Well, the "play" verb base takes the s-P conjugation, and has a zero classifier, so if we want to build a P mode form of this verb, we'll need to get our subject prefix from the chart in (3) above. The verb stem **ne'** was used in (5) because this is the P mode stem for this verb base. Since **na** in (5) is followed immediately by an s-P subject prefix, and since that subject prefix is not the 3 person prefix, Rule Disj-3 (with our new addition) applies to the structure in (5) to change **na** to **ni** and create the form **niséne'**.

This matter of improving Rule Disj-3 is the only new thing we needed to deal with here. Everything else about the forms in (4) should be completely clear to you. To help you, here are some review questions about these forms.

Why didn't Rule Disj-3 apply in the form **naazne'**? (Answer: In this word, the **na** is immediately followed by the 3 person s-P subject prefix, so part (c) of Rule Disj-3 does not apply. The other parts of Rule Disj-3 don't apply either, since **na** isn't followed by 4 person **j** or by the distributive plural **da** either.)

Why is there a long **aa** in the forms **naazne'** and **nidaazne'**? (Answer: Rule Disj-1 applied. Make sure you see why this rule does not apply to any of the other forms in (4).)

Why is there a ' in front of **ne'** in the forms **nisii'ne'** and **nidasii'ne'**? (Answer: Rule Subj-1 applied.)

Why is there a vowel **i** following the prefix **j** in the 4 forms? (Answer: Rule Conj-1 applied.)

Now, let's look at an example of the s-P conjugation pattern in the case of a barred-l classifier verb base. We cannot use the verb base that means "cut it out", because, as we've seen, that verb base is conjugated in the y-P pattern, so instead, let's use a new verb base. The verb base shown below means "investigate it":

(6)

Stem-set		Classifier: barred-l
I:	**kaah**	
P:	**káá'**	Lexical prefixes: **na** (outer)
F:	**kah**	Transitivity: transitive
R:	**kah**	
O:	**kaah**	Perfective: s-P

(Note the shortened vowel and the final **h** in the F mode stem. Also, this verb base is another case of a transitive verb with barred-l classifier. And, the meaning of this verb base is atelic, so it is reasonable that it has the prefix **na-**, which, incidentally, guarantees that the P mode conjugation used is s-P.)

Can you predict the P mode forms of this verb? Hint: don't forget that (a) this verb is transitive, and (b) we learned about some effects involving the barred-l classifier in Chapter 6....

Well, here are the actual forms:

(7)	sg	dpl	distr dpl
1	nisélkáá'	nisiilkáá'	nidasiilkáá'
2	nisíníłkáá'	nisoołkáá'	nidasoołkáá'
3		neiskáá'	nideiskáá'
4		nijiskáá'	nidajiskáá'

Let's look at a few of these and make sure that we understand what's going on.

The sandwich rule (Rule Subj-2) does not apply in the case of the 1sg form here. Why not? Because the 1sg prefix, which is **sé**, does not end in **sh** or **s**. Note, therefore, that the **ł** classifier is completely visible here in the 1sg P mode form, in contrast to the 1sg I mode form where it disappears between the **sh** subject prefix and the first consonant of the verb stem. However, the sandwich rule does apply to the 3 and 4 forms, because in these forms, the subject prefix does end in **s** (in fact, it is just **s**.)

Rule Subj-3 applies to the 1dpl forms in the usual way, changing the classifier **ł** to **l**.

Rule Subj-4, strictly speaking, does not apply to the 2dpl forms, since the 2dpl prefix doesn't end in **h**. However, the 2dpl forms don't look any different from the way they'd look if Subj-4 did apply, since the effect of that rule would have been to delete the **h** at the end of the subject prefix (if there had been one there) and leave the **ł** classifier alone. This means that with verb bases that take the barred-l classifier, we can't tell that the 2dpl s-P subject prefix is really **soo**, without an **h** in it.

Do you understand why the 3 forms have the diphthong **ei** in them? If not, here's the whole story on the form **neiskáá'**. This form is built this way:

(8) outer   object   subject cl verb
      prefix   prefix   prefix   stem

          na - y - s - ł - káá'

Why is there an object prefix **y** in this structure? Answer: Rule Str-1 put it there (the subject is 3, and the verb is transitive, so the 3 object has to be represented by **y** rather than by zero.) Rule Conj-2 applied to the **y** in this form (this **y** is preceded by the vowel **a** of **na**, and followed by the subject prefix **s**), changing it into the vowel **i**. This would give us "nais...", whereupon Rule Disj-2 changes the **ai** to **ei**. This, and also the sandwich rule (which deletes the **ł**), turns the structure in (8) into the actual word **neiskáá'**.

The other effects found in (7) are the same as what we've already seen (by now, many times.)

There is something that we should take note of. How many new rules did we need to learn in this chapter in order to be able to conjugate these two verb bases in the s-P mode? Answer: (almost) none! Except for the small addition to Rule Disj-3, the rules that we've already learned earlier have been enough to give us exactly the right forms! This should give us courage that we've come a significant way in our study, which indeed we have. Of course, there is still quite a way to go, and we will have to learn some more rules (but not very many!) Before moving on to verb bases with plain-l and d classifiers, let's gloat some more and see that we can conjugate the verb base that means "boil it" in the P mode. Recall that this verb base takes the s-P conjugation. (The rest of the information about this verb base can be found in Chapter 7(6).) Can you write out the forms? (Hint: look at Rule Subj-6.) Here they are:

(9)	sg	dpl	distr dpl
1	shéłbéézh	shiilbéézh	dashiilbéézh
2	shíníłbéézh	shoołbéézh	dashoołbéézh
3	yishbéézh		deishbéézh
4	jishbéézh		dajishbéézh

Do you see what happened? The verb stem contains the consonant **zh**, so all of the s's in chart (3) above turned into **sh**'s under the action of Rule Subj-6.

Incidentally, since the verb base here involves no lexical prefixes, we might ask about Rule Str-2: did any of these forms need the peg **yi**? The answer is: no. If the subject is 1 or 2, you can see from the chart in (3) that the subject prefix involves a whole syllable in front of the verb-stem syllable. If the subject is 4, the 4 prefix **j** (in object prefix position), which appears as **ji** (by Rule Conj-1), gives us a whole syllable, even if the subject prefix doesn't. What about the case where the subject is 3? Well, this verb is transitive, so Rule Str-1 required us to put in the object prefix **y** to represent the 3 person object. This prefix shows up as **yi** (by Rule Conj-1). So, even if we don't have the distributive plural prefix in there, we at least have the 3 person object **yi** in the verb, so no peg is needed.

(Warning: This was a trick issue. If the verb happened to be intransitive, something unexpected would happen. We'll study this situation at the end of this chapter.)

We can now turn to the case of the s-P conjugation for verb bases with plain-l and d classifiers. As we said earlier, we need a different set of subject prefixes. Here is the set we need:

(10)   s-P subject prefixes, plain-l/d classifiers:

	sg	dpl
1	sis	siid
2	síní	sooh
3	s	

Let's look at these a little and see if we can say anything about them that will help us memorize them.

First of all, the 2sg and 1dpl prefixes in this set are the same as the 2sg and 1dpl prefixes for the zero/barred-l s-P set. This is actually true in a more general way: for any P mode conjugation pattern, the 2sg and 1dpl subject prefixes don't depend on the classifiers. That is, for all four classifiers, the 2sg and 1dpl subject prefixes will be the same (for that P mode conjugation pattern.)

Second, the 3 prefix happens to be the same as the 3 prefix used with barred-l classifiers in the s-P conjugation.

Now, if we look at the 1sg prefix **sis**, we see something interesting. Remember that we said earlier that some of the s-P subject prefixes looked as though they were formed by placing an s in front of the corresponding I mode subject prefix? Suppose we try this trick with the 1sg case. The I mode prefix is **sh**, so if we put an s in front of it, we'd get a mess like **ssh**. If we imagined that Rule Conj-1 applied to this, it would turn into **sish**, which is almost what we have. What seems to have happened is that something like Rule Subj-6 applied to change the **sh** into s, only here, it isn't a consonant in the verb stem that made this change happen, it's the **s** that we tacked on the beginning (the **s** that tells us we're in the s-P conjugation) that made the **sh** change into **s**. (Incidentally, if the verb stem has one of the consonants that changes s's into sh's, all the s's in (10) change into sh's! In particular, the 1sg prefix **sis** becomes **shish**.)

Let's move on to the 2dpl prefix **sooh**. It almost looks as though this consists of an **s** followed by the I mode 2dpl prefix **oh**. The only slight curve is that the vowel in the s-P prefix **sooh** is long.

Finally, don't forget the following general fact that we mentioned earlier: in any P mode conjugation, the 1sg subject prefix used with plain-l and d classifiers ends in **s** or **sh**, and the 2dpl subject prefix used with plain-l and d classifiers ends in **h**. (In any P mode conjugation, the 1sg subject prefix used with zero or barred-l classifiers <u>never</u> ends in **s** or **sh**, and the 2dpl subject prefix used with zero or barred-l classifiers <u>never</u> ends in **h**.)

As a first example using the prefixes in (10), let's take the verb base meaning "work". We never presented this verb base completely, so let's do that here:

(11)

Stem-set		Classifier: plain-l
I:	**nish**	Lexical prefixes: **na** (outer)
P:	**nish**	
F:	**nish**	Transitivity: intransitive
R:	**nish**	
O:	**nish**	Perfective: s-P

Now here's an easy stem-set: the same stem is used for all the modes! This is not particularly common, but it occasionally happens, which makes it easy for us to learn these sets.

Note that we have an intransitive verb with a plain-l classifier (a typical arrangement.) Also, the fact that this verb has the atelic **na** prefix ("work" is an atelic activity) means that we'll use the s-P conjugation for the P mode.

You should have no trouble coming up with the P mode forms for this verb. Here they are:

(12)	sg		dpl	distr dpl
1	nishishnish	nishiilnish		nidashiilnish
2	nishínílnish	nishooɬnish		nidashooɬnish
3		naashnish		nidaashnish
4		nijishnish		nidajishnish

In the case of the plain-l/d s-P, the sandwich rule (Rule Subj-2) will apply to the 1sg and the 3 (and the 4) forms. Rule Subj-3 applies in the usual way to the 1dpl forms in (12), and Rule Subj-4 applies in the usual way to the 2dpl forms (you should compare what happens here with our discussion of these rules in connection with the I mode conjugation.)

Incidentally, the nondistributive P mode 3 subject form of this verb turns out accidentally to be the same as the I mode 1sg form: both forms are **naashnish**. But the structure is different. In the I mode, the first **sh** is the 1sg subject prefix, whereas in the P mode, the first **sh** is the 3 subject prefix (which actually "started out" as **s**, but got turned into **sh** by Rule Subj-6 in this case, because the verb stem **nish** contains the consonant **sh**.) Everthing else about the forms in (12) should be completely familiar by now.

Just for completeness, let's look at the s-P conjugation of a d classifier verb base. We saw in Chapter 6 that the verb base that means "crawl around" has a d classifier, but we didn't give the entire verb base. Here it is:

(13)

Stem-set		Classifier: d
I:	**na'**	
P:	**na'**	Lexical prefixes: **na** (outer)
F:	**nah**	
R:	**nah**	Transitivity: intransitive
O:	**nééh**	Perfective: s-P

You might have noticed that the F mode stem for this verb looks like the I mode stem, except that an **h** replaces the **'** at the end of the stem.

The P mode forms are easily built. Don't forget that the d classifier causes d-effect on the initial consonant of the verb stem, turning the simple **n** into the combination **'n**. Here are the forms:

(14)

	sg	dpl	distr dpl
1	nisis'na'	nisii'na'	nidasii'na'
2	nisíní'na'	nisooh'na'	nidasooh'na'
3		naas'na'	nidaas'na'
4		nijis'na'	nidajis'na'

There is nothing special we need to say about these forms, except to point out that the d classifier of this verb base becomes important here in the P mode. If the classifier had been zero instead of d, a different set of subject prefixes would have been used (namely, the prefixes in (3)), and some of the forms would have been different.

We are essentially finished with learning the s-P conjugation. However, there is one tiny complication that we should look at here. This has to do with verbs that lack any lexical prefixes. We already saw one such verb, the verb meaning "boil it", and we were able to conjugate it without difficulty. However, this verb never needed to have the peg element added in the P mode. The reason was that the verb was transitive. Why does being transitive make a difference? Because in the s-P conjugation, all the subject prefixes have a syllable in them except for the 3 prefix. So, the only s-P form that ever might have to have the peg added would be a 3 form. But if the verb is transitive, there already will be an extra syllable in front of the verb stem, namely, the syllable that is formed when Rule Conj-1 supplies the vowel **i** to the 3 object prefix **y**. We saw this happening in the case of the word **yishbéézh** "he/she boiled it". But if we were trying to conjugate an intransitive verb that has no lexical prefixes, it looks as though we'd need a peg for the (nondistributive) 3 forms.

As it happens, the real form is a little different. We can describe what happens by giving the following rule, which we are going to consider as an addition to Rule Str-2 (in the Appendix, this addition, as well as some others, are already shown as part of Rule Str-2):

(Add to Rule Str-2): If a verb base is conjugated in the s-P and has no prefixes, then the 3 subject prefix **z** or **s** becomes **si**. (Note: In this case, any non-zero classifier is <u>not</u> deleted, since it's not sandwiched in between the **s** and the consonant at the beginning of the stem.)

To illustrate this, let's look at a verb that means "stand". This verb will also teach us about some other things as well.

First of all, "stand" is our first example of a neuter verb, that is, a verb conjugated in only one mode, which, for this particular verb, happens to be the P mode. But notice: normally, the P mode is used to describe a completed event, in particular, an event that was completed either in the past or else before some other point of time. But in the case of this verb, there is no actual event - the verb is simply telling us about a position that a person is in, the position called "standing". (This verb is particularly useful in sentences that talk about where a person is standing.) It happens that in Navajo there are a number of verbs that describe positions and location like this, for people as well as for other sorts of entities. For people, typical positions are: "stand", "sit", and "lie down". These verbs are mostly neuter verbs that are conjugated in the P mode only. And, in fact, they are conjugated specifically in the s-P conjugation.

The "stand" verb base can be described as follows:

(15)

Stem-set P: **zį́**	Classifier: zero
	Lexical prefixes: (none)
	Transitivity: intransitive
	Perfective: s-P

Using the subject prefixes in (3), and remembering the addition to Rule Str-2 that we just learned, we get the following forms for this verb:

(16)

	sg	dpl	distr dpl
1	sézį́	siidzį́	dasiidzį́
2	sínízį́	soozį́	dasoozį́
3	sizį́		daazzį́
4	jizzį́		dajizzį́

Note that our addition to Rule Str-2 applies only to the form **sizį́** "he/she is standing". The other forms are no different from what we've already seen a lot.

There are some things we must mention about some of the forms in (16), however. In almost all written materials, when two identical consonants come directly next to each other, they are written with only one consonant. So, the word meaning "one is standing" would normally be found written as **jizį́** rather than **jizzį́**. Similarly, the distributive plural forms that mean "they're standing" and "those ones are standing" would normally be written **daazį́** and **dajizį́** instead of **daazzį́** and **dajizzį́**. This is an accurate reflection of the real pronunciation: the middle consonant in the word **jizzį́** is not actually pronounced any different from the middle consonant in the words **sizį́** or **sézį́**. Rather than add another rule to take care of this matter, let's just remember that we normally simplify the sequence of two identical consonants to one consonant. (Some written materials, in some cases, actually do write out two identical consonants next to each other.)

Here's a quick review question: Why is there a **dz** in the forms **siidzį́** and **dasiidzį́**? (Answer: Rule Subj-1 applied. Check the chart in Chapter 4(9) to see what happens when d-effect applies to **z**.)

Before moving on to the next part of our study of the P mode, let's briefly think about how we would recognize an s-P form if we see or hear one. If you're a Navajo speaker, of course, this is not really a problem: when you hear or read a word, you know what it means. But if you are first learning the Navajo language, or if your knowledge of the language is incomplete, or if you speak Navajo well but you're first learning the grammar of the verb, will you be able to look at a verb and tell if that verb is an s-P form? Mostly, you will: the subject prefixes in (3) and (10) don't look like any other subject prefixes, so if you see **sé** or **sis** (or **shé** or **shish**) right in front of the verb stem, you'll probably be right if you guess that you're looking at an s-P form where the subject is "I". The same is true if you see **síní** (or **shíní** - singular "you"), **sii** (or **shii** - "we"), or **soo** or **sooh** (or **shoo** or **shooh** - plural "you") in front of the verb stem. However, in the 3 person, you might get confused. We already discussed the fact that the word **naashnish** could mean "he/she/they (two) worked" (that is, 3 subject s-P conjugation of P mode), or it could mean "I am working" (that is, 1sg subject I mode.) And you might have noticed that the word **yishbéézh** in (9), which means "he/she/they (two) boiled it", can also mean "I am boiling it" - see Chapter 7(7). Is this going to be a common problem?

Well, perhaps not. In the case of the verb bases that mean "work" and "boil it", there are three situations involved that simultaneously make the 1sg I mode form and the 3 s-P mode form come out the same. First, the I mode stem and the P mode stem for these verb bases happen to be the same. Second, the verb stems for these verb bases have the sort of consonant in them that causes Rule Subj-6 to change the "real" 3 s-P subject prefix, which is **s**, into **sh**, thereby making it look like the I mode 1sg prefix **sh**. And third, the classifier is not zero, so the s-P 1sg subject prefix starts out as **s** rather than as **z**. If any one of these situations is not present, the I mode 1sg subject and s-P mode 3 subject forms will be different. For example, if the verb stem doesn't have the kind of consonant in it that causes Rule Subj-6 to apply, then the 1sg I mode will have **sh** in front of the verb stem, while the 3 s-P mode will have **s** (or **z**, if the classifier is zero) in front of the verb stem. As an example, look at the words shown in Chapter 6(6). How do we say "I am crawling around"? The word is **naash'na'**, with **sh** in front of the verb stem. Now, look at the forms in (14) above (in this chapter). How do we say "he/she/they (two) crawled around"? The word is **naas'na'**, with **s** (not **sh**) in front of the verb stem. The verb base that means "crawl around" has the same stem in the I mode and the P mode, but we still get two different words for "I'm crawling around" and "he (etc.) crawled around".

Still, if the Navajo language is a new experience for you, you might get confused. So what do you do? Well, if you see an **s** or **sh** directly in front of a verb stem, it will help to keep the following in mind:

(17)   (a) The 1sg I mode prefix is basically **sh**; it becomes **s** only if the verb stem has in it one or more of the consonants **s**, **z**, **dz**, **ts**, or **ts'** (these are the consonants in the left-hand column of Chapter 7(18). The 1sg I mode prefix is never **z** or **zh**.

        (b) The 3 s-P mode prefix is basically **s** if the classifier is not zero, and **z** if the classifier is zero. These become **sh** or **zh** only if the verb stem has in it one or more of the consonants **sh**, **zh**, **j**, **ch**, or **ch'** (these are the consonants in the right-hand column of Chapter 7(18).

So, if we see **z** or **zh** in front of the verb stem, do we have a 1sg I mode form or a 3 s-P mode form? (Answer: 3 s-P mode. Example: the word **naazne'**, which means "he/she/they (two) played" - see (4) above.) If we see an **s** in front of the verb stem and the verb does not have any of the consonants **s**, **z**, **dz**, **ts**, or **ts'** in it, which form do we have? (Answer: 3 s-P mode. Example: **naas'na'** "he/she/they (two) crawled around".). If we see an **sh** in front of the verb stem and the verb stem does not have any of the consonants **sh, zh, j, ch**, or **ch'** in it, which form do we have? (Answer: 1sg I mode. Examples: **naashné** "I'm playing", **naash'na'** "I'm crawling around".) If we see an **s** or **sh** in front of the verb stem and we happen to know that the classifier for that verb is zero, which form do we have? (Answer: 1sg I mode. Example: **naashné** "I'm playing")

In most cases, this will take care of the problem. If you still cannot tell whether you have a 1sg I mode form or a 3 s-P mode form, check the verb stem. And, of course, there are a few verb bases (like "work" and "boil it") where we do actually get the same word for both forms.

Well, with this, we have finished our first confrontation with the P mode. In fact, we have learned all we need to know about the s-P conjugation. Note that we only needed two small additions to two of our rules in order to get all the right forms! We are now ready to move onto the y-P conjugation of the P mode.

CHAPTER 9

THE y-P CONJUGATION:
ZERO AND BARRED-L CLASSIFIERS

Having learned the s-P conjugation, let's move directly to the y-P conjugation. We might mention that this chapter is the hardest chapter of the entire course. When you have mastered the material in this chapter, it will be downhill all the way for the rest of our study!

You remember that when we began our study of the P mode in Chapter 8, we learned that each P mode conjugation pattern has two sets of subject prefixes, one used when the classifier is zero or barred-l, and the other used when the classifier is plain-l or d. When we studied the s-P conjugation, we gave two charts of subject prefixes: Chapter 8(3) had the prefixes used for zero or barred-l classifiers, and Chapter 8(10) had the prefixes used for plain-l or d classifiers. When we come to the y-P conjugation, we expect that we'll need two charts again. However, the y-P conjugation is more complicated, and it will turn out that we're really going to need more than two charts. For this reason, we'll take it a little slower: we'll only study the case of zero and barred-l classifiers in this chapter. When we've mastered this case, we'll move on to the y-P conjugation of verb bases with plain-l and d classifiers in Chapter 10.

The problem that we face with the subject prefixes in the y-P conjugation is that these prefixes interact in special ways with any prefixes that precede them. For this reason, it will be best if we break up our study of these subject prefixes according to what kind of prefix, if any, immediately precedes it. We're going to start with the case that the y-P subject prefix is immediately preceded by a disjunct prefix. For this particular case, we can represent the subject prefixes as follows:

(1)   y-P subject prefixes, zero/barred-l classifiers, preceded by disjunct prefix:

	sg	dpl
1	v́v́	iid
2	v́íní	oo
3	v́v́	

There are things in this chart that we have to explain.

First, the 1sg and 3 prefixes are listed as "v́v́". Here, "v" means "vowel", and, of course, v́ means "high tone vowel". What we mean to say is that the 1sg prefix and the 3 prefix is just a long, high-tone vowel. But which vowel? What we do is this: we look at the vowel at the end of the disjunct prefix that precedes the subject prefix (remember: a disjunct prefix always ends in a vowel!), and we use <u>that</u> vowel as the v. If that vowel is short, we lengthen it (if it's already long, we leave it long.) If that vowel is low-tone, we make it high-tone (if it's already high-tone, we leave it high-tone.) The resulting long, high-tone vowel is the subject prefix, for 1sg and 3 subjects! We can summarize this by saying: "v́v́" means "make the vowel at the end of the preceding disjunct prefix long (if it isn't already long) and high-tone (if it isn't already high-tone)".

Another way of thinking of these two subject prefixes is that they are like a hole in the verb. The hole is filled with the vowel from the disjunct prefix just to its left. This vowel is made long and high-tone if it isn't already that way.

Let's illustrate this particular subject prefix with a few forms here; later on, we'll give complete charts of the y-P conjugation.

If you look at Chapter 7(16), you'll find the verb base that means "speak". We noted at the beginning of Chapter 8 that this verb base is conjugated in the y-P conjugation. Let's form the word that means "I spoke" or "he/she/they(two) spoke":

(2)　outer　　subject　cl　verb
　　　prefix　　prefix　　　stem

　　　yá　-　v́v́　-　ł　-　ti'

Now, the "v́v́" means "make the vowel at the end of the preceding disjunct prefix long and high-tone". The preceding prefix is an outer prefix, so it's a disjunct prefix, and the vowel at the end of it is **á** (the **á** of **yá**.) This vowel is already high-tone, so we just have to make it long. This gives us the form **yáałti'**, which is the correct form for "I spoke" or "he/she/they(two) spoke". (You should check that none of our other rules apply to this word.)

As another example, let's look at the verb base for "cry", shown in Chapter 7(1). Again, we noted at the beginning of Chapter 8 that this verb base takes the y-P conjugation. Let's build the y-P mode form for this verb with the distributive plural 3 subject:

(3)　distributive　subject　verb
　　　plural　　　prefix　　stem

　　　da　-　v́v́　-　cha

Since the distributive plural prefix is a disjunct prefix, we take our subject prefix in (3) from the chart in (1). Again, "v́v́" means "make the vowel at the end of the preceding disjunct prefix long and high-tone". This time, the vowel at the end of the preceding disjunct prefix is the **a** of **da**, which is short and low-tone. By making it long and high-tone, we get the word **dáácha**, which is the correct form

82

that means "they cried".

Let's move on now to the 2sg prefix, which is shown in the chart as **víní**. Here again, "v́" stands for "high-tone vowel". Again, what we do here is use the vowel at the end of the preceding disjunct prefix, and, if it is not high-tone, we make it high-tone. But be careful: if, by any chance, that vowel happens to be long, we'll shorten it: that is we'll just write one letter for the v́. One final point: don't forget to apply Rule Disj-2 if this rule is applicable!

As an example of this, let's look at the form that means "you (sg) spoke". This form is built like this:

(4) outer   subject   cl   verb
     prefix   prefix   stem

     yá   -   víní   -   ł   -   ti'

For v, we use the vowel at the end of the preceding disjunct prefix. This vowel is the **á** of **yá**. Since it is already short and high-tone, we don't have to change it. This would give us "yáíníłti'", except that we'll remember to apply Rule Disj-2 to get the actual form: **yéíníłti'** (we really need an extra clause in Rule Disj-2 to handle this case, so we'll add it in, in the Appendix.) Again, check through and see that no other rules apply.

We have examined how the 1sg, 2sg, and 3 subject prefixes in chart (1) work. The 1dpl and 2dpl prefixes in that chart work the same as corresponding prefixes in other conjugations - we don't need any new rules. This might lead us to think that we can write out a complete chart of all the y-P forms for some verb. But actually, we are not ready to do so. The reason is that the 4 person subject forms have the prefix **j** in object prefix position, and the object prefixes are conjunct prefixes, not disjunct prefixes. This means we cannot completely write out all the P mode forms until we study the subject prefixes that are used when there is a conjunct prefix immediately in front of them. So, let's get right to these prefixes.

We can describe these prefixes easily as follows. Suppose we're in the y-P conjugation and the classifier is zero or barred-l. Suppose the subject prefix is immediately preceded by a conjunct prefix. Suppose we try to use the subject prefixes given in (1) above. We'd need to figure out what vowel we should use for the "v" - remember, a conjunct prefix always ends in a consonant, so the preceding prefix doesn't give us a vowel to use. It turns out that we'll get the right subject prefixes if we use the following rule: use the vowel **i**.

But for convenience, let's actually write out these subject prefixes in a chart of their own, so we can see what they look like.

(5)   y-P subject prefixes, zero/barred-l classifiers, preceded by conjunct prefix:

	sg	dpl
1	íí	iid
2	ííní	oo
3	íí	

These prefixes are simply the prefixes in (1) except that we've replaced each "v́" with í.

Now, whenever we're building a verb in the y-P conjugation and the classifier is zero or barred-l, if the subject prefix is immediately preceded by a conjunct prefix, we can either say that the subject prefix is chosen from chart (1) except that we replace each "v́" with í, or we can say that the subject prefix is chosen from chart (5). It amounts to the same thing, of course, but when we're actually building verbs, we'll mostly just say that, in this case, we're getting our subject prefix from chart (5).

These prefixes are easy to use - we simply put them in whenever there's a conjunct prefix immediately to the left. We cannot illustrate all of them yet, because we have seen only two conjunct prefixes in our studies so far: the 4 person subject prefix **j** (which is placed in object prefix position) and the special 3 person object prefix **y**, used with transitive verbs when the subject and the object are both 3 person. In both cases, the subject prefix will be the one for 3 person, so that's the only prefix in chart (5) that we'll illustrate in this chapter. (But we won't have to wait long till we see the others.)

As our first example that uses a prefix from (5), let's form the word that means "one cried", using the **j** prefix. This word is built like this:

(6)   object   subject   verb
        prefix   prefix   stem

         j   -   íí   -   cha

Since **j** is in the object prefix position, and since object prefixes are conjunct prefixes, we choose the subject prefix from chart (5) rather than from chart (1). (Or we could have said: we use a prefix from chart (1), but we change any "v́" to an í.) This is why the subject prefix is íí here. If you check through the rules that we've learned, you'll see that none of them apply. The actual word is therefore simply **jíícha**.

As an example that illustrates the effect of the object prefix **y**, let's use the verb base that means "cut it out". This verb base can be found in Chapter 6(16); and we noted in Chapter 8 that this verb takes the y-P conjugation in the P mode. The word that means "He/she/they (two) cut it out (in the past)" is built like this:

(7) outer   object   subject   cl   verb
     prefix   prefix   prefix   stem

     ha - y - íí - ł - gizh

Remember: Rule Str-1 requires us to use the object prefix **y**, since this is a transitive verb and the subject and object are both 3 person. Again we have an object prefix, and since object prefixes are conjunct prefixes, the subject prefix is chosen from chart (5) rather than from chart (1) - this is why the 3 subject prefix appears as **íí** in (7). A check through our rules shows that none of them apply (not even Rule Conj-2, because the **y** is followed by a vowel, namely, **íí**.) The actual word is therefore just **hayííłgizh**.

Let's stop a moment and look at the prefixes in chart (1) and in chart (5) a little more.

First of all, the 1dpl and 2dpl prefixes are the same in the two charts. The 1dpl prefix is actually the same as the 1dpl prefix in the regular I mode conjugation. And the 2dpl prefix **oo** looks like the s-P 2dpl prefix **soo** without the **s**. There is something about this prefix that we should make note of: there is no **h** at the end. Remember that in Chapter 8 we said that this is always the case for P mode 2dpl prefixes used with zero or barred-l classifiers.

The 1dpl and 2dpl prefixes are easy: not only are they the same in charts (1) and (5), but we'll see in a moment that if there is no prefix in front of them, the same prefixes are still used (with Rule Str-3 kicking in.)

Next, we already learned that when a prefix in (1) is different from a prefix in (5), it's because the prefix in (1) has one or two "v́"'s in it which got changed to í's in (5). So, for example, if we compare the 1sg and 3 person prefixes in (1) with these prefixes in (5), we see that, in both cases, the prefix takes the form of a long, high-toned vowel. If a disjunct prefix precedes, we use the vowel of the disjunct prefix as the long high-toned vowel, whereas if a conjunct prefix precedes, we use **íí** as the long, high-toned vowel. We can sort of "explain" the conjunct situation by remembering that we learned about a rule that inserts a vowel after a conjunct prefix. Since a conjunct prefix always ends in a consonant, and since we need a long, high-toned vowel to be our subject prefix, which vowel should we use? Well, Rule Conj-1 would insert the vowel **i**, so we can say, if we want, that this **i** is used as our "v", so that "v́v́" turns into the **íí** which appeared in (5). For example, in explaining the word **jíícha** which we saw in (6), we could say that this word starts out as **jcha**, then Rule Conj-1 turns it into **jicha**, and finally the **i** is made long and high-tone, to give the final result **jíícha**. (Some people find games like this fun. If you like this sort of thing, perhaps it'll help you remember the forms. On the other hand, you might find it easier not to think this way, but instead just to use the charts in (1) and (5), or just remembering that the prefixes in (5) are the same as the prefixes in (1) except that **í** substitutes for "v́".)

Here's a question: can we make use of this "explanation" for the 2sg prefix in (5)? Will Rule Conj-1 apply?

Well, Rule Conj-1 won't apply, because this rule applies only if the conjunct prefix is directly followed by a consonant. But with this prefix, any conjunct prefix that precedes víní (whatever we think v́ might be) is followed by a vowel (either the v́, or else the first í of víní, depending on how we think of it.) This vowel would prevent Rule Conj-1 from applying. For this reason, maybe it's best not to play this game with the 2sg prefix. (For those of you who like to play clever games with sounds, you might try this trick: say that the 2sg prefix is actually v́yní (or maybe yní?) and use Rule Conj-2 to turn the y in this prefix into i.... This trick will look even better after you read Chapter 20.)

There still remains the case where the subject prefix is preceded by no other prefix at all. As we said a moment ago, the 1dpl and 2dpl prefixes remain the same, and Rule Str-3 applies in the usual way (you might want to review Chapter 7 about this.) In the case of the 1sg and 3 prefixes, what we actually find is: yí. Note that the high-tone is still there, but the vowel is short. This prefix looks like a special version of the peg that Rule Str-2 introduced, so we should perhaps write an addition to this rule for this case.

But before we do that, let's ask about the one prefix left: what if the 2sg prefix is preceded by nothing? In this case, we have no alternative: we simply have to remember that the actual form turns out to be yíní. One way to describe this might be to say that the prefix loses the v́ at the beginning of víní (in chart (1)), and Rule Str-3 comes along and supplies a y at the beginning of the prefix.

Since we have to remember the form of the 2sg prefix as well as the forms of the 1sg and 3 prefixes, let's write an addition to Rule Str-2 that tells us what these forms are. (Since Rule Str-2 is really the peg rule, the information about the 2sg prefix doesn't actually belong there, but it won't hurt to put it in so that it's together with the other two prefixes that have to be memorized.)

(Add to Rule Str-2): If a verb base is conjugated in the y-P, the classifier is zero or barred-l, and there are no prefixes, then the 1sg and 3 prefixes become yí, and the 2sg prefix becomes yíní.

Well, this actually says everything we need for the case that the subject prefix is preceded by no other prefix. However, it might be a good idea to give a chart of the actual subject prefixes that we use when there is no prefix in front of them. Here is such a chart:

(8)   y-P subject prefixes, zero/barred-l classifiers, preceded by no prefix:

	sg	dpl
1	yí	yiid
2	yíní	woo
3	yí	

In chart (8), we already put in the **y** and **w** at the beginning of the 1dpl and 2dpl (and 2sg) prefixes that are supplied by Rule Str-3.

Be careful! These charts are organized according to what (if anything) precedes the subject prefix. They are <u>not</u> organized according to, say, the kind of verb base we're looking at. For example, we might have a verb base that has no lexical prefixes. Does that mean that we'll always use chart (8)? Well, some of the time, we will; but if we want the 4 person subject form, then the **j** is a conjunct prefix, so we move to chart (5). Also, if the verb is transitive, and if the subject is 3, we'll need a 3 object prefix **y**, which is also a conjunct prefix, so again we'll move to chart (5). And finally, for the distributive plural forms, the verb will have the **da** in it, which is a disjunct prefix, so we'll use chart (1) to get the subject prefixes for those cases.

Before moving on to some more examples, let's take note of a few more facts about all these prefixes.

First of all, the 1sg prefix does not end in **sh** or **s**. Remember that in Chapter 8, we said that, in any P mode conjugation, the 1sg prefix does not end in **sh** or **s** if the classifier is zero or barred-l. (This also means that the sandwich rule (Rule Subj-2) won't apply to these forms.)

Second, the 1sg prefix and the 3 prefix are the same in each of the charts for the y-P, zero/barred-l conjugation. This means that, in this conjugation, we cannot tell the difference between a 1sg subject and a 3 subject on the basis of the subject prefix alone. In the case of an intransitive verb, the form for these two subjects will actually be the same. We already saw an example of this: the word **yááłti'** (see (2) above) means either "I spoke" or else "he/she/they (two) spoke". However, in the case of a transitive verb, Rule Str-1 will put the **y** object prefix into the verb if the subject is 3, but not if the subject is 1sg, so the forms of the verb will really be different for these two subjects. (We'll see examples in just a moment.)

And finally, we repeat that the 1dpl and 2dpl prefixes **iid** and **oo** are completely "normal". It doesn't matter what prefixes are in front of them (or even if there is a prefix in front of them at all) - you just put them in and apply whatever rules you have to, and the right form will come out. But since the 1dpl prefix here is the same as the 1dpl prefix in the regular I mode conjugation, we run into the following situation: if the subject is 1dpl, the only way to tell the difference between the I mode and the P mode (if we're in the y-P conjugation) is by the form of the verb stem! For those verb bases where the I mode stem and the P mode stem are the same, the 1dpl subject form of these two modes will be the same (if the y-P conjugation is used in the P mode.)

That's all there is to it!

Well, this may seem like a lot, but if we illustrate it, we'll see that it's actually pretty straightforward. We are now ready to look at the complete P mode conjugation of some verbs. Let's start with a verb base that uses the y-P conjugation where the classifier is zero. One such verb base is the one that means "dig it out". Here it is:

(9)

Stem-set		Classifier: zero
I:	**gééd**	
P:	**geed**	Lexical prefixes: **ha**
F:	**goł**	Transitivity: transitive
R:	**go'**	
O:	**gééd**	Perfective: y-P

You might make note of the fact that the long vowel **éé** found in the I mode stem turns into the short vowel **o** in the F mode stem (we've seen that a change like this is common.) Also, note the **ł** at the end of the F mode stem which replaces the **d** at the end of the I mode stem. This is also a typical change, as we mentioned earlier.

Do you think you can build the P mode forms for this verb? If you try to do so, remember that the verb is transitive, so you'll need to add in the object prefix **y** when the subject is 3. Also, don't forget that when the subject is 4, the prefix **j** appears in the object position (and prefixes in the object position are conjunct prefixes.)

If you can't stand the suspense, here are the forms:

(10)   sg   dpl   distr dpl

	sg	dpl	distr dpl
1	háágeed	haiigeed	hadasiigeed
2	háínígeed	haoogeed	hadasoogeed
3	hayíígeed		hadeizgeed
4	hajíígeed		hadajizgeed

Whoops!

Let's first look at the nondistributive forms and make sure we understand them. Then we have to say something special about the distributive plural forms.

The 1sg form is built like this:

(11)   outer   subject   verb
        prefix   prefix   stem

          ha   -   v́v́   -   geed

Question: Why is there no object prefix? (Answer: See Rule Str-1. The subject is 1 person, so the

3 person object prefix is zero.)

Question: Why is the subject prefix in (11) shown as ẃ? (Answer: The subject prefix is immediately preceded by an outer prefix, which is a disjunct prefix, so the subject prefixes in chart (1) are used.)

Now, what do we do about the ẃ? Remember what we said earlier: the v́v́ means "make the vowel at the end of the preceding disjunct prefix long and high-tone". What is the preceding disjunct prefix? It's **ha**. What vowel does this end in? It ends in **a**. Therefore, we make this a long and high-tone, that is, we change it into **áá**. None of our other rules apply, so this gives us our word: **háágeed** "I dug it out".

Next, look at the 2sg form, which is built like this:

(12) outer   subject   verb
      prefix   prefix   stem

      ha - v́íní - geed

Remember what the v́ means in this prefix: the vowel at the end of the preceding disjunct prefix has to be short and high-tone. In this case, the **a** at the end of **ha** becomes a high-tone vowel. This gives us our word **háínígeed** "you dug it out". (Rule Disj-2 doesn't change anything, because of the **h**.)

The 3 form (nondistributive) is built this way:

(13) outer   object   subject   verb
      prefix   prefix   prefix   stem

      ha - y - íí - geed

Question: Why is there an object prefix **y** in here? (Answer: See Rule Str-1.)

Question: Why is the subject prefix **íí**? (Answer: The object prefix **y** is a conjunct prefix, so the subject prefix is taken from chart (5).)

No further rules apply (make sure you see why Rule Conj-2 doesn't apply), and we get directly the form **hayíígeed** "He/she/they (two) dug it out".

The structure of the 4 person form is very similar to (13), except that the 4 person subject prefix **j** appears in the object position in the same place that contains **y** in (13). (If the subject is 4, then the 3 object is represented by zero, so there's no other object prefix - see Rule Str-1.)

The nondistributive 1dpl and 2dpl are completely regular. (Note that d-effect applied to **g** doesn't change it - see Chapter 4(9).)

If we turn now to the distributive plural forms, we see something weird: these forms are actually constructed according to the s-P conjugation, rather than the y-P conjugation! What's going on?

It turns out that for a moderate number of verbs that normally take the y-P conjugation, the perfective mode shifts into the s-P when the distributive plural **da** is used. This is sometimes called "perfective **da**-shift". The "dig it out" verb base is one such case. The question is: which verb bases shift this way?

This turns out to be a difficult question to answer, because it appears that the Navajo language is undergoing some change with respect to this shift: younger speakers are shifting less than older speakers. For some people, and for some verbs, it doesn't seem to matter whether they shift or not, whereas for other verbs, you either have to shift, or you cannot shift. As a start, we can say that the following principles seem to be true (see Kari 1976 for further discussion of this question.)

Firstly, if a verb base has an outer prefix that requires the use of the y-P conjugation, then that verb base can be expected to shift. (Recall that the outer prefix **ha**, meaning "up and out", requires the y-P, so verb bases with this prefix will usually shift.)

Secondly, if a verb base shifts, there are two patterns: either all the distributive plural forms shift, or else only the 3 and 4 person distributive plural forms shift. This seems to vary with speakers. The speakers on whose speech the forms in (10) are based shift for all distributive plural forms. However, the charts in YM suggest that for "dig it out", we could just as easily expect nonshifted forms in the 1dpl and 2dpl (these forms would just be **hadeiigeed** and **hadaoogeed**.)

Thirdly, some verb bases other than those with disjunct lexical prefixes that require the y-P also shift, or shift optionally. We will not give any principles here to predict which of these other verb bases shift, but we'll take note of these as we come to them in our studies.

Since there is variation on the matter of this shift, we will not represent the possibility of the shift in the verb base itself. But we'll note what happens whenever we run into particular cases of the shift.

Before continuing, you should make sure that you understand how the distributive plural forms in (10) are actually constructed. There is nothing new involved - all these forms are completely normal, providing that we take the subject prefix from the chart in Chapter 8(3). You might want to compare the forms in the last column of (10) with the forms in the last column of Chapter 8(7). (The verb in Chapter 8(7) has a different outer prefix and a different classifier, though. Make sure you see how these differences affect the forms.)

Now, let's look at another example of the y-P conjugation in action. This time, we'll take a verb base that has a barred-l classifier. The verb base meaning "cut it out", in Chapter 6(16), will be a good example (recall that in Chapter 8 we learned that this verb base is conjugated in the y-P pattern.) Here are the P mode forms for this verb:

(14)	sg		dpl	distr dpl
1	háátgizh	haiilgizh		hadeiilgizh
2	háíníłgizh	haootgizh		hadaootgizh
3		hayííłgizh		hadeishgizh
4		hajííłgizh		hadajishgizh

There is not much we have to say about these forms. The way the subject prefixes are formed works the same here as in the case of "dig it out" in (10). Note that Rule Subj-2 (the sandwich rule) does not apply to the 1sg form, since the 1sg subject prefix does not end in **s** or **sh**. Rule Subj-3 applies normally to change the classifier **ł** into an **l** in the 1dpl forms. Rule Subj-4 does not apply, since the 2dpl subject prefix does not end in **h**. The actual forms of the subject prefixes follow the same pattern as in the case of "dig it out" in (10). Perfective **da**-shift to the s-P conjugation is shown in the 3 and 4 distributive plural forms, whereas the 1dpl and 2dpl distributive plural forms are built according to the y-P pattern. (Note that Rule Subj-6 applied in the case of the distributive 3 and 4 forms to change the s-P 3 person subject prefix **s** into **sh**, since the verb stem contains the consonant **zh**.)

You might want to compare the P mode forms in (14) with the I mode forms of the same verb base, found in Chapter 6(7). A good exercise would be to compare each I mode form with the P mode form that has the same subject - this will help you learn the subject prefixes better. If you do this, you'll see that the 1dpl forms for the two modes differ only in the verb stem: in the I mode, the forms are **haiilgéésh** and **hadeiilgéésh**, and in the P mode the forms are **haiilgizh** and **hadeiilgizh**. Note also that the 2dpl forms have a short **o** in the I mode (**haołgéésh** and **hadaołgéésh**) but a long **oo** in the P mode (**haoołgizh** and **hadaoołgizh**.)

Now let's look at a prefixless verb in the y-P. An example of one such is "cry" (see Chapter 7(1) - recall from Chapter 8 that this verb takes the y-P.) Here are the P mode forms for this verb:

(15)	sg		dpl	distr dpl
1	yícha	yiicha		deiicha
2	yínícha	woocha		daoocha
3		yícha		dáácha
4		jíícha		dajíícha

Let's make sure we understand these forms.

For the nondistributive 1, 2, and 3 subject forms, we used the subject prefixes in chart (8) directly.

But for the nondistributive 4 form, since we have a prefix in object-prefix position, we shift to chart (5), which is why the **íí** pops up in **jíícha** (we already discussed this word - see (6) above.) Since this verb is intransitive, there is no object prefix in the 3 subject forms. The 1sg and (nondistributive) 3 forms end up being the same.

In the distributive forms, we find the **da** prefix, which is a disjunct prefix, so the subject prefixes used are those found in chart (1). (There is no shift to s-P in this verb. It is often the case that verbs with no lexical prefixes don't have any perfective **da**-shift.) The word **dáácha** "They cried" was discussed earlier (see (3)). In this word, the **áá** is derived in exactly the same way as the **áá** of **háágeed** "I dug it up".

Again, compare the chart of the P mode forms in (15) with the corresponding I mode forms of the same verb base found in Chapter 7(5). For this verb base, the I mode stem and the P mode stem are the same. Because of this, the only difference between "he/she/they (two) are crying" **yicha** and "he/she/they (two) cried" **yícha** is in the tone of the first syllable, and the only difference between "one is crying" **jicha** and "one cried" **jíícha** is in the length and tone of the first syllable. The 1dpl forms are the same in the two modes: **yiicha** and **deiicha**.

We are almost finished with the zero/barred-l case of the y-P conjugation. There is, however, one last detail we have to deal with. It turns out that there is an "irregularity" in the 3 object prefix **y** under certain circumstances. One of these circumstances involves the y-P conjugation, so we had better study this irregularity now. We need to describe what the irregularity is, and we need to learn when it occurs.

The simplest way of describing the irregularity is to say that, instead of marking a 3 object by means of the object prefix **y**, we sometimes double this prefix; that is, we put two **y**'s next to each other, like this: **yy**. (The way this ends up being spelled and pronounced will automatically be taken care of by our rules. We'll see an example very soon.)

Now, when does this happen? Well, one circumstance when we find this happening is when we've got a prefixless verb base, with a zero or barred-l classifier, that is conjugated in the y-P conjugation. When the 3 person **y** object prefix isn't preceded by any other prefix, we get this doubling. Let's formulate this as an addition to Rule Str-1:

(Add to Rule Str-1): Instead of using the 3 object prefix **y**, put two **y**'s next to each other (like this: **yy**) into the object prefix position in the y-P conjugation if the classifier is zero or barred-l, the subject is 3 person, there is no inner prefix following the 3 object prefix, and there is no prefix preceding the 3 object prefix.

This little twist has not come up in our examples yet because so far we haven't looked at a prefixless, transitive verb base that is conjugated in the y-P. (The verb base that means "boil it" is transitive and prefixless, but it's conjugated in the s-P. The verb base that means "cry" is prefixless and conjugated in the y-P, but it's intransitive. The verb bases that mean "dig it up" and "cut it out" are transitive and are conjugated in the y-P, but they have lexical prefixes.) So here's an example that illustrates this new twist: the verb base that means "chew it". The verb base is:

(16)

Stem-set		Classifier: zero
I:	'aał	
P:	'aal	Lexical prefixes: (none)
F:	'ał	
R:	'ał	Transitivity: transitive
O:	'aał	
		Perfective: y-P

(There's that shortened vowel in the F stem again! Also: the P mode stem is the only one which ends in l rather than in ł - it's not a misprint! This is a stem-set pattern that we'll talk about a little at the end of Chapter 13.)

The P mode forms of this verb come out as follows:

(17)   sg   dpl   distr dpl

1   yí'aal   yiit'aal   deiit'aal
2   yíní'aal   woo'aal   daoo'aal
3   yiyíí'aal   dayíí'aal
4   jíí'aal   dajíí'aal

Comparing this with the forms in (15), we see that there is a difference only in the 3 subject forms (so, as a consequence, the 1sg and nondistributive 3 forms are different for the "chew it" verb.) Naturally, there is no object prefix in the "chew it" verb for the 1, 2, and 4 subject cases, because Rule Str-1 says that the 3 object is marked as zero in those cases; and there is no object prefix in the "cry" verb for those subjects because "cry" is intransitive, so it never takes an object prefix in any form. (Actually, the j in jíí'aal is an object prefix, but it indicates that the subject is 4 person. There's no prefix in jíí'aal that indicates that the object is 3 person.)

The nondistributive 3 P mode form of "chew" is built like this:

(18) object   subject   verb
      prefix   prefix   stem

       yy   -   íí   -   'aal

Here, **yy** appears in the object prefix position because of the addition to Rule Str-1 that we just learned: we are in the y-P conjugation, the classifier is zero, the subject is 3 person, there is no inner prefix to the right of the object prefix, and there is no prefix to the left of the object prefix. The subject prefix is **íí**, because the object prefix to its left is a conjunct prefix, so the subject prefix is taken from chart (5).

What happens to the structure in (18)? Well, Rule Conj-1 comes along, notices that the first **y** in this structure is a conjunct prefix followed immediately by a consonant (namely, the second **y**!), and inserts an **i**. The result is **yiyíí'aal**, which is the actual word. (You should check that none of our other rules apply to the structure in (18).) Note that in order for Rule Conj-1 to work this way, we need to think of the **yy** at the beginning of (18) as two prefixes, so that the first **y** all by itself is a prefix that Rule Conj-1 can act upon. Incidentally, make sure you understand that Rule Conj-1 doesn't do anything to the second **y**.

The addition we gave above to Rule Str-1 might not be exactly right, however. The issue involves another case of variation, that is, a case where different people use slightly different forms of the same word. To see what's going on, let's look at the distributive plural 3 person form. (Note, incidentally, that there is no shift to the s-P in the distributive plural forms of this verb.) As things stand, this form is built as follows:

(19) distributive object   subject verb
      plural   prefix   prefix   stem

      da   -   y   -   íí   -   'aal

which gives us **dayíí'aal** directly (Rule Conj-2 doesn't apply because the **y** is followed by a vowel: **íí**.) Note that the addition to Rule Str-1 did not apply when we built (19) since there is a prefix to the left of the object prefix.

However, while forms like **dayíí'aal** are found in print, it is also possible to find forms like **deiyíí'aal** in print. And, in very careful speech, I have sometimes heard what sounded like **dayiyíí'aal**. These last two forms suggest that the distributive plural 3 form is really built like this:

(20) distributive object   subject verb
      plural   prefix   prefix   stem

      da   -   yy   -   íí   -   'aal

If we started with the structure in (20) instead of the structure in (19), Rule Conj-2 would apply to the first of the two **y** prefixes in the object prefix position. The result of applying it would be **daiyíí'aal**. Rule Disj-2 would now come along and change the **ai** to **ei**, which would give **deiyíí'aal**. And, instead of this, in the careful speech of some individuals, the regular part of Rule Conj-1 would

94

simply insert an **i** between the two **y**'s in (20) to give **dayiyíí'aal**. (Do you remember that, back in Chapter 7, we talked about the fact that for some speakers, when they pronounce verbs very carefully, the pronunciation seems to show that they do not use Rule Conj-2? This would be another case of the same thing.)

We could get the structure in (20) if our addition to Rule Str-1, which we gave a little bit earlier, were changed slightly to read:

(Add to Rule Str-1): Instead of using the 3 object prefix **y**, put two of these next to each other (like this: **yy**) into the object prefix position in the y-P conjugation if the classifier is zero or barred-l, the subject is 3 person, there is no inner prefix following the object prefix, and there is no lexical prefix preceding the object prefix.

This would create the structure in (20) rather than the one in (19), since **da** is not a lexical prefix. And, as we saw, if we start with (20), the actual words we form correspond to what we sometimes find in writing and in speech.

Which version of the addition to Rule Str-1 should we use? Perhaps the forms derived from (20) are a little more common, so it might be better to use the second version of the addition to Rule Str-1. But in the Appendix, we put the word "lexical" in parentheses. You should keep in mind that there is variation here, and you might as easily find words like **dayíí'aal** as you would find words like **deiyíí'aal** in print.

By the way, does it bother you that with this addition to Rule Str-1 we find that we are sometimes going to have two prefixes in the object prefix position? If so, please relax! It will turn out that there are other circumstances (not involving the 3 object prefix **y**) where we'll find two prefixes in the object prefix slot. This is something that is allowed (under certain circumstances) in the structure of Navajo verbs.

As we've said, the doubling of the 3 object prefix **y** occurs with prefixless verbs - that's why we wrote our statements of the addition to Rule Str-1 to say that there can't be an inner prefix following the object prefix in order for this to happen. If there are any inner prefixes in a verb, then the 3 object prefix **y** just stays **y**, in the ordinary way. We'll run into examples of this when we come to study verb bases that have inner prefixes. But as we learn more about other conjugations we'll occasionally run into other cases where the 3 object prefix **y** doubles to **yy**. The statement of Rule Str-1 in the Appendix includes these other cases as well.

Well, that's all we need to say about the forms in (17). (By the way, if you were wondering what that **t'** is doing in the 1dpl forms in (17), see Rule Subj-1 and Chapter 4(9).) In fact, this is everything we need to learn about the y-P conjugation for verb bases with zero or barred-l classifiers. (Whew!) As a dessert, let's give the complete conjugation of the verb that means "speak" in the P mode, just to see that we've really learned how to do this. (We already worked out two of the forms earlier - see

(2) and (4).) The verb base can be found in Chapter 7(16) - note that the perfective is indeed y-P, as we mentioned near the beginning of Chapter 8. Since we have an outer prefix in this base, most of the subject prefixes will come from chart (1). Here are the P mode forms for this verb:

(21)	sg	dpl	distr pl
1	yááłti'	yéiilti'	yádeiilti'
2	yéínííłti'	yáoołti'	yádaoołti'
3		yááłti'	yádaałti'
4		yájííłti'	yádajííłti'

In the form **yááłti'** "I spoke", we saw earlier that the **á** vowel which comes from the disjunct prefix **yá** is lengthened to **áá** (this vowel is also required to have high tone, but it happens to have already had high tone to start with.) And, since this verb is intransitive, the same form means "he/she/they (two) spoke".

In the form **yéínííłti'** "you (sg) spoke", we noted earlier that Rule Disj-2 applied. Note that the same rule also applies in the forms **yéiilti'** "we (two) spoke" and **yádeiilti'** "we spoke". Interesting point: the high tone on the **é** of **yéínííłti'** is required as part of the 2sg subject prefix (see chart (1)), but the high tone on the **é** in **yéiilti'** is there just as a left-over of the high tone on **yá** (review Rule Disj-2.) That's why there is no high tone on the **e** in **yádeiilti'** - there's no reason for there to be a high tone on it.

Why didn't Rule Subj-5 put a high tone on the **eii** of **yádeiilti'**? (Answer: **eii** isn't short.)

Why does the vowel **áá** have high tone in the form **yádááłti'**? (The 3 person subject prefix actually consists of this high tone (and the vowel length). See chart (1).)

The vowel **íí** popped out in the 4 person forms because the **j** prefix, which is in the object prefix position, is a conjunct prefix, requiring us to go to chart (5) for the subject prefix.

Why is there an **l** rather than an **ł** in the 1dpl forms? (See Rule Subj-3.)

Now, take a short break, and then proceed directly to Chapter 10, where we'll study the y-P conjugation for verb bases that have a plain-l or d classifier!

CHAPTER 10

THE y-P CONJUGATION:
PLAIN-L AND D CLASSIFIERS

Having learned the way that verbs with zero or barred-l classifiers are conjugated in the y-P, we turn next to verbs with plain-l and d classifiers. Again, we will break up our study of the subject prefixes into several cases. In Chapter 9, we found it convenient to give three charts of subject prefixes, representing the situation where the subject prefix was immediately preceded by a disjunct prefix (Chapter 9(1)), by a conjunct prefix (Chapter 9(5)), or by no prefix (Chapter 9(8)). For the plain-l and d classifiers, we will do the same thing. Let's get right to it and look at these charts. First, here's the chart for the subject prefixes for the y-P conjugation when the classifier is plain-l or d, for the case that the subject prefix is immediately preceded by a disjunct prefix:

(1)   y-P subject prefixes, plain-l/d classifiers, preceded by disjunct prefix:

	sg	dpl
1	vvsh	iid
2	víní	ooh
3	vv	

This chart resembles the chart in Chapter 9(1) in a number of ways, but there are also some differences. What we need to do first of all is to understand exactly what chart (1) above means. There is only one thing about (1) that we need to discuss: the symbol "vv", which is part of the 1sg subject prefix and which is the entire 3 subject prefix.

In Chapter 9(1), we used the symbol "w̋" to mean that the vowel at the end of the preceding disjunct prefix is to be made long and high-tone. The "vv" here (without the tone marks) means something similar. It means: make the vowel at the end of the preceding disjunct prefix long.

But what about the tone? Important: we will leave the tone as it is! That is, whenever we see the symbol "vv", if the preceding disjunct prefix ends in a short high-tone vowel, we'll lengthen the vowel and get a long high-tone vowel. If the preceding disjunct prefix ends in a short low-tone vowel, we'll lengthen the vowel and get a long low-tone vowel. If the preceding disjunct prefix ends in a long vowel already, we'll do nothing. This is all we need to know about the 1sg and 3 prefixes in (1).

The remaining three prefixes are straightforward. The 1dpl and 2dpl prefixes are completely ordinary, and the 2sg prefix is actually the same as in the case where the classifier is zero or barred-l.

We can illustrate the way the "vv" symbol works by building a few forms from a new verb base. Here is the verb base that means "dash up out" (that is, "run quickly up out of something"):

(2)

Stem-set		Classifier: plain-l
I:	**taał**	Lexical prefixes: **ha** (outer)
P:	**táál**	
F:	**tał**	Transitivity: intransitive
R:	**tał**	
O:	**taał**	Perfective: y-P

(There's that vowel shortening in the F stem again! And again the P mode stem is the only one that ends in l instead of ł; it's also the only one with a high tone vowel.)

Let's build the word that means "I dashed up out". Here is the structure of this word:

(3) outer   subject   cl   verb
     prefix   prefix   stem

     ha   -   vvsh   -   l   -   táál

Remember what the "vv" in (3) means: if the vowel at the end of the preceding disjunct prefix is short, then lengthen it. The preceding disjunct prefix in (3) is **ha**, and its vowel is indeed short. So, we'll lengthen it, which means that we'll get a word that starts like this: "haash....". To finish the story, we only need to remember that Rule Subj-2 (the sandwich rule) applies, so the word ends up being **haashtáál**.

(You might be wondering why we're using this "vv" in the subject prefix as a way of saying that the preceding vowel is lengthened. Why don't we just say that Rule Disj-1 lengthens the vowel? The answer is this: Rule Disj-1 only lengthens some vowels. For example, it does not lengthen a high-tone á. However, any vowel (with any tone) gets lengthened by the "vv" in the 1sg and 3 prefixes in chart (1). In later chapters, we'll see examples of verbs that have vowels lengthened by "vv" that Rule Disj-1 doesn't lengthen.)

We'd like to write out the complete set of P mode forms for this new verb base. However, to do this, we need to deal with the forms of the subject prefixes when there is a conjunct prefix preceding it. Why? Because we want to include the 4 person subject forms in our chart, and these involve the **j** prefix which is a conjunct prefix (remember, it's placed in the object prefix position). So, here is our second chart for this chapter, the chart that gives the subject prefixes for the y-P conjugation when the classifier is plain-l or d, for the case that the subject prefix is immediately preceded by a conjunct prefix:

(4)   y-P subject prefixes, plain-l/d classifiers, preceded by conjunct prefix:

	sg	dpl
1	eesh	iid
2	ííní	ooh
3	oo	

The situation here is different from the situation when the classifier is zero or barred-l. In that case, when the subject prefix is preceded by a conjunct prefix, what we did is substitute the vowel **i** for the v symbol in the subject prefix chart (remember?) Here, the 2sg prefix works this way, too. But the 1sg prefix seems to have been formed by substituting **e**, not **i**, for the v. And the 3 prefix was formed by substituting **o** for the v. If it helps to remember the prefixes in (4) by thinking of these different substitutions, then go ahead and think of them. But you might find it easier just to memorize the prefixes in (4) as they're listed.

The good news is that there is nothing new we need to learn in order to use these prefixes. We won't be able to illustrate all of the prefixes in (4) in this chapter because we haven't yet studied enough conjunct prefixes to build forms that would use them all. But don't worry: we'll see all of the prefixes in (4) in the next chapter. In this chapter, it's the 3 subject prefix **oo** in (4) that we will see. With this prefix (and the ones in (1)) we can build a complete set of P mode forms of the verb base that means "dash up out". Would you like to try to do this before looking at the forms below? If so, you might remember that since **ha** is an outer prefix that calls for the y-P conjugation, you can expect **da**-shift to the s-P conjugation in the distributive forms (we'll show this for the 3 and 4 person distributive plural subjects only.)

Here are the forms:

(5)	sg	dpl	distr dpl
1	haashtááł	haiiltááł	hadeiiltááł
2	háíníltááł	haooltááł	hadaooltááł
3	haaltááł		hadaastááł
4	hajooltááł		hadajistááł

Let's make sure we understand these forms.

We have already discussed the form **haashtááł** where the subject is 1sg - see (3) above and the discussion there.

Next, the only forms in (5) where there is a conjunct prefix preceding the subject prefix are the 4 person forms, where the 4 person prefix **j**, which is placed in the object prefix position, is the conjunct prefix. The nondistributive 4 person form is built this way:

(6)   outer   object   subject   cl   verb
        prefix   prefix   prefix   stem

        ha - j - oo - l - táál

Question: Why is the subject prefix **oo** used? Answer: The subject prefix is preceded by an object prefix, which is a conjunct prefix, so the subject prefix is taken from chart (4). Remember that a 3 person subject prefix is always used when the 4 person subject is indicated by **j**.

Incidentally, none of the rules we've learned make any changes in the structure in (6), so the word ends up as **hajooltáál**. You should read through our rules so far and make sure that none of them do anything to this structure.

Question: Why isn't the subject prefix **oo** used in the nondistributive 3 person form? Answer: There is no conjunct prefix in this form. The nondistributive 3 form is built like this:

(7)   outer   subject   cl   verb
        prefix   prefix   stem

        ha - vv - l - táál

The subject prefix in (7) is taken from chart (1), since the subject prefix in this form is preceded by an outer prefix, which is a disjunct prefix. And remember what the "vv" does. We check to see if the vowel at the end of the immediately preceding disjunct prefix is short, and if it is, we lengthen it. As in the case of the structure in (3), the vowel we're interested in is the **a** of **ha**, which is short. So, we lengthen it to **aa**. You should check that no other rules apply to the structure in (7), so the actual word is **haaltáál**.

The 2sg form is built and derived the same way as the 2sg form is built and derived in the case of a zero or barred-l classifier. We saw how this works in Chapter 9 - you might want to look at the 2sg forms in the charts in Chapter 9(10) and Chapter 9(14).

The other nondistributive forms in (5) are easy, so we won't discuss them in detail either.

Question (again!): Why is there a long **aa** in the forms **haashtáál** and **haaltáál**? (Answer: the **a** of **ha** is lengthened by the "vv" which is part of the 1sg subject prefix and which is the whole 3 subject prefix.)

Question: Why does the long **aa** in the forms **haashtáál** and **haaltáál** have a low tone? (Answer: this **aa** starts out as the **a** of **ha**, and this **a** has a low tone. The "vv" which is part of the 1sg subject prefix and which is the whole 3 subject prefix does not change the tone of the vowel that it lengthens.)

Question: Why don't we see an **h** as part of the subject prefix inside the form **haooltáál**? (Answer: See Rule Subj-4.)

Question: What happened to the **l** classifier in the form **haashtaal**? (Answer: See Rule Subj-2.)

The distributive plural forms are all straightforward, as soon as we realize that the speakers of the forms in (5) used perfective **da**-shift to the s-P conjugation in the 3 and 4 person distributive plural forms. As we said earlier, we expect the shift with this verb base since it contains the prefix **ha** which requires the y-P conjugation.

We are almost finished with the plain-l or d classifier case of the y-P conjugation. The only thing left is to study the subject prefixes that are used when they have nothing in front of them. Here is a chart for this situation:

(8)   y-P subject prefixes, plain-l/d classifiers, preceded by no prefix:

	sg	dpl
1	yish	yiid
2	yíní	wooh
3	yi	

We'll illustrate these in just a moment. But first, let's look a bit at the prefixes in the three charts that we've learned in this chapter. By comparing them with one another, and by comparing them with the prefixes that we learned in Chapter 9 for the case where the classifier is zero or barred-l, we'll make it easier to learn them.

First of all, the 2sg prefixes in the three charts above are exactly the same as the 2sg prefixes in the corresponding charts given in Chapter 9 for the zero/barred-l classifier case. This is always true for P mode conjugations: the 2sg subject prefix does not differ when different classifiers are used.

Next, the 2dpl prefix for the plain-l and d classifier case (in any of the charts above: they're the same) ends in **h**, so Rule Subj-4 will apply. Remember: in the P mode in general, the 2dpl subject prefix regularly ends in **h** when the classifier is plain-l or d. (The 2dpl subject prefix does not end in **h** when the classifier is zero or barred-l, in the P mode.) We might note that the 2dpl prefix in (1) and (4) looks like the s-P plain-l/d 2dpl prefix **sooh** with the **s** missing. It also resembles the I mode 2dpl prefix, differing from it only in that here in the y-P, the vowel is long. (The **wooh** in (8) is really just the same prefix **ooh**, with a **w** stuck on the beginning by Rule Str-3.)

The 1dpl prefix (in any of the charts above: they're the same) is the same as the 1dpl prefixes found in the corresponding charts given in Chapter 9 for the zero/barred-l classifier case. This is also always true for P mode conjugations: the 1dpl subject prefix does not differ when different classifiers are used. Also, this prefix is actually the same as the 1dpl prefix for the regular I mode conjugation. Finally, this prefix looks like the s-P 1dpl prefix **siid** with the **s** missing. (The **yiid** in (8) is really just the same prefix **iid**, with a **y** stuck on the beginning by Rule Str-3.)

Now let's look at the 3 prefixes. If we compare each chart in this chapter with the corresponding chart in Chapter 9, we see something interesting: the 3 prefixes in the three charts in Chapter 9 all have high tone, whereas this is not the case here in this chapter. For the plain-l or d classifier case, if there is a disjunct prefix in front of the 3 subject prefix, the tone of the disjunct prefix is the tone of the subject prefix; otherwise, we get a low tone. Also, if a conjunct prefix precedes the 3 subject prefix, we get a different vowel in the two cases: (high-tone) **íí** if the classifier is zero or barred-l, (low-tone) **oo** if the classifier is plain-l or d. If there is no prefix preceding the subject prefix, then the zero/barred-l case looks like the peg with a high tone on it, whereas the plain-l/d case simply looks like the peg (which normally has low tone.)

Finally, let's look at the 1sg prefixes. Comparing the charts in this chapter with the corresponding charts in Chapter 9, we can make the following simple statement. If the classifier is zero or barred-l, the 1sg prefix is the same as the 3 prefix; if the classifier is plain-l or d, the 1sg prefix is almost the same as the 3 prefix with **sh** following it (the only difference is that, if there's a conjunct prefix in front of it, we get the vowel **ee** in front of the **sh** rather than the **oo** that we see with the 3 subject prefix.) This **sh** is the "same" as the 1sg subject prefix in the regular I mode conjugation. Again, we have a general fact: the **sh** which we normally find as part of the 1sg subject prefix in most conjugation patterns mysteriously disappears in the P mode if the classifier is zero or barred-l, but is present in the P mode if the classifier is plain-l or d.

Well, all this might help you remember the actual prefixes. On the other hand, you might prefer just to memorize the charts in (1), (4), and (8).

Now, we've illustrated the prefixes in (1) and the **oo** prefix in (4). To illustrate the prefixes in (8), let's take a verb base that has no lexical prefix. We'll use the verb base that means "drink it" - it has a **d** classifier, so its subject prefixes will be chosen from the charts in this chapter. Here it is:

(9)

Stem-set		Classifier: d
I:	**dlą́**	Lexical prefixes: (none)
P:	**dlą́ą́'**	
F:	**dlį́į́ł**	Transitivity: transitive
R:	**dlį́į́h**	
O:	**dlį́į́h**	Perfective: y-P

(Did you notice the ł at the end of the F mode stem?)

Do you notice anything unusual about this verb base? Aha: the classifier is d, but even so, this verb is transitive! (Recall that d classifier verb bases are usually intransitive.)

Since this verb base has the d classifier, we expect d-effect to apply to the first consonant in the verb stem. If we check Chapter 4(9), we see that d-effect applied to **dl** just gives us **dl**; that is, there is no change. So, in the actual verb forms, the stem will begin with **dl**, and there won't be any other sign of a classifier. However, when building the P mode forms for this verb, the fact that the classifier is really d (rather than zero) becomes important. If the classifier were zero, we'd use the subject prefixes discussed in Chapter 9. But since the classifier is really d, we need to use the subject prefixes that we're learning in this chapter.

Can you create all the P mode forms? Here they are:

(10)   sg   dpl   distr dpl

	sg	dpl	distr dpl
1	yishdlą́ą́'	yiidlą́ą́'	deiidlą́ą́'
2	yínídlą́ą́'	woohdlą́ą́'	daoohdlą́ą́'
3		yoodlą́ą́'	dayoodlą́ą́'
4		joodlą́ą́'	dajoodlą́ą́'

The 1sg subject form in (10) (the word that means "I drank it") is very easy. Here is its structure:

(11)   subject   cl   verb
       prefix   stem

       yish - d - dlą́ą́'

The subject prefix in (11) was taken from chart (8), since it is not preceded by a conjunct prefix in this word. None of our rules apply, and we just get **yishdlą́ą́'**. (The d-effect caused by the d classifier makes no change here, as we said earlier.)

103

(But wait! We could have analyzed this word differently. Suppose we said that the 1sg subject prefix was really **sh** in the case that there is no prefix in front of it. If we did this, then the peg rule (Rule Str-2) would supply the **yi**, and we'd end up with the same form. Should we do this? Well, we could. It just seems odd to say that the 1sg subject prefix is **sh** preceded by all sorts of stuff if there is a prefix to its left but reduces to just plain **sh** if there is no prefix to its left. If you like this better, you can think of it this way, but it seemed simpler just to list in (8) the actual forms of the subject prefixes for the case that there is no prefix to its left.)

Next, let's build the word **yiidlą́ą́'** "We (two) drank it":

(12)   subject   cl   verb
         prefix   stem

         yiid   -   d   -   dlą́ą́'

In this form, d-effect applies twice to **dl** (once due to the classifier, once due to Rule Subj-1), but **dl** still just stays **dl** even after all that.

(Again, we could say that the subject prefix is **iid**, and then Rule Str-3 would supply that **y** that we see at the beginning of this word.)

Here are some questions about the 3 and 4 person forms in (10).

Question: Where did the **y** at the beginning of **yoodlą́ą́'** "He/she/they (two) drank it" come from? (Answer: See Rule Str-1. This **y** is the object prefix that indicates 3 person object when the subject is 3 person.)

Question: What are those **oo**'s in the 3 and 4 forms? (Answer: The **oo** is the 3 subject prefix which is used when there's a conjunct prefix in front of it. In **yoodlą́ą́'** and **dayoodlą́ą́'**, the **y** which is the 3 object prefix (see the previous question) is the conjunct prefix, and in **joodlą́ą́'** and **dajoodlą́ą́'**, the **j** which indicates 4 person subject (and which is in the object prefix position) is the conjunct prefix.)

To make sure you understand the last two questions, look at the way the word **yoodlą́ą́'** is built:

(13)   object   subject   cl   verb
         prefix   prefix   stem

         y   -   oo   -   d   -   dlą́ą́'

The subject prefix **oo** was taken from chart (4) because it is preceded by an object prefix (which is a conjunct prefix.) The **y** at the beginning of this word has nothing to do with the peg inserted into some verbs (not this one!) by Rule Str-2 or with the **y** that Rule Str-3 puts in at the beginning of some words (not this one!). The **y** in this word is a "real" prefix - the object prefix required by Rule Str-1.

The word **joodláá'** is built in a similar way.

Just to firm up our understanding of this conjugation, let's compare the forms in (10) with the forms for an intransitive d classifier prefixless verb base. Here is one such; it means "remain", "survive":

(14)

Stem-set		Classifier: d
I:	**dziih**	
P:	**dzíí'**	Lexical prefixes: (none)
F:	**dzih**	Transitivity: intransitive
R:	**dzih**	
O:	**dziih**	Perfective: y-P

(Again, the vowel in the F mode stem is short. And again, the P mode stem is the only one with high tone - it's also the only one that ends in '.)

As in the case of "drink it", the d classifier does not change the first consonant of the verb stem: the **dz** just stays **dz**. But we know that this verb has a d classifier (rather than a zero classifier) because, in the P mode, the subject prefixes used are the ones we're studying in this chapter rather than the ones we learned in Chapter 9.

Before trying to write out the P mode forms of this verb, can you answer the following question: In what forms of the P mode will this verb look different from the verb in (10)?

Answer: Only in the 3 subject forms. The verb in (10) is transitive, so in the 3 subject forms, that verb had in it the object prefix **y**. But this verb won't have this prefix. In the case of the other subjects (1, 2, and 4), the 3 object is indicated in the verb in (10) by zero (which means it has no object prefix), and, of course, the verb whose verb base base is in (14) won't have any object prefixes, since this verb is intransitive.

Okay, here are the P mode forms of "remain":

(15)	sg	dpl	distr dpl
1	yisdzíí'	yiidzíí'	deiidzíí'
2	yínídzíí'	woohdzíí'	daoohdzíí'
3		yidzíí'	daadzíí'
4		joodzíí'	dajoodzíí'

Question: Why is the vowel **aa** in **daadzíí'** "They remained" long? (Answer: Since **da** in this word is a disjunct prefix, the 3 subject prefix used in this word was taken from the chart in (1). This prefix turns out to be vv, so the vowel of **da** is lengthened.)

Question: Why is the subject prefix in **yisdzíí'** "I remained" **yis** instead of **yish**? (Answer: See Rule Subj-6. Note that the verb stem contains the consonant **dz**.)

In all other respects, the P mode forms of this verb are like the P mode forms of "drink it". Note, by the way, that the 4 person prefix **j** causes the vowel **oo** (see chart (4)) to pop out in the forms of this verb, just as it did in the case of the transitive verb "drink". Transitivity has nothing to do with it: it's the presence of something in the object-prefix position that did it.

Well, this takes care of our basic study of the y-P conjugation. We have not been able to illustrate all of the possible forms of the subject prefixes, however. For example, we have not yet studied any structure in which a conjunct prefix could precede a non-3 subject prefix. (The only conjunct prefixes that we've studied so far are the 4 person "subject" prefix **j** and the 3 person object prefix **y**, both of which are placed in the object-prefix position, and both of which only occur when the subject-prefix position has the 3 person prefix in it.) But we will see many examples of these fairly soon, so don't forget those other forms of the subject prefixes!

There are also some circumstances, involving certain particular prefixes that we haven't studied yet, where we will have to add a few little details to the story of the y-P conjugation. But what we've learned here is the basis even for those special cases (we'll clean those cases up in future chapters.) For most Navajo verbs that take the y-P conjugation, what we've learned already is enough to give us all the forms correctly.

(By the way: how many new rules did we need in order to form the words we studied in this chapter? None! We won't always be so lucky, but the fact is, we've already learned a large portion of the rules we need for the whole verb system.)

CHAPTER 11

OBJECT PREFIXES FOR TRANSITIVE VERBS

In our study so far, we have looked at forms (in the I and P modes) of some transitive verbs. However, we only looked at verbs where the object of the verb was 3 person. In this chapter and the next, we will learn how to form transitive verbs that have other kinds of objects.

What other kinds of objects can there be? Well, for some verbs, a 3 person object is actually the only one that we'd ever expect to find. These are verbs where the action is something that only makes sense if the object is some inanimate thing. For example, actions like "boil", "plant", or "buy" are actions that are not normally done to human beings. It is sort of hard to imagine that anybody ever would want to say things like "He boiled you" or "Jack planted me" (although perhaps there are some unusual circumstances where these might make sense.) For verb bases with meanings like these, what we've learned already is really enough, at least as far as the object is concerned.

However, there are other kinds of actions where it is easy to imagine one person doing the action to another person. For example, actions like "see", "hit", "rescue", "know", "feed", or "kiss" are actions that one person often would do to another. This means that languages have ways of saying things like "he saw you", "they rescued me", "I am feeding you", "you kissed us", and so forth. In sentences like these, the object is no longer 3 person. Since the object of a Navajo verb is indicated by putting a prefix into the verb itself, we need to study how these non-3 objects are represented.

The way that the object of a transitive verb is indicated is by putting a prefix into the object-prefix position. Now, we know that different sets of subject prefixes are used for different modes. However, object prefixes are easier: the same object prefixes are used for all modes.

The actual prefixes that are used to indicate objects of transitive verbs are listed in (1). Incidentally, since these are conjunct prefixes, all the object prefixes in (1) end in a consonant.

(1)

	sg	dpl
1	sh	nih
2	n	nih
3	y or b or zero	
4	hw	
unspec	'	

There are a number of things about this chart that we need to explain.

If you already know some Navajo, you might have noticed that the prefixes in (1) look the same as the prefixes that are used with nouns to indicate possession. Like those possessive prefixes, the 1dpl and 2dpl prefixes happen to be the same. This means that there will always be a possible ambiguity when this prefix is used: the verbs that mean, for example, "he saw us (two)" and "he saw you (two)" will end up being the same. However, in certain cases, we'll be able to tell more exactly what is meant: for example, if the subject prefix indicates that the subject is "we", and if we see **nih** as an object prefix, then the object can only be "you (two)". Why? Because the prefixes in (1) can never be used "reflexively", that is, they can never be used to refer to the same person or thing or group of persons or things as the subject. If you want to built a transitive verb where the object and the subject are the same, you have to use a special reflexive construction. We will study the reflexive construction in Chapter 26.

Chart (1) indicates nothing about plurality. Of course, there are different prefixes for "me" (1sg) and "us" (1dpl), for example, but what about objects involving groups of three or more? Also, in the 3 and 4 persons, even the difference between singular and duoplural doesn't exist (this is the same as the situation with subject prefixes.) In general, plurality of objects is usually not indicated in the verb at all. However, if it is necessary to emphasize that an object is plural, the distributive plural prefix **da** can be used (in its ordinary position.) This means that, potentially, there is an ambiguity: if **da** is present in a transitive verb, does it mean that the subject is plural, or does it mean that the object is plural? Well, in most cases, it means that the subject is plural. However, it is possible to use **da** to mean that the object is plural, in certain circumstances. We won't be able to study this matter further as part of our course; the main thing that we have to remember here is that there is no other general way of making the objects of transitive verbs plural.

The entry in (1) for 3 person object shows three possibilities for the prefix in this case. Back in Chapter 6, we learned a rule (Rule Str-1) that told us that the object prefix is zero in certain cases and **y** in others. So what's the mysterious **b** that we see in (1)? It turns out that a 3 object appears as **b** rather than as **y** or zero in certain situations. We will present these situations as additions to Rule Str-1. Here, we will learn one such addition:

(add to Rule Str-1): If a transitive verb has 3 subject and 3 object, the object is indicated by **b** if the verb is going to be used as an inverse form.

The problem with this addition is that we won't know what it actually means until we learn what is meant by "using a verb as an inverse form", so let's talk about this now.

The business of using a verb as an inverse form is really a matter of syntax; in fact, it's a piece of syntax that's been studied quite a lot. Let's take a brief look at it here, just so that we know what we're dealing with.

Normally, when a transitive verb is used, the subject of the verb is the topic, that is, the main person or thing that is being talked about. On the other hand, the object of the verb is a kind of extra entity, something new that's being added in. However, sometimes we want to use a transitive verb where the object is the topic of the conversation. In this case, we'd use an inverse form of the verb.

Now, in Navajo, the only time that an inverse form of a verb looks different from a "normal" form (the "normal" form is usually called the *direct* form) is when the subject and the object are both 3 person. In this case, the difference shows up in the way the object is marked in the verb: use **y** as the object prefix if the verb is going to be used normally (that is, if we want to use the direct form of the verb, because the subject is the topic), but use **b** as the object prefix if the verb is going to be used as an inverse (that is, if the object is going to be the topic.)

In all the examples that we've seen in earlier chapters, whenever we built a transitive verb with a 3 person subject and a 3 person object, we've actually built the direct form. Let's look at an example that illustrates the way the inverse form is built. We'll use a new verb base, one which means "carry him/her up out of something". This verb base will be handy because it's easy to give examples with this verb that illustrate the way that inverse forms are used in sentences. Here is this verb base:

(2)

Stem-set		Classifier: barred-l
I:	**teeh**	
P:	**tį**	Lexical prefixes: **ha** (outer)
F:	**tééł**	
R:	**tééh**	Transitivity: transitive
O:	**tééł**	Perfective: y-P

(This is another example where the vowel in the P mode stem looks different from the vowels in the other stems. And, don't forget to notice the ł at the end of the F mode stem!)

How would we form the word that means "he/she/they (two) carried him/her up (out of something)"? According to what we have learned in earlier chapters, this word is built this way:

(3)	outer prefix		object prefix		subject prefix		cl		verb stem
	ha	-	y	-	íí	-	ł	-	tį

Checking through our rules, we see that none (!) of them apply to change anything, so the actual word is: **hayííłtį**.

But this is the direct form. This word could be used by itself to mean, say, "he carried her up (out of something)". It also could be used in a sentence like:

(4)   Jack Jill hayíítį́.

This sentence means "Jack carried Jill up (out of something)". Note that in this sentence, the name that corresponds to the subject (**Jack**) appears first, and the name that corresponds to the object (**Jill**) appears second.

Here's another sentence using this word:

(5)   Jill hayííłtį́.

This sentence would mostly be used to mean "he carried Jill up", or "she carried Jill up", or "they (two) carried Jill up". The thing to notice about (5) is that the person mentioned by name, namely Jill, is probably not the topic: if there are two people involved in an event, and one is mentioned by name while the other is referred to by a pronoun (which means that he or she wouldn't be mentioned by a separate word at all in Navajo), the pronoun is probably the topic. Since the direct form of the verb is used in (5), the subject is the topic; since the subject is the topic, the subject is the person that is not mentioned in (5), which means that Jill is the object.

Now, let's build the inverse form of this verb. All we have to do to build the inverse form is use **b** instead of **y** as the 3 object marker:

(6)   outer   object   subject   cl   verb
      prefix   prefix   prefix   stem

      ha   -   b   -   íí   -   ł   -   tį́

Again, none of our rules do anything here, so the word just comes out as **habííłtį́**. By itself, this word might be translated something like: "he/she, he/she/they (two) carried him/her up (out of something)" (whew!) This will make more sense if we use this word in a sentence. If we say:

(7)   Jack Jill habííłtį́.

this means "Jack, Jill carried him up (out of something)". Note that now Jill is doing the carrying and Jack is getting carried; that is, the name that corresponds to the object comes first in (7), and the name that corresponds to the subject comes second. What is happening is this: when both the subject and the object are mentioned outside the verb, the expression that corresponds to the topic comes first. This is true for (7), where the object is the topic, and also for (4), where the subject is the topic.

Next, if we say:

(8)   Jill habííłtį́.

we mean, most likely, "Jill carried him/her up". Why? Since the participant that is mentioned outside the verb is probably not the topic, (8) is understood to mean that Jill is probably not the topic. But this means that Jill is the subject, since the verb is in the inverse form, which is the form used when the subject is not the topic (because the object is the topic.)

There are a number of other issues involving the usage of inverse forms. For many speakers, if a transitive verb is being used to talk about an event where one participant is a human being and the other participant is an animal or an inanimate thing, then the human being has to be considered the topic no matter which participant is the subject and which the object. It seems that these usages may be undergoing change; it is certainly true that different speakers have different habits with regard to the way in which they use inverse forms. You can read more about issues like this in YM 87 page 65, for example, but we won't say any more about it here. We can summarize our discussion of the usage of inverse forms this way:

(9)(a) direct form = subject is topic
        inverse form = object is topic

   (b) If both subject and object are mentioned outside the verb, the topic comes first.

   (c) If only one of the participants is mentioned outside the verb, the participant that is not mentioned outside the verb is the topic.

We won't list these rules in the Appendix, because these are rules of syntax, so they're not really part of our study (we're really only studying the forms of verbs here.) However, keeping these rules in mind will help you to understand how the inverse forms are used.

Incidentally, near the end of Chapter 9, we introduced another addition to Rule Str-1. That addition had to do with the fact that the prefix **y** sometimes doubles and becomes **yy**. In the case of the prefix **b**, nothing strange like that ever happens. In the inverse form, 3 subject and 3 object, the object prefix is always just plain **b**.

This is all we need to say about the 3 object prefixes listed in (1).

Before moving on to our study of the actual forms of verbs with object prefixes in them, you may be wondering about the prefix listed in (1) which is called "unspec". What is this prefix for? Rather than answering this question now, we will put off studying this prefix until Chapter 12. At that time we'll explain what this prefix is used for.

We'd like to start illustrating the prefixes in (1). In most cases, we can just go ahead and build new words, putting these prefixes in and applying our rules, and we'll get exactly the right forms. But for the complete story, we'll need a few new rules. For one thing, it turns out that Rule Conj-1 does not quite work in the normal way for the 4 person and the "unspec" prefixes. Besides that, there are other things we'll need to say about these two prefixes. For that reason, we are going to leave these two prefixes for the next chapter.

But we still have to learn a new rule for the other prefixes. This rule turns out to be a general fact about conjunct prefixes. Here it is:

Rule Conj-3: Let C stand for the consonant at the end of a conjunct prefix. If C is followed immediately by a 2sg subject prefix **ni**, then this **ni** is replaced by **í**, so the combination of the end of the conjunct prefix with the subject prefix looks like this: **Cí**. (Rule Conj-1 doesn't apply in this case.)

Rule Conj-3 will affect the forms of verbs in the I mode conjugation if the subject is 2sg and if there is a nonzero object prefix chosen from (1). In this case, the object prefix plays the role of the conjunct prefix in Rule Conj-3.

To illustrate the formation of words with the object prefixes, we will look at a number of examples. But we won't give complete charts. If you think about it, you'll realize that there are quite a lot of different forms that a transitive verb can have, since the subject and the object can each vary, which means that a complete chart would be pretty big. The examples that follow should give a complete picture, though, in the sense that any other form of the verbs shown are built in the same way as the forms in the examples.

Using the verb base that means "carry up (out of something)" shown in (2) above, let's first build some I mode examples with various objects. Here is the word meaning "I'm carrying you (sg) up":

(10)   outer   object   subject   cl   verb
        prefix   prefix   prefix   stem

        ha   -   n   -   sh   -   ł - teeh

In (10), the prefix **n** was chosen from (1) above to indicate that the object is 2sg, that is, "you (sg)". The subject prefix is the regular I mode subject prefix **sh** from Chapter 4(2), indicating that the subject is 1sg, that is, "I". The rest of the verb is built the usual way; make sure that you see that the verb stem in (10) is the I mode verb stem for this verb base. We chose this stem since we are building an I mode word.

Two rules apply to this word. First of all, Rule Conj-1 puts the vowel **i** in after the object prefix **n**, since this prefix is followed directly by a consonant. And secondly, the sandwich rule (Rule Subj-2) deletes the ł that is sandwiched in between the subject prefix **sh** and the first consonant of the verb stem. Applying these rules, we get the actual word that means "I'm carrying you up": **hanishteeh**.

(Why didn't Rule Disj-1 apply to **ha**? Answer: in the actual word, **ha** is not the pre-stem syllable, since the syllable that follows **ha** is the syllable **ni**, which is not the verb stem syllable.)

Next, let's switch the subject and the object and build the word that means "you (sg) are carrying me up":

(11) outer   object   subject   cl   verb
      prefix   prefix   prefix   stem

         ha   -   sh   -   ni   -   ł - teeh

In this case, our new rule, Rule Conj-3, applies, since the object prefix **sh** is a conjunct prefix, and this prefix is directly followed by the 2sg I mode prefix **ni**. No other rules apply, so the actual word that means "you're carrying me up" turns out to be: **hashíłteeh.**

Moving right along, let's look at the word meaning "he's carrying you (sg) up":

(12) outer   object   subject   cl   verb
      prefix   prefix   prefix   stem

         ha   -   n   -   (zero)   -   ł - teeh

Rule Conj-1 applies to this word: the object prefix **n** is a conjunct prefix, and it is followed directly by the consonant ł (the classifier.) When this vowel is put in, we get our word: **haniłteeh.**

It will be instructive to switch the subject and the object of this last word and build the word that means "you (sg) are carrying him up":

(13) outer   object   subject   cl   verb
      prefix   prefix   prefix   stem

         ha   -   (zero)   -   ni   -   ł - teeh

Note that the object prefix, representing a 3 object, is zero (that is, it isn't there), since the subject is not 3 person. In particular, Rule Conj-3 does not apply, since (13) doesn't actually have a conjunct prefix in it. In fact, no rule at all applies to (13), so the word is simply **haniłteeh.** But look: this is the same as the word we built using (12)! The word **haniłteeh** is actually ambiguous: it can either mean "he (or she) is carrying you up", or it can mean "you're carrying him (or her) up". The way the word "starts out" is different for these two meanings: (12) and (13) are different structures. But the actual spelling and pronunciation ends up being the same for both structures.

The next example illustrates a little matter for which we'll need another rule. Let's form the word that means "one is carrying me up" (using the 4 person subject). If you try to write down the structure, you'll see what the problem is: we want to use the object prefix **sh** to indicate that the object is "me". But we also want to use the prefix **j** (for 4 person subject), and this prefix also is supposed to go into the object prefix position! Can we have two prefixes in this position? And, if so, what order should they be in?

The answer is: yes, we can have two prefixes in the object prefix position. The ordering is handled by the following rule:

Rule Str-4: If the 4 person subject prefix **j** is used in the object prefix position together with another object prefix, the 4 person prefix **j** comes second (that is, the other object prefix precedes the **j**.)

With the help of Rule Str-4, we can build our word:

(14) outer   object   subject   cl   verb
      prefix   prefix   prefix   stem

      ha - sh - j - (zero) - ł - teeh

In this word, Rule Conj-1 applies twice, putting an **i** after the **sh** and also after the **j** (since both of these prefixes are conjunct prefixes, and each one is followed by a consonant in (14).) The word is therefore **hashijiłteeh**.

Other combinations are built the same way. What would be the word for "we (two) are carrying you (sg) up"? (Answer: **haniilteeh**. Note that Rule Conj-1 doesn't apply in this word, since the object prefix **n** is followed by a vowel, namely, the vowel of the subject prefix **iid**. And why is there an ordinary **l** instead of an **ł** in this word? See Rule Subj-3.) What about: "we (more than two) are carrying you (sg) up"? (Answer: **hadaniilteeh**.) What about: "you (two) are carrying me up"? (Answer: **hashołteeh**. Again, Rule Conj-1 doesn't apply here. Why isn't there an **h** after the **o** in this word? See Rule Subj-4.) What about: "you (more than two) are carrying me up"? (Answer: **hadashołteeh**.)

Let's collect all the I mode forms of "carry someone up" that we've seen in this chapter. These are not all the I mode forms that are possible, but they illustrate the way the object prefixes are used, and by collecting them here you can look at a bunch of them all together and, hopefully, see that these forms are not at all hard:

(15)   hanishteeh   "I'm carrying you (sg) up"
        hashíłteeh   "you (sg) are carrying me up"
        haniłteeh   "he/she's carrying you (sg) up"
        haniłteeh   "you (sg) are carrying him/her up"
        hashijiłteeh   "one is carrying me up"
        haniilteeh   "we (two) are carrying you (sg) up"
        hadaniilteeh   "we (pl) are carrying you (sg) up"
        hashołteeh   "you (two) are carrying me up"
        hadashołteeh   "you (pl) are carrying me up"
        haiłteeh   "he/she's carrying him/her up" (direct)
        habiłteeh   "he/she's carrying him/her up" (inverse)

(We tacked on the direct and inverse I mode forms for 3 person subject, 3 person object, so that you can see these as well. And while we're at it, what about "I'm carrying him/her up"? Aha - that's just what we learned back in Chapter 6 - we use zero as the object prefix. The form is just: **haashteeh** (Rule Disj-1 applied in this word.))

All the forms we've looked at have been in the I mode. Let's try some forms of this verb base in the P mode. Incidentally, this will allow us to see some of the forms of the subject prefixes that we listed in Chapter 9(5) but haven't seen yet.

First, "I carried you (sg) up":

(16) outer   object   subject   cl   verb
      prefix   prefix   prefix   stem

      ha   -   n   -   íí   -   ł   -   tį́

Make sure you understand how the pieces of this structure were chosen. The object prefix **n** came from (1) above - it represents the object "you (sg)". The subject prefix **íí** came from Chapter 9(5). Since the verb base uses the y-P conjugation, and since the classifier is barred-l, the subject prefixes used by this verb base are the ones we learned in Chapter 9. We're using the chart in Chapter 9(5) because the subject prefix is immediately preceded by a conjunct prefix (the object prefix **n**.) Note also that the P mode verb stem is used, since we're in the P mode. None of our rules apply, so the word comes out directly as: **hanííłtį́**.

A quick look at Chapter 9(5) will show us that the same word can also mean: "he/she carried you (sg) up". The reason is that the subject prefixes for 1sg and 3 are the same. You may remember that we mentioned in Chapter 9 that in the zero/barred-l y-P conjugation, the subject prefixes for 1sg and 3 subjects are always the same.

Next, let's do "you (sg) carried me up":

(17)

outer prefix		object prefix		subject prefix		cl		verb stem
ha	–	sh	–	ííní	–	ł	–	tį

This time, **sh** was chosen from (1) as the object prefix. Our subject prefix still has to come from Chapter 9(5): from Chapter 9, since the verb base is conjugated in the y-P and has a barred-l classifier, and Chapter 9(5) specifically, since the subject prefix is immediately preceded by a conjunct prefix (the object prefix **sh**.) No rules apply: we just get **hashííníłtį** as the word.

To verify your understanding: make sure you understand why the word for "he/she carried me up" is **hashííłtį**. Also, can you say why this word does <u>not</u> mean "I carried myself up"? (Answer: If the subject and the object are the same person, we have to use the special reflexive form which we'll study later.)

Here is a list of some P mode forms of this verb base. In this list are the words we built in (16) and (17), along with a few other P mode words. Make sure that you understand how each one is built, and how our rules work to give the actual forms of the words shown.

(18)

hanííłtį	"I carried you (sg) up"
hanííłtį	"he/she carried you (sg) up"
hashííníłtį	"you (sg) carried me up"
haniiltį	"we (two) carried you (sg) up"
hadaniiltį	"we (more than two) carried you (sg) up"
hashoołtį	"you (two) carried me up"
hadashoołtį	"you (more than two) carried me up"
hayííłtį	"he/she carried him/her up" (direct)
habííłtį	"he/she carried him/her up" (inverse)

Just to firm up this business, let's look at another verb base and build a few more verbs with various objects. Here is the verb base that means "carry him/her around":

(19)

Stem-set		
I:	**té**	Classifier: barred-l
P:	**tį**	Lexical prefixes: **na** (outer)
F:	**teeł**	Transitivity: transitive
R:	**teeh**	
O:	**teeł**	Perfective: s-P

116

There are some things to be said about this verb base.

First of all, it contains the atelic outer prefix **na**. We learned in Chapter 8 that this prefix requires the s-P conjugation in the perfective. This will give us a chance to see various object prefixes together with s-P subject prefixes.

More mysteriously, you may have noticed that the stem-set for this verb base is almost, but not quite, the same as the stem-set in the verb base that means "carry up" (in (2), near the beginning of this chapter.) The F, R, and O mode stems here have low tone, whereas the corresponding stems in (2) have high tone. With the I stems, the tone situation is reversed: high tone here, low tone in (2), and in addition, the vowel in the I stem here is short, whereas it is long in (2). The P mode stems of the two sets are the same. We will learn later that these two stem-sets are variations of each other. They both have to do with the notion of handling or carrying a single animate entity. (By the way, the fact that the object of both of these verb bases has to be a single animate entity is why we didn't give any examples using the 1dpl or 2dpl object prefixes with "carry up out of something".)

Later on we are going to learn about some of the ways that different verb bases can be related to each other. When two verb bases are related to each other, they will have some meaning in common (for example, the verb bases in (2) and (19) both have to do with carrying or handling an animate object.) In many cases, we'll see two related verb bases that have the same stem-set but different classifiers or different lexical prefixes. Sometimes, though, we'll have two related verb bases where slightly different stem-sets are found. Here is one common situation: we'll collect all the verb bases that are related to each other according to some sort of meaning, and we'll look at all the stem-sets in all these verb bases. What we'll find is that there are two stem-sets (that resemble each other) used in these verb bases, one stem-set with some verb bases, the other stem-set with other verb bases. In a case like this we'll say that the two stem-sets are related to each other.

Does this mean that we will have to memorize ten rather than five verb stems? Not exactly. Sometimes, only one mode will have different stems in related stem-sets (when this happens, it's the I mode that has different stems.) But even in cases where the stems are different for many of the modes, they are related by certain patterns which will help us remember them, such as the differences in tones that we saw between the stems in (2) and the stems in (19). But for now, do not worry any more about this - we'll clarify this later on, as we learn more and more verbs. Let's get back to the matter of the object prefixes as they are used with the verb base in (19).

In the I mode, the forms for "carry around" will be similar to the forms for "carry up out of something". Here are some words, which you should compare with the words that we constructed above in (10), (11), (12), (13), (14), and (15):

(20) nanishté   "I'm carrying you (sg) around"
      nashíłté   "you (sg) are carrying me around"
      naniłté   "he/she/they (two) are carrying you (sg) around"
      naniłté   "you (sg) are carrying him/her around"
      nashijiłté   "one is carrying me around"
      naniilté   "we (two) are carrying you (sg) around"
      nidaniilté   "we (more than two) are carrying you (sg) around"
      nashołté   "you (two) are carrying me around"
      nidashołté   "you (more than two) are carrying me around"
      neiłté   "he/she's carrying him/her around" (direct)
      nabiłté   "he/she's carrying him/her around" (inverse)

These words are formed the same way as the corresponding words that talk about carrying someone up out of something.

Question: Why didn't Rule Disj-3 apply to most of these words (to change **na** to **ni**?) Answer: except for two of the words in (20), **na** is neither followed by the distributive plural prefix nor by the **j** that indicates 4 person subject. In the I mode, these are the only circumstances where **na** would change to **ni** (at least, these are the only ones that we learned about in Chapter 5!) For the two words in (20) that have the distributive plural prefix in them, **na** is followed by the distributive plural prefix **da**, and in these two words the **na** does change to **ni**.

In Chapter 8, we added something to Rule Disj-3, but that addition, which has to do with s-P subject prefixes, doesn't change the story here. If you examine the statement of Rule Disj-3 in the Appendix, you'll see that there are more additions that we will learn. However, none of them apply to the words in (20).

But it's handy to remember the following principle: **na** (and **ná**) do not change to **ni** (or **ní**) when they are immediately followed by an object prefix. Since this is a handy thing to remember, we've added it at the end of the statement of Rule Disj-3 in the Appendix, as a convenience statement.

Incidentally, make sure you understand why there is a high-tone in the second syllable of the word **nashíłté** (see Rule Conj-3.)

At the end of (20) we put in the direct 3 person subject 3 person object word **neiłté** "he/she/they (two) are carrying him/her around", and the inverse form **nabiłté**, so that you can see these as well. Make sure you know how these words are built and how our rules work (you'll need Rule Conj-2 and Rule Disj-2 for the word **neiłté**.)

In the P mode, the "carry around" verb base will let us see some object prefixes together with s-P subject prefixes. The forms are easy, so we'll only look at one carefully. The word meaning "I carried you (sg) around" is built this way:

(21)   outer   object   subject   cl   verb
        prefix   prefix   prefix   stem

          na - n - sé - ł - tį́

Rule Conj-1 supplies **i** after the object prefix, to give us the word **naniséłtį́**. (If you speak Navajo, you might have noticed that this word can also mean something like "I carried you (sg) there (and back)". We'll look at meanings like this in Chapter 17.)

Before giving a few other P mode forms for this verb base, we need to mention something that is only partially new. Back in Chapter 7, we learned a "sibilant assimilation rule", namely Rule Subj-6. It turns out that the process that turns sounds like **sh** into sounds like **s** or vice-versa applies to conjunct prefixes as well as to subjects, with the following difference: with conjunct prefixes, the change is optional. Let's write this up as a new rule:

<u>Rule Conj-4</u>: If a conjunct prefix contains a **sh**, **zh**, or **j**, then this is preferentially changed to an **s**, **z**, or **dz** if either the verb stem or a prefix between the conjunct prefix in question and the verb stem contains one or more of the consonants **s**, **z**, **dz**, **ts**, or **ts'**. If a conjunct prefix contains an **s**, **z**, or **dz**, then this is preferentially changed to a **sh**, **zh**, or **j** if either the verb stem or a prefix between the conjunct prefix in question and the verb stem contains one or more of the consonants: **sh**, **zh**, **j**, **ch**, or **ch'**.

We stated Rule Conj-4 in a general way, to cover lots of cases, but here we are interested in this rule in connection with the 1sg object prefix **sh**. Rule Conj-4 says that this prefix will preferentially turn into **s** if either the verb stem has an **s**-like sound in it, or if some other prefix to the right of the object has an **s**-like sound in it. Now, in the s-P conjugation, the subject prefixes all have **s**'s or **z**'s in them, unless the verb stem contains sounds that changed these into **sh**'s or **zh**'s. So, except for this circumstance, in the s-P conjugation, the 1sg object prefix will usually be **s** rather than **sh**.

Now, here are a few other P mode forms of the verb in (19):

(22)   nasisíníłtį́   "you (sg) carried me around"
       nanistį́   "he/she/they (two) carried you (sg) around"
       nashijistį́   "one carried me around"
       neistį́   "he carried him around" (direct)
       nabistį́   "him, he carried him around" (inverse)

In the word **nasisíníłtį́**, Rule Conj-4 (if we choose to apply it) changes the 1sg object prefix to **s**, because of the subject prefix **síní**, which contains an **s**. In the word **nashijistį́**, to the right of the 1sg object prefix, there is one prefix with a **j** sound in it (namely, the 4 person prefix), and one prefix with an **s** sound in it (namely, the 3 subject prefix). Since the **j** is closer to the 1sg object prefix than the **s** is, it tends to "protect" the 1sg object prefix, so that we can get **sh** rather than **s**. However, we mentioned at the very end of Chapter 7 that some people change the 4 person **j** prefix to **dz** when there is an **s**-like sound in the verb stem. Those people are really applying our new Rule Conj-4 to the **j** prefix (which is a conjunct prefix, after all!), turning it into a **dz**. Such people can say **nasidzistį** instead of **nashijistį**. Note that in **nasidzistį**, Rule Conj-4 has applies both to the 4 person subject prefix **j** and to the 1sg object prefix **sh**. In general, there is variation from speaker to speaker as to whether Rule Conj-4 is applied or not (and even individual speakers sometimes pronounce the same word differently at different times.)

The examples we have been looking at should make it clear how to construct Navajo verbs that have object prefixes that indicate 1, 2, and 3 person. As we proceed through our study, we'll see more examples, in other modes and with other conjugations.

To finish our story, we need to look at the 4 person object prefix and the "unspec" object prefix. Since there is a fair amount of material that we need to look at in connection with these two prefixes, we'll give these two prefixes a chapter of their own.

CHAPTER 12

UNSPEC OBJECT AND 4 PERSON OBJECT PREFIXES; LEXICAL OBJECTS

In Chapter 11, we learned how Navajo transitive verbs represent objects that are not 3 person (we learned about 3 person objects back in Chapter 6.) In Chapter 11(1), we listed the object prefixes that are used in Navajo verbs. However, in our study, we postponed talking about the 4 person object prefix **hw**, and the "unspec" object prefix **'**. We will now study these two prefixes. Let's look first at the "unspec" prefix.

First of all, what exactly is an "unspec" object prefix? What is it used for? To understand this, let's start by looking at two English sentences:

(1)(a) I'm weaving a saddle blanket.
   (b) I'm weaving.

The first sentence (the one in (1a)) is an ordinary transitive sentence that describes an activity in which the subject (who happens to be the speaker) is doing some weaving and in which a saddle blanket is getting woven. If we compare this sentence with the sentence in (1b), we see something interesting. In English, we can (sometimes) leave out the object of a transitive verb. And notice what happens when we do this: we get a sentence that talks about a situation where the subject (again, the speaker in this particular sentence) is doing some weaving, but where there is no reference to what the weaver is weaving. Now, this doesn't mean that the speaker isn't weaving anything - you can't just be weaving, you have to be weaving something. What's happening with sentence (1b) is that by leaving out words that talk about the thing that the speaker is weaving, this sentence concentrates our attention on the activity of weaving. For sure, something is being woven, but the person who says (1b) isn't interested in what's being woven. Whoever says (1b) is only interested in the activity.

Now, how do we do this in Navajo? If we think for a moment, we'll see that in Navajo it is impossible to simply leave the object out. Why? Well, look first at this sentence:

(2)   Ak'idahi'nilí yishtł'ó.

This means about the same as sentence (1a). Suppose we leave out the word **ak'idahi'nilí** (which means "saddle blanket") in (2). What do we get? We get:

(3)   Yishtł'ó.

But this does <u>not</u> mean "I'm weaving". What (3) means is: "I'm weaving <u>it</u>". Why? Because the verb base that means "weave" is a transitive verb base. We learned back in Chapter 6 how transitive verbs indicate 3 person objects. The verb in (3) is an ordinary transitive verb, with a 3 person object indicated the ordinary way: by zero (see Rule Str-1). It's true that the exact object isn't specified in (3); but the 3 person object in Navajo is like a pronoun in English - there is some specific object, perhaps something that was just mentioned, that the speaker has in mind by saying (3). This is different from (1b), where the activity of weaving is being talked about, and the thing being woven is completely out of the picture. The issue is that in Navajo the object of a transitive verb is always somehow referred to in the verb, even if the way that it is referred to is by zero. In English, a sentence that corresponds to a Navajo transitive verb always has some extra word or words that refer to the object, even if it's only a word like "it" or "him" or "her". So, in English, we could leave this word out. But in Navajo, since the 3 person object in (3) is indicated by zero, there is no way that we can just "leave it out"!

So, we come back to our question: how do we say things like (1b) in Navajo? The answer is: we put a special prefix into the object slot of the verb. This prefix indicates that the object is unspecified, and that the verb is therefore really just talking about the activity. The prefix we use is the one called "unspec" in Chapter 11(1).

We want to illustrate this prefix, but we need to say something about our rules. It turns out that Rule Conj-1 doesn't work in its normal way with the unspec prefix. The reason for this is that the unspec prefix consists of a glottal stop, and the glottal stop behaves differently from other consonants. So what we'll do is this. We'll say that the unspec object prefix is an "irregular" prefix, and we'll give a special rule for it! (We'll put a note into Rule Conj-1 sending us to our new rule when the conjunct prefix we're looking at is the unspec object prefix.) In this chapter, we won't learn the entire rule - there'll be some additional parts coming in later chapters. But here is what we need to get started:

Rule Conj-5: If the unspec prefix ' is followed directly by a consonant, insert the vowel **a** between the ' and the consonant following it.

We can illustrate Rule Conj-5 using the verb base that means "weave it", which is:

(4)

Stem-set		Classifier: zero
I:	tł'ó	
P:	tł'ǫ	Lexical prefixes: (none)
F:	tł'óół	
R:	tł'óóh	Transitivity: transitive
O:	tł'óół	
		Perfective: s-P

(The P mode stem is the only one that has a nasal vowel. Did you notice the ł at the end of the F mode stem?)

First, let's see exactly how we say (1b) in Navajo. All we have to do is build our verb this way:

(5) object   subject   verb
     prefix   prefix   stem

      '   -   sh   -   tł'ó

Do you see how this word is built? We're using the unspec object prefix, in the regular object prefix position, to indicate that we're not interested in saying what the object is (we're just interested in the activity). The subject prefix is the usual 1sg prefix for the regular I mode conjugation, and the verb stem is the I mode stem chosen from the stem-set in (4). Rule Conj-5 that we just learned applies to (5), giving us this verb form: **ashtł'ó**. This word is the way we say (1b) in Navajo.

(Note that these days we usually do not write the glottal stop when it is at the beginning of a word. That's why when we write this word, the first letter we write is the vowel **a** that Rule Conj-1 inserted. But in some written materials, this word would be written **'ashtł'ó**, with the glottal stop at the beginning actually written in as **'**.)

Incidentally, since the unspec object prefix causes us to have a syllable in front of the verb stem syllable, we do not add a peg (see Rule Str-2). We did add the peg to the verb in (3), which is built this way:

(6) subject   verb
     prefix   stem

      sh   -   tł'ó

(Remember: the 3 person object is indicated by zero in (6); that is, physically, there is no object prefix in (6), even though the meaning of the word specifically includes a 3 person object.)

Let's write out the entire I mode conjugation of the verb base meaning "weave it" using the unspec object prefix. The meanings of these verbs correspond to the English verb **weave** with the object left out. That is, the words in the chart below mean things like "I'm weaving", "you're weaving", etc.

(7)	sg		dpl	distr dpl
1	ashtł'ó		iitł'ó	da'iitł'ó
2	ítł'ó		ohtł'ó	da'ohtł'ó
3		atł'ó		da'atł'ó
4		ajitł'ó		da'jitł'ó

There is one detail in the forms shown in (7) that our rules do not deal with yet. Can you find it?

123

Well, look at the 4 person subject distributive plural form **da'jitł'ó**. This word is built this way:

(8) distributive object subject verb
     plural   prefix prefix   stem

     da - '- j - (zero) - tł'ó

Note first that Rule Str-4, which we learned in Chapter 11, allows us to put two object prefixes into the verb as long as the 4 person subject prefix **j** comes second. This is what we did in (8): the unspec prefix and the 4 person subject prefix are both placed in the object prefix position, in the correct order. But this means that there are two places in (8) where a conjunct prefix is followed directly by a consonant: the unspec prefix **'** is followed directly by **j**, and the 4 person subject prefix **j** is followed directly by the first consonant of the verb stem. We would expect Rule Conj-1 to apply to both cases (although in the first case, we'd use our new Rule Conj-5 instead of Rule Conj-1), which would give us **da'ajitł'ó**. However, the word is usually spelled and pronounced **da'jitł'ó**. What's going on?

What is happening with this word is something else that has to do specifically with the unspec prefix, so let's write an addition to Rule Conj-5 to take care of it. The following will do it:

(add to Rule Conj-5): However, if the unspec prefix **'** is preceded by a vowel and if the syllable **'a** which we would get by adding the vowel **a** right after **'** would not be the pre-stem syllable, then no vowel is inserted after **'**. (In this case, the **'** will end up being followed directly by another consonant.)

In the word **da'jitł'ó**, the unspec prefix **'** is preceded by the vowel **a** of the distributive plural prefix **da**. This is the first condition in our addition to Rule Conj-5. But also, if we add in **a** to the right of **'** in this word, the syllable **'a** that we'd get by doing this would be followed by the syllable **ji**, which is not the verb-stem syllable. Thus, the **'a** syllable wouldn't be the pre-stem syllable. This means that the second condition of our addition to Rule Conj-5 is also satisfied. Since both conditions of the addition are satisfied, we don't insert any vowel at all after **'**. The result is that, in the actual word, **'** is followed directly by the consonant **j**.

We can rephrase this addition to Rule Conj-5 by saying this. If the unspec prefix **'** is preceded by a vowel (and followed by a consonant, of course), Rule Conj-5 adds in an **a** only if the syllable that it creates by doing this is going to end up being the pre-stem syllable. If this syllable wouldn't be the pre-stem syllable, then the **a** isn't added in. But be careful: it is not true that Rule Conj-5 only adds in an **a** when the syllable it creates will be the pre-stem syllable. If the unspec prefix isn't preceded by a vowel, then our new addition to Rule Conj-5 doesn't apply, and the **a** is still added in - you can see this happening with the word **ajitł'ó** in (7), where the **'** (at the very beginning of the word, so it's not actually written!) isn't preceded by a vowel (after all, it's at the beginning of the word.) In this word, Rule Conj-5 does add in the vowel **a**, even though the syllable **'a** that we get by doing this isn't the pre-stem syllable. It's only when the unspec prefix is preceded by a vowel that we add the **a** only when the pre-stem syllable is being created by doing this.

124

And here's yet another way of thinking about this addition to Rule Conj-5. We can say that (when the unspec prefix is followed by a consonant) Rule Conj-5 <u>always</u> adds in an **a** after the unspec prefix, which creates the syllable **'a**, but then this addition to the rule comes along and checks if the syllable **'a** is preceded by a vowel. If it is, it tries to remove the **a**. Now, if the syllable **'a** is the pre-stem syllable, then the **a** is protected - it can't be removed. But if the syllable **'a** isn't the pre-stem syllable, then the **a** does disappear. (But remember: there has to be a vowel preceding the unspec prefix for this to happen!)

It turns out that there are a few more special things we'll have to learn about in connection with the unspec prefix. When we learn about them (which will be in later chapters), we'll end up adding more things to Rule Conj-5. But what we've presented here is the basic part of this rule, so learn it well.

All of the other forms in (7) are completely straightforward, but let's point out a few things anyway, for review.

First of all, the prefix **'** is the first sound of many of the words in (7). As we already mentioned, this consonant is usually not written these days when it's at the beginning of a word. This means that the unspec prefix is "invisible" in the written form of many of the words in (7) - what we actually see is a word beginning with a vowel letter. This is what tips us off to the fact that there really is an extra **'** in these words. This **'** is important: as the unspec prefix, it's the signal that we're ignoring the object of the verb and talking only about the activity. But in the written forms of these words, the signal that we actually see is that the word begins with a vowel letter.

Next, look at the form for "you (sg) are weaving", which is **ítł'ó**. This word is completely regular - we mention it only because Rule Conj-2 applied. Remember that like all other object prefixes, the unspec prefix is a conjunct prefix.

It might be useful to compare the forms in (7) with the I mode forms of the same verb base when the object is a real 3 person object rather than an unspecified object. The forms are completely parallel to the forms we saw back in Chapter 7(7) (except that in Chapter 7(7) we had a verb base with a barred-l classifier whereas here we have a zero classifier.) Here they are (remember: these words mean things like "I'm weaving it", "you're weaving it", etc.):

(9)	sg	dpl	distr dpl
1	yishtł'ó	yiitł'ó	deiitł'ó
2	nitł'ó	wohtł'ó	daohtł'ó
3		yitł'ó	deitł'ó
4		jitł'ó	dajitł'ó

You should compare the forms in (9) with the forms in (7). The following points should be noted.

The 3 person object, 1dpl and 2dpl subject forms **yiitł'ó** and **wohtł'ó** begin with consonants **y** and **w** that were supplied by Rule Str-3, whereas the unspecified object, 1dpl and 2dpl subject forms **iitł'ó** and **ohtł'ó** begin with written vowel letters (they really begin with **'**, which is why Rule Str-3 didn't apply to these words!)

The distributive plural forms for the unspecified object words all have a written **'** inside them (right after the distributive plural prefix **da**), so the unspec prefix is visible. This **'** also "protects" the **a** vowel of **da** from being changed by other rules. (Which other rules? Rule Disj-1 and Rule Disj-2!) In the distributive plural forms for the 3 person object words, the **da** is not followed by **'** - and notice that the **a** vowel changes to **e** in the forms **deiitł'ó** and **deitł'ó** (review Rule Disj-2 and Rule Conj-2.)

To make sure we understand what verbs with the unspec prefix look like, let's move over to the P mode of the "weave it" verb base and build forms using the unspec object prefix (so these words will mean things like: "I weaved", "you weaved", etc.). These forms are very easy, so we won't go through any of them in detail.

(10)	sg	dpl	distr dpl
1	asétł'ǫ́	asiitł'ǫ́	da'siitł'ǫ́
2	asínítł'ǫ́	asootł'ǫ́	da'sootł'ǫ́
3		aztł'ǫ́	da'aztł'ǫ́
4		ajiztł'ǫ́	da'jiztł'ǫ́

As we see by looking at (4), this verb base takes the s-P conjugation, and the P mode verb stem is **tł'ǫ́**. The initial "a" in words like **asétł'ǫ́**, **asínítł'ǫ́**, etc. represents the vowel inserted by Rule Conj-5 (the **'** which triggered this vowel is not written, since it's at the beginning of the word.) The effect of our addition Rule Conj-5 is seen not only in the word **da'jiztł'ǫ́**, but also in the words **da'siitł'ǫ́** and **da'sootł'ǫ́**.

Let's look at another example of a verb with the unspec prefix in it. This time, we'll take the verb base that means "drink it", which is found in Chapter 10(9). The P mode forms of this verb base are shown in Chapter 10(10). But let's put the unspec prefix in and look at a few of the forms.

If we put the unspec prefix into the verb base that means "drink it", we'll form verbs that mean things like "I am drinking", "he drank", etc. In English, when we leave the object of "drink" unspecified this way, there is sometimes an unpleasant suggestion that we are talking about people drinking alcohol. In Navajo, the verbs that we'll form using the unspec prefix can also be used with this meaning. Although this meaning is unpleasant, it still seems like a good idea to look at these words, since this will give us a chance to see some forms of subject prefixes that we haven't yet seen.

If we build the I mode forms of this verb base with the unspec object prefix in them, we'll get words that are just like the words in (7), so let's skip to the P mode. The words we'll build will have meanings like "I drank", "you drank", etc. Before presenting the actual words, let's think about them a little. We're dealing with a verb base that has the d classifier and which is conjugated in the y-P conjugation. If the unspec prefix is used, that means that all the subject prefixes will have to come from the chart in Chapter 10(4), since every subject prefix will be preceded by a conjunct prefix (either ', or else **j**). Can you write out the forms?

Well, here they are:

(11)	sg	dpl	distr dpl
1	eeshdláá'	iidláá'	da'iidláá'
2	íínídláá'	oohdláá'	da'oohdláá'
3		oodláá'	da'oodláá'
4		ajoodláá'	da'joodláá'

There is nothing new that we need to study in order to build these words. Note that the nondistributive forms all begin with a written vowel, which means that they really begin with the unspec prefix '. Rule Conj-5 applied only to **ajoodláá'** (it put the **a** in at the beginning of this word) and the addition to Rule Conj-5 applied only to **da'joodláá'** (allowing the ' and **j** to be next to each other in this word), since in all the other forms the ' is followed directly by a vowel (the vowel at the beginning of the subject prefix.).

But we should take special note of the vowels at the beginning of the words **eeshdláá'**, **íínídláá'**, and **oodláá'**. These are the special vowels that appear when y-P subject prefixes for plain-1 and d classifier verb bases are used with a conjunct prefix (see Chapter 10(4).) (And don't forget: in writing, these words begin with vowel letters; but that's just a signal that they really begin with a glottal stop. That glottal stop is just the unspec object prefix, of course. The unspec prefix is the conjunct prefix that sent us to the chart in Chapter 10(4) in order to build these words.)

Well, we've looked at enough forms with the unspec prefix to see how words with this prefix are formed. But before turning to the 4 object prefix, there is something about the unspec prefix that we might want to think about.

What we've been doing is considering the unspec prefix to be an ordinary object prefix that has a special meaning, namely, the meaning that the object is being ignored. But there is another way that we could be analyzing the use of this prefix. We could say that adding this prefix to a transitive verb base creates a new, intransitive verb base.

For example, let's go back to the "weave" example. In (4) above we've got the verb base that we said means "weave it". Rather than saying that the unspec prefix is one of the object prefixes that this verb base can be used with, we could instead say that there is a different verb base, a verb base which means "weave" (that is, do the activity of weaving), which is as follows:

127

(12)

Stem-set	Classifier: zero
I: tł'ó	
P: tł'ǫ́	Lexical prefixes: ' (object)
F: tł'óół	
R: tł'óóh	Transitivity: intransitive
O: tł'óół	Perfective: s-P

In (12), we've put in the unspec object prefix as a lexical prefix, that is, a prefix that is part of the definition of this verb base. Is this a good thing to do? As we explore Navajo verbs further, we'll see examples of verb bases where we'll want to say that there has to be some particular object prefix in every verb built using that verb base. This suggests that the idea that a particular object prefix could be lexical (that is, part of the verb base) is something that we will want to accept.

Still, we might wonder if there is any advantage to separate out the verbs that mean "weave" (the activity only, without the object specified) from the verbs that mean "weave it" (some specified object). Here are two advantages to doing this.

First of all, the unspec prefix is commonly used only with certain transitive verb bases - verb bases that describe activities that are often spoken about as activities, without attention being paid to the objects. By regarding the verbs that mean "weave" as coming from a different verb base as the verbs that mean "weave it", we're calling attention to the fact that this is one of the activities that people talk about this way.

And secondly, we saw in the case of "drink it" versus "drink" that sometimes, when we use the unspec prefix, the verb can acquire a special meaning that it didn't have when used with an ordinary object. By creating a separate "drink" verb base, we can say that these special meanings are part of the meaning of the new verb base.

As it happens, YM regards those verbs with the unspec prefix as coming from a separate verb base. For example, the verb base in (12) is given a separate listing in the dictionaries from the verb base in (4).

Incidentally, note that in (12) we've specified the verb base as intransitive. The idea is that when we put the unspec prefix in, we cannot have any representation of a "real" object in the verb (the whole point of the unspec prefix is to get rid of that object!)

Well, from now on, let's be on the lookout for these lexical objects. So far, we've seen that the unspec object prefix can be a lexical object. Can any object prefix be lexical? The answer is probably: no. But we'll keep our eyes open for other possibilities as we go along.

Let's turn now to the second object prefix that we postponed to this chapter: the 4 object prefix **hw**. This prefix has the most complicated forms. Now, we might be tempted to say: is it worth spending a lot of time on complicated forms for a prefix that means 4 person object? After all, isn't this a relatively rare prefix? How often do we talk about actions where someone does something to a person that is referred to in the 4 person? Well, we do need to know how such forms are built. But, apart from that, it will turn out that this prefix is more common than you might think. There are two reasons for this.

First of all, in addition to meaning 4 person object, the prefix **hw** has another meaning: it can refer to an area or space (in YM, when **hw** means this, it's called the "3s" prefix.) We'll come back to this again in Chapter 21. (Note: this is different from the prefix **j**, which can only mean 4 person subject.)

And secondly, **hw** often occurs in verb bases as a lexical prefix. This usage is quite common. Because of this, it is not at all unusual to run into verb forms with **hw**.

So, we'd better learn the forms of this prefix well! The forms are varied enough that it is convenient to collect everything relating to this prefix into one special rule that applies just to this prefix. We'll put little notes into Rules Conj-1 and Conj-3 sending us to this rule if the conjunct prefix that we are looking at is the **hw** prefix.

Here is the rule (we'll need to add to it slightly in several later chapters.)

Rule Conj-6:

(a) If the object prefix **hw** is followed directly by a consonant, then this prefix becomes **ha** if the following syllable is the verb-stem syllable (which means that the syllable **ha** that we get this way is automatically the pre-stem syllable). But if the following syllable is not the verb-stem syllable, then **hw** becomes **ho** (which is automatically <u>not</u> the pre-stem syllable.) Exception: in the s-P conjugation, if the subject is 3, **hooz** or **hoos** is sometimes used instead of **haz** or **has**.

(b) If **hw** is followed directly by the 2sg subject prefix **ni**, then the **hw** and the **ni** together become **hó**.

(c) Normally, if **hw** is followed directly by the vowel **i(i)** or **e(e)**, then no special adjustment is made. If **hw** is followed directly by the vowel **a(a)** or **o(o)**, then the **w** of **hw** disappears and we just get **ha(a)** or **ho(o)**.

(d) (Exceptions to part (c):) However, in the y-P, zero/barred-l conjugation, when **hw** is followed by the 1 or 3 subject prefix **íí**, this combination of **hw** followed by **íí** regularly becomes **hóó**. (But **hw** followed by the 2sg prefix **ííní** in the y-P conjugation is **hwííní**; that is, part (c) applies normally in this case.) Also: in the y-P, plain-l/d conjugation, if the subject is 1sg, **hoosh** is sometimes used instead of **hweesh**.

(whew!)

The way to think about the parts of Rule Conj-6 is this: parts (a), (b), and (c) are "regular" - these parts give the basic principles of how the **hw** prefix will appear. Part (d) is exceptional: it describes the form of this prefix in some particular cases. Later on, we will need to add to part (d) in order to take care of a few more special cases involving conjugation patterns that we haven't learned yet.

An easy way to illustrate the forms of the **hw** prefix is to look at a verb base that has this prefix as a lexical prefix. Here is one, the verb base that means "talk about" or "tell about":

(13)

Stem-set		Classifier: plain-l
I:	**ne'**	Lexical prefixes: **hw** (object)
P:	**ne'**	
F:	**nih**	Transitivity: intransitive
R:	**nih**	
O:	**ne'**	Perfective: y-P

We have all the information we need to conjugate this verb base in the I and P modes. First, let's look at the I mode forms:

(14)	sg	dpl	distr dpl
1	hashne'	hwiilne'	dahwiilne'
2	hólne'	hołne'	dahołne'
3		halne'	dahalne'
4		hojilne'	dahojilne'

Let's note the following.

In the forms **hashne'**, **halne'**, and **dahalne'**, part (a) of Rule Conj-6 applies: the **hw** prefix becomes **ha** because it is followed directly by a consonant, and the next syllable is the verb-stem syllable (so we see **ha** being the pre-stem syllable in these words.) For example, the form **halne'** is built like this:

(15)	object prefix		subject prefix	cl	verb stem
	hw	-	(zero) -	l	- ne'

In this form, **hw** is followed directly by the classifier **l** (which is a consonant.) The next syllable is (l)**ne'**, which is the verb-stem syllable, so Rule Conj-6 tells us that **hw** becomes **ha**. And remember: since the next syllable is the verb-stem syllable, the syllable **ha** in this word (and in the other word in (14) where **hw** becomes **ha**) is the pre-stem syllable.

In the forms **hojilne'** and **dahojilne'**, part (a) of Rule Conj-6 applies again. When we build these words, **hw** is followed by the consonant **j**, as we see here:

(16)　object　　subject　　cl　　verb
　　　 prefix　　 prefix　　　　　stem

　　　 hw - j　-　(zero)　-　l　-　ne'

In this form, we have two object prefixes, in the correct order, with **j** coming second (as required by Rule Str-4.) But here, the next syllable after the **hw** syllable is not the verb-stem syllable (it's the syllable **ji**), so **hw** becomes **ho** rather than **ha**. When **hw** becomes **ho** by part (a) of Rule Conj-6, the syllable **ho** is never the pre-stem syllable.

The form **hólne'** "you (sg) are talking" illustrates part (b) of Rule Conj-6 at work. This word is built this way:

(17)　object　　subject　　cl　　verb
　　　 prefix　　 prefix　　　　　stem

　　　 hw　-　ni　-　l　-　ne'

Part (b) of Rule Conj-6 applies directly here, since **hw** is followed by the 2sg subject prefix **ni**.

(Part (b) of Rule Conj-6 tells us what happens to the special prefix **hw** in those situations where a normal conjunct prefix would have had Rule Conj-3 apply to it. Note that, as in the normal case, we lose the **n** of the **ni** prefix, and we get a high tone. What makes **hw** different is that the vowel is **ó** instead of **í**.)

When building the forms **hwiilne'** "we (two) are talking" and **hołne'** "you (two) are talking", part (c) of Rule Conj-6 comes into play. For example, to form "you (two) are talking", we do this:

(18)　object　　subject　　cl　　verb
　　　 prefix　　 prefix　　　　　stem

　　　 hw　-　oh　-　l　-　ne'

In (18), **hw** is followed by the vowel **o**, so by part (c) of Rule Conj-6, the **w** of **hw** disappears, and we just get **h** followed directly by **o**, giving us **hołne'**. (Rule Subj-4 also applied in this word.)

(Note that in this word, the syllable **ho** is the pre-stem syllable! However, the **o** in this syllable wasn't put in there by part (a) of Rule Conj-6. The **o** in this syllable is part of the subject prefix - it was there already.)

Now let's do the P mode for this verb. You might want to try building the forms yourself. If you do, don't forget that this verb base is conjugated in the y-P conjugation, the classifier is plain-l, and there always is a conjunct prefix in front of the subject prefix (namely, either **hw** or else **j**), so the subject prefixes will all come from the chart in Chapter 10(4). Also, there is no **da**-shift to the s-P conjugation with this verb.

Well, here are the forms:

(19)	sg	dpl	distr dpl
1	hweeshne'	hwiilne'	dahwiilne'
2	hwíínílne'	hoołne'	dahoołne'
3	hoolne'		dahoolne'
4	hojoolne'		dahojoolne'

The 4 subject P mode forms are similar to the 4 subject I mode forms: **hw** is followed by **j**, and the next syllable is not the verb-stem, so part (a) of Rule Conj-6 turns **hw** into **ho**. In all the other forms, **hw** is followed by the vowel at the beginning of the subject prefix, so part (c) applies, either causing the **w** to drop when it's followed by **oo** in the forms **hoolne'** and **hoołne'** (and **dahoolne'** and **dahoołne'**), or else leaving the **hw** as is when it's followed by the vowels **ee** or **ii** in the forms **hweeshne'**, **hwíínílne'**, **hwiilne'**, and **dahwiilne'**.

Just to see what happens in the y-P conjugation when the classifier is zero or barred-l, let's look at one more verb base. Again, we'll pick a verb base that has **hw** as a lexical prefix. Here is the verb base that means "sing":

(20)

Stem-set		Classifier: zero
I:	**taał**	
P:	**táál**	Lexical prefixes: **hw** (object)
F:	**tał**	
R:	**tał**	Transitivity: intransitive
O:	**taał**	Perfective: y-P

(In this verb base, we see that the P mode stem is the only one with a high tone vowel; it's also the only one that ends in **l** rather than in **ł**. By now, we've seen a number of verb bases where the P mode

132

stem has something different about its vowel, or ends in a different consonant, than the other stems.)

The I mode forms for this verb are essentially the same as the forms shown earlier in (14) (the only difference is that here the classifier is zero.) However, the P mode forms for this verb won't look like the forms in (19). Why? Because the classifier here is zero, which means that the subject prefixes will be the ones we learned about in Chapter 9, rather than the ones we learned in Chapter 10 (which are used when the classifier is plain-l or d, as in (19).)

In creating the P mode forms for this verb, we'll need to keep part (d) of Rule Conj-6 in mind. As in the case of the forms in (19), the subject prefixes that we need are the ones that are used when preceded by a conjunct prefix, since every subject prefix will be preceded either by **hw** or else by **j**. These prefixes are found in Chapter 9(5).

Here are the forms:

(21)	sg	dpl	distr dpl
1	hóótáál	hwiitáál	dahwiitáál
2	hwíínítáál	hootáál	dahootáál
3	hóótáál		dahóótáál
4	hojíítáál		dahojíítáál

The only forms in this chart that show anything new are the forms that mean "I sang" and "he/she sang" (and also the distributive plural form that means "they sang".) These two forms are the same, since this verb is intransitive and since the subject prefix is the same for 1sg and 3 in the y-P conjugation for zero or barred-l classifiers. The forms are built like this:

(22)	object prefix	subject prefix	verb stem
	hw -	íí -	táál

(Check the chart in Chapter 9(5) for the subject prefix **íí**.) Part (d) of Rule Conj-6 applies to this structure, so the actual word is **hóótáál**.

The other forms in (21) are created the same way as corresponding forms in other charts that we've seen earlier in this chapter. We might point out that the word **hootáál** that means "you (two) sang" differs from the word **hóótáál** "I sang" or "he/she sang" only in the tone of the first syllable. However, these words are built in very different ways. We just saw how **hóótáál** was built: the **óó** that we find in that word is the result of part (d) of Rule Conj-6. However, in **hootáál**, the **oo** (with low tone) is just the subject prefix that we got from Chapter 9(5). Here's how we build this word:

(23) object   subject   verb
      prefix   prefix   stem

       hw   -   oo   -   táál

Part (c) of Rule Conj-6 wipes out the **w** from the prefix **hw**, giving us the word **hootáál**.

Here's a review question: why does the (nondistributive) 4 person form in (19) start with **hojoo-** (in the word **hojoolne'**), while the (nondistributive) 4 person form in (21) starts with **hojíí-** (in the word **hojíítáál**)?

Answer: When the subject is 4 person, the subject prefix that we have to use is the one for 3 person. In the y-P conjugation, when the classifier is plain-l, the 3 person subject prefix is **oo** when preceded by a conjunct prefix (Chapter 10(4).) But when the classifier is zero, the 3 person subject prefix is **íí** when preceded by a conjunct prefix (Chapter 9(5).) The **oo** of **hojoo-** (in **hojoolne'**) and the **íí** of **hojíí-** (in **hojíítáál**) are just these subject prefixes. (They have nothing to do with the **hw** prefix!)

Well, this takes care of what we need to know about the unspec object prefix and the **hw** object prefix. Before moving on to the next chapter, though, let's spend a moment thinking about the forms of the **hw** object prefix as compared with other prefixes that involve an **h**. In previous chapters we've seen verb forms built from verb bases that have an outer prefix with the shape **ha** (take a look at the forms in Chapter 6(7), for example.) Verbs with this prefix are all going to have **h**'s in them at or near the beginning of the verb. Now, verbs, that have the **hw** object prefix in them are also all going to have **h**'s in them. If we see a verb with an **h** in it, how can we tell whether we have the outer **ha** prefix or the object **hw** prefix?

There are quite a few ways in which these two prefixes differ. One way to see the difference is to compare the forms in Chapter 6(7) with the forms in (14) above: both of these are tables of I mode forms, but if you compare them form by form, you'll see lots of differences. For example, the 1sg I mode form with the **ha** prefix starts like this: **haash-** (see Rule Disj-1), while the 1sg I mode form with the **hw** prefix starts like this: **hash-** (see Rule Conj-6 part (a).) The 2sg I mode form with the **ha** prefix starts like this: **hani-**, whereas Rule Conj-6 part (b) makes the 2sg I mode form with the **hw** prefix start like this: **hó-**. Continuing in this way, you can see that the two prefixes actually lead to very different forms. You might also want to compare the P mode forms in Chapter 9(14), which involve the **ha** disjunct prefix, with the P mode forms in (21) above, which show the **hw** prefix.

If you look at these forms, you might have noticed some general facts. It seems that if a verb has the **ha** disjunct prefix, then the **h** has to be followed by at least one **a**. If we see a verb form with an **h** followed by a **w** or by an **o**, then we are probably dealing with the **hw** prefix and not the **ha** prefix. On the other hand, it is possible for both the **ha** prefix and the **hw** prefix to appear as an **h** followed by an **a**. However, a close look at the rules shows us that we can still tell the difference: by Rule Conj-6 part (a), **hw** appears as **ha** only if the next syllable is the verb-stem syllable; but by Rule Disj-

1, if the next syllable is the verb-stem syllable, the **ha** prefix appears as **haa** (with a long **aa**) and not **ha** (with a short **a**.) In other words, if we see a verb where the pre-stem syllable is **ha** (with short **a**), then this **ha** is actually the **hw** object prefix, whereas if we see a verb where the pre-stem syllable is **haa** (with a long **aa**), then this **haa** is the **ha** disjunct prefix.

(We should also remember that since **ha** is an outer prefix, it will appear before the distributive prefix **da** (if this prefix is in the verb), whereas **hw** always comes after the **da**.)

Well, it looks as though we should have no trouble distinguishing between these two prefixes. Unfortunately, **ha** and **hw** are not the only verb prefixes in Navajo that have an **h** in them - we will learn about others later on. But hopefully, we'll still be able to tell what prefix is involved when we see an **h** in the verb somewhere before the verb stem.

Let's end this chapter with a reminder. We've run into something new in this chapter that is worth stressing: the idea that an object prefix can be a lexical prefix. Another way of saying this is: it is possible to have a verb base where any verb built from that verb base has to have a particular object prefix in it. This means that something we said in Chapter 2 now turns out to be wrong. We said in Chapter 2 that lexical prefixes appear in two positions in the diagram shown in Chapter 2(6): they are either outer prefixes or inner prefixes. What we now see is that there is a third position where we can find a lexical prefix, and that is the object prefix position. This also means that there are two kinds of conjunct lexical prefixes: lexical prefixes in the object position, such as the unspec prefix in (12) or the **hw** prefix in (13) and (20), and lexical prefixes that are inner prefixes. (We have not yet seen any examples of inner prefixes, but we will soon.)

And finally, the fact that there are lexical object prefixes means that there are two possibilities whenever we see an object prefix in a verb: either that prefix is there to actually tell us about an object, as in the verbs in Chapter 11 (see especially (15), (18), (20), or (22)), or the prefix is there because it's part of the verb base, as in the verbs in (14), (19), or (21) of this chapter.

CHAPTER 13

VOICED FRICATIVE VERB STEMS

In this chapter we are going to study the forms of verbs whose stems begin with certain consonant sounds. We will see that, for these verbs, the sound at the beginning of the verb stem might not be the same when we compare different forms of the same verb.

To get started, we need to make a list of the consonants that are involved. These consonants are all in the following chart:

(1)

voiced fricative	unvoiced fricative
z	s
zh	sh
l	ł
y	h
w	h
gh	h

In (1), we've listed some consonants in two columns. The idea is that each consonant in the left column is paired with the consonant in the same row in the column on the right. In other words, **z** is paired with **s**, **zh** is paired with **sh**, etc. Note that three different consonants are paired with the consonant **h**.

At the top of the left column in (1) is the heading "voiced fricative". This is a technical name for the sounds in that column. Similar, the term "unvoiced fricative" is a technical name for the sounds in the second column in (1). Here's what these terms mean.

First of all, all the sounds listed in either column in (1) involve some sort of hissing noise (although the hissing is much lighter for the sounds in the first column, and for some speakers, with the sounds **l**, and especially **w** and **y**, the hissing may be just about gone.) Hissing sounds like these are called *fricatives* by linguists, because the hissing is caused by friction between air and some part of the mouth.

Next, can you see what the difference is between the sounds in the first column and the sounds in the second? If you put your fingers on your throat while you say all the sounds in (1), you'll feel the difference right away in your fingertips. When you say the sounds in the first column, you'll feel a vibration - this vibration is produced by your vocal cords. For the sounds in the second column, there

136

is no such vibration. When linguists talk about sounds that have this vibration, they call those sounds *voiced*. Sounds that don't have this vibration are called *unvoiced* or *voiceless* (these two terms mean the same thing.) So, the sounds in the first column of (1) are hissing sounds (that is, fricatives) that have the vibration produced by the vocal cords (that is, they are voiced), while the sounds in the second column are hissing sounds (fricatives) that don't have the vibration by the vocal cords (they are unvoiced.)

Now, if you look through the examples of verb stems that we've seen so far, none of them begin with any of the consonants listed in either column in (1). For verbs whose stems begin with consonants other than the ones in (1), we don't have to deal with the special issues that we are about to study. But there are some verb stems in Navajo that do begin with fricatives, and for those, we need to learn some new things.

It happens that no Navajo verb stems ever begin with any of the consonants in the second column in (1) (the unvoiced fricatives.) However, there are verb stems that begin with the consonants in the first column in (1), that is, with voiced fricatives. But we will see that sometimes these consonants change into the consonants in the second column, so that we can find actual words where the stems start with unvoiced fricatives. Whenever we find such a word, it will turn out that the verb stem really had started with a voiced fricative to begin with, and some process changed that voiced fricative into a voiceless one. Whenever this change happens, the voiced fricative (in the first column of (1)) will change into the unvoiced fricative that it is paired with in the second column; that is, a **z** will change into an **s**, a **zh** will change into an **sh**, and so forth.

(Do you remember that when we discussed d-effect back in Chapter 4 we said that the consonants **s, sh, ł,** and **h** didn't appear in the left-hand column of Chapter 4(9) because these consonants can never be in a position to have d-effect apply to them? Well, here is the reason for this: no Navajo verb stems begin with these consonants!)

So, in this chapter, we are going to study the forms of Navajo verbs whose stems begin with voiced fricatives. Let's call these verbs "voiced fricative verbs".

To study voiced fricative verbs, it will turn out to be easiest if we deal with the four classifiers separately. To start with, let's note that we don't have to deal with the d classifier at all. Can you see why? (Look at Chapter 4(9).)

Remember that the effect of the d classifier is to cause the first consonant of the verb stem to undergo d-effect. If you look at Chapter 4(9), you'll see that after d-effect has applied, the result is never a fricative! That is, none of the sounds listed in the second column of Chapter 4(9) are found in the chart in (1) above. Therefore, for verbs with d classifiers, there is nothing new that we need to learn about in this chapter.

So, let's move on to another classifier. It will be useful to look at the plain-l classifier next. As it happens, we don't have to learn anything new in order to deal with voiced fricative verbs that have the plain-l classifier. But even so, it will turn out to be a good idea to see what the forms of such a verb look like. Let's examine the forms of the cheerful verb that means "dance". Here is the verb base:

(2)

Stem-set		Classifier: plain-l
I:	**zhish**	
P:	**zhiizh**	Lexical prefixes: **'** (object)
F:	**zhish**	Transitivity: intransitive
R:	**zhish**	
O:	**zhish**	Perfective: y-P

(Another case where the P mode stem has a vowel different from the other stems, and also ends in a consonant different from the other stems! The P mode stem has a long vowel, whereas the other stems all have a short vowel. And the P mode stem ends in **zh**, whereas the other stems end in **sh**.)

Note that this verb base has a lexical unspec object. The I mode forms are going to look like the forms in Chapter 12(7), except that there is a plain **l** classifier. No new rules are needed to build the I mode forms - can you build them?

Here they are:

(3)	sg	dpl	distr dpl
1	ashzhish	iilzhish	da'iilzhish
2	ílzhish	ołzhish	da'ołzhish
3		alzhish	da'alzhish
4		ajilzhish	da'jilzhish

The P mode forms of this verb are also easy to build - they don't require any new study, either.

Question: Which chapter should we look in to find the subject prefixes for this verb in the P mode? Answer: Since the perfective conjugation is indicated in (2) as being the y-P, the subject prefixes will be found either in Chapter 9 or Chapter 10. Since the classifier for this verb is plain-l, it's Chapter 10 where we'll find the subject prefixes.

Question: Which chart in Chapter 10 should we use? Answer: Since the verb base in (2) shows that there is a lexical object prefix, every verb form will contain a conjunct prefix (either the lexical **'**, or else this **'** together with the 4 person **j**.) That is, a subject prefix in this verb will always be preceded by some conjunct prefix. Therefore, all the subject prefixes for this verb will be taken from the chart in Chapter 10(4).

Well, by now, you should be able to write out all the P mode forms of this verb. These forms will look like the forms in Chapter 12(11), except that here we'll see a plain-l classifier, whereas in Chapter 12(11) we had a d classifier.

Here are the P mode forms of this verb:

(4)	sg	dpl	distr dpl
1	eeshzhiizh	iilzhiizh	da'iilzhiizh
2	íínílzhiizh	oołzhiizh	da'oołzhiizh
3		oolzhiizh	da'oolzhiizh
4		ajoolzhiizh	da'joolzhiizh

Incidentally, you should make sure that you understand how Rules Subj-2, Subj-3, and Subj-4 work in the forms in (3) and (4). There is nothing new here - it's all just the same as we've seen before.

Since there is nothing to learn about voiced fricative verbs if the classifier is either d or plain-l, you may be wondering what all the fuss is about. Well, when we look at voiced fricative verbs with the other two classifiers, we'll find that there is something new to learn.

So let's look at voiced fricative verbs where the classifier is zero. For such verbs, it turns out that, in certain forms, the voiced fricative at the beginning of the verb stem changes into the unvoiced fricative that is paired with it in chart (1) above. Here is a rule that says when this happens:

Rule Subj-7: If a verb stem begins with a voiced fricative, this sound is devoiced if the classifier of the verb base is zero and if the verb stem is immediately preceded by any subject prefix ending in **sh** or **s** or **h**.

What do we mean when we say "this sound is devoiced"? We mean that the voiced fricative, which is going to be in the first column of (1) above, changes into the sound that it is paired with in the second column.

To illustrate this, let's use the verb base that means "carry a ropelike thing around". Here is this verb base:

(5)

Stem-set		Classifier: zero
I:	**lé**	
P:	**lá**	Lexical prefixes: **na** (outer)
F:	**leeł**	
R:	**leeh**	Transitivity: transitive
O:	**lééł**	Perfective: s-P

As it happens, this verb base involves a stem-set with an irregularity. Since this stem-set is an important one, let's use it even so; besides, it will be good to see what sorts of irregularities can be found in Navajo verbs (there are not many irregularities like this, by the way.)

Before getting to that, though, we can at least see that we are dealing with stems that start with a voiced fricative: they all start with **l**. Be careful: This **l** is part of the stem. Since the stems start with an **l**, there'll often be an **l** in the words that we build using this verb base. But this **l** is not a classifier! The classifier in this verb base is indeed zero. Keep this in mind as we work out the forms of this verb. In particular, rules like Rule Subj-2, Rule Subj-3, and Rule Subj-4 do not apply to any of the forms of (5).

We can illustrate the operation of Rule Subj-7 by looking at the I mode forms of this verb base. (We'll assume that the ropelike thing that the subject is carrying around is always 3 person.) Here are the forms:

(6)	sg		dpl	distr dpl
1	naashłé		neiilyé	nideiilyé
2	nanilé		naohłé	nidaohłé
3		neilé		nideilé
4		nijilé		nidajilé

There are three words in (6) where the stem is immediately preceded by a subject prefix that ends in **sh** or **h**. These are the words **naashłé** "I'm carrying it around", **naohłé** "you (two) are carrying it around", and **nidaohłé** "you (pl) are carrying it around". In these words, the **l** at the beginning of the verb stem changed into an **ł**. In the other words in (6), we see the plain **l** that is the real first consonant of the verb stem for this verb.

Can you see an irregularity in two of the words in (6)? It's in the forms **neiilyé** and **nideiilyé**. In these words, the subject prefix is the 1dpl prefix **iid**. We learned in Rule Subj-1 that the **d** at the end of **iid** is supposed to cause the first consonant of the verb stem to undergo d-effect. Now, if we look up the chart in Chapter 4(9), we see that when d-effect applies to **l**, the **l** should turn into **dl**.

However, with this verb, we see that after a 1dpl subject prefix, the **l** turned into **ly** instead. This irregularity is a peculiar property of this particular stem-set - the **l** at the beginning of the stem becomes **ly** when preceded by the 1dpl prefix. (We'll see, though, that under other circumstances when d-effect applies, the **l** does become **dl**. We will learn about those other circumstances later. By the way: we mentioned this verb stem briefly in Chapter 4. Do you remember?)

Apart from this irregularity, and the new fact that Rule Subj-7 changes the **l** to **ł** in some of the forms, everything in (6) should be familiar to you by now.

If we compare the forms in (6) with the forms in (3), we'll see something interesting. Look at the word that means "I'm dancing": **ashzhish**. The **sh** in this word which indicates that the subject is 1sg is followed by the consonant **zh**. Now, **zh** is a <u>voiced</u> fricative (it's in the first column of (1).) Compare this with the word that means "I'm carrying it (a ropelike thing) around": **naashłé**. Here, the **sh** that indicates that the subject is 1sg is followed by **ł**, which is an <u>unvoiced</u> fricative (it's in the second column of (1).) Looking at all the other forms in (6), we know that the verb-stem in the word **naashłé** "really" starts with a voiced **l** (no Navajo verb stems start with unvoiced fricatives.) So what's the difference between the two verbs: why did the **l** devoice to **ł** in **naashłé**, while the **zh** did not devoice (to **sh**) in the word **ashzhish**? The answer is: the classifier! The word **ashzhish** has a plain-l classifier. Even though this classifier was wiped out in the word **ashzhish** by the sandwich rule, it protected the **zh** at the beginning of the verb stem from getting devoiced - note that Rule Subj-7 requires that the verb base that you're working with has a zero classifier. The "dance" verb base doesn't have a zero classifier (it has a plain-l classifier), so Rule Subj-7 cannot apply, even if the sandwich rule erases the actual **l**. However, in the word **naashłé** the classifier is indeed zero, so Rule Subj-7 kicked in and devoiced the **l** at the beginning of the verb stem to **ł**.

Incidentally, this means that something we said back in Chapter 6 is not exactly right. Do you remember that we said that, because of the sandwich rule, it is impossible to tell from a 1sg I mode form what the classifier of a verb is? Well, that's still true most of the time; but if the verb stem begins with a fricative, then we sometimes <u>can</u> tell what the classifier is. Here's the idea: if we're looking at a verb where the subject is 1sg, and inside the verb we see this: ...**shC**..., where the **sh** is (or is the last consonant of) the 1sg subject prefix, and C is a fricative, then if C is voiced (that is, if C is in the first column of (1) above), the classifier has to be plain-l. (It can't be d, because C wouldn't be a fricative if d-effect had applied to it. It can't be zero, because of Rule Subj-7. And, we will learn in a moment that it can't be barred-l either.) If we see ...**shC**... where the **sh** is the 1sg subject prefix and C is a voiceless fricative, then the classifier is either zero or barred-l. (It can't be d because C is a fricative, and it can't be plain-l, because if it were, the C would not have been devoiced. Remember: no Navajo verb stems begin with an unvoiced fricative, so if we see an unvoiced fricative at the beginning of a verb stem, it must have started out as a voiced fricative and some rule (either Rule Subj-7 or else the rule we're going to learn in a moment) must have devoiced it.) Of course, if we see ...**shC**... in a 1sg verb and C isn't a fricative at all, then we're back to the (more common) situation that we talked about in Chapter 6, where we just cannot tell what the classifier is without looking at other forms of the verb.

Rule Subj-7 gives the correct results for all modes, not just the P mode. It might be fun to look at the P mode forms of the verb in (5), just to make sure that we know how they're formed. Since this verb takes the s-P conjugation, we'll use the subject prefixes in Chapter 8; and since the classifier is zero, the chart we want is Chapter 8(3). We get the following forms:

(7)

	sg		dpl	distr dpl
1	nisélá		nisiilyá	nidasiilyá
2	nisínílá		nisoolá	nidasoolá
3		neizlá		nideizlá
4		nijizlá		nidajizlá

Note that since the 1sg subject prefix for a zero classifier P mode conjugation never ends in **sh** or **s**, and since the 2dpl subject prefix for a zero classifier P mode conjugation never ends in **h**, Rule Subj-7 has no opportunity to apply to a zero classifier P mode form. All of the l's in (7) are real l's - none of them were changed into ł's. (Note that the 3 person s-P subject prefix **z** does not trigger Rule Subj-7. Only subject prefixes that end in **sh**, **s**, or **h** will cause this rule to act. You might have noticed that these sounds are themselves unvoiced fricatives, whereas **z** is a voiced fricative....)

Let's now look finally at the case where the classifier is barred-l. For this case, it might be easiest if we started by looking at the actual forms. After looking at them, we'll work out the rule that we need.

In the barred-l case, we're going to have to separate the verb stems that start with **z** or **zh** from the verb stems that start with the other voiced fricatives. As our first example, let's look at a verb where the stem starts with **y**. We'll use the verb base that means "melt it". (This verb base is used if you're melting snow or ice; a different verb base is preferred if you're melting something else.) Here it is:

(8)

Stem-set		Classifier: barred-l
I:	yį́į́h	
P:	yį́į'	Lexical prefixes: (none)
F:	yįh	
R:	yįh	Transitivity: transitive
O:	yį́į́h	Perfective: y-P

(The F mode stem has a shortened vowel. The P mode stem is the only one that ends in a glottal stop.)

Let's examine the I mode forms for this verb. Here they are:

(9)	sg	dpl	distr dpl
1	yishhį́įh	yiilyį́įh	deiilyį́įh
2	niłhį́įh	wołhį́įh	daołhį́įh
3		yiłhį́įh	deiłhį́įh
4		jiłhį́įh	dajiłhį́įh

Note that the verb stem as it appears in the words in (9) begins with **h** except when the 1dpl subject prefix **iid** is used. We can describe this situation using the following rule:

Rule Subj-8: If a verb stem begins with a voiced fricative and if the classifier of the verb base is barred-l, then this voiced fricative is devoiced, except if the classifier is preceded by a 1dpl subject prefix ending in **d**, in which case Rule Subj-3 applies normally and there is no change to the voiced fricative at the beginning of the verb stem.

Rule Subj-8 applies even if the sandwich rule gets rid of the actual ł. We see this in the form **yishhį́įh** "I'm melting it" in (9).

Note on spelling: In the word **yishhį́įh** "I'm melting it", there are two **h**'s next to each other. The second **h** stands for the usual "h" sound, while the first **h** is part of the combination **sh**, which has a sound of its own. When two **h**'s come together like this, many people prefer to write an **x** for the real "h" sound, so they would spell this word this way: **yishxį́įh**. But they wouldn't use an **x** in the other words in (9), since the **h**'s in the other words are not themselves immediately preceded by another **h**.

The effect of Rule Subj-8 is to make barred-l voiced fricative verbs look as though the verb stem begins with an unvoiced fricative. We mentioned that for most of the verbs in (9), the stem begins with **h**. This may give the impression that we have a verb stem that "really" begins with **h**. However, when we look at the 1dpl forms, we see that the **h** mysteriously changes into **y**. What we are saying is that, despite the fact that this **y** only pops up when there is a 1dpl subject, this **y** is the real first consonant of the verb stem. The **h** that we usually see at the beginning of the verb stems for the forms of this verb is the result of the barred-l classifier causing the **y** to devoice.

Incidentally, the 1sg form in (9) shows that the 1sg prefix **sh** is directly in front of an unvoiced fricative (**h** in this case.) Recall our discussion earlier: if we see a verb whose subject is 1sg, and we see that the **sh** of the 1sg subject prefix is in front of an unvoiced fricative, we know that the classifier is either zero or barred-l. In the case of **yishhį́įh**, the classifier is barred-l, but we don't see the classifier in this word, because the sandwich rule got rid of it.

Rule Subj-8 gives the correct result for all modes, by the way. Try writing out the P mode forms of "melt it"; you should get the following forms:

(10)   sg   dpl   distr dpl

1   yíłhį́į́'   yiilyį́į́'   deiilyį́į́'
2   yínížhį́į́'   wooɫhį́į́'   daooɫhį́į́'
3   yiyíížhį́į́'   dayíížhį́į́'
4   jíížhį́į́'   dajíížhį́į́'

There is nothing new that we have to learn about these forms. If you understood how the I mode forms of this verb base work, then these P mode forms should be clear.

Now let's see what the story is if a barred-l verb base has verb stems beginning with **z** or **zh**. Rule Subj-8 still applies, but more happens. Again, let's look at an actual verb, and then we'll give the rule. We'll take the verb base that means "brush it" or "comb it" (this verb stem can also mean "shell it", that is, shell corn.) Here it is:

(11)

Stem-set		Classifier: barred-l
I:	zhóóh	
P:	zhóó'	Lexical prefixes: (none)
F:	zhoh	
R:	zhoh	Transitivity: transitive
O:	zhóóh	Perfective: y-P

Here are the I mode forms of this verb. You should examine them carefully and compare them with the I mode forms of "melt it" in (9).

(12)   sg   dpl   distr dpl

1   yishshóóh   yiilzhóóh   deiilzhóóh
2   nishóóh   wohshóóh   daohshóóh
3   yishóóh   deishóóh
4   jishóóh   dajishóóh

Do you see what has happened here? When the classifier is preceded by a 1dpl subject prefix, we still have the normal situation. In all other cases, (which are cases where the barred-l classifier simply devoices the voiced fricative at the beginning of the verb stem), not only does the **zh** devoice to **sh**, but the ł classifier disappears! We can deal with this by adding a statement to Rule Subj-8:

(add to Rule Subj-8): If the verb stem begins with **z** or **zh**, then when this consonant devoices to **s** or **sh**, the barred-l classifier (that is, the ł) is dropped. Incidentally, this prevents Rule Subj-4 from applying.

The effect of this rule is quite striking, in the following sense. Look at the words in (12), but ignore the 1dpl forms. Not only does the verb stem seem to start with an unvoiced fricative, but the classifier seems to be zero! There's no trace of a barred-l. However, when that 1dpl subject prefix is put in, all of a sudden we see an **l** popping out, and the **sh** at the beginning of the verb stem turns into a **zh**! (At least with "melt it", we could see the barred-l classifier in many of the forms.)

Of course, by looking at the forms in (12) and thinking about what we've learned, we can tell that we have a barred-l classifier even if we ignore the 1dpl forms. Why? Because while a zero classifier verb whose stem begins with **z** or **zh** would change the **z** or **zh** to **s** or **sh** in at least some forms (namely, the 1sg and 2dpl forms) by Rule Subj-7, in the other forms, we'd see a **z** or **zh**, not an **s** or **sh**. That is, for a zero classifier verb, Rule Subj-7 is the rule that controls what's going on, and by that rule, we get devoicing only when the subject prefix ends in **sh**, **s**, or **h**. For a barred-l classifier verb, Rule Subj-8 is the rule that is in effect, and in this case we get devoicing all the time except when the subject prefix is 1dpl.

By the way: note that in the word that means "I'm brushing it", we have a double **sh**: **yishshóóh**. Do you remember how, back at the end of Chapter 8, we talked about how many people write only one consonant when two identical consonants come together? Well, this applies to words like **yishshóóh**, too: you may see this word spelled **yishóóh**. But this is also the way the word that means "he/she/they (two) is/are brushing it" is spelled! So be careful: if you see **yishóóh**, the writer might mean either "I'm brushing it" or else "he/she/they (two) is/are brushing it" - you'll have to use the context to decide which. And, as we mentioned in Chapter 8, these two words are actually pronounced about the same, so if you hear someone say this word, you'll have to use the context to decide if the person means "I'm brushing it" or "he/she/they (two) is/are brushing it".

By the way, would you like to see the P mode forms of "brush it"? Rule Subj-8, with its new addition, applies the same way as in the I mode. Here are the forms:

(13)	sg	dpl	distr dpl
1	yíshóó'	yiilzhóó'	deiilzhóó'
2	yíníshóó'	wooshóó'	daooshóó'
3		yiyííshóó'	dayííshóó'
4		jííshóó'	dajííshóó'

Make sure that you understand these forms. There is nothing new here.

Well, that's all there is to the voiced fricative verbs. However, there is a special reason to rejoice: not only have we finished this chapter, but we've finished our discussion of all the rules of the type "Rule Subj-(number)". There are no more rules that tell us anything about the forms of subject prefixes, classifiers, and the beginnings of verb stems! Of course, we'll see more examples of the effects of Rules Subj-1 to Subj-8 in other modes and other conjugation patterns; but (except for occasional irregularities - we can never avoid those!) there will be no more processes to learn about that have to do with this part of the Navajo verb.

Unfortunately, we're not quite finished with the other three groups of rules. However, we have learned about the most important processes that are involved. The rest should be easy!

Before moving on to the next chapter, this might be a good place to mention something that we've been occasionally noticing all along. In this chapter, we learned that fricatives come in pairs: voiced and unvoiced. We learned about this because verb stems that begin with voiced fricatives sometimes change their form and start with the corresponding unvoiced fricative instead. But there is a pattern involving stem-sets that has to do with verb stems that end in fricatives, and since we now know that fricatives come in pairs, we can describe this pattern easily: for some of the stem-sets that we've looked at, all the stems except the P mode stem end in one particular unvoiced fricative, while the P mode stem ends in the corresponding voiced fricative. An example of this can be seen in this chapter: look at the stem-set in (2). All the stems except the P mode stem end in **sh**, but the P mode stem ends in **zh**. Back in Chapter 7(19) there is a stem-set where all the stems except the P mode stem end in **s**, but the P mode stem ends in **z**. And in Chapter 9(16) we saw a stem-set where all the stems except the P mode stem end in ł, but the P mode stem ends in **l**. If you look back through our studies you can find some more examples of this. But watch out! There are cases where this pattern is not found. For example, in the stem-set in Chapter 7(6), all the stems end in a fricative, but the P mode and the I mode and the O mode stems end in a voiced fricative (**zh**), whereas only the F and R mode stems end in the corresponding unvoiced fricative (**sh**). Still, keeping this pattern in mind will help you to memorize a fair number of important stem-sets.

A somewhat similar pattern is this: there are stem-sets where all the stems except the P mode stem end either in a vowel or in **h**, whereas the P mode stem ends in the glottal stop '. The stem-set in (8) in this chapter is like that, and so is the stem-set in Chapter 10(14). This is a little different from the pattern described just above, since the glottal stop ' is not a fricative at all, but it's another example of the pattern where the P mode stem is different in some special way from the stems of the other modes.

But note: these stem-set patterns have nothing to do with the main topic of this chapter! What we've been learning here has to do with verb stems that start with voiced fricatives. If a verb stem starts with a voiced fricative, we've learned that this voiced fricative interacts with the classifier and with the subject prefix. But if a verb stem ends in a fricative, that fricative never interacts with the classifier or the subject prefix (they are too far away!)

CHAPTER 14

THE FUTURE MODE

At this point, we have studied quite a bit of the harder parts of the Navajo verb. So let's relax a little, and treat ourselves to an important but relatively easy new mode. Compared with the complications of the I and especially the P mode, the F mode is quite straightforward.

To form an F mode form of any verb, we'll use the F mode stem from the stem-set of that verb, together with the subject prefixes for the F mode. Here are those prefixes:

(1)

	sg	dpl
1	**d-eesh**	**d-iid**
2	**d-íí**	**d-ooh**
3	**d-oo**	

Each subject prefix in the F mode has two parts. The first part is simply the consonant **d**. (We'll call this the *F mode d*.) The second part is something that looks a little like the subject prefixes of other modes.

In fact, you may have noticed that the second part of the subject prefixes in (1) look very much like the subject prefixes used in the y-P conjugation when the classifier is plain-l or d and when there is a conjunct prefix preceding the subject prefix; in fact, only the 2sg prefix is different. But in the F mode, the prefixes shown in (1) are used for all verbs. It doesn't matter what the classifier is. And there is only one F mode conjugation. (Actually, there is a second F mode conjugation that we'll study in Chapter 20, but its subject prefixes are almost the same as the ones in (1).)

The F mode 2sg subject prefix is indeed strange. All the other 2sg subject prefixes that we've seen have the syllable **ni** in them, but in the F mode, there is no **ni** in the 2sg subject prefix. However, things are not quite that crazy. Look up Rule Conj-3: under certain circumstances, a **ni** that indicates a 2sg subject disappears and a high tone appears instead. For example, we've seen words like **itł'ó** ("you (sg) are weaving") or **hólne'** ("you (sg) are talking") or **hashíłteeh** ("you are carrying me up"), where the 2sg subject is indicated by a high tone only. In the F mode, the 2sg subject prefix has a high tone (in fact, it's the only F mode subject prefix with a high tone), so if we want, we can say that this high tone is what's telling us that the subject is 2sg.

The reason we separated the two parts of each F mode subject prefix by a hyphen in the chart in (1) is that the two parts are actually put in two different positions inside the verb. The second part of the prefix (the part that really looks like a subject prefix) is put in the usual subject prefix position. The F mode **d** is put <u>before</u> any inner prefixes that might be in the verb, but <u>after</u> any object prefixes. If we diagram the Navajo verb the way we've been doing in these lessons, we can say that the F mode **d** goes in the position shown in the following diagram:

(2) outer   distributive object   inner   subject   cl   verb
     prefixes   plural   prefix   prefix   prefix   stem
                                 ⇑
                          F mode d

Now, so far, we have not yet studied any verb bases that have inner prefixes. This means that for all the verb bases that we've seen so far, the F mode **d** will be right next to the second part of the subject prefix. For such verbs, the actual subject prefixes in the F mode will therefore end up looking like this:

(3)

	sg	dpl
1	**deesh**	**diid**
2	**díí**	**dooh**
3	**doo**	

However, when we start studying verb bases that have inner prefixes (we'll do that in the next chapter, in fact), we'll see that for those verb bases, the inner prefix separates the **d** of the F mode subject prefixes from the second part of the F mode subject prefixes.

Here is something important: the F mode **d** is itself a conjunct prefix. This makes sense: it is placed in between two other positions that contain conjunct prefixes. Object prefixes (which are put to the left of the F mode **d**) are conjunct prefixes, and so are inner prefixes (which are put to the right of the F mode **d**), so it's reasonable for the F mode **d** to be a conjunct prefix as well. This means that whenever we're in the F mode, we'll have to pay attention to rules that have to do with conjunct prefixes to see if the F mode **d** makes them operate.

We almost do not have to learn anything new (except for the prefixes in (1)) in order to form F mode verbs. Rules Subj-1 through Subj-8 work the same for the F mode as they do for the I and the P modes. All of the effects that we've seen earlier, such as dropping out a classifier that is sandwiched in between **sh** or **s** and the verb stem, or the various forms of the 1dpl or 2dpl subject prefixes when the classifier is barred-l or plain-l, or the effects involving voiced fricative verbs, work the same in the F mode as in the other modes. However, there are one or two little adjustments that sometimes need to be made, and we haven't seen these yet. Rather than giving rules, though, let's actually look at the

F mode forms of a verb and see if we can find any little problems that we need to take care of.

Let's start with the F mode forms of the verb base that means "cry" (see Chapter 7(1) for this verb base.) These forms mean things like "I'll cry", "you'll cry", etc.:

(4)	sg	dpl	distr dpl
1	deeshchah	diichah	dadiichah
2	dííchah	doohchah	dadoohchah
3		doochah	dadoochah
4		jidoochah	dazhdoochah

Except for one of the forms listed in (4), there isn't anything new (or even anything hard!) in (4). For example, the words **deeshchah**, **dííchah**, **diichah**, **doohchah**, and **doochah** are all built this way:

(5)	F-mode	subject	verb
	d	prefix	stem
	d -	(whatever) -	chah

where "whatever" is simply the second part of each of the five subject prefixes in (1). None of our rules apply in any of these cases (except for Rule Subj-1 in the case of **diichah**, although d-effect has no effect in this case) - the structure built according to the pattern in (5) is just the actual word.

(Note, by the way, that the only difference between **dííchah** "you (sg) will cry" and **diichah** "we (two) will cry" is the tone of the first syllable. This will often be the case in the F mode, but for other verbs, there will also be differences between these two forms that have to do with d-effect or with classifier effects (see Rule Subj-1 and Rule Subj-3).)

The forms **dadiichah**, **dadoohchah**, and **dadoochah** are built this way:

(6)	distributive	F-mode	subject	verb
	plural	d	prefix	stem
	da -	d -	(whatever) -	chah

Again, none of our rules apply (except for Rule Subj-1 in **dadiichah**). You should make sure you understand why Rule Disj-1 doesn't change the vowel in the prefix **da** in these words.

And the form **jidoochah** is built like this:

(7) object   F-mode   subject   verb
     prefix   d   prefix   stem

      j   -   d   -   oo   -   chah

In the case of this word, Rule Conj-1 applies normally to insert the vowel **i** after the **j**.

There is one word left in (4), the word **dazhdoochah**. Can you see what happened here? The **j** that indicates 4 person subject somehow got changed into a **zh** and Rule Conj-1 didn't apply for some reason, so no vowel got inserted. To get the correct form of this word, we need to add something to our rules.

The thing to do at this point is to go back to Chapter 12 and review our discussion of an addition that we made to Rule Conj-5 having to do with the unspec prefix **'**. If you look at the word **da'jitł'ó**, which is diagrammed in Chapter 12(8), you'll see that under certain circumstances, Rule Conj-5 does not insert any vowel after the **'** even if a consonant does follow it. Now, the same fact is true about the 4 subject prefix **j**. It happens that under the same circumstances when we don't insert a vowel after the unspec prefix **'**, we also don't insert a vowel after the 4 person **j**. However, in addition to this, when the **j** winds up right next to a consonant to its right, it turns into the sound **zh**.

In general, the 4 subject prefix **j** does not have a lot of irregularities. However, this business of sometimes changing into **zh** is a kind of irregularity, and we'll learn later that there are a few other special changes that involve the 4 subject prefix **j**. So, what we are going to do is create a new Rule Conj-7 in which we'll collect all the irregularities that have to do with this prefix. What we need so far is:

Rule Conj-7: If the 4 subject prefix **j** is preceded by a vowel and followed by a consonant, and if the syllable **ji** that we'd get if Rule Conj-1 applied would not be the pre-stem syllable, then no vowel is inserted after the **j**, and, in this case, the **j** is changed to **zh**.

We'll also put a note into Rule Conj-1 sending us to this new rule if it applies.

Let's now look at the word **dazhdoochah** and see how all this works. This word is built like this:

(8) distributive   object   F-mode   subject   verb
        plural   prefix   d   prefix   stem

      da   -   j   -   d   -   oo   -   chah

In this word, the 4 subject prefix **j** is preceded by a vowel (the vowel **a** at the end of the disjunct prefix **da**). Also, the syllable following the **j** is **doo**, which is not the verb-stem syllable, so if Rule Conj-1 were to put in an **i** after the **j**, the syllable **ji** wouldn't be the pre-stem syllable. These are the conditions for our new Rule Conj-7 to apply: this rule says that no vowel is inserted after the **j**, and moreover, the **j** changes into **zh**. No other rule applies to this word, so we end up with **dazhdoochah**, the correct form.

With Rule Conj-7, we have most of what we need to form F modes of the verb bases that we've seen so far. However, before we turn ourselves loose on all those unsuspecting verbs, we need to take care of two additional little effects.

The first effect has to do with the following idea: we just learned that under certain circumstances, we do not put a vowel in after the 4 person prefix **j**. In Chapter 12, we learned that under these same circumstances we do not put a vowel in after the unspec object prefix **'**. Now, what happens if we have <u>both</u> of these prefixes in a verb, and the circumstances are such that we aren't supposed to put a vowel in after them?

We can see what happens by looking at the F mode of a verb that has the unspec object prefix in it. So, let's form the F mode verbs that have to do with weaving. We'll use the verb base in Chapter 12(4), but we'll put the unspec object prefix in, in order to form verbs that mean things like "I'll weave", "you'll weave", etc., where we're talking about the action only and ignoring the thing that gets woven. (Or, alternatively, we could say that we're forming the F mode of the verb base in Chapter 12(12).) You might want to try and write out the forms first, before looking at the following chart:

(9)	sg		distr dpl
		dpl	
1	adeeshtł'óół	adiitł'óół	da'diitł'óół
2	adíítł'óół	adoohtł'óół	da'doohtł'óół
3	adootł'óół		da'dootł'óół
4	azhdootł'óół		dazh'dootł'óół

All of the forms in (9) except for one of them are taken care of by the rules we've learned. The nondistributive forms all begin with the written vowel **a**, which means that they really begin with the **'** sound that indicates the unspec object. The fact that the vowel **a** is inserted is something we learned about in Chapter 12. For example, the word **adeeshtł'óół** ("I'll weave") is built like this:

(10)	object prefix	F mode d	subject prefix	verb stem
	' -	d -	eesh -	tł'óół

Rule Conj-5 that we learned in Chapter 12 inserts the vowel **a** after the **'** prefix. (Since the **'** prefix is not preceded by a vowel, we really do put the **a** in, even though the resulting **'a** syllable isn't the pre-stem syllable.) No other rules apply, so we get **adeeshtł'óół** as the actual word (leaving out the

' from the written form at the beginning of the word.)

Most of the distributive plural forms are also taken care of by the rules we've learned. The addition to Rule Conj-5 that we learned in Chapter 12 explains why we don't see any vowel between the unspec ' and the F mode **d** in these forms. For example, the word **da'dootł'óół** ("they'll weave") is built like this:

(11) distributive object   F mode   subject   verb
      plural   prefix   d   prefix   stem

       da   -   '   -   d   -   oo   -   tł'óół

Since the object prefix ' is preceded by a vowel (the **a** of **da**), and since the next syllable is **doo**, which is not the verb stem syllable, no vowel is added in after the ' even though the next sound is a consonant. (If we had added in the **a** after the ', the syllable **'a** wouldn't have been the pre-stem syllable in this word.)

What happens if we have both the unspec prefix and the 4 person subject prefix in the object prefix position? This is the situation that we find with the word **azhdootł'óół** ("one will weave"). This word is built this way:

(12) object   F mode   subject   verb
      prefix   d   prefix   stem

      ' - j - d - oo - tł'óół

Remember that we learned in Chapter 11 that when we want to build a verb that has the 4 subject prefix **j** in the object prefix position together with another object prefix, the other prefix precedes the **j** (review Rule Str-4.) In the F mode, there is nothing different about this, so in (12) we see the ' and the **j** both sitting in the object prefix position, with the ' coming first. To create the actual word, we just use Rule Conj-5 and Rule Conj-7. First of all, we insert the vowel **a** after the ', since ' is followed by a consonant and not preceded by a vowel. And secondly, we use the new Rule Conj-7 that we just learned to change the **j** into **zh**, since the **j** is preceded by the vowel **a** and is followed by a syllable (namely, **doo**) that is not the verb stem (so if we had created the syllable **ji**, this syllable wouln't have been the pre-stem syllable.)

Now, in building the word **azhdootł'óół**, we didn't insert a vowel after the **j** in (12), but we did insert a vowel after the '. What happens if the circumstances are such that we have both ' and **j** in a word and we don't insert a vowel after either of them? This is exactly the situation that we see in the word **dazh'dootł'óół** ("those ones will weave"). It looks as though some sort of switch has happened with this word - the ' comes after the **zh**! To help see what's going on, let's start with a diagram of how this word is built:

(13) distributive object   F mode   subject   verb
         plural   prefix   d   prefix   stem

         da - ' - j - d - oo - tł'óół

If we apply our rules, what happens? Well, the ' is preceded by a vowel and followed by a syllable which is not the verb stem, so we won't insert any vowel after it. But what happens to the **j**? It's not preceded by a vowel, so if we don't do something to stop it, Rule Conj-1 will come along and try to put the vowel **i** after it. Since this would give the wrong result (we'd get something like "da'jidootł'óół"), we'd better do something quick! What we'll do is add a statement to Rule Conj-5 and also to Rule Conj-7. We'll add this statement to Rule Conj-5 because the unspec prefix ' is involved. We'll add the same statement to Rule Conj-7 because the 4 person subject prefix **j** is also involved. Here is the statement:

(Add to Rule Conj-5 and to Rule Conj-7): If a verb has both the unspec ' and the 4 person **j** as object prefixes, if ' is preceded by a vowel, if **j** is followed by a consonant, and if the syllable which follows **j** is not the verb-stem syllable, then no vowels are inserted either after ' or after **j**, and the ' followed by the **j** together become **zh'**.

So this addition to Rule Conj-5 and to Rule Conj-7 switches the order of the **j** prefix (which has turned into **zh**) and the ' prefix. We'll see later that there are certain other circumstances in which the order of two prefixes has to be switched, but in general, this is a relatively unusual process in the Navajo verb.

This is important: the addition we've just put into our rules only switches the two particular object prefixes mentioned, namely, the unspec object prefix and the 4 person subject prefix. Whenever we have another pair of object prefixes, no switch occurs. So, for example, if **j** is preceded by some object prefix other than ', we don't switch the prefixes.

Note on pronunciation: we've seen that in the F mode if a verb has the unspec object prefix, we sometimes get the ' right next to the F mode **d**. In (9), this happens with the distributive plural forms; but with other verb bases, it could even happen with other forms as well. Now, when ' is followed directly by **d** in these words, some people pronounce this combination almost the same, or even exactly the same, as the consonant **t'**. So, for example, some people pronounce the word **da'diitł'óół** as though it were written **dat'iitł'óół**. Not only that, but occasionally words like this are actually spelled with the letters **t'**. This means that you have to be aware, if you see something like **dat'iitł'óół** in print, that you're really supposed to be thinking that you're seeing **da'diitł'óół**.

Well, this takes care of everything we'll need to know about ' and **j** for the F mode. Rule Conj-7 (with its new addition) and the addition to Rule Conj-5 that we've learned will create the right forms of the words. But you might want to keep in mind that nothing in these additions actually mentions the F mode. We will see some other situations not involving the F mode where these additions apply.

There is a second small effect that happens with some F mode forms that we need to look at. This effect has to do with the outer prefix **na**. Remember that back in Chapter 5 we learned that the outer prefix **na** (and also **ná**) sometimes becomes **ni** (or **ní**). What happens in the F mode? To see, let's pick one of the verb bases that we've learned that has the outer prefix **na** in it, and write out the F mode forms for it. Let's take a nice easy one, the verb base that means "work" (see Chapter 8(11). Here are the forms:

(14)	sg	dpl	distr pl
1	nideeshnish	nidiilnish	nidadiilnish
2	nidíílnish	nidoołnish	nidadoołnish
3		nidoolnish	nidadoolnish
4		nizhdoolnish	nidazhdoolnish

We see from this that **na** becomes **ni** in all the F mode forms for this verb base. Rule Disj-3 that we gave in Chapter 5, even as amended in Chapter 8, doesn't tell us about this, so we're going to have to add more information to this rule. The following addition should do it:

(Add to Rule Disj-3): (...the **na** or **ná** is immediately followed by):

(d) the F mode **d**.

(e) a cluster of consonants consisting of **zh** or **'** or **zh'** followed directly by the F mode **d**.

(Here's an idea. We've noticed that **na** becomes **ni** when followed by the 4 person prefix **j**, and now we see that **na** becomes **ni** when followed by the F mode **d**. How about this: **na** becomes **ni** when it's followed by a conjunct prefix...? Well, no: look at the forms in Chapter 11(20): for many of those forms, **na** is followed by an object prefix, and **na** stays **na**. This shows that we have to be careful when we try to create a rule. If we do it wrong, the rule will give wrong answers! We are listing specific cases in Rule Disj-3 because this seems the best way of learning the facts about these prefixes.)

This will take care of all the cases we've seen so far. In the F mode of the "work" verb base, **na** is followed either by the F mode **d** (which is taken care of by part (d) of our new version of Rule Disj-3), or else by **zhd**, which is taken care of by part (e).

As we learn about more about Navajo verbs, we'll find that we have to add a little more to Rule Disj-3. But if you learn the way **na** behaves in each new structure that we study, it won't be hard.

Well, believe it or not, this is all we need to know to build the F mode forms of all the verb bases we've seen so far. If you feel like spending some time, you could go through all the chapters that we've had up till now and write out the F mode for every verb base that we've presented. We won't do that here, but just to show that there are no further problems, let's write out the F mode forms for a few additional verb bases that have various different characteristics.

First, let's look at a transitive verb with 3 person object. Look at the verb stem that means "boil it" (see Chapter 7(6)). Can you write out the F mode forms of this verb? How will these forms differ from the F mode forms of "cry" that we saw above in (4)?

(There are two differences to watch out for. Firstly, "boil it" is transitive, so when the subject is 3 person, the 3 person object will have to be indicated by putting in a **y** in the object prefix position. And secondly, "boil it" has a barred-l classifier rather than the zero classifier of "cry".)

Here are the forms:

(15)	sg	dpl	distr dpl
1	deeshbish	diilbish	dadiilbish
2	dííłbish	doołbish	dadoołbish
3		yidoołbish	deidoołbish
4		jidoołbish	dazhdoołbish

Here are some things to note about these words.

The F mode stem **bish** is used in (15). You might recall that in both the I mode and the P mode, the stem for this verb base is **béézh**.

The barred-l classifier is behaving in exactly the same way in (15) as we've seen many times now with other modes and with other verb bases. You might want to compare the way the barred-l classifier shows up in (15) with the way it shows up in Chapter 7(7) (the same verb base in the I mode.)

In the word **yidoołbish** ("he/she/they (two) will boil it"), the **y** at the beginning of the word is the object prefix that indicates a 3 person object when the subject is 3 person (see Rule Str-1.) The vowel **i** after this **y** was inserted by Rule Conj-1. You should compare this word with the word **doochah** ("he/she/they (two) will cry"), where there is no **yi** at the beginning ("cry" is intransitive, so there is never any object.)

Can you explain why we find **ei** in the word **deidoołbish** ("they'll boil it") but not in the word **dadoochah** ("they'll cry")?

How about the F mode of a transitive verb with an outer prefix? Let's write out the F mode of "carry him/her up out of something" (see Chapter 11(2) for the verb base).) If the object is 3 person, we get:

(16)   sg   dpl   distr dpl

1   hadeeshtééł   hadiiltééł   hadadiiltééł
2   hadííłtééł   hadoołtééł   hadadoołtééł
3   haidoołtééł   hadeidoołtééł
4   hazhdoołtééł   hadazhdoołtééł

If you have understood everything up till now, you will understand everything about the words in (16). There is nothing new here.

What if we want to build F mode forms for this verb where the object is not 3 person? Again, there is nothing special about this: just put the appropriate object prefix (see Chapter 11(1)) into the object prefix position. Here are a few words that can be built this way:

(17)   hanideeshtééł   "I'll carry you up"
        hashidííłtééł   "you'll carry me up"
        hanidoołtééł   "he/she/they (two) will carry you up"

        (etc.)

To convince ourselves that there is no special problem with the **hw** object prefix, let's look at the F mode of a verb that has a lexical **hw** in it. We'll take the verb that means "talk about", which will also illustrate that nothing new happens in the F mode if the classifier is plain-l (see Chapter 12(13) for this verb base.) The F mode forms are:

(18)   sg   dpl   distr dpl

1   hodeeshnih   hodiilnih   dahodiilnih
2   hodíílnih   hodoołnih   dahodoołnih
3   hodoolnih   dahodoolnih
4   hozhdoolnih   dahozhdoolnih

Why does the **hw** prefix show up as **ho** in all of these forms? (Answer: in all the forms in (18), the **hw** is followed by a consonant, and the next syllable is the syllable of the F mode subject prefix, which is not the verb-stem syllable. By Rule Conj-6 part (a), **hw** becomes **ho**.)

To show that nothing new happens in the F mode with voiced fricative verbs, let's write out the F mode forms of the verb that means "carry a ropelike thing around" (see Chapter 13(5)):

(19)	sg	dpl	distr pl
1	nideeshłeeł	nidiilyeeł	nidadiilyeeł
2	nidííłeeł	nidoohłeeł	nidadoohłeeł
3	neidooleeł		nideidooleeł
4	nizhdooleeł		nidazhdooleeł

We see that the l at the beginning of the verb stem becomes ł in the words **nideeshłeeł** ("I'll carry it around"), **nidoohłeeł** ("you (two) will carry it around"), and **nidadoohłeeł** ("you (pl) will carry it around") because in these words the voiced fricative l is preceded by **sh** or **h**. Note also the irregular d-effect in the 1dpl forms (review the discussion of this verb base in Chapter 13.)

By the way, how did the **ei** get in the word **neidooleeł** ("he/she/they (two) will carry it around")?

Well, this should do it for the F mode. In the next chapter, we'll expand our study to include verb bases with something totally new: inner prefixes!

CHAPTER 15

THE INNER PREFIX D
AND OUTER OBJECTS

In this chapter, we are going to expand our knowledge of the Navajo verb in two important ways.

First of all, we'll make our first acquaintance with inner prefixes. While many Navajo verb bases do not have inner prefixes, many others do, and we need to start learning how these work. Some inner prefixes have irregularities associated with them. But here's the good news: although inner prefixes are very important, there aren't many different ones, so if we take it slow, we can master them.

Secondly, we'll start learning verb bases that have more than one lexical prefix. So far, all the verb bases we've seen have either no lexical prefixes or else have exactly one lexical prefix. However, there are many Navajo verb bases with two, three, or even four or more lexical prefixes. The great expressive power of the Navajo verb is due largely to being able to create verb bases with different combinations of lexical prefixes, so we need to start getting familiar with how this works. Mostly, we won't have any trouble with the actual forms of the verbs: the rules and principles we've learned so far carry over to the bigger verbs with little or no change.

In this chapter we're going to start our work by learning about one particular inner prefix. The inner prefix we'll learn is simply: **d**. This is probably the most common inner prefix in the Navajo language, and it has the additional pleasant feature of being relatively well-behaved: there is very little new that we need to learn in order to form verbs that have the inner prefix **d** in them.

To get started, let's actually build verb forms from the following verb base, which means "melt it" (i.e. "liquify it by heating"):

(1)

Stem-set		Classifier: barred-l
I:	yį́įh	
P:	yį́į'	Lexical prefixes: **d** (inner)
F:	yįh	
R:	yįh	Transitivity: transitive
O:	yį́įh	Perfective: y-P

Before proceeding: did you notice that this verb base has the same stem-set as the verb base in Chapter 13(8)? That verb base also meant "melt it", but there are differences in usages between the two verb bases. For example, the verb base in Chapter 13(8) seems to be preferred if you're letting snow or ice melt, whereas the verb base in (1) above is preferred if, say, you're heating some gold in order to melt it (to make jewelry, for example.)

Now, can we actually make verbs out of the verb base in (1)? We can, and we don't need any new rules! Let's start with the I mode. If you want to try to write out the forms yourself first, you might want to keep the following points in mind.

The verb base in (1) is a voiced-fricative verb with a barred-l classifier, so the part of Chapter 13 that dealt with this classifier will come into play (see especially Rule Subj-8.)

Since an inner prefix is a conjunct prefix, every verb form built using the verb base in (1) has a conjunct prefix in it. Therefore, don't forget to check the rules called Rule Conj-(number).

The verb base in (1) is transitive. The thing that you are melting is going to be 3 person, so don't forget Rule Str-1.

If you've tried to write out the I mode forms of this verb, you should have gotten something like this:

(2)	sg	dpl	distr dpl
1	dishhį́įh	diilyį́įh	dadiilyį́įh
2	dííłhį́įh	dołhį́įh	dadołhį́įh
3		yidiłhį́įh	deidiłhį́įh
4		jidiłhį́įh	dazhdiłhį́įh

As in the case of the verb in Chapter 13(8), some people write **dishxį́įh** instead of **dishhį́įh**, in order to avoid writing two **h**'s next to each other.

Officially, there is nothing new here. However, here are some review questions to help you understand some of the forms.

Question: Why does the stem in most of the forms in (2) begin with **h**? (Answer: Rule Subj-8 applied. Review the discussion of Chapter 13(9).)

Question: Why does the form that means "you (sg) are melting it" start out **dí-**? (Answer: Rule Conj-3 applied.)

Question: Is the **yi** at the beginning of **yidiłhį́įh** ("he/she/they (two) is/are melting it") the peg? (Answer: No! This **yi** is the 3 object prefix **y**, with the vowel **i** added in by Rule Conj-1. The peg is only used to supply a pre-stem syllable. In the word **yidiłhį́įh**, there already is a pre-stem syllable (the syllable **di**).)

Question: Why does the form that means "those ones are melting it" begin with **dazh** rather than with **daji**? (Answer: Read Rule Conj-7 carefully. The word **dazhdiłhį́į́h** is built like this:

(3) distributive object inner cl verb
     plural prefix prefix stem

       da - j - d - ł - yį́į́h

In (3), the 4 person prefix **j** is preceded by a vowel (the **a** of the distributive plural **da**) and the syllable which follows **j** is not the verb-stem syllable (it's the syllable **di**, as soon as Rule Conj-1 puts that **i** in), so no vowel is inserted after the **j**, and in addition, the **j** becomes **zh**. Note that the inner prefix **d** is what makes this happen. In the verb bases we've seen before, the **j** in words like this would have been followed directly by the verb-stem syllable, so if we apply Rule Conj-1 the syllable **ji** that we'd get would be the pre-stem syllable, and this exception would not have applied. For words built from those verb bases we just get **daji-**. By the way, we learned about **j** becoming **zh** in connection with our study of the F mode, but here it's happening in the I mode. Do you see why? It's that inner prefix!

Well, this should be enough about the words in (2). Here's something to keep in mind about the I mode forms of verbs with inner prefixes: the 2sg form won't have **ni** as the subject prefix. Instead, there'll be that high tone on the vowel that was inserted by Rule Conj-3 right after the inner prefix. Up till now, we've only seen this high tone when we had transitive verbs with various object prefixes in them (see, for example, the word that means "you (sg) are carrying me up" in Chapter 11(15).) What we need to remember is that this is also going to happen whenever a verb has an inner prefix, whether or not there is any object, since the inner prefix will trigger Rule Conj-3.

Let's look at the P mode forms of the verb base in (1). These are easy. If you want to write out the forms, answer the following question first: Where can we find the correct subject prefixes to use? (Answer: Since we're using the y-P conjugation and since this verb base has a barred-l classifier, the subject prefixes are somewhere in Chapter 9. Since the verb base has an inner prefix (which is a conjunct prefix), all the subject prefixes will be from the chart in Chapter 9(5).)

Here are the P mode forms for this verb base:

(4)   sg   dpl   distr dpl

	sg	dpl	distr dpl
1	díłhį́į́	diilyį́į́	dadiilyį́į́
2	díínłhį́į́	doołhį́į́	dadoołhį́į́
3	yidíłhį́į́		deidíłhį́į́
4	jidíłhį́į́		dazhdíłhį́į́

If you understood the construction of the I mode forms of this verb, these P mode forms should have no surprises for you. Incidentally, do you understand why **j** becomes **zh** in the word **dazhdííłhíí'**?

And: why isn't the **y** prefix doubled in **yidííłhíí'**? After all, we're in the y-P mode, the classifier is barred-l, and there's no prefix to the left of this object prefix. Well, when we first came upon those doubled **yy**'s back in Chapter 9, we mentioned that this was something that happened with prefixless verb bases. An inner lexical prefix would prevent this doubling just as an outer lexical prefix would. Here we've got the inner **d**, so we just get an ordinary single **y** as the object prefix.

What about the F mode? Let's build one word carefully. We'll take the word that means "I'll melt it". This word is built as follows:

(5) F mode   inner   subject cl   verb
     d   prefix   prefix   stem

     d - d - eesh - ł - yįh

Note the positioning of the prefixes: the inner prefix comes after the F mode **d**.

To create the actual word, we note that Rule Conj-1 will insert an **i** between the two **d**'s (since the F mode **d** is a conjunct prefix). Also, Rule Subj-8 and the sandwich rule both apply. The result is: **dideeshhįh** (sometimes spelled **dideeshxįh**.)

(Were you wondering why we say that the inner prefix comes after the F mode **d** rather than the other way, since both of these prefixes are just **d**'s? When we look at other inner prefixes, we'll see that they (usually!) come after the F mode **d**, so we're just saying the same thing about the inner prefix **d**.)

It's now easy to write out the entire F mode for this verb:

(6)	sg	dpl	distr dpl
1	dideeshhįh	didiilyįh	dadidiilyįh
2	didííthįh	didoołhįh	dadidoołhįh
3		yididoołhįh	deididoołhįh
4		jididoołhįh	dazhdidoołhįh

(The distributive plural F mode forms of verb bases that have the inner prefix **d** are always going to have three **d**'s in them! First, there's the **d** of **da** (for the distributive plural), then there's the F mode **d**, and finally there's the inner prefix **d**.)

We've worked out the entire I, P, and F modes of this new verb base that has an inner prefix in it, and we didn't need any new rules! This should help convince you that we've really learned a lot about the way Navajo verbs are constructed.

Let's look at another verb base, this time one with a plain-l classifier (so the P mode will be a little different.) The following verb base means "step":

(7)

Stem-set		Classifier: plain-l
I:	**'éés**	
P:	**'eez**	Lexical prefixes: **d** (inner)
F:	**'is**	
R:	**'is**	Transitivity: intransitive
O:	**'éés**	Perfective: y-P

(Did you notice that all the stems end in **s**, except for the P mode stem, which ends in **z**?)

Since the stems in (7) all have either an **s** or a **z** in them, Rule Subj-6 will apply.

The I mode forms of this verb base are just like the I mode forms of "melt it", shown in (2). Here are the I mode forms for "step":

(8) sg   dpl   distr dpl

1   dis'éés   diil'éés   dadiil'éés
2   díl'éés   doł'éés   dadoł'éés
3   dil'éés   dadil'éés
4   jidil'éés   dazhdil'éés

Question: Why isn't there any **yi** at the beginning of the word **dil'éés** ("he/she/they (two) is/are stepping")? (Answer: this verb is intransitive, so there is no object prefix.)

Note that the only difference between **díl'éés** "you (sg) are stepping" and **dil'éés** "he/she/they (two) is/are stepping" is in the tone of the first syllable.

The P mode of this verb will have forms a little different than the forms in (4), because the classifier is plain-l. We'll use the subject prefixes in ... (where? in Chapter 10(4).) We get:

(9) sg   dpl   distr dpl

1   dees'eez   diil'eez   dadiil'eez
2   dííníl'eez   dooł'eez   dadooł'eez
3   dool'eez   dadool'eez
4   jidool'eez   dazhdool'eez

Note that when we are working with a verb with an inner prefix, we can easily see all the subject prefixes that are listed in Chapter 10(4).

The F mode is straightforward:

(10)   sg   dpl   distr dpl

1   didees'is   didiil'is   dadidiil'is
2   didííl'is   didooł'is   dadidooł'is
3   didool'is   dadidool'is
4   jididool'is   dazhdidool'is

Again, we didn't need any new rules. It looks like our studies so far have paid off well! However, before we get too smug, we'd better notice that so far, the verb bases we've looked at have used the y-P conjugation. It turns out that with the s-P conjugation, there is something new we need to learn.

What happens is this. If a verb base has **d** as an inner prefix, then in any verb we build using that verb base, this **d** will be followed directly by the subject prefix. Now, in the s-P conjugation, the inner prefix **d** contracts with the s-P subject prefixes, and we need to learn these contracted forms. What we'll do is simply list them. As in the case of the P mode generally, we need to divide the story up into two cases: when the classifier is zero or barred-l on the one hand, and when the classifier is plain-l or d on the other.

If the classifier is zero or barred-l, instead of having the inner prefix **d** followed by the prefixes in the chart in Chapter 8(3), we get the following contracted forms:

(11)   inner **d** contracted with s-P subject prefixes,
        zero/barred-l classifiers:

	sg	dpl
1	dé	deed/disiid
2	díní	disoo
3	deez or dees	

In (11), the choice between **deez** and **dees** for the 3 person form is the same as in the normal s-P case: use **deez** if the classifier is zero, and use **dees** if the classifier is barred-l.

In the case of the 1dpl and 2dpl forms, there is variation. For the 1dpl case, the form **deed** is common, but the uncontracted form **disiid** (and occasionally also the form **diid**, by the way) occur, too. For the 2dpl, the form **disoo**, which is the one shown in (11), seems to be the most common, but I've occasionally also heard **sidoo** (with the **s** in front of the **d.**)

If the classifier is plain-l or d, similar contractions occur. Instead of the inner prefix **d** being followed by the prefixes in the chart in Chapter 8(10), we find the following contracted forms:

(12)   inner **d** contracted with s-P subject prefixes,
        plain-l/d classifiers:

	sg	dpl
1	**désh**	**deed/disiid**
2	**díní**	**disooh**
3	**dees**	

Note the high-tone **é** in the 1sg form **désh** - this is different from the ordinary 1sg plain-l/d s-P prefix, which is **sis**. (Also, since there is no other **s** in the prefix, the 1sg part of this form reverts to **sh.**)

Something else worth noting: if we're in the y-P conjugation and we have an inner prefix **d**, a verb with a 2sg subject will have **dííní** in it (see (4) and (9) for examples.) But if it's the s-P conjugation that we're in, we'll see **díní** instead.

We can illustrate these forms easily with some new verb bases. Here is the verb base that means "fall":

(13)

Stem-set		
I: geeh	Classifier: zero	
P: go'	Lexical prefixes: **d** (inner)	
F: goh	Transitivity: intransitive	
R: goh		
O: geeh	Perfective: s-P	

(This verb base is used mainly to mean a person falling from a standing position to the ground on which he/she was standing, say, as a result of tripping. Did you notice that the stem-set in (13) is another one of those stem-sets where the P mode stem ends in a glottal stop while all the others end in **h**?)

For practice, let's do all three modes that we've learned so far.

In the I mode, there is nothing new. The forms are very similar to the forms for "step" that we saw above in (8). The I mode forms for "fall" are:

(14)   sg   dpl   distr dpl

1   dishgeeh   diigeeh   dadiigeeh
2   dígeeh   dohgeeh   dadohgeeh
3   digeeh   dadigeeh
4   jidigeeh   dazhdigeeh

In the P mode, we'll use our new contracted forms. Since the classifier is zero, the forms we need are the ones in (11). We get:

(15)   sg   dpl   distr dpl

1   dégo'   deego'   dadeego'
2   dínígo'   disoogo'   dadisoogo'
3   deezgo'   dadeezgo'
4   jideezgo'   dazhdeezgo'

What if we want to diagram the way these are built? Well, for the word **dégo'** "I fell", we can do something like this:

(16) inner   subject   verb
      prefix   prefix   stem

        d - sé - go'
          \   /
           dé

Make sure you understand how all the P mode forms are built. There are no mysteries.

In the F mode, there is nothing special. For practice, let's write out the F mode forms of "fall" anyway:

(17)   sg   dpl   distr dpl

1   dideeshgoh   didiigoh   dadidiigoh
2   didíígoh   didoohgoh   dadidoohgoh
3   didoogoh   dadidoogoh
4   jididoogoh   dazhdidoogoh

To illustrate the contracted forms in (12), here's a verb base with a plain-l classifier. This verb base means "start to work":

(18)

Stem-set		Classifier: plain-l
I:	**níísh**	
P:	**nish**	Lexical prefixes: **d** (inner)
F:	**nish**	
R:	**nish**	Transitivity: intransitive
O:	**níísh**	
		Perfective: s-P

By now, we should be happy with the I mode and F mode forms of verbs like this, so let's only write out the P mode. Using the contracted forms in (12), we get:

(19)   sg   dpl   distr dpl

1   déshnish   deelnish   dadeelnish
2   dínílnish   dishoołnish   dadishoołnish
3   deeshnish   dadeeshnish
4   jideeshnish   dazhdeeshnish

Note the effect of Rule Subj-6, due to the **sh** at the end of the verb stem.

Incidentally, did something about this verb seem familiar to you? We already learned the verb base that means just "work" - see Chapter 8(11). Here, we have a verb base with a related meaning. Note that the stem-set in (18) is very similar to, but not exactly the same as, the stem-set in Chapter 8(11). Does this situation remind you of something else that we already saw? Go back to Chapter 11, and compare the verb base in Chapter 11(2), which means "carry someone up out of something" with the verb base in Chapter 11(19), which means "carry someone around". We mentioned in our discussion there that the stem-sets for these two verb bases are very similar, but not exactly the same. The two "work" stem-sets are like this, too. What's going on?

We already suggested in Chapter 11 that sometimes we'll see stem-sets coming in pairs like this. Since we've just run into this again, let's learn some things about such pairs.

First of all, whenever we have such a pair, the P mode stems of the two sets are always the same. For the stem-sets that had to do with carrying someone, the P mode stems for both sets was **tį**. For the two stem-sets that have to do with working, the P mode stems for both sets is **nish**. For this reason, reference books on Navajo often list verb stems by the P mode stem. For example, the stems are listed in YMM 92 by the P mode form.

166

Secondly, when there are two related stem-sets like the examples we've seen, there is a connection between the stem-set that is actually used in a particular verb base and the rest of the verb base. Here is what this connection is. When stem-sets come in pairs, one of the stem-sets in the pair is reserved just for those verb bases that have the atelic outer prefix **na** as one of their lexical prefixes. For now, we'll say that the other stem-set is used for any other verb bases, but we'll see later that it's slightly more complicated than that. We'll find it convenient to give names to the two stem-sets in each pair. The stem-set that is used in atelic verb bases with **na** will be called a *continuative aspect stem-set*, or sometimes just a *continuative stem-set*. The other stem-set will be called a *momentanous aspect stem-set*, or just a *momentaneous stem-set*. These terms are used in YM, so you should be familiar with them.

For example, in the case of carrying someone, the stem-set in Chapter 11(2) is the momentaneous stem-set, whereas the stem-set in Chapter 11(19) is the continuative stem-set. Note that the verb base in Chapter 11(19) has the atelic outer prefix **na** in it, whereas the verb base in Chapter 11(2) doesn't have this prefix. If you think about the meanings of these verb bases, you'll see that the base in Chapter 11(2) is telic but the base in Chapter 11(19) is atelic. While you're carrying someone up out of, for example, a hole, you haven't finished it yet, and when you do finish carrying him/her up out of the hole, you can't continue doing it, because you're finished - the person is out of the hole. But carrying someone around is something that you can keep doing and that you can stop doing at any time. Verb bases with continuative stem-sets have to be atelic. Verb bases with momentaneous stem-sets tend to be telic, but sometimes more complicated things happen.

In the case of the verb bases that have to do with working, we have the same thing. Simply working is atelic - you can keep on working, and you can stop at any time. But to start to work is different: once you've started, you can't keep on starting! The verb base in Chapter 8(11) has the atelic prefix **na** in it, so this verb base uses the continuative stem-set that has to do with working. But the verb base in (18) above doesn't have the atelic **na** in it, and, in fact, it doesn't express an atelic action, as we just saw. This verb base uses the momentaneous stem-set that has to do with working.

The combination of atelic **na** with the continuative aspect stem-set is a fixed arrangement that's pretty common in the Navajo language. We've already seen a number of verb bases that have this combination, and as you continue your study of the Navajo language, you'll run into many more verb bases structured this way. Because this combination is so common, there's another piece of terminology you should know: when a verb base has the atelic **na** as a lexical prefix together with a continuative aspect stem-set, YM says that the verb base has the *continuative aspect*. That is, they use the term *continuative aspect* to describe the verb base as well as to describe the version of the stem-set in that verb base.

But remember: not all stem-sets come in pairs like this! There are also cases of pairs of stem-sets where the two sets are related in a different way than what we've just described. And, for a few common stem-sets, there are actually more than two sets that are related. We'll see more of this as our study progresses, and we'll summarize the most common arrangements in Chapter 27. But, at this time, you should start to become aware of related stem-sets.

Well, let's get back to our main task. Have we finished with the inner prefix **d**? Well, almost. There is one more rule we need to learn about in this chapter. But in order to do so, it will be convenient to start looking at verb bases with more than one lexical prefix. We want to do this anyway, since so many Navajo verb bases have more than one lexical prefix.

Most of the time, when we have a verb base with more than one lexical prefix, there is nothing new involved. We simply apply all the relevant rules to all the parts of the verb that each rule deals with. To see that this is not particularly hard, here's the verb base that means "pray":

(20)

Stem-set		Classifier: plain-l
I:	**zin**	
P:	**zin/ziįd**	Lexical prefixes: **so** (outer), **d** (inner)
F:	**ziįł**	Transitivity: intransitive
R:	**ziįh**	
O:	**zin**	Perfective: y-P

Here we have a verb base with an outer prefix **so** (a new prefix for us, but that's okay), and also with the inner prefix **d**. Can we build verbs using this base? Sure we can! We simply have to keep a number of things in mind.

First of all, the stems all start with **z**, so we've got a voiced fricative verb here, with plain-l classifier. This means that our discussions in Chapter 13 will be relevant. Also, the **z** in the stems will trigger Rule Subj-6.

Next, since this verb base has the inner prefix **d**, what we've learned so far in this chapter will apply to this verb base.

Finally, since this verb base also has an outer prefix, we'll have to make sure we check the rules that have to do with disjunct prefixes. As it happens, though, we'll soon see that the **so** prefix is never followed by a consonant followed by the verb stem syllable (because of the inner prefix!), so **so** is never the pre-stem syllable in any form of this verb base. We'll also see that **so** is never followed by a vowel. This means that neither Rule Disj-1 nor Rule Disj-2 could apply to any of the forms. Since the other rules that have to do with disjunct prefixes only apply to certain specific prefixes, we see that we're never going to have to change the form of this prefix.

So, what are the forms? Starting with the I mode, we have:

(21)	sg		dpl	distr dpl
1	sodiszin		sodiilzin	sodadiilzin
2	sodílzin		sodołzin	sodadołzin
3		sodilzin		sodadilzin
4		sozhdilzin		sodazhdilzin

(Would you be surprised to learn that some people say **sozdilzin** instead of **sozhdilzin** for "one is praying"? They've applied the optional Rule Conj-4.)

The only thing to note here is that, since there is an outer prefix in this verb, the condition for changing the 4 person prefix **j** to **zh** is present in the form **sozhdilzin**: the **j** is preceded by the vowel **o** of **so**, and the syllable following the **j** is not the verb stem syllable (because of the inner prefix) so if we had created the syllable **ji**, it wouldn't have been the pre-stem syllable.

For review: How can we tell, just by looking at the word **sodiszin** "I'm praying", that this verb has a plain-l classifier? (Answer: It's because of the **sz** - the plain-l classifier protected the **z** from getting devoiced. Review Chapter 13.)

And note that in every word in (21), the **so** prefix is followed by a consonant, and the syllable following **so** is not the verb stem syllable. Thus, as we mentioned, we expect that there won't be any change to this syllable. This is exactly what we find.

In the P mode, we have:

(22)	sg		dpl	distr dpl
1	sodeeszin		sodiilzin	sodadiilzin
2	sodíínílzin		sodoołzin	sodadoołzin
3		sodoolzin		sodadoolzin
4		sozhdoolzin		sodazhdoolzin

We're using the P mode stem form **zin** to build the words in (22) (apparently, an alternative P mode stem **zįįd** is sometimes found for this stem-set.) As in the I mode, the syllable **so** never changes. The forms are completely regular.

In the F mode, we have:

(23)   sg   dpl   distr dpl

1   sodideeszįįł   sodidiilzįįł   sodadidiilzįįł
2   sodidíílzįįł   sodidoołzįįł   sodadidoołzįįł
3   sodidoolzįįł   sodadidoolzįįł
4   sozhdidoolzįįł   sodazhdidoolzįįł

Look at what we've accomplished: we've conjugated our first verb with two lexical prefixes, and we didn't have to learn anything new to do it!

As another example, let's look at a transitive verb base with two lexical prefixes. If you do not speak Navajo, some of the forms of this verb will be tongue-twisters for you, because there are a lot of **d**'s. Here is the verb base we want - it means "make/light/start/build it (a fire)". (This verb base only refers to making or starting a fire, not making or starting anything else!)

(24)

Stem-set:	Classifier: barred-l
I: **jeeh** P: **jéé'** F: **jah** R: **jah** O: **jeeh**	Lexical prefixes: **di** (outer), **d** (inner)
	Transitivity: transitive
	Perfective: y-P

The outer and inner prefixes both have **d**'s in them, which is why various forms of this verb will have a lot of **d**'s....

Starting with the I mode, we have:

(25)   sg   dpl   distr dpl

1   didishjeeh   didiiljeeh   didadiiljeeh
2   didíłjeeh   didołjeeh   didadołjeeh
3   diidiłjeeh   dideidiłjeeh
4   dizhdiłjeeh   didazhdiłjeeh

Do you understand why there's **ii** in the word **diidiłjeeh** "he/she/they (two) is/are making it (the fire)"? It's because this verb is transitive - the object is 3 person (it refers to the fire that is being made). So the word **diidiłjeeh** is built like this:

(26) outer   object   inner cl   verb
      prefix   prefix   prefix   stem

          di - y - d - ł - jeeh

Rule Conj-2 applies here: since **y** in (26) is followed by a consonant (the inner prefix **d**) and preceded by a vowel (the **i** of the outer prefix **di**), the **y** turns into **i**. This is how that **ii** got in there.

Of course, by Rule Str-1, we only find the object prefix **y** in the forms where the subject is 3 person. In the word **diidiłjeeh**, we end up with **ii**, as we just saw. In the word **dideidiłjeeh** "they are making it (the fire)", the object prefix **y** shows up in the form of the diphthong **ei**, as we've already seen many times. In the words where the subject is 1, 2, or 4 person, the 3 person object prefix is zero; that is, there is no object prefix at all.

And, keep in mind that the first **di** in these words is an outer prefix. This means, for example, that when we put the distributive plural prefix **da** into the verb, the **da** comes after the outer prefix **di**.

The P mode forms come out looking like this:

(27)   sg   dpl   distr dpl

1   didííłjéé'   didiiljéé'   didadiiljéé'
2   didííníłjéé'   didoołjéé'   didadoołjéé'
3   diidííłjéé'   dideidííłjéé'
4   dizhdííłjéé'   didazhdííłjéé'

(The entry for this verb in YM suggests that some speakers shift to the s-P conjugation in the distributive plural forms when the subject is 3 or 4 person.)

Make sure you understand what happened to the 3 person object prefix **y** in the words in (27) that have a 3 person subject. (The story is the same as in the I mode.)

The F mode forms are (watch out for those **d**'s!):

(28)   sg   dpl   distr dpl

1   didideeshjah   dididiiljah   didadidiiljah
2   dididííłjah   dididoołjah   didadidoołjah
3   diididoołjah   dideididoołjah
4   dizhdidoołjah   didazhdidoołjah

Whew! There may be a lot of **d**'s in there, but all the forms are built in exactly the same way as we've seen all along. Can you say which **d** is which in a word like **didadidiiljah**? (Answer: The first **d** is the **d** of the outer prefix **di**. The second **d** is the **d** of the distributive plural prefix **da**. The third **d** is the F mode **d**. The fourth **d** is the inner prefix **d**.)

At this point, it will be useful to learn about another kind of outer prefix that is found with quite a few Navajo verb bases. To illustrate this, we're going to take a verb base that doesn't happen to have an inner prefix. In fact, the verb base we'll look at next seems to be exactly the same as the verb base in Chapter 8(11) (the verb base that means "work"), but with an additional outer prefix. The thing is, the additional outer prefix actually seems to be a kind of object. The meaning of the verb base we have in mind is "work on it":

Rather than giving the verb base first, it will be easier if we start by looking at all the I mode forms of this verb. Here they are:

(29)	sg		dpl	distr dpl
1	binaashnish	bineiilnish		binideiilnish
2	binanilnish	binaołnish		binidaołnish
3		yinaalnish		yinidaalnish
4		binijilnish		binidajilnish

The verbs in (29) mean things like "I'm working on it", "you're working on it", etc. (By the way, the **ni** in **binijilnish** and in the distributive plural forms is just about always pronounced as **n** only.)

If you compare the forms in (29) with the forms in Chapter 6(12), you'll see that the forms in (29) look just like the forms in Chapter 6(12) except that for most of the forms in (29) we've tacked on a prefix **bi**. But: when the subject is 3 person, the prefix we added isn't **bi**, it's **yi**. Does this remind us of anything?

Well, we know that if we have an ordinary transitive verb and the object is 3 person, we put the prefix **y** in the object prefix position if the subject is 3 person. But we use **b** as the object only if the verb is going to be used as an inverse (see Chapter 11). And, if the subject isn't 3 person, we don't put any prefix into the object prefix position at all. (Now would be a good time to review Rule Str-1.)

What's happening here is similar, but not exactly the same. The **bi** in most of the forms in (29) actually is a kind of object - in fact, it corresponds to the "it" in the English sentence "I'm working on it". But it's placed into the outer prefix position instead of the usual object prefix position. (How do we know this? Because it precedes the outer prefix **na**.) Also, when the subject isn't 3 person, we actually have to put something in, which is different from the way an object works in an ordinary transitive verb. If we just used "zero" for the object, the way we would with an ordinary transitive verb, the forms would look the same as the forms in Chapter 6(12), and we wouldn't know that we meant to say "I'm working on it" instead of just saying "I'm working"! This is why we put in **bi**. But

172

if the subject is 3 person, then the rule is the same as for an ordinary object: use **yi** as the object if the verb is direct, and use **bi** as the object if the verb is inverse.

In order to deal with all of this, we're going to have to add some information to our rules. But first, let's write down the verb base that means "work on it". Here it is, but you'll see that we've put in a special symbol having to do with this new object. We'll explain this symbol in a moment.

(30)

Stem-set	Classifier: plain-1
I:　　nish P:　　nish	Lexical prefixes: **Pi** (outer), **na** (outer)
F:　　nish R:　　nish	Transitivity: intransitive
O:　　nish	Perfective: s-P

There are two new things here.

First of all, this verb base has two outer prefixes. Whenever this happens (it is not unusual), the two outer prefixes will always be placed in the verb in one particular order. When we present verb bases with two outer prefixes, we'll list the outer prefixes in the order in which they are placed in the verb.

Secondly, the first of the two outer prefixes is listed as **Pi**. The "P" in this prefix stands for "pronoun". The idea is that whenever we list a P like this as part of a prefix, we're saying that any object prefix can be placed in the position of the P. The actual object prefixes that can be used are the same as the ones that are usually put into the object prefix position - you can find a chart showing them in Chapter 11(1). But whenever we use the P symbol, it is going to mean that even when the subject is 1, 2, or 4 person, a 3 person object has to be represented using the prefix **b**. To make sure that this happens, we'll need to add something to Rule Str-1. Here is the addition that we need:

(add to Rule Str-1): A 3 person object listed as P is represented by **b** if the subject is 1, 2, or 4 person.

We're also going to use the term *outer object* to mean an object which is part of an outer prefix. The verb base in (30) is our first example of a verb base with an outer object.

Now, in the case of the verb base in (30), our new addition to Rule Str-1 tells us that a 3 person object has to show up as **b** if the subject of the verb is 1, 2, or 4 person. If the subject is 3 person, then Rule Str-1 applies as before: we get **y** for the direct form of the verb and **b** for the inverse form.

This should take care of what we need to know about verb bases like (30). But just to make sure,

173

let's build one of the verbs in (29) and see that the form comes out right. The word that means "I'm working on it" will be built like this:

(31)   outer   subject   cl   verb
        prefixes   prefix   stem

        bi - na - sh - l - nish

Why is **b** used as the "P" in this form? Because the outer object (which corresponds to the "it" in "I'm working on it") is 3 person, and the subject is not 3 person (the subject is 1 person), so our new addition to Rule Str-1 tells us to use the object prefix **b**.

Note that in the forms built out of this verb base, **bi** (or **yi**) is always followed by a consonant (namely, the **n** of **na**) and that the next syllable is never the verb stem syllable (the next syllable is either **na**, or else what **na** turns into), so we don't have to change anything about this prefix.

Incidentally, when we gave the verb base in (29), we said that this verb base was intransitive. Why?

Because no object prefix ever appears in the usual object prefix position when this verb is conjugated. The part of the verb that refers to the "it" (in, for example, "I'm working on it") is the **b** of the outer object prefix **bi**. As far as the ordinary object prefix position is concerned, this verb is like any ordinary intransitive verb - we never put anything in that position.

We won't write out the P mode and F mode forms of this verb, because there is nothing special about them. As long as you remember to use **yi** instead of **bi** when the subject is 3 person, all you have to do is take the P mode and F mode forms of "work" and tack on a **bi** to the front.

Now that we've learned that there is such a thing as outer object prefixes in Navajo, let's look at another verb base. This one has an outer object prefix, and an inner prefix. Moreover, it's transitive. The meaning of this base is "wrap it around it", or "bandage it with it".

(32)

Stem-set		Classifier: zero
I:	**dis**	
P:	**diz**	Lexical prefixes: **Pik'í** (outer), **d** (inner)
F:	**dis**	
R:	**dis**	Transitivity: transitive
O:	**dis**	Perfective: s-P

Before writing out forms, let's think a little about structure. This verb base is listed as transitive, which means that we'll be looking for object prefixes (in the usual object prefix position.) But this verb base also has an outer object prefix. Does this mean that there are two objects in this verb?

Yes! In fact, we can say what these objects refer to. The ordinary object prefix refers to the thing (for example, the bandage) that is used as wrapping. The outer object refers to the thing that gets covered by the wrapping or by the bandage. Another way of saying this is: the meaning of this verb base is "wrap it (object) around it (outer object)", or "bandage it (outer object) with it (object)".

What about the actual forms of this verb? Well, there still is nothing new we have to learn! We'll get the right forms of this verb as long as we remember to: (a) represent the ordinary (3 person) object as zero except when the subject is 3 person; (b) represent the object as **y** when the subject is 3 person; (c) use **b** in the 3 person outer object prefix when the subject is 1, 2, or 4 person; (d) use **y** instead of **b** in the outer object prefix when the subject is 3 person; (e) use the proper contracted forms in the P mode (since we have an inner prefix **d** and the s-P conjugation); (f) apply the other rules we've learned in the usual way. You really should try this before looking at the forms below.

Okay. Here's the I mode:

(33)	sg	dpl	distr dpl
1	bik'ídísdis	bik'ídiidis	bik'ídadiidis
2	bik'ídídis	bik'ídóhdis	bik'ídadohdis
3	yik'íididis		yik'ídeididis
4	bik'ízhdídis		bik'ídazhdidis

Here's the P mode:

(34)	sg	dpl	distr dpl
1	bik'ídédiz	bik'ídeediz	bik'ídadeediz
2	bik'ídínídiz	bik'ídisoodiz	bik'ídadisoodiz
3	yik'íideezdiz		yik'ídeideezdiz
4	bik'ízhdeezdiz		bik'ídazhdeezdiz

And here's the F mode:

(35)	sg	dpl	distr dpl
1	bik'ídideesdis	bik'ídidiidis	bik'ídadidiidis
2	bik'ídidíídis	bik'ídidoohdis	bik'ídadidoohdis
3	yik'íididoodis		yik'ídeididoodis
4	bik'ízhdidoodis		bik'ídazhdidoodis

175

Simple!

Were you wondering why there is a high tone on the third syllable of the I mode forms **bik'ídísdis** "I'm bandaging it with it", **bik'ízhdídis** "one is bandaging it with it", and **bik'ídóhdis** "you (two) are bandaging it with it"? Review Rule Subj-5.

Review the chart in (11) above for the contracted subject prefixes that you see in (34).

Incidentally, when the 3 person object prefix **y** is changed into **i** by that exception to Rule Conj-1, keep in mind that this new **i** is always low tone. This is why the second **i** in the **íi** inside the words **yik'íididis**, **yik'íideezdis**, and **yik'íididoodis** does not have a high tone. The first **í** in the **íi** inside these words does have a high tone, because that **í** is simply the last vowel in the outer prefix **bik'í/yik'í**, and this vowel happens to have a high tone.

We are going to end this chapter with a look at one more verb base. This verb base exhibits something new that we do have to learn about inner prefixes. It has to do with the unspec object prefix. The verb base in (36) means "uncover it by digging". The "it" that is uncovered is represented as an outer object. There is no ordinary object prefix, which is why the verb base is listed as intransitive.

(36)

Stem-set		Classifier: barred-l
I:	**gééd**	Lexical prefixes: **Páá** (outer), **'** (object), **d** (inner)
P:	**geed**	
F:	**goł**	Transitivity: intransitive
R:	**go'**	
O:	**gééd**	Perfective: y-P

Perhaps you noticed that the stem-set in (36) is exactly the same as the stem-set in Chapter 9(9), where we gave a verb base that meant "dig it out". This stem-set has to do with digging.

(Suppose you were to learn that this stem-set was one of a pair of related stem-sets that have to do with digging. Is this stem-set momentaneous or continuative?

Answer: momentaneous. To dig something out, or to uncover something by digging, are both actions that aren't finished until they are finished, and when they are finished, you can't continue to do them (because there's no more to do). There is a continuative stem-set that has to do with digging which can be used to form a verb base (using the atelic outer prefix **na**) that means "go around digging things", which is an action that can be stopped at any time, or that can be continued as long as you want. This continuative stem-set is very similar to, but not exactly like, the stem-set in (36) and in Chapter 9(9) - but the P mode stem is the same: **geed**.)

The verb base in (36) is our first verb base with three lexical prefixes! Note that one of these is the unspec object prefix **'**. (If we want to think about what this prefix might mean, we can say that it refers to whatever we have to dig away in order to uncover the thing that we're really interested in. We can think of this verb base as meaning "dig (something unspecified) so as to uncover it (outer object)".)

When we build the I mode and P mode forms of this verb, we still don't have anything new to learn! First, here is the I mode of this verb:

(37)	sg	dpl	distr dpl
1	bą́ą́'díshgééd	bą́ą́'diilgééd	bą́ą́da'diilgééd
2	bą́ą́'díłgééd	bą́ą́'dółgééd	bą́ą́da'dołgééd
3	yą́ą́'díłgééd		yą́ą́da'díłgééd
4	bą́ą́zh'díłgééd		bą́ą́dazh'díłgééd

Look at the forms in (37) except for the 4 person forms. Note that we have not inserted any vowel after the unspec prefix **'**. Why not? Well, in Chapter 12 we learned as part of Rule Conj-5 that when **'** is preceded by a vowel and when the next syllable is not the verb stem syllable, we don't insert any vowel after **'**. This is exactly what we have here. In all these forms, the **'** is preceded either by the outer prefix **bą́ą́** (or **yą́ą́**), or else by the distributive plural prefix **da**, and these prefixes all end in vowels. Also, because the inner prefix **d** is in there, the syllable which follows the **'** is never the verb stem syllable. This means that if we added in the vowel **a** to create the syllable **'a**, this syllable wouldn't be the pre-stem syllable. Therefore, Rule Conj-5 tells us not to add any vowel after the **'**.

In the 4 person forms, note the switch of the positions of the **j** (which turns into **zh**) and the **'**. We learned about this when we studied the F mode in Chapter 14, but here it's happening in the I mode. Why? Because the conditions for it to happen are present here. Let's diagram the way that the word **bą́ą́zh'díłgééd** "one is uncovering it by digging" is built:

(38) outer   object   inner   cl   verb
     prefix   prefix   prefix   stem

      bą́ą́ -   '   - j - d - ł - gééd

We have two object prefixes in (38), the unspec prefix **'** and the 4 person subject prefix **j**, in the correct order as specified by Rule Str-4. Rule Conj-1 will apply in the regular way to insert an **i** after the inner prefix **d**. But in the case of the conjunct prefixes **'** and **j**, the addition to Rule Conj-5 we learned in Chapter 14 applies. The **'** is preceded by a vowel at the end of a disjunct prefix, the **j** is followed by a consonant, and the next syllable is not the verb stem syllable. So, even though we're not in the F mode, we still have the same effect: the ' followed by the **j** together become **zh'**.

Incidentally, Rule Subj-5 also applies to (38) to put a high tone on the **i** which was inserted after the **d**. Note that this **i** is a short vowel in the pre-stem syllable, and the syllable which precedes it (which is **bą́ą́**) ends in a high tone vowel. What other forms in (37) did Rule Subj-5 apply to? (Answer: **bą́ą́'díshgééd**, **yą́ą́'díílgééd**, and **bą́ą́'dółgééd**.)

Let's move on to the P mode forms. Here they are:

(39)	sg	dpl	distr dpl
1	bą́ą́'díílgeed	bą́ą́'diilgeed	bą́ą́da'diilgeed
2	bą́ą́'díínílgeed	bą́ą́'doołgeed	bą́ą́da'doołgeed
3	yą́ą́'díílgeed		yą́ą́da'díílgeed
4	bą́ą́zh'díílgeed		bą́ą́dazh'díílgeed

(The entry for this verb in YM suggests that some speakers switch to the s-P in the distributive plural forms when the subject is 3 and 4 person.)

There is nothing new here. However, let's take note of the following interesting effect. The conjugation is the y-P, with a barred-l classifier. Now, in this conjugation, the subject prefixes for 1sg and for 3 person subjects are the same. Moreover, this verb is intransitive: there is no object prefix **y** that pops in when the subject is 3 person. In cases like this that we've seen earlier, the 1sg form and the 3 form are exactly the same (for example, look at the 1sg and 3 forms in Chapter 9(15) or Chapter 9(21).) But here, these forms are different. The reason is that there's an outer object: when the subject is 3 person, **y** is used as the outer object instead of **b**. This can only occur with a 3 person subject, so the **y** in **yą́ą́'díílgeed** tells us that the subject is 3 person and not 1sg. In **bą́ą́'díílgeed**, the **b** tells us that the subject is almost certainly 1sg. (Actually, **bą́ą́'díílgeed** could conceivably also be an inverse form. The context in which the word was being used would have to make it clear if an inverse form was intended. For many speakers, it would be impossible for this to be an inverse form, since the subject of this verb is (almost certainly) a person and the outer object is (almost certainly) an inanimate thing.)

When we move to the F mode, something new happens. Here are the forms:

(40)	sg	dpl	distr dpl
1	bą́ą́di'deeshgoł	bą́ą́di'diilgoł	bą́ą́dadi'diilgoł
2	bą́ą́di'díílgoł	bą́ą́di'doołgoł	bą́ą́dadi'doołgoł
3	yą́ą́di'doołgoł		yą́ą́dadi'doołgoł
4	bą́ą́zhdi'doołgoł		bą́ą́dazhdi'doołgoł

The unspec object prefix ' has moved to the right of the F mode **d**!

At the risk of weighing Rule Conj-5 down with exceptions and additions, we'll add yet another provision to this rule to take care of this effect:

(add to Rule Conj-5): If the unspec object prefix ' is preceded by a vowel, if it is directly in front of a consonant C_1, and if to the right of C_1 there is a consonant C_2 which is part of a conjunct prefix and which starts a syllable which is not the verb-stem syllable, then ' hops over to the right and is placed just in front of C_2. (We can call this process "unspec-hopping".)

In reality, the requirement that the unspec prefix has to be preceded by a vowel just really means that the unspec prefix isn't the first thing in the verb. (Do you see why? If the unspec prefix is preceded by a disjunct prefix, that disjunct prefix will end in a vowel. If the unspec prefix is preceded by a conjunct prefix, some rule will end up adding in a vowel to separate that conjunct prefix from the unspec prefix.)

If the unspec prefix is the first piece of a verb, Rule Conj-5 will insert that **a** vowel after it and the prefix won't hop. Otherwise, it will hop if there's a place for it to hop to. That place is the consonant C_2 described in our addition to Rule Conj-5.

To see how this works, let's build the word **yáádadi'doołgoł** "they'll uncover it by digging". The structure of this word is:

(41) outer distributive object F mode inner   subject   cl   verb
    prefix plural prefix d prefix prefix stem

    yáá - da - ' - d - d - oo - ł - goł

Question: Why is **yáá** used instead of **báá** in (41)? (Answer: the subject is 3 person, so a 3 person object is represented by **y** rather than by **b** in a direct form.)

Question: Why is the subject prefix **oo**? (Answer: This is the 3 person subject prefix for the F mode, apart from the F mode **d**.)

Now, Rule Conj-1 applies in the usual way to insert an **l** between the two **d**'s. But since we have an unspec object prefix in this structure, we will want to ask about Rule Conj-5: what does it do? Well, nothing will be inserted after the '. Why? Because ' is preceded by a vowel (the **a** at the end of **da**) and the next syllable is **di**, which is not the verb stem syllable. At this point, ' is right in front of the F mode **d**.

But now, our new addition to Rule Conj-5 (the unspec-hopping part of the rule) comes into play. To the right of the F mode **d**, there is another **d** (the inner prefix - so it's a conjunct prefix), and this

179

second **d** starts the syllable **doo**, which is not the verb-stem syllable. Our new addition says: the **'** hops to the right and appears just in front of the inner prefix **d**. (So: the F mode **d** plays the role of C_1 in our new addition, and the inner prefix **d** plays the role of C_2.)

At this point, we can still ask what Rule Conj-5 tells us about the form of the unspec prefix. Since the **'** is preceded by a vowel (the vowel **i** inserted after F mode **d** by Rule Conj-1), since it is followed by a consonant (the inner **d**), and since the next syllable isn't the verb-stem syllable (it's the syllable **doo**), Rule Conj-5 tells us not to insert any vowel after **'**. Since none of our other rules apply, the resulting word is exactly **yą́ądadi'doołgoł**. (If you think about the conditions in the unspec-hopping part of Rule Conj-5, you'll see that it always turns out this way: after **'** gets hopped, no vowel is inserted after it.)

(As you see, Navajo verbs can sometimes get kind of long. But this doesn't mean that they get harder - they don't!)

Before continuing, there are a few things we need to say about the process of unspec-hopping.

First of all, we've been studying Navajo verbs based on the idea that each piece of the verb has a position that it has to be placed in in order for the verb to be correct. Mostly, Navajo verbs are really structured this way. But our principle of unspec-hopping shows us that something else can occasionally happen: the unspec prefix is normally placed in the object prefix position, but now we see that in certain cases it moves to the right so that it ends up in a different position. This kind of movement process is not common, but we'll see as we go along that it occurs with a few other prefixes as well, especially when the verb gets to have a lot of prefixes in it. Of course, each time we run into a new case of a movement like this, we'll write up a rule that explains when the movement happens and where the prefix in question is moved to.

But rules like this, which move prefixes to different positions, bring up another issue. Up till now, all our rules have been about the <u>form</u> of prefixes - that is, they've told us how a particular prefix is spelled and pronounced in a particular circumstance. But now we see that we'll occasionally have rules that move prefixes around. This brings up the following scary possibility: suppose some rules tell us that the form of a prefix would be different depending on where in the verb structure it's placed. If a rule moves this prefix around, what form does it take, the form it would take in the original position or the form it would take in the position that it's moved to? In general, the answer is: it takes the form it would take in the position that it's moved to. What this means for us is simply this: if we have a rule that moves a prefix, we should try to apply that rule before we apply any rules that tell us anything about the form of the prefix. For example, whenever we see a verb structure that has the unspec prefix in it, we should check the unspec-hopping part of Rule Conj-5 (and apply it if it applies) before we check any of the other parts of Rule Conj-5. This isn't exactly what we did earlier when we analyzed the structure in (41): we said something about Rule Conj-5 not inserting a vowel before we looked at the unspec-hopping part of the rule. But this was a mistake: the unspec prefix wasn't in its correct position yet!

So, to summarize: we are going to have a small number of rules that move prefixes. For any movement rule like this, we will try to apply the movement rule before we try to apply any rules that tell us about the forms of prefixes. So far, we've learned exactly one movement rule: the unspec-hopping part of Rule Conj-5. Each time we learn a new movement rule (there are not many of them), we'll mention it, so that we'll remember that we need to try to apply it before we figure out what the forms of the prefixes are. We'll also put notes in the statement of the rules in the Appendix indicating which are the movement rules.

(In the last chapter we learned about a special case where ' and **j** change positions. That was a movement process also. But it was less drastic than unspec hopping, since the two prefixes still end up in the object prefix position, and since the forms of these prefixes always end up the same, namely **zh'**. We didn't pay much attention to whether the forms of the prefixes were determined after the movement or not, since the whole business was described in one rule, but you can see that even in that case we want to say that the movement happens first and then the forms are determined.)

The unspec-hopping part of Rule Conj-5 is all that we need in order to take care of effects that can happen when a verb has the inner prefix **d**. All regular forms (in all the modes) that involve the inner prefix **d** will now be built correctly by the rules that we've learned.

What about other inner prefixes? We'll be learning about them in later chapters. Most of what we've learned in this chapter will carry over without change, but each new inner prefix will involve a small number of special adjustments that we'll have to deal with. We'll do this one prefix at a time. It will not be difficult.

Incidentally, by now we've met quite a few **d**'s that can appear in Navajo verbs. There's the **d** of the distributive plural prefix **da**; there's the F mode **d**; there's the inner prefix **d**; and we even saw an outer prefix that has a **d** in it (see the verb base in (24) above.) If you see a Navajo verb and there's a **d** (or several of them) in front of the verb stem, will you be able to tell what these **d**'s are? We talked a little about recognizing the distributive plural prefix **da** back in Chapter 5 - this prefix always appears either with an actual **a** in it, or else it will appear as **de**, but only if it's followed by an **i** or by **ii**. Outer prefixes with **d**'s are not that common - after a while, you'll probably learn all the ones that you're likely to run into. But F mode **d** and inner prefix **d** are both quite common, and sometimes it's not easy to tell them apart. The special vowels that we see in the F mode subject prefixes can sometimes help tip us off that we have an F mode form, but some of these vowels show up elsewhere as well, such as the P mode. Suppose, for example, that you saw the word **sodoolzin**, and suppose that you didn't know this verb at all. The fact that there's a plain **l** in front of the **z** would make it possible that this is a y-P 3 person subject form, which would make the **d** an inner prefix. But then again, maybe this is just an F mode form, and the **d** is the F mode **d**, with the **oo** the usual F mode 3 person subject prefix? Without knowing more about this verb, you'd have no way of telling! This means that if you wanted to look this verb up in YM 87, for example, you'd have to try both guesses. To use YM 87, you need to know the 1sg I mode form of the verb. If you guess that **sodoolzin** is a P mode form with **d** an inner prefix, you might try to build an I mode form like **sodiszin**, which would be completely correct, of course, and which you'd find listed in the dictionary. But if you thought that **sodoolzin** was an F mode form, you might build something weird like "soszin" as the 1sg I mode form, which, of course, is wrong, and you'd never find it in the dictionary. Perhaps a better idea would be to try to find the verb using its stem, which is easy to do in YMM 92. But this has its own pitfalls - you'd first check **zin** in Appendix II of YMM 92, and then if you persuaded yourself that you really did need to look under the stem listed as **yįįd** (!), you'd find the verb quickly enough. The best approach, of course, is to already know what the verb means. If you know at least that **sodoolzin** means "he/she/they (two) prayed", you'll know that you don't have an F mode form (the meaning doesn't involve the future!), so the **d** is probably an inner prefix. It can't be the **d** of **da**, since it's followed by the vowel **o**. In fact, since the meaning of this word suggests an event in the past, you could guess that this is a P mode form. Then, seeing the **oo** followed by the plain **l**, you'll realize that the **oo** is probably preceded by a conjunct prefix. (Why? Look at the charts of subject prefixes in Chapter 10.) This strongly suggests that the **d** is the inner prefix **d** (there are no other conjunct prefixes with **d**'s in them.) With this information, you can try constructing other forms of the verb, and ultimately find it in a dictionary, for example, in YM 87, by looking up **sodiszin**.

CHAPTER 16

SOME IRREGULAR VERBS

In the last chapter we took a look at some fairly complicated verbs - at least, they were complicated in the sense that there were lots of things involved in conjugating them: up to three lexical prefixes, ordinary objects and outer objects, adjustments involving classifiers and subject prefixes, unspec-hopping, and so on. What we saw was that by using the rules we've developed, everything came out exactly right. This might lead us to think that every form of every verb in the Navajo language can be built using these rules.

Well, this is almost true! However, there are some verbs that are really irregular. Fortunately, there aren't many of these, but just as in other languages, some of the irregular verbs are also some of the most common ones. In this chapter, we'll study a number of particular irregular verbs, partly because these verbs are important in their own right, but mainly because we want to have a look at some of the kinds of irregularities that can be found in Navajo verbs.

Let's start with a verb base that means "want" or "think". This verb is used only in one mode, the I mode. You may remember that verbs that have only one mode are called neuter verbs, so the verb base given in (1) can be thought of as a neuter verb base:

(1)

Stem-set I: **zin**	Classifier: zero
	Lexical prefix: **n** (inner)
	Transitivity: either

(Since this verb is conjugated only in the I mode, there is no entry in (1) that talks about which conjugation is used in the P mode!)

Now, there are two things that are unfair about this verb base. First of all, this is a neuter verb that is conjugated in the I mode only. It happens that the Navajo verb system has some special conjugations that apply to neuter verbs that are conjugated only in the I mode - but we haven't studied them yet! Since we won't study them until Chapter 21, how will we know that the verb in (1) is irregular?

The other unfair thing about (1) is that it has an inner prefix which we haven't yet studied, namely **n**. Again, we won't be able to see the irregularity if we don't know how this inner prefix works in regular verbs.

However, this verb is so common and so important that we want to look at it here. And it is actually irregular - we'll point out the irregularities as soon as we look at the actual forms.

But first: we listed the transitivity as "either". What's going on?

Well, this verb has a number of different usages. In some usages, it's transitive, and in other usages it's intransitive. For example, when it means "want" and we want to express or suggest an object which is the thing that the subject wants, the verb is transitive. But when it means "think" and we indicate what the subject is thinking, it's intransitive.

Something you might want to do at this time: use our rules exactly as we have learned them and try to build I mode forms for this verb. Treat the inner prefix **n** exactly as though it were the inner prefix **d** which we studied in the last chapter. And don't forget that we have a voiced fricative verb with a zero classifier.

If you do this, you'll get something close to, but not exactly like the real forms, which are:

(2)	sg	dpl	distr dpl
1	nissin	niidzin	daniidzin
2	nínízin	nohsin	danohsin
3		nízin/yinízin	danízin/deinízin
4		jinízin	dazhnízin

Can you see the irregularity? The **ni** syllable which comes from the inner prefix **n** has a high tone when the subject prefix is 2sg or 3 - but it has a low tone if the subject prefix is 1sg, 1dpl, or 2dpl! Also: Rule Conj-3 didn't apply - there is a separate **ni** syllable for the 2sg subject prefix. When we learn about the special neuter I mode conjugations, we'll see that there are indeed some special patterns involving **n**'s and tones. However, the forms in (2) are really irregular - they don't correspond to any of the regular neuter patterns. You should simply memorize the forms in (2).

By the way: why did we list two forms for the nondistributive 3 person subject and two forms for the distributive 3 person subject? (Answer: The intransitive and transitive forms are different. If the verb is being used as a transitive verb, when the subject is 3 person, the 3 person object has to be represented by **y** (Rule Str-1), so we have the words **yinízin** "he/she/they (two) want it" and **deinízin** "they want it". When the words are being used intransitively, this **y** isn't there (there is no object prefix), so we get **nízin** "he/she/they (two) think" and **danízin** "they think".)

Would it surprise you that some people say **daznízin** instead of **dazhnízin**? (It shouldn't - see Rule Conj-4.) Would it surprise you that some people write **nisin** instead of **nissin**? (It shouldn't - see the note on double consonants in the discussion after Chapter 8(16).)

One final thing to keep in mind about this verb: there are other Navajo verbs that are built using the verb base (1) as a starting point. (More lexical prefixes are added.) These other verbs are conjugated the same way - they have the same irregularities as the ones shown in (2).

The next irregular verb we'll look at is the verb that means "eat it". Let's start by giving the verb base with this meaning, and then we'll talk about the irregularities.

(3)

Stem-set		Classifier: zero
I:	yá	
P:	yą́ą́'	Lexical prefixes: (none)
F:	yį́į́ł	Transitivity: transitive
R:	yį́į́h	
O:	yą́ą́'	Perfective: y-P

Notice the stems: they begin with a **y**. This means that we are dealing with a voiced fricative verb, and this is where one of the irregularities comes in. According to what we learned in Chapter 13, the **y** at the beginning of the verb stems of this verb should turn into **h** when it is immediately preceded by **sh** or **h** - but that's not what happens! Instead, when preceded by **sh**, the **y** turns into **sh**, and when preceded by **h**, the **y** turns into **s**. (When the **y** turns into **sh** because there's an **sh** right in front of it, the double **shsh** is just about always written as a single **sh**.)

And this is not all - there's a second irregularity: whenever d-effect applies to the **y** at the beginning of any of the stems in (3), the **y** turns into **d**. For the part of the verb system we've learned so far, this irregularity comes into play exactly when the subject prefix is 1dpl.

(We already saw another verb that has an irregular d-effect - do you remember it? Look at the verb base in Chapter 13(5) and the discussion there about it.)

As long as you keep these irregularities in mind, you'll be able to construct the verbs that are made using the verb base in (3). In the I mode, you should get:

(4)	sg		dpl	distr dpl
1	yishą́		yiidą́	deiidą́
2	niyą́		wohsą́	daohsą́
3		yiyą́		deiyą́
4		jiyą́		dajiyą́

In (4), we spelled **yishą́** "I'm eating it" with a single **sh**, since that's the way you'll probably see it in print.

In the P mode, we get:

(5)	sg	dpl	distr dpl
1	yíyą́ą́'	yiidą́ą́'	deiidą́ą́'
2	yíníyą́ą́'	wooyą́ą́'	daooyą́ą́'
3		yiyííyą́ą́'	deiyííyą́ą́'
4		jííyą́ą́'	dajííyą́ą́'

(Why didn't the **y** at the beginning of the stem turn into an **s** in the 2dpl forms in (5)? Answer: the subject prefix does not end in **h** in the P mode when the classifier is zero (or barred-l). For a similar reason, the 1sg form in (5) doesn't have any **sh** at all in it - the **y** at the beginning of the verb stem stays **y**.)

In the F mode, we have:

(6)	sg	dpl	distr dpl
1	deeshį́į́ł	diidį́į́ł	dadiidį́į́ł
2	dííyį́į́ł	doohsį́į́ł	dadoohsį́į́ł
3		yidooyį́į́ł	deidooyį́į́ł
4		jidooyį́į́ł	dazhdooyį́į́ł

Note: Some people say (and write) **doohshį́į́ł** and **dadoohshį́į́ł** in the F mode instead of **doohsį́į́ł** and **dadoohsį́į́ł**.

By the way, this is one of those transitive verbs which can be commonly used with the unspec object prefix **'**. The very same irregularities described above and illustrated in (4), (5), and (6) will be present if the unspec object prefix is used. Let's write out the P mode for "eat" when the object is unspecified. (These verbs mean things like "I ate", "you ate", etc.)

(7)	sg	dpl	distr dpl
1	ííyą́ą́'	iidą́ą́'	da'iidą́ą́'
2	ííníyą́ą́'	ooyą́ą́'	da'ooyą́ą́'
3		ííyą́ą́'	da'ííyą́ą́'
4		ajííyą́ą́'	da'jííyą́ą́'

(For practice, why not write out the I mode and F mode forms for "eat" with the unspec object prefix?)

Our third irregular verb is the verb that means "see it". Here we have to be careful about meaning, because Navajo is more precise than English. In English, **see** can mean many things. The verb base we'll give in (8) means only "perceive it by vision". It doesn't even mean "catch sight of it", which in Navajo is expressed by a different (and regular) verb. It also doesn't mean "go to visit", which is something that the English verb **see** can sometimes mean.

The Navajo verb base that means "see it" in the sense of "perceive it visually" is used only in the I mode. Here is the verb base:

(8)

Stem-set: I: **'į́**	Classifier: zero
	Lexical prefixes: (none)
	Transitivity: transitive

Again, since this verb is not conjugated in the P mode, we didn't put an entry into (8) concerning the conjugation used in the P mode.

(In modes other than I, the verb base that means "catch sight of it" corresponds to the English verb **see**.)

The irregularity in this verb has to do with the subject prefixes that it uses. Here is the story: even though the mode we're conjugating this verb in is the I mode, and even though the classifier is zero, the subject prefixes used are the ones normally used in the y-P conjugation (of the P mode!) when the classifier is plain-l or d, except that the 2dpl subject prefix for this verb has a short **o** (that is, the prefix is **oh**) rather than a long **oo** (as in the actual y-P prefix **ooh**).

So, what are the forms of this verb? Here they are, if the object is 3 person:

(9)	sg	dpl	distr dpl
1	yish'į́	yiit'į́	deiit'į́
2	yíníʼį́	woh'į́	daoh'į́
3		yoo'į́	dayoo'į́
4		joo'į́	dajoo'į́

Note how the vowel **oo** pops out as the 3 person subject prefix when there is a conjunct prefix (the 3 person object prefix **y** in **yoo'į́** "he/she/they (two) see it" and the 4 person subject prefix **j** in **joo'į́** "one sees it".) This shows that we really do have the same subject prefixes that we learned about in Chapter 10!

How do you think we say "I see you" in Navajo? (Remember, the **you** of "I see you" is an object, so it'll show up in the verb as the object prefix **n** - see Chapter 11(1). This object prefix is a conjunct prefix - so what will the subject prefix look like?)

Answer: Yup - it's actually **neesh'į̱**! Other combinations with other object prefixes are formed similarly, using the forms of the subject prefixes that we usually see in the y-P conjugation when the classifier is plain-l or d, except that the 2dpl subject prefixes have a short **o**. (You can find these prefixes in the chart in Chapter 10(4), by the way.)

We can see more of these prefixes if we put the unspec object prefix into this verb. (If we do this, the meaning of the verbs that we get can be something like "be able to see", just as in English.) Since the unspec object prefix is a conjunct prefix, the subject prefixes in Chapter 10(4) (with a short **o** in the 2dpl prefix) are used. Here are the forms that mean "I see", "you see", etc.:

(10)	sg	dpl	distr dpl
1	eesh'į̱	iit'į̱	da'iit'į̱
2	íínî'į̱	oh'į̱	da'oh'į̱
3		oo'į̱	da'oo'į̱
4		ajoo'į̱	da'joo'į̱

(Review the forms in Chapter 12(11) if you need to reacquaint yourself with words that look like this.)

Our fourth irregular verb is the verb that means "say". This verb is also used only in the I mode; if you want to express the concept of "say" in another mode, another, regular verb is substituted for it.

If we want to give the verb base for this verb, we could, I suppose, do something like this:

(11)

Stem-set: I: **ní**	Classifier: zero
	Lexical prefixes: **d** (inner), if subject is not 3 person; none, if subject is 3 person
	Transitivity: intransitive

But the forms are so irregular that we cannot easily say in (11) what's going on with the lexical prefixes. Here are the actual I mode forms, which you should simply memorize:

(12)	sg		dpl	distr dpl
1	dishní		dii'ní	dadii'ní
2	diní		dohní	dadohní
3		ní		daaní
4		jiní		dajiní

So what are the irregularities?

First of all, some forms have an inner **d** prefix, and some do not.

Secondly, the word **diní** "you (sg) say" does not have a high tone on the **i** of **di** - that is, Rule Conj-3 didn't apply.

And thirdly: the word **ní** "he/she/they (two) say" has no pre-stem syllable! (The peg rule did not apply.)

It turns out that there is a fourth irregularity involving this verb. This fourth irregularity doesn't show up in the ordinary I mode forms given in (12), but it shows up in a set of transitive verb forms that are related to the words in (12). To understand these words, let's first remind ourselves about the verb base which means "work on it" that we studied in Chapter 15 (see Chapter 15(29) and Chapter 15(30).) This verb base looks the same as the ordinary "work" verb base (given in Chapter 8(11)) except that an object was added in. This object appeared in the form of an outer object, that is, an object prefix which is placed inside an outer prefix, in the outer prefix position. We can say that the intransitive verb "work" could be made to take an object by putting that object in as an outer object. But there was something about the form of that object that we had to learn: when the object is 3 person and the subject is 1, 2, or 4 person, we used **b** as the object rather than zero. We represented this special fact by using the symbol "P" for the object pronoun part of the outer prefix.

Now, some intransitive Navajo verbs can have objects added to them in a different way: the object is put in the usual object prefix position, rather than in the outer prefix position. We've already seen something a little like this: the verb base that means "want" or "think", that we studied earlier in this chapter, could be either intransitive or transitive. However, for some verbs, including the verb "say", the situation is different: we have a basically intransitive verb, and we want to attach an object to it.

So what's the problem? Mostly, there isn't any, except that if we just go ahead and put ordinary object prefixes into the ordinary object prefix position, we run into a problem when the subject is 1, 2, or 4 person, and when the object is 3 person: the usual object prefix in this case is zero, so how will we know that it's there? That is, how will we know that we don't have the intransitive verb rather than the transitive verb with a 3 person object?

The way this is handled is that in cases like this, the 3 person object is represented not by zero, but by **b**. In other words, we do the same thing that we'd do if the object were an outer object.

Let's illustrate this by giving a verb base related to (11) that has an object like this. The following verb base means "say to him/her":

(13)

Stem-set	Classifier: zero
I: **ní**	Lexical prefixes: P (object), **d** (inner) or no inner prefix (as in (11))
	Transitivity: transitive

This should be compared to Chapter 15(30), which is still intransitive (no prefixes are put into the ordinary object prefix position). With the verb base in (13), we do actually put prefixes into the ordinary object prefix position. But we've listed "P" as a lexical prefix (in the ordinary object position) to indicate that, instead of zero, we use **b** to represent a 3 person object when the subject is 1, 2, or 4 person.

Now, why are we talking about this verb base? Because there is a new irregularity that shows up with the verb base in (13). (Note: the use of **b** instead of zero to represent a 3 person object is not an irregularity. It's simply something that happens with certain verb bases that are transitive versions of other verb bases.)

To see the irregularity, let's write out the I mode of (13). We'll write the forms showing a 3 person object.

(14)	sg	dpl	distr dpl
1	bidishní	bidii'ní	dabidii'ní
2	bidiní	bidohní	dabidohní
3		yiłní	deiłní
4		bijiní	dabijiní

Do you see the irregularity? It has to do with the 3 person subject form, the form that shows up as **ní** in (12). When the object is added in, a barred-l classifier is put in, too! This happens only when the subject is 3 person (it does not happen when the subject is 4 person, even though the 3 person subject prefix is used in this case); and it happens with any object prefix (for example, "he/she says to me" is **shiłní**.) This is the fourth irregularity with the "say" verb that we mentioned above.

(By the way: How do we know that the **b**'s and the **y**'s in (14) are in the regular object prefix position, rather than being outer objects? Answer: Look at the distributive plural forms. The distributive plural prefix **da** precedes the object prefixes in the right-hand column of (14). If the objects were outer objects, they would come in front of **da** rather than after **da**.)

We said above that a regular verb base is used for "say" if we need to use another mode. In case you're curious, here is that other, regular verb base for "say":

(15)

Stem-set	Classifier: zero
I: **niih** P: **niid**	Lexical prefixes: **d** (inner)
F: **niił** R: **niih**	Transitivity: intransitive
O: **ne'**	Perfective: y-P

This verb is completely regular. The inner prefix **d** in (15) is treated exactly as we learned in Chapter 15. This verb even has an I mode. However, in the I mode, the irregular verb in (11)-(12) is more commonly used.

There is a transitive version of (15), too, which means "say to him/her":

(16)

Stem-set	Classifier: zero
I: **niih** P: **niid**	Lexical prefixes: P (object), **d** (inner)
F: **niił** R: **niih**	Transitivity: transitive
O: **ne'**	Perfective: y-P

This is all we need to say about the "say" verbs.

Our fifth and last irregular verb is a little different. What we want to illustrate here is something that we'll run into from time to time: an irregularity having to do with the vowels that go with a particular inner prefix.

So far, we've learned one inner prefix, the prefix **d**, which we studied in Chapter 15. In that chapter, we learned everything we need to know about this prefix when the verb is regular. However, every so often, we'll run into a verb with this inner prefix where some forms are irregular. We'll simply have to memorize these irregular forms for those verbs when we encounter them.

Here is an illustration of one such verb. The following verb base means "fill something up with it":

(17)

Stem-set		Classifier: barred-l
I:	**bin**	
P:	**bįįd**	Lexical prefixes: **ha** (outer), **d** (inner)
F:	**bį́į́ł**	Transitivity: transitive
R:	**bį́į́h**	
O:	**bin**	Perfective: y-P

(The (ordinary) object of this verb refers to the material that is being placed inside the container that is getting filled. The container that is getting filled is not actually referred to anywhere in this verb! It can be referred to, if necessary, by putting an extra postposition (the postposition **bii'** or **yii'**) in front of the verb.)

This verb is regular in all modes except for the P mode. In the P mode, rather than using the usual y-P zero/barred-l subject prefixes that we'd use when there's a conjunct prefix (see Chapter 9(5)), we get a few forms with the vowel **ee**:

(18)	sg	dpl	distr dpl
1	hadéélbįįd	hadeelbįįd	hadadeelbįįd
2	hadíínłbįįd	hadoołbįįd	hadadoołbįįd
3		haidéélbįįd	hadeidéélbįįd
4		hazhdéélbįįd	hadazhdéélbįįd

If we look at the combination of the inner prefix **d** with the subject prefixes, we see that the words in (18) have the following prefixes:

(19)

	sg	dpl
1	>déé	>deed
2	dííní	doo
3	>déé	

In (19), the irregular forms are marked with the symbol ">". If you compare (19) with what we saw in, for example, Chapter 15(4), you'll see that the regular forms for the inner prefix **d** combined with the y-P subject prefixes in the zero/barred-l classifier case are just:

(20)

	sg	dpl
1	**díí**	**diid**
2	**dííní**	**doo**
3	**díí**	

These are simply the subject prefixes listed in Chapter 9(5) with a **d** in front of each. So where do the irregular forms in (19) with the **éé** or **ee** vowels come from?

Well, they're just irregular. We'll have to remember that when we conjugate "fill something up with it" in the P mode, we get the forms in (18), with the irregular **d**-plus-subject-prefix combinations of (19), instead of the usual forms. As you learn more Navajo verbs, you'll occasionally run into other verbs with an inner **d** prefix that have the forms in (19) in the y-P conjugation. You'll also run into irregular forms like this with other inner prefixes. There are also verbs that have irregularities that are similar to those in (19) but not exactly the same; for example, some verbs have **ee** vowels when the subject is 1sg and 3 person, but the normal **ii** vowel when the subject is 1dpl. There are also a few verbs that have irregularities like this in the I mode.

(In the next few chapters, we're going to see several instances where we have to add information about conjugation patterns into verb bases. We might want to do that here, too: we could add into (17) a statement that in the P mode, the combination of the inner prefix **d** with the subject prefixes come out looking like (19).)

This is all that we will study in this chapter. We've seen some important irregular verbs, but, unfortunately, these are not the only ones - later on, we'll learn several others. One very important irregular verb is the verb that means "make it". This verb has some features that resemble prefixes and conjugation patterns that we haven't yet studied, so we won't go through the forms here. However, this verb is so important that you might want to look its forms up in YM and memorize them, if you haven't already done so.

Another very important Navajo irregular verb is the verb that means "go". We are going to devote an entire chapter to this verb, namely the next chapter.

CHAPTER 17

INTRODUCTION TO MOTION VERBS,
"GO",
AND VERB THEMES

In our studies so far, we've run into several cases where we had different verb bases with related meanings. For example, in Chapter 8(11) we have the verb base that means "work", in Chapter 15(18) we have the verb base that means "start to work", and in Chapter 15(30) we have the verb base that means "work on it". To understand fully the very expressive Navajo verb system, we need to study in a deeper way how verb bases can be related to each other. For example, are there rules that say if you have a verb base with a certain kind of meaning, you can create a different verb base whose meaning is related to the first one in some particular way? It will turn out that sometimes there are rules like that, but sometimes different verb bases simply have to be memorized. So far, all we've done is noted some particular examples as we've come upon them. What we need to do is make a systematic vocabulary study of verbs, and see what kinds of patterns there are. But there is a problem with this: the Navajo verb system is so rich that we won't be able to learn anywhere near all the vocabulary patterns there are. What we'll do instead is learn a few important ones that will form a basis for the learning that will continue after you are finished with this book. With the examples of vocabulary structure that we'll look at here, you should be able to expand your understanding of the Navajo verb vocabulary on your own.

To represent vocabulary patterns when we find them, we're going to introduce a new kind of statement which we'll call a *vocabulary principle*. In this chapter, we'll look at one group of verbs and we'll learn two vocabulary principles for that group.

In order to make vocabulary studies of verbs, it will be necessary to classify verbs into different kinds according to their meaning. The reason we need to do this is that the variations in meaning that we want to express depend on the kind of action that we're talking about. For example, if we have an action that has to do with something or somebody moving from one place to another, we might want to know how we could add in something to the verb that tells us that this motion involves starting in an enclosure and then going outside. But if we have an action like "work", it wouldn't make sense to try to add such a meaning. In this chapter, we're going to look only at verbs whose meaning involves something or somebody moving from one place to another. These verbs are called *verbs of motion*, or *motion verbs*.

Be careful! The term "motion verb" might lead you to think that any verb that expresses an action that has some motion in it is a motion verb. This is not the way we're using the term "motion verb"! For example, if you're working, you're probably doing a lot of moving around. Is **work** a motion verb? No! Why? Because the word **work** isn't specifically talking about somebody moving from one place to another. The person who is working might be moving around a lot, but that doesn't make it working. What makes it working is the effort involved and the purpose of the action, not the particular changes of place being made by the person who is working. In fact, it is sometimes possible to work while doing very little motion, or maybe no motion at all.

So, what are some examples of motion verbs?

Let's start with some English examples. In English, it is convenient to separate motion verbs into intransitive and transitive motion verbs. Intransitive motion verbs involve the subject of the verb going from one place to another. Here are some English sentences with intransitive verbs of motion in them.

(1)   John went to the store.
        Sally came back.
        The chairman entered the chapter house.
        Sam ran out of the hogan.
        Officer Chee flew to Washington.
        Bill rafted down the Colorado River.

If you look at the sentences in (1), you'll see that there is a lot of information in them about the motion that the subjects of the sentences make. Some of this information is in the verb itself. For example, the verb **entered** tells us that the motion involves going from outside something to inside something. The verb **ran** tells us something about the speed with which the subject used his legs in order to move. The verb **flew** tells us that the subject moved through the air, but we also guess that the subject probably used a special device (such as an airplane) to make his motion. The verb **rafted** specifically tells us that a raft was used.

Apart from the information provided by the verb, there is also information provided by other words in the sentences. For example, the phrase **to the store** tells us that the place that John moved to was the store. The word **back** tells us that Sally had been around earlier, had left, and then made a motion that had her ending up in the place where she started. The phrase **out of the hogan** tells us that Sam started out inside the hogan and ended up outside of it. The phrase **down the Colorado River** tells us something about where the rafting trip was.

Let's look at a few examples of English sentences with transitive verbs of motion. When the motion verb is transitive, it's the object of the verb that's going from one place to another.

(2)   John put the ball in the box.
        Officer Leaphorn drove Officer Chee to the airport.
        Bill threw the rock across the canyon.
        Sam dropped the hammer.

Again, certain kinds of information are provided by the verb. Since these verbs are transitive, they can give information about what the subject did in order to get the object to move. For example, **drove** tells us that Officer Leaphorn moved Officer Chee by arranging for him (Officer Chee) to be in a car that the he (Officer Leaphorn) was the driver of. The verb **threw** indicates that Bill got the rock to move by holding it, moving his hand quickly, and letting go while his hand was moving, whereas **dropped** simply means that Sam let go of the hammer so that it fell. And, as in the case of the sentences in (1), additional information is provided by other words in the sentences in (2).

In Navajo, the situation is partially similar to English and partially different. One way that Navajo is similar to English is that there are different verb stems that indicate different ways of getting oneself to move, like walking, running, flying, and so forth (these verb stems form intransitive verbs.) And there are also different verb stems for getting other things to move, like putting, throwing, or dropping (these verb stems form transitive verbs.) But Navajo is different from English in that some of the information that is indicated in the sentences in (1) and (2) by words outside the verb is indicated in Navajo by various combinations of lexical prefixes that are part of the verb. Also, Navajo uses different verb stems for certain kinds of information that English doesn't use different verbs for - we'll see examples of this later on. Finally, the kinds of information that can be expressed easily in Navajo do not match up exactly with the kinds of information that can be expressed easily in English - again, we'll see examples of this in a little bit. What we need to study is: What are the kinds of information that can be expressed by Navajo motion verbs, and how are these kinds of information expressed?

Before starting our study, a word of warning: motion verbs are more complicated than other kinds of verbs. It will take us several chapters to study them properly. In this chapter, we'll make a good start, but there'll be a lot more to come later on.

(You may be wondering why we'd do our first serious vocabulary study with a class of verbs that is so complicated. The reason is that motion verbs are not only very important, but also very common. The verbs we'll be learning about are a daily part of ordinary Navajo speech.)

In the rest of this chapter, we're going to learn "one" new intransitive motion verb. (Why those quotes around the "one"? Because there'll actually be quite a few verb bases for that "one" verb.) But we'll also see that some of the verb bases that we've studied earlier are also motion verbs, and those verb bases will end up being examples of things we're learning about, too. Our "one" new intransitive motion verb will be the Navajo verb that means "go".

Well, we're already going to have to deal with some special problems!

First of all, instead of giving, say, a verb base that means "go" (in some sense of going - we'll have to see what kinds of goings there are!), we'll need to give three verb bases. Why? Because in Navajo, there are three separate, totally different stem-sets that are used to mean "go" depending on the number of people who are going! There is a stem-set that means "one person is going", there is a stem-set that means "two people are going", and there is a stem-set that means "more than two people are going". When talking about verb bases that mean "go", we'll refer to these three types of verb bases as singular, dual, and plural verb bases (or singular, dual, and plural go-verbs.)

(But don't worry! This split into three kinds of going is not something that we'll have to deal with in general. Most motion verbs in Navajo don't come in singular, dual, and plural versions like this - most motion verbs just have one version. If you already know Navajo, you might have noticed that the Navajo verbs that mean "run" also come in separate singular, dual, and plural forms, but almost all other motion verbs use the same verb bases no matter how many people or things are moving.)

Next, it turns out that the singular go-verbs are irregular! (The dual and plural go-verbs are all regular (what a relief!))

Since we have complications like this, let's start out by choosing an arrangement of lexical prefixes that is familiar to us from earlier chapters. In the following three verb bases, we'll use the atelic outer prefix **na** that we've seen many times already. And what about the stem-sets? If you remember our discussion in Chapter 15 about momentaneous and continuative stem-sets, you'll know that we need to use continuative stem-sets in the verb bases we're about to give.

What do these verb bases mean? Based on the kinds of meanings that we've seen with other verb bases that have atelic **na** in them, we'd expect these verb bases to mean something like "go around (randomly)". Well, these verb bases can mean this, but they also have some other meanings which we'll discuss in a moment. But first, let's look at the actual forms.

Here is the singular go-verb with the atelic **na** prefix:

(3)

Stem-set	Classifier: zero
I: **-á** P: **yá**	Lexical prefixes: **na** (outer)
F: **-aał** R: **-aah**	Transitivity: intransitive
O: **-a'**	Perfective: s-P

In the stem-set given in (3), all the stems except for the P mode stem are shown starting with a hyphen. The reason this is done is to call attention to the fact that there are major irregularities with these stems. (We'll learn what these irregularities are in just a moment.) In the P mode, the behavior of the stem is almost regular, so we listed it in (3) in a normal way.

Here is the dual verb base that corresponds to (3):

(4)

Stem-set		Classifier: zero
I:	'aash	
P:	'áázh	Lexical prefixes: **na** (outer)
F:	'ash	
R:	'ash	Transitivity: intransitive
O:	'aash	Perfective: s-P

And here is the plural verb base that corresponds to (3):

(5)

Stem-set		Classifier: d
I:	kai	
P:	kai	Lexical prefixes: **na** (outer)
F:	kah	
R:	kah	Transitivity: transitive
O:	kai	Perfective: s-P

Note that the verb base in (5) has the d classifier. This means that when you conjugate this verb in the P mode, make sure you use the subject prefixes that go with the d classifier (see Chapter 8(10).)

Before we discuss the actual forms that we can get, let's think about subject prefixes. What subject prefixes could we use with the verb base in (3)? Since the meaning of this verb base is that one person is going, we'd expect that we could never use the dpl subject prefixes with this verb. This turns out to be (practically) true - only the 1sg, 2sg, and 3 subject prefixes can be used with the verb in (3) (of course, we can also add the 4 person subject prefix (in object prefix position) if we want to.) We also expect that we won't find the distributive plural prefix **da** used with (3).

Now, what about the verb base in (4)? Obviously, we'd have no difficulty using the 1dpl, 2dpl, or 3 prefixes (the 3 prefix can be used to mean a group of two, remember?) But we'd expect that the 1sg or 2sg prefixes would be impossible with (4), since the 1sg and 2sg prefixes talk about singular persons whereas the verb base in (4) means that a group of two is going. Now, mostly, this is so, but it turns out that there is a special sentence pattern where a dual verb base can be used with a 1sg or a 2sg subject prefix: if we want to express something like "Person 1 went with Person 2", we use the dual verb base, since two people are going, but the subject prefix is a singular subject prefix (referring only to Person 1) - Person 2 is then expressed the same way as in English, by using a word that means "with". But we won't make a study of this pattern here - we're only noting that such combinations are possible. Since the verb in (4) is regular, we'll have no trouble actually building the forms, even if the subject prefix is one that we wouldn't expect. But when we write out conjugations of the verb base in (4) (or any other dual go-verb), we'll omit the strictly singular subjects. For practice, try to create the correct forms of these yourself (they're completely easy.)

What about the verb base in (5)? It turns out that here too we normally only get the 1dpl, 2dpl and 3 person subject prefixes, but that in the special pattern we mentioned above we can indeed get a 1sg or 2sg subject prefix with a plural verb. When we write out conjugations of (5) (or of any plural go-verb), we'll again leave out the strictly singular subjects. But before we get any further, we need to say something about the distributive plural **da**.

In the verbs we've seen so far, the **da** prefix is used with 1dpl, 2dpl, or 3 person subject prefixes to indicate that more than two persons are doing the action. In the case of plural go-verbs, the verb automatically means that more than two persons are doing the action. For this reason, typically, **da** is not used with such verbs. However, sometimes **da** is added in anyway - this is done to suggest that the various people don't form a close-knit group, but are being thought of as separate from one another.

Let's get back to (3) and talk about its irregularities. What we're going to say here applies not only to (3), but to any verb base that uses the stem-set of (3) or the related momentaneous stem-set. (Remember: the stem-set shown in (3) is the continuative stem-set.) But these irregularies only apply to these singular "go" stems, not to verb stems from unrelated stem-sets with other meanings. We'll describe the irregularities by examining the possible subject prefixes one by one. Here is our first irregularity.

(6)   (Irregularity involving the 1sg subject prefix) When used with a 1sg subject prefix that ends in **sh**, drop the hyphens in the stems and just follow the **sh** of the subject prefix with the vowel of the stem.

(Note that for all the stems that start with a hyphen, the letter that follows the hyphen is a vowel.)

As an example of this, let's build the 1sg subject I mode form of (3). This word can mean "I'm going around randomly". Its structure is as follows:

(7)   outer   subject   verb
        prefix   prefix   stem

        na   -   sh   -   -á

To combine the subject prefix **sh** with the stem **-á**, we just drop the hyphen in **-á** and put the rest of the stem (which is just **á**) together with the subject prefix, like this: **shá**. To build the whole word, we only have to remember to apply Rule Disj-1 (none of our other rules apply.) The actual word is therefore: **naashá**.

Our next irregularity is:

(8)   (Irregularity involving the 2sg subject prefix) When used with any 2sg subject prefix (no matter what its shape is), replace the hyphens in the stems by **n**.

As an example, the 2sg subject I mode form of (3), which can mean "you (sg) are going around randomly", is built like this:

(9)   outer   subject   verb
      prefix   prefix   stem

        na   -   ni   -   -á

Since the subject prefix is 2sg, we first replace the hyphen in the stem with **n**, which gives us **ná** as the new version of the stem. Putting everything together, we get as the actual word: **naniná**. (Check that none of our rules apply so nothing else is changed.) Note that the **n** that replaces the hyphen when (8) operates is a kind of extra **n** that's in the verb in addition to the **n** in the 2sg subject prefix **ni**. (But this **n** is put in even when the 2sg subject prefix doesn't have an **n** in it itself.)

Our next irregularity is:

(10)   (Irregularity involving the 3 subject prefix) When used with any 3 subject prefix (no matter what its shape is), replace the hyphens in the stems by **gh**, except when using the F mode stem, where the hyphen is replaced by **g**.

The 3 subject I mode form of (3), which can mean "he/she is going around randomly", has this this structure:

(11)   outer   subject   verb
       prefix   prefix   stem

         na   -   (zero)   -   -á

Since the subject prefix is 3, and since we are not using the F mode stem, we replace the hyphen in -á with **gh**, giving us **ghá** as the new version of the stem. The actual word is: **naaghá** (Rule Disj-1 applied, of course.)

There is another irregularity associated with the stems that start with hyphens. We cannot illustrate this irregularity yet, since it involves d-effect, and we haven't yet seen any circumstances where d-effect could occur with these stems. In fact, the only case where we've seen d-effect applying to a stem is when the stem is preceded by a 1dpl subject prefix, and these singular go-verbs don't occur with duoplural subjects. But we'll learn later that there are other circumstances when d-effect can really apply to these stems. Since we're listing irregularities, let's list this one, too, for completeness. It turns out that the P mode stem also has an irregularity involving d-effect, so let's throw that into our statement as well.

(12) (Irregularities involving d-effect) When d-effect applies to a stem that begins with a hyphen, replace the hyphen by **d**. When d-effect applies to the singular go-verb P-mode stem **yá**, this stem changes into **dzá**.

We suggested that the P mode stem, shown as **yá**, was almost but not entirely regular, and we've just learned that this stem behaves irregularly when d-effect applies. This stem has one other irregularity. This other irregularity affects some of the forms that we'll look at right here, so we'd better learn it:

(13) (Irregularity involving the P stem **yá**) When **yá** is preceded by the s-P 3 person subject prefix **z**, the **z** disappears.

That's all there is to it! We can now write out all the forms of the verb bases in (3), (4), and (5), at least for the three modes that we've learned so far. Here are the forms for the singular go-verb given in (3). Since we only have singular subjects, let's collapse the three modes we know into one chart.

(14)   I   P   F

1sg   naashá   niséyá   nideeshaał
2sg   naniná   nisíníyá   nidíínaał
3(sg) naaghá   naayá   nidoogaał
4(sg) nijighá   nijiyá   nizhdoogaał

(In the 3 and 4 person, the subject prefix is not in itself specifically singular, but because we have a singular go-verb here, the meaning is necessarily singular. That's why we put in "sg" in the labels of the 3 and 4 person rows. But we put it in in parentheses, to remind ourselves that the singularness is from the verb base, not from the subject prefix.)

We already discussed the way the I mode forms of this verb are built, except for **nijighá**. This word has the following structure:

(15)   outer   object   subject   verb
        prefix   prefix   prefix   stem

        na   -   j   -   (zero) -   -á

The description of the irregularity given in (10) above tells us that -á becomes **ghá** here, since we're using a 3 person subject prefix. Rule Conj-1 inserts an **i** after the **j**, and Rule Disj-3 changes **na** to **ni** (make sure you understand why these rules apply the way they do!) This gives us **nijighá**.

The P mode forms **niséyá** and **nisíníyá** are regular. In the case of **naayá** and **nijiyá**, the statement in (13) tells us what's going on: since we're in the s-P conjugation, we'd expect the 3 person subject prefix to be **z**, but (13) tells us that with this verb, this **z** disappears, so we get **naayá** instead of "naazyá", and **nijiya** instead of "nijizyá".

The F mode forms show irregularities that are similar to the I mode forms. The main thing to note is that, in the F mode, when the subject prefix is 3 person, the hyphen in the verb stem is replaced by **g**, not by **gh**, so we get the **gaał** of **nidoogaał** and **nizhdoogaał** as the verb stem.

The I, P, and F mode forms of the dual and plural go-verbs in (4) and (5) are regular. Let's list them, for completeness. First, the dual go-verb in (4):

(16)   I   P   F

1dpl   neiit'aash   nishiit'áázh   nidiit'ash
2dpl   naoh'aash   nishoo'áázh   nidooh'ash
3(dpl) naa'aash   naazh'áázh   nidoo'ash
4(dpl) niji'aash   nijizh'áázh   nizhdoo'ash

(Why to the P mode forms have **sh**'s and **zh**'s in the subject prefixes? Answer: Rule Subj-6 applied, since the verb stem has **zh** in it.)

(We labelled the rows in (16) "duoplural", but with this verb stem, we only have dual meaning (that is, two persons are going).)

Here are the forms for the plural go-verb in (5):

(17)   I   P   F

1dpl   neiikai   nisiikai   niikah
2dpl   naohkai   nisoohkai   nidoohkah
3(dpl) naakai   naaskai   nidookah
4(dpl) nijikai   nijiskai   nizhdookah

The forms in (16) and (17) are completely regular - make sure you understand how they were built.

This is all we need to say about the forms of the three go-verbs that we gave in (3), (4), and (5). But there is something about the meanings of these verbs that we need to talk about.

First of all, we already said that these verbs can mean something like "go around (randomly)". But in addition to this, there is another kind of meaning that they can express. To see what this is, let's look at the following English sentence:

202

(18)   John went to Window Rock.

If we want to describe the meaning of (18), we could say, perhaps, that it means something like: "John made a trip to Window Rock". Now, what exactly is the movement described by (18)? We might think that (18) tells us that at a certain moment John was at a certain place (not Window Rock), and then he moved in such a way that at a later moment he was at Window Rock. Well, okay, but if we say (18) and we really mean that John made a trip to Window Rock, we probably are thinking that he not only went to Window Rock, but he also came back. We can call this the *round-trip meaning of "go"*.

Now, in addition to meaning "go around randomly", the verbs in (3), (4), and (5) can also be used to indicate this kind of round trip meaning that sentences like (18) often have. So, if we wanted to say in Navajo that John made a trip to Window Rock, in the sense that he moved from here to there, then perhaps did something there, and finally came home, we can say:

(19)   John Tségháhoodzánígóó naayá.

It seems, therefore, that the verbs in (3), (4), and (5) have at least two meanings: "go around (randomly)" and "go (round-trip)". (You might have noticed that the round-trip meaning is particularly common when these verbs are used in the P mode.) Actually, these verbs have more meanings besides these two. You may know that, especially in the I mode, these verbs can be used simply to mean "be" when a location is meant. For example, to say "John is at Window Rock", we can say:

(20)   John Tségháhoodzánádi naaghá.

(In some sense, this is sort of using the word **naaghá** in its "going around randomly" meaning: when we say (20), it's as though we're saying that what John is doing in Window Rock is he's just going around inside Window Rock, perhaps doing things, perhaps not.)

There are also a number of idiomatic expressions that use these verbs. A very common one is to use the verb together with the postposition **baa** (or **yaa**, if the subject is 3 person!) to mean "do it". But we won't attempt to give a complete list of all the usages of the verbs in (3), (4), and (5). For now, we'll stop with what we've already mentioned. At this point, we want to ask a different kind of question.

We said earlier that we want to start making a vocabulary study of motion verbs. So far, we've looked at a group of verb bases that carry one group of meanings associated with the notion of going. Does this have anything to do with motion verbs in general?

Well, look at how the verb bases in (3), (4), and (5) were built. We took a continuative stem-set whose meaning had to do with motion, we added the atelic outer prefix **na**, and we got a verb base

203

that means "perform the motion represented by the stem-set either in a random way, or else in a round-trip way". Now, it turns out that, more or less, we can do this with any continuative stem-set whose meaning has to do with motion!

In fact, we've already seen at least three verb bases where this is exactly what we did! Let's take a quick look at them.

Look at the verb base in Chapter 11(19), which means "carry him/her around". The stem-set in that verb base happens to be a continuative stem-set. (Can you find the momentaneous stem-set that goes with it? Look at Chapter 11(2)....) The meaning of this stem-set all by itself might be described as something like: "move (or take or carry) an animate being". What we did in Chapter 11(19) is the same as what we did in (3), (4), and (5): we combined the stem-set with the atelic outer prefix **na**, and we got a verb base where the motion is randomly round about.

You might be asking: Wait a second! The verb bases in (3), (4), and (5) are intransitive, while the verb base in Chapter 11(19) is transitive. What's going on?

Well, we saw in (1) and (2) that English verbs of motion can be either intransitive or transitive. The same is true of Navajo. The stem-sets used in (3), (4), and (5) refer to an intransitive kind of moving (where a subject just moves), while the stem-set in Chapter 11(19) refers to a transitive kind of moving (where a subject makes an object move).

You might be asking: Wait another second! The verb bases in (3), (4), and (5) can have a round-trip meaning. What about the verb base in Chapter 11(19)?

Well, that verb base can also have a round-trip meaning! For example, if I say

(21)   Ákǫ́ǫ́ naniséltį́.

this can mean "I took (carried) you there" (for example, I took you to the doctor's, maybe when you were a baby), in the sense that I took you there and also brought you back afterwards.

Can you find another motion verb built the same as (3), (4), (5), or Chapter 11(19)? (Answer: Look at Chapter 13(5). The stem-set in that verb base is continuative; it happens to be transitive; and the verb base we get can mean not only "carry it (a ropelike thing) around", but also "carry it (a ropelike thing) to a place in a round-trip way".)

Can you find a third motion verb like this? (Answer: Go back to Chapter 8(13). This verb base is intransitive, so it's more like (3), (4), and (5) than the ones in Chapter 11 and 13. It also has both the random-motion and the round-trip motion meanings.)

We are now almost in a position to state the first real principle of Navajo vocabulary building. There is one detail that we've ignored.

To see what it is, let's go back to the stem-set in (3) above. Suppose we're given this stem-set, we're told that it's continuative, and we're told what it means. Can we build the verb base in (3) out of it?

If we want to build the verb base in (3), what do we need to say? What do we need to say about any verb base? First of all, we need the stem-set - but that's given to us. What else do we need?

Well, we need to know if there are any lexical prefixes. But that's not a problem here, because we're specifically building a verb base using the atelic outer prefix **na** (and no other lexical prefix.)

We need to know what the perfective conjugation should be. But that's not a problem, because we know that if the verb base has the atelic outer prefix **na** as one of its lexical prefixes, then the perfective conjugation has to be the s-P (we learned this back in Chapter 8, remember?)

We need to know whether the verb base is transitive or intransitive. But that's not a problem, because when we look at the meaning of the stem-set that we're given, we can tell whether it means that the subject moves, or whether it means that the subject makes the object move.

So what else do we need to know? The classifier!

The fact is, we cannot know what the classifier is just from the information we've got so far. For example, the verb bases in (3) and (4) above and the one Chapter 13(5) were built with the zero classifier, but the verb base in Chapter 11(19) was built with the barred-l classifier, and the verb base in (5) above and also the one in Chapter 8(13) were built with the d classifier.

What this means is this: rather than starting out with a particular continuative stem-set, we have to start out with a continuative stem-set together with a classifier. If we have that much information, we can then create a real verb base that has the random-motion/round-trip-motion meaning by having atelic outer **na** as the only lexical prefix, having the transitivity be whatever the meaning requires, and using the s-P conjugation in the P mode.

Here is a kind of game we can play that might help sort this out.

Let's go back to the verb bases in Chapter 11(19) and Chapter 11(2). We can say that there is some material in these verb bases whose meaning is: "move/take/carry an animate being". What exactly is that material?

Well, the stem-sets in those two verb bases have this meaning, but we also need the classifier (as we've just seen). If we want to collect the information needed later on, we may as well also add in the transitivity. If we put all of this together, we'll get something that looks like this:

(22)

Momentaneous stem-set		Continuative stem-set	
I:	**teeh**	I:	**té**
P:	**tį́**	P:	**tį́**
F:	**tééł**	F:	**teeł**
R:	**tééh**	R:	**teeh**
O:	**tééł**	O:	**teeł**
Classifier: barred-l			
Transitivity: transitive			

Now, (22) is not a verb base. It has too much information and also too little information to be a verb base: on the one hand, there are two stem-sets in (22), but on the other hand, there is no information about lexical prefixes or P mode conjugation. But (22) does have a meaning: "move (or take, or carry) an animate being". This means that maybe we should consider structures like (22) to be part of Navajo vocabulary, even though such a structure doesn't by itself describe any particular verb.

In YM, structures like (22) are called *verb themes*. The importance of verb themes is that we can give rules that tell us how to build real verb bases starting with verb themes. We've been using one such rule in this whole chapter. Let's write this rule out in a slightly more precise way. The following will be our first example of a vocabulary principle. When we give these principles, we'll number them Vocabulary-(number).

Vocabulary-1: If you have a verb theme whose meaning involves motion, you can build a verb base whose meaning involves motion that goes around randomly as well as round-trip motion by constructing that verb base as follows:

Stem-set: use the continuative stem-set of the verb theme	Classifier: use the classifier of the verb theme
	Lexical prefixes: **na** (outer)
	Transitivity: use the transitivity of the verb theme
	Perfective: s-P

This is exactly what we did in all the examples that we've been looking at. The verb bases that we learned in this chapter, based on our new go-verbs, were built using Vocabulary-1, and this is also the way the verb bases in Chapter 8(13), Chapter 11(19), and Chapter 13(5) were created. And not only that: whenever we run into a new verb theme that has to do with motion, we can use Vocabulary-1 to build a new verb base out of that verb theme with the random-motion/round-trip-

206

motion meanings!

A note: Vocabulary-1 is different from the kinds of rules we've been seeing all along, the rules numbered Rule Str-(number) or Rule Subj-(number) or Rule Disj-(number) or Rule Conj-(number). The difference is this: the rules we've seen so far have to do with building an individual word out of the pieces that make it up. The principle we've called Vocabulary-1 has to do with building a verb base. We can think of Vocabulary-1 as a principle that tells us how to come up with verbs that have a certain kind of meaning, while the rules we've been learning all along tell us about the form of the actual words.

To show how useful vocabulary principles can be, let's give another one involving motion verbs and see what we get when we use it to build verb bases.

Vocabulary-2: If you have a verb theme whose meaning involves motion, you can build a verb base whose meaning is that the motion starts (in the P mode, the meaning is that that motion is about to happen) by constructing that verb base as follows:

Stem-set: use the momentaneous stem-set of the verb theme	Classifier: use the classifier of the verb theme
	Lexical prefixes: **d** (inner)
	Transitivity: use the transitivity of the verb theme
	Perfective: s-P

To be honest, the verb bases that you get using Vocabulary-2 are used much more frequently in the P mode than in any of the other modes. In fact, the P modes of the verb bases that we get using Vocabulary-2 with the ordinary "go" themes are among the most common "go" words in Navajo. Let's form these words, and then we'll see how to use them.

To use a principle like Vocabulary-2, we need to have verb themes. If the meaning we're interested in is just plain "go", we've already given part of the information (in the verb bases in (3), (4), and (5)), but we were using continuative stem-sets earlier, and here we need momentaneous ones. Just to practice our verb theme format, let's write out verb themes for "go". As we know now, we need three of these, depending on how many people are going. The verb theme for one person going is:

(23)

Momentaneous stem-set	Continuative stem-set
I: -ááh	I: -á
P: yá	P: yá
F: -ááł	F: -aał
R: -ááh	R: -aah
O: -a'	O: -a'
Classifier: zero	
Transitivity: intransitive	

A reminder: the irregularities described in (6), (8), (10), (12), and (13) earlier apply to the momentaneous stems of this theme as well as to the continuative stems.

The verb theme for two persons going is:

(24)

Momentaneous and continuative stem-set
I: 'aash
P: 'áázh
F: 'ash
R: 'ash
O: 'aash
Classifier: zero
Transitivity: intransitive

Here is something easy: in this theme the continuative and momentaneous stem-sets are the same!

The verb theme for more than two persons going is:

(25)

Momentaneous stem-set	Continuative stem-set
I: **kááh**	I: **kai**
P: **kai**	P: **kai**
F: **kah**	F: **kah**
R: **kah**	R: **kah**
O: **kááh**	O: **kai**
Classifier: d	
Transitivity: intransitive	

For this verb theme, the two stem-sets are different only in the I and O modes.

Now, if we use Vocabulary-2, we end up forming the following verb bases. For one person going, we have:

(26)

Stem-set	
I: **-ááh**	Classifier: zero
P: **yá**	Lexical prefixes: **d** (inner)
F: **-ááł**	Transitivity: intransitive
R: **-ááh**	
O: **-a'**	Perfective: s-P

For two persons going, we have:

(27)

Stem-set	
I: **'aash**	Classifier: zero
P: **'áázh**	Lexical prefixes: **d** (inner)
F: **'ash**	Transitivity: intransitive
R: **'ash**	
O: **'aash**	Perfective: s-P

And, for more than two persons going, we have:

(28)

Stem-set		Classifier: d
I:	**kááh**	
P:	**kai**	Lexical prefixes: **d** (inner)
F:	**kah**	
R:	**kah**	Transitivity: intransitive
O:	**kááh**	Perfective: s-P

Let's write out the I, P, and F mode forms of these. The irregularities described in (6), (8), and (10) will come into play for the singular verb in the I and F modes. Also, the irregularity described in (13) will play a role in the P mode for the singular verb. Since the three verb bases have an inner prefix **d** and are conjugated in the s-P pattern, we'll need to use the contracted forms that we learned in Chapter 15 (see Chapter 15(11) and Chapter 15(12)) for the P mode (for all three verb bases.)

For one person going, the forms are:

(29)   I   P   F

	I	P	F
1sg	disháah	déyá	dideesháál
2sg	dínááh	díníyá	didíínáál
3(sg)	digháah	deeyá	didoogáál
4(sg)	jidigháah	jideeyá	jididoogáál

In **disháah** and **dideesháál**, the principle in (6) above applied: the vowel of the verb stem comes directly after the **sh**. In **dínááh** and **didíínáál**, the rule in (8) put the **n**'s in; but note that in **dínááh** Rule Conj-3 still applied normally. The **gh**'s in **digháah** and **jidigháah**, and the **g**'s in **didoogáál** and **jididoogáál** are due to the principle in (10). In **deeyá** and **jideeyá**, the rule in (13) removed the **z**'s that we would have expected, but otherwise we still have the contracted forms of Chapter 15(11). (Instead of **deez**, we have **dee**, because the **z** dropped out by (13).)

For two persons going, the forms are:

(30)   I   P   F

	I	P	F
1dpl	diit'aash	deet'áázh	didiit'ash
2dpl	doh'aash	dishoo'áázh	didooh'ash
3(dpl)	di'aash	deezh'áázh	didoo'ash
4(dpl)	jidi'aash	jideezh'áázh	jididoo'ash

(The **s**'s and **z**'s of Chapter 15(11) turned into **sh**'s and **zh**'s in the P mode here, because of the **zh** in

210

the verb stem.)

And for more than two persons going, the forms are:

(31)   I   P   F

1dpl   diikááh   deekai   didiikah
2dpl   dohkááh   disoohkai   didoohkah
3(dpl) dikááh   deeskai   didookah
4(dpl) jidikááh   jideeskai   jididookah

Again, the forms in (30) and (31) are completely regular - you should make sure that you understand how each of them is formed.

The meaning of the verb bases (26), (27), and (28) is basically "start to go". As in the case of the verb bases in (3), (4), and (5), there are a number of idiomatic expressions which use these verbs. All of the forms listed in (29), (30), and (31) can be used in idioms, and perhaps also in other circumstances. But when ordinary "go" is meant, the most commonly used forms are the P mode ones. The meaning of the P mode forms in (29), (30), and (31), as these forms are actually used, is something like "be about to go" or "intend to go" (or even "be on one's way", although to emphasize this meaning there's another way of saying it.) This means that these P mode words very often correspond to the English verb **go** when it is used in combinations like **am going**, **are going**, or **is going**. An example:

(32)   Na'nízhoozhígóó déyá. "I'm going to Gallup"

That is, I plan to go to Gallup, or I'm about to set off for Gallup, or I'm on my way to Gallup.

Note that the action in (32) could be described as being in the present or the future. This is unusual for a P mode verb. Usually, P mode verbs in simple sentences refer to actions in the past. This special non-past meaning is something that we find with the P modes of motion verbs built according to Vocabulary-2.

The P mode forms in (29), (30), and (31) are used when the motion is simple going, but we can apply Vocabulary-2 to other motion verb themes to build verb bases whose P modes have this kind of meaning. For example, if we take the verb theme in (22) above and use Vocabulary-2, we get the following verb base:

211

(33)

Stem-set		Classifier: barred-l
I:	**teeh**	
P:	**tį́**	Lexical prefixes: **d** (inner)
F:	**tééł**	
R:	**tééh**	Transitivity: transitive
O:	**tééł**	
		Perfective: s-P

The general meaning of this verb base is "start to move/take/carry an animate being". But if we build the P mode forms of (33), we'll get verbs that mean things like "am taking (carrying)", "are taking (carrying)", or "is taking (carrying)" (where the object of the taking or the carrying is an animate being.) For example, we could use this verb to say something like "She's taking the baby to the clinic today". Here is a Navajo way of saying this:

(34)   Dííjį́ awéé' azee'ál'į́įgóó yideestį́.

The verb **yideestį́** "he/she/they (two) is/are carrying him/her" is built from (33) in a completely regular way. For review, let's discuss how it is built. Here is its structure:

(35)   object   inner   subject   cl   verb
        prefix   prefix   prefix   stem

        y   -   d   -   s   -   ł   -   tį́

Question: Why is there an object prefix **y**? (Answer: This is a transitive verb, the subject is 3 person, and the object is also 3 person, so Rule Str-1 tells us that the object is represented by the prefix **y**.)

Question: Why is the subject prefix **s** and not **z**? (Answer: the classifier is barred-l.)

Question: Where did the **ee** in **yideestį́** come from? (Answer: The inner prefix **d** contracts with s-P subject prefixes. The contracted form of **d** with the 3 person subject prefix **s** is **dees**.)

Question: What happened to the classifier **ł** in **yideestį́**? (Answer: The sandwich rule got rid of it.)

So Vocabulary-2, like Vocabulary-1, allows us to make up lots of new verb bases.

As a final example, we might ask: can we create verbs that mean "crawl" with the kind of present/future meaning that we had in (32) or (34)? For example, how would we ask a baby "Where are you crawling?" We'd just say this:

(36)   Háágóó díní'na'?

Where did the word **díní'na'** come from? Well, its structure is just:

(37)   inner   subject   cl   verb
        prefix   prefix   stem

        d - síní - d - na'
          \ /   \ /
          díní   'na'

Recall that the d classifier causes d-effect on the verb stem, creating **'na'** from **na'** (review Chapter 6.) Also, **d** contracts with **síní** to give **díní** (see Chapter 15(12).)

Here's a question about (37): where did we get the verb stem? Well, since we used Vocabulary-2, we must have gotten it from the momentaneous stem-set that means "crawl". Whoops - we haven't seen the momentaneous stem-set that means "crawl"! Did we make a mistake?

No. Recall that the P mode stem is the same for the momentaneous stem-set and for the continuative stem-set of a verb theme. The stem-set back in Chapter 8(13) is the continuative stem-set (why?), but since it's the P mode stem that we need for (37), we know that we can go ahead and use **na'**.

But just in case you're curious, here's the verb theme that means "crawl":

(38)

Momentaneous stem-set		Continuative stem-set	
I:	**nééh**	I:	**na'**
P:	**na'**	P:	**na'**
F:	**nah**	F:	**nah**
R:	**nah**	R:	**nah**
O:	**nééh**	O:	**nééh**
Classifier: d			
Transitivity: intransitive			

Note that in this verb theme only the I mode has different stems for the two stem-sets.

So, the verb base in Chapter 8(13) is formed from (38) by using Vocabulary-1. If we use Vocabulary-2 instead, we get the verb base:

(39)

Stem-set		Classifier: d
I:	nééh	
P:	na'	Lexical prefixes: **d** (inner)
F:	nah	
R:	nah	Transitivity: intransitive
O:	nééh	
		Perfective: s-P

The P mode forms of (39) will express the sort of present/future meaning that we saw in (32) and (34). This is exactly what we did to get the verb in (36).

Well, this is enough of a beginning for our vocabulary study of motion verbs. We will continue with motion verbs in the next chapter, but first, here's something that might cheer you up. With principles like Vocabulary-1 and Vocabulary-2 (and others that we'll learn and yet others that you'll discover on your own), we're able to build lots of new verb bases. But, all the forms of all the verb bases that we build are constructed according to the rules that we've learned. In fact, we have studied almost all of the rules that describe how the parts of the Navajo verb are formed! With what we've learned so far, we can already build thousands, and perhaps millions of verbs!

Now, take a break, and get set for some more ways of making verb bases for motion verbs.

CHAPTER 18

MORE ABOUT MOTION VERBS, AND THE N-I AND N-P CONJUGATIONS

In Chapter 17, we studied two patterns for building verb bases for motion verbs. These were described in Vocabulary-1 and Vocabulary-2. These vocabulary principles tell us that if we start with a verb theme, we can create a verb base with a certain kind of meaning by building it in some particular way. In this chapter, we'll look at some more vocabulary principles for motion verbs. We will also learn about two new conjugation patterns.

If you look at the verb bases built by Vocabulary-1 and Vocabulary-2, you'll notice that both of them involve lexical prefixes. In the first case, the atelic outer prefix **na** is used, and in the second case, the inner prefix **d** is used. Are there any patterns for motion verbs that involve no lexical prefixes?

There are. In fact, here is a new vocabulary principle:

Vocabulary-3: If you have a verb theme whose meaning involves motion, you can build a *completive* verb base by constructing it as follows:

Stem-set: use the momentaneous stem-set of the verb theme	Classifier: use the classifier of the verb theme
	Lexical prefixes: (non)
	Transitivity: use the transitivity of the verb theme
	Perfective: y-P

The way that Vocabulary-3 tells us to construct verb bases is clear. What is not clear is, what is a "completive" verb base?

Well, we'd like to say that a completive verb base is a verb base with a certain kind of meaning. But the fact is, the meanings of the verb bases created by Vocabulary-3 are a bit elusive. The reason is that the verb bases built this way are almost never used alone. Instead, they are used in certain combinations with other words. The best way to think of it is that the word *completive* in Vocabulary-3 is a label for the kind of verb bases that we're getting rather than a description of the meaning. We'll then have some additional rules that say things like: take a completive verb base and combine it with something, and you'll get a phrase that means such-and-such.

(The word *completive* is the term used in the dictionary parts of YM to label the verb bases created by Vocabulary-3. It seemed useful to use it here as well, so that if you see it in YM, you'll recognize what they're talking about.)

In fact, let's give an example of a principle that uses completive verb bases. Since this principle builds our Navajo vocabulary, let's still consider it a vocabulary principle even though it starts with a verb base rather than with a verb theme.

Vocabulary-4: If you combine a completive verb base (that is, a verb base built by Vocabulary-3 from a verb theme of motion) with the postposition **biih** (or **yiih**, when the subject is 3 person), you get an expression whose meaning involves motion from the outside to the inside of something. The **b** (or **y**) in **biih** (or **yiih**) refers to the thing inside of which the motion ends.

To illustrate this, let's carefully go through all the steps and see what we get.

Let's start with ordinary going. In Chapter 17 we learned the verb themes that mean "go" - remember that "go" is exceptional in that there are three such themes, depending on the number of people who are going. We'll take the momentaneous stem-set from each one and build three verb themes using Vocabulary-3. These will then be completive verb bases that mean "go".

If one person is going, Vocabulary-3 gives us:

(1)

Stem-set		Classifier: zero
I:	-ááh	
P:	yá	Lexical prefixes: (none)
F:	-áál	
R:	-ááh	Transitivity: intransitive
O:	-a'	Perfective: y-P

(Don't forget that those hyphens are there in the verb stems to remind us about the special irregularities that these stems have.)

If two persons are going, we get:

216

(2)

Stem-set		Classifier: zero
I:	**'aash**	
P:	**'áázh**	Lexical prefixes: (none)
F:	**'ash**	
R:	**'ash**	Transitivity: intransitive
O:	**'aash**	Perfective: y-P

And if more than two persons are going, we get:

(3)

Stem-set		Classifier: d
I:	**kááh**	
P:	**kai**	Lexical prefixes: (none)
F:	**kah**	
R:	**kah**	Transitivity: intransitive
O:	**kááh**	Perfective: y-P

At this point, let's look at the actual forms of the verbs built using these verb bases. By now, you should be able to create these forms in your sleep, but since these verbs are so important, and since the singular go-verb is irregular, we'll write them out.

Here are the I, P, and F mode forms built from the verb base in (1):

(4)	I	P	F
1sg	yisháah	yíyá	deesháál
2sg	nináah	yíníyá	díínáál
3(sg)	yigháah	yíyá	doogáál
4(sg)	jigháah	jííyá	jidoogáál

Make sure you understand the irregular shapes of the verb stem in the I and F modes. And you should also know that the **yi** in the words **yisháah** and **yigháah** was supplied by the peg rule.

All the P mode forms in (4) are regular (the only irregularities of the P mode "go" stem **yá** involved either the s-P conjugation or d-effect, and we don't have either of these here.) Since this verb is intransitive and since the P mode is conjugated using the y-P conjugation, the 1sg and 3(sg) P mode forms are the same.

Here are the I, P, and F mode forms built from (2):

(5)   I   P   F

1dpl   yiit'aash   yiit'áázh   diit'ash
2dpl   woh'aash   woo'áázh   dooh'ash
3(dpl) yi'aash   yí'áázh   doo'ash
4(dpl) ji'aash   jíí'áázh   jidoo'ash

All forms are regular. The **yi** of **yi'aash** was put in by the peg rule.

(Review question: where did the **y** of **yiit'aash** and **yiit'áázh**, and the **w** of **woh'aash** and **woo'áázh** come from? Answer: Look at Rule Str-3.)

Here are the I, P, and F mode forms built from (3):

(6)   I   P   F

1dpl   yiikááh   yiikai   diikah
2dpl   wohkááh   woohkai   doohkah
3(dpl) yikááh   yikai   dookah
4(dpl) jikááh   jookai   jidookah

If you were wondering about the low tone on the **yi** of **yikai** (as compared with the high tone on the **yí** of **yí'áázh**) or about the **oo** of **jookai**, remember that (3) has a d classifier....

Now that we've got the actual verb forms, we can use Vocabulary-4 to create expressions whose meaning is "go into it" (or, in more colloquial English, "get into it". For example, we can say things like:

(7)   Chidí biih yíyá.

which means "I got into the car". In this sentence, the **b** of **biih** is actually a pronoun that refers to the car. If we already knew we were talking about a car, we could just say **biih yíyá**, meaning "I got into it."

Incidentally, (7) would not be used to mean "he/she got into the car", even though the verb **yíyá** could also be used if the subject is 3 person. Can you see why? How <u>would</u> you say this? (It has to do with the word **biih**.)

Note on pronunciation: in combinations such as the one described in Vocabulary-4, people tend to pronounce the **biih** (or **yiih**) and the verb so close together that it almost seems as thought the **biih** or **yiih** becomes a prefix to the verb. We could call it an outer prefix (which would make the **b** or the **y** an outer object) if we want, although there is something about it that makes it different from the outer prefixes that we've seen. Do you see what that difference is? It's that real outer prefixes always end in vowels, whereas **biih** and **yiih** end in a consonant, the consonant **h**. Nevertheless, these expressions are often pronounced in a way that makes **biih** and **yiih** almost seem to become prefixes of the verb. One effect of this is that when the verb itself begins with a **y**, some people drop this **y** after **biih** or **yiih**. For example, some people say the sentence in (7) as though it were written:

(8)   Chidí biihíyá.

Pronunciation adjustments like this often happen (especially in faster speech) when verbs are combined with other words this way. You should be on the lookout for them.

As in the case of the vocabulary principles we learned in Chapter 17, Vocabulary-3 and Vocabulary-4 can be used with any motion verb theme to create new phrases. The phrases created by Vocabulary-4 will all have meanings involving motion into something. For example, if we take the verb theme in Chapter 17(38), we can create expressions that mean "crawl into it". We'll use the momentaneous stem-set in Chapter 17(38), the d classifier, and no lexical prefixes, and we'll use the y-P conjugation if we want a P mode form (that's what Vocabulary-3 tells us to do), and then we'll combine the words we get with **biih** or **yiih** (that's what Vocabulary-4 tells us to do.) To make sure you understand this process, here is the completive verb base that means "crawl":

(9)

Stem-set		Classifier: d
I:	nééh	Lexical prefixes: (none)
P:	na'	
F:	nah	Transitivity: intransitive
R:	nah	
O:	nééh	Perfective: y-P

Vocabulary-3 built (9) out of the verb theme in Chapter 17(38). For practice, you should write out the completive I, P, and F mode forms of "crawl" using (9).

Now, all we have to do in order to express the idea "crawl into it" is to take the words built from (9) and put them together with **biih** or **yiih**. For example, here is a sentence (taken from YM 87) illustrating what can be said using such a combination:

(10)   Tł'óo'di awéé' hashtł'ish yiih yi'na'.

This means "The baby crawled into the mud outside."

If we start with a transitive verb theme, Vocabulary-3 and Vocabulary-4 will allow us to create expressions that correspond to the English expression "put it into it". For example, we've seen some verb bases that use a stem-set that has to do with moving a ropelike thing - look at Chapter 13(5). We haven't actually given a verb theme that means "move a ropelike thing", so let's do that here:

(11)

Momentaneous stem-set		Continuative stem-set	
I:	lé	I:	lé
P:	lá	P:	lá
F:	lééł	F:	leeł
R:	lééh	R:	leeh
O:	lééł	O:	lééł
Classifier: zero			
Transitivity: transitive			

You may remember that in Chapter 13 we mentioned an irregularity involving the stems in (11): when preceded by a 1dp subject prefix, the **l** at the beginning of the stem becomes **ly**. This happens with the momentaneous stems, too.

Now, Vocabulary-3 and Vocabulary-4 tell us that if we want to build an expression that means "move it (a ropelike thing) into it", we first build the completive verb base for this meaning using the momentaneous stem-set in (11), the zero classifier (because that's what is shown in (11)), no lexical prefixes, and the y-P conjugation (if we want the P mode). We then combine the verbs constructed from this verb base with the word **biih** or **yiih**. For example, we can say "I put the rope in the box" like this:

(12)   Tł'óół tsits'aa' biih yílá.

The word **yílá** is a P mode form with a 1 sg subject prefix. Can you describe how it was formed? For practice, write out the verb base that Vocabulary-3 creates from the verb theme in (11) and then show how the word **yílá** is built from that verb theme.

Suppose we want to talk about putting an animate entity into something. We'll start with the verb theme in Chapter 17(22) instead of the verb theme in (11) above, but otherwise we'll do the same thing, following the instructions in Vocabulary-3 and Vocabulary-4. The following funny sentence was taken from YM 87:

(13)   Ashkii yázhí bá'ólta'í asdzą́ą́ bibéeso bizis ch'ał yiih yiyííłtį́.

This means "The little boy put a frog into the woman teacher's purse."

Make sure that you understand exactly how the words **yílá** in (12) and **yiyíiltį** in (13) are structured.

This might be a good time to start looking a bit at an important fact about certain transitive motion verb themes that you may have noticed. The verb theme in Chapter 17(22) and the verb theme in (11) above both have as their meaning "move it", but they differ in that the verb theme in Chapter 17(22) means specifically that the thing that is getting moved is an animate entity (a person or an animal), while the verb theme in (11) means specifically that the thing that is getting moved is a ropelike thing. Now, there are about a dozen verb themes in Navajo that mean "move it", where the "it" that is getting moved is required to be something with a particular shape or characteristic. Some examples of the meanings expressed by these themes are:

(14)   (a)   move an animate being
       (b)   move a ropelike thing
       (c)   move a compact solid thing
       (d)   move a sticklike thing
       (e)   move something (especially a liquid) that is in a container
       (f)   move a bunch of more than one thing

              (etc.)

The list in (14) is not complete, but it will give you an idea of the kinds of things that are involved. What's important about (14) is the following.

First of all, each of the meanings listed in (14) differs from the others in that what is moved has some sort of special characterization, either by its nature (as in (14)(a)), its shape (as in (14)(b), (c), and (d)), the way it's handled (as in (14)(e)), or by how many there are (as in (14)(f)). (Incidentally, the meanings in (14)(a), (b), (c), and (d) only apply to the action of moving <u>one</u> thing. When a plurality of things is involved, meanings like (f) have to be used.)

Second, in Navajo, each meaning in (14) is expressed by a different verb theme. We've learned the verb themes that express (14)(a) and (14)(b). We'll run into some of the others from time to time, but you will have to know all of them eventually.

Third, there are transitive verb themes of motion besides the verb themes that express meanings like (14). For example, there are transitive verb themes that have meanings like:

(15)   (a)   move something by rolling it
       (b)   move something by dragging it

              (etc.)

221

We need to divide up the transitive verb themes of motion in Navajo into several groups, because sometimes different groups have different vocabulary principles that apply to them. For now, the particular group of transitive verb themes of motion that we'll be interested in the most are the ones that have meanings like (14). We'll call these verb themes *classificatory motion verb themes*, because the verb theme classifies the object of the verb (the thing that gets moved) according to some characteristic.

One thing we can say right now: If we use Vocabulary-3 and Vocabulary-4 with a classificatory verb theme, the result will be an expression that usually corresponds to an English phrase like "put it into it". The difference between the meanings of expressions like this that are made from different classificatory verb themes has to do with the kind of thing that is getting put.

This doesn't mean, though, that we can't use Vocabulary-3 and Vocabulary-4 with other (non-classificatory) transitive verb themes as well. But if we do that, the meaning that comes out is a little different. To illustrate what happens, here is the transitive verb theme that means "move it by rolling it":

(16)

Momentaneous stem-set		Continuative stem-set	
I:	máás	I:	maas
P:	mááz	P:	mááz
F:	mas	F:	mas
R:	mas	R:	mas
O:	máás	O:	maas
Classifier: barred-l			
Transitivity: transitive			

(The two stem-sets differ only in the I and O modes. Did you notice that the P mode stem is the only one that ends in a **z**?)

Let's apply Vocabulary-3 to create a completive verb base:

(17)

Stem-set		Classifier: barred-l
I:	**máás**	
P:	**mááz**	Lexical prefixes: (none)
F:	**mas**	
R:	**mas**	Transitivity: transitive
O:	**máás**	Perfective: y-P

Now, Vocabulary-4 tells us that we can form verbs from (17) and combine them with **biih** or **yiih**. For example, we can say:

(18)   Jooł hashtł'ish biih yíłmááz.

How would we say (18) in English? Like this: "I rolled the ball into the mud." The verb **yíłmááz**, which is one of the forms we can build from (17) (which is based on the verb theme in (16)), tells us that the way the ball moved was that it rolled. In English, we usually express meanings like this by using some other verb (like **roll**) instead of **put**. When we need to refer to verb themes like (16) (or 15)) that have meanings describing the way that the object moves, we will call them *transitive manner-of-motion verb themes*.

Let's stop a moment and see where we've come so far in this chapter. We learned Vocabulary-3, a vocabulary principle that builds certain verb bases from motion verb themes. These verb bases are called completive verb bases. The words built from these verb bases are rarely used by themselves, but there are a number of important combinations that they are a part of. One of these is described by Vocabulary-4, where the motion is from the outside to the inside of something. We worked out some particular combinations, first using the intransitive verb themes that mean "go" and "crawl" - these gave us ways of saying "get into it" and "crawl into it" in Navajo. We then looked at some transitive examples. If a classificatory transitive verb theme is used, we get ways of saying "put it into it". If we use a manner-of-motion verb theme, we can express various other kinds of ideas - our example was "roll it into it".

Incidentally, this story tells us about one way English and Navajo are different. In English, when we use the verb **put,** there is no indication of the kind of thing that is getting put. But in Navajo, the choice of the classificatory verb theme gives information about the thing that is getting put. For example, if you overhear somebody say:

(19)   He put it in the box.

you'll have no information about what was put into the box. But if you overhear somebody say:

(20)   Tsits'aa' yiih yiyíílá.

you'll know something about the thing that got put into the box: it was something ropelike.

(If you know Navajo, you'll know that (11) can also be used for moving certain other kinds of things besides ropelike things, such as for example things that come in pairs, so (20) might also mean that a pair of something got put into the box.)

In the rest of this chapter, we're going to look at a few more kinds of verb bases that can be formed from motion verb themes. But the verb bases we're going to study will involve new conjugation patterns in the I and P modes, so let's talk about these first.

So far, we've learned about one conjugation pattern for the I mode. We called this pattern the regular I mode conjugation. But for the P mode, we learned two conjugation patterns, the y-P and the s-P conjugations. However, there are conjugation patterns besides these. Verbs of motion sometimes use a special I mode conjugation pattern called the *n-I* (in YM, this is called the *ni-Imperfective*) and a special P mode conjugation pattern called the *n-P* (in YM, this is called the *ni-Perfective*). The idea is that there will be a vocabulary principle that builds verb bases from verb themes of motion where the I and P modes have these special conjugations. (Note: The n-I and the n-P go together: for any verb base, either its I mode is conjugated using the n-I pattern and its P mode is conjugated using the n-P pattern, or else neither its I mode nor its P mode use these special conjugations.)

First, let's learn the forms of the n-I and the n-P. What we need to learn are the subject prefixes. For the n-I, the subject prefixes are as follows:

(21)   Subject prefixes, n-I conjugation:

	sg	dpl
1	**nish**	**niid**
2	**ní**	**noh**
3	(see (24))	

If the subject is 1 or 2 person, the subject prefix looks as though the regular I mode subject prefix was preceded by some sort of conjunct prefix **n** - there's even the high tone on 2sg **ní**! But the 3 person subject is different - we'll learn it in just a moment, but first, let's look at the subject prefixes for the n-P. If the classifier is zero or barred-l, the subject prefixes are:

(22)   Subject prefixes, n-P conjugation, zero/barred-l classifiers:

	sg	dpl
1	ní	niid
2	víní/ííní/yíní	noo
3	ní	

And if the classifier is plain-l or d, the subject prefixes for the n-P conjugation are:

(23)   Subject prefixes, n-P conjugation, plain-l/d classifiers:

	sg	dpl
1	nish	niid
2	víní/ííní/yíní	nooh
3	(see (24))	

The n-P subject prefixes look as though they are derived from the y-P prefixes by some sort of process involving an **n**. First of all, the 2sg prefixes are actually the <u>same</u> as the y-P prefix: the choice between **víní**, **ííní**, and **yíní** is exactly the same for the n-P conjugation as it is for the y-P conjugation: use **víní** if the subject prefix is immediately preceded by a disjunct prefix, use **ííní** if it's immediately preceded by a conjunct prefix, and use **yíní** if it's not preceded by any prefix.

The 1dpl and 2dpl n-P subject prefixes look like the y-P subject prefixes with an **n** in front of them.

Like the y-P conjugation, if the classifier is zero or barred-l, the 1sg and 3 subject prefixes are the same: **ní**. But the form of this prefix is not what we'd get if we preceded the y-P prefix with a conjunct prefix **n** (what <u>would</u> we get?) - it looks more like an **n** combined with the form of the y-P prefix used when it's not preceded by anything. Similarly, the 1sg prefix used when the classifier is plain-l or d is not what we'd get if we preceded the y-P prefix with a conjunct prefix **n** - it too looks like an **n** combined with the form of the y-P prefix used when it's not preceded by anything. And, if the classifier if plain-l or d, the 3 subject prefix is the same as the 3 subject prefix in the n-I conjugation.

What is this 3 subject prefix? Here it is:

(24)

	If the 3 subject prefix is preceded by:	the 3 subject prefix is:
	an outer prefix	zero
	distr pl **da**	zero or **í**
	an object prefix	**í (hw+í --> hó)**
	an inner prefix	**ee**
	no prefix at all	**yí**

This seems a little complicated, but actually it'll be easy to learn if you take each case step by step. In this chapter, we won't see all the cases listed in (24) - we'll only see the case where this 3 subject prefix is either preceded by an object prefix, or else is not preceded by any other prefix. In Chapter 19, we'll see examples where there's an outer prefix or **da** in front of this 3 person prefix. The case where this 3 person subject prefix is preceded by an inner prefix is not very common, so you can probably leave that row out of your study of (24) until later.

In the case of the 3 subject prefix being preceded by the distributive plural prefix **da**, there seems to be some variation. The charts in YM 92 suggest that **í** is preferred to zero as the 3 subject prefix in this case.

When the 3 subject prefix is preceded by an object prefix, the form of the subject prefix is **í**. As shown in parentheses, if the object that precedes this **í** is **hw**, the combination of **hw** and **í** comes out as **hó**. We'll add this fact to Rule Conj-6 (as shown in the Appendix.)

There is something else to learn about the n-P. You may remember that in Chapter 9 we came upon the fact that, sometimes, in the y-P conjugation, if the distributive plural prefix **da** is used, the conjugation switches to s-P, especially if the subject is 3 person. Well, in the case of the n-P conjugation, this can happen, too. In fact, if the classifier is plain-l or d, we just about always switch to the s-P if the subject is 3 person. If the classifier is zero or barred-l, we can say at least that this switch is common if the subject is 3 person.

Let's look at some real verbs using these new conjugation patterns. We can do this by learning a new vocabulary principle:

Vocabulary-5: If you have a verb theme whose meaning involves motion, you can build a verb base whose meaning expresses the arrival at the end of the motion by doing the following:

Stem-set: use the momentaneous stem-set of the verb theme	Classifier: use the classifier of the verb theme
	Lexical prefixes: (none)
	Transitivity: use the transitivity of the verb theme
	Conjugation: n-I, n-P

In Vocabulary-5, for the first time, we are talking about verb bases where we have to say something about a conjugation pattern for one of the modes other than the P mode. To do this, we changed the name of the "Perfective" entry: rather than calling it "Perfective", we called it "Conjugation". In fact, it is a good idea to decide that this entry for any verb base should be called "Conjugation" rather than "Perfective". The reason is that there are a number of verb bases where we have to say more about the way the verb is conjugated than just giving its perfective mode conjugation. For most verb bases, we won't have to do this: the only thing that the "Conjugation" slot will contain will be a note that the verb base is conjugated in the y-P or s-P conjugations, just as we've seen all along. (The other modes for such verb bases are all conjugated in the regular conjugation for those modes.) But for the verb bases created by Vocabulary-5, we need to note that both the I mode and the P mode have special conjugations. In Chapter 20 we'll learn about other verb bases where we have to say something about the conjugation of modes other than the P mode. So, for most verb bases, there is no real change here - we're only changing the name of that last box in our verb base charts - but for a smaller group of verb bases, there will be more information in that last box than just information about the P mode. And remember the following general convention: when a mode is not listed in the "Conjugation" slot, then use the regular conjugation for that mode.

Here's something interesting: if you compare Vocabulary-3 with Vocabulary-5, you'll see that they create verb bases that are the same except for the conjugation pattern in the I and P modes. This means that the words built from completive verb bases in the modes other than I and P (for example, the F mode) are automatically also going to be words that could have been built from the verb bases created by Vocabulary-5. We'll see an example in just a moment.

The meanings of the verb bases created by Vocabulary-5 always have to do with arrival at the end point of the motion. To see how this actually works out, let's look at some examples.

We'll start with the verb themes that mean just plain "go". These themes are given in Chapter 17(23), Chapter 17(24), and Chapter 17(25). Using Vocabulary-5, we create the following verb bases:

(25)

Stem-set		Classifier: zero
I:	**-ááh**	Lexical prefixes: (none)
P:	**yá**	
F:	**-ááł**	Transitivity: intransitive
R:	**-ááh**	
O:	**-a'**	Conjugation: n-I, n-P

(26)

Stem-set		Classifier: zero
I:	**'aash**	Lexical prefixes: (none)
P:	**'áázh**	
F:	**'ash**	Transitivity: intransitive
R:	**'ash**	
O:	**'aash**	Conjugation: n-I, n-P

(27)

Stem-set		Classifier: d
I:	**kááh**	Lexical prefixes: (none)
P:	**kai**	
F:	**kah**	Transitivity: intransitive
R:	**kah**	
O:	**kááh**	Conjugation: n-I, n-P

(Of course, (25) is used when one person is going, (26) is used when two people are going, and (27) is used when more than two people are going.)

Before talking about the meaning of these three verb bases, let's look at the forms. Again, since these verbs are so common, we'll write out all the forms for the three modes that we've learned so far. The forms we get from the verb base in (25) are:

(28)	I	P	F
1sg	nishááh	níyá	deesháál
2sg	nínááh	yíníyá	díínááł
3(sg)	yíghááh	níyá	doogááł
4(sg)	jíghááh	jiníyá	jidoogááł

228

Note first that the forms in the F column of (28) are exactly the same as the forms in the F column of (4) above. (The verb base in (25) is different from the verb base in (1) only in the way the verb is conjugated in the I and P modes.)

Next, in the I mode, the alternate forms of the stem follow the usual pattern of irregularities for the singular go-verbs. But you should compare the I mode forms here in (28) with the I mode forms in (4). The 1sg form is different in that, in the n-I, there is an **ni** at the beginning (the regular I just has the **yi** supplied by the peg rule.) In the 2sg, 3, and 4 forms, the only difference is a difference of tone: in the regular I mode forms the first syllable has low tone, whereas in the n-I forms the first syllable has high tone.

Make sure you understand how the I mode forms in (28) were built. The 1sg and 2sg forms are easy: just use the subject prefix listed in (21) with the appropriate form of the stem. For the 3(sg) form, we used the subject prefix listed in (24) for the case "no prefix at all" (meaning, no prefix precedes the 3 subject prefix) - this prefix is **yí**. For the 4(sg) form, we used the subject prefix listed in (24) for the case "object prefix" (meaning, an object prefix precedes the 3 subject prefix) - this prefix is just **í**. The object prefix in **jígháah** is, of course, **j**.

The P mode forms are straightforward. They use the subject prefixes in (22), with no special problems involved. Even so, it's a good idea to compare the P mode forms in (28) with the P mode forms in (4). Note, for example, that the 2sg forms are the same (the n-P 2sg subject prefix is the same as the y-P 2sg subject prefix, as we mentioned earlier.) For the other forms, there are those **n**'s in the n-P forms.

Here are the verbs built from the verb base in (26):

(29)	I	P	F
1dpl	niit'aash	niit'áázh	diit'ash
2dpl	noh'aash	noo'áázh	dooh'ash
3(dpl)	yí'aash	ní'áázh	doo'ash
4(dpl)	jí'aash	jiní'áázh	jidoo'ash

Again, the F mode forms of (29) are the same as the F mode forms in (5). In the I mode, the 1dpl and 2dpl forms in (29) have those **n**'s at the beginning, and the 3 and 4 forms differ from the 3 and 4 forms in (5) only in the tone of the first syllable. As in the case of the singular go-verb, the **yí** of **yí'aash** is the form of the 3 person subject prefix supplied by (24) for the case that this prefix is not preceded by anything else, and the **í** following the **j** in **jí'aash** is the form of the 3 person subject prefix supplied by (24) for the case that this prefix is preceded by an object prefix (**j**, in this word.)

The verbs built from (27) are as follows:

(30)   I   P   F

	I	P	F
1dpl	niikááh	niikai	diikah
2dpl	nohkááh	noohkai	doohkah
3(dpl)	yíkááh	yíkai	dookah
4(dpl)	jíkááh	jíkai	jidookah

Comparing these with the words in (6), we see that the F forms are the same, and the I forms in (30) have extra **n**'s in the front for the 1dpl and 2dpl forms, and high tones on the first syllables of the 3 and 4 forms. The 3 and 4 person subject forms of the P mode in (30) illustrate the fact that the 3 person subject prefix in the n-P conjugation is the same as the 3 person subject prefix in the n-I conjugation if the classifier is plain-l or d. A result of this is that the n-P form **yíkai** differs from the y-P form **yikai** only in the tone of the first syllable.

We still haven't said much about the meaning of the verb bases created by Vocabulary-5, but now that we have some actual words, we can illustrate the meaning a little. The verbs in (28), (29), and (30) can be used with expressions of location to mean something like "arrive at ..." or "get to ...". So, for example, we can say:

(31)   Shimásání baghandi níyá. "I got to my grandmother's house."

(32)   Bill dóó Sally Tségháhoodzánídi ní'áázh. "Bill and Sally got to Window Rock."

The F mode forms in (28), (29), and (30) can be used with this meaning too:

(33)   Yiską́ą́go áadi diikah. "We'll get there tomorrow."

The place words in (31), (32), and (33) end in the suffix **-di**, a suffix which indicates location, rather than, for example, **-góó**, which would indicate real motion. These verbs can be used with motion expressions that end in **-góó**, too:

(34)   Kóhoot'éédą́ą́' Hoozdogóó niikai. "Last year, we went to Phoenix."

In (34), there is more of a sense of motion. But a sentence like (34), and also sentences (31), (32), and (33), involve one-way motion. Compare these sentences with the sentence in Chapter 17(19), where **-góó** is used with a round-trip motion verb. Sentence (34), for example, might be used to introduce some statements about what we did in Phoenix when we got there. On the other hand, the sentence in Chapter 17(19) refers to the whole trip.

And don't forget that the verb in Chapter 17(19) was built using Vocabulary-1, so it has the atelic outer prefix **na**, it uses a continuative verb-stem, and in the P mode it's conjugated in the s-P. The verbs in (31), (32), (33), and (34) here have no lexical prefixes, they use momentaneous verb-stems, and in the P mode they're conjugated in the n-P.

Here's something interesting: the verbs in (28), (29), and (30) can be used without any actual expression of location, as in:

(35)   Bill níyá.

If this is done, a very common meaning is that the place where Bill ended up is: here. In other words, (35) means something like "Bill got here", or "Bill has come". This points up another difference between Navajo and English. In English, a distinction is made between the verb **go** and the verb **come**: we use the verb **come** in English instead of **go** if the end point of the motion is near the speaker, or is a location that the speaker identifies with. This particular distinction does not exist in Navajo - "go" and "come" are expressed using the same verbs.

Here is a usage that it's good to learn about here. Suppose we use Vocabulary-5 to build a verb base that expresses arrival or end-point of motion. Sometimes, we want to identify the end point of the motion by means of a human being, that is, by saying that the person or thing that moved ended up at the place where some person is. To express this, we combine the verbs with the postposition **baa**. Here, the **b** refers to the human being who is located at the place where the motion ended, the person who defines the end of the motion. In the case of the go-verbs, combining the verb with **baa** gives a meaning somewhat like: "go to see". An example:

(36)   Shaa yíkai. "They came to see me."

Sentence (36) also illustrates that the person represented in the postposition in this construction doesn't necessarily have to be 3 person - that person can be anybody. (And don't forget: if the person is 3 person, use **yaa** instead of **baa** if the subject of the verb is 3 person.)

We can use Vocabulary-5 with motion verb themes other than "go", of course. If we use it with "crawl", for example, we can say things like:

(37)   Ed baa nish'na'.

which means something like "I crawled over to Ed." Note how we're using the postposition **baa** here because we're defining the end of the motion by means of a human being: the place where I ended up after my crawl is the place where Ed is.

What about the word **nish'na'** in (37)? We simply conjugated "crawl" in the P mode using the n-P conjugation. Since the classifier is d (look at the verb theme in Chapter 17(38)), we used the 1sg subject prefix from the chart in (23).

Vocabulary-5 can be used with transitive verb themes, too. For example, we can say things like:

231

(38)   Łééchąą yázhí shimásání baghandi níłtį́.

This means something like "I took the puppy to my grandmother's house." Here are two things to notice about (38).

First, since the thing that got taken is an animate entity (in this case, an animal), we used the verb theme in Chapter 17(22). This is one of the classificatory verb themes - it's the one used when the thing that is moved is a person or animal.

Second, (38) talks about a one-way motion. It expresses the idea that the puppy ended up at my grandmother's house. I might want to use a sentence like (38) if I'm going to continue talking about things having to do with the puppy being at my grandmother's house, for example, if I go on to say that I showed her the puppy, or that she played with him. This should be compared with sentences like the one in Chapter 17(21), which express round-trip motion. You should make sure you understand the differences between the way the verb in Chapter 17(21) is built (using Vocabulary-1, so it has the atelic outer prefix **na**, a continuative verb-stem, and it's conjugated in the s-P, since the mode is P), and the way the verb in (38) is build (using Vocabulary-5, so it has no lexical prefixes, it uses momentaneous verb-stems, and the P mode is conjugated in the n-P.)

Here's something quite important that you definitely want to remember: if we apply Vocabulary-5 to a transitive classificatory verb stem, and if we use the postposition **baa** (or any other form of this postposition), the meaning usually corresponds to the English verb "give". For example:

(39)   Ed tł'óół naa yinílá. "Ed gave you (sg) the rope."

(40)   Mósí shaa níłteeh. "Give me the cat."

The choice of classificatory verb theme depends on what kind of thing is being given, and the object of **baa** (the pronoun prefix in this word) is the person to whom that thing is being given.

Incidentally, sentence (40) illustrates something we've never mentioned but that you've probably noticed long ago. To express an imperative (that is, a command or a request), use the I mode with a 2 person prefix. Of course, sentence (40) could also mean something like "You're giving me a cat", but the imperative meaning is common. You may also have noticed that the F mode can be used this way, too, especially if the request is for an action somewhat in the future. Here's something easy: in Navajo, there is no special imperative form (so we won't have to learn one!)

Earlier, we mentioned that when verbs are used together with other words in combinations with special meanings, those other words are sometimes pronounced almost like prefixes attached to the verbs. In the case of the "give" combinations, the postposition **baa** (or **shaa** or **naa** or **yaa** or whatever) is sometimes pronounced this way. This can lead to changes in the pronunciation. For example, when the verb begins with a **y**, the vowel of the postposition can coalesce with the **y** and we get something like **ei**. So, (39) is often pronounced as though it were written:

(41)   Ed tł'óół neinílá.

Something we should remember: in English, we normally wouldn't call **give** a verb of motion. But in Navajo, the most normal way of expression the idea of giving is by applying Vocabulary-5 to a transitive classificatory verb theme and expressing the person being given to by means of the postposition **baa**. This illustrates how two languages sometimes express the same thing using extremely different kinds of structures.

What if we apply Vocabulary-5 to a transitive verb theme of motion that isn't a classificatory verb theme? Well, let's try it with the verb theme in (16) above. We can say things like:

(42)   Yas shaa nííłmáás. "Roll the snowball over to me"

If you wanted to say that (42) involves a notion of giving, you could think of it as having a meaning like "give me the snowball by means of an action that involves rolling it".

(You may have noticed that, literally, (42) says something like "Roll the snow over to me". How do we know that we're talking about a snowball? Well, we're guessing that we are, since the snow is getting rolled!)

Well, this is enough about Vocabulary-5 for now. You should keep in mind, though, that the verb bases created by Vocabulary-5 will reappear in more combinations. Just as Vocabulary-4 used the verb bases created by Vocabulary-3 as "input", there will be further vocabulary principles that will use the verb bases created by Vocabulary-5 as input - these verb bases will be the foundation for other verb bases or expressions. In fact, you might want to start making your own list of combinations that use the verb bases created by Vocabulary-3 and Vocabulary-5 - there are quite a few verbs of motion that you can learn to build this way.

A note on terminology: In YM 87, but <u>not</u> in YMM 92, the term *terminative* is used as a name for the verb bases created by Vocabulary-5. (In YMM 92, it seems that there is no special name for this particular group of verb bases, and the word *terminative* is used for a different group of verb bases.)

Since we've been talking about the n-I and n-P conjugations, there is a detail that we should add here, for completeness. Back in Chapter 15 we learned about unspec-hopping: if the unspec prefix ' is right in front of a consonant C_1, then it will hop to the right and place itself in front of another consonant C_2 if C_2 starts a conjunct prefix. It happens that this hopping will also take place if C_2 is the **n** that starts a subject prefix (if this **n** also starts a syllable of its own.) Since there are a bunch of subject prefixes like this in the n-I and n-P conjugations, we'll find that unspec-hopping can move the unspec prefix and attach it just to the left of the **n**'s at the beginning of these prefixes. But we won't illustrate this here (we need a fairly big verb for this to happen) - we'll give an example at the end of our study, in Chapter 27. (Incidentally, the unspec prefix usually does not hop to the **n** in the middle of the 2sg P mode prefixes, although one or two charts in YM 87 suggest that there may be some variation here.)

Before taking a break, here's something to think about. The n-I and n-P conjugations involve (usually) putting an **n** into the verb. Will you be able to tell the difference between this **n** and the **n** that is part of the outer prefix **na**? Here are some differences between them that will help you know, if you see an **n** in the verb somewhere before the verb stem, whether it's the **n** of the n-I or n-P conjugation or the **n** of **na**.

If the syllable that starts with the **n** is the pre-stem syllable, then the outer prefix **na** will either show up as **naa** (as in words like **naashné** or **naané**), or else the **a** of **na** will coalesce with another vowel, and you'll see things like **nei** or **neii** or **nao** (think of words like **neilé, neii'né, naohné**.) But if you look at (21), (22), and (23), you'll see that the **n** of the n-I and n-P conjugations is followed directly by **i** or **ii** or **o** or **oo**. In fact, you should note that the **n** of these conjugations (at the beginning of the subject prefixes) always starts the pre-stem syllable. So, for example, you might see **ni**... as the pre-stem syllable if the word is being conjugated in the n-I or n-P, but this cannot happen if the **n** is from **na**. It's true that **na** sometimes turns into **ni**, but if you check Rule Disj-3, you'll see that this cannot happen if the **na** syllable is the pre-stem syllable.

The **j** that indicates 4 person subject has to come before the **n** of the n-I or n-P conjugations, but after the **n** of **na**. The same is true of the **da** prefix that indicates distributive plural.

Actually, it's not all that difficult to tell **na** and the **n** of the n-I or n-P forms apart. Unfortunately, we are going to learn about some more n's in Chapter 21, so the issue will get a little harder. It will help later on if you learn the n-I and n-P forms very well not only so that you'll recognize these forms, but also so that you'll be able to tell when you're looking at something different.

Now, take a short break, and we'll see you in Chapter 19!

CHAPTER 19

MORE OUTER PREFIXES
AND MORE MOTION

In this chapter, we're going to look at two outer prefixes that are important in the world of motion verbs. One of these outer prefixes has quite a few special forms that we need to learn, so we will spend some time on it. Let's start with that one: its basic form is **'a**.

The important thing to notice about **'a** is that it begins with a glottal stop. Why is this important?

Well, for one thing, there is the matter of spelling: whenever this prefix is at the very beginning of a verb (which will happen quite often), we won't actually write the glottal stop. Instead, we'll spell the word starting with the first vowel. Remember, in Navajo, words never really begin with vowels, even if they're written that way. If you see a word that's written starting with a vowel, there's really a glottal stop there in front of that vowel. However, when we mention this prefix all by itself in this chapter, we'll always write in the glottal stop, to remind us that it's there.

Next, remember that we've already seen a prefix involving a glottal stop - the unspec object prefix. (In fact, that prefix consists entirely of just the glottal stop.) One potential problem for us is that we might confuse the unspec prefix and the new **'a** prefix that we're studying here. We'll see later that much of the time we won't have any difficulty telling them apart. But if we think back, we'll remember that the unspec prefix has a lot of special properties compared with other object prefixes (look at Rule Conj-5.) These special properties are really due to the glottal stop, so we won't be surprised to learn that **'a** will have quite a few special properties, too.

Before getting to this, let's say something about the meaning of **'a**. With motion verb themes, **'a** will add a meaning that is similar to the meaning of the English word **off** as it's used in sentences like "John went off to Phoenix" or "Karen took the baby off to the doctor's". (Meanings like this can sometimes also be expressed in English using **away** instead of **off**: "John went away to Phoenix", "Karen took the baby away to the doctor's".) The prefix **'a** can sometimes be used with non-motion verbs also. In such cases, the meaning usually involves something disappearing or "going off" somewhere, even if the meaning of the verb as a whole isn't a motion meaning.

In a little bit, we'll write up a vocabulary principle that makes use of this **'a** prefix for motion verbs. But first, let's get to work and learn the forms of the **'a** prefix. Since there are so many special facts we need to learn about **'a**, we're going to write up a special rule, which we'll call Rule Disj-4, just for this one prefix. Rule Disj-4 will have a number of different clauses in it. Each one will deal with a particular situation - it'll say what form **'a** takes when it's in that situation. The actual situations involved will be, mostly, familiar to us. However, there are an annoyingly large number of these situations that we'll have to list, so, to make it all easier to learn, we'll write up the statement of each clause of Rule Disj-4 separately and then discuss it. All the clauses of the rule can be found collected together in the Appendix. For any situation not covered by one of the clauses of Rule Disj-4, the form of the prefix will be just **'a**.

The first clause deals with the same situation as Rule Disj-1:

<u>Rule Disj-4(a)</u>: Whenever **'a** is followed by a consonant and the syllable **'a** would be the pre-stem syllable, change **'a** into **'ii**.

To illustrate this, we need a verb base with **'a** in it. Rather than giving one (we'll soon learn a vocabulary principle that will create many of these for us), let's just trust that we can use **'a** with a momentaneous motion verb stem. If we want to build an I mode form that means something like "I'm going off", we could create this structure:

(1) outer   subject   verb
     prefix   prefix   stem

       'a   -   sh   -   -ááh

The form of the verb stem after the 1sg subject prefix **sh** is just **ááh** (see Chapter 17(6)). In this word, **'a** is followed by a consonant (**sh**), and the next syllable is the verb-stem syllable, so, by Rule Disj-4(a), **'a** becomes **'ii**. The actual word is therefore: **iisháah**, with **'ii** as the pre-stem syllable.

The next clause of Rule Disj-4 deals with almost the same situations as Rule Disj-2:

<u>Rule Disj-4(b)</u>: If **'a** is followed by **ii** or **o** or **oo**, then **'a** becomes just **'**.

We can see this if we build, for example, the following I mode form, which could mean "We (two) are going off":

(2) outer   subject   verb
     prefix   prefix   stem

       'a   -   iid   -   'aash

In (2), **'a** is followed by **ii**, so Rule Disj-4(b) applies, and **'a** just becomes **'**. After applying d-effect to the **'** of **'aash** (Rule Subj-1), we get as our word: **iit'aash**.

Rule Disj-2 also talks about what happens if a disjunct prefix is followed by a short **i**. One common situation where this occurs is that the 3 person object prefix **y** follows the disjunct prefix (see Rule Conj-2.) If we're looking at **'a**, this case is covered by a separate clause of Rule Disj-4, our third clause, in fact:

<u>Rule Disj-4(c)</u>: If **'a** is followed by the 3 person object prefix **y** and this **y** is followed directly by a consonant (so that Rule Conj-2 would normally turn the **y** into **i**), the combination of **'a** and **y** becomes **'ii**.

To illustrate this, we'll need a transitive verb. Suppose we believe that we can use **'a** with a momentaneous classificatory verb stem to create a meaning like "carry it off/away". We could form an I mode word that should mean, say, "he/she/they (two) is/are carrying it off", like this (we'll use the ropelike verb theme, since we know it):

(3) outer   object   subject   verb
     prefix   prefix   prefix   stem

     'a   -   y   -   (zero) - lé

In (3), the 3 person object prefix **y** is followed directly by a consonant (the **l** of **lé**). Since it is also preceded by the vowel (the **a** at the end of **'a**), we'd expect Rule Conj-2 to change **y** into **i**. But **y** is preceded by the special outer prefix **'a**, which has its own rule, namely Rule Disj-4, so we check Rule Disj-4 and find that part (c) tells us that **'a** and **y** together become **'ii**. Since no other rules apply, the word we get is: **iilé**.

There is another group of cases we have to consider: in the y-P conjugation, some of the subject prefixes that are used when preceded by a disjunct prefix start with the special symbol v́v́ or v́ or vv. Now, since **'a** is an outer prefix, it's a disjunct prefix, so we'll have cases where **'a** is followed by such symbols. When we learned about these (back in Chapters 9 and 10), we explained how they work. But with the prefix **'a**, something special again happens. We'll put this information into part (d) of our new rule:

<u>Rule Disj-4(d)</u>: In the y-P conjugation, the following special changes occur:

If **'a** is followed directly by v́v́, the result is **'íí**.

If **'a** is followed directly by v́íní, the result is **'ííní**.

If **'a** is followed directly by vv, the result is **'ee**.

You might have noticed that the first two changes described above in Rule Disj-4(d) will happen automatically if you pretend that, in the y-P conjugation, the prefix **'a** somehow changes to **'i**. In fact, the same is true of Rule Disj-4(c): if **'a** were to change into **'i** before the 3 person object prefix **y** and **y** is followed by a consonant, then if Rule Conj-2 applied normally we'd end up with the **'ii** that Rule Disj-4(c) says we should get. Rule Disj-4(a) also seems to suggest that **'a** is behaving as though it were **'i**. The third part of Rule Disj-4(d) is still strange, but if you recall that a high-tone **í** sometimes changes to **é** (see Rule Disj-1), you can perhaps believe that the **'ee** we get in the third part of Rule

Disj-4(d) came from 'i also. These facts taken together suggest that maybe we should say that the basic form of the prefix we're studying is 'i rather than 'a, and that 'i turns into 'a in some cases. There is nothing wrong with doing it that way, but by doing it the way we did we can discuss this prefix using the same conditions that we've been discussing for all the other outer prefixes. (If we say that the prefix is basically 'i and that 'i turns into 'a sometimes, we'd end up having to say something like "the prefix 'i becomes 'a when the conditions of Rule Disj-1 and Rule Disj-2 aren't present.) Still, thinking about this prefix as though it were 'i in some cases may help you to remember its forms. On the other hand, you might find it easier just to memorize the forms given in the various parts of Rule Disj-4 rather than playing this game.

To illustrate Rule Disj-4(d), we may as well write out an entire y-P conjugation of some verb base. So, let's give our vocabulary principle for motion verbs right now and get all the verb bases we need.

Vocabulary-6: If you have a verb theme whose meaning involves motion, you can build a verb base where the meaning involves motion "off" or "away" by doing the following:

Stem-set: use the momentaneous stem-set of the verb theme	Classifier: use the classifier of the verb theme
	Lexical prefixes: 'a (outer)
	Transitivity: use the transitivity of the verb theme
	Conjugation: y-P

(Another way of thinking of this is: start with the completive verb base built from the verb theme, and then add in the outer prefix 'a as a lexical prefix.)

The word we analyzed in (1) above is therefore one of the verbs built using the verb base that Vocabulary-6 creates from the verb theme in Chapter 17(23). What is this verb base? Here it is:

(4)

Stem-set		Classifier: zero
I:	-ááh	Lexical prefixes: 'a (outer)
P:	yá	
F:	-áát	Transitivity: intransitive
R:	-ááh	
O:	-a'	Conjugation: y-P

Since we've got this verb base, let's write out its I, P, and F mode forms.

But wait: are there any more clauses of Rule Disj-4 that we'll need before we do this? No! It turns out that there really is another clause in Rule Disj-4, but that clause refers specifically to one special situation that we don't run into with this verb base. That situation is the case where **'a** is followed directly by the unspec object prefix. We'll learn that clause a little later on, but first let's do some go-verbs. We can build all the verbs that the verb base in (4) gives us just using the parts of Rule Disj-4 that we've learned. Here they are:

(5)

	I	P	F
1sg	iisháád	ííyá	adeesháá̜ł
2sg	anináád	ííníyá	adíínáá̜ł
3(sg)	iigháád	ííyá	adoogáá̜ł
4(sg)	ajigháád	ajííyá	azhdoogáá̜ł

We already studied the word **iisháád**; the word **iigháád** is similar.

The words **ííyá** and **ííníyá** illustrate the cases of Rule Disj-4(d) where **'a** is followed by v́v́ and by **víní**.

For all of the other words in (5), none of the clauses of Rule Disj-4 apply, so the prefix appears in its original form **'a**. Make sure you understand that for each form in (5) that begins with **a** (which is really **'a**, of course), the **'a** is followed by a consonant (so clauses (b) and (d) do not apply), the **'a** is not followed by a 3 person object prefix (so clause (c) doesn't apply), and the next syllable is not the verb stem syllable (so clause (a) doesn't apply.)

Since the go-verbs are so important, let's write out the forms of the dual and plural go-verbs that are built using the verb bases created by Vocabulary-6. For the dual go-verb, this verb base is:

(6)

Stem-set		Classifier: zero
I:	**'aash**	
P:	**'áázh**	Lexical prefixes: **'a** (outer)
F:	**'ash**	
R:	**'ash**	Transitivity: intransitive
O:	**'aash**	Conjugation: y-P

and its forms are:

(7)	I	P	F
1dpl	iit'aash	iit'áázh	adiit'ash
2dpl	oh'aash	oo'áázh	adooh'ash
3(dpl)	ii'aash	íí'áázh	adoo'ash
4(dpl)	aji'aash	ajíí'áázh	azhdoo'ash

Clause (b) of Rule Disj-4 operated in the case of the words **iit'aash**, **iit'áázh**, **oh'aash**, and **oo'áázh**, where the **'a** prefix is followed immediately either by the **ii** of the 1dpl subject prefix **iid** (in I and P) or by the **o** of the I mode 2dpl subject prefix **oh** or by the **oo** which is the y-P 2dpl subject prefix. Clause (a) is responsible for the **ii** in **ii'aash** ('a is followed by the consonant ', and the next syllable is the verb-stem syllable, so **'a** becomes **'ii**). Clause (d) applied in the case of **íí'áázh** ('a is followed by the 3 person y-P subject prefix **v́v́** in this word.) In the case of the remaining words in (7), none of the clauses of Rule Disj-4 applied so the prefix appears in its basic form **'a**.

The plural verb base created for "go" by Vocabulary-6 is:

(8)

Stem-set		Classifier: d
I:	**kááh**	
P:	**kai**	Lexical prefixes: **'a** (outer)
F:	**kah**	Transitivity: intransitive
R:	**kah**	
O:	**kááh**	Conjugation: y-P

and the words built from (8) are:

(9)	I	P	F
1dpl	iikááh	iikai	adiikah
2dpl	ohkááh	oohkai	adoohkah
3(dpl)	iikááh	eekai	adookah
4(dpl)	ajikááh	ajookai	azhdookah

Do you understand how the word **eekai** "they went off" is built? Its structure is:

(10) outer   subject   cl   verb
      prefix   prefix   stem

      'a   -   vv   -   d   -   kai

240

The subject prefix **vv** is the 3 person subject prefix for the y-P conjugation, plain-l or d classifier, when preceded by a disjunct prefix (see the chart in Chapter 10(1).) According to Rule Disj-4(d), **'a** combined with this **vv** gives **'ee**. This is how we get **eekai**.

(Review question: Where did the **oo** of **ajookai** come from? Answer: Look at the chart in Chapter 10(4). Remember: **j** is a conjunct prefix.)

We have given examples that illustrate clauses (a), (b), (c), and (d) of Rule Disj-4. There is one more clause which we need to add to this rule. This clause tells what happens if the **'a** prefix is followed immediately by the unspec object prefix. This combination is not particularly common, but it's not all that rare, either, and since we've already learned about the unspec object prefix, we may as well complete our knowledge of **'a** by learning this fifth clause now. On the other hand, the story here is a little complicated, so if you want, you can skip this section (go directly down to the discussion of Vocabulary-7 below) and come back to it later.

When the **'a** prefix is followed immediately by the unspec object prefix, we need to divide up our rule into sub-clauses that have to do with different situations that the unspec object prefix finds itself in. Take a deep breath, and here we go:

Rule Disj-4(e): If **'a** is followed immediately by the unspec object prefix, then:

(i) If Rule Conj-5 would insert **a** after the unspec object prefix **'**, the resulting combination **'a'a** changes to **'e'e**.

(ii) If the unspec object prefix **'** is followed by a consonant C and Rule Conj-5 would not insert any vowel after **'**, then **'a'C** changes to **'i'C**.

(iii) If the unspec object prefix **'** is in the kind of position where Rule Conj-5 would create the combination **zh'C** (where C is a consonant), then **'azh'C** changes to **'izh'C**.

(iv) If the unspec object prefix **'** is followed directly by a 2sg subject prefix **ni** so that Rule Conj-3 applies, then the resulting combination **'a'í** becomes **'i'í**.

(v) If the unspec object prefix **'** is followed by a (long or short) vowel (of either high or low tone), then **'a'** becomes **'v'**, where v is the vowel that follows the unspec object prefix; in other words, the vowel that follows the unspec **'** substitutes for the **a** of **'a**. However, the syllable **'v** (that **'a** turned into) always has a short vowel and low tone. (Here's a simpler way of saying this: if **'a'** is followed by a vowel, the **a** is changed to match that vowel.)

(Whew!)

But this is not quite as bad as it seems.

First of all, if you think about it, part (i) of Rule Disj-4(e) only applies if the syllable started by the unspec object prefix is the verb-stem syllable. Why? Because according to Rule Conj-5, if the next syllable is not the verb-stem syllable, and the unspec object prefix is preceded by a vowel (which it is in this case, since the preceding prefix is the **'a** prefix), then Rule Conj-5 doesn't insert that **a**, so part (i) above wouldn't apply. This means that we can remember part (i) as follows: if the combination of the **'a** prefix and the unspec object prefix is immediately in front of the verb-stem syllable (so that the syllable starting with the unspec object prefix would be the pre-stem syllable), then what we get is **'e'e**. This might be easier than the way we phrased it above, so in the Appendix we'll add this statement in as well.

Next, parts (ii) and (iii) go together: **'a** becomes **'i** whenever the unspec object prefix that follows it doesn't have a vowel after it. Part (iv) could be considered another case like this (if you think about the **n** of **ni** as though it were still there), or else you could think of part (iv) as a special case of part (v) because the **í** vowel after the unspec object prefix is "echoed in advance" by the first **i** in the combination **'i'í**.

Let's look at an example to see these effects. The following verb base is not a motion verb, but it will be a handy verb to provide us with examples of various effects described in Rule Disj-4(e). This verb base means "have a bite to eat" - its literal construction suggests a meaning like "swallow (something unspecified) away":

(11)

Stem-set		Classifier: barred-l
I:	**neeh**	
P:	**na'**	Lexical prefixes: **'a** (outer), **'** (object)
F:	**nah**	Transitivity: intransitive
R:	**nah**	
O:	**neeh**	Conjugation: y-P

Can you use the various clauses of Rule Disj-4, especially Rule Disj-4(e), to write out the I, P, and F mode forms of this verb base?

For the I mode, we have the following forms:

(12)	sg	dpl	distr dpl
1	e'eshneeh	i'iilneeh	ada'iilneeh
2	i'iłneeh	o'ołneeh	ada'ołneeh
3		e'ełneeh	ada'ałneeh
4		i'jiłneeh	ada'jiłneeh

Let's analyze a few of these words to make sure we understand what's going on.

First, the word "I'm having a bite" is structured like this:

(13) outer   object   subject   cl   verb
      prefix   prefix   prefix   stem

      'a   -   '   -   sh   -   ł   -   neeh

Since the unspec object prefix ' is followed by a consonant (**sh**), and since the next syllable is the verb-stem syllable, Rule Conj-5 would insert an **a** after the unspec '. This would create **'a'a** at the beginning of this word - but Rule Disj-4(e) part (i) says that in exactly this circumstance, we get **'e'e** instead.   As we pointed out, another way to say this is that the syllable which follows the combination of the **'a** prefix and the unspec object prefix is the verb-stem syllable in this word, so that combination has to become **'e'e**.   Either way, this, together with the sandwich rule, gives us **e'eshneeh** from (13).

The structure of the word **e'ełneeh** "he/she/they (two) is/are having a bite" is similar - for practice, write out a description of how this word is built.

Next, let's look at "you (sg) are having a bite". Here is the structure of this word:

(14) outer   object   subject   cl   verb
      prefix   prefix   prefix   stem

      'a   -   '   -   ni   -   ł   -   neeh

Rule Conj-3 applies here to change **'ni** into **'í**. Rule Disj-4(e) part (iv) then says that the **'a'í** that results from this becomes **'i'í**. Since none of our other rules apply, the word ends up as **'i'íłneeh**.

The word that means "one is having a bite" has the structure:

(15) outer   object   subject   cl   verb
      prefix   prefix   prefix   stem

      'a   -   '   -   j   -   (zero)   -   ł   -   neeh

Rule Conj-1 applies in the normal way to insert an **i** after the **j**, but no vowel is inserted after the unspec ', since it is preceded by a vowel (the vowel at the end of the outer (disjunct) prefix in front of it) and since the next syllable is not the verb-stem syllable. By Rule Disj-4(e) part (ii), **'a'j** becomes **'i'j**. This gives us the word **i'jiłneeh**.

What about "we (two) are having a bite"? Here is its structure:

(16) outer   object   subject   cl   verb
      prefix   prefix   prefix   stem

       'a   -   '   -   iid   -   ł   -   neeh

In (16), the unspec ' is followed by a vowel, so Rule Disj-4(e) part (v) says that 'a is changed to match that vowel. Since the vowel after unspec ' is ii, the a of 'a is changed to i. This (together with Rule Subj-3) gives us **i'iilneeh**.

We won't write out the structure of **o'ołneeh**, but you should do so for practice. Rule Disj-4(e) part (v) applies in the case of this word, too: the **'a** prefix becomes **'o** to match the **o** that follows the unspec object prefix **'**.

Question: Why doesn't any part of Rule Disj-4(e) apply to the distributive plural forms in (12)? (Answer: the distributive plural prefix **da** comes between the **'a** outer prefix and the unspec object prefix, so the **'a** prefix is not immediately followed by the unspec object prefix.) Make sure that you understand that none of the other clauses of Rule Disj-4 apply to these forms either, so the prefix appears simply in its original **'a** form.

Here's something about the distributive plural forms in (12) that you should notice: when the distributive plural prefix **da** is used, the unspec object prefix follows the **da** (we learned this already, of course), while the new **'a** prefix precedes the **da** (as it should, since its an outer prefix.)

Can you write out the P mode forms of this verb? Here they are:

(17)   sg   dpl   distr dpl

1   i'ííłna'   i'iilna'   ada'iilna'
2   i'ííníłna'   o'oołna'   ada'oołna'
3   i'ííłna'   ada'ííłna'
4   i'jííłna'   ada'jííłna'

In most of the nondistributive forms, the unspec ' is followed by a vowel, so part (v) of Rule Disj-4(e) applies. For example, in the word which means "I had a bite" (and also: "he/she/they (two) had a bite"), which has this structure:

(18) outer   object   subject   cl   verb
      prefix   prefix   prefix   stem

       'a   -   '   -   íí   -   ł   -   na'

the unspec object prefix is followed by **íí**, so **'a** becomes **'i**, which is how we get **i'íítna'**.

(Review question: Why is the subject prefix in (18) **íí**? Answer: we're in the y-P conjugation, the classifier is barred-l, and the subject prefix is preceded by a conjunct prefix (the unspec object prefix), so we take our subject prefixes from the chart in Chapter 9(5).)

The only nondistributive form in (17) which doesn't work like this is the 4 person subject form, where the story is about the same as the corresponding I mode form (which we analyzed in (15) above.) Part (ii) of Rule Disj-4(e) applies in this case.

As in the I mode, the distributive plural forms are easy: the outer prefix **'a** is not followed directly by the unspec object prefix (it's separated from it by the distributive plural prefix **da**), so Rule Disj-4(e) does not apply at all. None of the other clauses of Rule Disj-4 apply either, so **'a** appears as **'a**.

How about the F mode of this verb? The forms are:

(19)	sg	dpl	distr dpl
1	i'deeshnah	i'diilnah	ada'diilnah
2	i'díítnah	i'doołnah	ada'doołnah
3		i'doołnah	ada'doołnah
4		izh'doołnah	adazh'doołnah

Parts (ii) or (iii) of Rule Disj-4(e) apply to the nondistributive forms in (19). For example, the word that means "you (two) will have a bite" is built like this:

(20)	outer prefix	object prefix	F mode d	subject prefix	cl	verb stem
	'a	- '	- d	- ooh	- ł	- nah

Since the unspec object prefix is preceded by a vowel and since the next syllable is not the verb-stem syllable, Rule Conj-5 doesn't insert a vowel after it. This is the condition for part (ii) of Rule Disj-4(e), so **'a** changes to **'i**. With this change (and also Rule Subj-4) we get **i'doołnah**.

(The word that means "he/she/they (two) will have a bite" is also **i'doołnah**, but the structure starts out a little different. For practice, diagram the structure of this word.)

Well, this is all we need to say about the form of **'a**. Let's look at a few more examples. The following vocabulary principle will give us an important group of expressions where we find verbs with this prefix.

<u>Vocabulary-7</u>: If you combine a verb base built by Vocabulary-6 from a verb theme of motion with the word **yah,** you get an expression whose meaning involves motion from the outside to the inside of an enclosure.

For example, if we apply Vocabulary-7 to the I mode 2 person subject forms of the go-verbs created by Vocabulary-6 (shown in (5), (7), and (9) above), we get Navajo expressions that correspond to the English command "come in":

(21)   Yah anináάh.   (to one person)
        Yah oh'aash.   (to two persons)
        Yah ohkááh.   (to more than two persons)

If you do not speak Navajo, you might think that the meanings of the expressions created by Vocabulary-7 is the same as the meanings of the expressions created by Vocabulary-4 back in Chapter 18, but actually, the meanings are not quite the same. As a rough statement of the difference we might say this: the expressions created by Vocabulary-4 involve moving into a "tight" place, whereas the expressions created by Vocabulary-7 involve moving into a relatively large enclosure, such as a house or room. There is also a grammatical difference between these expressions. The word **biih** has a pronoun in it (the **b**, which changes to **y** when the subject of the expression is 3 person) which refers to the thing you end up inside of. However, the word **yah** has no pronoun in it (this word never changes.) Of course, if you want to say where someone ended up when he went into something, that information can be added:

(22)   Ken hooghan góne' yah ííyá. "Ken went into the hogan."

As in the case of the other vocabulary principles that we've studied that have to do with verbs of motion, Vocabulary-7 can be used with any motion verb theme, including transitive ones. We'll give an example involving our familiar "move a ropelike thing" verb theme, but for practice, since the **'a** prefix has so many special forms, let's actually write out the I, P, and F mode conjugations of the verb base that Vocabulary-6 creates from this verb theme. (Write out the structure of this verb base yourself, as an exercise.) Here is the I mode:

(23)   sg   dpl   distr dpl

1	iishłé	iilyé	adeiilyé
2	anilé	ohłé	adaohłé
3		iilé	adeilé
4		ajilé	adajilé

We actually analyzed the word **iilé** already, in (3) above. None of the clauses of Rule Disj-4 apply to **anilé, ajilé,** or the distributive plural forms. Rule Disj-4(a) applies in the case of **iishłé,** and Rule Disj-4(b) applies in the case of **iilyé** and **ohłé.**

(Review question: Why did the **l** become **ł** in some of the words in (23)? Answer: See Chapter 13.)

Next, the P mode:

(24)	sg	dpl	distr dpl
1	íílá	iilyá	adeiilyá
2	íínílá	oolá	adaoolá
3		ayíílá	adeizlá
4		ajíílá	adajizlá

Do you understand that none of the clauses of Rule Disj-4 applies in the case of **ayíílá**? This word is built as follows:

(25)	outer prefix	object prefix	subject prefix	verb stem
	'a	- y	- íí	- lá

The object prefix **y** represents the 3 person object (see Rule Str-1) - remember, this verb is transitive. Since this **y** is a conjunct prefix, the 3 person subject prefix that we use is **íí**.

Now, clause (a) of Rule Disj-4 doesn't apply to (25) since the syllable that immediately follows **'a** is not the verb-stem syllable. Clause (b) doesn't apply since **'a** is not followed by a vowel. Clause (c) doesn't apply since the **y** in (25) is not followed by a consonant (another way of saying it: Rule Conj-2, that might have turned this **y** into **i**, wouldn't apply here). Clause (d) doesn't apply because **'a** is not followed by any of the special v symbols. And clause (e) doesn't apply because **'a** is not followed by the unspec object prefix.

The other forms in (24) are straightforward, and should be easy for you to analyze. Note that we see the shift to the s-P conjugation in the 3 (and 4) person distributive plural forms. There is something we can say about this. First, whenever **'a** is a lexical outer prefix in a verb base, it requires that verb base to take the y-P conjugation in the P mode. This is certainly the case for the verb bases built by Vocabulary-6, but it happens that any verb base that has **'a** as a lexical prefix takes the y-P. Now, we learned back in Chapter 9 that when a verb base has a lexical outer prefix that requires the y-P, we can expect shifting to the s-P in the distributive plural forms, especially for 3 and 4 person subjects. So, the shift that we see in (24) is something we'd expect.

Finally, here are the F mode forms of this verb:

(26)	sg	dpl	distr dpl
1	adeeshłééł	adiilyééł	adadiilyééł
2	adííléél	adoohłééł	adadoohłééł
3		iidoolééł	adeidoolééł
4		azhdoolééł	adazhdoolééł

For all forms in (26) except one, none of the clauses of Rule Disj-4 apply. The one form where this rule does apply is the form that means "he/she/they (two) will take/carry it (something ropelike) away". This word is built like this:

(27)	outer prefix	object prefix	F mode d	subject prefix	verb stem
	'a -	y -	d -	oo -	lééł

Again, the **y** in (27) is the 3 person object prefix required here since the verb is transitive and the subject is 3 person. In this word, this **y** is followed by a consonant and preceded by a vowel, so Rule Conj-5 would turn it into an **i**. In exactly this situation, Rule Disj-4(c) applies to change the **'ai** (or **'ay**) into **'ii**.

Well, these are the forms of this verb. An example showing Vocabulary-7 applied to this verb is:

(28)   Ashkii yázhí tł'iish hooghan góne' yah ayíílá.

This means "The little boy brought (carried) a snake into the hogan."

Before moving on, it might be useful to compare the words in (23), (24), and (26) with words in which the first prefix is the unspec object prefix. We said near the beginning of this chapter that there might be some possibility of confusing the **'a** prefix with the unspec object prefix, since they both have a glottal stop in them. Do these two prefixes create forms that are very different? Let's check this out, mode by mode.

First, look at Chapter 12(7), which shows the I mode forms for "weave", and compare these forms with the ones in (23). The distributive forms are very different: the unspec object prefix follows **da** (in the distributive plural forms of Chapter 12(7) we can see a written ' in there to the right of **da**, so the words have **da'** in them) but outer **'a** precedes **da**, so we get a combination **ada** instead. Among the nondistributive forms, the 1sg and 3 person subject forms are also different: if the prefix is the unspec object, we get words starting with **a**, whereas if the prefix is outer **'a**, the words start with **ii**. And if the subject is 2sg, they are also different: the unspec object prefix gives us words starting with **í**, whereas the outer **'a** prefix gives us words starting with **ani**. However, the remaining nondistributive forms look the same for the two cases. If the subject is 4, they both start with **aji**, if the subject is 1dpl, they both start with **ii**, etc. This means that if you're looking at an I mode form with a 4 person subject that starts with **aji**, or I mode forms with 1dpl or 2dpl subjects that start with **ii** or **o**, you won't automatically know whether the verb has an unspec object prefix or an outer **'a** prefix. To tell which one you've got, you'd have to look at one of the other forms. If you speak Navajo, this is not a problem: just ask yourself how the same verb would go if the subject was "I". If the answer starts out **ash**, then you've got a verb with the unspec object prefix, but if the answer starts out **iish**, then the verb has the outer **'a** prefix. If you don't speak Navajo, you've got a problem. Probably the best thing to do would be to make up two 1sg I mode forms corresponding to these two possibilities and then look them up in YM 87 to see which one you'll find.

(Of course, if you're looking at a verb like this in a text, and the word **yah** is immediately in front of it, that's a good bet that the expression was built by Vocabulary-7, so the verb will have the outer **'a** in it. There are a number of other combinations like this that use the verb bases built by Vocabulary-6, so if you see them, they would also provide a clue that you're looking at the outer **'a**.)

If you want to compare the P mode forms in (24) with words involving the unspec object prefix, you need to look at a different verb than "weave" in Chapter 12 because that verb takes the s-P conjugation. So, take a look at the words in Chapter 16(7), which are P mode forms of "eat". Again, the distributive plural forms of "eat" and of "take it (a ropelike thing) away" are different, because of the different positions of outer **'a** and the unspec **'** with respect to **da**. But the nondistributive forms look mostly the same - only the 3 person word **ayíílá** starts out in a different way from the word "he/she/they (two) ate", which is **ííyą́ą́'**. But this is only due to the fact that **ayíílá** is transitive - if you looked at an intransitive verb, like **ííyá** "he/she went off" (see (5) above), then the verbs start out the same in this case, too. So what does this tell us? If you're looking at a P mode verb that starts out **íí** or **ajíí** or **ii** or **oo**, you cannot tell just from the form of the verb whether it's got outer **'a** or unspec **'** in it as a prefix. If you speak Navajo, all you have to do is create a distributive plural form of the same verb, and you'll see where the prefix is. If it's to the left of **da**, it's outer **'a**, and if it's to the right of **da**, it's the unspec object. But if you don't speak Navajo, you'll have to guess both possibilities and try to find them in the dictionary.

The situation in the F mode is similar to the situation in the P mode. If you compare the words in (26) with the words in Chapter 14(9), you'll see that the distributive plural forms are clearly different, but that the nondistributive forms look the same, except when **'a** is used with a transitive verb and there's that 3 person object prefix **y** in there. The solution is the same: when in doubt, create other forms of the verb, if you can, and if you can't, guess possible forms for the 1sg I mode form and try to find the word in YM 87.

Well, this ends our somewhat long story about the **'a** prefix. Before moving on to our next prefix, though, here's something that might help with a famous irregular verb.

At the end of Chapter 16 we mentioned that the Navajo verb base that means "make it" is quite irregular. If you've learned its forms, you may have noticed that this verb base seems to have an outer prefix with the shape **'á**, that is, an outer prefix that looks the same as the one we've just been studying except that there's a high tone on it. Does this prefix act the same as ordinary **'a**? A good exercise would be to look at the forms of the irregular "make it" verb and see whether the various parts of Disj-4 apply to **'á** as well. Here's what you will find.

Under the conditions of Rule Disj-4(a), **'á** doesn't change - it stays **'á**.

Under the conditions of Rule Disj-4(b), **'á** "transfers" its high tone to the first vowel that follows it. In other words, **'á** followed by **ii** becomes **'íi**, **'á** followed by **o** becomes **'ó**, and **'á** followed by **oo** becomes **'óo**. You might want to compare this with parts (b) and (c) of Rule Disj-2 - the similarity should suggest that the prefix **'á** sometimes acts as though it were **'í** (just as the prefix **'a** sometimes acts as though it were **'i**, as we saw.)

Under the conditions of Rule Disj-4(c), **'á** followed by **y** (when followed by a consonant) becomes **'íi**.

It's not clear what Rule Disj-4(d) should say about **'á** when it is followed by **v́v́**, **v́**, or **vv**, since the subject pronoun prefixes for the "make it" verb are irregular in the P mode (for example, they have low tones).

You cannot use the simple "make it" verb to see what Rule Disj-4(e) would do to **'á**, but more complicated versions of that verb show that Rule Disj-4(e) affects **'á** the same way that it affects **'a**, except that the result has a high tone on it.

There are a few other verb bases that have an outer prefix **'á**, but mostly, for those verb bases, this prefix occurs in a position where none of the parts of Rule Disj-4 would apply, so the prefix actually appears as **'á** in the word.

Well, that's enough about this prefix!

To relax a little, let's look at another (easy!) outer prefix that can be used with motion verbs. This second prefix is used in an arrangement that also involves the n-I and n-P conjugations that we learned last chapter, so it'll provide us with a review of those conjugations. Here is a vocabulary principle:

Vocabulary-8: If you have a verb theme whose meaning involves motion, you can build a verb base where the meaning involves motion out (horizontally) of something by doing the following:

Stem-set: use the momentaneous stem-set of the verb theme	Classifier: use the classifier of the verb theme
	Lexical prefixes: **ch'í** (outer)
	Transitivity: use the transitivity of the verb theme
	Conjugation: n-I, n-P

(Another way of saying this is: take the verb base created by Vocabulary-5 and add in the outer prefix **ch'í** as a lexical prefix.)

So, using this prefix with some of the verb themes that we've looked at, we can create verb bases that mean things like "go out", "crawl out", "take/carry it (an animate thing) out", "take/carry it (a ropelike thing) out", "roll it out", etc. Let's just make sure we know what the actual words look like by taking one verb theme and writing out all the forms for the three modes that we've studied - how about the "move it (an animate being)" theme. The verb base created by Vocabulary-8 will be this one:

(29)

Stem-set:		Classifier: barred-l
I:	**teeh**	
P:	**tį**	Lexical prefixes: **ch'í** (outer)
F:	**tééł**	
R:	**tééh**	Transitivity: transitive
O:	**tééł**	Conjugation: n-I, n-P

What do the I mode forms look like? If you want to try writing them out first, remember, we're using the n-I conjugation! And don't forget the special rule given in Chapter 18(24) for the 3 person subject prefix. You should get something like this:

(30)   sg   dpl   distr dpl

1	ch'íníshteeh	ch'íniilteeh	ch'ídaniilteeh
2	ch'íníłteeh	ch'ínółteeh	ch'ídanołteeh
3	ch'ííłteeh		ch'ídeíłteeh
4	ch'íjíłteeh		ch'ídajíłteeh

Let's note a few things about these words before moving on to the P mode.

First of all, Rule Subj-5 applies in at least one of these forms. Can you see which one or ones?

(Rule Subj-5 would have applied in words like **ch'íníłteeh** and **ch'íjíłteeh** if the **í** in the **ní** or **jí** syllable had started out low tone. However, in the n-I conjugation, this vowel is already high tone.)

Second, let's look at the word that means "he/she/they (two) is/are carrying him/her out", which is built like this:

(31) outer   object   subject   cl   verb
      prefix   prefix   prefix   stem

      ch'í - y - í - ł - teeh

Since the subject and object are both 3 person, we use the object prefix **y**. The subject prefix **í** is chosen from Chapter 18(24), based on the fact that in (31) the subject prefix is preceded by an object prefix. As things stand, none of our rules apply, so we'd get **ch'íyíłteeh**. However, words like this are usually written **ch'ííłteeh**. The issue here is that the y is dropped because it's in between two i's. However, there seems to be some inconsistency in this matter: when an **y** comes between two **i**'s, sometimes the **y** is written, sometimes not. Generally, when the 3 person object prefix **y** comes between two **i**'s, the **y** is dropped. We won't make this an official rule, but you should keep this fact in mind. Later on, we'll run into another (!) prefix which also is just a **y** - and that other **y** is usually not dropped between two **i**'s.

The P mode forms are straightforward:

(32)   sg   dpl   distr dpl

1   ch'íníłtį   ch'íniiltį   ch'ídaniiltį
2   ch'ííníłtį   ch'ínoołtį   ch'ídanoołtį
3   ch'ííníłtį   ch'ídeistį
4   ch'ízhníłtį   ch'ídajistį

Are you wondering about the high-followed-by-low tone on the **íi** of the word **ch'ííníłtį** "he/she/they (two) carried him/her out"? If so, go back to Chapter 15 and review the discussion that follows the words in Chapter 15(34). The story here is the same. This word has the following structure:

(33) outer   object   subject   cl   verb
      prefix   prefix   prefix   stem

      ch'í - y - ní - ł - tį

Rule Conj-2 changes the **y** in this position into low-tone **i**. The high-tone **í** in front of it is just the vowel at the end of the outer prefix **ch'í**.

You might want to compare (33) with the structure of the word **ch'ííníłtį** "you (sg) carried him/her out":

(34) outer   subject   cl   verb
      prefix   prefix   stem

      ch'í - víní - ł - tį́

Question: Why isn't there any object prefix in (34)? (Answer: The object is 3 person and the subject is 2sg. When the object is 3 person and the subject is not 3 person, then the object is marked with zero - that is, there is no object prefix.)

Back in Chapter 9 we learned what to do with the v́ in (34). This simply is the vowel at the end of the preceding prefix. (And, if that vowel isn't already high-tone, we make it high-tone.) So, the first í of íí in **ch'íiníłtį́** is the í of **ch'í** (which is the v́), and the second í of íí in this word is the first í in **víní**.

As is usual for n-P verbs, (32) shows us switching to the s-P in the distributive 3 and 4 persons.

If you've understood the I and P mode forms, the F mode should be easy:

(35)   sg   dpl   distr dpl

1   ch'ídeeshtééł   ch'ídiiltééł   ch'ídadiiltééł
2   ch'ídííłtééł   ch'ídoołtééł   ch'ídadoołtééł
3   ch'íidoołtééł   ch'ídeidoołtééł
4   ch'ízhdoołtééł   ch'ídazhdoołtééł

The íi in **ch'íidoołtééł** arises the same way as it did in the P mode form **ch'íiníłtį́** that we analyzed in (33).

Since the object of these verbs can be any human, we can also put in other object prefixes and say things like **ch'íshiníłtį́** "he/she/they (two) carried me out", **ch'ínidadiiltééł** "we'll carry you (sg) out", etc.

To illustrate another part of the rule in Chapter 18(24), let's write out the n-P conjugation for a verb with a plain-l or d classifier. We can take our old friend "crawl" - we won't write out the verb base that means "crawl out" (you should do it for practice), but here are the P mode forms for it:

(36)   sg   dpl   distr dpl

1   ch'ínísh'na'   ch'ínii'na'   ch'ídanii'na'
2   ch'ííní'na'   ch'ínooh'na'   ch'ídanooh'na'
3   ch'é'na'   ch'ídaas'na'
4   ch'íjí'na'   ch'ízhdaas'na'

Do you understand how the **é** vowel came to be in the word **ch'é'na'** "he/she/they (two) crawled out"? This word is structured like this:

(37) outer   subject   cl   verb
      prefix   prefix   stem

      ch'í - (zero) - d - na'
                          \ /
                         'na'

Why is the subject prefix zero? Look at Chapter 18(23) and (24): in the n-P conjugation, with plain-l/d classifiers, the 3 subject prefix is zero if it is preceded by an outer prefix, which is what we've got in (37).

So why does **ch'í** become **ch'é**? Look at Rule Disj-1. In (37), **ch'í** is followed by a consonant (the consonant ') and the next syllable is the verb-stem syllable, so Rule Disj-1 says that the **í** of **ch'í** becomes **é**. (Another way of saying it: if **ch'í** is followed by a consonant, and if this syllable is going to be the pre-stem syllable in the verb, it shows up as **ch'é**.)

(And, don't forget that Rule Subj-5 applies in a couple of the forms in (36).)

This is all we are going to say about Vocabulary-8 here. However, since the "go" verbs are so important, you should apply Vocabulary-8 to the verb themes for ordinary going, and come up with I, P, and F mode words that mean "go out" or "come out". The singular go-verb will have its usual irregularities, exactly like the words built from other verb bases that use this theme. The change from **ch'í** to **ch'é** also occurs in a few forms (even one form of the singular verb - do you see why?)

This should do it for this chapter. But keep in mind that there are other vocabulary principles besides Vocabulary-7 that create expressions using the words that result from Vocabulary-6. And there are other vocabulary principles besides Vocabulary-8 that make use of the n-I and n-P conjugations of motion verbs. Keep a lookout for them as you encounter more Navajo verbs.

CHAPTER 20

THE LONG-VOWEL CONJUGATIONS

In this chapter we are going to learn about a new group of conjugations for the I, P, and F modes. We will also learn some vocabulary principles that involve these new conjugations. Quite a few Navajo verbs are conjugated using the patterns we are going to learn, so studying them will allow us to expand our knowledge of the Navajo verb system in an important way.

We are calling these conjugations the "long-vowel conjugations", because many (not all!) of the subject prefixes have a long vowel in them. Actually, the long-vowel is almost always **ii**, so we could have called these the **ii**-conjugations instead, but "long-vowel" seemed like an easier name.

Let's start right in with the long-vowel-I conjugation. The subject prefixes for this conjugation are best learned if we divide them up into two sets, one to be used if preceded by a disjunct prefix and the other to be used otherwise. Here they are:

(1)   long-vowel-I subject prefixes,
        when not preceded by a disjunct prefix:

	sg	dpl
1	iish	iid
2	ii	ooh
3	ii	

(2)   long-vowel-I subject prefixes,
        when preceded by a disjunct prefix:

	sg	dpl
1	ish	iid
2	i	ooh
3	i (but yii after da)	

Did you notice the 2sg prefixes? No, that's not a misprint: in the long-vowel-I conjugation, the 2sg subject prefix is the same as the 3 person subject prefix! It doesn't have any "ni" syllable as part of it, and there's no high tone either!

In this new conjugation pattern, the 1dpl and 2dpl prefixes are "easy" - we've seen **iid** a lot as a 1dpl subject prefix, and the 2dpl **ooh** is also familiar - in fact, it's the same as the regular I mode 2dpl prefix

255

except for having a long vowel in it: **oo**. But the other three prefixes are new - and they have different forms according to whether a disjunct prefix is in front of them or not.

Question: What happens if these subject prefixes aren't preceded by any prefix at all? Answer: Since, in this case, the subject prefixes are not preceded by a disjunct prefix, we'll use the forms of the prefixes shown in chart (1). Rule Str-3 will then supply a **y** in front of most of them (and a **w** in front of **ooh**.)

It will turn out that the forms of the prefixes in (1) are going to be much more common than the forms in (2). The reason is that the majority of outer prefixes in Navajo are never actually used in verb bases that take the long-vowel conjugation. We will, of course, see distributive **da** in front of the 1dpl, 2dpl, and 3 person subject prefixes. In the case of **iid** and **ooh**, Rule Disj-2 kicks in so that the vowel of **da** coalesces with the vowel in the subject prefix in the way that we've already seen a lot of times. In the case of the 3 person subject prefix, when **da** immediately precedes it, the form used is always **dayii**. For most of the few combinations in which the long-vowel subject prefixes do find themselves with a disjunct prefix immediately to the left, (2) gives the correct forms (with just **i** as the 3 person subject prefix.) There are a very very small number of irregular outer prefixes where the forms are slightly different.

We are almost ready to give examples of a long-vowel-I conjugation. But there are two details that we need to add.

First, you may remember that Rule Str-1 has a special statement that says that a 3 person object prefix **y** is doubled (like this: **yy**) if we're in the y-P conjugation, the classifier is zero or barred-l, the subject is 3 person (not 4 person!), there is no inner prefix following it, and there is no prefix (or no lexical prefix) in front of it. Now, the same thing happens in the long-vowel-I conjugation under the same conditions, except for the business about the classifier. So, let's add this to Rule Str-1:

(add to Rule Str-1): Instead of using the 3 object prefix **y**, put two of these next to each other (like this: **yy**) into the object prefix position in the long-vowel-I conjugation if the subject is 3 person, the form is the direct form, there is no inner prefix following it, and there is no (lexical) prefix preceding it.

We'll see examples of this in just a moment.

The second detail concerns the object prefix **hw**. In Rule Conj-6 we gave a list of statements that show what this prefix looks like in a number of different circumstances. In the case of the long-vowel-I conjugation, we have to make an additional statement, which we'll add into part (d) of Rule Conj-6:

(add to Rule Conj-6(d)): In the long-vowel-I conjugation, when **hw** is followed by the 1sg subject prefix **iish** or the 2sg/3 prefix **ii**, the combination can become **hoosh** or **hoo**.

We won't see any examples of this till the end of this chapter, but we thought we'd put the statement of this princple here in order to make our presentation of the long-vowel-I conjugation complete.

Let's illustrate the long-vowel-I with some actual words. We'll use a new verb base - the verb base in (3), which means "make one cut in it":

(3)

Stem-set		Classifier: zero
I:	**gish**	
P:	**gish**	Lexical prefixes: (none)
F:	**gish**	Transitivity: transitive
R:	**gish**	
O:	**gish**	Conjugation: long-vowel-I, s-P, long-vowel-R, long-vowel-U, long-vowel-O

Before going on, note first that the stem-set for this verb base uses the same stems for all the modes. We are going to say something about this stem-set in a little while - for now, let's just enjoy the fact that this stem-set is so easy.

Next, this verb base uses the long-vowel conjugations in the I, R, U, and O modes, but not in the P or F modes. These two modes are perfectly ordinary - the s-P conjugation is used in the P mode, and the regular F mode conjugation is used in the F mode. Since we haven't learned the regular R, U, or O modes yet, we won't learn the long-vowel versions of those modes here, either. Instead, when we come to study those modes (in Chapter 23), we'll learn the regular and the long-vowel conjugations together.

But we can certainly write up the I mode for the verb base in (3) using what we've said about the long-vowel conjugation. Can you do it without looking at the forms? If you try it, your words should come out looking like these:

(4)	sg	dpl	distr dpl
1	yiishgish	yiigish	deiigish
2	yiigish	woohgish	daoohgish
3		yiyiigish	dayiigish
4		jiigish	dajiigish

(You might find **deiyiigish** for the 3 person distr dpl form. Remember our discussion of this point in Chapter 9?)

There isn't much to say about the forms in (4). Just to make sure, note that "he/she/they (two) are making a cut in it" is built like this:

(5) object   subject   verb
    prefix   prefix   stem

    y - y - ii - gish

The 3 person object **y** is doubled because we are in the long-vowel-I conjugation, the subject is 3 person, we're building a direct form (rather than an inverse form), the object isn't followed by any inner prefix, and there isn't any prefix in front of the object. Rule Conj-1 inserts an **i** between the two **y**'s. Nothing else happens, so the word is **yiyiigish**.

What about the word that means "one is making a cut in it"? The structure is:

(6) object   subject   verb
    prefix   prefix   stem

      j - ii - gish

Since the subject (3 person) is not preceded by a disjunct prefix, we use the form **ii** found in (1). No rules apply, and we get **jiigish**.

And, just to make sure, what about "you (sg) are making a cut in it"? The structure is:

(7) subject   verb
    prefix   stem

    ii - gish

Again, since there is no disjunct prefix in front of the subject prefix, we get our subject prefix from (1). In this case, the word is stranded with a vowel at the beginning, so Rule Str-3 comes along and puts a **y** in front of the whole verb. That's how we get the word **yiigish**.

Incidentally, you might note that the doubling of the **y** in **yiyiigish** is how we can tell that there really is an object in this word. Compare this with **yiigish** meaning "you (sg) are making a cut in it", and also the **yiigish** that means "we (two) are making a cut in it". The **yiy** of **yiyiigish** helps us to know that the subject of this word is 3 person ("he/she/they (two)"), rather than 2sg or 1dpl.

Since the P and F modes of the verb base in (3) are regular, we won't write them out (you should do so yourself, for practice.) This verb base has no lexical prefixes, so those modes are particularly easy.

Let's look at the verb base in (3) a little more, though. You might recall that many chapters ago we saw another verb base involving cutting. In fact, that verb base meant "cut it out" (in the sense of "remove it by cutting"). You'll find most of that verb base in Chapter 6(16) - the only thing not shown there is the perfective conjugation used, which is the y-P.

Now, if we compare the stem-set in Chapter 6(16) with the stem-set in (3) above, we see that they are not exactly the same. Is this another example of a pair of stem-sets where one is momentaneous and one is continuative?

No! To see this, let's first ask: Is the stem set in Chapter 6(16) likely to be momentaneous or continuative? Well, since the verb base means "cut it out", which is a telic action (when you've finished cutting it out, you cannot keep on cutting it out), we'd guess that it's got a momentaneous stem set. This happens to be correct.

Now, what about the stem set in (3)? Here are two things to notice.

First, (3) means "make one cut in it". Now, this is also telic! (Once you've made one cut in something, you can't keep on making one cut in it.) In fact, if anything, it's a particularly fast kind of cutting: the action lasts only for a brief bit of time - it's almost instantaneous.

Second, remember that when we have a pair of related stem-sets, one momentaneous and one continuative, the P mode stems are always the same. But the P mode stem in (3) is different from the P mode stem in Chapter 6(16): here we have **gish**, and there we had **gizh**!

What's going on is that the stem-set in (3) is not part of a pair of which the other set is the one in Chapter 6(16). Instead, the stem-set in (3) is a special kind of derived stem-set. This kind of derived stem-set is used specifically for actions that are almost instantaneous. The name used in YM for this kind of stem-set is: *semelfactive stem-set* (or: *semelfactive aspect stem-set.*) We'll use this term here, too.

The way to think of this is this: given a verb theme, it is sometimes possible to derive a new verb theme from it by using a semelfactive stem-set that is derived from the stem-sets of the original verb theme. When this is done, certain kinds of verb bases can then be built from this new verb theme. Let's write this up as two vocabulary principles. We'll say that the new verb theme is the *semelfactive verb theme* derived from the original one.

Vocabulary-9: Given a (normal) transitive verb theme, a semelfactive verb theme can sometimes be derived from it by doing the following:

> Stem-set: use the semelfactive stem-set, which is created as follows: all modes have as stem the F mode stem of the momentaneous stem-set of the given verb theme.
>
> Classifier: use the same classifier as the given verb theme.
>
> Transitivity: transitive

The meaning of the derived semelfactive verb theme is of a single, instantaneous piece of action of the type referred to by the given verb theme.

Before writing up the next vocabulary principle, there are some very important things to say about Vocabulary-9.

All of the vocabulary principles we've learned up till now have been quite general. Given some situation, you could be pretty sure that if you created something in the way specified by the principle, you'd get something real. But Vocabulary-9 is different.

First of all, not every ordinary verb theme can have a semelfactive verb theme derived from it. For one thing, it has to make sense to want to talk about a single, instantaneous kind of whatever action the original verb theme specifies. But apart from this, there still might not be a semelfactive version of that theme. In other words, given a verb theme, we cannot predict whether or not it'll have a semelfactive version. The best we can do is simply learn more and more examples of particular semelfactive verb themes.

So what's the point of Vocabulary-9? Simply this: it tells us about a possibility - it tells us that there are certain things we can expect. Every time we learn a new semelfactive theme, we'll be able to say: Ah - that's another example of one of those semelfactive things.

But before continuing, we have more warnings.

For most semelfactive stem-sets, all modes have the same stem, and that stem is identical to the F mode stem of the momentaneous stem-set of the original verb theme. But there are exceptions - a few semelfactive stem-sets involve different stems for different modes. In fact, there is a particular group of stem-sets that work a little differently than the way we described it in Vocabulary-9 above. We'll say a bit more about this at the end of our study, in Chapter 27, but in general, be on the lookout for the occasional semelfactive stem-set that doesn't follow the rule given above.

Similarly, most semelfactive themes use the same classifier as the original theme, but occasionally there is a change. As an example: the verb base in Chapter 6(16) uses a barred-l classifier, whereas the verb base in (3) uses a zero classifier. What gives?

Well, this is an exception. As it happens, there are a lot of verb bases that are built using the "cutting"

260

verb theme, and some of them do use a zero classifier, although a lot of the usual ones use the barred-l, like "cut it out". We simply have to remember that "make one cut in it" uses the zero classifier. However, this is indeed an exception - in most cases, a semelfactive stem-set is used with the same classifier as the ordinary stem set that it was derived from.

Now, let's write up our second vocabulary principle, the one that tells us about a kind of verb base we can build using a semelfactive verb theme.

Vocabulary-10: Given a semelfactive verb theme, we can build a verb base that means "make one instance of an action upon it" by doing the following:

Stem-set: use the stem-set of the semelfactive verb theme	Classifier: use the classifier of the semelfactive verb theme
	Lexical prefixes: (none)
	Transitivity: transitive
	Conjugation: long-vowel-I, s-P, long-vowel-R, long-vowel-U, long-vowel-O

Vocabulary-10 is a bit more trustworthy than Vocabulary-9: If you've got a semelfactive verb theme, there is a reasonable chance that there really is a verb theme built according to the scheme shown in Vocabulary-10. But it still would be a good idea to be sure before making up any new words. The best thing is to think of Vocabulary-9 and Vocabulary-10 as going together. Whenever you see a verb base that has the structure shown in Vocabulary-10, you can check if its stem-set is related to a momentaneous one with a similar (usually, more general) meaning.

The verb base we saw in (9) followed the pattern laid down by these two vocabulary principles, except for the classifier, as we mentioned. Starting with the stem-set in Chapter 6(16), Vocabulary-9 builds a semelfactive verb theme - note that **gish** is the F mode stem in the stem-set in Chapter 6(16); and we simply have to remember the irregularity of using a zero classifier with this new stem-set. The verb base in (3) now follows the structure shown in Vocabulary-10.

Here's another example. In (8) we have the verb theme that refers to the action of sucking (this theme doesn't seem to have a continuative stem-set):

(8)

Momentaneous stem-set	
I:	ts'ǫǫs
P:	ts'ǫ́ǫ́z
F:	ts'ǫs
R:	ts'ǫs
O:	ts'ǫǫs
Classifier: zero	
Transitivity: transitive	

Vocabulary-9 suggests that there might be a semelfactive verb theme that looks like this:

(9)

Semelfactive stem-set	
I:	ts'ǫs
P:	ts'ǫs
F:	ts'ǫs
R:	ts'ǫs
O:	ts'ǫs
Classifier: zero	
Transitivity: transitive	

As it happens, there actually is such a verb theme. It means something like "perform one very quick sucking action on it"

Since we have (9), Vocabulary-10 suggests that there is a verb base like this:

(10)

Stem-set		
I:	ts'ǫs	Classifier: zero
P:	ts'ǫs	Lexical prefixes: (none)
F:	ts'ǫs	Transitivity: transitive
R:	ts'ǫs	
O:	ts'ǫs	Conjugation: long-vowel-I, s-P, long-vowel-R, long-vowel-U, long-vowel-O

There is indeed such a verb base. It can be used to mean "kiss him/her (once)". (It can have some other meanings, too.)

The I mode forms look a lot like (4) above. Let's write them out, just to make sure we know what a long-vowel-I conjugation looks like.

(11)   sg   dpl   distr dpl

1   yiists'ǫs   yiits'ǫs   deiits'ǫs
2   yiits'ǫs   woohts'ǫs   daoohts'ǫs
3   yiyiits'ǫs   dayiits'ǫs
4   jiits'ǫs   dajiits'ǫs

The P and F modes should be completely familiar by now. Even though they don't involve long-vowel conjugations, let's write them out, too, as a review. The P mode is:

(12)   sg   dpl   distr dpl

1   séts'ǫs   siits'ǫs   dasiits'ǫs
2   sínits'ǫs   soots'ǫs   dasoots'ǫs
3   yizts'ǫs   deizts'ǫs
4   jizts'ǫs   dajizts'ǫs

(If it's been awhile since you've seen an s-P conjugation with no lexical prefixes, you might want to compare these words with the words in Chapter 8(9).)

And the F mode is:

(13)   sg   dpl   distr dpl

1   deests'ǫs   diits'ǫs   dadiits'ǫs
2   díits'ǫs   doohts'ǫs   dadoohts'ǫs
3   yidoots'ǫs   deidoots'ǫs
4   jidoots'ǫs   dazhdoots'ǫs

(Note that Rule Subj-6 was used in some of the forms of this verb.)

Vocabulary-10 creates verb bases in which the I mode is conjugated in the long-vowel conjugation, but the P and F modes are regular. But there are other vocabulary principles that create verb bases that use the long-vowel conjugation patterns of the P and F modes, too. Let's learn these conjugations now, and then we'll look at some examples.

The long-vowel-P conjugation resembles the y-P (there aren't any **s**'s like the ones in the s-P subject prefixes, and there aren't any **n**'s like the ones in the n-P subject prefixes.)

As always with the P mode, we have to separate things by classifier. Let's first look at the case where the classifier is zero or barred-l. For the long-vowel conjugation, we'll separate these prefixes further: we'll do the same thing that we did with the long-vowel-I mode prefixes. That is, we'll make two charts, one for the case that the subject prefix is not preceded by a disjunct prefix, and the other for the case that it is preceded by a disjunct prefix:

(14)   long-vowel-P subject prefixes,
       zero/barred-l classifier,
       when not preceded by a disjunct prefix:

	sg	dpl
1	ii	iid
2	(see (16))	oo
3	ii	

(15)   long-vowel-P subject prefixes,
       zero/barred-l classifier,
       when preceded by a disjunct prefix:

	sg	dpl
1	i	iid
2	ini	oo
3	i (but **yii** after **da**)	

As in the case of the long-vowel-I subject prefixes, we'll find the prefixes in (14) a lot more common than the ones in (15). Note that if there is no prefix preceding the subject prefix, we'll use the forms of the subject prefixes in (14), which means that Rule Str-3 will put a **y** or a **w** in at the beginning of the word.

There is one tiny complication concerning the 2sg subject prefix for the long-vowel-P when not preceded by a disjunct prefix:

(16)   long-vowel-P, 2sg subject prefix,
             not preceded by a disjunct prefix:

when preceded by an object prefix:	**iini**
otherwise:	**ini**

Note that **ini** is used not only when there is no prefix to its left, but also when it is preceded by an inner prefix.

The strangest thing about the subject prefixes in (14), (15), and (16) is that they all have low tones. In the y-P, s-P, and even the n-P conjugations, the 1sg, 2sg, and 3 person subject prefixes (at least for the zero/barred-l classifier case) have high tones. You should think of the low tone in the corresponding long-vowel subject prefixes as a special feature of the long-vowel-P conjugation.

The doubling of the object prefix **y** to **yy** happens in the long-vowel-P conjugation as well as in the y-P (and long-vowel-I) conjugation. This means we'll need another addition to Rule Str-1:

(add to Rule Str-1): Instead of using the 3 object prefix **y**, put two of these next to each other (like this: **yy**) into the object prefix position in the long-vowel-P conjugation if the classifier is zero or barred-l, the subject is 3 person, the form is the direct form, there is no inner prefix following it, and there is no (lexical) prefix preceding it.

We also need to add a statement about **hw** to Rule Conj-6, but first let's finish the subject prefixes for the long-vowel-P conjugation by giving the subject prefixes when the classifier is plain-l or d. Here they are:

(17)   long-vowel-P subject prefixes,
        plain-l/d classifier,
        when not preceded by a disjunct prefix:

	sg	dpl
1	**iish**	**iid**
2	(see (16))	**ooh**
3	**ii**	

(18)   long-vowel-P subject prefixes,
       plain-l/d classifier,
       when preceded by a disjunct prefix:

	sg	dpl
1	**ish**	**iid**
2	**ini**	**ooh**
3	**i** (but **yii** after **da**)	

Certain patterns in these prefixes are by now very familiar. The **sh** at the end of the 1sg prefix and the **h** at the end of the 2dpl prefix in the plain-l/d case (and the absence of these elements in the zero/barred-l case) is a pattern that we've seen a lot already - any P mode conjugation has this pattern. Note also that the 2sg and 1dpl prefixes don't depend on the classifier (that is, they're the same for all four classifiers), which is also something that is true for every P mode conjugation pattern.

For completeness, let's now add that piece about the **hw** prefix in the long-vowel P mode conjugation to Rule Conj-6:

(add to Rule Conj-6(d)): In the long-vowel-P conjugation, when **hw** is followed by the 1sg subject prefix **ii** or **iish** or the 3 prefix **ii**, the combination can become **hoo** or **hoosh** or **hoo**.

(In case you were wondering: would the object prefix **y** double in the P mode forms when the classifier is plain-l or d? We'd expect it to. The only thing is, there don't seem to be any transitive prefixless verb bases with plain-l or d classifiers that are conjugated in the long-vowel-P conjugation.)

So that this is not completely abstract, let's illustrate some of these prefixes with a new verb base. The verb base in (19) means "see it", in the sense of "catch sight of it". (This verb base is particularly commonly used in the P and F modes. The I mode equivalent of the English verb "see" is more commonly expressed in Navajo using the irregular verb that we discussed back in Chapter 16 - see Chapter 16(8), Chapter 16(9), and Chapter 16(10).)

(19)

Stem-set		Classifier: barred-l
I:	**tsééh**	
P:	**tsá**	Lexical prefixes: (none)
F:	**tsééł**	
R:	**tsééh**	Transitivity: transitive
O:	**tsééł**	Conjugation: long-vowel conjugation in all modes

The I mode forms of this verb are much like the ones in (4) and (11) - write them out yourself for practice.

The P mode forms will use the prefixes in (14) and (15) (and (16).) Here is the P mode of this verb:

(20)   sg   dpl   distr dpl

1   yiiłtsą   yiiltsą   deiiltsą
2   yiniłtsą   wooltsą   daooltsą
3   yiyiiłtsą   dayiiłtsą
4   jiiłtsą   dajiiłtsą

How do these differ from ordinary y-P forms? Well, first of all, the tones of the subject prefixes in (20) are all low for the 1sg, 2sg, 3 (and 4) subjects - in an ordinary y-P conjugation, with a barred-ł (or zero) classifier, these prefixes would have high tone. And second, the 1sg form has a long **ii** in it. (In the ordinary y-P conjugation, if the verb doesn't have any lexical prefixes, the 1sg form would start with **yí**, with a short **í**.)

Test your understanding of the rule in (16) above by building the word that means "you saw me". (You should get **shiiniłtsą**. The 2sg subject prefix is **iini** in this word because it is preceded by the object prefix **sh**. In a little while we'll see examples of the 2sg subject prefix preceded by an inner prefix - in that case, (16) tells us that the 2sg prefix is **ini**, not **iini**.)

To illustrate the subject prefixes in (17) and (18), we need to look at the P mode conjugation of a verb base that has a plain-ł or a d classifier. The following verb base has a d classifier - this verb base means "become black", and also "get sunburned":

(21)

Stem-set		Classifier: d
I:	**zhį́į́h**	
P:	**zhį́į́'**	Lexical prefixes: (none)
F:	**zhį́į́ł**	
R:	**zhį́į́h**	Transitivity: intransitive
O:	**zhį́į́h**	Conjugation: long-vowel conjugation in all modes

We learned in Chapter 6 that the d classifier causes the first consonant of the verb stem to undergo d-effect. In the case of (21), this means that the stems in all the modes will really start with **j**. Keeping this in mind, can you write out the P mode? (In fact, can you also write out the I mode?)

So far, all the examples that we've seen of long-vowel conjugations (in both the I and in the P modes) have been examples of transitive verbs. Since the verb base in (21) is intransitive, let's write out the I mode as well as the P mode. The I mode is:

(22)	sg	dpl	distr dpl
1	yiishjį́įh	yiijį́įh	deiijį́įh
2	yiijį́įh	woohjį́įh	daoohjį́įh
3		yiijį́įh	dayiijį́įh
4		jiijį́įh	dajiijį́įh

The 3 subject forms in (22) should be compared with the 3 subject forms in (4) and (11). Since there is never an object prefix in any of the words in (22), the word that means "you (sg) are getting sunburned" and the word that means "he/she/they (two) is/are getting sunburned" will have to be the same, since the 2sg and the 3 subject prefixes are the same for the long-vowel-I conjugation. (The word that means "we (two) are getting sunburned" is also the same, but that's because the consonant at the beginning of the verb stem doesn't change any when we apply the d-effect caused by the **d** of **iid**.) Note also that the distributive plural 3 person form has **dayii** in it, which is what regularly happens in the long-vowel-I.

For the P mode, which is what we were aiming for all along, we get the following forms:

(23)	sg	dpl	distr dpl
1	yiishjį́į'	yiijį́į'	deiijį́į'
2	yinijį́į'	woohjį́į'	daoohjį́į'
3		yiijį́į'	dayiijį́į'
4		jiijį́į'	dajiijį́į'

Again, there are some differences between forms like the ones in (23) and regular y-P forms. There's the long **ii** in the **yiish** of **yiishjį́į'**, for example, and there are the low tones in the **yini** part of **yinijį́į'**. The forms **yiijį́į'** "he/she/they (two) got sunburned" and **jiijį́į'** "one got sunburned" are quite different from ordinary y-P conjugation forms. An ordinary y-P 3 person subject form would start out **yi-** if the classifier is d and the verb is intransitive. And the ordinary y-P 4 person form would have **joo** in it.

The verb bases in (19) and (21) use long-vowel conjugations in all modes. To finish our story (for now, at least), we need to look at the long-vowel version of the F mode.

The long-vowel-I and the long-vowel-P conjugations involved learning new subject prefixes. In the case of the F mode, the long-vowel conjugation actually uses the same subject prefixes as the ordinary F mode conjugation. The difference is that if we are conjugating a verb in the long-vowel-F, we'll add in a special element just in front of the F mode **d**. It is easy to describe what this element looks like. If there are no additional prefixes to the left of this element, then it will appear as **yi** (so that the whole F mode word will start out **yid-**.) If there's a disjunct prefix to its left, the element appears as **i**, so that we'll see the sequence **-id-** in the word. If there's a conjunct prefix to its left (which at this point can only be an object prefix), then the element appears as **ii**, so we get the sequence **-iid-** in the word.

We could write these facts up as some sort of rule about the long-vowel F mode conjugation, but instead we're going to play one of those games that we've occasionally mentioned. The reason we're going to do this is that, not only is this game very easy, but in fact it'll make life easier for us when we get to Chapter 24. So, let's write up the following principle for the long-vowel F mode conjugation:

(24)   In the long-vowel-F conjugation, place the prefix **y** just in front of F mode **d**:

Let's call this prefix the *long-vowel-F prefix* or the *long-vowel-F y*. Since this prefix is located in a position that can have conjunct prefixes to its left and to its right, it makes sense to consider the long-vowel-F **y** a conjunct prefix. And note: we now have two conjunct prefixes that have the form **y**: the 3 person object prefix, and the long-vowel-F prefix. Let's see what forms the long-vowel-F **y** actually takes in various circumstances.

If the long-vowel-F **y** is the first thing in the verb, Rule Conj-1 will put a **i** right after it (since the **y** will be immediately followed by a consonant, namely, F mode **d**), so the words will actually start out like this: **yid-**.

If the long-vowel-F **y** is immediately preceded by a disjunct prefix (which will end in a vowel, of course), then Rule Conj-2 will change the long-vowel-F **y** into **i**. Note that in the past we've seen Rule Conj-2 change the 3 person object prefix **y** into **i**. But exactly the same process affects our new **y** prefix in exactly the same way.

But what if the long-vowel-F **y** is immediately preceded by a conjunct prefix? This can happen, since an object prefix would be placed to its left. In this case, we have to learn a new rule. We'll add this rule in as another part of Rule Conj-2. Since it tells us what happens when a conjunct **y** is sandwiched in between two consonants, we'll sometimes call this part of Rule Conj-2 the "sandwiched y" rule. Here it is:

(add to Rule Conj-2:) If a conjunct prefix **y** is in between two consonants, then change the **y** to **ii**.

With this addition, the long-vowel-F **y** will end up having the correct form in all cases.

This is almost the entire story of the long-vowel F mode conjugation. As it happens, there is a special adjustment that sometimes happens when the 4 person subject **j** or the 3 person object **y** is in object position. Let's write up a special "structure" rule to take care of this adjustment. This rule has two parts - here they are (we'll illustrate them in a moment.)

<u>Rule Str-5</u>:

(a) If the 4 person subject prefix **j** (in object position) is preceded by another prefix and followed directly by the long-vowel-F prefix, then the long-vowel-F prefix and **j** interchange positions.

(b) If the 3 person object prefix **y** is preceded by another prefix and followed directly by the long-vowel-F **y** prefix, then the two **y** prefixes merge and become one **y**.

Part (a) of Rule Str-5 moves prefixes around, so remember: we should apply this rule (if we can!) before we try to figure out what the forms of the various prefixes actually end up being. We'll put a note in the Appendix indicating that this is a movement rule, to help us remember this.

Can you use (24) and Rule Str-5 to build the F mode forms of "see it"? Let's see if we can't come up with one word first. The word that means "I'll see it" will have the following structure:

(25)	long-vowel-F prefix	F mode d	subject prefix	cl	verb stem
	y	- d -	eesh -	ł -	tséél

Question: Why isn't there an object prefix in this word? (Answer: Look at Rule Str-1.)

The only really new thing about (25) is that there's that long-vowel-F prefix in there, just in front of the F mode **d**.

So, what does the word actually look like? (Remember, Rule Conj-1 applies.) The word is: **yideestséél** (the sandwich rule as well as Rule Subj-6 also applied.)

Next, let's try the word that means "he/she/they (two) will see it". The structure is:

(26)	object prefix	long-vowel-F prefix	F mode d	subject prefix	cl	verb stem
	y	- y -	d -	oo -	ł -	tséél

By Rule Str-1, we're using the 3 person object prefix **y** in (26), since the subject is also 3 person. But this means that the long-vowel-F prefix in (26) is sandwiched in between the consonant **y** (the 3 person object prefix) and the consonant **d** (the F mode **d**), so our new sandwiched **y** rule changes it into **ii**. None of our many other rules apply to (26), so the word is just **yiidoołtséél**.

270

(Words built like (26) show us that we've got to let the sandwiched **y** rule turn a **y** into **ii** before we give Rule Conj-1 a chance to apply! Our note in Rule Conj-1 (in the Appendix) about checking to see if Rule Conj-2 applies can remind us of this. Incidentally: you might want to check that the doubled **y**'s that Rule Str-1 sometimes gives us as the 3 person object prefix is always followed by a vowel, so the sandwiched **y** rule never can apply to the second of these two **y**'s.)

Make sure you understand the order of the prefixes in (26). When we learned about the F mode, we learned that F mode **d** goes in just to the right of any object prefix and just to the left of any inner prefix. In the long-vowel-F conjugation, we have an additional prefix, the long-vowel-F prefix, which is always placed immediately to the left of the F mode **d**. This means that this prefix will follow object prefixes, if there are any. Of course, it'll also follow any disjunct prefixes.

Question: Why didn't our new Rule Str-5 apply to (26)? Answer: The 3 person object **y** in (26) is not preceded by any other prefix.

Let's do just one more F mode word using the "see it" verb base. Here's how we build the word that means "those ones will see it":

(27)

distributive plural	object prefix	long-vowel-F prefix	F mode d	subject prefix	cl	verb stem
da -	j -	y -	d -	oo -	ł -	tséél

What happens to the structure in (27)? Well, in (27) we've got a 4 person **j** preceded by a prefix (the distributive plural **da**), and followed immediately by the long-vowel-F prefix. By Rule Str-5(a), the **j** and the long-vowel-F prefix interchange positions. This means that the structure for this word turns into this:

(28)

distributive plural	long-vowel-F prefix	object prefix	F mode d	subject prefix	cl	verb stem
da -	y -	j -	d -	oo -	ł -	tséél

Well, with (28) as our structure, what does the word look like? The old part of Rule Conj-2 will change the **y** into an **i**, whereupon Rule Disj 2 will apply (since **da** is followed by a vowel), and so will Rule Conj-7. The word is: **deizhdoołtséél**. (Some people may say **deizdoołtséél**, because of the **ts** in the verb stem.)

The three F mode forms of "see it" that we've worked out should give you an idea of how the long-vowel F mode conjugation goes. Can you write out the entire F mode for this verb? Here it is:

(29)   sg   dpl   distr dpl

1	yideestsééł	yidiiltsééł	deidiiltsééł
2	yidííltsééł	yidooltsééł	deidooltsééł
3		yiidooltsééł	deidooltsééł
4		jiidooltsééł	deizhdooltsééł

Make sure you understand why Rule Str-5 doesn't apply in the case of the word **jiidooltsééł**. This word has almost the same structure as **yiidooltsééł** in (26) - the only difference is that the object prefix position is filled with **j** instead of **y**.

Make sure you understand all those **dei-** forms in the distributive plural. The **i** in this **ei** combination is actually the long-vowel-F prefix. Note also that Rule Str-5(b) applies in the case of the word that means "they'll see it": the object **y** and the long-vowel-F **y** coalesce into a single **y**, which becomes **i** (by Rule Conj-2), so the word starts with the same **dei** as the other distributive plural words in (29).

(Occasionally, you might find **deiidooltsééł** rather than **deidooltsééł** for "they'll see it". To get this form of this word, all we have to do is assume that there is no part (b) of Rule Str-5. This makes for simpler grammar. Keep in mind, though, that YM show these words as having **deid-** in them rather than **deiid-**.)

The F mode forms for the verb base in (21) should now be easy. Since this verb is intransitive, the 3 person forms will be a little different from the ones in (29). Here is the F mode of this verb (so these words mean "I'll get sunburned", "you'll get sunburned", etc.):

(30)   sg   dpl   distr dpl

1	yideeshjį́į́ł	yidiijį́į́ł	deidiijį́į́ł
2	yidííjį́į́ł	yidoohjį́į́ł	deidoohjį́į́ł
3		yidoojį́į́ł	deidoojį́į́ł
4		jiidoojį́į́ł	deizhdoojį́į́ł

Actually, the 3 person distributive plural form isn't any different for transitive and intransitive verbs. Have you noticed that this is true in the long-vowel-I and long-vowel-P conjugations, too?

The nondistributive 3 person form is a little different, though. Since there is no object prefix in the word **yidoojį́į́ł** "he/she/they (two) will get sunburned", Rule Conj-1 inserts a short **i** after the long-vowel-F prefix (we don't see a long **ii**.)

Well, this is all we need to learn about the actual forms of the long-vowel conjugations at this time. We'll learn about long-vowel versions of the other modes when we come to study those other modes.

To see that what we've learned allows us automatically to build the forms of more complicated verbs, let's look at the I, P, and F mode forms of the following verb base, which means "learn it":

(31)

Stem-set		Classifier: barred-l
I:	**'aah**	
P:	**'ą́ą́'**	Lexical prefixes: **Pí** (outer), **hw** (object)
F:	**'ą́ą́ł**	Transitivity: intransitive
R:	**'ą́ą́h**	
O:	**'ą́ą́ł**	Conjugation: long-vowel conjugation in all modes

The outer object pronoun in this verb refers to what is being learned. For this reason, it is just about always 3 person, which means it will normally appear as **b**, except when the subject is 3 person, when it changes to **y**.

We listed this verb as "intransitive" in (31). Can you explain why? (The reason is that with this verb we never put any prefix into the ordinary object prefix position for the purpose of referring to anything. The **hw** in the object prefix position is lexical - that is, it's always there. The **it** of **learn it** is referred to by the pronoun in the outer prefix.)

In the case of this verb, all the printed forms I've ever seen show the change of **hwii** to **hoo** in the cases covered by the additions to Rule Conj-6(d) that we learned earlier in this chapter. This verb will allow us to demonstrate these changes.

First, the I mode:

(32)	sg	dpl	distr dpl
1	bíhoosh'aah	bíhwiil'aah	bídahwiil'aah
2	bíhooł'aah	bíhooł'aah	bídahooł'aah
3		yíhooł'aah	yídahooł'aah
4		bíhojiił'aah	bídahojiił'aah

The **hoo** in **bíhoosh'aah**, **bíhooł'aah** (meaning "you (sg) are learning it"), **yíhooł'aah**, and **yídahooł'aah** are due to the first addition to Rule Conj-6(d) that we learned earlier in this chapter when we studied the forms of the long-vowel-I conjugation. All the other forms of the **hw** prefix are taken care of by the parts of Rule Conj-6 that we learned back in Chapter 12. For example, the **oo** of **bíhooł'aah** "you (two) are learning it" is just the subject prefix. When **hw** is followed by **oo**, it becomes **h** (see Rule Conj-6(c).)

In the P mode, we'll use the prefixes in (14) and (15). We'll also use the addition to Rule Conj-6(d) that we learned in connection with the P mode. The forms are:

(33) sg   dpl   distr dpl

1   bíhooł'ą́ą́'   bíhwiil'ą́ą́'   bídahwiil'ą́ą́'
2   bíhwiinił'ą́ą́' bíhooł'ą́ą́'   bídahooł'ą́ą́'
3   yíhooł'ą́ą́'   yídahooł'ą́ą́'
4   bíhojiił'ą́ą́'   bídahojiił'ą́ą́'

Note that we have that long **ii** in **bíhwiinił'ą́ą́'** because the 2sg subject prefix is preceded by an object prefix (the **hw** prefix) - see (16) for this condition. The long-vowel-P 2sg subject prefix has the form **ini** in all other cases.

Which forms in (33) have **hoo** in them because of the addition to Rule Conj-6(d) that had to do with the P mode? (Answer: **bíhooł'ą́ą́'** (meaning "I learned it"), **yíhooł'ą́ą́'**, and **yídahooł'ą́ą́'**. But in the word **bíhooł'ą́ą́'** (meaning "you (two) learned it"), the **oo** is the 2dpl subject prefix, and as we just saw it is completely normal for **hw** to become **h** in front of **oo**.)

How about the F mode of "learn it"? Here are the forms:

(34) sg   dpl   distr dpl

1   bíhwiideesh'ááł   bíhwiidiil'ááł   bídahwiidiil'ááł
2   bíhwiidííł'ááł   bíhwiidooł'ááł   bídahwiidooł'ááł
3   yíhwiidooł'ááł   yídahwiidooł'ááł
4   bíhwiizhdooł'ááł   bídahwiizhdooł'ááł

The **ii** that follows **hw** in all these forms is the long-vowel-F prefix - since this prefix is preceded by the object prefix **hw** in all these words, it comes out as **ii** because of the sandwiched **y** rule.

How is the word **bíhwiizhdooł'ááł** built? Well, we start out like this:

(35) outer   object   long-vowel-F   F mode   subject   cl   verb
     prefix prefix   prefix   d   prefix   stem

     bí - hw - j - y - d - oo - ł - 'ááł

The two object prefixes are placed in the correct order in (35) by Rule Str-4. Since we've got a 4 person subject **j** in the object prefix position, we use the 3 person subject prefix **oo**.

Now, Rule Str-5(a) applies to (35): **j** is preceded by another prefix (in this case, the lexical object

hw) and immediately followed by the long-vowel-F prefix, so the **j** and the long-vowel-F prefix have to be interchanged. This gives us the following structure:

(36) outer   object   long-vowel-F   object   F mode   subject   cl   verb
      prefix   prefix   prefix   prefix   d   prefix   stem

         bí - hw - y - j - d - oo - ł - 'áál

Note that when we interchanged **j** and the long-vowel-F prefix in this word, the long-vowel-F prefix ended up in between the two object prefixes!

From (36) to the actual word **bíhwiizhdooł'áál** is easy - the sandwiched **y** rule, together with exactly one of our other rules (which one?) applies to (36) to give us this word.

<u>Note on pronunciation and spelling</u>: The prefix **bí** (but not **yí**!) is often, or even usually, pronounced **bó** when followed by **hoo**. In fact, we often see it spelled this way in print. For example, "I learned it" is often spelled **bóhooł'ą́ą́'**, "you (sg) are learning it" is often **bóhooł'aah**, etc.

At this point, let's talk a little about vocabulary. We've seen some examples of verb bases where all the modes are conjugated in the long-vowel conjugation. In YM, such verb bases are called *transitional aspect verb bases*. Transitional aspect verb bases with no lexical prefixes (like (19) and (21)) are called *simple transitional aspect verb bases*. The verb base in (31) is transitional aspect (because it uses the long-vowel conjugation in all modes), but not simple transitional aspect (because it has lexical prefixes.)

We can write up a vocabulary principle like this, if we want to:

<u>Vocabulary-11</u>: Given a verb theme we may be able to form a simple transitional verb base from it by doing this:

Stem-set: use the momentaneous stem-set of the verb theme	Classifier: use the classifier of the verb theme
	Lexical prefixes: (none)
	Transitivity: use the transitivity of the verb theme
	Conjugation: long-vowel conjugation in all modes

The problem with Vocabulary-11 is that it's even more flaky than Vocabulary-9 - there's really no way of knowing which verb themes can be used in the transitional aspect. There's also no clear way of saying what the resulting verb bases mean. To some extent, we can say that transitional aspect verb bases, especially simple ones, have a meaning that involves acquiring some condition, or making something acquire some condition. For example, there is a family of simple transitional aspect words that mean "come to have a certain color" - the verb base in (21) is like this, and there are also simple transitional aspect verb bases that mean things like "become white", "become yellow", etc. Also, there are transitive versions of these - simple transitional aspect verb bases that mean things like "blacken it", "whiten it", "make it yellow", etc. Other simple transitional aspect verb themes have to do with acquiring a condition other than a color - one example of this is a simple transitional aspect verb base that means "stand up", which can be thought of as the action of acquiring the condition of being standing. (And even the non-simple transitional aspect verb base in (31) can be thought of as involving acquiring a condition: to learn it means to acquire the condition of knowing or understanding it.) But there are a few simple transitional aspect verb bases, like the one in (19) that means "see it" or "catch sight of it", where it is hard to explain how their meaning fits the idea of acquiring a condition. (Maybe "see it" means to acquire the condition of perceiving it visually?) So, the best thing to do is simply take note of the fact that there are such things as simple transitional aspect verb bases, and to learn them as you meet them.

There are many vocabulary principles that involve long-vowel conjugations. Before leaving this chapter, let's learn one more. The principle we are going to learn applies to motion verbs, so it's also a continuation of our study of that group of verbs. Here is the principle:

Vocabulary-12: If you have a verb theme whose meaning involves motion, you can create an expression which refers to the start of the motion by combining the word **dah** with a verb built from the verb base whose structure is as follows:

Stem-set: use the momentaneous stem-set of the verb theme	Classifier: use the classifier of the verb theme
	Lexical prefixes: **d** (inner)
	Transitivity: use the transitivity of the verb theme
	Conjugation: long-vowel conjugation in all modes except F

Let's study the forms of these verbs first, and then we'll talk a bit about what they mean.

Let's start with the verb themes that refer to simple going. To save time and space, we won't write out the verb bases that Vocabulary-12 creates from the verb themes (you can see the themes themselves in Chapter 17(23), Chapter 17(24), and Chapter 17(25).) But let's write out the forms of the verb. Keep in mind that we're going to use the momentaneous verb stems, the inner prefix **d**, and the long-vowel conjugations, except in the F mode, where we use the ordinary (regular) conjugation. For the singular go-verb, we have:

(37)   I   P   F

	I	P	F
1sg	diisháah	diiyá	dideesháál
2sg	diináah	diniyá	didíínáál
3(sg)	diigháah	diiyá	didoogáál
4(sg)	jidiigháah	jidiiyá	jididoogáál

Let's make sure we understand how these words are formed.

In the I mode, the subject prefixes are all from chart (1) above, since the subject prefixes in (37) are always preceded by an inner (hence, conjunct) prefix, which means that they are not preceded by a disjunct prefix. In addition, the irregularies that we've already seen lots of times with the singular go-verb are present. For example, the **n** in **diináah** is due to one of those irregularities (see Chapter 17(8)), as is the **gh** in **diigháah** and **jidiigháah** (see Chapter 17(10).)

In the P mode, the subject prefixes are taken from (14) and (16). There are no object prefixes in this verb, so the 2sg subject prefix is **ini** (see (16).) Note all the low tones in the subject prefixes.

The F mode forms in (37) are not formed according to the long-vowel conjugation, but according to the regular F mode conjugation. This means that the F mode words in (37) are actually the same as the F mode words in Chapter 17(29) which were formed from a different verb base that also used the inner **d** prefix and the momentaneous go-verb stem-set.

Before going on to the dual and plural go-verb forms created by Vocabulary-12, there is something that we should say about pronunciation and writing.

According to Vocabulary-12, when we use the words in (37), we combine them with the word **dah**. For example, we say things like:

(38)   Kinłánígóó dah diiyá.   "I set off for Flagstaff."

Now, we already mentioned several times that when a verb is combined with another word (like **dah**) to form an expression, the other word is pronounced almost as though it were a prefix to the verb. In the case of those words in (37) that have the 4 person subject prefix in them (the words that start with **j**), this leads to the following development.

The word **dah** ends in an **h**. But suppose we ignore the **h** for a moment, and think of **da(h)** as an outer prefix. What would happen? Well, the **j** in the words **jidiigháah**, **jidiiyá**, and **jididoogáál** would be preceded by the vowel **a** (we're ignoring the **h**, remember?), and the syllable following the **j** (the syllable **dii** or **di**) is not the verb stem syllable, so Rule Conj-5 would not insert any vowel after the **j**, and moreover the **j** would turn into **zh**, which means we'd end up with words like "da-zhdiigháah", "da-zhdiiyá", and "da-zhdidoogáál". But there is in fact an **h** in there - what could its

277

effect be? The answer is this: it changes the **zh**'s into **sh**'s. The final result of all this is, instead of pronouncing these expressions as though they were written like this:

(39)   dah jidiighááh, dah jidiiyá, dah jididoogááł

people usually pronounce these expressions as though they were written like this:

(40)   dashdiighááh, dashdiiyá, dashdidoogááł

In fact, these expressions are very often written as in (40) rather than (39), so be prepared to see spellings like these! The tricky thing about the spellings in (40) is this: you see (and hear) an **sh** in the word, but this **sh** is a "version" of the prefix **j**. And, at the same time, the word begins with **da**, which you somehow have to recognize is really the word **dah**. In most cases, when you see or hear **dash** at the beginning of a verb, and this syllable isn't the pre-stem syllable, it's probably the word **dah** followed by a verb form that starts with **j**.

Having discussed all of this, let's now write out the dual and plural go-verbs created by Vocabulary-12. The dual words are:

(41)   I   P   F

1dpl   diit'aash   diit'áázh   didiit'ash
2dpl   dooh'aash   doo'áázh   didooh'ash
3(dpl) dii'aash   dii'áázh   didoo'ash
4(dpl) jidii'aash   jidii'áázh   jididoo'ash

(And, of course, people usually say **dashdii'aash**, **dashdii'áázh**, and **dashdidoo'ash** instead of **dah jidii'aash**, **dah jidii'áázh**, and **dah jididoo'ash**.)

The plural words are:

(42)   I   P   F

1dpl   diikááh   diikai   didiikah
2dpl   doohkááh   doohkai   didoohkah
3(dpl) diikááh   diikai   didookah
4(dpl) jidiikááh   jidiikai   jididookah

(How do people usually pronounce the 4 person forms in (42) when they are combined with **dah**?)

Like the vocabulary principles that we learned earlier which made use of verb themes of motion, Vocabulary-12 can be used with any motion verb theme to create a meaningful expression.

Le'ts say something about how these words are used.

When Vocabulary-12 is applied to an intransitive motion verb theme, the meaning tends to be something like the translation given for sentence (38) above. In English, expressions with this meaning, more or less, are: "set off", "leave", "start off", etc. This is true even if the verb isn't one of the plain "go" verbs. Here's an example based on our "crawl" theme:

(43)   T'óó hooghanjigo dah diish'na'.

This means something like "I started crawling home", or "I set off for home, crawling".

If a transitive classificatory verb theme is used as input to Vocabulary-12, the expressions we get can mean "start to go off while carrying it/him/them", or perhaps "make off with it/him/them". But in addition, such expressions can simply mean "lift it/him/them up". For example, we can form a sentence like:

(44)   Díí awéé' shá dah diiłteeh.

which means "Lift the baby (up) for me." The word **diiłteeh** is based on the classificatory verb theme that means "move an animate being" (see Chapter 17(22).)

Transitive manner-of-motion verb themes can also be used, with a meaning of starting the motion or getting the motion underway. An example:

(45)   Díí yas dah diiłmááz. "I got this snowball started rolling."

You might want to compare Vocabulary-12 with Vocabulary-2, discussed in Chapter 17. In both cases, an inner **d** prefix is used, along with momentaneous verb stems, and in both cases, the meaning has to do with starting the motion. However, the verbs created by Vocabulary-2 have a special present/future meaning in the P mode. Also, those verbs are used in a number of special idiomatic expressions. They are less often used to refer overtly to the actual starting of motion. On the other hand, the expressions created by Vocabulary-12 are in fact regularly used to refer directly to the beginning of movement.

Note that the verb bases created by Vocabulary-12 use the long-vowel conjugation in all modes except the F mode. This makes these verb bases a little different from the ones created by Vocabulary-11. Even so, YM includes the verb bases created by Vocabulary-12 in the group they call transitional aspect verb bases. They use the term *transitional inceptive* to describe specifically the expressions created by Vocabulary-12.

(One thing you may have discovered about YM is that they give names to many groups of verb bases that are constructed in particular ways and have particular meanings. As we come to various of these constructions and describe them with vocabulary principles, we'll mention the name used by YM for those constructions so that you'll be able to find out more about them in the YM reference works.)

Let's finish off this chapter with some comparison games, to help us remember the various patterns of prefixes that we've learned so far.

Vocabulary-12 creates verb bases in which the inner prefix **d** is combined with long-vowel conjugations. It is instructive to compare what the long-vowel conjugations look like with what the regular conjugations look like with that **d** in there. For example, in the I mode, if the subject is 1sg, a verb in the regular conjugation has **dish** in it, but a verb in the long-vowel conjugation will have **diish** in it. Here is a little chart of possibilities:

(46)

Subject	Regular I mode with inner **d**	Long-vowel I mode with inner **d**
1sg	dish	diish
2sg	dí	dii
3	di	dii
1dpl	diid	diid
2dpl	doh	dooh

You should be able to understand why each of these has the shape that it does.

Here are prefix forms for the P-mode. We've put in forms for s-P as well as y-P, as a review.

(47)

Subject	y-P with inner **d**	Long-vowel P with inner **d**	s-P with inner **d**
1sg (zero/barred-l)	díí	dii	dé
1sg (plain-l/d)	deesh	diish	désh
2sg	dííní	dini	díní
3 (zero/barred-l)	díí	dii	deez/dees
3 (plain-l/d)	doo	dii	dees
1dpl	diid	diid	deed/disiid
2dpl(zero/barred-l)	doo	doo	disoo
2dpl(plain-l/d)	dooh	dooh	disooh

Again, make sure you understand why each of these combinations has the shape that it does.

The chart in (48) below has some of the same information arranged differently. The first column in (48) gives several possibilities for inner **d** combined with a 1sg subject prefix in the P mode. The second column describes what the conjugation pattern is. Can you cover up the second column and say what the conjugations are? Can you cover up the first column and give the subject prefixes?

(48)

P mode 1sg subject prefixes preceded by inner **d**	Conjugation
díí	y-P (zero/barred-l)
dii	long-vowel (zero/barred-l)
dé	s-P (zero/barred-l)
deesh	y-P (plain-l/d)
diish	long-vowel (plain-l/d)
désh	s-P (plain-l/d)

And here's the same game for the 2sg subject prefix:

(49)

P mode 2sg subject prefixes preceded by inner **d**	Conjugation
dííní	y-P
dini	long-vowel
díní	s-P

For practice: write up charts like (48) or (49) for the 3 person subject prefixes, the 1dpl prefixes, and the 2dpl prefixes in the P mode.

Exercises like this will help you recognize what you're seeing and hearing when you examine a particular verb. For example, if you see a verb that means "you (sg) (did something)" (so you think the verb is probably in the P mode), and you see **dini** (with low tones) in there, you'll guess that you're looking at a verb conjugated in the long-vowel P conjugation. This means that if you want to find the verb in YM 87 (which means you want to find its 1sg I mode form), you'll guess something with **diish** in it as the 1sg I mode form. (It happens that if a verb uses the long-vowel conjugation in the P mode, it'll use the long-vowel conjugation in the I mode, too. In Chapter 27 we'll survey the most common conjugation patterns for Navajo verb bases.)

Here's another kind of problem you might be faced with: suppose you see a verb that has **diish** in it, and you're pretty sure that the **sh** is the 1sg subject prefix and the **d** is the inner prefix **d**. What can you tell about the verb? Answer: The verb is either in the long-vowel I mode or else in the long-vowel P mode, but if it's the long-vowel P mode, then the classifier is plain-l or d. (Study the charts in (46), (47), and (48) until you understand why this is so!)

For practice: pick any of the combinations in the charts above and ask the same question. That is, try to figure out what you can about the mode, conjugation, and even classifier of a verb based on seeing a particular combination of **d** with a subject prefix. For example, if you see **dii** in a verb (low-tone **ii**, no **sh** after it), what possible forms could this be?

Well, this finishes our study of the long-vowel conjugations in the I, P, and F modes. It's time to move on to our next topic.

CHAPTER 21

THOSE PESKY N'S,
AND THE CONJUNCT HIGH TONE

If you have been faithfully working on your Navajo vocabulary, you may have noticed that a lot of verbs have **n**'s in them somewhere before the verb stem. We've already learned about one outer prefix that has an **n** in it, namely the prefix **na**. We've also learned about the special n-I and n-P conjugations (in Chapter 18) - most of the subject prefixes for these conjugations have **n**'s in them. But there are other **n**'s that can show up in a verb. In this chapter, we're going to learn about most of them. There are a number of different **n**'s involved, so we have a bit of work to do.

First of all, it is possible for **n** all by itself to be an inner lexical prefix for a verb base. Do you remember that in Chapter 15 we learned that **d** all by itself can be an inner prefix? The situation with **n** is roughly the same. In fact, we almost don't have to learn anything new in order to create most of the actual forms of such verbs. Let's look at such a verb base right away. The following verb base means "card it (wool)":

(1)

Stem-set		Classifier: barred-l
I:	**chaad**	
P:	**chaad**	Lexical prefixes: **ha** (outer), **n** (inner)
F:	**chał**	
R:	**cha'**	Transitivity: transitive
P:	**chaad**	Conjugation: y-P

(You might remember that when the outer prefix **ha** is present in a verb base, the perfective conjugation for that verb base is expected to be the y-P conjugation.)

You do not need to know anything new to create the I-mode forms of this verb base. Try to do so yourself, before looking at the actual forms, which are:

(2)   sg   dpl   distr dpl

	sg	dpl	distr dpl
1	hanishchaad	haniilchaad	hadaniilchaad
2	haniłchaad	hanołchaad	hadanołchaad
3		hainiłchaad	hadeiniłchaad
4		hazhniłchaad	hadazhniłchaad

By now, you should know all the rules involved in building these forms, so we won't discuss any of them. You might want to compare the forms in (2) with the forms in Chapter 15(2), where the I mode forms of a verb base with inner **d** are shown. (That verb base doesn't have an outer prefix, but you shouldn't have any trouble relating the forms there with the forms in (2).)

You should also have no trouble creating the P-mode forms of the verb base in (1), provided you remember that since this verb base has the outer prefix **ha** in it, we expect perfective da-shift to take place. Assume that the da-shift only happens when the subject is 3 or 4 person. Can you write out the P-mode forms? Here they are:

(3)	sg		dpl	distr dpl
1	hanííłchaad	haniilchaad		hadaniilchaad
2	hanííníłchaad	hanoołchaad		hadanoołchaad
3		hainííłchaad		hadaneeshchaad
4		hazhnííłchaad		hadazhneeshchaad

But wait! Are you wondering where the vowel **ee** in the forms **hadaneeshchaad** and **hadazhneeshchaad** came from? The answer is that the inner prefix **n** contracts with the subject prefixes of the s-P conjugation in much the same way that the inner **d** prefix does. We'll study the forms carefully in just a moment - for now, you might want to review the contracted forms for the inner **d** prefix (see Chapter 15(11) and Chapter 15(12).) Note that when the subject prefix is 3 person and there's an inner **d** in the verb, we get the prefix **deez** or **dees** in the s-P conjugation. With an inner **n**, we get **neez** or **nees**.

To build the F-mode forms of a verb base with an inner **n** prefix we need to learn about something new. For fun, try to write out the F-mode forms of the verb base in (1) (don't forget to put the F-mode **d** and the inner prefix **n** in the right order!), and compare your forms with the correct ones shown below:

(4)	sg		dpl	distr dpl
1	hadínéeshchał		hadíníilchał	hadadíníilchał
2	hadínííłchał		hadínóołchał	hadadínóołchał
3		haidínóołchał		hadeidínóołchał
4		hazhdínóołchał		hadazhdínóołchał

Do you see the difference between what you wrote and the forms in (4)? If you did your work correctly, the only difference is that there are some mysterious high tones in the forms in (4).

Here's what's going on. It is possible for a high tone all by itself to be a conjunct prefix! When this happens, we will call this high tone the *conjunct high tone*. Now, whenever a verb base has an inner prefix **n** in it, it turns out that in the F mode this conjunct high tone suddenly appears automatically in between the F mode **d** prefix and the inner **n**. This is a peculiar structural fact about the way F mode forms are built when there is an inner **n** prefix, so it looks like we're going to need another structure rule. Here it is:

<u>Rule Str-6</u>: If a verb base has an inner **n** prefix in it, then, in the F mode, insert a conjunct high tone just in front of the inner **n**.

What this rule tells us is that when we want to build a structure that represents, say, the word that means "I'll card it", which we would expect to look like this:

(5) outer   F mode   inner   subject   cl   verb
     prefix   d   prefix prefix   stem

      ha   -   d   -   n   -   eesh - ł - chał

Rule Str-6 comes along and puts in that "conjunct high tone" in front of the inner **n**, so we get a structure like this:

(6) outer   F mode   inner   subject   cl   verb
     prefix   d   prefix prefix   stem

      ha   -   d - high-tone - n   -   eesh - ł - chał

What Rule Str-6 doesn't tell us is what to do with this high tone! We need a new conjunct prefix rule.

 (The reason we're separating the idea of putting a conjunct high tone into an F mode verb form from the idea of what that tone actually does is that, as we'll see in a little bit, a conjunct high tone can be part of a verb for reasons other than Rule Str-6. For example, some verb bases have a conjunct high tone as a lexical prefix.)

The actual effect of a conjunct high tone is, as you may have guessed, to put a high tone on certain vowels. But to describe what actually happens, we will need to talk about different cases. The first thing that we need to know is that whenever a verb has a conjunct high tone in its structure, there will be a conjunct prefix to its left. (This isn't exactly a rule - it's simply a fact!) For example, in the structure diagrammed in (6), the conjunct high tone has the F mode **d** to its left - remember that the F mode **d** is a conjunct prefix. This means that whenever a structure contains a conjunct high tone, part of that structure will look like this:

(7)   some conjunct
        prefix

        ...   C   -   high-tone   ....

where "C" stands for the consonant at the end of the conjunct prefix that immediately precedes the conjunct high tone. What actually happens depends on what follows the conjunct high tone. So let's give our rule, which we'll divide up into cases according to what follows the conjunct high tone. We'll give this rule in a fairly complete form, although for the verb base that we're looking at, we won't need all this detail.

<u>Rule Conj-8</u>:

(a) Suppose a conjunct high tone is part of a structure like this:

        some conjunct
        prefix

        C   -   high-tone   -   V

(Here "C" is the consonant at the end of the preceding conjunct prefix. This case is where the conjunct high tone is immediately followed by a vowel, represented by "V".) Then:

    if V is a short vowel, it acquires a high tone (if it doesn't already have one)

    if V is a long vowel or diphthong, then the <u>first</u> vowel letter of V acquires a high tone (if it doesn't already have one)

(b) Suppose a conjunct high tone is part of a structure like this:

        some conjunct
        prefix

        C_1 -   high-tone   - C_2

(Here "C_1" is the consonant at the end of the preceding conjunct prefix. This case is where the conjunct high tone is immediately followed by a consonant, represented by "C_2".) What happens now depends on what follows C_2. In either case, Rule Conj-1 or Rule Conj-5 or Rule Conj-6 will insert a vowel in between C_1 and C_2. The first effect of the conjunct high tone is that this vowel acquires a high tone (if it doesn't already have one.) Now, if the syllable following C_2 is the verb-stem syllable (so that the syllable starting with C_1 is the pre-stem syllable), then nothing else happens. But if the syllable following C_2 is not the verb-stem syllable (so that the syllable starting with C_1 is not the pre-stem syllable), then the vowel of that syllable acquires a high tone as well, according to the same pattern as described in part (a).

Let's see how Rule Conj-8 works in the structure shown in (6).

First, do we have case (a) or case (b)? Well, in (6), the conjunct high tone is followed immediately by the consonant **n** (the inner prefix **n**, in fact), so we have case (b). We know that Rule Conj-1 will insert an **i** in between the F mode **d** and the inner **n**, so the first thing that part (b) of Rule Conj-8 tells us is that this **i** acquires a high tone and becomes **í**. Next, the syllable following the inner prefix **n** is not the verb-stem syllable, so part (b) of Rule Conj-8 tells us that the vowel of the next syllable also acquires a high tone, according to the pattern described in part (a). What is the vowel of the next syllable? It's **ee**, which is a long vowel. Part (a) of Rule Conj-8 tells us that the first vowel letter of this vowel acquires a high tone - this means we end up with **ée**. Thus, when we apply Rule Conj-8 to (6) (and also one of our old familiar rules - which one?), we end up with the actual word, which is **hadínéeshchał**.

Since we're in the F mode, all the vowels that follow the inner **n** in the forms in (4) will be long. (Why? Because all these vowels are the vowels that are part of the F mode subject prefixes, and these happen to all be long vowels.) This means that the effect of the conjunct high tone will be the same for all the F mode forms, except for when the subject is 2sg. (Why? Because in this case the subject prefix is already a long vowel which is high tone all the way: **íí**.) What we see is a long vowel where the first part is high tone and the second part is low tone. This is sometimes called a "falling tone", since the tone goes from high to low as the vowel is pronounced. Because of Rule Conj-8, we often see a syllable with a falling tone following the syllable that "really" carries a conjunct high tone. But remember: this only happens with syllables that aren't the verb-stem syllable. Rule Conj-8 never changes the tone of the verb-stem syllable!

It would probably be a good idea to compare Rule Conj-8 with Rule Subj-5. Rule Subj-5 allows the high tone at the end of (for example) a disjunct prefix to raise the tone of the vowel in the next syllable, but only if that vowel is short and only if that next syllable is the pre-stem syllable. Rule Subj-5 cannot do anything at all to any long vowel, no matter what its position. Rule Conj-8 can raise the tone of the first part of a long vowel - but Rule Conj-8 is triggered by one very specific thing, namely, the conjunct high-tone.

The fact that the F mode forms of verbs with the inner **n** prefix have a conjunct high tone is the one special fact that forced us to learn all this new material in order to be able to create forms of verbs that have the inner **n**. This is almost all we need to know about the inner **n**. The only thing left is something that we mentioned briefly in our discussion of the P mode forms in (3) earlier: just as the inner **d** prefix normally contracts with the s-P subject prefixes, the inner **n** prefix also normally contracts with the s-P subject prefixes. The actual contracted forms are very similar to the ones for inner **d** in Chapter 15(11) and Chapter 15(12). Here are charts for the contracted forms of the inner **n**:

(8)   inner **n** contracted with s-P subject prefixes,
        zero/barred-l classifiers:

	sg	dpl
1	né	need
2	níní	noo/sinoo
3	neez or nees	

(For the 3 person subject forms, we use **neez** if the classifier is zero, and **nees** if the classifier is barred-l. This is the same situation that we already learned about in connection with the inner **d** prefix.)

(9)   inner **n** contracted with s-P subject prefixes,
        plain-l/d classifiers:

	sg	dpl
1	nésh	need
2	níní	nooh/sinoo
3	nees	

Let's illustrate these contracted forms. To display the zero/barred-l classifier case, here's a verb base that means "herd them (animals)":

(10)

Stem-set	Classifier: barred-l
I: kaad P: kaad	Lexical prefixes: **na** (outer), **n** (inner)
F: kał R: ka'	Transitivity: transitive
O: kaad	Conjugation: s-P

The I and F mode forms of this verb are straightforward, so we won't give them here. Actually, the P mode forms are also straightforward, but let's write them out so that we can see the contractions in (8):

(11)   sg   dpl   distr dpl

1   nanélkaad   naneelkaad   nidaneelkaad
2   naníníłkaad nanoołkaad   nidanoołkaad
3   neineeskaad   nideineeskaad
4   nazhneeskaad   nidazhneeskaad

Something to notice: the outer prefix **na** does not change to **ni** in the forms in (11) that don't have the distributive plural prefix. We learned in Rule Disj-3 that **na** becomes **ni** when it is followed by the F mode **d**; and, although we haven't actually discussed this, it turns out that **na** becomes **ni** when it is followed by inner **d** as well (we've listed this case in the Appendix along with the cases we've seen.) However, **na** does not become **ni** when followed by inner **n** (or by any combinations involving **n**, such as **'n** or **zhn** or **zh'n**.) Keep this in mind when you write out the I mode and F mode forms of this verb (which you should do for practice.)

To illustrate the contracted forms for the plain-l/d classifier case, let's use the following verb base, which means "to squat down":

(12)

Stem-set		Classifier: plain-l
I:	**jííd**	
P:	**jííd**	Lexical prefixes: **n** (inner)
F:	**jííł**	
R:	**jííh**	Transitivity: intransitive
O:	**jííd**	Conjugation: s-P

Here are the P mode forms:

(13)   sg   dpl   distr dpl

1   néshjííd   neeljííd   daneeljííd
2   níníljííd   shinoołjííd   dashinoołjííd
3   neeshjííd   daneeshjííd
4   jineeshjííd   dazhneeshjííd

(The charts in YM 87 show the alternate 2dpl subject prefix **sinoo** for this verb. Note also that Rule Subj-6 applied.)

There are verb bases with the inner **n** prefix as a lexical prefix which are conjugated using the long-vowel conjugation in some of the modes. We don't have to learn anything new in order to work out the forms of such verbs. The actual forms look much the same as the forms we saw in Chapter 20 when we looked at verbs with the inner **d** prefix that were conjugated in the long-vowel conjugation, except, of course, that instead of a **d** there's an **n** there. Just to see a few forms, though, here's a vocabulary principle that creates some important verb bases like this:

Vocabulary-13: If you have a verb theme whose meaning involves certain kinds of actions or processes, you can build a verb base which has the meaning that the subject is starting that action, or that that process is starting, by doing the following:

Stem-set: use the momentaneous stem-set of the verb theme	Classifier: use the classifier of the verb theme
	Lexical prefixes: **Pi** (outer), **'** (object), **n** (inner)
	Transitivity: intransitive
	Conjugation: long-vowel conjugation in all modes except F

Note: when building a verb base using Vocabulary-13, if the original verb theme is transitive, then the outer object (the P in the outer prefix Pi) is used to represent the object of the action. If the original verb theme is intransitive, then the outer object is used to represent the subject, and when you build the verb, the actual subject prefix used is always the 3 person one.

Like some of the vocabulary principles we've seen, you cannot use Vocabulary-13 with any random verb theme. What you'll need to do is notice the actual cases of verbs built by Vocabulary-13 as you come across them. You'll see, however, that quite a few verb bases can be built this way.

We won't go through the complete conjugation of an example, but if you want to look at some forms, try using Vocabulary-13 with the verb theme that means "melt it" or "thaw it". You'll find the momentaneous stem-set and classifier for this theme inside the verb base in Chapter 13(8) - Vocabulary-13 will give you a verb base that means "start to melt it". (The verb theme is transitive, so the "P" in the verb base you build refers to the thing that is getting melted.) If you follow our rules carefully, you should be able to create all the forms of this verb correctly. To get you started: "I am starting to melt it" is **bi'niishhį́įh** (or: **bi'niishxį́įh**), and "he started to melt it" is **yi'niiłhį́į'**. When working out the forms for this verb, pay attention to the part of Rule Conj-5 that talks about unspec-hopping. You'll see this happening in the F mode for this verb; for example, "we (three or more) will start to melt it" is **bidadí'níilyįh**. The chart in YM 87 shows unspec-hopping happening even in one P mode form. (How do you say "you (sg) started to melt it"? How about **bini'niłhį́į'**? As we mentioned at the end of Chapter 18, unspec-hopping usually doesn't place the unspec prefix immediately in front of the **n** in the middle of the 2sg P mode subject prefix. But with words like this one it seems to be okay, possibly because the inner **n** makes this particularly easy to pronounce.)

Note on terminology: We mentioned in Chapter 20 that YM uses the word *transitional* to describe verb bases that are conjugated in the long vowel conjugations either in all modes or in all modes except F. They use the term *inchoative transitional* to refer to verb bases built by Vocabulary-13.

Verb bases with other prefix combinations also exist. For example, there are verb bases that have an inner **d** and an inner **n** prefix simultaneously.

Important fact: when both inner **d** and inner **n** are in a verb base, then the inner **d** prefix always precedes the inner **n**.

We won't give a rule for this since this is a fact about the way verb bases are constructed rather than a fact about the way actual forms are built starting from a verb base, but it's well worth remembering.

We also hinted earlier that some verb bases can have a conjunct high-tone as a kind of lexical element. Can a verb base have an inner **d**, an inner **n**, and a lexical conjunct high-tone? Yes! Will our rules give the correct forms for such a verb base? Let's see. Here is a verb base that means "start to herd them (animals)":

(14)

Stem-set		Classifier: barred-l
I:	**kaad**	
P:	**kaad**	Lexical prefixes: **d** (inner), high-tone (inner), **n** (inner)
F:	**kał**	Transitivity: transitive
R:	**ka'**	
O:	**kaad**	Conjugation: s-P

In this verb base we listed the conjunct high-tone as an "inner prefix", although it isn't exactly a prefix by itself. By the way, does the stem-set look familiar? If you examine the verb bases in (10) and (14), you might conclude (correctly!) that they both come from the same verb theme, and that the momentaneous stem-set and the continuative stem-set for this theme are the same. (Why is the stem-set in (14) the momentaneous stem-set? Why is the stem-set in (10) the continuative stem-set?)

Using what you know, try to write out all the I mode, P mode, and F mode forms of this verb. To see if you got the right answers, here are the I mode forms of this verb:

(15)	sg	dpl	distr dpl
1	díníshkaad	díníilkaad	dadíníilkaad
2	díníłkaad	dínółkaad	dadínółkaad
3		yidíníłkaad	deidíníłkaad
4		jidíníłkaad	dazhdíníłkaad

291

Rule Conj-8 is responsible for the falling tone on the **íi** syllable of (**da**)**díníilkaad**. It's also responsible for a few other high tones (which ones?)

Here are the P mode forms:

(16)	sg	dpl	distr dpl
1	dínéłkaad	dínéelkaad	dadínéelkaad
2	díníníłkaad	dínóołkaad	dadínóołkaad
3		yidínéeskaad	deidínéeskaad
4		jidínéeskaad	dazhdínéeskaad

Again, note those falling tones on **ée** and **óo** in some of these forms. That's Rule Conj-8 at work again.

Finally, here are the F mode forms:

(17)	sg	dpl	distr dpl
1	didínéeshkał	didíníilkał	dadidíníilkał
2	didínííłkał	didínóołkał	dadidínóołkał
3		yididínóołkał	deididínóołkał
4		dizhdínóołkał	dadizhdínóołkał

Rule Str-6 doesn't have any work to do in the F mode forms of this verb since there already is a conjunct high-tone just in front of the inner **n**.

Study the forms of this verb, which illustrate the effects of Rule Conj-8 as well as the contracted forms in the P mode.

Did you notice something odd about the 4 person F mode forms? The **j** prefix seems to have undergone the kind of hopping that we learned earlier happened with the unspec object prefix (see Chapter 15). This is a new effect that we haven't seen before. What's causing it is the fact that there are lots of lexical prefixes. Let's add a clause to Rule Conj-7 that deals with this:

(Add to Rule Conj-7): If **j** is followed by both the F mode **d** and the inner **d**, then **j** hops over the F mode **d** and is placed immediately in front of the inner **d** (and the first clause of this rule applies as well) if one of the following situations is also true: (a) there is at least one additional inner prefix in the verb; or (b) at least one of certain prefixes are present in the verb somewhere to the left of the **j**. The prefixes that trigger part (b) include outer **'a** and the seriative prefix **h** (discussed in Chapter 24.)

(We can call this effect "**j**-hopping". We'll add a note in the appendix reminding us that this is a movement process so we have to remember to try to apply it before working out the actual forms of the prefixes in a verb.)

In the case of the 4 person forms in (17), our new addition is triggered by the fact that, in addition to the F mode **d** and the inner **d**, the verb in (17) also has an inner **n** prefix.

Incidentally, it seems that when verbs start getting big and complex, there is greater variation from one speaker to another. You may run into cases where different speakers or different writers create forms that deviate slightly from what our new addition to Rule Conj-7 would predict. This is no problem if you already speak Navajo, but if you don't, you should be prepared for such variation. In learning new words, you should learn the forms that your teacher uses, or that are used by the people that you talk with.

At the end of Chapter 20, we did a little survey of some of the kinds of forms you'd see when a verb has an inner **d** prefix. Practically the same facts hold for inner **n**, except that with verbs that have **n**'s in them, there is an additional possibility: remember that in Chapter 18 we learned about the n-I and the n-P conjugations, and most of the subject prefixes for these conjugations involved an **n**. Because Navajo has those conjugations, it is possible for an **n** to be found in a verb for more reasons than the reasons for finding a **d** in a verb. Let's briefly look at some of the possibilities.

In the I mode, we have the following possibilities for prefix combinations involving **n**'s. (This chart assumes that there is no conjunct high-tone and no high tone due to Rule Subj-5. If either of these are present, of course, then there will be a high tone on more of the vowels in this chart.)

(18)

Subject	Regular I mode with inner **n**	Long-vowel I mode with inner **n**	n-I mode
1sg	nish	niish	nish
2sg	ní	nii	ní
3	ni	nii	(Chapter 18(24))
1dpl	niid	niid	niid
2dpl	noh	nooh	noh

Note that the forms for the regular I mode with inner **n** are almost the same as the forms for the n-I conjugation - the only difference is when the subject is 3 person, in which case the regular I mode has a prefix **ni** in there whereas the n-I mode has something else (review the information on the n-I mode conjugation and note that, in this conjugation, the 3 person subject prefix never has an **n** in it.) This means you should pay particular attention to the difference between a verb base that has an inner **n** and a verb base that is conjugated in the n-I conjugation - they'll look almost the same in the I mode (but they'll have more differences in other modes.) Remember especially: a verb base with an inner n will have that **n** in there in all forms of all modes, but a verb base that's conjugated in the n-I mode (and the n-P mode) won't have any extra **n** in any of its forms for the modes other than I or P.

Let's compare the various possibilities for the P mode:

(19)

Subject	y-P with inner **n**	Long-vowel P with inner **n**	s-P with inner **n**	n-P
1sg-zero/barred-l	**níí**	**nii**	**né**	**ní**
1sg-plain-l/d	**neesh**	**niish**	**nésh**	**nish**
2sg	**nííní**	**nini**	**níní**	**-íní**
3-zero/barred-l	**níí**	**nii**	**neez/nees**	**ní**
3-plain-l/d	**noo**	**nii**	**nees**	(Chapter 18(24))
1dpl	**niid**	**niid**	**need**	**niid**
2dpl-zero/barred-l	**noo**	**noo**	**(si)noo**	**noo**
2dpl-plain-l/d	**nooh**	**nooh**	**(si)nooh**	**nooh**

Note that in the P mode, the four conjugation patterns displayed in (19) are reasonably different from each other, at least for the 1sg, 2sg, and 3 subject cases. For the duoplural subjects, they are much more alike. (The same can be said for the I mode.)

This is all we need to say about the inner **n** prefix at this time. However, by now you may have run across Navajo verbs that have **n**'s in them in a conjunct prefix position but where the verb forms don't fit any of the patterns we've seen so far. Let's take a brief look at a few of these.

First, there are many neuter verbs that have **n**'s in them. (Remember: a neuter verb is a verb that is conjugated in only one mode. By the way, in YM, ordinary verbs that aren't neuter verbs are called *active verbs*.) When a neuter verb is conjugated only in the P mode, the forms are (in most cases) the same as the P mode forms we've seen all along for ordinary verbs. But there are many neuter verbs that are conjugated only in the I mode, and these sometimes have special subject prefixes involving an **n**.

The situation with I mode neuter verbs is actually a bit complex. Different I mode neuter verbs are often conjugated quite differently. Many I mode neuters can be grouped into classes, each with a particular conjugation pattern, but others (such as the "want"/"think" verb that we learned in Chapter 16) are special cases. We will not be able to study the entire range of these verbs here. What we'll do is look at a few representative cases. If you are learning Navajo as a new language, what you need to do is, first of all, learn the forms of each I mode neuter individually, and then group them into classes that will help you remember the forms. (We'll suggest a few classes here.) The good news, of course, is that these verbs are conjugated only in this one mode.

To get started, here is a chart giving a framework for the subject prefixes for a considerable number of I mode neuter verbs:

(20)   Common subject prefixes for I mode neuter verbs:

	sg	dpl
1	**nish**	**niid**
2	**ní**	**noh**
3	(see (21))	

This looks a lot like the chart we gave back in Chapter 18(21) for the n-I conjugation subject prefixes. The difference has to do with the 3 person prefix. In the case of neuter verbs, the possibilities for this prefix are different than for ordinary ("active") verbs. In fact, for the neuter verbs, we cannot give a nice rule the way we did in Chapter 18(24) - different neuter verbs work differently, which means that the 3 person form really has to be learned for each neuter verb. Here are the most common possibilities (the ones shown in (21) are not the only ones, though!):

(21)

If the 3 subject prefix is preceded by:	the 3 subject prefix can be:
an outer prefix	zero
distr pl **da**	zero or **ni**
an object prefix	**í** (**hw+í-->hó**) or zero
an inner prefix	zero or **ni**
no prefix at all	**ni**

One principle that seems to be true: if a neuter verb has a lexical outer prefix, then the form of the 3 subject prefix is usually zero rather than any of the other options. But, as we said, different neuter verbs can be different with regard to the 3 subject prefix, so be prepared to memorize those forms! And, unfortunately, some I mode neuters don't have their other prefixes exactly as shown in (20), either. Even so, it is probably a good idea to regard (20) and (21) as a starting point for learning I mode neuter verb forms.

As we mentioned earlier, the subject prefixes shown in (20) and (21) resemble the subject prefixes for the n-I conjugation. Since (21) is different from Chapter 18(24), we will not call the conjugation shown in (20) and (21) the n-I conjugation. When we find an I mode neuter that has the forms shown in (20) and (21) we'll say that it is conjugated in the neuter n-I conjugation. But keep in mind that because of the options listed in (21), saying that a verb base is conjugated in the neuter n-I conjugation doesn't give all the information we need. We still have to learn what the actual 3 subject prefix is for that verb base.

Some neuters have a conjunct high tone in them. When this happens, Rule Conj-8 will tell us where the actual high tones are found in the word.

Since we're talking about neuter verbs, this might be a good place to briefly mention something important about the prefix **hw**. We learned in Chapters 11 and 12 that **hw** is an object 4 person prefix. We also learned that this prefix can be a lexical prefix as part of a verb base. Now, it turns out that with a fair number of intransitive verbs, including quite a few neuter verbs, **hw** can be used as a subject prefix - that is, it can be used to refer to the subject of the verb. The **hw** prefix is used this way when the subject is some sort of area or a place, such as a building or a landscape feature. (We briefly mentioned this meaning in Chapter 12; recall that YM uses the term *3s prefix* for **hw** when it has this meaning. The "s" in the term "3s" stands for "space".) Important: when it's used this way, the **hw** prefix is still placed in the object prefix slot. Mostly, Rule Conj-6 still tells us how its forms look, but for a number of neuters, when the **hw** syllable is the pre-stem syllable, the form we see is **hoo** rather than **ha** - you will have to be alert to this possibility.

Let's look at a few examples of neuter n-I verbs. Here's a verb base that means "be tall/long":

(22)

Stem-set I: **neez**	Classifier: zero
	Lexical prefixes: (none)
	Transitivity: intransitive
	Conjugation: neuter n-I (3 = **í** after an object prefix, otherwise **ni**)

In the "Conjugation" slot we simply listed the facts about the 3 subject prefix that we need to know in order to conjugate this verb.

Try writing out the forms of this verb - there is enough information in (22) for you to do so! Then compare what you've written with the following:

(23)	sg	dpl	distr dpl
1	nisneez	nii'neez	danii'neez
2	níneez	nohneez	danohneez
3		nineez	danineez
4		jíneez	dajíneez

This is one reasonably common pattern for neuter verbs. This pattern includes a number of verbs whose meanings correspond to English adjectives of size. But for comparison, look at the following related verb base whose meaning can be roughly described as: "be tall/long to a certain degree":

(24)

Stem-set I: nééz	Classifier: barred-l
	Lexical prefixes: high-tone (follows subject **n**'s)
	Transitivity: intransitive
	Conjugation: (almost:) neuter n-I (3 = **ni** always)

The fact that the conjunct high-tone in this verb follows the **n**'s of the subject prefixes suggests that these **n**'s should perhaps be analyzed as inner lexical prefixes. One of the actual forms of this verb also suggests this in another way. Here are the forms - can you find the unexpected one?

(25)	sg		dpl	distr dpl
1	nísnééz		níilnééz	daníilnééz
2	níníłnééz		nółnééz	danółnééz
3		níłnééz		daníłnééz
4		jiníłnééz		dazhníłnééz

The 2sg form in (25) starts out **níní-**!

It happens that for a number of I mode neuters, we'll find a 2sg form in **nini-** or **níní-** instead of the **ní-** that chart (20) promises. We'll simply have to keep alert to these possibilities.

For your information: there's a third I mode neuter verb base related to the ones in (22) and (24). The structure of this third base is the same as the one in (24) except that there's an additional lexical prefix, namely, the outer prefix **'á** (with high tone.) The conjugation of this verb base is the same as for (24), so that, except for one form (which one? (see Rule Conj-7)), the actual written forms are exactly the same as the ones in (25) with an **á** added on in front. The meaning of this third verb base can be roughly described as "be tall to a particular degree".

In case you were wondering about the difference in meaning between (22), (24), and the third verb base described in the previous paragraph, it's this. The verb base in (22) is used when you want to say that something is simply long, or a person is in fact tall. The verb base in (24) is used when the length of something or the tallness of a person has to be referred to without actually saying that that thing or person is in fact long or tall - a typical situation for using this verb base is in a question that asks for a person's height. The third verb base is used when the actual degree of tallness is what's important - a typical situation for using this verb base is in a comparative statement. For example, if you want to say "Dan is tall", you'd say **Dan nineez** - in this case, Dan is definitely tall. If you want to ask "How tall is Dan", you'd say **Dan haa nííłnééz?** - because you can ask how tall he is even if in fact he isn't tall. If you want to say "Dan is taller than Bill", you'd say **Dan Bill yiláahgo áníłnééz** - because the degree of Dan's tallness is important (we're saying it exceeds the degree of Bill's tallness.)

Many neuter verbs whose meanings correspond to adjectives of size (or some other quantifiable characteristic) come in triples like this. Often, the second and third members of the triple have a different classifier than the first one, just as we saw in the case of the three "tall" verb bases above. The conjugations of these triples follow the example of the "tall" verb bases exactly. So I mode neuters like this constitute one of the groups (or maybe, three of the groups!) that you should keep in mind when you learn new neuter verbs.

For something a bit different, here is a neuter verb base that means "look like":

(26)

Stem-set I: **lin**	Classifier: zero
	Lexical prefixes: **na** (outer), **hw** (object)
	Transitivity: intransitive
	Conjugation: neuter n-I (3 = zero; 3 = **í** after **j**)

Don't forget to check Rule Conj-6 when writing out the forms of this verb. You should get:

(27)	sg	dpl	distr dpl
1	nahonishłin	nahoniidlin	nidahoniidlin
2	nahonílin	nahonohłin	nidahonohłin
3	nahalin		nidahalin
4	nahojílin		nidahojílin

Note that in this verb, the 3 subject prefix is zero when preceded by the lexical object prefix **hw**, but the 4 person subject prefix, which is placed (as usual) in the object position, causes the 3 subject prefix to become **í**.

As your Navajo vocabulary increases, you will run across more and more different examples of neuter verbs that are conjugated in some version of the I mode. A few of them have a real inner **n** prefix, but, as we hinted earlier, when dealing with neuter verbs its sometimes hard to tell the difference between a real inner **n** prefix and the **n**'s that are part of the subject prefixes of the neuter n-I conjugation. You will run across a few neuters with an inner **n** where the subject prefixes combined with this **n** show this pattern: (1sg:) **neesh**, (2sg:) **nini**, (3:) **nee**, (1dpl:) **niid**, and (2dpl:) **nooh** - these might remind you of the irregular P mode pattern we looked at at the end of Chapter 16. (You will also find a few neuters that have **d**'s instead of **n**'s in patterns similar to this.)

And there are other special patterns you'll find among the neuters. For example, there is a group of neuters (many of which denote colors, or certain other perceptually salient characteristics) that have a **ł** prefix which combines with the subject prefixes like this: (1sg:) **łinish**, (2sg:) **łiní**, (3:) **łi**, (1dpl:) **łiniid**, (2dpl:) **łinoh** - these words all have the zero classifier, but the **ł** prefix actually turns into a plain-l classifier when the subject is 3 person and the word has other prefixes in it (conjunct or disjunct), including the distributive plural prefix. Other neuter patterns exist, too. Unfortunately, as we said, we cannot give the sort of general analysis of I mode neuters that we're able to give for active verbs, so you'll have to learn each new neuter verb on its own, although the examples we've looked at should provide a good framework for starting to see groups of neuters.

Before we move onto another topic, let's end our exploration of Navajo neuter verbs by looking at a few verb bases that have to do with being. Navajo has a number of these, and each has its own 3 person prefix facts. First, here is a verb base that is used only with certain other words; YM translates it as "be in a condition":

(28)

Stem-set I: **t'é**	Classifier: zero
	Lexical prefixes: (none)
	Transitivity: intransitive
	Conjugation: neuter n-I (3 = zero)

Because there are no lexical prefixes, and because the 3 prefix is always zero, the peg rule will operate in one of the forms of this verb. Here are the forms:

(29)	sg	dpl	distr dpl
1	nisht'é	niit'é	daniit'é
2	nít'é	noht'é	danoht'é
3		yit'é	daat'é
4		jit'é	dajit'é

Incidentally, when we use the **hw** prefix (with the "area" meaning) with this verb base, the form we get is: **hoot'é**. (You may have heard someone asking about the weather by saying **Tł'óo'di haash hoot'é?** which means, more or less, "What's it like outside?") Recall that we said that the **hw** prefix sometimes appears as **hoo** when its used this way with a neuter verb and its syllable is the pre-stem syllable.

A very common verb base related to the one in (28) has the outer prefix **'á** as a lexical prefix - this is one of the ordinary verbs that means "be". You might think that the only difference between this verb base and the one in (28) is this prefix, but if you look carefully at the forms, you'll see that there's another difference as well:

(30)

	sg	dpl	distr dpl
1	ánísht'é	ániit'é	ádaniit'é
2	ánít'é	ánóht'é	ádanoht'é
3		át'é	ádaat'é
4		ájít'é	ádajít'é

Looking at (30), we'd certainly blame the high tones on the subject prefix syllables on Rule Subj-5, and this is in fact correct for most of the cases. But how did the high tone get on the syllable **jí** in the word **ádaajít'é**? Clearly, for this verb, the 3 subject prefix takes the form **í** when preceded by the 4 person subject prefix **j** (otherwise, it's still zero, just as in the verb base in (28).) This sort of unpredictability is typical of the more commonly used neuter verb bases.

For completeness, let's give the verb base that means "be" when applied to persons:

(31)

Stem-set I: **lį́**	Classifier: zero
	Lexical prefixes: (none)
	Transitivity: intransitive
	Conjugation: neuter n-I (3 = **í** after an object prefix, otherwise **ni**)

And here are the forms, which are probably completely familiar to you:

(32)	sg		dpl	distr dpl
1	nishłį́		niidlį́	daniidlį́
2	nílį́		nohłį́	danohłį́
3		nilį́		danilį́
4		jílį́		dajílį́

The conjugation facts for (31) are the same as for (22), by the way. For these two verb bases, did the idea that the 3 person prefix **ni** becomes **í** when immediately preceded by an object prefix seem slightly familiar? This is exactly what happens to the 2sg subject prefix **ni** when Rule Conj-3 operates on it! With a little work, we can extend Rule Conj-3 so that it will apply this way to the 3 person **ni** in (22) and (31); and, with a little more fiddling, we can get those **í**'s that appear as 3 person subject prefixes in the n-I and n-P conjugations this way, too, by assuming that there's a **ni** prefix in there to start with. But this has to be done carefully: not every pre-stem **ni** syllable undergoes this process (for example, if **n** is an ordinary inner **n** in an active verb, this doesn't happen - see the 3 and 4 person nondistributive forms in (2) near the beginning of this chapter.) The different conjugation facts for different neuters make this task harder, too. So, let's leave this idea as an exercise....

This is all we are going to say about the neuter verbs in Navajo. As we've seen, there are quite a few **n**'s among them.

If you are working through this book for the first time, you might want to skip the next section and jump directly to the verb base in (47) (a relatively common verb with an inner **n** prefix that shows some irregularites.). However, at some point in your study you will need to find out about the **n**'s that we are about to discuss, which are different from the **n**'s we've seen so far but which we're including here, since we've been surveying **n**'s in this chapter. If you skip this section, make sure you come back to this material later on.

If you review what we have covered in this chapter, you'll see that in the (ordinary) n-I conjugation, subject prefixes for 1 and 2 persons have **n**'s in them, but the subject prefix for 3 person never has an **n** in it. This sometimes (but not always!) happens with the neuter n-I conjugations. On the other hand, if a verb base has an inner **n** as a lexical prefix, this **n** is there all the time - every verb form has it. The special pattern we are going to look at next has I mode forms that are similar to the n-I conjugation, in that when the subject is 1 or 2 person, there's an **n** in there, but when the subject is 3 person, there isn't any **n** there. (We will see that there are no **n**'s in the other modes at all (mostly!))

The verb bases we want to look at appear to also have an inner prefix **y** in them; in addition, many of them have the conjunct high-tone as part of their structure. These two elements are present in all the modes, so the best thing to say that they are lexical prefixes that are part of the verb base just like any other lexical prefixes we've seen so far. However, the I modes of these verbs show those **n**'s that we've mentioned, and, as we'll see in a moment, all this material combines with the subject prefixes in a special way. We said that in the other modes there is (mostly) no trace of the **n**, but again there are a few unusual combinations with the subject prefixes. So here's what we'll do: we'll say that verb bases like this have a special inner prefix that looks like this: **yn**, with or without a conjunct high-tone (depending on the verb base), and we'll simply list the forms that show how this prefix combines with the various subject prefixes. Incidentally, some of the verbs that have this prefix have peculiarities in addition to what we'll say here, so it will be best to plan to memorize some occasional extra facts about some of the verbs of this sort, just as we have to do with neuter verbs.

Here are two facts about these verb bases worth keeping in mind. First, almost all the verb bases that have both the **yn** inner prefix and the conjunct high-tone are transitive. This means that when the subject is 3 person, such verbs will have an object prefix in them. And second, it is mostly the case that if the verb base has the conjunct high-tone as well as the **yn** inner prefix, then its P mode conjugation will be the y-P, whereas if the verb base has the **yn** inner prefix but doesn't have the conjunct high-tone, its P mode conjugation will be the s-P. There are occasional exceptions to this, but you won't have any trouble figuring out what the forms should be for those exceptions.

Let's start with the I mode of this type of verb. As we said a moment ago, to make things as simple as possible, we'll just list the combinations of the subject prefixes with the **yn** element. First, if there is no conjunct high tone, we get the following combinations:

(33)   I mode subject prefixes combined with **yn** inner prefix:

	sg	dpl
1	(i)inish/oosh	(i)iniid
2	(i)iní	(i)inoh
3	(o)o	

(The longer forms are used when immediately preceded by a conjunct prefix.)

Two forms are shown for the 1sg combination. Apparently, speakers differ in which form they use; also, apparently, some verbs with the **yn** prefix prefer one or the other of these forms.

If there's a conjunct high-tone in the verb base, the combinations look like this:

(34)   I mode subject prefixes combined with **yn** inner prefix and conjunct high-tone:

	sg	dpl
1	(í)ínísh	(í)íníid
2	(í)íní	(í)ínóh
3	ó	

(The longer forms are used when immediately
preceded by a conjunct prefix.)

You may occasionally find **óosh** instead of **íinish** as the 1sg subject form for some verbs.

The strange thing about the combinations in (33) and (34) is is that in the 3 person, not only does the **n** disappear, but an **o** vowel appears. This 3 person **o**, together with the loss of the **n** in the 3 person, is a special feature of the **yn** prefix.

(You may have noticed that if we assume that a conjunct high-tone was sitting to the left of the **n**'s in the 1 person and 2 person forms, then the high tones in the prefixes in (34) would be created exactly as described by Rule Conj-8.)

Here is a common verb base that uses this conjugation. This verb base means "read it" or "count it/them":

(35)

Stem-set	Classifier: barred-l
I: ta'	
P: ta'	Lexical prefixes: high-tone (inner), **yn** (inner)
F: tah	
R: tah	Transitivity: transitive
O: ta'	Conjugation: y-P

Can you write out the I mode forms of this verb? You'll need to review Rule Str-3, since the structure of some of the forms starts with a vowel. Using the forms shown in (34) (since this verb base has a conjunct high-tone), you should get the following:

(36)	sg	dpl	distr dpl
1	yíníshta'	yíníilta'	deíníilta'
2	yínílta'	yínólta'	deínólta'
3		yólta'	dayólta'
4		jólta'	dajólta'

Make sure that you understand that the **y** at the beginning of the nondistributive 1 person and 2 person forms was put in there by Rule Str-3, but that the **y** in the 3 person forms is a real prefix: it's the 3 person object prefix for the direct form.

An easy way to see the longer forms in (34) is to take the verb base in (35) and add the unspec object prefix. The verb base you'll get by doing this is commonly used; it can mean "read" (i.e. read in general, without saying what you're reading), but it's also often used to mean "go to school". For example, the word that means "I'm reading" or "I'm going to school" is **íínishta'**. You should have no trouble working out the remaining I mode forms.

The verb base we just looked at had the conjunct high-tone. Here is a verb base that has the **yn** prefix but not the conjunct high tone. This verb base means "behave kindly" or "be nice":

(37)

Stem-set	Classifier: zero
I: **baah** P: **ba'**	Lexical prefixes: **j** (inner), **yn** (inner)
F: **baał** R: **baah**	Transitivity: intransitive
O: **baah**	Conjugation: s-P

(This verb base has an inner prefix, namely **j**, that we've never seen before, but we won't let that bother us, will we?)

This time, we'll use the forms in (33). The I mode comes out like this:

(38)	sg	dpl	distr dpl
1	jiinishbaah/jooshbaah	jiiniibaah	dajiiniibaah
2	jiiníbaah	jiinohbaah	dajiinohbaah
3		joobaah	dajoobaah
4		jijoobaah	dajijoobaah

(You may have noticed that the first **j** in the form **dajijoobaah** didn't turn into **zh**. Apparently, when the consonant following the 4 person **j** prefix is itself a **j**, this change doesn't happen. We'll put a little note into Rule Conj-7 about this.)

Let's now move on to the P mode forms for verb bases with the **yn** inner prefix. We'll do the y-P conjugation first.

Here is a chart showing the combinations of the **yn** prefix with subject prefixes for the case that the classifier is zero or barred-l. Since verb bases with the **yn** prefix but without the conjunct high-tone are conjugated in the s-P, we'll assume in this chart that there's a conjunct high-tone present. The forms are:

(39)   y-P conjugation, zero/barred-l classifier, subject prefixes combined with **yn** inner prefix and conjunct high-tone:

	sg	dpl
1	**í (íí) {v́v́}**	**yíid (íid)/yíníid (ííníid)**
2	**íní (ííní) {v́íní}**	**wóo (óo)/yínóo (íínóo)**
3	**í (íí) {v́v́}**	

(The forms in parentheses are used when preceded by a conjunct prefix.
The forms in curly brackets are used when preceded by a disjunct prefix.)

Let's say a few things about the form of the prefixes shown in (39).

The prefixes for the 1sg, 2sg, and 3 subjects in (39) are actually exactly the same as the prefixes for the ordinary y-P conjugation.

(By the way, this means that if the subject is 3 person and there is a 3 person direct object, we will find that the object pronoun **y** is doubled when not preceded by a (lexical) prefix, as is ordinarily the case with the y-P conjugation when there's no lexical inner prefix. In this case, there actually are lexical inner prefixes in the verb base (the conjunct high-tone and the **yn**), but these seem to disappear in the 1sg, 2sg, and 3 subject cases. Just to make sure, we'll add a little note to Rule Str-1 that mentions this case.)

The prefixes for the 1dpl and 2dpl subjects differ from the regular y-P prefixes. First of all, there's that falling tone, which is normal when there's a conjunct high-tone in there. Secondly, the **y** at the beginning of the 1dpl prefix and the **w** at the beginning of the 2dpl prefix are there not only when there is no prefix to the left of the subject prefix, but at least also when preceded by the distributive plural prefix **da**. (Some written forms suggest that the **y** and **w** at the beginning of these prefixes disappear when preceded by other disjunct prefixes.) And thirdly, the 1dpl and 2dpl cases have alternate forms with **n**'s in them.

Starting with the verb base in (35), it's easy to use (39) to build the P mode forms. Here they are:

(40)   sg   dpl   distr dpl

1   yíłta'   yíilta'   dayíilta'
2   yíníłta'   wóołta'   dawóołta'
3   yiyííłta'   dayííłta'
4   jííłta'   dajííłta'

Verb bases with the **yn** inner prefix and the conjunct high tone (and therefore take the y-P conjugation) that have a plain-l or d classifier are relatively rare. The combinations that seem to be found for those few verbs are the following:

(41)   y-P conjugation, plain-l/d classifier, subject prefixes combined with **yn** inner prefix and conjunct high-tone:

	sg	dpl
1	éésh {yéésh}	yíid (íid)
2	íní (ííní) {víní}	wóoh (óoh)
3	éé {yéé}	

(The forms in parentheses are used when preceded by a conjunct prefix.
The forms in curly brackets are used when preceded by a disjunct prefix.)

A verb base that displays these forms is the following one, which means "curse him/her out":

(42)

Stem-set		Classifier: d
I:	dziih	
P:	dzíí'	Lexical prefixes: high-tone (inner), **yn** (inner)
F:	dzih	
R:	dzih	Transitivity: transitive
O:	dziih	Conjugation: y-P

The P mode forms of this verb appear to be:

(43)   sg   dpl   distr dpl

	sg	dpl	distr dpl
1	yéésdzíí'	yíidzíí'	dayíidzíí'
2	yínídzíí'	wóohdzíí'	dawóohdzíí'
3		yéédzíí'	dayéédzíí'
4		jéédzíí'	dajéédzíí'

Let's move on to the combinations of the **yn** prefix with the s-P subject prefixes. Most verb bases that have this arrangement do not have the conjunct high-tone, so that's the only case we'll look at here. The actual forms are relatively easy.

(44)   s-P conjugation, zero/barred-l classifier, subject prefixes combined with **yn** inner prefix:

	sg	dpl
1	(i)isé	(i)isiid
2	(i)isíní	(i)isoo
3	**ooz** or **oos**	

(The longer forms are used when immediately preceded by a conjunct prefix.)

The 1 and 2 person combinations are the ordinary s-P subject prefixes preceded by an element **(i)i**. But in the 3 person combination, there's that **o**-based vowel again.

Let's just write out the P mode forms for the verb base in (37):

(45)   sg   dpl   distr dpl

	sg	dpl	distr dpl
1	jiiséba'	jiisiiba'	dajiisiiba'
2	jiisíníba'	jiisooba'	dajiisooba'
3		joozba'	dajoozba'
4		jijoozba'	dajijoozba'

If you have a verb base without an inner prefix (except for the **yn**), the s-P forms will start out with **yi** for 1 and 2 person.

You can probably guess what the combinations are if the classifier is plain-l or d. Here is a chart:

(46)   s-P conjugation, plain-l/d classifier, subject prefixes combined with **yn** inner prefix:

	sg	dpl
1	(i)isis	(i)isiid
2	(i)isíní	(i)isooh
3	oos	

(The longer forms are used when immediately
preceded by a conjunct prefix.)

We won't illustrate these here - the actual forms are straightforward.

The F mode forms of verbs with the **yn** inner prefix are also quite easy. They resemble the F mode forms for the long-vowel F conjugation. In fact, if the verb base in question doesn't have a conjunct high-tone, the forms are the same as the long-vowel F conjugation: an element **y** is placed directly in front of the F mode **d**. Exactly as in the long-vowel F conjugation, this element becomes long **ii** if there is a conjunct prefix immediately preceding it (remember the sandwiched **y** rule?), short **i** if there is a disjunct prefix immediately preceding it (that's Rule Disj-2 at work), and (by Rule Conj-1) **yi** if no other prefix precedes it. (The conjunct prefix that precedes this element will almost always be an object prefix, but occasionally something else can happen - we'll see an example in just a moment.) If the verb base has a conjunct high-tone, then this **y** element becomes **íí** or **í** or **yí** instead, and the vowel which follows the F mode **d** also takes a high tone as described by Rule Conj-8. We won't write out a complete set of forms (you should do that yourself), but, for example, starting with the verb base in (35), the word that means "I'll read it" or "I'll count it" is **yídéeshtah**. If we add the unspec object prefix to this, in order to create the word that means "I'll read" or "I'll go to school", we get **íídéeshtah**. The F mode forms of the verb base in (42) work exactly the same way.

In the case of the verb base in (37), there's a slight complication that has to do with the inner prefix **j**. This prefix wants to be to the left of any conjunct **d**'s around, so in the F mode, the inner **j** hops to the left of the F mode **d**. Since this **j** is a conjunct prefix, when we put **y** immediately to the left of the F mode **d**, it will become **ii**, by the sandwiched **y** rule.. Thus, the F mode forms of the verb base in (37) all have the syllable **jiid** inside them; for example, the word that means "I'll be nice" is **jiideeshbaał**. (Since the **j** inner prefix is relatively rare, we won't add in a special rule to take care of this movement, which means that officially we've got an irregularity in this verb. For practice: write out a structure rule that moves an inner **j** prefix to the left of any conjunct **d** prefix.)

(In order to say "one will be nice", some people say **jijiidoobaał** and some say **jiizhdoobaał**. Do you see what is happening? Can you suggest an addition to Rule Conj-7 to deal with this?)

This is all we are going to do with the **yn** inner prefix. Be on the lookout for more verbs with this prefix. Some of them have slight irregularities, which you simply will have to memorize. And you might want to keep in mind that there are some neuter verbs that have the **yn** prefix.

Since the F mode forms of these **yn** verbs involve a **y** element, and since there seems to be a **y** element in a lot of the forms in all the other modes, we might want to see if we can derive the various forms of the subject prefix combinations by applying our various rules, based on our assumption that there's a conjunct prefix **y** in there. The rules we've learned (mostly, it's the sandwiched **y** rule that comes into play) give the right answers for some of the combinations (you might want to check through and see which combinations work out correctly this way), but for others additional rules have to be made up; for example, we probably would want to say that the **y** prefix turns into **oo** if the syllable that would begin with this **y** would be the pre-stem syllable - this would be enough to take care of the s-P prefixes in (44) and (46). But we'd still have to deal with the **n** element that shows up in the I mode, and sometimes a bit in the y-P conjugation, for these verb bases - it appears and disappears in strange ways. For our purposes in this book, it seemed that the best thing to do for learning the forms of these verbs is to list out the actual combinations, and that's what we've done. But you might see discussions in other books or articles where these verbs are analyzed by saying that each form has a **y** element and some forms also have an **n** element that appears and disappears according to some special rules.

Well, this is (almost) all we are going to study in this chapter about **n**'s that you might find among the prefixes of a Navajo verb. Unfortunately, we haven't seen the whole story yet. Here are a few final comments to help you along at this point.

First of all, there are some outer prefixes involving **n**'s that we haven't seen. One important one is **ni**, which has a meaning that has to do with stopping an action or a motion. Verb bases with this outer prefix always use the n-I and n-P conjugations, so the forms of those verbs often have two **n**'s in them before the verb-stem syllable. If you want to write out the actual forms for such a verb base, you need to know that Rule Disj-1 changes **ni** to **nii** when the conditions for that rule are present. With that piece of information, you know enough to be able to create forms for verb bases with this outer prefix. But if you do, keep in mind that some of the forms that have outer **ni** in them will look like the forms we've seen for verb bases that have outer **na** (because **na** sometimes changes into **ni**!) You'll be able to tell **ni** and **na** apart, though, because **na** sometimes shows up as **na** or **naa** or **ne** (the last one in front of an **i** vowel), whereas **ni** never does. For example, if the next prefix is the 3 person object prefix **y**, an outer **na** prefix becomes **nei**, but an outer **ni** prefix becomes **nii**.

And, it is possible to get verb bases that have even more **n**'s in them. For example, there are verb bases that have the outer **ni** prefix that we just mentioned and also the inner **n** prefix. Since such verb bases use the n-I and n-P conjugations, we'll get a lot of **n**'s in the I and P modes! Believe it or not, the rules we've learned will give us the correct forms even for big verbs like that (we've really learned quite a lot.)

Two other outer prefixes with **n**'s in them are so important that we'll devote an entire chapter to them

(the next chapter, in fact.)

As a cool-down, let's finish this chapter by looking at the forms of one particular common verb base that has an inner **n** together with a few irregularities. This verb base means "look at it":

(47)

Stem-set		Classifier: barred-l
I:	**'į**	Lexical prefixes: **n** (inner), high-tone (inner)
P:	**'įį'**	
F:	**'įįł**	Transitivity: transitive
R:	**'iih**	
O:	**'įį'**	Conjugation: y-P with some irregular vowels

(You probably recognize the I mode verb-stem as being the same as the verb-stem for the verb base that means "see it", which we learned about in Chapter 16.)

Here are the I mode forms. Do you notice one irregularity?

(48)	sg	dpl	distr dpl
1	nísh'į	níil'į	daníil'į
2	nínił'į	nół'į	danół'į
3		yinił'į	deinił'į
4		jinił'į	dazhnił'į

The irregularity is that Rule Conj-3 didn't apply: the **n** that is part of the 2sg I mode prefix **ni** is still there (Rule Conj-8 gave it its high tone). We saw earlier a neuter verb with a 2sg form like this - look at the words in (25). In that case, we noted that the **níni-** form is regularly found with the particular kind of neuter verb base we were looking at (verb bases that correspond to adjectives of size or a quantifiable characteristic, where the degree of the size was uncertain.) But in (48) we have an active verb. Possibly, it is the fact that the 2sg prefix **ni** is immediately preceded by the conjunct high-tone which prevents Rule Conj-3 from applying - a small number of other verbs with a conjunct high tone and an inner **n** also don't allow Rule Conj-3 to apply. Except for this, the forms in (48) are completely regular.

In the P mode, we see some irregular vowels which are similar to the ones we saw back in Chapter 16(19) in connection with the inner **d** prefix. With this verb, which doesn't have an inner **d** but does have an inner **n** (and a conjunct high tone), we see an **éé** vowel appearing if the subject prefix is 1sg or 3, but not if the subject prefix is 1dpl. The P mode forms are:

310

(49)	sg	dpl	distr dpl
1	néél'įį'	nííl'įį'	danííl'įį'
2	nínít'įį'	nóoł'įį'	danóoł'įį'
3		yinéél'įį'	deinéél'įį'
4		jinéél'įį'	dazhnéél'įį'

There's another irregularity in (49): the 2sg form does not correspond to a y-P conjugation form with an inner **n** (check the chart in (19) earlier in this chapter). The **níní-** we see in (49) looks like the s-P conjugation, but we certainly don't have the s-P conjugation with this verb (there's no **s** in sight anywhere in (49).) Again, the conjunct high-tone is probably a factor in these irregularities, but rather than suggesting a rule let's just go ahead and memorize the forms.

The F mode forms of this verb are completely regular, so we won't write them out. A few other verb bases that use the "see" stem-set found in (47) also tend to have some irregularities in the I and P modes. Be on the lookout for them.

CHAPTER 22

"MORE" AND "BACK"

In this chapter we are going to learn about two very important outer prefixes. These two prefixes resemble each other somewhat (and they both have **n**'s in them), but they are also some important differences between them. Let's get right to the first one.

The first outer prefix is a prefix that can be added into almost any verb base to create a new verb base. The meaning that this prefix adds is "more" or "again". In other words, when we add this prefix in, the new word will mean that the action or event described by the word is happening (or has happened, or will happen) some more, or is happening again. The basic form of this prefix is **nááná**. Let's formulate what we've just said as a vocabulary principle:

Vocabulary-14: Starting with almost any verb base, a new verb base can be built whose meaning is that the action or event of the original verb base happens again or happens more by doing the following two things:

> (a) Add the outer prefix **nááná** into the verb base as a lexical outer prefix. If there are other lexical outer prefixes already in the verb base, then **nááná** will be the last outer prefix (that is, it will come after the other outer prefixes.)

> (b) For certain common verb bases, the classifier undergoes the process of classifier shift.

Vocabulary-14 is our first example of a vocabulary principle that builds a verb base out of another verb base. Rather than trying to explain how Vocabulary-14 works by giving a chart, we just listed the changes that have to be made to the verb base. But to understand Vocabulary-14, we need to explain what the process of *classifier shift* is.

There are a number of circumstances in the grammar of Navajo verbs where the classifier of a verb base changes in a particular way. Adding in the **nááná** prefix is the first example we've seen where this can happen. We're using the term *classifier shift* as our name for this change of classifier. What actually happens is that the zero classifier changes into the d classifier, the barred-l classifier changes into the plain-l classifier, but the other two classifiers don't change. Here is a chart that shows these changes:

(1)

classifier before classifier shift	classifier after classifier shift
zero	d
barred-l	plain-l
plain-l	plain-l
d	d

So, only two of the four classifiers actually get changed by this process - the other two remain the same. (Unfortunately, as you've probably noticed, the two classifiers that change are the most popular ones!)

There is nothing particularly hard about classifier shift as such. The tricky part is that it doesn't always happen! In fact, this is one of those processes where speakers sometimes differ. If you are learning the Navajo language as a new language, here's what you should keep in mind about Vocabulary-14. There are a number of verbs, including some very common ones, where all speakers shift the classifier according to (1). There are many verbs, including other relatively common ones, where few or no speakers shift the classifier. For some verbs, some speakers shift and others don't. We'll also see that classifier shift happens as part of other grammatical processes, but different grammatical processes require classifier shift with different groups of verbs. In the case of Rule Vocabulary-14, the situation seems to be as follows. First, very few, and possibly no verb bases with the barred-l classifier actually undergo classifier shift. And second, the most common zero-classifier verb bases shift to the d classifier, while the less common ones don't shift. So, in practice, when learning about Vocabulary-14, you only have to pay attention to the zero-classifier verb bases and remember which ones shift.

In general, the actual situation with regard to classifier shift has not been fully studied. As always, if you are learning the Navajo language, follow the example of your teacher and of the people that you usually speak Navajo with.

Before getting back to the **nááná** prefix, there is something else we should say about classifier shift: there are some verbs where something irregular happens when we shift the classifier. Let's look at the most important examples of this.

First of all, on a few occasions during our study, we ran into a classificatory motion verb theme that has to do with moving ropelike things; in fact, you can find this verb theme in Chapter 18(11). Now, all the verb stems for this theme begin with **l**, and we learned that whenever any 1dpl subject prefix is placed immediately to the left of one of these stems, instead of the **l** changing to **dl** (which is the usual d-effect result - remember that Rule Subj-1 says that the 1dpl prefix causes d-effect when it's immediately followed by the verb-stem), for this particular verb theme the **l** is changed into **ly**. Now, the classifier for this verb theme is zero, so if it undergoes classifier shift, the new classifier will be d; remember that a d classifier causes d-effect on the first consonant of whatever verb stem it is in front of. So, what happens when the verb theme in Chapter 18(11) shifts to the d classifier? Do all the **l**'s at the beginning of the verb stems become **ly**'s? No! In most cases, they just become **dl**'s, in a completely regular way. So, for these verb stems, we don't actually have an irregularity when classifier shift happens (which in this case causes d-effect, since the classifier becomes d), even though we do have an irregularity when the verb stem is immediately preceded by a 1dpl subject prefix (which also (normally) causes d-effect when the classifier is zero).

Next, what happens with the verb "eat"? Remember that in Chapter 16 we learned that this verb has a number of irregularities. The verb stems all begin with **y**, but when the verb stem is preceded by a 1dpl subject prefix, this **y** turns into a **d**. Since this verb also has a zero classifier, if it undergoes classifier shift, the new classifier becomes d. What happens to the verb stems? The answer for this verb is that the effect of the d classifier on the verb stems is the same as the effect of the 1dpl subject prefixes: the **y** at the beginning of the stems turns into **d**.

Finally, and perhaps most important, what happens to the singular go-verb when classifier shift happens? Chapter 17(12) gives us the answer. The original classifier for this verb theme is zero. Under classifier-shift, the classifier becomes d. By Chapter 17(12), when there's a d classifier in there trying to change the first consonant of the verb stem by d-effect, the hyphen at the beginning of a singular go-verb stem is replaced by a **d**. Chapter 17(12) also tells us that the singular go-verb P mode stem, which is **yá**, becomes **dzá** when d-effect applies to it. Since the P mode stem is the only one that doesn't begin with a hyphen, this gives us all the information we need about how d-effect words with the singular go-verb stem-set.

And speaking of P modes: for any verb that starts out with a zero or a barred-l classifier, if the verb undergoes classifier shift, this will automatically mean that in the P mode the set of subject prefixes will change. For example, if the verb is conjugated in the y-P conjugation, then instead of using the prefixes we studied in Chapter 9, we'll use the prefixes we studied in Chapter 10. Similar changes happen for the other conjugations, of course.

To finish our study of Vocabulary-14, there are two things we have to say about the prefix **nááná**.

First of all, under certain circumstances, a shortened form of the prefix **nááná** is used. This shortened form is **náá**. The circumstances when the shortened form is used are easy to state and to learn, so let's write up a rule. We're going to call this a structure rule rather than a rule about a disjunct prefix, because even after the rule applies, we'll still have to check the ordinary disjunct prefix rules to get the right forms.

Rule Str-7: The outer prefix **nááná** shortens to **náá** when it is immediately followed by a consonant and the next syllable is not the verb-stem syllable. However, if the consonant that follows **nááná** is the 3 person object prefix **y**, and if this **y** is itself immediately followed by a consonant, then the original longer form is used. Also, the following special combinations are used:

When **nááná** is immediately followed by the y-P/n-P 2sg subject prefix or by a **yn** prefix that begins **yíní**, we can get **nááyíní**. When **nááná** is immediately followed by a long-vowel 1sg, 2sg, or 3 prefix that begins **(i)i**, we usually get **nááyii**. When **nááná** is immediately followed by the 3 person object prefix **y**, and the **y** is immediately followed by the 3 subject n-P zero/barred-l prefix **ní**, we usually get **nááyíní**.)

Here's something you can check for yourself. If the position of the prefix **nááná** is such that its second syllable is the pre-stem syllable of the verb, then the long form is always used. (But be careful: sometimes the long-form is used when its second syllable isn't the pre-stem syllable: for example, we get the long form whenever the 3 person object prefix **y** is the next element in the verb and this **y** is itself followed directly by a consonant. We simply have to read Rule Str-7 carefully and apply it exactly when it says we should. However, the short form **náá** is never used if its syllable would be the pre-stem syllable.)

This rule is pretty easy (it's easier than it looks.) When it applies, there'll be this **náá** prefix sitting in the outer prefix position (after any other outer prefixes the verb might have), which then behaves like any normal outer prefix. If this rule doesn't apply, the outer prefix added by Vocabulary-14 will just be **nááná**.

There is one more detail we need to learn concerning this prefix. Actually, it's not about this prefix exactly - it's about the prefixes **na** and **ná**. We learned earlier that these prefixes sometimes change into **ni** and **ní**, depending on what follows them; in fact, we have a huge rule, called Rule Disj-3, that tells us when this happens. It turns out that if **na** or **ná** is immediately followed by our new prefix, either in the form **nááná** or in the form **náá**, then they change to **ni** and **ní**. We'll add a statement to Rule Disj-3 that says this.

Incidentally, you may know that **nááná** exists as an independent word, meaning "again" or "more". You may also know that the **náá** prefix can be sometimes used with words other than verbs, with the same sort of meaning.

Note on terminology: In YM, the **nááná** and **náá** prefixes are called the *semeliterative* prefixes. We'll use this term here, too.

With what we've learned, we can construct any verb form from any verb base that is created by Vocabulary-14. In previous chapters, we wrote out complete conjugations of many verb bases in the three modes that we've learned so far - for the majority of these, we could apply Vocabulary-14 and write out complete conjugations showing our new semeliterative prefix in there. To save time and space, we won't do this - in any case, the forms are very easy. What we'll do is give a few examples of particular words, just to demonstrate what can happen.

Going back to the very first verb we started studying back in Chapters 4 and 5 (the verb that means "play"), how do we say "I'm playing some more", or "I'm playing again"? The word that means this is **nináánáshné**. How was this word built? Here is its structure:

(2) outer   subject   verb
     prefix   prefix   stem

  na - nááná - sh - né

Why did we put in the longer form (**nááná**) of the semeliterative prefix? Because, even though the next sound is a consonant (**sh**), the next syllable is the verb-stem syllable. Note that this prefix is the last of the outer prefixes (that is, it comes after **na**), as required by Vocabulary-14.

Starting from the structure in (2), we see that Rule Disj-3 changes the **na** prefix to **ni**. Note that Rule Disj-1 doesn't do anything to **nááná**, even though this prefix is followed by a consonant and the next syllable is the verb stem syllable. (Why not? Because Rule Disj-1 doesn't do anything to a high-tone **á**.) This gives us the actual word **nináánáshné**.

Question: Did classifier shift happen? Answer: no. If classifier shift had taken place, we'd have a d classifier in there, which would have changed the verb stem **né** into **'né**. Since there's no glottal stop in there in front of **né**, we know that this is one of the many verbs that don't undergo classifier shift when we add in the **náá** (or **nááná**) prefix.

Incidentally, if you think about this example and you reread Rule Disj-1, you'll probably realize that whenever the semeliterative is used in a position that satisfies the basic condition for Rule Disj-1, then the long form **nááná** is the form that will be used.

Here is another example. The word that means "We (two) are boiling it some more" or "We (two) are boiling some more stuff" is **náánéiilbéézh**. The structure of this word is:

(3) outer   subject   cl   verb
     prefix   prefix   stem

  nááná - iid - ? - béézh

This time, we used the original long form **nááná** of the prefix because the next sound isn't a consonant at all. Part (a) of Rule Disj-2 applies to this word, changing **nááná** into **nááné**.

Question: What is the classifier in this word? If you check the verb base that means "boil it" (see Chapter 7(6)), you'll see that its classifier is barred-l. Did classifier shift take place? Well, if it didn't, we'd get the correct form of the word - note that Rule Subj-3 would apply to change the ł classifier to l. But if classifier shift did take place, then the classifier would now be plain-l, and Rule Subj-3 would still give us the (same) correct word. In other words, we cannot tell from this word whether or not classifier shift has taken place! To find out whether or not classifier shift takes place for this verb base, change the subject to one that clearly reveals the classifier, such as "you (sg)". But even better: remember that with Vocabulary-14, classifier shift just about never occurs when the classifier is barred-l. (So, how do we say "you (sg) are boiling some more stuff"? It's just **náánílbéézh**. We use the short form of the semeliterative prefix because it's followed by a consonant (the **n** of the 2sg subject prefix **ni**) but the next syllable isn't the verb stem syllable. Rule Subj-5 puts the high tone on the **ni**, of course.)

If you reread Rule Disj-2 and think about the example illustrated in (3), you'll probably realize that whenever the semeliterative is used in a position that satisfies the basic condition for Rule Disj-2, then the long form **nááná** is the form that will be used.

On the other hand, the short form of the semeliterative, that is **náá**, will be used if, for example, the semeliterative is immediately followed by prefixes such as the distributive plural **da**, the F mode **d**, the inner **d**, the inner **n**, or an object prefix other than the **y**. And, as we saw a moment ago, it will also be used if the next prefix is the 2sg I mode subject prefix **ni** (and in this case Rule Subj-5 will put a high tone on the 2sg subject prefix.) If the next prefix is the 3 person object prefix **y**, then the short form is used if the **y** is itself followed by a vowel, as in the word **nááyółta'** "he/she is reading it again" (see Chapter 21(35) and Chapter 21(36)). But the long form is used if the **y** is immediately followed by a consonant (which means that Rule Conj-2 changes the **y** into an **i**), as in the word **náánéílbéézh** "he/she is boiling it some more" or "he/she is boiling more (stuff)" (see Chapter 7(6) and Chapter 7(7).

Incidentally, did you notice the high tone on the **í** in this word? This looks like the sort of effect created by Rule Subj-5, but be careful: we don't have an actual syllable with a short vowel here! Do you remember back in Chapter 7 when we discussed the word **yáołti'** (see Chapter 7(16) and Chapter 7(17)) - we said that Rule Subj-5 doesn't apply because the **o(h)** isn't a separate syllable - the disjunct prefix **yá** and the subject prefix **o(h)** coalesced into one syllable? In the word **náánéílbéézh** we have the same situation, so why are we getting that high tone on the **í**?

The answer is that the 3 person object prefix **y** is a bit special. We know that Rule Conj-2 changes the **y** into an **i** in words like this, but we've already seen that sometimes careful speakers don't actually do this -they leave the **y** in there, so that an actual **yi** syllable appears in the word. If we have that **yi** syllable in there, then Rule Subj-5 would indeed apply normally to put a high tone on it. What's happening is that this high tone is there even when we do change the **y** into an **i**. What we'll do is, we'll add a note to Rule Conj-2 that mentions this effect.

Getting back to the semeliterative: what form of this prefix is used if it's immediately followed by one of those subject prefixes that starts with **v́v́** or **vv**? According to Rule Str-7 above, it should be the long form, and that's in fact what we get. An example: by using Vocabulary-7 (see Chapter 19) with the singular go-verb, we can construct an expression that means "I went in" - this expression is **yah ííyá** (make sure you understand how we got this!) Now, suppose we want to say "I went in again". Using Vocabulary-14, we add the semeliterative prefix, perform classifier shift (the go-verbs routinely undergo classifier shift when Vocabulary-14 applies to them), and we get **yah anáánáásdzá**. To make sure that you understand this, note that the verb **anáánáásdzá** is built like this:

(4) outer   subject   cl   verb
     prefix   prefix   stem

'a - nááná - vvsh - d - yá
                    \ /
                    dzá

Since we've actually shifted the classifier, we find that, instead of a zero classifier, we've got that **d** in the classifier slot in (4). The semeliterative prefix is in the outer prefix slot in (4), following the other outer prefix, which is the **'a** put in there by Vocabulary-6. The subject prefix is taken from the chart in Chapter 10(1), since we have a d classifier and there is a disjunct prefix to its left. The effect of the vv is to lengthen the **á** at the end of the **nááná** prefix. Rule Subj-6 also applies to this word, because of the **dz** in the verb stem, and we get our word.

Let's finish our study of the semeliterative by noting a few general facts.

If the short form of the semeliterative is used, then it happens that none of our rules will ever change its form - it will always show up in the actual verb as **náá**. If the long form **nááná** is used, then none of our rules will ever change the form of the first syllable of this prefix - only the second syllable is ever changed (as we just saw in some of our examples.) Does this mean that if we see the syllable **náá** in a verb somewhere to the left of the verb-stem then this syllable is automatically the semeliterative prefix (or the first syllable of the semeliterative prefix)? Most of the time this will be the case. But suppose you see the syllable **náá** in a verb, and this syllable is the pre-stem syllable. Then this **náá** cannot be the semeliterative. Do you see why? (If the next syllable is the verb-stem, then the semeliterative would have to appear in its long form **nááná**.) So, we can say these two things: if the semeliterative is used, then the syllable **náá** will definitely appear in the verb and the syllable following this syllable is definitely not the verb-stem syllable. And, if the syllable **náá** is in a verb but it's not the pre-stem syllable, then this **náá** is very probably the semeliterative prefix (or part of it.)

This is all that we're going to say about the semeliterative prefixes. Be on the lookout for them as you continue your Navajo studies. Rule Str-7 will give correct forms, but occasionally you may run into a form that is different from the one that this rule would give you. Again, when verbs get big and less common, speakers sometimes differ in the way they build their verbs.

Let's move on to the second of our outer prefixes. This prefix is **ná**. We've already learned almost all we need to know about the forms of this prefix (see Rule Disj-3). Here, we'll learn one additional important fact about the forms of this prefix, plus a few details. We'll also look at what it means.

First, what does this prefix mean? In many verb bases, this prefix carries with it the meaning "back", in the sense of returning to a place where the subject had previously been. In fact, here is a vocabulary principle:

<u>Vocabulary-15</u>: For verb bases whose verb themes are themes of motion, a new verb base can be created whose meaning is the same as the original one except that the motion is said to be back to a starting point by doing the following two things:

(a) Add the outer prefix **ná** as a lexical outer prefix. If there are other lexical outer prefixes in the verb base, then **ná** will be the last outer prefix, except that if the semeliterative prefix is also in the verb base, then **ná** immediately precedes the semeliterative.

(b) For certain common verb bases, the classifier undergoes the process of classifier shift.

Note that, like Vocabulary-14, Vocabulary-15 creates a new verb base from an old verb base.

In Vocabulary-15, classifier shift operates the same as we've seen earlier, with the shifts shown in (1). As in the case of the semeliterative, not all verb bases undergo classifier shift when Vocabulary-15 is applied to them - you'll have to pay attention to which verbs undergo it and which verbs don't.

Vocabulary-15 can be applied to pretty much any verb base that involves a verb theme of motion. But it can also be applied to some other verb bases as well. If a verb base describes an event in which something changes its form or condition in a reversible way, then **ná** can often be added to create a verb base whose meaning involves the reverse change, where something goes back to a previous form or previous condition. Also, verb bases that describe changes of condition where the new condition is viewed as the normal condition for the subject very often have the **ná** prefix as a lexical prefix. An example of such a verb base is the one that means "wake up". To wake up is to change from a condition of being asleep to a condition of being awake. Since being awake is the normal state for a person, this verb base has the **ná** prefix in it. The transitive verb base that means "to wake him/her up" also has **ná** in it, for the same reason. We'll look at these verb bases in a little bit.

Terminology: the **ná** prefix introduced by Vocabulary-15 is called the *reversionary prefix* in YM. We'll use this term as well. (But the **ná** prefix can sometimes have other meanings. In YM, the term "reversionary" is not used when these other meanings are involved. However, what we are going to learn about the forms of this prefix will still be correct even for the other meanings that this prefix can have.)

The prefix **ná** changes into **ní** in ways that are completely parallel to the ways that the prefix **na** changes into **ni**, and we've already seen many examples of **na** becomeing **ni**. However, in the case of **ná**, there is an additional process that we have to learn about.

The issue is this. If **ná** is immediately preceded by another outer prefix, then sometimes **ná** contracts with that outer prefix. We have to learn how this contraction works and what the forms are.

The first fact about this contraction process is this: only certain outer prefixes contract with **ná**. However, the ones that contract are among the most common ones, so we really need to deal with this.

The second fact is that this contraction appears to be optional. However, for a considerable number of common verbs, the most usual forms are the contracted forms. If no contraction occurs, then it will be easy for you to recognize the structure of the form. But the contracted forms are very common, so we need to study them.

The third fact has to do with when these contractions occur. It happens that these contractions can be made when **ná** is in exactly those positions in a verb where the shortened form of the semeliterative prefix would be used. For this reason, we won't give a new rule - in the Appendix, we'll write Rule Str-7 so that it talks about the contraction of the reversionary prefix as well as the short form of the semeliterative prefix.

(One particular case worth remembering: if **ná** is the pre-stem syllable, then it won't contract!)

Let's look a bit at the actual contractions. Below is a list of those outer prefixes that we've seen so far in our studies that contract with **ná**:

(5)

Outer prefix	Prefix contracted with **ná**
ch'í	**ch'éé**
ha	**háá**
Pi	**Péé**
Pí	**Péé**

The contracted forms all have long, high-tone vowels. But note carefully: the contracted forms do not have an **n** in them - the **n** of the prefix **ná** has disappeared! And remember: these contractions only occur if the outer prefix and the prefix **ná** are right next to each other.

Question: What happens if the outer prefix **na** is followed immediately by **ná**? It turns out that this is another situation where **na** changes to **ni** - we'll add this to Rule Disj-3. And, although you might not believe it, it is possible to have a verb where the prefix **ná** is immediately followed by **ná**. In this case, the first **ná** becomes **ní**, except in one particular circumstance that we'll mention at the end of this chapter. We'll see examples of **náná** becoming **níná** in the next chapter.

Let's look at a few example words. We can apply Vocabulary-15 to the verb base in Chapter 11(2) to create a verb base that means "carry someone back up out of something". For example, the word that means "I'm carrying him/her back up out of something" is **hanáshteeh**. It has the following structure:

(6)   outer   subject   cl   verb
       prefix   prefix   stem

       ha - ná - sh - ł - teeh

Note that the reversionary prefix appears after the other outer prefix **ha**. The sandwich rule is the only one of our rules that applies to this word.

Why isn't there any contraction in this word? Because, although **ná** is immediately followed by a consonant, the next syllable is the verb-stem syllable, which means that **ná** is the pre-stem syllable in this word. (If we had used the semeliterative in this position, we would have used the long form.)

On the other hand, the word that means "You're carrying him/her back up out of something" would normally be **háánílteeh**. This word has the structure:

(7)   outer   subject   cl   verb
       prefix   prefix   stem

       ha - ná - ni - ł - teeh
          \ /
          háá

(Rule Subj-5 applied.) This time contraction is possible (and usual). Remember: if we had used the semeliterative instead of the reversionary in (7), we would have used the short form.

Because we sometimes get contractions like this and sometimes don't, it will be useful to get an overview of verb forms with the reversionary prefix, so let's write out the entire I mode for the verb that means "carry him/her back up out of something":

(8)   sg   dpl   distr dpl

1   hanáshteeh   hanéiilteeh   háádeiilteeh
2   háánílteeh   hanáołteeh   háádaołteeh
3   hanéíłteeh   háádeiłteeh
4   háájíłteeh   háádajiłteeh

(Some of you might say **hanáłteeh** for "you (two) are carrying him/her up out of something".)

Make sure you understand why contraction occurs in some of these forms and not in others - it might help to review the discussion earlier about the places where the short form of the semeliterative is found instead of the long form. These are the places where the reversionary can contract.

You might want to write out the P and F mode forms of this verb base (with the reversionary). If you are unsure about the forms you've made up, you can check them against the forms given in the charts in YM 87 (look up "reversionary" in the grammar section.)

Earlier we mentioned that the verb bases that mean "wake up" and "wake him/her up" have the **ná** prefix in them. In order to get a little more practice with this prefix, let's look at the verb base that means "wake him/her up":

(9)

Stem-set		Classifier: barred-l
I:	**zííd**	
P:	**zid**	Lexical prefixes: **ch'í** (outer), **ná** (outer)
F:	**ził**	Transitivity: transitive
R:	**zi'**	
O:	**zííd**	Conjugation: n-I, n-P

You might want to review Chapter 13 before trying to build verbs using this verb base. Let's look at two examples here.

How would we say "He/she will wake him/her up"? This word would be built as follows:

(10) outer   object F mode subject cl   verb
      prefix   prefix   d   prefix   stem

      ch'í - ná - y - d - oo - ł - ził

Since **ná** is followed by the 3 person object prefix **y** which is itself followed by a consonant, we expect that there won't be any contraction in this word (reread Rule Str-7!) Rule Conj-2 changes that **y** into **i**, which means that Rule Disj-2 will now apply to **ná**. Also, some of the effects we learned about in Chapter 13 apply here as well. The actual word is therefore **ch'ínéidoosił**.

Compare this with the word that means "You (sg) will wake me up". (This word can also be used as an imperative: "Wake me up!") The structure is:

(11)

outer prefix		object prefix		F mode d		subject prefix		cl		verb stem
ch'í	-	ná	-	sh	-	d	-	íí	-	ł	-	ził

This time, since **ná** is followed by a consonant and the next syllable (which is actually **shi** in the real word because of Rule Conj-1) is not the verb-stem syllable, we expect contraction to happen. The word therefore ends up being: **ch'ééshidíísił.**

If you work through more verbs created from the verb base in (9), you'll see that very many of them have the contracted form of the outer prefixes. Because of this, forms of this verb sometimes don't have quite as many n's in them as you might think, even though the I and P modes are conjugated using the n-I and n-P conjugations. For example, "I woke him/her up" is **ch'ééníssid** - the **n** in this word is the **n** in the 1sg subject prefix for the n-P conjugation. The **n** of the **ná** prefix disappeared inside the contracted form **ch'éé.**

Incidentally, in case you're curious: the verb base that means "wake up" (not "wake him up", but "wake up all by oneself") is almost the same as the verb base in (9). The only difference is that the classifier is d instead of barred-l (and, of course, the "wake up" verb base is intransitive, not transitive.)

So here are some important things to remember. If a verb base has the **ná** prefix in it and also one of the common outer prefixes that can contract with it, you will often see syllables like **ch'éé** or **háá** or **béé** or **yéé** (for example) in the forms of that verb, but only if the next syllable isn't the verb-stem syllable (that is, only if the syllable you're looking at isn't the pre-stem syllable). The reverse is almost always true, too: if you see one of these syllables in a verb and this syllable is not the pre-stem syllable, then there's a very good chance that what you're looking at is a contracted form of some outer prefix with **ná.**

It is possible to have a word that has both the reversionary and the semeliterative prefixes in it. As you can tell from Vocabulary-15, when this happens, the reversionary prefix comes before the semeliterative prefix. For example, the word that means "I will go back again" is **nínáádeeshdááł.** The structure of this word is:

(12)

outer prefix		F mode d		subject prefix		cl		verb stem
ná	-	náá	-	d	-	eesh	-	d	-	-ááł

Rule Disj-3 changes **ná** in this word to **ní.** The d classifier is the result of classifier shift, which always happens with the go-themes. And remember: with this irregular verb, when d-effect applies to a verb-stem that begins with a hyphen, the hyphen is simply replaced by a **d.**

It is probably a good idea to write out all the forms you can for the verb bases that mean "go back" and "go back again". Start by reviewing Vocabulary-5 in Chapter 18. Then note that in the singular case, the I mode stem will be **dááh**, the P mode stem will be **dzá**, and the F mode stem will be **dááł**, as we just saw. The dual verbs will have the stems **t'aash**, **t'áázh**, and **t'ash** for these three modes. The stems for the plural go-verb will look the same as they always did (why?). And don't forget to use the correct P mode subject prefixes; for example, "I went back" (or "I came back" or "I got back") is **nánísdzá** (remember, we're using the n-P conjugation.) Note, by the way, that **ná** does not change to **ní** if it's immediately followed by an n-P or n-I subject prefix. (We'll add a hint about this to Rule Disj-3 in the Appendix, for greater comprehensiveness.)

Incidentally, in words that have the reversionary, the semeliterative, and another outer prefix in front of the reversionary, there usually isn't any contraction. For example, using the intransitive "wake up" verb base that we mentioned a moment ago, we can form a word that means "I woke up again" by putting the semeliterative prefix into the verb along with the **ch'í** prefix and the reversionary **ná** prefix that are both already in that verb base. We get the word **ch'ínínáánísdzid**, which has the following structure:

(13)   outer   subject   cl   verb
          prefix   prefix   stem

     ch'í - ná - náá - nish - d - zid

This might be our first verb form with three outer prefixes - make sure you understand why these three prefixes are in the order that they are. Since this form is in the P mode, we use the verb stem **zid** - see (9). We also mentioned that the intransitive version of (9) takes the d classifier; that, together with the fact that this verb base is conjugated in the n-P conjugation, explains why the 1sg subject prefix is **nish** in (13). Make sure you know why the short form of the semeliterative is used in (13). Although the reversionary in (13) is in the kind of position where we would expect it to contract with **ch'í**, this contraction is not carried out, because the semeliterative is also there.

The only thing you should keep in mind, in addition to what we've studied here, is that there are a few more outer prefixes (in addition to the ones listed in (5)) that contract with **ná**. Be on the lookout for them. (You can read about them in YM.)

(Let's mention one of these other outer prefixes here. Believe if or not, there is an outer prefix which has the form **ná** and which means something like "up". This prefix, which can occur with verb themes of motion (in certain combinations with other prefixes), can appear directly in front of the reversionary prefix, which is also **ná**, of course. When the reversionary prefix is in a position to contract according to Rule Str-7, these two prefixes contract to **náá**, which looks exactly like the semeliterative prefix! This doesn't happen all that often, but it does happen - there are words that have this arrangment inside them. For example, "I picked it up" (a ropelike thing) is **nídiilá** - this word has the **ná** that means "up" in it. If we put the reversionary prefix into this word, we get a word

324

that means "I picked it back up" (a ropelike thing): **náádiidlá**. In this word, the **ná** that means "up" and the reversionary **ná** contracted to **náá**. For your information: verb bases that mean "pick it up" can be formed from classificatory motion themes by using this outer prefix **ná** (the one meaning "up") together with the inner prefix **d**, and using the long-vowel conjugation in all modes except F.)

This is all we need to say about the prefix **ná**; or, at least, this is all we need to say about this prefix in this chapter.... But why worry? The next chapter will come soon enough.

CHAPTER 23

THE ITERATIVE, USITATIVE, AND OPTATIVE MODES

In this chapter we are going to learn how to conjugate verbs in three of the remaining four modes. (We'll study the progressive mode in Chapter 25.)

Back in Chapter 3, we said some general things about the way the mode of a Navajo verb is indicated: each mode has a special set of subject prefixes, and for any verb base, there is a special verb stem for each mode. We've learned all that we need to know about the subject prefixes for the I, P, and F modes, and we've seen lots of examples. What we need to do next is learn the subject prefixes for the I, U, and O modes.

But before we do that, let's think for a moment about the F mode. We learned that the F mode involves not only a special set of subject prefixes, but also a special conjunct prefix (the one we called the "F mode **d**") that is placed in a particular position in the verb. When we listed the F mode prefixes back in Chapter 14, we listed the F mode **d** as though it was part of the subject prefixes (see Chapter 14(1)). But by now you understand that the F mode **d** can be separated by other conjunct prefixes from the prefixes that go into the subject prefix position. This means that the F mode **d** is really a separate prefix - it has to be in there whenever you want the verb to be in the F mode, but it's separate from the subject prefixes that are used in the F mode. The reason that it's useful to think about the F mode arrangement in this way is that something similar happens in the R mode. (The U mode and the O mode are simpler - they just involve using ordinary subject prefixes and a particular verb stem.)

So let's start with the R mode. Here is a set of instructions that tell you how to build an R mode form from any verb base.

(1) <u>Instructions for building R mode forms</u>:

    (a) Use the R mode stem from the stem-set as the verb stem.

    (b) For the subject prefix, follow these principles:

        (i)   For the regular R mode, use the same subject prefixes as are used for the regular I mode.

        (ii)   For the long-vowel R mode, use the same subject prefixes as are used for the long-vowel I mode.

(c) Add the outer prefix **ná** into the verb structure. If there are already other outer prefixes in the verb base, then this new **ná** prefix will be the last outer prefix. We will call this prefix the *R mode ná*.

(d) Classifier shift may occur.

This looks complicated, but in practice it works out pretty easily. Let's first study each part of these instructions, and then we'll look at examples.

Part (a) tells us that to form an R mode verb we need to use the R mode stem. There is nothing surprising about this - for any mode, we use the verb stem that corresponds to that mode. However, here is something interesting. You might think that you'll need to memorize an extra verb stem for every stem-set that you learn. But we've got some good news: for practically every stem-set in Navajo, if you know the I and F mode stems, you can figure out what the R mode stem is going to be! Let's learn how to do this.

If you know the I and F mode stems for a particular stem-set, the first thing you need to do is to compare these two stems with each other. There are two possibilities:

(2)   Possibility 1:   The F mode stem ends in a ł and the I mode stem doesn't end in an ł.

      Possibility 2:   Either the F mode stem doesn't end in an ł, or else both the I mode and the F mode stems end in ł.

When you've seen which of these two possibilities the I and F mode stems fall into, you can figure out the R mode stem as follows:

(3) Rule for the R mode stem:

If the I and F mode stems fall into the Possibility 1 case, build the R mode stem by taking the F mode stem and changing the ł at the end of the F mode stem into an **h**. Exception: If the I mode stem ends in a **d**, then change the ł at the end of the F mode stem into a glottal stop: **'**.

If the I and F mode stems fall into the Possibility 2 case, then the R mode stem is the same as the F mode stem.

Examples of all these cases can be found by hunting through the stem-sets that we've seen throughout our study. For example, in the stem-set in Chapter 11(2), the I mode stem is **teeh** and the F mode stem is **tééł**. This is an example of Possibility 1: the F mode stem ends in ł, but the I mode stem doesn't end in ł (it ends in **h**.) Our rule tells us that we can get the R mode stem by taking the F mode stem and changing the ł at the end of it into **h**. This gives us **tééh** - and you can check in Chapter

11(2) that this is indeed the R mode stem for this stem-set.

To illustrate the exception for this part of the rule, look at the stem-set in Chapter 9(9). The I mode stem is **gééd**, and the F mode stem is **goł**. We have Possibility 1 here, because the F mode stem ends in **ł** but the I mode stem doesn't. However, since the I mode stem ends in **d**, our rule tells us that we get the R mode stem by taking the F mode stem and changing the **ł** into **'**, rather than into **h**. This gives us **go'** as the R mode stem, which agrees with what we see in Chapter 9(9).

To see an example of Possibility 2, look at the stem-set in Chapter 8(13). The I mode stem is **na'** and the F mode stem is **nah**. Since the F mode stem doesn't end in **ł**, our rule tells us that the R mode stem is the same as the F mode stem, which is exactly what is shown in Chapter 8(13).

Another example showing Possibility 2 is found in Chapter 9(16). For the stem-set that we see there, the I mode stem is **'aał** and the F mode stem is **'ał**. This time, the F mode stem does end in **ł**, but we don't have Possibility 1 because the I mode stem also ends in **ł**. Since we have Possibility 2, our rule tells us again that the R mode stem is the same as the F mode stem, and again this is exactly what we see in Chapter 9(16).

(Another way of thinking of the two possibilities in (2) is this. Possibility 1 is the case where the F mode stem has a **ł** added on. Possibility 2 is where the F mode stem doesn't have a **ł** added on. Possibility 2 includes the case where the stems "really" end in **ł**, so the **ł** at the end of the F mode stem wasn't added on - it was there all along.)

If you look through all the stem-sets we've seen, you will note that for every one of those stem-sets, our rule gives us the correct form of the R mode stem. This means that when you learn vocabulary, you don't have to memorize the R mode stems for verbs if you learn the I and F mode stems. (Unfortunately, you do have to also memorize the P mode stems - there is no rule that will tell you what the P mode stem is if you know the I and F mode stems. But you've probably been memorizing the I, P, and F mode stems already for the verbs you've been learning. Of course, if you already speak Navajo, then you already know all these stems.)

The next part of our instructions for building R mode forms is part (b). We don't have to say much about this. The actual subject prefixes used in the R mode are the same as the ones used in the I mode, so we don't have any new prefixes to learn. The only thing we should say is that there is no such thing as an n-R conjugation. If a verb base is conjugated in the n-I pattern for its I mode, it will be conjugated in the regular R mode conjugation, which means that it will use the regular I mode subject prefixes in its R mode forms. The n-I subject prefixes are never used to create R mode forms.

Let's skip to the fourth part of our instructions for building R mode forms, part (d). (We'll get to part (c) in a moment.) There is actually nothing new we need to say here. The situation is similar to the situation with the reversionary and semeliterative prefixes: not all verb bases actually undergo classifier shift, so for each verb base you learn, you'll have to remember if it undergoes classifier shift

328

or not. It is worth remembering that, mostly, verbs with the barred-l classifier don't undergo classifier shift in the R mode.

The only thing left to talk about is the third part of our instructions for building R mode forms, that is, part (c). Because of what we learned in the last chapter, we don't actually have much new to learn about this. But since we're suddenly dealing with a new prefix that looks exactly the same as one we've already studied (the reversionary), we'd better say a few things about this.

First of all, as far as its forms are concerned, the R mode **ná** prefix operates pretty much the same as the reversionary **ná** prefix we studied in Chapter 22. For example, the R mode **ná** changes to **ní** according to Rule Disj-3. Also, some sources say that the R mode **ná** can contract with a preceding outer prefix (if the preceding outer prefix is one of the ones that contract this way) under the circumstances described in Rule Str-7. However, remember that this contraction is optional. As it happens, it seems that the R mode **ná** tends to contract less often than the reversionary prefix. In fact, even the reversionary prefix itself prefers not to contract when it is followed by the R mode **ná**. Only uncontracted R mode forms are shown in the charts in YM 87 for either of these cases.

Next, the outer prefixes **na** and **ná** become **ni** and **ní** when followed immediately by R mode **ná** - we'll add a note to Rule Disj-3 about this. Note that it if we are forming an R mode word from a verb base that has the reversionary prefix in it, we're going to have reversionary **ná** followed directly by R mode **ná**.

With all these **na**'s and **ná**'s that we have, it is possible to have not only two, but even three syllables like this next to each other, all in a position for Rule Disj-3 to change them into **ni** or **ní**. But when this happens, they don't all change! Instead, the last **ná** in the sequence stays **ná** - it does not change - but the others (to its left) do change. We'll add a special note to Rule Disj-3 that has this information in it. (Incidentally, if there is a sequence like this, the last prefix in the sequence will end up being **ná** (with high tone.) The prefix **na** (with low tone) is never preceded by another **na** or **ná**.)

This is actually all we need to know to built R mode forms of verbs, but to make sure we understand how everything works, let's write out some R mode forms.

First, let's write out the complete set of R mode forms for a very simple verb. We'll take the verb base meaning "drink it" (see Chapter 10(9)). Here are the forms:

(4)	sg	dpl	distr dpl
1	náshdlį́į́h	néiidlį́į́h	nídeiidlį́į́h
2	nánídlį́į́h	náohdlį́į́h	nídaohdlį́į́h
3	néídlį́į́h		nídeidlį́į́h
4	níjídlį́į́h		nídajidlį́į́h

(Some of you might say **náhdlį́įh** for "you (two) repeatedly drink it".) Examine these forms and note that **ná** becomes **ní** as expected before the 4 person prefix **j** and before the distributive plural prefix **da**. Rule Conj-2 applied to the nondistributive form with 3 person subject - remember that a transitive verb requires an object pronoun if the subject is 3 person, and we can see our usual **y** in there, masquerading as the vowel **i**. Of course, the special R mode verb stem is used in all the forms in (4). And, importantly, the subject prefixes that are used in (4) are exactly the regular I mode subject prefixes.

(The high tone of the first **í** vowel in **néídlį́įh** is another example of the effect we talked about in the last chapter: Rule Subj-5 seems to have applied even though we don't have a separate short-vowel syllable. Recall that we added a note to Rule Conj-2 to take care of this situation.)

Next, let's look at the verb base in Chapter 19(29), the verb base that means "take/carry him/her out". The R mode forms are:

(5)	sg	dpl	distr dpl
1	ch'ínáshtééh	ch'ínéiiltééh	ch'ínídeiiltééh
2	ch'ínáníłtééh	ch'ínáołtééh	ch'ínídaołtééh
3	ch'ínéíłtééh		ch'ínídeiłtééh
4	ch'íníjíłtééh		ch'ínídajiłtééh

In (5), we followed the charts in YM 87 and used uncontracted forms.

You might want to compare (5) with Chapter 19(30). Not only is the verb stem in (5) different (the R mode stem is used in (5), of course) and not only do the forms in (5) all have the R mode **ná** prefix in them, but the subject prefixes used in (5) are different! In Chapter 19(30), the subject prefixes are the ones used for the n-I conjugation, since that's the I mode conjugation used for this verb base. But in (5), the regular I mode subject prefixes are used.

As a third example, let's write out the R mode forms for "play" - this will give us a chance to see what happens when the R mode **ná** is preceded by the prefix **na**. We can find the R mode verb stem in Chapter 6(15). The forms are:

(6)	sg	dpl	distr dpl
1	nináshneeh	ninéii'neeh	ninádeii'neeh
2	nináníneeh	nináohneeh	ninádaohneeh
3	nináneeh		ninádaaneeh
4	ninájíneeh		ninádajineeh

The forms in (6) illustrate that when Disj-3 applies to the prefix sequence **na - ná**, the second prefix (which is R mode **ná**) doesn't change, even when followed by **j** or **da**. The result is that all the forms in (6) begin with **niná** (or **niné**, which came from **niná**, of course.)

As a final example we'll write out the R mode forms of the verb base that means "kiss him/her" (see Chapter 20(10). Since this verb base is conjugated in the long-vowel R conjugation, we'll use the long-vowel I mode subject prefixes. Whenever the subject prefix is immediately preceded by R mode **ná**, we'll use the form of the subject prefix that is required when the immediately preceding prefix is a disjunct prefix. Here we go:

(7)	sg	dpl	distr dpl
1	néists'ǫs	néiits'ǫs	nídeiits'ǫs
2	néits'ǫs	náoohts'ǫs	nídaoohts'ǫs
3		náyiits'ǫs	nídayiits'ǫs
4		níjiits'ǫs	nídajiits'ǫs

Rule Disj-2 applied in a number of these forms, as did Rule Disj-3.

Something to note: We do not have a high tone on the short **i** in the words **néists'ǫs** and **néits'ǫs** - the first syllable of these words has a falling tone, not a high tone all the way through the syllable. In other words, the long-vowel subject prefixes **ish** and **i** behave in a normal way: the vowels in these prefixes join with the vowel at the end of the preceding prefix to form a single syllable, and Rule Subj-5 does not apply. This is different from what we saw when there was a short **i** that came from the 3 person object prefix **y** by Rule Conj-2 (for example, in the word **néídlį́į́h** that we talked about just a bit ago.)

Here are some other situations to keep in mind.

It is possible to have two copies of the syllable **ná** (with high tone) next to each other in a verb structure: the first **ná** could be, for example, either the reversionary prefix or else that special prefix we mentioned briefly at the end of Chapter 22 that means "up"; the second prefix would be the R mode **ná**. If these two prefixes are the first ones in the verb, then all the R mode forms will start with **níná** (or **níné**), similar to the forms shown above in (6). If these two prefixes are themselves preceded by another prefix, say for example, **ch'í**, then all the R mode forms will start with **ch'íníná** (or **ch'íníné**), with the reversionary prefix preferring not to contract.

It is even possible to have a verb whose structure has three **ná**'s in a row: the first **ná** could be the prefix that means "up", the second **ná** could be the reversionary prefix, and the third **ná** could be the R mode **ná**. In this case, what happens is that the first two **ná**'s change to **ní** but the third one doesn't. Assuming that there are no other prefixes in front of these, all the R mode forms of such a verb would start out **níníná** (or **níníné**).

If a verb base has the special **yn** inner prefix that we learned about in Chapter 21, then in the R mode the subject prefixes look exactly the same as the I mode subject prefixes for verbs that have the **yn** prefix (just make sure you use the form that is appropriate when preceded by a disjunct prefix when R mode **ná** immediately precedes it.) So, for example, "I repeatedly read it (or count it)" is **néíníshtah**, "he/she repeatedly reads it (or counts it)" is **náyółtah**, etc. (See Chapter 21(35) for this verb base.)

This should do it for the R mode. However, before moving on to the other modes, let's just say a word about recognizing R mode forms. Since there are a number of **ná** prefixes in the Navajo language, seeing a **ná** prefix in the verb doesn't automatically mean that the verb is in the R mode - you also have to have an I mode subject prefix, and also the verb stem has to be the R mode verb stem for that verb base. In Chapter 22, we saw some verb forms which had the reversionary **ná** prefix in them, but none of those forms had the R mode verb stem. Also, if the mode wasn't I, then the subject prefix wasn't an I mode prefix either. Remember: in order for a verb to be in the R mode, the verb has to have three things in it: (1) the R mode **ná**, (2) a subject prefix from an I mode conjugation (not the n-I conjugation), and (3) the R mode verb stem.

Let's now move on to the U mode. As it happens, we will say very little about this mode. Given what we've learned, the U mode forms of any verb base are very easy to create. In fact, here are instructions for doing so:

(8) <u>Instructions for building U mode forms</u>:

    Follow parts (a) and (b) of the instructions (in (1)) for building R mode forms. Leave out parts (c) and (d).

So, one way of saying it is that the U mode forms of any verb are the same as the R mode forms of that verb except that the R mode **ná** is missing, and the original classifier is used (if classifier shift applied in the R mode.)

A useful thing to do is to compare the U mode with the I mode for any verb. For a verb that does not take the n-I conjugation, the only difference between the I mode forms and the U mode forms for that verb is the verb stem: the U mode forms take the same verb stem as the R mode (that is, the U mode forms use the R mode stem), whereas, of course, the I mode forms take the I mode stem. If the verb uses the n-I conjugation in the I mode, there's a second difference between the I mode and the U mode: the subject prefixes are different. (In this case the subject prefixes used for the U mode are the regular I mode prefixes.)

Because the U mode forms can be related closely to the R mode and I mode ones, we won't go through a study of these forms. You should be able to form and recognize them easily. But just to illustrate one case, let's write out the U mode forms of the verb base that means "drink it":

(9)   sg   dpl   distr dpl

1   yishdlį́į́h   yiidlį́į́h   deiidlį́į́h
2   nidlį́į́h   wohdlį́į́h   daohdlį́į́h
3   yidlį́į́h   deidlį́į́h
4   jidlį́į́h   dajidlį́į́h

You should compare these forms not only with the R mode forms in (4) above, but also with the I mode forms of this verb. You'll need to build the I mode forms yourself: find the verb base in Chapter 10(9), and use the I mode verb stem, which is **dlą́**. Except for the different verb stem, the I mode forms look the same as the U mode forms in (9).

The last mode we are going to study here is the O mode. O mode forms are created by using the O mode verb stem from the stem-set of the verb base, and by using special subject prefixes. The subject prefixes will require a bit of attention. Before getting to them, let's say a word about the O mode verb stems.

Unfortunately, unlike the case of the R mode, if we know the I, P, and F mode stems of a stem-set, we cannot predict the O mode stem. However, we can say the following: for a substantial majority of stem-sets, the O mode verb stem is the same as the I mode verb stem. However, other possibilities are far from rare. In most cases, when the O mode stem is different from the I mode stem, the O mode stem is the same as either the P, F, or R mode stem. Occasionally, an O mode stem is different from any other of the stems - an example is the O mode stem for the singular go-verb (see Chapter 17(23)) - will say something more about this stem a little later. If you do not speak Navajo, the thing to do is to learn those cases where the O mode stem is different from the I mode stem. If you don't know a particular stem-set, you're statistically safe in guessing that the O mode stem is the same as the I mode stem.

To learn to build O mode words, we need only learn the special subject prefixes used in the O mode. For the regular O mode conjugation, we'll give these prefixes in two charts - one for the case that the subject prefix is not immediately preceded by a disjunct prefix, the other for the case that the subject prefix is immediately preceded by a disjunct prefix.

(10)   regular O mode subject prefixes - when not immediately preceded
        by a disjunct prefix:

	sg	dpl
1	**ósh**	**ood**
2	**óó**	**ooh**
3	**ó**	

(11)   regular O mode subject prefixes - when immediately preceded by
        a disjunct prefix:

	sg	dpl
1	osh	ood
2	óó	ooh
3	o	

There are a number of odd things about these prefixes. Let's take a closer look at them.

First of all, all the O mode subject prefixes have some sort of **o** vowel in them. This vowel can be regarded as the special sign of the O mode.

Secondly, the 2sg subject prefixes don't have an **n** in them. Like the 2sg prefix used in the F mode, the O mode 2sg subject prefix is a long, high-tone vowel, appropriately enough **óó** (since O mode prefixes all have those **o**'s in them.)

And thirdly, there is something strange about the 1sg and 3 prefixes: when preceded by a conjunct prefix or by no prefix, these subject prefixes have a high tone, but when preceded by a disjunct prefix, they have a low tone.

(That low tone on the 1sg and 3 prefixes in (11) remains low even if the prefix is immediately preceded by a disjunct prefix that ends in a high tone - in other words, Rule Subj-5 doesn't apply, which is the normal situation. Remember that we saw the same thing with some of the long-vowel subject prefixes when we looked at long-vowel R mode forms earlier.)

Don't forget to apply Rule Str-3 when the O mode subject prefix doesn't have any other prefix to its left. The effect of this rule will be to add in a **w** at the beginning of the word.

To illustrate the prefixes in (10) and (11), let's write out O mode forms for a few verbs. We'll start with the verb base that means "cry" (see Chapter 7(1)). Here are the forms:

(12)   sg   dpl   distr dpl

1	wóshcha	woocha	daoocha
2	wóócha	woohcha	daoohcha
3	wócha		daocha
4	jócha		dajócha

The nondistributive forms are all built using the prefixes in (10), since the subject prefix is preceded either by nothing, or, in the case of the 4 person subject, by the conjunct prefix **j**. The distributive forms are built using the prefixes in (11), except for the one form where the 4 person **j** prefix is in there immediately to the left of the 3 person subject prefix. This is why the nondistributive 3 person form **wócha** has a high tone on its **o** whereas the **o** in the 3 person distributive form **daocha** has low tone: the **o** in **daocha** is from (11), whereas the **ó** in **wócha** is from (10).

The "cry" verb is intransitive. If we look at a transitive verb with no lexical prefixes like "boil it" (see Chapter 7(6)), the only difference will be in the case that the subject is 3 person. The O mode forms for "boil it" with 3 person subject are **yółbéézh** and **dayółbéézh** - the **y**'s in these words are the 3 person object prefix, and the high-tone **ó** in both of them is the 3 person subject prefix from (10).

Let's take a verb base with a disjunct lexical prefix - the "work" verb base in Chapter 8(11) will do. The O mode forms are:

(13)	sg	dpl	distr dpl
1	naoshnish	naoolnish	nidaoolnish
2	naóólnish	naoołnish	nidaoołnish
3		naolnish	nidaolnish
4		nijólnish	nidajólnish

Again, the 4 person **j** prefix causes the subject prefix to switch to the chart in (10) - otherwise, all the subject prefixes are from (11), since there's a disjunct prefix immediately to the left of the subject prefix.

We mentioned earlier that if an O mode 1sg or 3 prefix is preceded by a disjunct prefix that ends in a high-tone vowel, the O mode prefix does not acquire a high tone. This can be seen from the 1sg O mode form of the verb base that means "wake him/her up" (see Chapter 22(9)), which is **ch'ínáossííd**.

If a verb base has a lexical inner prefix, or a lexical object, then all the subject prefixes in the O mode will come from (10). As an example, look at the verb base in Chapter 15(36), the one that means "uncover it by digging". The O mode forms of this verb are:

(14)	sg	dpl	distr dpl
1	bą́ą́'dóshgééd	bą́ą́'doolgééd	bą́ą́da'doolgééd
2	bą́ą́'dóółgééd	bą́ą́'doołgééd	bą́ą́da'doołgééd
3		yą́ą́'dółgééd	yą́ą́da'dółgééd
4		bą́ą́zh'dółgééd	bą́ą́dazh'dółgééd

You should have no trouble building O mode forms for most other verb bases that use the regular O mode conjugation. The only problematic cases are verb bases that have the special **yn** inner prefix that we learned about in Chapter 21. In Chapter 21 we simply gave charts showing how this prefix combines with the I mode and P mode subject prefixes. We would like to do the same for the O mode, but the information in YM and elsewhere is not completely clear. What we will do is give a chart that seems to be correct for the case that the conjunct high-tone is also present. When this is not present, O mode forms are, apparently, rare or nonexistent. As in the case of the I and P modes, there are alternate forms that are found for some of the combinations.

(15)   O mode subject prefixes combined with **yn** inner prefix and conjunct high-tone:

	sg	dpl
1	(í)ínósh/óosh	óod/{wóod}
2	(í)ínóó/óó	óoh/{wóoh}
3	óo/ó	

(The longer forms are used when immediately preceded by a conjunct prefix.
The forms in curly brackets are used when immediately preceded by a disjunct prefix.)

As an example, here are O mode forms for the verb base that means "read it" or "count it" (see Chapter 21(35):

(16)	sg	dpl	distr dpl
1	yínóshta'	wóolta'	dawóolta'
2	yínóólta'	wóolta'	dawóolta'
3	yólta'		dayólta'
4	jólta'		dajólta'

If the unspec object prefix is added in (in order to create the meaning "read" or "go to school", the entry in YM 87 shows forms with the shorter 1sg, 2sg, and 3 prefixes given in (15). The O mode forms for verbs with the **yn** inner prefix need to be studied further.

This takes care of our discussion of the regular O mode conjugation. There is, however, also a long-vowel O mode conjugation, which has its own subject prefixes. Fortunately, those prefixes are easy - we can show them in one chart. Here it is:

(17)   O mode subject prefixes, long-vowel conjugation:

	sg	dpl
1	oosh	ood
2	oó	ooh
3	oo	

These prefixes are used in all cases (so when there is no other prefix to their left, Rule Str-3 prefixes a **w** to them.) Note that all the prefixes in (17) have a long **oo** in them. Only the 2sg prefix has a high tone, and this high tone is only on the second **o**, so that the tone on the whole 2sg prefix is in fact a rising tone.

As an example, here are the O mode forms built from the verb base that means "kiss him/her" (Chapter 20(10)). (That verb base uses the long-vowel conjugation for all its modes except the P and the F mode.)

(18)   sg   dpl   distr dpl

1   woosts'ǫs   woots'ǫs   daoots'ǫs
2   woóts'ǫs   woohts'ǫs   daoohts'ǫs
3   yoots'ǫs   dayoots'ǫs
4   joots'ǫs   dajoots'ǫs

Before leaving the O mode, we need to say something about a few special cases.

We learned in Chapter 19 that the outer prefix **'a** sometimes has unexpected forms when it is followed by certain prefixes. When **'a** is immediately followed by the 1sg O mode prefix **osh** or the 3 O mode prefix **o** (from chart (11)), the combination comes out **'oosh** or **'oo**, and when **'a** is immediately followed by the 2sg prefix **oó** (also from chart (11)), we get **'oó**. We'll add a note to Rule Disj-4 about these cases.

Actually, some other outer prefixes also show special adjustments when immediately followed by O mode subject prefixes. In particular, at least the more common outer prefixes that end in **i** or **í** lose their **i** vowel and the tone of the combination undergoes an adjustment. For example, when **nitsí** is immediately followed by an O mode subject prefix, the five combinations (with the five prefixes in (11)) come out as (1sg:) **nitsóosh**, (2sg:) **nitsóó**, (3:) **nitsóo**, (1dpl:) **nitsóod**, and (2dpl:) **nitsóoh** - note the long vowels in the 1sg and 3 combinations, suggesting that the **í** has changed into **ó**. With the outer prefix **ni**, which has a low tone (see the end of Chapter 21) we get the combinations (1sg:) **noosh**, (2sg:) **noó**, (3:) **noo**, (1dpl:) **nood**, and (2dpl:) **nooh**. Many prefixes that end in **i** or **í**, such as **ch'í** and **Pí**, work exactly the same as **nitsí** and **ni**, but there are a few other outer prefixes that end in **i** or **í** that don't change their form - they just combine their basic form with the prefixes in (11) without any changes, which is the usual situation that we've seen with outer prefixes that end in **a** or **á**.

We also need to say something about the singular go-verb O mode stem. Back in Chapter 17, we learned about the irregularities of the singular go-verb stems. As it happens, the O mode stem, which we represented as **-a'** in our stem-set charts, has slightly different irregularities. When preceded by a 1sg subject prefix, the O mode stem works the same as the I mode stem; so, for example, using the completive verb base (see Chapter 18(1)), the 1sg O mode form is **wósha'**, which is what we'd expect. But when the 2sg or the 3 person subject prefixes are used, the O mode stem **-a'** becomes **ya'** - we don't see any **n** for the 2sg case and we don't see any **gh** or **g** for the 3 case. So, again using the completive verb base, we have **wóóya'** for the 2sg O mode form and **wóya'** for the 3 O mode form. (Of course, the same irregularities occur in the O mode forms of any verb base built around the singular go-verb.)

By the way, the irregularities we learned about in Chapter 16 for the verb that means "eat" apply to the O mode without any change.

This is all we need to say about the way the O mode is formed. To close, let's think about how we can recognize an O mode form (regular or long-vowel) when we see one.

In general, recognizing O mode forms should be easy because of the **o** vowel in the pre-stem syllable. We might want to suggest a "rule": pre-stem **o** vowel means O mode. Unfortunately, there are quite a few cases where we've already seen an **o** vowel in the pre-stem syllable but where we haven't been in the O mode. Can you remember them?

The most important case like this is the regular I mode prefix for the 2dpl subject, which is **oh** (remember?) This is different from the regular O mode 2dpl prefix, but only in the length of the vowel - the regular O mode 2dpl prefix is **ooh**. Since for many verbs the verb stem will be the same in the I and O modes, the only difference between the I mode word with 2dpl subject and the O mode word with 2dpl subject will be this length.

But there are quite a few other circumstances when an **o** vowel can immediately precede the verb stem syllable. For example, if the verb is conjugated in the y-P conjugation and the classifier is plain-l or d, then it is possible to see or hear the vowel **oo** immediately preceding the verb stem if the subject is 3 (or 4) person (review Chapter 10.) For many verbs, the stem will tell you that you're in the P mode and not in the O mode, but this isn't always the case (sometimes the stems for these modes are the same.) In the F mode, a form where the subject is 3 or 4 person will always have the vowel **oo** in the pre-stem syllable, but F mode forms are pretty easy to recognize (because they all have the F mode **d** in them, as well as an F mode stem.) Another important situation that can lead to a pre-stem **o** vowel is the case where the verb has the prefix **hw** in it - review Rule Conj-6, especially part (d). Then there are those 3 person (and 4) person forms (in the I and sometimes the P modes) of verbs that have the **yn** inner prefix - review our study of these in Chapter 21.

However, the best way to recognize O mode forms is to learn about how such forms are used. The O mode is only used in certain special arrangements and with special meanings, often with particular words such as **laanaa** and **lágo**. If you see or hear a verb that you think is being used this way, and there's an **o** vowel preceding the verb stem, you probably have an O mode verb. But if you see or hear a verb that is being used in a more ordinary way, then it could very likely not be an O mode verb even if you do see or hear an **o** vowel preceding the verb stem.

CHAPTER 24

THE SERIATIVE

In this chapter we're going to learn about a new inner prefix, called the *seriative prefix*. We are devoting an entire chapter to this prefix because its forms are a little complicated. But first, let's say a word about the meaning of this prefix and how it fits into the Navajo verb system.

The seriative prefix is often found with verb themes of motion. The meaning that this prefix adds is that the motion happens over and over again in a sequence. If the verb theme is intransitive, a common meaning is that a number of people perform the motion one at a time, one after another. Another meaning that an intransitive verb theme with the seriative can have is that the subject performs the motion over and over again. With a transitive verb theme, the seriative often means that the subject moves a number of things individually, one after another. It happens reasonably often that a person takes a bunch of things out of a house or a room one at a time (because the items are too big or heavy to take out all together), or that someone loads something into a car one at a time, or that someone puts a group of objects in a particular place one at a time. When we want to speak about such activities in Navajo, the seriative is used.

(You might remember that back in Chapter 11 we pointed out that there isn't a general way of indicating that the object of a transitive Navajo verb is plural. But with transitive motion verbs, if the subject is moving a number of items one after another in a sequence, then using the seriative prefix helps to show that the object of the verb is plural.)

In addition, the seriative prefix is found as a lexical prefix for certain verb bases even if the meaning doesn't directly involve the kind of one-at-a-time-in-a-series motion that we just talked about. The general situation is similar to the situation with the reversionary: just as the reversionary has a specific meaning with verbs of motion (where it means motion back, or returning), but can also be a part of other verb bases where there isn't actual motion involved (like "wake up"), the seriative has a specific meaning with verbs of motion (repeated motion one-at-a-time), but can also be part of other verb bases. For example, the verb base that means "buy" has the seriative in it.

To have something concrete to start with, let's write up a vocabulary principle:

Vocabulary-16: Given a verb base that is constructed from a verb theme of motion, it may be possible to create another verb base that means that the motion described by the original verb base is performed over and over again in a series. This is done by adding the seriative inner prefix into the verb base as a lexical prefix. If the original verb base was conjugated in the n-I, the new verb base is conjugated in the regular I conjugation. If the original verb base was conjugated in the n-P or y-P, the new verb base is conjugated in the s-P. Otherwise, the conjugation patterns are not changed.

We'll see examples of Vocabulary-16 when we look at the actual forms of the seriative prefix, which we'll do in a little bit. But first, let's think about the conjugation patterns of verb bases that have the seriative in them. According what we wrote above, it seems that if we use Vocabulary-16 to build a verb base with the seriative in it, then the conjugation pattern of the verb base will change so that the new verb base uses the regular I mode conjugation and the s-P conjugation in the P mode. Actually, this is not quite true: if the original verb base used the long-vowel I and long-vowel P conjugations, then the new verb base (with the seriative) still uses the long-vowel conjugations for these modes. However, except for the long-vowel case, the seriative prefix does want its verb bases to take the regular I mode and the s-P conjugations. Here is something to keep in mind: when the seriative is part of a verb base that is not built from a verb theme of motion (like the verb base that means "buy", for example), these non-motion seriative verb bases are mostly also conjugated using the regular I and s-P conjugations. But there are exceptions! Be on the lookout for them.

Our study of the seriative is going to be just a little bit complicated. There are a number of reasons for this. One reason is that the seriative prefix has two different forms, and we need to know when each form is used. Another is that the seriative is placed in different positions in the verb, and we need to know when each position is used. But there's another kind of problem: by now, we've learned about so many pieces of Navajo verb grammar (six modes (some having more than one conjugation pattern), outer prefixes, inner prefixes, object prefixes, etc.) that there are lots of different combinations that we could illustrate. Because there are so many combinations, we won't be able to give examples of what happens in every possible combination, but we want our study to be able to deal with any situation, including situations that we don't give examples of.

What we are going to do is write a big rule with four parts, called Rule Conj-9, that describes what the seriative looks like and where it is placed. To start, we'll say that the basic form of the seriative is **h**, and that its basic position is that it precedes any other inner prefixes and also precedes F mode **d**(!), but it follows any object prefixes that may be in the verb. Starting with these two basic facts about the seriative, here is the rule that will tell us what happens when the seriative is found in various circumstances.

Rule Conj-9:

(a)   Form: If the seriative prefix is immediately preceded by a conjunct prefix, then the form of the prefix changes from **h** into **y**. (This applies to the prefix when it is placed at its actual position in the word, that is, after part (d) of this rule moves it around. Remember: if prefixes have to be moved, we always move them before we try to figure out what they look like.) Check to see if the sandwiched **y** part of Rule Conj-2 applies.

(b)   When the seriative (either in the form **h** or in the form **y**) is immediately followed by a subject prefix of the s-P conjugation, the seriative contracts with the subject prefix.

(c)   The seriative in the form **h** undergoes pre-stem vowel harmony.

(d)   Position: If the seriative is preceded by an object prefix (not counting 4 person **j**) and followed by one or more conjunct prefixes, then the seriative hops to the right over all the conjunct prefixes and is placed just to the right of the last conjunct prefix. If the only object prefix that precedes the seriative is 4 person **j** and the seriative is followed by a conjunct **d** prefix, then the **j** moves to the right of the seriative. (See also Rule Conj-7, which will apply after this part of Rule Conj-9 has applied.) If this rule positions the seriative immediately to the right of a conjunct prefix of the form **n**, and if the seriative is followed by a vowel, then the seriative is deleted.

This rule is pretty thick; not only that, but it also has some parts that need further explanation. For example, part (c) talks about a mysterious process called "pre-stem vowel harmony". What we're going to do is look at a series of examples that illustrate the various parts of Rule Conj-9. As we come to each part, we'll explain everything that needs to be explained. But you probably want to keep the following basic facts about part (d) in mind right from the beginning. The main idea is that the position of the seriative prefix is likely to change if two conditions are met: the seriative is immediately followed by another conjunct prefix, and the seriative is immediately preceded by an object prefix. So, for example, if you see a verb structure where the seriative is immediately followed by the subject prefix, then you can safely ignore part (d) - the position won't change. Similarly, if you're working on a verb structure where there is no object prefix at all, you can ignore part (d) - the position won't change.

Let's start by looking back at Chapter 18. In Chapter 18(17) there is a completive verb base built from the verb theme of motion shown in Chapter 18(16). We then used Vocabulary-4 to build expressions using the verb base in Chapter 18(17) that mean "roll it into it". Let's use our new Vocabulary-16 to build a verb base out of the one in Chapter 18(17). We can then form expressions that mean "roll them one after another into it" by adding the extra word **biih** (or **yiih**) to verbs built from this verb base.

(1)

Stem-set	Classifier: barred-l
I: **máás** P: **mááz**	Lexical prefixes: **h/y** (inner)
F: **mas** R: **mas**	Transitivity: transitive
O: **máás**	Conjugation: s-P

Note that the original completive verb base in Chapter 18(17) used the y-P conjugation in the P mode, but the verb base in (1), created by Vocabulary-16, uses the s-P.

In (1) we represented the seriative prefix as **h/y** to remind ourselves that although the basic form of the seriative is **h**, it often changes into **y**.

Let's see if we can use Rule Conj-9 to build I mode forms from the verb base in (1). We can ignore part (b) of that rule, since that part only has to do with the P mode. We'll assume that part (c) of that rule deals with something weird that doesn't have anything to do with this verb base (this is essentially true). Also, part (d) only comes into play when there are other conjunct prefixes to the right of the seriative, and we don't have any of those here. So, we should be able to do the I mode easily.

If the subject is 1sg, the structure of the word is:

(2) inner   subject   cl   verb
     prefix   prefix   stem

       h   -   sh   -   ł - máás

Part (a) tells us that when the seriative **h** is preceded by a conjunct prefix, it turns into **y**, but in (2) there aren't any prefixes at all in front of the seriative, so we won't change its form. So, starting with (2), Rule Conj-1 inserts **i** after **h**, the sandwich rule gets rid of the **ł** classifier, Rule Subj-6 applies, and we get **hismáás** as our word, which is exactly correct.

If the subject is 2sg, then the subject prefix will be **ni**. Rule Conj-3 will apply, and our word becomes **hiłmáás**.

What if the subject is 4 person? The structure will look like this:

(3) object   inner   subject   cl   verb
     prefix   prefix   prefix   stem

       j   -   h?   -   (zero) -   ł - máás

Part (a) of Rule Conj-9 now tells us that the form of the seriative has to change into **y** because it's immediately preceded by that **j**, which is a conjunct prefix, of course. (That's why we wrote the question mark after the **h** in (3) - we were suggesting that the basic form, which is **h**, might not be the actual form used in this word.) This means that we really have:

(4) object   inner   subject   cl   verb
     prefix   prefix   prefix   stem

       j   -   y   -   (zero) -   ł - máás

Now what? Since the seriative **y** is sandwiched in between two cononants, the sandwiched **y** part of Rule Conj-9(a) changes the **y** into **ii**. Thus, the word is: **jiiłmáás**.

Continuing in this way, we can get the entire set of I mode forms. Try it, and compare your answers with the following:

(5)	sg		dpl	distr dpl
1	hismáás		hiiłmáás	dahiiłmáás
2	hííłmáás		hołmáás	dahołmáás
3		yiyiiłmáás		dayiiłmáás
4		jiiłmáás		dajiiłmáás

Why is there an **h** (instead of a **y**) in the words **dahiiłmáás** and **dahołmáás**? Because Rule Conj-9(a) only changes **h** into **y** when it is immediately preceded by a conjunct prefix. A preceding disjunct prefix does not have this effect.

There is one form in (5) that you might have gotten wrong, namely the 3 person nondistributive form **yiyiiłmáás**. If we followed our instructions exactly, this should have come out as "yiiłmáás", but instead we see that doubling of the y's again. In Rule Str-1 we listed some cases where this happens, so we'll add a special note to that rule about this case as well. The situation here is a little different from the previous cases where we found this doubling. In the previous cases, in order for the 3 person object to double, it had to be necessary that there aren't any conjunct prefixes after it. In this case, the 3 person object **y** is actually followed by a conjunct prefix (namely, the seriative.) However, when the seriative **y** changes into **ii** by the sandwiched **y** rule, the effect is almost as though the seriative "disappears", at least for the purposes of the process described in Rule Str-1 that doubles the 3 person object prefix **y**.

Here's something to keep in mind. When the sandwiched **y** rule applies, the resulting **ii** in the verb often makes the verb look a lot like a long-vowel verb form. In fact, words like **yiyiiłmáás** and **jiiłmáás** look the same as they would look if they were built using the long-vowel I mode conjugation. Now, it happens that there aren't any long-vowel forms just like this (the long-vowel conjugations actually can be used with motion verb themes like the one used in (1) - we already saw some examples of long-vowel conjugations with verbs of motion back in Chapter 20 - but there is always some other inner prefix in there, usually inner **d**.) So this is something you need to be on the lookout for. Since a seriative verb form can often look like a long-vowel form (when the seriative prefix becomes **y** and then **ii** by Rule Conj-9(a) and Rule Conj-2), whenever you see or hear a verb that has an **ii** in it, you have to be careful - it might be long-vowel verb, but then again it might be a regular I mode form with the seriative prefix.

Let's move on to the P mode - this will give us a chance to study the effects of Rule Conj-9(b). What we need to do first is give a table showing the contractions of the seriative prefix with the s-P subject prefixes. So here we go:

(6)   seriative **h** contracted with s-P subject prefixes,
        zero/barred-l classifiers:

	sg	dpl
1	**hé**	**heed**
2	**híní**	**hisoo**
3	**heez** or **hees**	

(As we've seen in other cases involving the s-P conjugation, for the 3 person, **heez** is the form we get when the classifier is zero, and **hees** is the form used when the classifier is barred-l.)

(7)   seriative **h** contracted with s-P subject prefixes,
        plain-l/d classifiers:

	sg	dpl
1	**hésh**	**heed**
2	**híní**	**hisooh**
3	**hees**	

In the case of s-P contractions involving inner **d** and inner **n**, we've learned that we sometimes find variations. The same is true with seriative **h** - in fact, especially if the classifier is plain-l or d, we often find uncontracted forms where the syllable **hi** precedes the ordinary s-P subject prefix.

You are almost in a position to write out the P mode forms of the verb base given in (1). All you need to know in addition to what we've said is the following: seriative **y** does not contract with the 3 person subject prefix. Now, try to write out the complete set of P mode forms for this verb, and compare your results with the following:

(8)	sg	dpl	distr dpl
1	héłmááz	heelmááz	daheelmááz
2	híníłmááz	hisoołmááz	dahisoołmááz
3	yiyiismááz		dayiismááz
4	jiismááz		dajiismááz

The 1 and 2 person forms in (8) should be completely clear. Just to make sure we understand things, let's look at the 3 person nondistributive form in (8). The structure of this word is:

(9)   object   inner   subject   cl   verb
      prefix   prefix   prefix   stem

      y - h? - s - ł - mááz

Rule Conj-9(a) changes seriative **h** into **y** in this structure, since it's immediately preceded by the 3 object prefix **y**, which is a conjunct prefix. This **y** does not contract with the 3 person subject prefix **s**. Since seriative **y** is sandwiched in between two consonants (3 person object **y** and 3 person subject **s**), it changes into **ii**. The (regular) sandwich rule gets rid of the ł classifier, and, apparently, the 3 person object is doubled (so we need to add something again to Rule Str-1). This gives us exactly the correct form of the word: **yiyiismááz**.

If you saw or heard the word **yiyiismááz**, would you think it's a long-vowel form? The beginning of the word (the **yiyii-** part) looks like the beginning of a long-vowel I mode or long-vowel P mode word. In this case, though, that **s** in there is a tip-off that we have something different - a long-vowel I or P mode form wouldn't have such an **s** (unless it was a form of the 1sg prefix **sh**, but then the doubled **y** at the beginning wouldn't make sense).

Moving to the F mode, we'll have a chance to see some of part (d) of Rule Conj-9 at work. There is enough information in that rule (together with what you already know from previous chapters) to get all the F mode forms of this verb exactly right. If you write them out, check your answers with the following forms:

(10)   sg   dpl   distr dpl

1   hideeshmas   hidiilmas   dahidiilmas
2   hidííłmas   hidoołmas   dahidoołmas
3   yidiyoołmas   deidiyoołmas
4   hizhdoołmas   dahizhdoołmas

To make sure, let's figure out how the 3 and 4 person forms in (10) were constructed.

The structure of the nondistributive 3 person form in (10) is as follows:

(11)   object   inner   F mode   subject   cl   verb
       prefix   prefix   d   prefix   stem

       y - h? - d - oo - ł - mas

First of all: why is there an inner prefix in front of the F mode **d**? Normally, inner prefixes follow F mode **d** in F mode forms. However, a peculiarity of the seriative prefix is that, in the F mode, its basic position is indeed to the left of the F mode **d**, as we mentioned earlier. If there were other inner prefixes in this word, they would appear in their normal position, to the right of the F mode **d**.

When faced with a structure like (11), the first thing to do is look at Rule Conj-9(d) and figure out if any of the prefixes have to be moved to a different position. We didn't do that with the I mode and the P mode forms we looked at earlier because none of those forms had a conjunct prefix of any sort to the right of the seriative. But here the seriative is followed by F mode **d**, so we better check out Rule Conj-9(d). In fact, since the seriative in (11) is not only followed by F mode **d** but preceded by an object prefix, Rule Conj-9(d) tells us that the seriative hops to the right of the F mode **d**, giving us the following structure:

(12) object F mode inner subject cl verb
     prefix   d   prefix prefix   stem

       y - d - h? - oo - ł - mas

With the prefixes positioned correctly, we check Rule Conj-9(a) and find that the seriative changes into **y**, since it's immediately preceded by F mode **d**, which is a conjunct prefix. This gives us:

(13) object F mode inner subject cl verb
     prefix   d   prefix prefix   stem

       y - d - y - oo - ł - mas

Rule Conj-1 now routinely inserts an **i** right after the object prefix **y** and another **i** right after F mode **d**. This gives us the actual word **yidiyoołmas**. Note that the sandwiched **y** rule does not apply to this word, since the seriative **y** is followed by a vowel in (13).

The 4 person form in (10) starts out with a structure somewhat similar to (11), namely:

(14) object inner F mode subject cl verb
     prefix prefix   d   prefix   stem

       j - h? - d - oo - ł - mas

Checking Rule Conj-9(d) carefully, we see that we have a special case. The seriative in (14) is indeed followed by a conjunct prefix of the form **d**, and also preceded by an object prefix. But if the object prefix is 4 person **j**, we don't hop the seriative - instead, we hop the 4 person **j** over to the right of the seriative. This gives us the following:

(15) inner object F mode subject cl verb
      prefix prefix   d   prefix   stem

      h - j - d - oo - ł - mas

The labels over the prefixes in (15) are beginning to look quite weird - specifically, the seriative, which is really an inner prefix, looks like it's in a very strange position. Still, this is the way words like this one are actually built. (The fact that the position of some of these prefixes can move around like this has led some linguists to think that prefixes like the seriative, the object prefixes, and the F mode **d** are really separate words rather than prefixes that are attached to the verb. However, in written Navajo, expressions like the one diagrammed in (15) are always written as single words.)

In any case, let's finish up our word. There is an instruction in Rule Conj-9(d) telling us to check Rule Conj-7 to make sure we do the correct thing with the **j** prefix. In this case, Rule Conj-7 tells us to change **j** into **zh**. We should also check Rule Conj-9(a) to see if the form of the seriative should be changed - in the case of (15), we don't change it, since there aren't any conjunct prefixes to the left of the **h** (which is why we put "h" in (15) rather than "h?" as we did in some other structures when we thought the **h** might get changed into **y**.) Rule Conj-1 operates in the usual way to insert an **i** after the **h**, and we end up with our word: **hizhdoołmas**.

(But: for words like this, I have occasionally seen forms in print that begin **jidiyoo-**. In order to get this kind of form, we'd consider the **j** prefix to be an ordinary object prefix and we wouldn't apply the special instruction in Rule Conj-9(d) that moves **j** to the right of the seriative in cases like this. Instead, we'd create the word exactly the same way that we did when we started out with the structure in (11). Apparently, some people, at certain times, use this form, so we have another case of variation. We've already mentioned that the more complicated a verb becomes, the more likely it is that you'll find different speakers saying it different ways.)

Since we've now learned the R, U, and O modes, we can write out the forms of (1) for those modes as well. Rule Conj-9(d) will never apply in those modes, since for this verb base there won't be any conjunct prefixes to the right of the seriative. We won't write out all the forms for these other modes; if you're careful, you should get the correct forms for all the U and O mode words based on what we've done. In the case of the R mode, though, there is one form where the mysterious part (c) of Rule Conj-9 comes into play. Let's look at that now, so we can learn what "pre-stem vowel harmony" is about. The form is the 1sg R mode form, which has the following structure:

(16) R mode inner   subject cl verb
      ná   prefix   prefix   stem

      ná - h - sh - ł - mas

Make sure you remember the principles for building structures like (16). Since we're in the regular

R mode, the subject prefix is taken from the regular I mode set of subject prefixes, plus we've added in the R mode **ná**, which is a disjunct prefix.

Now, starting with (16), parts (a), (b), and (d) of Rule Conj-9 don't make any changes to our word. We expect the (ordinary) sandwich rule to apply normally and remove the ł classifier. When Rule Conj-1 inserts **i** after **h**, Rule Subj-5 puts a high tone on this **i**, and Rule Subj-6 changes the subject prefix **sh** into **s**, we'd expect to end up with "náhísmas". But the usual form of this word is **náhásmas**. What's going on?

What's going on is a process that we are going to call *pre-stem vowel harmony*. The effect of this process is to make the vowels in two adjacent syllables the same. What we'll do is give a basic rule that gives the general principles for when this happens. Then, we'll list the particular cases that we need to know about.

(17)   <u>General Rule for Pre-stem Vowel Harmony</u>

(a)   In order for the process of pre-stem vowel harmony to occur, the following two conditions must be true:

(i)   The syllable consisting of seriative **h** followed by a vowel must be the pre-stem syllable.

(ii)   The seriative must be immediately preceded by a disjunct prefix.

(b)   The effect of the process of pre-stem vowel harmony is to make the vowel preceding the seriative **h** and the vowel following it the same. (That's why we're calling this process "vowel harmony".)

Unfortunately, the rule in (17) only gives the general setting for our study. To describe exactly what happens and when, we have to, first of all, list the cases of pre-stem syllables beginning with **h** when vowel harmony really occurs, and secondly, list the actual effects.

Lets start with the first task. We know that in order for pre-stem vowel harmony to occur, the syllable beginning with seriative **h** has to be the pre-stem syllable. However, not every pre-stem syllable undergoes pre-stem vowel harmony. Here are the ones that do undergo it:

(18)   <u>Pre-stem syllables that undergo vowel harmony</u>:

(a)   Any pre-stem syllable created when Rule Conj-1 inserts the vowel **i** after the seriative **h** when **h** is immediately followed by a consonant.

(b)   Optionally, the syllables **hé**, **hésh**, **heed**, **heez**, and **hees** created when **h** contracts with subject

349

prefixes of the s-P conjugation. (The syllables with long **ee** in them seem to undergo vowel harmony less frequently than the ones with short **é**. The syllable **heed** seems to undergo it less frequently than the syllables **heez** and **hees**.)

Important: one pre-stem syllable that does <u>not</u> undergo pre-stem vowel harmony is the syllable **hí** created by Rule Conj-3.

The example that we just ran into (the R mode word **náhásmas**) is an example of (18a) - the vowel that Rule Conj-1 inserted after **h** was changed from **i** (or **í**) into **á**. Before proceeding, you might want to check the examples of words with the seriative prefix in them that we've seen in this chapter. If you do, you should see that none of the I mode and F mode forms we looked at could undergo pre-stem vowel harmony, either because the syllable beginning with **h** wasn't one of the ones listed in (18), or because the syllable beginning with **h** wasn't immediately preceded by a disjunct prefix, or because the seriative took the form of **y** (or **ii**) so there wasn't any seriative **h** in the word at all. In the case of the P mode, there is one word that is a candidate for pre-stem vowel harmony: the word **daheelmááz** in (8). We listed this word with the original **ee** vowel because the **heed** syllable undergoes vowel-harmony the least frequently, so we allowed ourselves to ignore the issue when we looked at the P mode. For speakers who use vowel harmony when saying this word, the word is **dahaalmááz**.

We now have to explain exactly which vowels change and what they change to when vowel harmony occurs. This is a bit tricky because in addition to the change in the vowel that follows seriative **h**, sometimes the vowel that the preceding disjunct prefix ends in also changes! What we'll do is list the most frequently encountered cases in a chart. To make it clear, we'll start by listing the forms only for the case of pre-stem syllables of the form (18a). Then we'll say something very easy that will handle the (18b) cases.

(19)   Vowel-harmony effects:

disjunct prefix	plus **h** (pre-stem)	gives
any disjunct prefix ending in **a**	**h**	-aha (exception: **'a+h='ahi**)
any disjunct prefix ending in **e**	**h**	-ehe
any disjunct prefix ending in **i**	**h**	-ehe

Don't forget that, in addition to these vowel harmony effects, Rule Subj-5 will put a high tone on the vowel following **h** if the preceding vowel has a high tone. Incidentally, the preceding vowel (the vowel at the end of the preceding disjunct prefix) is allowed to be long or short, high tone or low tone. (The vowel following **h** is always short in the (18a) case.)

Note that in the case of disjunct prefixes ending in **i**, the vowel of the disjunct prefix changes to **e**; this matches the vowel that follows the **h**, which is also changed to **e**.

If the pre-stem syllable is one of the ones listed in (18b), the same vowel changes occur. However, if the pre-stem syllable starts out with a long vowel, then the new vowel in the pre-stem syllable is long, too; and if the pre-stem syllable starts out with a high tone, then the new vowel in the pre-stem syllable has a high tone, too. (Said differently: the length and tone of the pre-stem syllable doesn't change.) If the preceding disjunct prefix starts out ending in **i** , then that **i** changes into **e**, the same as in the cases covered by (19). In this case, since there already is an **e** vowel after the **h**, the vowel of the preceding disjunct prefix is the only vowel that changes.

Let's get back to our example, the word whose structure is given in (16). In this word, the seriative appears in its **h** form, and the syllable that starts with this **h** is a pre-stem syllable whose vowel is created by Rule Conj-1. Thus, this syllable falls under the case of (18a). Not only that, but in this word, this pre-stem syllable is immediately preceded by a disjunct prefix that ends in **á**. By the first row in (19), the pre-stem syllable undergoes vowel harmony, changing its vowel to **a**. Rule Subj-5 puts a high tone on this vowel, so the word ends up starting with the syllables **náhá**.

As another example: we can apply Vocabulary-16 to the verb base we get by applying Vocabulary-8 (see Chapter 19) to the "roll" verb theme in Chapter 18(16) - this will give us a verb base that means something like "roll them out one after another". How would we say "I'm rolling them out one after another"? Careful: the verb base created by Vocabulary-8 uses the n-I and n-P conjugations. What about the verb base created from it by Vocabulary-16?

OK - the word that means "I'm rolling them out one after another" is **ch'éhésmáás**. How did we get this word? Its structure is:

(20) outer inner subject cl verb
      prefix prefix prefix   stem

      ch'í - h - sh - ł - máás

The conjugation pattern we're using here is the regular I conjugation, not the n-I conjugation (reread Vocabulary-16), which is why the subject prefix is just **sh**. Rule Conj-9(d) doesn't apply (there are no conjunct prefixes in (20) following the seriative.) Rule Conj-9(b) doesn't apply (we're in the I mode, not the P mode.) Rule Conj-9(a) doesn't apply (the seriative in (20) is not preceded by a conjunct prefix.) However, Rule Conj-9(c) does apply: the syllable beginning with seriative **h** is the syllable created by Rule Conj-1, so that syllable is an instance of (18a). By the last row in (19) (together with Rule Subj-5), this word will start out **ch'éhé**. (Of course, Rule Subj-6 and the sandwich rule also applied to this word.)

Note that the outer prefix **'a** that we studied in Chapter 19 is an exception: it does not cause pre-stem vowel harmony with the seriative prefix. For example, "I'm rolling them away one after another" is **ahismááS**.

Incidentally: as you might have guessed from the word **náhásmas**, the prefix **ná**, and also the prefix **na**, do not change to **ní** (or **ni**) when followed by the seriative. In fact, these two prefixes never change when followed by the seriative, whether or not the seriative starts a pre-stem syllable, and whether the seriative has the form **h** or the form **y**.

We have looked at almost everything we need in order to conjugate verbs that have the seriative prefix in them. We'll look at a few more examples, just to fill in some blanks and firm up our understanding. But before doing that: did you notice anything at all familiar about the idea of pre-stem vowel harmony? Do you think you might have seen something like this already?

If you check Rule Disj-4(e)(i), you'll see an effect that looks suspiciously similar to the vowel harmony effects listed in (19). The story is that the unspec object prefix also undergoes pre-stem vowel harmony! However, the specific facts are a bit different for that prefix as compared to seriative **h**. For example, if seriative **h** starts a syllable of the (18a) sort and is preceded by the outer prefix **'a**, the result is **'ahi**, whereas, as we see from Rule Disj-4(e)(i), if unspec **'** starts a syllable like this and is preceded by outer **'a**, the result is **'e'e**. But there are other effects involving the unspec prefix that look like (19). We'll survey them briefly in Chapter 27.

One thing we haven't looked at is contractions of the seriative in its **y** form with s-P subject prefixes. Here are tables showing these contractions:

(21)   seriative **y** contracted with s-P subject prefixes,
        zero/barred-l classifiers:

	sg	dpl
1	**yé**	**yeed**
2	**yíní**	**yoo**
3	(no contraction)	

(22)   seriative **y** contracted with s-P subject prefixes,
plain-ł/d classifiers:

	sg	dpl
1	**yésh**	**yeed**
2	**yíní**	**yooh**
3	(no contraction)	

For the 3 person subject, these tables say "no contraction". What this means is that when forming a word with the 3 person subject in the s-P conjugation, if the seriative is in there and if its form is **y**, then it's treated exactly the same as we've learned, without any special contraction. We have already seen an example of this - look at (9) earlier.

To see an example that shows the contractions with the **y** form of the seriative, let's have a look at the verb base that means "make a series of payments". Here is that verb base:

(23)

Stem-set	Classifier: zero
I: **lé** P: **la'**	Lexical prefixes: **ni** (outer), **'** (object), **h/y** (inner)
F: **lééł** R: **lééh**	Transitivity: intransitive
O: **lééł**	Conjugation: s-P

You might have noticed that the stem-set in (23) is almost the same as the momentaneous stem-set of the "move a ropelike object" verb theme (see Chapter 18(11).) We have already noticed a few peculiarities about that verb theme (for example, the irregularity when it's preceded by a 1dpl subject prefix.) Another peculiarity is that for certain verb bases that use it, the P mode stem is **la'** rather than **lá**. The verb base in (23) is one of those. (Yet another peculiarity is the fact that in the stem-sets of this verb theme, the O mode stem is not the same as the I mode stem - instead, it's the same as the F mode stem.)

Since the seriative is always going to be preceded by the unspec object prefix **'** in words built from (23), part (a) of Rule Conj-9 will always kick in. The result is that none of the actual words built from (23) have the **h** form of the seriative. Instead, we'll see those **y**'s, and also, of course, those **ii**'s.

Let's start with the I mode. If you try writing the forms out, you might wonder about what happens when the subject is 2sg: does Rule Conj-3 apply? The answer is that it does. With that information, write the forms and compare them with:

(24)   sg   dpl   distr dpl

1	ni'iishłé	ni'iyiilyé	nida'iyiilyé
2	ni'iyłé	ni'iyohłé	nida'iyohłé
3		ni'iilé	nida'iilé
4		ni'jiilé	nida'jiilé

Let's look at a few of these forms.

First of all, the word meaning "I'm making a series of payments" has this structure:

(25)   outer   object   inner   subject   verb
       prefix   prefix   prefix prefix   stem

       ni   –   '   –   h?   –   sh   –   lé

Rule Conj-9(d) doesn't apply, so we don't have to rearrange any of the prefixes. Rule Conj-9(a) changes the form of the seriative to **y**. Since this **y** is now sandwiched in between the consonant **'** (the unspec object prefix) and the consonant **sh** (the subject prefix), the sandwiched **y** rule changes the **y** to **ii**. The only other thing that happens is that Rule Subj-7 changes the **l** at the beginning of the verb stem to **ł**. This gives us our word **ni'iishłé**. No problem here.

Next, let's look at "you (sg) are making a series a payments". The structure is:

(26)   outer   object   inner   subject   verb
       prefix   prefix   prefix prefix   stem

       ni   –   '   –   h?   –   ni   –   lé

Now there is an issue with Rule Conj-3. The issue is this: If we let Rule Conj-9(a) not only change the seriative **h** into **y** but then into **ii** (since it's in between the consonant **'** and the consonant **n**), then Rule Conj-3 would not be able to apply, and we'd get the wrong answer. So here's what we have to say. Rule Conj-3 is a "powerful" rule: the 2sg prefix **ni** really wants to change into a high tone whenever there's a conjunct prefix to its left. It doesn't want the seriative to slip out of this by losing its consonantal quality and becoming **ii**! So what happens is that as soon as the seriative becomes **y** (which it has to, since it's preceded by a conjunct prefix), Rule Conj-3 zips in and creates the syllable **yí**. To insure that this happens, we'll add a note to our sandwiched **y** rule clause in Rule Conj-2 that will prevent it from applying if the **y** is followed by 2sg **ni**. All that is needed now to finish our word is for Rule Conj-1 to insert the **i** after the **'**, and we get **ni'iyílé**.

But wait! We should be using Rule Conj-5 instead of Rule Conj-1 to figure out what (if anything) is inserted after the unspec **'** prefix. Now, that rule, as we've learned it so far, tells us that if **'** is preceded by a vowel (which it is in (26)) and if the syllable that follows is not the verb stem syllable (which is also true in this case: the syllable that follows ' is **yí**), then no vowel should be inserted! What's going on?

As it happens, the situation is a bit unclear. In some cases, when the unspec prefix ' is followed by seriative **y**, we'll see **'y** written, which is what Rule Conj-5 says ought to happen. But usually an **i** is inserted - in fact, in the word **ni'iyílé**, I've always seen that **i** in there. Since **y** is a special sort of consonant (it has some of the qualities of a vowel), we'll blame the problem on the **y** - we'll add a note to Rule Conj-5 that will officially say that we should insert an **i** when ' is followed by **y**. But sometimes such an **i** isn't inserted, so the question is, can we tell when it's inserted and when it isn't? The following seems to be true: if the ' got to be in front of the **y** because of unspec hopping (see Rule Conj-5), then don't insert the **i** (otherwise, insert it.) We'll see an example of this in just a moment.

One other thing. Towards the end of Chapter 19 we ran into an example of a word where the most usual spelling of the word involved dropping a **y** between two **i**'s. (The word we were looking at was **ch'íílteeh**, an n-I form with 3 person subject and 3 person object.) Could that happen with any of the words in (24)? If we dropped the **y** in the word for "you (sg) are making a series of payments", we'd get **ni'iílé**, with a "rising" tone. I've never seen this word written this way, but I wouldn't be surprised if you ran into such a spelling. I actually have seen the word for "we (two) are making a series of payments" written **ni'iilyé** (instead of **ni'iyiilyé**.) A spelling like this makes this word look like a long-vowel form, which is why I like the longer spelling with the **y** better, but you should be prepared to find such alternate spellings in printed Navajo texts.

Well, we've spent quite a bit of time on the I mode of this verb! What we were really interested in originally was the P mode, in order to see the contractions with seriative **y**, so let's get to those forms right away. With what we've learned about the seriative, together with the extra fact about inserting an **i** between unspec ' and seriative **y**, we can get exactly the right forms by using the contractions in (21). Here we go:

(27)	sg	dpl	distr dpl
1	ni'iyéla'	ni'iyeelya'	nida'iyeelya'
2	ni'iyíníla'	ni'iyoola'	nida'iyoola'
3		ni'iizla'	nida'iizla'
4		ni'jiizla'	nida'jiizla'

The 3 (and 4) person forms are constructed in much the same way as the corresponding forms we saw back in (8) and (9). The thing to remember is that when the subject is 3 person, seriative **y** doesn't contract with the s-P subject prefix, so whenever there's a prefix in the object prefix position, the sandwiched **y** rule changes the **y** into **ii**. But when the subject is 1 or 2 person, seriative **y** can contract with the s-P subject prefix and we get forms that are by now familiar to us from out previous experience with such contractions.

And note: since unspec hopping never happened in any of the forms in (27) (in fact, nothing got moved around in any of those forms), we do insert an **i** between **'** and **y** (when they're next to each other) in these forms.

Just to make sure our knowledge of the seriative is firm, let's write out the F mode forms of (23). Since this verb base has a lexical prefix in its object prefix position, Rule Conj-9(d) will move the seriative in all F mode forms (because of the F mode **d**.) We get:

(28)	sg	dpl	distr dpl
1	nidi'yeeshłééł	nidi'yiilyééł	nidadi'yiilyééł
2	nidi'yííłééł	nidi'yoohłééł	nidadi'yoohłééł
3	nidi'yoolééł		nidadi'yoolééł
4	nizhdi'yoolééł		nidazhdi'yoolééł

Can you see how these forms got created? Let's look at the word that means "I'll make a series of payments". Its structure starts out being:

(29)	outer prefix	object prefixes	inner prefix	F mode d	subject prefix	verb stem
	ni	- ' -	j	- h? -	d	- eesh - lééł

Two rules apply to change the position of the prefixes. Rule Conj-9(d) moves the seriative to the right of F mode **d** (because (at least!) the unspec object prefix is to its left); this gives us:

(30)	outer prefix	object prefixes	F mode d	inner prefix	subject prefix	verb stem
	ni	- ' -	j	- d -	h? -	eesh - lééł

But then the unspec-hopping part of Rule Conj-5 applies to (30), which moves the unspec prefix over to the right:

(31)	outer prefix	object prefix	F mode d	object prefix(!)	inner prefix	subject prefix	verb stem
	ni	- j -	d	- ' -	h? -	eesh - lééł

Rule Conj-9(a) changes the form of the seriative to **y**; but the sandwiched **y** rule doesn't apply since the seriative in (31) is followed by a vowel. Since unspec ' got to be next to seriative **y** by unspec hopping, we won't insert that **i** between them. Checking Rule Conj-7 for what to do about the 4 person prefix **j**, we see that we just change it into **zh** (we don't move it anywhere.) A simple application of Rule Conj-1 (to add in an **i** after F mode **d**) and of Rule Subj-7 (to change the **l** at the beginning of the verb stem to **ł**), and we have our word: **nizhdi'yeeshłééł**.

You should definitely write out all the R and O mode forms of this verb. For the R mode, you need to know that this verb base undergoes classifier shift in the R mode. Apart from this, you'll have no trouble. The R mode forms resemble the I mode ones, of course, because the same subject prefixes are used. You'll get forms like **niná'iishdlééh, niná'iyídlééh**, etc. In the O mode, you'll use the subject prefixes that are used when there's a conjunct prefix to the left of the subject prefix. Since the unspec object prefix will always be in there, the seriative will always have the form **y** (since the O mode subject prefixes all start with a vowel, the sandwiched **y** rule won't apply). You'll get forms like **ni'iyóshłééł, ni'iyóólééł**, etc.

To illustrate some more combinations, let's look at a verb base that has more lexical prefixes in it. We'll start with a new vocabulary principle that doesn't involve the seriative:

Vocabulary-17: Starting from a classificatory verb theme we can build a verb base that means "take it down (from a peg or shelf)" as follows:

Stem-set: use the momentaneous stem-set of the verb theme	Classifier: use the classifier of the verb theme
	Lexical prefixes: **na** (outer), **'** (object), **d** (inner)
	Transitivity: transitive
	Conjugation: long-vowel conjugation in all modes except F

Our plan is to add the seriative to verb bases created by Vocabulary-17, but before doing so, let's point out two things about these verb bases.

First: the outer prefix **na** used in Vocabulary-17 is not the atelic **na** that we've seen many times! The **na** here is a different prefix whose meaning is approximately "down". But don't worry: this prefix not only has a different meaning from the atelic **na**, but it also behaves differently, so you won't get confused. For example: atelic **na** requires its verb base to use the s-P conjugation, whereas the **na** that means "down" usually uses the y-P. (Here, it uses the long-vowel P but that's really because Vocabulary-17 builds transitional verb bases - review Chapter 20 about this.) Also, atelic **na** uses the continuative stem-set of a verb theme, whereas "down" **na** uses the momentaneous one.

Second: The verb bases created by Vocabulary-17 all have the unspec object prefix as a lexical prefix. But these verb bases are transitive - this means that a "real" object prefix (representing the actual object) is also going to go into the object prefix position. Because of the meanings of these verb bases, the only object prefix you'll really see (in most cases) is the 3 person **y**, which will be in the verb if the subject is also 3 person. When this **y** and the unspec object are both in the verb, it turns out that the unspec prefix is required to come first. Since, in these verbs, the **y** will be directly followed either by the inner **d** of the verb base or by F mode **d**, the sandwiched **y** rule will apply, so the combination of the two object prefixes and the following **d** will appear as **'iid**. (With verbs like this, no unspec hopping will happen when that 3 person **y** is in there - that syllable **'iid** will really be there in the actual word.) We'll add something about this unusual situation to Rule Str-4.

We won't write out the forms of any actual verb base created by Vocabulary-17; except for what we've already said, there is nothing new about them. However, let's have a look at a verb base that we get by applying Vocabulary-16 to a verb base created by Vocabulary-17. For our classificatory verb theme, let's stick with our "move a ropelike object" theme - we'll get a verb base that means "take down ropelike things one at a time (from a peg or shelf)". Note that the conjugation patterns for the verb base with the seriative will be the same as the conjugation pattern of the verb base without the seriative: we'll use the long-vowel conjugation in all the modes except for the F mode.

For the I mode, here are the forms:

(32)	sg	dpl	distr dpl
1	nahi'diishłé	nahi'diilyé	nidahi'diilyé
2	nahi'diilé	nahi'doohłé	nidahi'doohłé
3		neidi'yiilé	nideidi'yiilé
4		nahizh'diilé	nidahizh'diilé

If you've been following our discussion carefully, you will realize that the unspec object prefix has undergone unspec hopping in every one of the forms in (32)! As an example, let's start with "I'm taking ropelike things down one at a time". The structure of this word starts out like this:

(33)	outer prefix	object prefix	inner prefixes	subject prefix	verb stem
	na	- ' -	h? - d -	iish -	lé

Now, we've got a conflict between two rules that move prefixes around. On the one hand, Rule Conj-9(d) wants to move the seriative to the right (it's preceded by an object prefix and followed by a conjunct prefix.) On the other hand, the unspec hopping part of Rule Conj-5 wants to move the unspec prefix to the right. As it happens, unspec hopping wins out. The structure changes to:

(34)　outer　inner　object　inner　subject　verb
　　　　prefix　prefix　prefix　prefix　prefix　stem

　　　　na　-　h?　-　'　-　d　-　iish　-　lé

Rule Conj-9(d) no longer applies (there's no object prefix in front of it.) In fact, no part of Rule Conj-9 applies - the seriative just shows up as **h**. One simple application of Rule Conj-1, and we get the word **nahi'diishlé**.

You might want to compare this situation to the case where the seriative is immediately preceded by 4 person **j** - in that case, **j** can move to the right (and the seriative itself isn't moved.) If the seriative is immediately preceded by the unspec object prefix, and if unspec hopping could move that unspec prefix away, we have something similar: we have to let unspec hopping apply before we try Rule Conj-9(d). (We'll add a note to Rule Conj-9(d).) To see that the unspec prefix has to immediately precede the seriative in order to hop first, compare the word in (33)-(34) with the 3 person nondistributive form in (32). This latter word starts out as follows:

(35)　outer　　object　　inner　　subject　verb
　　　　prefix　　prefixes　prefixes　prefix　　stem

　　　　na　-　'　-　y　-　h?　-　d　-　ii　-　lé

This time, the seriative is immediately preceded by the 3 person object prefix, so Rule Conj-9(d) gets to move the seriative before anything else happens - the result is:

(36)　outer　　object　　inner　　subject　verb
　　　　prefix　　prefixes　prefixes　prefix　　stem

　　　　na　-　'　-　y　-　d　-　h?　-　ii　-　lé

Unspec hopping now moves the unspec object prefix:

(37)　outer　object　inner　object　inner　subject　verb
　　　　prefix　prefix　prefix　prefix　prefix　prefix　stem

　　　　na　-　y　-　d　-　'　-　h?　-　ii　-　lé

(The column headings in (37) look really weird! When the prefixes get moved around like this, terms like "object prefix" and "inner prefix" begin to lose their significance.)

The seriative becomes **y** (Rule Conj-9(a)), the 3 person object **y** becomes **i** (Rule Conj-2), the **a** vowel at the end of the outer prefix **na** becomes **e** (Rule Disj-2), an **i** is inserted after the inner **d** (Rule Conj-

1) (and no **i** is inserted after **'**, since it got to be in front of the seriative **y** by means of unspec hopping), and....? And that's it! We get **neidi'yiilé**.

The rest of the forms of this verb in all modes can now be written out - we've learned everything necessary to do so. We won't give all these forms here, but just to show that there's no problem with the seriative appearing together with the long-vowel P conjugation, here are the P mode forms:

(38)

	sg		dpl	distr dpl
1	nahi'diilá	nahi'diilyá		nidahi'diilya
2	nahidi'nilá	nahi'doolá		nidahi'doolá
3		neidi'yiilá		nideidi'yiilá
4		nahizh'diilá		nidahizh'diilá

When Rule Vocabulary-16 applies normally, a verb base that is conjugated in the n-I and n-P conjugations changes its conjugation pattern - the new verb base with the seriative is conjugated in the regular I conjugation and in the s-P conjugation, as we've seen. However, there are a few verb bases, not created by Vocabulary-16, that have the seriative in them and that are (unexpectedly) conjugated in the n-I and n-P patterns. These present no problems - our rules operate exactly as we've learned them. (Note, though, that since seriative **h** or seriative **y** is a conjunct prefix, the 3 person I mode subject prefix, and also the 3 person n-P subject prefix if the classifier is plain-l or d, will be **ee** when immediately preceded by the seriative - see Chapter 18(21) and Chapter 18(24). Also: remember that those **n**'s that are part of some of the subject prefixes in the n-I and n-P conjugations are not conjunct prefixes! This means, for example, that we shouldn't be tempted to move the seriative to the right of those **n**'s.)

There are just a few verb bases that have an inner **n** as well as the seriative. It seems that if Rule Conj-9(d) moves the seriative to the right of the inner **n**, and if a vowel follows (so that the sandwiched **y** rule wouldn't apply), then the seriative **y** is simply dropped out. An example is the word **néidínóo'ish** "he/she will sew it", an F mode form built from a verb base with outer **ná**, the seriative, inner **n**, zero classifier, and verb stem **'ish** (in all modes.)

This is all we need to learn about the seriative. Before leaving this chapter, note that verb forms with the seriative in them are very easy to recognize if the seriative is in its **h** form - usually, you'll see the syllable **hi**, which cannot be mistaken for a form of the outer prefix **ha** or of the object prefix **hw**. If pre-stem vowel harmony has happened, the seriative might end up looking like **he**, which is also easy to tell apart from any form of outer **ha** (which would be **haa** in pre-stem position, by Rule Disj-1) or of **hw** (which would be **ha** in pre-stem position.) But if pre-stem vowel harmony produces a syllable **ha** or **há** for the seriative, you'll want to be careful - it'll look the same as, for example, the object prefix **hw** (possibly with a high tone on it due to Rule Subj-5.) To tell whether you had seriative **h** or object **hw**, you'd have to look at other forms of the verb. Also, seriative **h** followed directly by a 2dpl subject prefix looks the same as the object prefix **hw** followed directly by a 2dpl subject prefix, so if you see a 2dpl word with **ho** or **hoo** in it, you'd have to look at other forms of the word to tell the difference. On the other hand, seriative **h** followed by a 1dpl prefix **iid** comes out **hiid**, whereas **hw** followed by this 1dpl prefix comes out **hwiid**, so we can easily tell them apart.

We already mentioned that when seriative **y** becomes **ii** by the sandwiched **y** rule, the verb form often looks very similar to, or even identical to, a long-vowel form. Becoming very familiar with long-vowel forms and seriative forms is probably the best way to learn to distinguish them. When seriative **y** doesn't change into **ii**, its position in the word (there will have to be a conjunct prefix to its left) makes it clear that it's really seriative **y** and not, say, the 3 person object prefix **y**.

CHAPTER 25

THE PROGRESSIVE MODE

In our studies so far we have looked at all the modes in the Navajo verb system except for the progressive mode. In this chapter we'll learn about this last mode. The actual forms of the subject prefixes are pretty easy, but before we get to them we need to say something about the way this mode fits into the verb system.

If we think of all possible Navajo verb bases as one huge collection, the fact is that many Navajo verb bases are not conjugated in the Pg mode at all. However, certain verb bases built from verb themes of motion can be conjugated in this mode, and for those verb bases, this mode is an important and often-used one. There are also non-motion verb bases that have Pg mode forms. Some of them use the Pg mode a lot, but for a significant number of those non-motion verbs, the Pg mode is used only to indicate a special meaning, often something like "walking along while engaging in the action".

But there is another way of looking at the Pg mode. To explain this other way, let's first remember that all the verb bases we've seen so far fall into two categories. The first one (which we called the *active* verb bases back in Chapter 21) are the "normal" ones. These are verb bases that have forms for the I, P, F, R, U, and O modes. Then there is a second group of verb bases: these are the neuter verb bases, and they have forms in only one mode. (It turns out that any neuter verb has forms either in the I mode only or in the P mode only, depending on the particular verb. We've seen examples of each of these in our studies.) Now, we could say that there's a third group of verb bases: these will be verb bases that are conjugated only in the Pg mode. If we say this, then any Pg mode verb form will be regarded as having been built from its own special verb base in this third group.

Saying that Pg mode forms are found only for a special group of verb bases may seem like a strange thing to do, but there are some reasons why it's not a bad idea - we'll see one of the reasons in a moment. But whether you think this is a good idea or not, you should be aware that the YM materials take this approach. For example, progressive (Pg mode) forms are listed as separate vocabulary items - they are not viewed as forms of other nonprogressive verbs. YM even have a special term for those verb bases that are conjugated in the Pg mode only: they call them *cursive* verb bases. (Actually, they really use the term *cursive aspect*, but we can view the term *cursive* as naming the group of verb bases that are conjugated in the Pg only.) We'll use that term here, too.

A reason why it's convenient to say that the Pg mode forms of a verb constitute a special verb base all by itself is that there are restrictions on the kinds of lexical prefixes that can be used when the Pg mode is used. For example: just about any verb theme of motion can be the basis for Pg mode forms. But many common prefix arrangments that are found with verbs of motion are not used in the Pg mode. For example: many outer prefixes cannot be used as part of any verb that's conjugated in the Pg mode. But some can: the reversionary and semeliterative prefixes that we studied in Chapter 22 can be used in a Pg mode verb, and so can the seriative that we just learned about in Chapter 24.

(Some inner prefixes are also possible.) By viewing Pg mode verbs as coming from a separate class of verb bases (the cursive verb bases), we can simply say that a cursive verb base can never have certain outer prefixes.

So what does a cursive verb base look like? Before we get to anything like a vocabulary principle, we need to talk about verb stems.

There is something odd about the verb stems used in the Pg: the verb stem used for the nondistributive forms is different from the verb stem used for the distributive forms! In fact, we can give a rule that tells us what these verb stems are:

(1)   Pg mode stem rule: For a nondistributive form, the verb stem used in the Pg mode is the F mode stem of the momentaneous stem set. For a distributive form, the verb stem used in the Pg mode is the I mode stem of the momentaneous stem set.

A nice thing about (1) is that we won't have to memorize any new verb stems in order to build Pg mode forms.

(You might think that it's odd that stems from the momentaneous stem set are used in the Pg mode. If you think about the way the Pg mode is used, you'll probably say that Pg verbs are very atelic, so we'd expect continuative stems to be used. Perhaps, but the fact is, the momentaneous ones are the ones that are really used.)

Now, the rule in (1) is another example of a situation where you'll find variation. It seems that some Navajo speakers use the momentaneous F mode stem even for the distributive forms of the Pg mode. I have seen examples of this in print; also, this has been reported by others working with the Navajo language. It may be the case that using the F mode stem for all the Pg mode forms is something that younger speakers do. Do not be surprised if you find examples of this.

OK - let's get started with a vocabulary principle that will give us lots of Pg mode verbs.

Vocabulary-18: Given a motion verb theme, we can build a cursive verb base, whose meaning is that the motion is currently going on, as follows:

Stem-set: use rule (1) above applied to the verb theme	Classifier: use the classifier of the verb theme
	Lexical prefixes: (none)
	Transitivity: use the transitivity of the verb theme
	Conjugation: Pg mode only

Vocabulary-14, Vocabulary-15, and Vocabulary-16 can be used quite freely to create many more verb bases starting with the verb bases created by Vocabulary-18.

To illustrate verbs built using Vocabulary-18, we need to know what the subject prefixes are for the Pg mode. So let's get to them right now.

Just as the verb stem is different for the nondistributive and the distributive Pg mode forms (at least for some speakers), the subject prefixes are different, too. So, in order to give the subject prefixes, we'll need several charts.

Let's start with the subject prefixes used in the nondistributive Pg mode forms. We'll give these in three charts: one for the case that the subject prefix is not preceded by any other prefix, the second for the case that the subject prefix is immediately preceded by a conjunct prefix, and the third for the case that the subject prefix is immediately preceded by a disjunct prefix.

(2)   Pg mode subject prefixes, when preceded by no other prefix:

	sg	dpl
1	yish	yiid
2	yí	woh
3	yi	

(3)   Pg mode subject prefixes, when preceded by a conjunct prefix:

	sg	dpl
1	eesh	iid
2	íí	ooh
3	oo	

(4)   Pg mode subject prefixes, when preceded by a disjunct prefix:

	sg	dpl
1	vvsh	iid
2	v́v́	oh
3	vv	

Let's point out a few things about these prefixes.

First of all, if there are no prefixes in the verb except for the subject prefixes, the chart in (2) shows us that the forms will look just like I mode forms except for the 2sg case. (So, for the other cases, the way we'll know that we have a Pg mode word is by the verb stem.) If the subject is 2sg, the Pg mode **yí** prefix looks just like the 1sg and 3 subject prefix that we see in the y-P conjugation when there's no other prefix. Again, the verb stem will tell us whether we have a P mode word or a Pg mode word.

The prefixes in (3) should look familiar - they're exactly the same as the subject prefixes used (together with the F mode **d**) in the F mode. (The fact that the nondistributive Pg mode stem is also the F mode stem is now beginning to look particularly interesting. Historically there may have been a connection between the Pg mode and the F mode.)

In the prefixes shown in (4), the notations vv and v́v́ have the same meaning that they did back in Chapters 9 and 10 when we learned about the y-P conjugation.

With these prefixes, we can form all the nondistributive Pg mode forms. Since motion verbs are among the most common verbs that have Pg modes, and since the go-verbs are so important, let's write out the Pg mode forms for the three cursive bases that Vocabulary-18 gives us if we start with the three go-verb themes (the singular, dual, and plural themes that we learned about in Chapter 17). We'll get words that mean "I'm going (now)" or "I'm on my way (at this moment)", etc. (If you want to write these out yourself, don't forget that the singular go-theme involves some irregularities.) Here are the forms of these verbs:

(5)	singular	dual	plural
1	yisháá	yiit'ash	yiikah
2	yínáá	woh'ash	wohkah
3	yigááł	yi'ash	yikah
4	joogááł	joo'ash	jookah

Important: did you see that the 3 person irregularity in the Pg mode of the singular go-verb is the same as the irregularity in the F mode (there's a **g** in **yigááł**) rather than being the same as the I mode (where we find a **gh**)? Review Chapter 17(10): this is what happens when a 3 person subject prefix is used with the F mode stem. Since the F mode stem is the one we're using here in the Pg mode, we get that **g**.

(And, you know that those **oo**'s in the 4 person forms are from the chart in (3), since **j** is a conjunct prefix.)

We can illustrate the prefixes in (4) by applying Vocabulary-15 from Chapter 22 (that's the one that adds in the reversionary prefix **ná** in order to indicate that the motion is back to the starting point) to the verb bases whose forms we wrote out in (5). This will give us the following useful words, which mean things like "I'm going back (right now)" or "I'm on my way back (at this moment)":

(6)   singular   dual   plural

1   nááshdááł   néiit'ash   néiikah
2   náádááł   náoht'ash   náohkah
3   náádááł   náát'ash   náákah
4   níjoodááł   níjoot'ash   níjookah

(Some of you might say **náh'ash** and **náhkah** for the 2 person dual and plural forms.)

The go-verb themes undergo classifier shift when the reversionary prefix is used - that's why we see all those **d**'s in the singular forms in (6) (see Chapter 17(12) about this.)

Something to notice: since **ná** ends in a high-tone vowel, the effect of vv and the effect of v́v́ end up being the same - we get **náá** in both cases. This means that the word that means "you (sg) are on your way back" and the word that means "he/she is on his/her way back" look and sound the same.

The forms in (5) and (6) haven't given us a chance to see the prefixes in (3), except for the 3 person one. We also need to learn the distributive Pg subject prefixes. Let's start by looking at the distributive prefixes. Since the distributive plural prefix **da** will always be there, the only issue is whether or not a conjunct prefix is in the verb. If there's no conjunct prefix, we find the following prefixes:

(7)   Pg mode subject prefixes with distributive plural **da**, no conjunct prefixes:

1	**deíníid**
2	**deínóh**
3	**deí**

Since any disjunct prefix other than the distributive plural prefix has to precede the distributive plural prefix **da**, if the verb has any other disjunct prefixes, they will precede the prefixes shown in (7). If there are no other prefixes, then the prefixes in (7) are the only ones in the verb in front of the classifier and verb stem.

Do the 1 and 2 person forms in (7) look a bit familiar? They're exactly what we get if we put the distributive **da** prefix in front of those prefixes that we learned about in Chapter 21 that combine the special **yn** inner prefix, the conjunct high-tone, and the I mode subject prefix (see Chapter 21(34).) But the 3 person form in (7) is different - it looks like an n-I form, in fact.

If there is a conjunct prefix in the verb, the following prefixes are used instead of (7):

(8)   Pg mode subject prefixes, preceded by a conjunct prefix, when distributive plural **da** will also
        be used:

1	**íiníid**
2	**íinóh**
3	**ée/í**

The 1 and 2 person prefixes in (8) again look exactly the same as the corresponding prefix combinations that we find when we combine the **yn** inner prefix, the conjunct high tone, and the subject prefixes. In the 3 person chart in (8), **ée** is used when immediately preceded by an inner prefix and **í** is used when immediately preceded by an object prefix. However, when the 3 person object prefix **y** is used, the combination **da + y + í** usually comes out **deí**.

Earlier, when we looked at the rule that gives the verb stems used for the Pg mode (the rule in (1)), we pointed out that some speakers (perhaps, younger speakers) don't use a different stem for the distributive forms. A similar kind of variation is found with the subject prefixes. Some speakers, probably younger ones, use the nondistributive subject prefixes in charts (2), (3), and (4) even for the distributive forms.

We now know all we need to know about the Pg mode. Let's look at the complete Pg mode for a motion verb other than the go-verbs that we wrote out earlier. If we use the "roll it" motion verb-theme in Chapter 18(16), we can get a cursive verb base by applying Vocabulary-18. Here are the Pg mode forms for this verb theme - we'll be conservative and use the special distributive verb stem and subject prefixes:

(9)	sg	dpl	distr dpl
1	yismas	yiilmas	deíníilmáás
2	yíłmas	wołmas	deínółmáás
3		yoołmas	deíłmáás
4		joołmas	dajíłmáás

In the form **yoołmas** "he/she is rolling it along (now)", the **y** is the 3 person object (this is a transitive verb), which is why the **oo** 3 person subject prefix from chart (3) is used. Note the verb stem in the nondistibutive forms: **mas**, which is the momentaneous F mode stem for the "roll it" verb theme. In the distributive forms, the verb stem is **máás**, which is the momentaneous I mode stem for this verb theme.

Let's write out one more set of Pg mode forms, to illustrate more of the prefixes listed in (3) and (8). There's a verb theme that means "move by hopping or hobbling" - this verb theme is almost always found together with the seriative inner prefix. To form the Pg mode, we need to know that the F mode stem is **chah** and the I mode stem is **chééh** for this verb theme. The classifier is d. (The P mode stem is **cha'**, in case you want to look it up in YMM 92.) Since the seriative prefix will be in all the forms of this verb, we'll used the prefixes in (3) and (8) to build the Pg mode. Again being conservative, we get the following forms:

(10)	sg		dpl	distr dpl
1	heeshchah	hiichah		dahííníchééh
2	hííchah	hoohchah		dahíínóhchééh
3		hoochah		dahéechééh
4		jiyoochah		dajiyéechééh

In the forms **jiyoochah** and **dajiyéechééh**, Rule Conj-9(d) doesn't move anything around, since the seriative is not followed by a conjunct prefix. Rule Conj-9(a) changes the form of the seriative to **y** in these words since it's immediately preceded by the conjunct prefix **j**.

A minor detail about Pg forms with inner prefixes: when inner **n** is present, the charts in YM 87 show shortened forms for the 1 and 2 person distributive Pg prefixes: **daníid** and **danóoh** - note that these are what we'd get if we used the nondistributive Pg subject prefixes together with distributive **da** and inner **n**, except that the conjunct high-tone is still in there.

As you can see, Pg forms are very easy to build. Sometimes they can be a bit hard to recognize, though. Study the charts in (2), (3), and (4) until you're very familiar with the forms that the subject prefixes can take. In addition, with the nondistributive forms, a tip-off is the use of the F mode verb stem without the F mode **d**. With the (conservative) distributive forms, the special subject prefixes involving the **n**'s will give it away. Study the forms in the examples in this chapter until you feel you can recognize Pg mode forms easily.

CHAPTER 26

THE REFLEXIVE, RECIPROCAL, AND PASSIVE

In this chapter we are going to study some constructions that are used to express certain kinds of special situations that have to do with the participants of an action. The first construction we will study involves forms called *reflexive* forms. These are the forms used when the subject of an action (the one who performs the action) is the same as the object (the one upon whom the action is performed.)

To start, let's look at ordinary transitive verbs. Normally, the object of the verb is represented by a prefix placed in the ordinary object position. However, you may remember that when we started learning about those object prefixes back in Chapter 11, we mentioned that something special has to be done if the object is the same person as the subject. The following rule tells us what to do.

(1)   <u>Rule for building the reflexive forms of a transitive verb</u>

If we have a transitive verb base, we can build forms that indicate that the object is the same as the subject by doing the following:

(a)   Add **'á** as an outer prefix into the verb. If there are other outer prefixes already in the verb base, then **'á** follows them, except that **'á** precedes the semeliterative and the R mode **ná**. Special note: **'á** follows these prefixes under certain circumstances. For example, if the semeliterative or R mode **ná** is in the verb and there are additional outer prefixes as well, then **'á** can move to the right so that it follows all the other outer prefixes, including these two prefix types. (But **'á** never comes to the right of the distributive plural prefix **da**.)

(b)   Add **d** as an inner prefix into the verb.

(c)   Apply classifier shift.

(d)   When a transitive verb base is made reflexive by this rule, the verb base officially becomes intransitive. (That is, no object prefixes are placed into the object prefix slot. In particular, the 3 person object prefix **y** is not put into the verb even if the subject is 3 person.)

Let's take a look at each of these four parts, and then we'll look at actual forms.

We don't have to say much about the special reflexive outer prefix **'á**. The instructions in (1a) above tell us where to put this prefix. As we've seen in our study of the unspec object prefix, the 4 person subject prefix, and the seriative prefix, some prefixes can appear in different positions depending on various circumstances. The reflexive outer prefix **'á** is another prefix like that. The rule is pretty easy - normally, this prefix follows any other outer prefixes but precedes the semeliterative and the R mode **ná**. But if there are other outer prefixes already in the verb (and occasionally under other circumstances), reflexive **'á** can follow the semeliterative and the R mode **ná** (there seems to be some variation with this positioning). Here's something easy: the form of reflexive **'á** never changes. (You might have noted that since a verb with reflexive **'á** in it will also have at least an inner **d** prefix by (1b), the reflexive **'á** will never be in one of those sensitive positions where we might expect its form to change. For example, it never is a pre-stem syllable.)

By the way: **na** and **ná** do not change to **ni** or **ní** when immediately followed by the reflexive **'á** prefix.

The second part of our reflexive rule, part (b) of (1), tells us to add an inner **d** prefix into the verb. This is also easy. But what if there are already inner prefixes in the verb? Well, in that case, the reflexive forms simply have an additional inner prefix! If there are other inner prefixes, then the reflexive inner **d** is placed in the same position as any ordinary inner **d**; for example, if the verb has an inner **n** prefix, then the reflexive inner **d** precedes the inner **n**, since all inner **d**'s precede inner **n**'s. (We mentioned this fact in Chapter 21.)

What if the verb already has an inner **d**? It appears that for such verbs we can sometimes find reflexive forms that have two inner **d**'s next to each other (in a case like this, there'll be three **d**'s in F mode forms (when the F mode **d** is added) and there'll be four **d**'s in the distributive F mode forms since the distributive plural prefix **da** has a **d** in it.) However, sometimes, if the reflexive is added to a verb base that already has an inner **d** in it, we don't get an extra **d** - we simply find one inner **d** prefix even in the reflexive forms. For such verbs, the signal that we have a reflexive form is only the **'á** prefix, together with the classifier shift. (We'll say something about classifier shift in a moment.)

If the reflexive inner **d** is immediately followed by an s-P subject prefix, we get the same contractions that we learned about a long time ago (in Chapter 15) when we first studied the inner **d** prefix.

We do have something important to say about the third part of our reflexive rule, part (c) of (1). The content of this part is easy - the verb base undergoes classifier shift - see Chapter 22(1) for a statement of what classifier shift is. But we've seen cases of classifier shift before, and there's something different about classifier shift with reflexives. When we ran into classifier shift before (which was in connection with the reversionary and semeliterative prefixes, and also in connection with the R mode), we noted that classifier shift doesn't always happen. In those earlier cases the classifier shifts mostly with a certain number of common zero-classifier verbs, but it usually doesn't shift with barred-l classifier verbs, or even with the less common zero classifier verbs. But classifier shift always happens when reflexive forms are built! This is not a problem - in fact, it's less of a problem than classifier shift in those earlier cases. With the reversionary, semeliterative, and R mode cases, we need to memorize which verbs undergo classifier shift. But with the reflexive, we don't have to memorize any facts like that, since any reflexive verb shifts its classifier.

Important: remember that when the classifier shifts, we change the subject prefixes that are used in the P mode. This means that the reflexive forms of the P mode of transitive verbs will often use different subject prefixes than the nonreflexive forms.

The fourth part of our rule, part (d) of (1), just reminds us that if we use the reflexive construction to indicate that the object of a transitive verb is the same as the subject, that means that the reflexive construction gives us all the information we need about the object. We won't need any other information about the object, so we don't ever put an object prefix into the verb.

We're now ready to build real reflexive verbs. We could write out entire conjugations in all the modes for verbs with the reflexive construction, but since the forms are straightforward and no new rules are involved, we won't do so. (There are some helpful charts in YM 87.) Instead, we'll just build a few reflexive words as examples.

There is a transitive verb base that means "scratch it". This verb base uses the zero classifier, and has no lexical prefixes. In the I and P modes, the verb stem is **ch'id**. So, "I'm scratching it" is **yishch'id**, "he/she is scratching it" is **yich'id**, and "they are scratching it" is **deich'id**. If we build the reflexive versions of these words, we'll get a word that means "I'm scratching myself", which is **ádíshch'id**, a word that means "he/she is scratching himself/herself", which is **ádích'id**, and a word that means "they are scratching themselves", which is **ádadich'id**. You probably have realized that the second high tone in the words **ádíshch'id** and **ádích'id** is the result of Rule Subj-5. Note also that there is no 3 person object **y** prefix in the words that mean "he's scratching himself" and "they're scratching themselves" - remember that the reflexive construction tells us all we need to know about the real object, and therefore a reflexive verb is officially intransitive (it doesn't take any object prefixes.) Incidentally, the word **ádích'id** can also mean "you (sg) are scratching yourself" - can you see why?

In the P mode, if we don't use the reflexive, we get words like the ones that mean "I scratched it" which is **yích'id**, "he/she scratched it" **yiyíích'id**, or "they scratched it" **deiyíích'id**, etc. (This verb base uses the y-P conjugation, as you see.) When we use the reflexive constructions, we'll get words that mean "I scratched myself" **ádeeshch'id**, "he/she scratched himself/herself" **ádooch'id**, "they scratched themselves" **ádadooch'id**, etc. Note how the subject prefixes changed. The original verb base has the zero classifier, so in the y-P conjugation we use the subject prefixes that we learned in Chapter 9. But when we use the reflexive construction with this verb, the classifier shifts to d, so in the P mode we use the subject prefixes that we learned in Chapter 10. Also, we again see that in the reflexive forms we don't have any prefix in the object prefix position.

In the R mode forms of this verb, the reflexive **'á** precedes the R mode **ná**, so we get forms like **ánídíshch'i'** for "I (generally) scratch myself". (The F mode stem for this verb is **ch'ił**, so by the rule we learned in Chapter 23(3), the R mode stem will be **ch'i'**.)

For a more complicated example, let's look at a few forms built from a transitive verb base that means "kick him/her repeatedly" or "give him/her a kicking". This verb base has the outer prefix **ná** in it as well as the inner prefix **n**. The classifier is zero, and the P mode uses the s-P conjugation. The verb stem is **tał** in all modes except for the P mode, where it's **táál**. Some ordinary nonreflexive forms are, in the I mode, **nánishtał** ("I'm giving him/her a kicking"), **néinitał** ("he/she is giving him/her a kicking"), etc., and in the P mode **nánétáál** "I gave him/her a kicking"), **néineeztáál** ("he/she gave him/her a kicking"), etc. If we want to use reflexive forms instead, we'll get I mode forms like **ná'ádinishtał** ("I'm giving myself a kicking") and **ná'ádinitał** ("he/she is giving himself/herself a kicking") and P mode forms like **ná'ádinéshtáál** ("I gave myself a kicking") and **ná'ádineestáál** ("he/she gave himself/herself a kicking"). In these forms we can see the reflexive **'á** following the other outer prefix (**ná**). We also see that the reflexive inner **d** appears in front of the inner **n**, which is the usual position of the inner **d** when there's also an inner **n** in the verb. In the R mode we see the reflexive hopping to the right of R mode **ná**, since there's another outer prefix in the verb: "I (generally) give myself a kicking" is **níná'ádinishtał**.

(Review question: why does the first **i** in the word **néinitał** have a low tone? Answer: read the note in Rule Conj-2 about high tones on the **i** that comes from the 3 person object prefix **y**. In **néinitał**, the next syllable isn't the verb stem syllable.)

Since these words are a bit big, let's write out the structure of one of them. The word that means "I gave myself a kicking" has the following structure:

(2) | outer prefix | inner prefix | subject prefix | cl | verb stem |

ná - 'á - d - n - sis - d - táál

Make sure you understand the positioning of these prefixes. The outer prefix **ná** is part of the verb base. The reflexive outer prefix **'á**, which was added in by the rule in (1) above, follows the other outer prefix, because the reflexive outer prefix normally follows other outer prefixes except for the semeliterative and the R mode **ná**. The inner prefix **n** is also part of the verb base. The reflexive inner prefix **d** precedes it, because an inner **d** always precedes an inner **n**. The classifier of the original verb base is zero, but it shifts to d because of the reflexive. This d classifier causes d-effect on the first consonant of the verb stem, but since the verb stem begins with a **t**, there's no actual change. The 1sg subject prefix is **sis** rather than **sé** (we're in the s-P conjugation) since the classifier is d instead of zero. Inner **n** contracts with **sis** to give **nésh** (see Chapter 21(9)), and Rule Conj-1 inserts an **i** after the inner **d**. This gives us our word **ná'ádinéshtáál**.

(For practice, diagram the structures of the other words built from this verb base and make sure you understand how the actual forms are derived.)

We won't say anything more about the reflexive construction as described in (1). However, we do have to say more about reflexives forms in general. The reason is that the reflexive construction in (1) only talks about creating verb forms where the object is the same as the subject. But there are other possibilities having to do with two participants of an action being the same. For example, we've seen verbs that have outer objects, that is, object pronoun prefixes inside of outer prefixes (we started learning about these in Chapter 15) - what if we want to create a form that tells us that an outer object is the same as the subject? Let's look at this situation briefly.

When we have an outer object, the part of the outer prefix that is occupied by an object pronoun prefix is represented as "P". We've seen verb bases with outer prefixes like Pi or Pik'í, for example. Normally, the "P" part of a prefix like this is occupied by one of the ordinary object prefixes that we learned about in Chapter 11. But if we want to indicate that the "P" is the same as the subject, what we do is, we combine the reflexive outer prefix 'á with the reflexive prefix d (which is normally an inner prefix) - this creates the syllable 'ád. Now, we'll put this syllable into the "P" position. But when we do this, we also have to apply classifier shift to the verb. Here's an example of this, taken from YM 87.

There is a verb base that means "pierce him/her with it". This verb base is formed from the same verb theme as the verb base in Chapter 15(36) - it has the same stem-set and classifier as that verb base, and it's also transitive. However, it has a different set of lexical prefixes; in fact, it has only one lexical prefix: the outer prefix Pighá. Also, it has a different conjugation pattern: it's conjugated in the n-I and n-P conjugations. Something important to note: with this verb base, the object (the prefix in the ordinary object position) refers to the thing that is being used to pierce somebody. The "P" in the outer prefix is the prefix that refers to the person being pierced. The following sentence taken from YM 87 (evidently, a memory from World War II) illustrates this verb in use:

(3)   Nááts'ózí ła' béésh shigháiníłgeed. "A Japanese person ran a knife through me"

Notice that the person who was pierced, namely "me", is represented by the sh prefix in the outer object position - it's playing the role of "P" in Pighá in the word shigháiníłgeed. The 3 person object prefix y (which appears as the i in front of the n in shigháiníłgeed - Rule Conj-2 is responsible for this) refers to the knife that was used to do the piercing.

Now, how would we say "He pierced himself with it"? We'll put 'ád in for the P and we'll shift the classifier from barred-l to plain-l. We'll still use the n-P conjugation, with 3 person subject - check Chapter 18(23) and Chapter 18(24) for the subject prefix. And, we'll still have the 3 person object y prefix in there (to stand for the "it" in "he pierced himself with it".) The actual word is: ádigháílgeed. (When the reflexive 'ád is used as the "P" with certain outer prefixes, a short i immediately following the reflexive acquires a high tone.) Note the plain l in this word; also, the 3 person subject prefix changed from ni (in the word in (3) to í, since the classifier changed. The form í is used because it's immediately preceded by the object prefix y, which was omitted in writing but it's still there nevertheless.

So, one thing to remember is that when we use reflexive 'ád as the "P" in an outer prefix, we sometimes can have an object prefix in the ordinary object position, if the verb base is such that it makes sense to do so. In the case of the word **ádíghá(y)ílgeed**, there are three kinds of participants in the action. First, there's the person doing the piercing - this person is represented by the 3 person subject prefix **í**. Next, there's the person getting pierced, represented by the outer object. Since this is the same person as the subject, we use the reflexive **'ád** as the outer object. But there's a third participant: the implement used to do the piercing. This third participant is represented by an ordinary object prefix - the "**y**" in this word.

Another thing to remember about reflexives in general is that reflexives really want the classifier to shift. In fact, they want the classifier to shift so much that even when the reflexive is a possessive on a noun well outside the verb, the classifier shifts! To illustrate using another example taken from YM 87, let's start by thinking about a verb base constructed from a classificatory verb theme. The verb theme in question is the one that means "move a compact rigid object". We have not seen this (very common!) verb theme yet, but the P mode verb stem for it is **'á** and the classifier is zero. If we use this verb theme with the outer prefix **ha** meaning "up and out" (we've seen this prefix before), we can get a transitive verb base that means "take/pull it up out of something". To say "he pulled it up out of something", we have the word **hayíí'á**. This is a completely regular y-P conjugation form - it's got the 3 person object prefix **y** in there, as well as the 3 person subject prefix **íí** used when there's a conjunct prefix in front of it.

Now, here's a sentence that means "He pulled his own tooth out":

(4)   Áwoo' hayoot'á.

The word **áwoo'** in (4) has a reflexive possessive prefix. (With many nouns, and some postpositions, the reflexive prefix is just **'á** rather than **'ád**.) This is enough to make the verb undergo classifier shift! The classifier is now **d**, which causes d-effect on the **'** at the beginning of the verb stem **'á** - that's why we see **t'** in the verb **hayoot'á** in (4). Notice also that we have a different 3 person subject prefix: **oo**. This is the subject prefix used in the y-P conjugation when the classifier is d (and when there's a conjunct prefix to its left.)

A similar kind of situation, also involving classifier shift, is when a verb is used together with a postposition that has a reflexive object. Here is an example, also from YM 87, that means "he made it for himself":

(5)   Ádá áyiilyaa.

In (5), the postposition **-á** which means "for" has the reflexive **'ád** as its object. The word **áyiilyaa**, which means "he made it", has undergone classifier shift. To see this, we have to first note that the ordinary way of saying "he made it" is **áyiilaa**. This is a form of the very irregular verb base that means "make it" - you have probably learned the forms of this verb by now (you can find them under the entry for "I'm making it", which is **áshłééh**, in YM 87.) This verb base has a zero classifier. But in (5), since there's a postposition out there with a reflexive object, the verb undergoes classifier shift, which means that the classifier becomes d. Now, d causes d-effect on the first consonant of the verb stem, but in the case of this verb, the **l** irregularly becomes **ly**.

With this, we're finished with our study of how reflexive forms are built. In order to recognize reflexive forms when we see or hear them, keep in mind the following. First, a reflexive form will always have a prefix **'á** somewhere in it. Secondly, a verb that is being used reflexively (even in the extended sense illustrated in (4) and (5)) will always have either a plain-l or a d classifier. Finally, there usually will be a **d** in there, either as an inner prefix (if the ordinary object is the same as the subject), or else right after the **'á** (if it's an outer object that's the same as the subject.)

We are now going to look briefly at several other constructions that have to do with special cases involving the participants of an action. All the constructions we'll look at have one thing in common with the reflexives: they all involve classifier shift.

First, let's take a look at the construction called the *reciprocal*. This construction is used when the verb expresses the idea that a group of persons do something to each other. Because of this meaning, this form is most often used with a plural subject. But it can also be used with singular subjects under certain circumstances, for example, if we use the postposition that means "with" to indicate who the subject is mutually doing the action with.

The following is the basic rule for building reciprocal forms:

(6)   Rule for building the reciprocal forms of a transitive verb

If we have a transitive verb base, we can build forms that indicate that the persons denoted by the subject, or the subject together with someone else, perform an action on each other, by doing the following:

(a)   Use the special reciprocal prefix **'ah** as the object pronoun prefix.

(b)   Apply classifier shift to the verb base.

Building reciprocal forms is very easy. The special prefix **'ah** never undergoes any change. Rule Conj-1 applies completely normally to insert an **i** after **'ah** when there is a consonant immediately following.

We can use the verb base in Chapter 21(47) to illustrate some reciprocal forms. For example, we know that the word **yiníł'į** can mean "they (two) are looking at it". If we want to say "they (two) are looking at each other", we'll just apply the rule in (6), which will give us **ahiníl'į**. In this word, we see the prefix **'ah** in the object prefix position. We also see a plain **l** in there: the classifier has shifted from barred-l to plain-l.

If we're talking about a group of more than two people, then "they are looking at it" is **deiníł'į́**. To say "they are looking at each other" (if there are more than two people), we simply have **da'ahiníl'į́**.

(And note in these two examples: the **'ah** prefix represents the object, so we don't find the 3 person object prefix **y** in these reciprocal forms.)

Here is another example. There's a verb theme whose basic meaning is "kill a plurality of beings". The P mode stem for this verb theme is **gháá'**, and the classifier is zero. This verb theme can be used with the reciprocal object prefix but with no other lexical prefixes to mean not only "kill each other" but also "fight". So, how would we say "I fought with him"? (To answer this, you need to know that the P mode uses the y-P conjugation.) It's simply: **bił aheeshgáá'**. Note that the subject prefix (**eesh**) tells us that the classifier is no longer zero (it's changed to d, of course, which is why the verb stem begins with **g** instead of **gh**.)

The reciprocal prefix can also be used as the "P" in an outer prefix, as well as with postpositions. But there are some complications. For one thing, sometimes, instead of **'ah**, we find **'ał** or **'ahił** as the prefix. And for another, unlike the reflexive, the reciprocal doesn't require the verb to undergo classifier shift when it's a "P" or the object of a postposition. On the other hand, sometimes there is classifier shift in these cases. This matter needs further study - we'll say no more about it here.

Reciprocal forms should be easy to recognize, since there'll be that **'ah** in there. However, you might have noticed that sometimes a reciprocal form can look the same as a form with a completely different structure. For example, suppose you have run into an I mode form that begins **ahish-**. In the I mode, the **sh** pretty much has to be the 1sg subject prefix. But what about the **ahi-** in front of it? This could be the reciprocal object **'ah**, with **i** inserted after it by Rule Conj-1. But another possibility is that the **a** is the outer prefix **'a**, and that the **hi** is the seriative **h** with **i** inserted after it by Rule Conj-1. Since there really are verb bases that have this combination of prefixes in them, this question could come up. Other forms in the I mode, and in other modes as well, will look the same for these two possibilities. How can we tell the difference? We have to look at more forms. A good trick is to look at distributive forms. The distributive **da** will always precede an object prefix, so if we've got reciprocal **'ah** in the object prefix position, a distributive form will have **da'ah** in it. But if the **a** of **ahi** is the outer prefix **'a**, then the distributive **da** will follow the outer prefix **'a**, so the forms will have **ada** in them. (Also, if **h** is the seriative, we might see forms where there's a **y** or **ii** in there instead of the **h**. This could never happen if the **h** was part of the reciprocal prefix **'ah**.)

This is all we will say about the reciprocal construction. Let's finish our chapter will a look at a number of constructions that correspond (somewhat) to the passive construction in English.

First of all, there's a construction that can be used with any transitive verb if the object of the verb is a person. When this construction is used, the subject is considered to be unexpressed or unmentioned. To see how these are used, let's first look at some English. Let's start with a simple English sentence like:

(7)   Jack carried Jill up out (of something).

Suppose we want to tell someone that an event like the one mentioned in (7) happened, only for some reason we didn't want to say explicitly that it was Jack who did it. In English, we can use a passive construction and say:

(8)   Jill was carried up out (of something).

The Navajo construction we're going to look at next corresponds to sentences like (8) in English. This construction can be used, as we said, with any transitive verb, provided that the object of the verb is a person. In the YM materials, this construction is called the *agentive passive* construction; in YM 87 it's also referred to as *Passive B*. (There's another construction called *Passive A* that we'll get to in a moment.) Here is the rule for building it:

(9)   <u>Rule for building the agentive passive of a transitive verb</u>

If we have a transitive verb base, then we can build verb forms that do not mention the subject (that is, passive verb forms) as follows, provided that the object that we are mentioning is a person or a group of people:

(a)   Use the 3 person subject prefix.

(b)   Use "P" in the object prefix position.

(c)   Insert the unspec object prefix ' into the object prefix position as well. (The unspec object will follow the "P" object.)

(d)   Add the inner prefix **d** to the verb base.

(e)   Apply classifier shift.

When we do this, the "P" prefix refers to the (human) object that we are mentioning. We could think of the 3 person subject prefix as referring to the "invisible" subject; another way of viewing it, though, is to think of the unspec object prefix as actually indicating that the <u>subject</u> is not specified. Whichever way you think of it, the rule in (9) will give you the forms, and, of course, our rules will apply to these passive forms in the usual way. For example, the unspec object is treated according to Rule Conj-5. And don't forget that by calling the prefix in the (ordinary) object position a "P" prefix, we mean that if the object is 3 person, we will definitely use the prefix **b**. (We don't use **y**!)

As an example, we can translate (8) into Navajo. To do this, recall that (7) is:

(10)   Jack Jill hayííłtį́.

(We saw some forms of the verb base that **hayííłtį** is built from back in Chapter 11.) To say (8), we need a verb built from the same verb base as **hayííłtį** but following the rule in (9). Let's diagram the structure of the word we're trying to build:

(11) | outer | object | inner | subject | cl | verb |
      | prefix | prefix | prefix | prefix | | stem |

ha - b - ' - d - oo - l - tį

How did we get (11)? Well, the verb base gave us the outer prefix **ha** and the P mode verb stem **tį**. It also gave us a barred-l classifier, but (9e) tells us that for the agentive passive we have to shift the classifier, so the classifier in (11) is plain-l. (9a) tells us to use the 3 person subject prefix, which, in the y-P conjugation (which is what we have for this verb base) is **oo** when the classifier is plain-l. (9b) tells us that the object is a "P" prefix, which means that we've got **b** in the object position in (11), since we have a 3 person object (Jill). (9c) tells us to put in the unspec object prefix after the "P" prefix, and (9d) tells us to add in an inner **d** prefix. This gives us exactly the structure in (11).

Applying our rules, the word we get from (11) is **habi'dooltį**. So, the translation of (8) is:

(12) Jill habi'dooltį.

Of course, any "P" prefix can be used. For example, the word that means "I was carried up out (of something)" is **hashi'dooltį**, etc.

Part (d) of (9) tells us to add in an inner **d** prefix. This is similar to the reflexive rule (1), where part (b) told us to do the same thing. We mentioned earlier that in the case of the reflexives, if the verb base we're working with already has an inner **d**, then in many common cases we don't add in a second **d**. Exactly the same is true for the agentive passives. And, of course, if the verb base already has an inner prefix of a different sort, such as **n**, then for the agentive passive we add in the inner **d**, and we position it in exactly the same place as an ordinary inner **d** (which would be to the left of an inner **n**.)

The agentive passives built by (9) are extremely regular. They can be built in any mode, of course. The only thing you have to remember is that they can only be used if you're talking about a human or a group of humans who have undergone (or will under go, or are undergoing) some action. Also: they can only be used if the person who has undergone the action would be normally represented by a prefix in the ordinary object position.

Agentive passives are very easy to recognize. Because the object prefix position of an agentive passive is filled by a "P", there always will be a visible or audible prefix in there, even in the 3 person case, where there'll be a **b** in the object position. The unspec prefix, the inner **d**, and the plain-l or d classifier will make it clear that we've got an agentive passive. If the verb base starts out without any inner prefixes, then any agentive passive form will have a syllable like **bi'd** or **shi'd** or **ni'd** or

378

nihi'd or **ho'd** in it, followed by a subject prefix. If the verb base did have an inner prefix to start with, the unspec prefix may hop to the right, so you won't see it in front of the **d** this way, but it'll still be in there in front of that other inner prefix. Don't forget that you'll get an ordinary 3 person subject prefix with these forms, but that in the P mode it'll be the 3 person subject prefix that goes with the plain-l and d classifiers.

The three constructions we've looked at so far in this chapter all apply only to transitive verb bases where the object can be a person or a group of persons. The reflexive construction deals with the case that the object is the same person or group as the subject. The reciprocal construction deals with the case that the object is the same group as the subject (or a group containing the subject) but where each person acts on a different one. The agentive passive deals with the case where the object is a person but we want to ignore the subject. Our next construction specifically deals with transitive verbs where the object is not a person or a group of persons. It's meaning is similar to the agentive passive: we use it when we want to ignore the subject. But in Navajo, when the object is not a person, we cannot use the agentive passive construction to express this. Instead, we use what YM call the *simple passive* construction (in YM 87 it's also referred to as *Passive A.*) Building simple passive forms is very easy - here is our rule:

(13)   Rule for building the simple passive of a transitive verb

If we have a transitive verb base, then we can build verb forms that do not mention the subject (that is, passive verb forms) as follows, provided that the object that we are mentioning is nonhuman:

(a)   Use the 3 person subject prefix.

(b)   Use no object prefix.

(c)   Apply classifier shift.

As you can see from (13), simple passive forms do not have any special prefixes - in fact, they have fewer prefixes than the normal transitive verbs, since the object prefix is missing. The chief signal of a simple passive form is the shift of the classifier.

An example: remember the verb that means "boil it" or "cook it" from Chapter 7(6)? If we use that verb as an ordinary transitive verb, we could say something like:

(14)   Gohwééh yiłbéézh.

which would mean "he/she is boiling (the/some) coffee". We could use (14) if we had already been talking about a specific person and we wanted to say that that person is now boiling coffee. On the other hand, here is a different sentence:

(15) Gohwééh yiłbéézh.

This means "the coffee is being boiled" (that is, someone is boiling the coffee.) The verb in (15) is in the simple passive form - note that the only signal of this is the plain **l** appearing in (15) in the classifier position. Sentence (15) would be used if we're interested in the coffee - we know someone's boiling it, but we don't particularly care who.

(Important: the **y**'s at the beginning of **yiłbéézh** and **yilbéézh** are (invisibly) different. The **y** in **yiłbéézh** is the 3 person object prefix, referring to the coffee (in (14)), whereas the **y** in **yilbéézh** is the peg element, inserted by our peg rule (Rule Str-2.))

The construction of the simple passive is, well, very simple. But this doesn't mean that there aren't some issues here. One is that the rule in (13) is so simple that, sometimes, it's impossible to tell that you have a passive form. For example, if we use our "boil" verb and build P mode forms, we see that the word **yishbéézh** could be either an ordinary transitive verb that means "he/she boiled it", or a simple passive form that means "it was boiled". In this form, we cannot tell whether we have a barred-l classifier with the 3 person object prefix, or the plain-l classifier with the peg. Check our prefixes and rules to see that this is so.

To complicate matters a bit, there's something similar to the passive that we need to mention. In the case of many transitive verb bases, there exists a different verb base which is intransitive and which expresses a meaning somewhat similar to the simple passive of the transitive verb base. When this is the case, the difference in the structure of the two verb bases will only involve the classifier, but the pattern is different than with classifier shift. In fact, the most common pattern of this sort involves a transitive verb base with the barred-l classifier and an intransitive verb base with the zero classifier. We can illustrate this with the "boil" verb base. In Chapter 7(6) we have the transitive verb base that means "boil it" - this verb base takes the barred-l classifier. (The "Conjugation" slot is missing from Chapter 7(6) because we hadn't studied that part of the verb yet in Chapter 7, but for "boil it" all we need to indicate is that this verb base uses the s-P conjugation.) There is also an intransitive verb base, meaning "boil" (in the sense of being in a state of boiling, not in the sense of causing something unspecified to boil) whose structure is exactly the same except that the classifier is zero. Using this intransitive verb base, we can say things like:

(16) Gohwééh yibéézh.

This sentence means "The coffee is boiling".

The meaning in (16) is a little different from the meaning in (15). The sentence in (15) suggests that someone is boiling the coffee, even though whoever is doing it is left unspecified. But in (16), there's no suggestion that anyone is actually doing anything - the coffee is simply in a state of boiling, for whatever reason.

A P-mode version of (16) is easy to recognize:

(17)   Gohwééh shibéézh.

Remember that in the s-P conjugation, if the subject is 3 person and there is no prefix, then instead of using the ordinary peg, the subject prefix changes from **z** to **si**. (Rule Subj-6 also applied here.)

There are actually quite a few transitive/intransitive verb base pairs like this. In fact, there are pairs of verb themes that pattern this way. For example, we've seen a number of verb bases created from the "roll it" verb theme in Chapter 18(16). There's another verb theme, an intransitive one, whose meaning is simply "roll" (that is, move by rolling) which is exactly the same as the "roll it" verb theme except that the classifier is zero instead of barred-l. Intransitive motion verb bases can be built from this verb theme using the vocabulary principles that we've learned. For example, if someone threw me out of a saloon, I can say:

(18)   Tł'óo'jį' ch'ínímááz. "I went rolling outside"

To form the word **ch'ínímááz** we applied Vocabulary-8 in Chapter 19 to the intransitive version of the verb theme in Chapter 18(16) - note the zero classifier.

As your knowledge of Navajo vocabulary gets deeper, you'll run into more and more cases of pairs of verb bases, or pairs of verb themes, that differ only in the classifier, where one is transitive and the other is intransitive. In such cases, intransitive verb bases are often used as much, or even more, than the simple passive of the corresponding transitive bases.

Let's close this chapter with a very brief look at something else, something related to the simple passive, which will also display something new about the unspec object prefix. The rule in (13) was written out so as to apply to a transitive verb base. Sometimes, a similar process can be applied to an intransitive verb base. When this is done, however, we usually or always find the unspec object prefix added in as well. It is not clear how freely this can be done - more research is needed on this matter. But, for example, there are words like:

(19)   Na'a'né.

This word is built from the verb base that means "play" (remember?) Classifier shift changed the classifier from zero to d - we see this because the **n** at the beginning of the verb stem became **'n**. Also, the unspec object prefix **'** was put in. The meaning of (19) is something like: "playing is going on". Just as the passive forms of a transitive verb base have the effect of ignoring the subject, forms like (19) have this effect as well - we're saying that there's an activity of playing happening, but we're ignoring (or not saying) who's doing the playing.

Just as sometimes, instead of a simple passive, a related verb base with a different classifier can be used (as in the case of **yibéézh**), we also find some cases of intransitive verb bases that are related to other intransitive verb bases with different classifiers, but with the unspec prefix also added in. An example is the word:

(20)   Na'anish.

which means "work is going on". In (20), we see a form with the zero classifier (remember that the ordinary "work" verb base has the plain-l classifier.) And, again, the word in (20) has the unspec object prefix in it.

Here's a question: since (19) and (20) have the unspec object prefix in them, what is unspecified? Since these verbs are intransitive, there is no object around that could be unspecified. It would appear that the unspec object prefix is being used to say that the subject is unspecified. In general, the unspec object prefix cannot be used with intransitive verb bases to indicate that the subject is unspecified. However, in a number of particular situations it can in fact be used this way; the situations illustrated by (19) and (20) are two examples of this. We also saw that the unspec object prefix forms a part of the agentive passive construction - possibly, in that construction, it is there to indicate that the subject is unspecified (but there, it's a transitive verb base that we're dealing with).

To end our chapter, here is another common situation where the unspec object prefix seems to indicate that the subject of an intransitive verb is unspecified. We add the unspec object prefix in to certain intransitive verbs of motion, and then use these verbs with the postposition that means "with". The object of this postposition refers to a person - the whole construction is used to indicate that that person is moving by means of an unspecified conveyance. Here is an example of this arrangement:

(21)   Bił na'a'eeł.

This means "he/she is floating around (on a conveyance)", or "he/she is going boat-riding". The word **na'a'eeł** is build from an intransitive verb theme of motion that means "float". The verb stem **'eeł** is the continuative (and also, it turns out, the momentaneous) I mode stem of this verb theme, which is combined with our old friend atelic **na**, but also with the unspec object prefix. The classifier is zero. (There is a corresponding transitive verb theme, meaning "float it" or "move it by floating") that has the same verb stems but the barred-l classifier instead of the zero classifier.) The **b** prefix attached to the postposition in (21) refers to the person who is on the boat or raft. Strictly speaking, the subject of **na'a'eeł** is the unspecified boat or raft that the person is on. (If you want to look this up in YMM 92, the P mode stem of these verb themes is **'ééł**.)

CHAPTER 27

SOME FINAL TOPICS

If you've gotten this far in this book, you have learned almost everything you need to know about the way Navajo verbs are structured. Except for some relatively uncommon situations, you have learned all the rules that describe the way a Navajo verb is built out of its parts. You have also learned about the categories that determine the form of a Navajo verb, and you have learned the fundamental framework for the verb vocabulary. In this chapter, we are going to fill in some gaps by discussing very briefly a number of issues that we haven't seen in our studies but that you might run into as your knowledge of Navajo increases. By now, you should be able to learn a great deal from even a brief presentation of these issues. We won't be able to cover absolutely everything that you might see, but the topics we will deal with should take care of most of it. We also will review a few things, and suggest ideas for further study.

THE S-I CONJUGATION

We have learned two conjugation patterns for Navajo verbs in the I mode. There is a third pattern, called the s-I (YM calls it the si-imperfective), that occurs with a small group of verb bases. This pattern is very easy - here are the subject prefixes for the s-I conjugation:

(1)   s-I subject prefixes:

	sg	dpl
1	**shish**	**siid**
2	**sí**	**soh**
3	zero	

These prefixes resemble the subject prefixes used in the s-P conjugation. They look like the regular I mode prefixes preceded by an **s**, except that there's no added **s** in the 3 person case. We could blame the **sh** at the beginning of the 1sg prefix on Rule Subj-6 or Rule Conj-4, due to the "real" 1sg part of the prefix, which is **sh**. Similarly, we could blame the high tone in the 2sg prefix on Rule Conj-3, if we pretend that the added **s** was a conjunct prefix.

By the way, like the s-P prefixes, these prefixes (the nonzero ones!) also cause a preceding **ná** to change to **ní**. (Low-tone **na** apparently doesn't ever occur together with this conjugation.)

Something to note: any verb base that uses the s-I conjugation for the I mode uses the s-P conjugation for the P mode.

Speaking of other modes: we learned back in Chapter 23 that the R and U modes use I mode subject prefixes: if a verb base uses either the regular or the long-vowel I mode conjugation, then the R and U modes use the same subject prefixes as the I mode, whereas if a verb base uses the n-I conjugation, then the R and U modes use the regular I mode subject prefixes. What if the verb base uses the s-I conjugation? It appears that those verb bases use the s-I subject prefixes for their R and U modes. For this reason, we'll say that those verb bases are conjugated in the s-R and s-U conjugations for the R and U modes.

We can briefly illustrate an s-I form using the following vocabulary pattern: start with a classificatory transitive motion verb theme, use no lexical prefixes, use the momentaneous stem-set of the verb theme, and use the s-I and s-P (and s-R and s-U) conjugations. If the verbs you get are then combined with the word **dah**, the result is a phrase that means "set it/them up on a shelf". For example, using the verb theme in Chapter 18(11), we can form an expression that means "I'm setting it (a ropelike thing) up on a shelf" as follows:

(2)   Dah shishłé.

The prefixes in (1) are very well behaved - we don't need to learn any new rules in order to build forms that have those prefixes in them.

CONJUGATION COMBINATIONS

For each mode, we've learned two, three, or (in the case of the P mode) four conjugation patterns. You may have realized that if we look at any actual verb base, we won't find an arbitrary combination of conjugation patterns - instead, only certain combinations are found. For example, we learned back in Chapter 18 that the n-I and n-P conjugations are used together - you'll only find one of them if you also find the other one. Also, we just learned that if a verb base uses the s-I conjugation, then it has to use the s-P one. Here is a list of all the combinations of conjugation patterns that are possible for Navajo verbs. (When a mode is not listed for a combination, that means that the regular conjugation for that mode is used.)

(3)   Possible conjugation combinations for Navajo verb bases:

   (a)   y-P
   (b)   s-P
   (c)   n-I and n-P
   (d)   s-I and s-P and s-R and s-U
   (e)   long-vowel in all modes
   (f)   long-vowel in all modes except the F mode
   (g)   s-P and long-vowel in all other modes except the F mode
   (h)   y-P and long-vowel in all other modes except the F mode

We've run across examples of all these combinations except for (3h). There are a few verb bases whose meanings involve hitting with a single blow (using various kinds of implements) that take this combination - for examples, look up **nídiishne'** "I'm hitting it once with a solid roundish object", **nídiishkaad** "I'm giving him/her one slap", or **nídiishhaał** "I'm hitting him/her (once) with a club" in YM 87. These verb bases all have the outer prefix **ná** and the inner prefix **d**, and they use the momentaneous stem-set. And, as we said, they use the conjugation pattern in (3h).

When describing any verb base, we need to say which of the combinations listed in (3) is the one that applies to that verb base. It would be handy to have some sort of mnemonic abbreviations for these combinations so that we could indicate a combination briefly and still know which one was meant. In YMM 92 there is a system for doing this in which the I and P modes only are listed, with "Ø" used to indicate the regular I mode conjugation and also the y-P conjugation, and "yi" used to indicate the long-vowel conjugation. For example, (3a) is listed as Ø/Ø, (3b) as Ø/si, (3c) as ni/ni, etc. (As you know, YM use the terms *si* and *ni* to refer to the s-P and n-P conjugations.) This system wouldn't be able to distinguish between (3e) and (3f) - but in YMM 92 verbs that use (3e) are analyzed differently from the way we did (YMM 92 classifies those verbs as though they used the regular I and y-P conjugations, but with a special inner prefix.) If we want to use our analyses as the basis for classifying the combinations of conjugations (which means we'll end up with the classes listed in (3)), we'd need to change this a bit. A possible set of terms is suggested below:

(4)   Suggested terms for conjugation pattern combinations:

term	combination
simple	y-P
S	s-P
N	n-I, n-P
double-S (DS)	s-I, s-P, s-R, s-U
full-long-vowel (FLV)	long-vowel in all modes
long-vowel (LV)	long-vowel in all modes except F
S-long-vowel (SLV)	s-P and long-vowel in all other modes except F
Y-long-vowel (YLV)	y-P and long-vowel in all other modes except F

(I've suggested abbreviations for the last five terms in this chart.)

Using terms like these we can write verb bases in an abbreviated way. For example, we could diagram the verb base that means "give him/her one slap" (mentioned above) by writing something like:

(5)   **ná**+O+**d**+zero+mom:**kaad**+YLV

The expression in (5) means that the verb base has the outer prefix **ná**, the verb base is transitive (the

"O" means the object prefix position is used for actual objects), the verb base has the inner prefix **d**, the classifier is zero, the stem-set is the momentaneous stem-set whose P mode stem is **kaad**, and the conjugations are the ones in the combination listed in (3h).

When using shorthand notations like the one in (5) for verb bases, it's probably best to list the stem-set by the P mode stem, since that stem is the same for most related stem-sets - we'll say more about this below. Also, that's the stem that is used to index stem-sets in YMM 92. Of course, a notation like this assumes that you either know the actual stems for the various modes, or else that there's a list of these handy somewhere.

In listings like the one in (5), if we want to diagram an intransitive verb base, we'll simply leave the "O" out. We will use "P" instead of "O" if the prefix in the object position has to use the **b** prefix to indicate a 3 person object in the cases when a normal transitive verb uses no object prefix.

Be aware, though, that the terms in (4) are new - you won't find them elsewhere (yet).

PRE-STEM VOWEL HARMONY

In Chapter 24 we learned that the seriative prefix in its **h** form undergoes pre-stem vowel harmony. We also mentioned that the unspec object prefix **'** undergoes a similar kind of process, but the details are different. Let's look at the pre-stem vowel harmony effects for the unspec object prefix and compare them with the seriative.

First of all, the unspec object prefix never contracts with the s-P subject prefixes the way the seriative prefix does. This means that if we look at Chapter 24(18) which lists the kinds of syllables involving the seriative that undergo pre-stem vowel harmony, and if we ask about the kinds of syllables involving the unspec object prefix that undergo pre-stem vowel harmony, we won't have anything that corresponds to Chapter 24(18b). The only syllables involving the unspec object prefix that we need to look at are the ones where Rule Conj-1 would have inserted an **i** if it weren't for Rule Conj-5, which inserts an **a** instead.

Now, one of the differences between the seriative and the unspec object prefixes is just this: when seriative **h** needs a vowel after it, the vowel is **i**, whereas when unspec **'** needs a vowel after it, the vowel is **a** (except in certain circumstances that never involve pre-stem position.) This means that when unspec **'** is preceded by a disjunct prefix that ends in **a** and we see the combination **a'a** in our verb, we don't notice anything in particular - this is exactly what we'd expect. But when seriative **h** is preceded by a disjunct prefix that ends in **a** and we see **aha** in our verb, we say "Aha! There was vowel-harmony here." (Sorry for that pun.) But the interesting thing is, the actual vowels look the same for the two prefixes! In fact, in all cases except one important one, the vowel patterns look the same for the two prefixes. Here is a chart:

(6)

Vowel at end of preceding disjunct prefix	combination with seriative h	combination with unspec object '
a	aha	a'a
e	ehe	e'e
i	ehe	e'e

If the vowel at the end of a preceding disjunct prefix is **e** or **i**, then for both prefixes we have to say that pre-stem vowel-harmony occurred, because the vowel after the **h** or the **'** is different from what it would have been if there hadn't been any prefix at all. If the vowel at the end of a preceding disjunct prefix is **a**, then for the seriative we have to say that pre-stem vowel harmony occurred (because there's an **a** after the **h** instead of an **i**) but for the unspec object prefix we don't have to say this, since we'd expect an **a** after the **'** anyway. That's why we could get away with talking about the unspec object prefix in half of Chapter 12 (and lots of places after that, too) without mentioning vowel-harmony. But as we see in (5), the unspec prefix undergoes vowel harmony, and the actual vowels we see are the same as for the seriative.

The one important case where the seriative and the unspec prefixes behave differently is the case when the preceding disjunct prefix is the special outer prefix **'a** that we studied in Chapter 19. What we get in pre-stem position is:

(7) **'a + h = 'ahi**   but   **'a + ' = 'e'e**

In the seriative case, we mentioned this as an exception in Chapter 24(19). In the unspec object case, we listed this as one of the cases in Rule Disj-4.

This should explain the vowels that you'll run into for various verb forms that have these prefixes in them. But remember: this vowel-harmony story is only valid for the situation that the seriative **h** or the unspec **'** starts a pre-stem syllable. If the syllable started by the seriative or the unspec prefix is further to the left in the verb, then, mostly, none of this happens - you'll usually see the vowels that you expected. However, as we learned in Chapter 19, if the unspec prefix is immediately preceded by the outer prefix **'a**, there are some special effects: review Rule Disj-4(e)(v). Occasionally, vowel harmony effects involve other prefixes; for example, we learned in Chapter 20 that when **bí** is immediately followed by **hoo**, it is often pronounced **bó**. You may occasionally run across one or two other situations besides these where the vowel at the end of a disjunct prefix is changed this way to match a vowel in a following syllable. As in the cases we've seen, this might happen when the consonant immediately following the disjunct syllable is **'** or **h**.

CONJUNCT PREFIXES

In our studies we've learned quite a lot about the conjunct prefixes that occur in Navajo verbs. We've become familiar with the object prefixes, and we've also studied a number of inner prefixes: **d, n,** the seriative, and also the special **yn** prefix. (We also saw one example of a verb base that has an inner **j** prefix.) For the vast majority of Navajo verb stems, these are the only conjunct prefixes you'll run into. But there are others, and some of the others have their own special behavior. Let's briefly say some things about two of them.

Some verb bases have a lexical prefix which consists just of the consonant **dz**. This prefix, found only with certain verb bases, has a meaning associated with it that involves a sudden or sharp movement. The **dz** prefix has a number of unusual properties which we'll look at now.

The first thing that's unusual about this **dz** prefix is that although it's meaning has nothing to do specifically with any participant of the action (it describes a characteristic of the action itself), grammatically this prefix is an object prefix! It is always placed in the object prefix position, rather than the inner prefix position. This means that in the F mode, it always precedes F mode **d**. Also, when it occurs in the F mode together with the seriative, Rule Conj-9(d) moves the seriative to the right, just as if an ordinary object prefix were in there. When the **dz** prefix is used with the long-vowel F mode conjugation, so that the F mode **d** is preceded by long-vowel-F **y**, this **y** becomes **ii**, just as though an object prefix were in front of it (and therefore we see **dziid** in those verb forms.) In the n-I conjugation, when the subject is 3 person, the subject prefix is **í** when it's preceded by **dz** (which is what we'd get if there's an object prefix just in front of it) rather than **ee** (which is what we'd get if there were an inner prefix just in front of it.)

Verb bases that have the prefix **dz** in them are always intransitive - there is never a "real" object prefix in the verb (although it's perfectly okay to have outer objects in verb bases with **dz**.) However, the 4 person prefix **j** can occur together with **dz**. When these two prefixes occur together, in most cases, they will fuse together and form the combination **yj**.

Another thing about the form of the **dz** prefix: if the subject is 1sg and the subject prefix is one of the usual ones that has the consonant **sh** just in front of the verb-stem or classifier, then **dz** usually changes to **j**. (Apparently, this change is optional.) An alternate change that seems to be possible in this situation: **dz** remains **dz**, but the subject prefix is changed so that there's an **s** in there instead of an **sh**. These changes remind us of Rule Conj-4 effects. It's important to remember them, because if you want to look up a **dz** verb in YM 87, you'll be using the 1sg form of the I mode, which means you may need to look up a verb form with a **j** in it.

For example, there's a verb base whose meaning is "let fly a kick" whose structure can be diagrammed as follows, using the shorthand we suggested earlier:

(8)   **'a+dz**+zero+mom:**táál**+simple

In the I mode, the 1sg form (the word that means "I'm letting fly a kick") will be **ajishtaał** (the I mode stem is **taał**.) If the subject isn't 1sg, the prefix reverts to **dz**, so that "you (sg) are letting fly a kick" is **adzítaał**, "we (all) are letting fly a kick" is **adadziitaał**, etc. If the subject is 4 person, the 4 person **j** and the **dz** prefix fuse to form **yj**, as we said - the behavior of the outer **'a** prefix in front of this **yj** is the same as if it were in front of, say, the 3 person object prefix **y**, so the word that means "one is letting fly a kick" is **iijitaał**.

When preceded by a vowel (at the end of a preceding disjunct prefix, say) and when the next syllable isn't the verb-stem syllable, **dz** undergoes the same kind of process as unspec **'** and 4 person **j**: no vowel is inserted after it and **dz** changes into **z** (or **zh** if there's a 1sg **sh** in the verb). In the same sort of position, the combination **yj** (4 person **j** combined with **dz**) becomes **yzh**. This can be seen in F mode forms of the verb base mentioned above: "he/she'll let fly a kick" is **azdootał**, "those ones will let fly a kick" is **adeizhdootał**, etc.

When not preceded by any other prefix, the **yj** combination appears as **yij** (that's just Rule Conj-1 at work) and, in the F mode, we irregularly see **jiizhd-**. For examples of this, and also for more examples illustrating the facts about this prefix that we've already mentioned, look up the words **jishtaał**, **jiinishdliih** (this word also has the **yn** inner prefix!), **nizhnists'in** (which has the structure **ni+dz+barred-l+mom:ts'in+N**), and **yáájiishdon** (which has the structure **yá+ná+dz+barred-l+mom:don+FLV**) in YM 87.

The second conjunct prefix we want to say something about is the prefix **y**. There are several conjunct prefixes that have this form. The first one we met was the 3 person object prefix (the one used when the subject is also 3 person and we're using the direct form of the verb.) But we've met other **y**'s also. For example, we've seen the long-vowel **y** that we find in the long-vowel F mode conjugation, there is the **y** element that forms part of the **yn** inner prefix, there's the seriative **y**, and there's the **y** that forms part of the contracted prefix **yj** that we find when the 4 person **j** prefix combines with the **dz** prefix that we just learned about. All of these **y**'s are subject to Rule Conj-2.

Are there any other conjunct **y**'s around? It depends on how we want to analyze things. For example, go back and look at the subject prefixes for the long-vowel I mode conjugation. The fact that the 1sg, 2sg, and 3 person prefixes have a long **ii** when not preceded by a disjunct prefix but a short **i** when preceded by a disjunct prefix looks like a Rule Conj-2 effect. Suppose we said that the long-vowel I mode conjugation involves a conjunct prefix **y** that's placed just to the left of the ordinary I mode subject prefixes. What would we have to add to our analysis in order to get the right forms? We'd have to add at least the following three items into our rules somewhere:

First, long-vowel **y** becomes **ii** not only when it's sandwiched in between two consonants, but also when it's followed by a consonant but not preceded by any prefix at all.

Second, when followed by a vowel, long-vowel **y** disappears; but the vowel that it was followed by is lengthened if it's short. (We'd need some sort of rule like this to explain why the 2dpl long-vowel

I subject prefix has a long **oo** in it.)

Third, the regular 2sg I mode prefix **ni** is replaced by zero when it follows long-vowel **y**.

In our presentation, it seemed easier just to list the forms of the subject prefixes the way we did rather than to make our rules even more complicated than they are. But some people prefer to analyze prefixes this way, and you may see ideas like this in various articles. In fact, we already mentioned that in YM the long-vowel I mode conjugation is sometimes called the yi-Ø conjugation - that "yi" refers to the idea of a conjunct **y** prefix being in there.

Are there any verb bases that simply have an inner **y** prefix without any other complications? Possibly. There are a few verb bases where all the forms of the verb can be explained if we assume that there's an inner **y** prefix that has the following properties:

(9)   Properties of inner **y**:

    (a)   If the syllable that would begin with inner **y** would be the pre-stem syllable, then replace that syllable with **oo**. (Note: this is just a vowel - there's no consonant in this element!)

    (b)   In the F mode, inner **y** is positioned to the left of F mode d.

    (c)   After parts (a) and (b) have applied, Rule Conj-1 and Rule Conj-2 apply normally.

An example: there is a verb base, meaning "earn it", or "win it", or "charge for it", that can be diagrammed as O+y+barred-l+mom:bá+S using our new shorthand. The 1sg I mode form is **wooshbįįh**, if you want to look it up in YM 87. The **woosh-** at the beginning of this word comes from (9a) changing the inner **y** into **oo**, which then causes Rule Str-3 to supply the **w** at the beginning of the word. The other I mode forms are also correctly produced. In the P mode, the forms look exactly like the ones given in Chapter 21(44), and in the F mode, the forms look just like long-vowel forms. In fact, if you compare the forms of verbs like this one with the forms of verbs that have the **yn** prefix, you'll probably realize that, at least for some verb bases, the **yn** prefix really is a combination of the inner **y** prefix (with the properties given in (9)) together with an additional **n** prefix that occurs only in certain forms and whose occurrance sometimes seems to be irregular, as we suggested back in Chapter 21.

But things can sometimes get more irregular. To see an illustration of what can happen, let's take a look at a pretty common verb base that might have two inner **y**'s! The verb base we want is the one that means "forget it". (In actual use, the postposition Paa is used with the verbs formed from this verb base. The "P" in this postposition refers to what was forgotten. The verb base itself is intransitive, meaning no object prefixes are used.) We'll start by looking at particular words built from this verb base.

In the I mode, the 1sg form is **yooshnééh**, and the 2sg and 3 person forms are both **yoonééh**. What do we conclude just from this? It looks like we have a long-vowel conjugation, except that there's a mysterious **oo** vowel in there instead of the **ii** that we'd expect. If we blame this vowel on an inner **y** that (9a) turned into **oo**, we still have that **y** at the beginning of these words, which must be an additional prefix of some sort - there's no other explanation for why it's there. If we say that there's a single inner prefix **y** in this verb base, then some of the other forms of this verb come out correctly with our current rules, but for the words we just saw we'd need to say (for example) that when any of the long-vowel subject prefixes that begin (normally) with **ii** follow the inner **y** in this verb, we find **oo** instead of **ii**.

The P mode of this verb appears to follow an s-P pattern that is normal for a verb with a (single) inner **y** prefix, except that the forms with a 3 person subject, such as the form **yooznah** that means "he/she forgot", have a **y** in them in addition to the **oo** vowel (which presumably was created by (9a) above.) Note that this **y** is not a 3 person object prefix (we find it in the 4 person P mode form **jiyooznah** as well.)

The F mode forms have two visible **y**'s in them. For example, "I'll forget it" is (**baa**) **yidiyeeshnah**. (One of the **y**'s seems to have undergone hopping of some sort.) We might want to say that we've got a long-vowel F mode pattern here, an idea that fits with the (apparent) long-vowel I mode; but then the conjugation pattern of this verb doesn't fit into any of the combinations shown in (3) and (4) earlier, since the P mode isn't long-vowel. All in all, it is hard to explain the forms of this verb in a straightforward way. It should, therefore, be properly regarded as irregular.

Another common verb base that seems to have irregularities involving a conjunct inner **y** prefix is the verb base that means "get it" (in the sense of "acquire it".) Look its forms up in YM 87 - the I mode form with 1sg subject is **shóosht'eeh**. Again, there are complications, but different ones than the ones we've seen with the "forget it" verb base. Verb bases like these two are probably best viewed as irregular. If you are learning Navajo as a new language, you should just memorize their forms rather than to try to create them on the basis of rules.

This is all we are going to say here about conjunct prefixes. As you continue with your studies, you'll occasionally come across other effects involving conjunct prefixes that go beyond what we've studied. But what we've covered in this book should provide you with a framework for thinking about these less common effects.

STEM-SETS

When we first started our study, we learned that each verb base had a stem-set which provided a verb stem for each of the modes. After a while, we learned about pairs of related stem-sets, called the momentaneous stem-set, and the continuative stem-set, the latter used when the verb base has the atelic outer prefix **na** in it. Later, we learned that sometimes a semelfactive stem-set can be formed from the momentaneous stem-set. And in our study of the Pg mode, we decided that it makes sense to consider the Pg mode verbs as verb bases all by themselves, which might mean that the verb stems used in that mode could be thought of as forming a stem-"set" (for one mode only!), which we can call a cursive stem-set. So, we now see that stem-sets come in families. Let's spend a little time thinking about families of stem-sets. And in particular: are there any kinds of stem-sets that we haven't seen yet?

There are, but before getting to that, we need to fix up our treatment of semelfactive stem-sets. In Chapter 20, we said that, at least for the regular cases, a semelfactive stem-set consists of stems all of which are the same as the momentaneous F mode stem. This does give quite a few correct semelfactive stem-sets, but it's not the whole story. To see what the problem is, you should first review the rule in Chapter 23(3) for forming R mode stems from F mode stems. What we need to think about here is that all F mode stems can be divided into two groups: some F mode stems have added on a ł at the end of the stem which isn't there in the other stems, whereas many F mode stems don't have this additional ł. For the F mode stems that don't have an added ł, our original rule for the semelfactive is correct: the semelfactive set consists of stems all of which are the same as the momentaneous F mode stem. But if the F mode stem has an added ł, the situation is different. If the ł at the end of the F mode stem doesn't replace a **d** at the end of the I mode stem, then the semelfactive stem-set consists of stems all of which are the same as the momentaneous R mode stem, except that the semelfactive F mode stem is the same as the momentaneous F mode stem - it has the additional ł. If the ł at the end of the F mode stem does replace a **d** at the end of the I mode stem, then the R and F mode stems of the semelfactive set are the same as the R and F mode stems of the momentaneous set, and the other semelfactive stems are the same as these except that the ' at the end of the R mode stem (or the ł at the end of the F mode stem) reverts to being a **d**.

Here's an example of the latter situation (which is more frequent than the case which doesn't involve a **d** at the end of the stems). We'll start with a transitive verb theme that means "shake it", which we can represent as follows:

(10)

Momentaneous stem-set	
I:	gháád
P:	gháád
F:	ghał
R:	gha'
O:	gháád
Classifier: zero	
Transitivity: transitive	

There are a number of verb bases that use this theme, such as the easy verb base that can be diagrammed as O+zero+mom:**gháád**+simple, which means simply "shake it". Our new rule will create a semelfactive stem-set (in fact, a semelfactive verb theme) which looks like this:

(11)

Semelfactive stem-set	
I:	**ghad**
P:	**ghad**
F:	**ghał**
R:	**gha'**
O:	**ghad**
Classifier: zero	
Transitivity: transitive	

Note that all the stems in (11) have a short, low-tone **a**, just like the momentaneous F and R mode stems. However, the I, P, and O mode stems in (11) end in **d**, while the semelfactive F and R mode stems in (11) are the same as the momentaneous F and R mode stems in (10). We can now apply Vocabulary-10 to (11) to create the verb base in (12) that means "give it a shake":

(12)   O+zero+sem:**gháád**+SLV

Note how we represented the stem-set in the shorthand expression in (12). We used the momentaneous P mode stem (which is **gháád**) as the name of the family of stem-sets that we're working with, even though this particular stem doesn't appear anywhere in (11)! The idea is that "sem:**gháád**" means "use the semelfactive stem-set that is derived from the momentaneous stem-set whose P mode stem is **gháád**".

Even with our new rules, there remain some semelfactive stem-sets that are not correctly built. Fortunately, there are only a few of these. They should be learned as special cases when you come across them.

Let's get back to our question: are there more kinds of stem-sets besides the ones we've seen so far?

There are two parts to the answer to this question. The first part is that there are some other stem-set types that, like the semelfactive, are derived from the more basic momentaneous stem-set by means of a rule. Let's look at one of them now.

The stem-set we want is called the *repetitive* stem-set in the YM materials. The stems of this stem-set are the same as the momentaneous ones, except that the momentaneous R mode stem is also used in the I and (usually) O modes. (But if the momentaneous R mode stem ends in a ' which replaced a **d**, then the I and O mode repetitive stems go back to ending in a **d**.) Although we didn't say anything about it at the time, we've actually seen a verb base that has a repetitive stem-set. The verb base in question is the one in Chapter 26 that meant "give him/her a kicking". Using our new shorthand for verb bases, we can diagram this verb base as follows:

(13)   **ná+O+n+zero+rep:táál+S**

The momentaneous R mode stem that goes with **táál** is **tał**, so this verb base uses this stem for the I and O modes as well.

A repetitive stem-set is used with verb bases that have certain specific prefix combinations. One of these combinations is the one illustrated by the verb base in (13): for certain verb themes whose meanings have to do with physical action that one person can inflict on another person or on a physical object, a transitive verb base that means that the subject does a series of these actions can be built by using the outer **ná** and inner **n** prefixes, the repetitive stem-set (and, of course, the classifier) of the verb theme, and the S conjugation pattern. For practice: write out a vocabulary-principle that describes this pattern.

(Incidentally: the verb **nánéts'ǫ́ǫ́z** "I gave kisses to him/her" that we saw back on page 1 (!) was built from a verb base with this pattern. In our shorthand, this verb base, which means "give him/her a series of kisses", has the structure **ná+O+n+zero+rep:ts'ǫ́ǫ́z+S**. You can find the verb theme that this is based on in Chapter 20(8).)

There are a few other derived stem-set types like this, but we won't go through them here. As your Navajo vocabulary increases, you'll gradually pick them up.

The second part of our answer to the question about whether there are any more stem-set types that we need to learn about involves looking at families of stem-sets in a more fundamental way. When we look at the stem-set types that we've seen up to this point, the following picture emerges: the basic stem-set is the momentaneous one, and the others are in some sense "derived" from the momentaneous stem-set. In the case of the semelfactive, cursive, and repetitive stem-sets, we have given rules that (except for some irregular cases) tell what the actual stems are. (For the semelfactive, see Vocabulary-9 in Chapter 20, together with the improvements given in our discussion earlier in this section; for the cursive, see Chapter 25(1); and for the repetitive, see the comments above.) This means that we don't really have to memorize additional stem-sets in order to use them - learning the momentaneous one is enough. But in the case of the continuative, the forms are not easily predictable, so these have to be learned separately.

However, this picture is not exactly right. Another situation is often found with many verbs, including quite a few common ones: one stem-set is used (usually with no lexical prefixes) to form common, basic verb bases with straightforward meanings, but a different stem-set is used in circumstances where we normally would say that a momentaneous stem-set would be required (for example, with prefix combinations that mean things like "start to" or "begin".) In cases like this, the YM materials use the term "momentaneous" for the stem-set that appears in the momentaneous-type verb bases, but for the stem-set used in the basic (prefixless) verbs, they have several different terms, depending on the conjugation pattern of the verb. If the prefixless verb base uses the simple conjugation pattern, they use the term *durative* for the stem-set in those basic verbs, whereas if the prefixless verb base uses the S pattern, they prefer the term *conclusive* for the stem-set. In addition, if a prefixless verb base uses the FLV combination, they say its stem-set is of the *transitional* type, although for such cases, related verb bases that have typically momentaneous meanings usually use the same stem-set. We've seen examples of all of these: the stem-set in the "cry" verb base (Chapter 7(1)), in the "eat it" verb base (Chapter 16(3)), and in the "drink it" verb base (Chapter 10(9)) are all durative stem-sets; the stem-sets in the "boil it" (Chapter 7(6)) and "weave it" (Chapter 12(4)) verb bases are conclusive stem-sets; and the stem-sets in the "see it" (Chapter 20(19)) and "become black" (Chapter 20(21)) verb bases are transitional stem-sets. As in the case of related momentaneous and continuative stem-sets, when we compare related momentaneous and durative stem-sets, or related momentaneous and conclusive stem-sets, we find that there isn't an easy rule that will tell us how to get one from the other - we simply have to learn both.

Do we need to have new terms such as "durative" or "conclusive"? Why can't we just say that the durative and conclusive stem-sets are continuative? Well, we could, but there are advantages to having separate terms. For example: the pairs of stem-sets that are called momentaneous and continuative are used differently from the pairs of stem-sets that are called momentaneous and durative (or conclusive). The biggest difference is this. When we have a pair of stem-sets where one is momentaneous and one is continuative, the momentaneous one is the basic one, and the continuative one is used in certain special circumstances (with atelic **na**). When we have a pair of stem-sets where one is momentaneous and one is durative or conclusive, it's the durative or the conclusive one that's the basic one (often used in verb bases with no lexical prefixes) and the momentaneous one is the one used only in circumstances that specifically require a momentaneous stem-set. And, separating the duratives from the conclusives helps us to remember the associated conjugation patterns for the prefixless verb bases that they form.

The fact that there are so many terms for different kinds of stem-sets may give the impression that the average family of stem-sets is fairly big, and that to learn all the stems in such a family is a major task for the memory. But this is not so. For most families of stem-sets, there will be one basic set, (called momentaneous, durative, conclusive, or transitional.) In addition, there will be at most one other stem-set whose forms are hard to predict from the basic one (but in almost all cases, the P mode stem for this second stem-set will be the same as the P mode stem for the basic stem-set.) If the basic set is momentaneous, the other, unpredictable set will typically be the continuative, whereas if the basic set is durative or conclusive, the other, unpredictable set will typically be the momentaneous. In addition, there may be other stem-sets that are predictable (that is, sets for which a rule can be given), such as the semeliterative, repetitive, or cursive.

Incidentally, just how different is a momentaneous stem-set from a continuative, durative, or conclusive stem-set? For many families of stem sets, only the I, and usually O mode stems are different. Assuming the most regular situation with regard to the O mode stems (that is, where the O mode stem is the same as the I mode stem for any set), this means that, for such a family, you only have to memorize a total of four stems: the momentaneous I mode stem, the continuative (or durative or conclusive) I mode stem, the P mode stem (which is the same for both sets), and the F mode stem (which is the same for both sets.) The R mode stems can then be worked out using our regular rule in Chapter 23(3), and the O mode stems will be the same as the I mode stems. If the family also includes semelfactive, repetitive, or cursive sets, our rules will tell you what they look like.

For a few of the more common families of stem-sets, though, there will be more work involved. We've seen a few cases where a continuative stem-set and a momentaneous stem-set only had their P mode stems in common (for example, see Chapter 17(22).) But even in those cases, the stems in the two sets are not different in crazy ways; in Chapter 17(22), for example, the F and R mode stems for the two sets differ only in the tone. So, even for these harder families, the burden to one's memory is not great.

How important is it to know the terms for the different stem-set types? Possibly, it is not important at all. In fact, the way YM use these terms is fairly complex - you may have good reason not to want to learn them! But it seemed like a good idea to go through at least the basic set-up of the way these terms are used. For one thing, it's a good idea to be a bit familiar with terms that you'll run across in your studies. For another, it's good to get an idea of what you'll find in a family of stem-sets. For example, it should be a relief to know that, even if you're looking at a particularly rich family of stem-sets, you won't ever have to memorize, say, fifteen or twenty (or more!) actual stems.

Well, we are coming close to the whole story. Let's add just one easy comment.

It often happens that the verb stem used with a neuter verb is related to some other stem-set (one with stems for all modes.) YMM 92 lists these neuter "sets" along with their related set. (A neuter stem "set", like a cursive stem "set", has only a stem for one mode in it, namely, the one mode that the neuter verb bases built using that stem are conjugated in.) Typically, the neuter stem cannot be derived from the basic stem-set by some sort of rule - it's simply one more stem that you'll have to memorize for those families that have one.

We'll end this section by giving a new, but very useful, term.

We have decided that it's a good idea to name a family of stem-sets by giving the P mode stem from the basic set in that family. This stem is called the *root* of the family of stem-sets. For example, the root of the stem-sets in (10) and (11) is **gháád**. As we already said, in our shorthand for describing verb bases we're using the root to name the family of stem-sets from which the particular set used by that verb base is taken. To indicate which particular set we want, we place the term describing the stem-set just in front of the root, separated from it by a colon. So, the stem-set in (10) is denoted **mom:gháád**, meaning the momentaneous stem-set in the family of stem-sets whose root is **gháád**.

Similarly, the stem-set in (11) (which is found in the verb base in (12)) is denoted sem:**gháád**, meaning the semelfactive stem-set in the family of stem-sets whose root is **gháád**. Keep in mind that in YMM 92 verb bases are indexed by the root of their stem-set.

PRE-STEM SYLLABLE EFFECTS

During our study we have come upon a number of cases where the syllable that immediately precedes the stem syllable (the syllable that we're calling the pre-stem syllable) behaves in a special way. For fun, let's collect what we know about this special syllable.

First: there has to be a pre-stem syllable. If the structure of the verb doesn't provide one, the peg rule (Rule Str-2) provides one.

The vowel changes that Rule Disj-1 describes for disjunct prefixes happen exactly when the disjunct prefix syllable is the pre-stem syllable.

The outer prefix **'a** becomes **'ii** when its syllable is the pre-stem syllable.

A short low tone vowel acquires a high tone if it's preceded by a disjunct prefix that ends in a high tone vowel, but only if its the vowel of the pre-stem syllable.

When a vowel is needed after the object prefix **hw**, that vowel is **a** (or **oo** in some positions) exactly when the syllable formed by that vowel is the pre-stem syllable. (It's **o** otherwise.)

The conjunct prefixes **'**, **j**, and **dz** always have a vowel inserted after them if the syllable formed by the inserted vowel is the pre-stem syllable. (Recall that if these prefixes are preceded by a vowel, no vowel is inserted after them if an inserted vowel would not be the vowel of the pre-stem syllable.)

The prefixes **'** and **j** never hop to the right so far that they would start the pre-stem syllable.

The prefix **ná** is prevented from contracting with a preceding outer prefix if it's the pre-stem syllable. (But don't forget that it's also prevented from a contraction like this if it's followed by a vowel.)

The long form of the scmeliterative prefix (that is, **nááná**) is used if it (actually, its second syllable) is going to be the pre-stem syllable. (But this is also the case if it's followed by a vowel.)

When a vowel is needed after the object prefix **'** or the seriative prefix **h**, then vowel harmony occurs if the syllable of the inserted vowel is the pre-stem syllable.

The inner prefix **y** becomes the vowel **oo** when the syllable that would be formed by inserting a vowel after the **y** would be the pre-stem syllable.

These effects are handy to remember because they'll help you figure out the parts of a verb, especially a big one. They are especially helpful in identifying the prefix that immediately precedes the classifier or the subject prefix.

While we're on the subject of the pre-stem syllable: it's also good to keep in mind that the vowel in the pre-stem syllable is sometimes part of the subject prefix and sometimes not. For example, if the subject prefix is **sh**, or zero, or **z**, say, then the pre-stem vowel comes from somewhere else - either it's inserted by the peg rule, or it's inserted after a conjunct prefix, or it's the vowel in a disjunct prefix. Other subject prefixes are entire syllables, like **ni**, **ní**, **sé**, or even pieces with more than one syllable in them, like **síní** or **víní**, etc. - with these subject prefixes, the vowel of the pre-stem syllable is the vowel in the subject prefix. Finally, there are subject prefixes that involve one syllable but that start with vowels, like **iid**, **eesh**, **íí**, vv, etc. In these cases, the consonant that starts the syllable comes from somewhere else but the pre-stem vowel is either the vowel in the subject prefix or else it comes from the vowel in the subject prefix combined in some fashion with the vowel of a preceding disjunct prefix. It's a good idea to keep these different possibilities in mind - this will help you identify the parts of a Navajo verb.

DISJUNCT PREFIXES

Earlier, we included some comments about conjunct prefixes, pointing out that we have seen examples of all the common conjunct prefixes and that we have learned essentially everything that we need to know about how conjunct prefixes work. In this section, let's briefly look at disjunct prefixes.

The disjunct prefixes we've seen have been, first of all, the distributive plural prefix **da**, and secondly, a certain number of outer prefixes. As in the case of the conjunct prefixes, we've learned just about everything we need to know about the grammatical principles that have to do with these prefixes. But, unlike the situation with the conjunct prefixes, we have not seen anywhere near all the disjunct prefixes themselves. The way we've described the structure of the Navajo verb, the distributive plural prefix is the only disjunct prefix that we haven't called an outer prefix. There aren't any other special disjunct prefixes like the distributive plural, but there are quite a few outer prefixes found in Navajo verb bases, and we've only seen a small selection of them. It'll be useful to mention a few facts here, to help guide you in your future study.

First of all, unlike inner prefixes like **d** or **n**, which seem to not have clear or specific meanings by themselves (or, as analyzed in YM, may have very different meanings in different verb bases), most outer prefixes have specific meanings. Sometimes the meaning is a bit abstract, as in the case of atelic **na**, and sometimes the meaning is extremely concrete, as in the case of **ch'í** (meaning "horizontally out of something"). When learning a new outer prefix, you should learn the meaning associated with the prefix.

Next, let's say something about the structure of outer prefixes. We have come across outer prefixes

398

with two different kinds of structure. On the one hand, we've learned about some outer prefixes, like **na, ha, nitsí**, etc., that are simple one-syllable or two-syllable units. But we've also seen others that have a "P" prefix element inside them, like **Pą́ą́, Pi,** etc. For most of these, the "P" prefix is followed by a unit that is identifiable as a postposition; for example, the **-ą́ą́** of **Pą́ą́** looks like the sort of element that would be the stem of a postposition, although this particular stem doesn't seem to actually be ever used as an independent postposition. In the case of **Pi** and **Pí**, the YM materials don't want to say that the single **i** or **í** vowel is a postpositional stem (they look too much like vowels that would be inserted automatically, like the vowels inserted by Rule Conj-1!), so they say that these prefixes are cases of a *null postposition*, that is, a postposition that isn't pronounced as anything but that is nevertheless there, in a sort of hidden way.

It turns out that there's a third kind of structure that we find among the outer prefixes. This third structure is formed by taking the stem of a noun, and, usually, changing its form a bit. These noun-stems are then used as outer prefixes, either by themselves or else with a "P" prefix indicating a possessor.

Here's an example of this third kind of outer prefix. The noun **łeezh** means "soil" or "clay". From this noun we get the outer prefix **łe** - it is used to indicate action that affects the ground or involves motion into the ground or into soil or ashes. An example of a verb base with this prefix is (in our new shorthand): **łe+'+zero+mom:geed**+simple, meaning "dig (a cellar or a pit, in the ground)" - you'll recognize the stem-set from previous "dig" verb bases that we've seen.

Another example: from the noun **azéé'**, meaning "mouth" we have an outer prefix of the form **Piza**, meaning "into P's mouth". For example, the verb base **Piza+O+h/y+zero+mom:lá+S** means "put them (ropelike things) one after another into P's mouth". (This verb can be used to talk about feeding spaghetti to somebody.)

In general, these noun-based outer prefixes behave exactly like any other outer prefixes; for example, Rule Disj-2 changes the **a** at the end of **Piza** into **e** in the F mode form **yizeidiyoolééł** "he/she will feed him/her something spaghetti-like". Similarly, in the word **bizahashłé** ("I'm feeding him/her something spaghetti-like") we see pre-stem vowel harmony at work - there's an **a** after the **h** instead of an **i**. But sometimes prefixes of this sort seem to act as though they are separate words: their form doesn't change, and effects like vowel harmony don't happen. Example: in YM 87, the word that means "I'm digging a pit/cellar", built from the verb base mentioned above, is shown as **łe'ashgééd**, without vowel harmony. Cases like this need to be investigated further.

Some outer prefixes were introduced by special vocabulary principles, such as the semeliterative **nááná** and the reversionary **ná**, and two of them, the R mode **ná** and the reflexive **'á**, are part of the grammatical inflection system. These prefixes have special rules that position them with respect to other outer prefixes and with respect to each other, but these are the only outer prefixes that have special positioning rules like this. All the other outer prefixes that you'll come across are "ordinary" ones, like the outer prefixes we saw when we first began our study.

Another issue that we've come across: we learned that some outer prefixes require particular conjugation pattern combinations. For example, atelic **na** requires the S combination (see (4) above), **'a** requires the simple combination, and **ch'í** requires the N combination. The full facts about this sort of requirement can sometimes be slightly more complicated than we've seen. For example, we already came across an outer prefix **na** different from atelic **na** - this other **na**, which occurs less commonly than atelic **na** (it only occurs in certain combinations, and with certain verb themes) means something like "down" - and it requires the simple conjugation combination rather than the S combination. In this case, we seem to have two entirely different outer prefixes (they have unrelated meanings) that happen to be pronounced the same.

A trickier case is the outer prefix **ha**, meaning "up and out of something". When we first came upon this prefix, we learned that it requires the simple combination. But in fact, it can also be used with the S combination - but only if the "out" part of the meaning has to do with moving out of something fairly large (like a canyon), where that the action doesn't have the feel of extraction from a tight or constraining situation.

Despite minor complications like this, very many outer prefixes occur only with one particular conjugation pattern combination. For those prefixes, it is a good idea to learn what its conjugation combination is, along with its form and meaning.

Finally, let's say something about the form of disjunct prefixes.

We've given two general rules, Rule Disj-1 and Rule Disj-2, that describe how the form of a disjunct prefix changes in certain circumstances. We also gave two additional rules that deal with particular prefixes have special forms in various circumstances. As you learn more and more outer prefixes, you mostly won't have to add anything to these. However, you will occasionally come across a situation not described by these rules. When learning a new outer prefix, you might want to ask the following questions about that prefix:

(14)

(a) What form does the prefix take when it's in the context described by Rule Disj-1?

(b) What form does the prefix take when it's in the context described by Rule Disj-2?

(c) What form does the prefix take when it's immediately followed by v́v́?

(d) What form does the prefix take when it's immediately followed by v́íní?

(e) What form does the prefix take when it's immediately followed by vv?

(f) What form does the prefix take when it's immediately followed by an O mode subject prefix?

You will find that for most new outer prefixes that you learn, the answers to these questions will be correctly given by the rules we've learned. But a few outer prefixes will be a bit different - the questions in (14) will help you organize the facts for those prefixes. (And, some outer prefixes never occur in some of the situations described by the questions in (14), so you won't have to worry about those.)

VERB BASES AND VERB THEMES

We first mentioned the term *verb base* back in Chapter 2 when we wanted to separate the parts of a verb that tell us the kind of action involved (these were the parts of the verb in the verb base) from the parts of a verb that tell us who or what is involved and when the action takes place. During our study, our concept of what a verb base consists of kept growing. Here is what we finally came up with. A verb base consists of: a stem-set, a classifier, a group of lexical prefixes (possibly none), a statement of whether the verb base is transitive or intransitive, and, finally, a conjugation pattern for the verb base. Any Navajo verb base (at least, any regular one!) is completely defined by this information. (That is, the forms of the actual verbs are defined by this information. We also have to say what the verb base means! Occasionally, this can get a bit involved. For example, if we have a verb base with an ordinary object as well as an outer object, we have to say what each of these objects is, that is, how each one is connected to the action.)

In Chapter 17, we introduced the concept of a *verb theme*. This notion corresponds to an element of vocabulary that has a basic meaning describing a kind of action, but not indicating all the specific details about the action that a verb base conveys. Formally, we said that a verb theme consists of: a family of related stem-sets, a classifier, and a statement of transitivity. We also mentioned that it is often possible to get related verb themes, a transitive one and an intransitive one, where these two themes differ only in the classifier - maybe this means that, at least sometimes, the family of stem-sets alone (without the transitivity and without the classifier) is a kind of verb theme. But this is all we said about the structure of verb themes. Here are two more comments about verb themes that we'd like to make.

First of all, when we presented verb themes, we listed two stem-sets in the family of stem-sets (sometimes we listed one.) We can still do this, but we should keep in mind what we said earlier in this chapter about stem-sets. In a fair number of cases, there are more stem-sets possible - we've looked at the semelfactive, repetitive, cursive, and neuter stem-sets as stem-sets that are (sometimes) associated with the basic ones. It's probably a good idea to decide that a verb theme includes all the stem-sets are are related to each other. In an earlier section we defined the notion of a "root" - we can refer to the entire family of stem-sets by giving the root. If we want to refer to a particular stem-set based on a given root, all we have to do is add in the term that describes that stem-set (that is, momentaneous, or semelfactive, or whatever.) - this is what we've been doing in our abbreviated diagrams of verb bases.

Getting back to verb themes, there is a second issue that we should look at. In some cases, we will want to allow a verb theme to contain prefixes. The reason we'd ever want to do this is that we might find that a particular family of stem-sets can represent a certain meaning, but that for every verb base built from it with that meaning there always is some particular lexical prefix in the verb base. This is something that really happens; in fact, we can illustrate this situation using examples we've already seen.

In Chapter 7(19) there is a verb base meaning "think". What is the verb theme that this verb base is built upon? We might say that it's the family of stem-sets that includes the stem-set in Chapter 7(19) (which we can represent as the root **kééz**), together with the zero classifier and with a statement that this verb theme is intransitive. If we say this, then we'd say that the verb base in Chapter 7(19) was constructed by taking one of the stem-sets from this verb theme (perhaps the momentaneous one), adding in the outer prefix **nitsí** (which, by the way, is really two prefixes: **ni** and **tsí**), and using the S conjugation pattern. (The conjugation pattern wasn't actually listed in Chapter 7(19) - we hadn't gotten that far yet!) So what's wrong with this?

Well, it turns out that all the verb bases that are constructed using the **kééz** stem-sets and that have meanings involved thinking also have the outer prefix **tsí** in them. This suggests that, if the verb theme is supposed to be a distillation of the basic meaning, then the outer prefix **tsí** should be part of the verb theme. If we do this, we'll say that, to build the verb base in Chapter 7(19), we'll start with the "think" verb theme, which already gives us the outer prefix **tsí** along with a family of stem-sets, a classifier, and a transitivity. To form the verb base, we'll add another outer prefix (**ni**, preceding **tsí**), we'll choose the momentaneous stem-set, and we'll use the S conjugation pattern.

When a prefix is part of a verb theme, we say that the prefix is *thematic*. Some prefixes, such as outer **tsí**, seem to be always thematic: we only find them associated with particular roots, where the combination of the prefix and the root have a certain basic meaning. Some prefixes, such as atelic outer **na**, are never thematic: whenever we find them in a verb base, they are there to add an extra meaning to the basic meaning provided by the verb theme (which means they aren't themselves part of the verb theme.) But some prefixes can be thematic in some verb bases and nonthematic in others. An example is the inner prefix **d**. Mostly, this prefix is not thematic. For example, we've seen a number of vocabulary principles (Vocabulary-2 in Chapter 17 and Vocabulary-12 in Chapter 20 are only two examples) where inner **d** is added to the material from a verb theme to create a verb base with a certain added meaning. Since the same verb themes can be used (with their same basic meanings) with other vocabulary principles that don't add in an inner **d** prefix, we certainly don't want to say that those verb themes have an inner **d** in them. However, there are a few verb themes that do seem to contain a thematic inner **d**. An example: the very same stem-sets based on the root **kééz** that, when combined with outer **tsí** create a verb theme that means "think", can be combined with inner **d** to create a verb theme that means "cough"! A number of verb bases whose meaning involves coughing are built using this verb theme - they all have stem-sets based on **kééz**, and they all have the inner **d** prefix (and, of course, none of them have the outer **tsí** prefix!)

So, inner **d** (and also inner **n**, by the way) are usually not thematic, but there are certain cases where these prefixes are indeed thematic. Inner **j**, on the other hand, appears to be always thematic (we saw a verb base with inner **j** in Chapter 21(37).) Keeping thematic prefixes in mind when you run into them will help you organize your understanding of the Navajo verb vocabulary.

VOCABULARY PRINCIPLES

During our study we have listed a number of vocabulary principles that describe how verb bases can be built either from verb themes or from other verb bases. If you have been deepening your Navajo language studies along with reading this book, you probably realize that the vocabulary principles we've covered hardly scratch the surface. As your knowledge of the Navajo verb vocabulary increases, you will come upon many new ways of building verb bases. You might want to write out your own versions of the vocabulary principles involved whenever you come upon them. Here, let's take a brief look at some patterns of vocabulary building.

In Chapter 19 we learned three vocabulary principles, called Vocabulary-6, Vocabulary-7, and Vocabulary-8, that added information to verbs of motion. The kind of information added by each of these principles had to do with the path of the motion: they convey the notion either of motion away, or of motion into, or of motion out of.

Let's look at the structure of Vocabulary-6 and Vocabulary-8. These principles each create a verb base by starting with material provided by a verb theme of motion, adding an outer prefix, and specifying a conjugation combination. Vocabulary-7 is different: it adds a word to the verbs created by Vocabulary-6. So, one thing we see immediately is that sometimes new vocabulary is created by combining a special word with the verbs formed from a verb base that is already present in the vocabulary. But the structure of Vocabulary-6 and Vocabulary-8 is important: there are very many combinations like the ones described in those principles, combinations where one or several prefixes, together with a particular conjugation combination, are added to a stem-set and classifier provided by a verb theme, that build verb bases that express particular meanings. For motion verb themes, there are many such patterns that give information about the path of the motion. Many patterns like this also exist for non-motion themes - these add all sorts of different meanings to the basic meaning of the verb theme.

Patterns like this are hidden behind some of the verb bases that we've seen elsewhere in our study. For example, in Chapter 15(36) we have a verb base that means "uncover it by digging". It turns out that the outer prefix P**ą́ą́**, the unspec object prefix **'**, the inncr prefix **d**, the use of a momentaneous stem-set, and the simple conjugation combination all taken together form a vocabulary pattern that expresses the meaning "uncover it" (where the "it" is represented by the "P" in the outer prefix.) While this pattern does not create a vast number of verb bases, it can be used with material from verb themes whose meanings involve action of the sort that could be used to uncover things. The result is to create verb bases whose meaning is to uncover something by means of that action. There are quite a few patterns like this, with all sorts of meanings, in the Navajo verb system. Be on the lookout for them.

A somewhat different situation is illustrated by Vocabulary-14 (the semeliterative) and Vocabulary-15 (the reversionary) in Chapter 22 and Vocabulary-16 (the seriative) in Chapter 24. These vocabulary principles start out with entire verb bases, and, by adding prefixes (and sometimes making certain other changes to the verb base), add extra pieces of meaning. Vocabulary principles like these are (somewhat) independent of the kinds of vocabulary principles we talked about in the two previous paragraphs, the ones that give information about the path of a motion or that carry meanings like "uncover it". What we mean is that the semeliterative, reversionary, and seriative can be used (at least sometimes) as part of the same verb base together with those other patterns. Of course, they can also be used with simpler verb bases that don't have patterns like that. The semeliterative, reversionary, and seriative are also somewhat independent of each other - more than one of them can simultaneously be part of the same verb base.

Another kind of vocabulary principle is the kind that adds meaning that has to do with starting or ending an action. We've run into a few cases of this in our study. Vocabulary-12 in Chapter 20 describes one pattern that is used to convey the notion of beginning, commonly found with motion verbs. But back in Chapter 15(18) we saw a verb base that means "start to work" - in that verb base, the inner prefix **d**, the momentaneous stem-set of the verb theme, and the S conjugation combination are used together to indicate the beginning of the action. (Vocabulary-2 in Chapter 17 uses a similar arrangement as the one found in Chapter 15(18), but that vocabulary principle is really a special case, used specifically with motion verbs.) There are roughly half-a-dozen vocabulary patterns found in Navajo for expressing the idea of an action starting - different verb themes seem to prefer different such patterns. (These are called *inceptive* patterns in YM.) There are also patterns indicating that an action is ending (*terminatives*), etc.

Still another kind of vocabulary principle involves the creation of verb bases from a single verb theme that differ from each other in the way an action unfolds. An example: compare the verb base in Chapter 20(10), whose structure is O+zero+sem:**ts'óóz**+SLV and which means "kiss him/her (once)", with the verb base that we mentioned above whose structure is **ná**+O+n+zero+rep:**ts'óóz**+S and which means "give him/her kisses". They are both formed (ultimately) from the verb theme in Chapter 20(8), but they differ in that one involves giving a single kiss while the other involves giving a series of kisses. This sort of difference is called (in YM and elsewhere) *aspect*. We analyzed the verb base in Chapter 20(10) by saying that we built it by applying Vocabulary-9 and Vocabulary-10 to the verb theme in Chapter 20(8), and you may have written out a vocabulary principle that will build the second "kiss" verb base from that verb theme as well. So, be on the lookout for vocabulary principles that create verb bases that differ among themselves in having different aspects.

(Another note on terminology: at least in YMM 92, the term *subaspect* is used for patterns like inceptives and terminatives, as well as for the semeliterative, reversionary, and seriative patterns. A complication is that YMM 92 also uses the term *aspect* to refer to stem-set types as well as to refer to the kind of vocabulary patterns we mentioned in the previous paragraph.)

In Part C of the Appendix we have listed all the vocabulary principles that we've covered in this book.

In addition to the numbered ones that were presented formally, we also included several that were described informally. These vocabulary principles were listed using the same shorthand that we've developed in this chapter for verb bases. The way to do this is easy: for any vocabulary principle, we simply list the parts of the verb base that the principle adds. So, for examle, Vocabulary-8 (Chapter 19) can be described by saying that you take a motion verb theme and add to it the material in the following expression:

(15) **ch'í+mom:+N**

The expression in (15) tells us to add a certain outer prefix (namely, **ch'í**), to use a certain stem-set (the momentaneous one), and to use a certain conjugation pattern (namely, N.) To get a real verb base, we have to supply a root (which indicates the family of stem-sets we're using), and a classifier. If the verb theme is transitive, we'll also put in the "O" symbol in the correct position for the object prefix.

To practice this notation, let's give another vocabulary principle. To form verb bases that mean "close something" or "shut something", apply the expression in (16) to certain verb themes whose meaning involve physical actions that could be used to close things:

(16) **dá+'+d+mom:+N**

Note: the verb bases built using (16) are intransitive.

One of the verb themes that this pattern can be used with consists of the family of stem-sets whose root is **kaal** and whose classifier is the barred-l classifier - this theme has a meaning which is described in YMM 92 as "execute a chopping motion with a rigid object". For practice, use our shorthand to describe the verb base created by applying (16) to this verb theme. (The meaning of this verb base is, by the way, "close (a door or a house)" - since this verb base is intransitive, the door or the house that is getting closed isn't referred to in the verb.) Then, write out as many forms of this verb base as you can. To help you out: the 1sg I mode form is **dádi'nishkaał** - note that the unspec prefix hopped to the n-I subject prefix, an effect that we talked about at the end of Chapter 18. Incidentally, the 3 person I mode form of this verb illustrates that the 3 person n-I prefix is **ee** when preceded by an inner prefix - the form is **dá'deełkaał**. The rules we've learned will give you all the correct forms of this verb.

In the case of many languages, learning vocabulary is often thought of as the same thing as learning words. While this is never exactly the case for any language, in the case of Navajo verbs, it is important to keep in mind that a major part of learning vocabulary is learning the kinds of patterns of which we've seen a few (only a few!) examples. As you learn new patterns, you'll notice that in almost all cases the actual forms of verbs are correctly given by our rules. This means that if you've learned the material in this book well, you shouldn't have any trouble either recognizing the various forms of verbs or creating them. Of course, there are always a few exceptional cases here and there, and these have to be learned individually.

If you have studied the material in this book all the way to this point, you will have learned a great deal about the way Navajo verbs are structured. You now should be able to move ahead and develop an advanced knowledge of the expressive power of this rich language.

APPENDIX

PART A: THE RULES

Here are the rules that we have learned in our study of Navajo verbs. There are four kinds of rules - we have collected each kind together. For each part of each rule, we have indicated the chapter in which that part of the rule was introduced.

Rules that involve movement are indicated by the phrase: a MOVEMENT rule. (Remember, movement rules should be tried before rules that determine form.)

RULES INVOLVING GENERAL STRUCTURE

Rule Str-1: If the subject of a transitive verb is 1, 2, or 4 person, then a 3 person object is represented by zero (Chapter 6), except for objects represented using the symbol "P" (outer objects (Chapter 15) and ordinary objects in certain verb bases (Chapter 16)), where the 3 person object is represented by the object prefix **b** in these cases. If the subject of a transitive verb is 3 person, then a 3 person object is represented by the object prefix **y** for the direct form, and by the object prefix **b** for the inverse form (Chapters 6 and 11.) Instead of using the 3 object prefix **y**, put two of these next to each other (like this: **yy**) into the object prefix position if the subject is 3 person, the form is the direct form, there is no inner prefix following it, and there is no (lexical) prefix preceding it, in any of the following circumstances:

(a)   In the y-P conjugation (including verb bases with inner **yn**) and the classifier is zero or barred-l (Chapter 9, Chapter 21.)

(b)   In the long-vowel-I conjugation (Chapter 20.)

(c)   In the long-vowel-P conjugation and the classifier is zero or barred-l (Chapter 20.)

(d)   If the 3 object prefix is followed by **ii** created from the seriative y by the sandwiched y rule (Rule Conj-2), in the I and s-P conjugations (Chapter 24.)

Rule Str-2: (The peg rule:) if a verb form has no syllable preceding the verb-stem syllable (either from the subject prefix or from any other prefix), then put in the prefix **yi** (Chapter 7.) However, if a verb base is conjugated in the s-P and has no prefixes, then the 3 subject prefix **z** or **s** becomes **si** (and in this case, Rule Subj-2 does not apply) (Chapter 8.) (Also: if a verb base is conjugated in the y-P, the classifier is zero or barred-l, and there are no prefixes, then the 1sg and 3 prefixes become **yí** (and the 2sg prefix becomes **yíní**) (Chapter 9.))

<u>Rule Str-3</u>: If a verb form is stranded with an initial vowel, prefix **y** to the verb if the initial vowel is **i** or **ii**, and prefix **w** to the verb if the initial vowel is **o** or **oo** (Chapter 7.)

<u>Rule Str-4</u>: If the 4 person prefix **j** is used in the object prefix position together with another object prefix, the 4 person prefix **j** comes second (that is, the other object prefix precedes the **j**) (Chapter 11.) If the unspec object prefix **'** is used in the object prefix position together with the 3 person object prefix **y**, the unspec object prefix **'** precedes the object prefix **y** (Chapter 24.)

<u>Rule Str-5</u>: (Chapter 20)

(a)   (A MOVEMENT rule:) If the 4 person subject prefix **j** (in object position) is preceded by another prefix and followed directly by the long-vowel-F prefix, then the long-vowel-F prefix and **j** interchange positions.

(b)   If the 3 person object prefix **y** is preceded by another prefix and followed directly by the long-vowel-F **y** prefix, then the two **y** prefixes merge and become one **y**.

<u>Rule Str-6</u>: If a verb base has an inner **n** prefix in it, then, in the F mode, insert a conjunct high tone just in front of the inner **n** (Chapter 21.)

<u>Rule Str-7</u>: The semeliterative outer prefix **nááná** shortens to **náá** when it is immediately followed by a consonant and the next syllable is not the verb-stem syllable. However, if the consonant that follows **nááná** is the 3 person object prefix **y**, and if this **y** is itself immediately followed by a consonant, then the original longer form is used. The prefix **ná** can contract with certain preceding outer prefixes under the same circumstances as the ones when the short form **náá** of the semeliterative prefix is used. Note also the following special combinations:

When **nááná** is immediately followed by the y-P/n-P 2sg subject prefix or by a **yn** prefix that begins **yíní**, we can get **nááyíní**. When **nááná** is immediately followed by a long-vowel 1sg, 2sg, or 3 prefix that begins **(i)i**, we usually get **nááyii**. When **nááná** is immediately followed by the 3 person object prefix **y** and the **y** is immediately followed by the 3 subject n-P zero/barred-l prefix **ní**, we usually get **nááyíní**.) Contracted forms of the prefix **ná** can be used in these cases.

RULES INVOLVING SUBJECT PREFIXES AND CLASSIFIERS

<u>Rule Subj-1</u>: Whenever the **d** at the end of a 1dpl subject prefix is immediately followed by the first consonant of the verb stem, then that **d** causes d-effect on the first consonant of the verb stem. (The **d** itself disappears.) (Chapter 4)

<u>Rule Subj-2</u>: (The sandwich rule:) the barred-l classifier (that is, the ł in the "cl" position) and the

plain-l classifier (that is, the **l** in the "cl" position) disappear when sandwiched in between any subject prefix that ends in **sh** or **s** and the first consonant of the verb stem (Chapter 6.)

Rule Subj-3: The **d** at the end of any 1dpl subject prefix disappears when immediately followed by a plain-l classifier. It also disappears when immediately followed by a barred-l classifier, except that in this case, the barred-l, that is, the **ł**, changes to a plain **l** (Chapter 6.)

Rule Subj-4: If a 2dpl subject prefix ends in **h**, this **h** disappears when immediately followed by the barred-l classifier (**ł**). It also disappears when immediately followed by the plain-l classifier (**l**), but the **l** changes into a **ł** in this case (Chapter 6.)

Rule Subj-5: If the pre-stem syllable has a short vowel in it, then it acquires a high tone if the syllable immediately preceding it has a high tone on the vowel that it ends with (Chapter 7.)

Rule Subj-6: If the verb stem contains one or more of the consonants **s, z, dz, ts,** or **ts'**, then any **sh** or **zh** that occurs in a subject prefix is replaced by **s** or **z** respectively. If the verb stem contains one or more of the consonants **sh, zh, j, ch,** or **ch'**, then any **s** or **z** that occurs in a subject prefix is replaced by **sh** or **zh** respectively (Chapter 7.)

Rule Subj-7: If a verb stem begins with a voiced fricative, this sound is devoiced if the classifier of the verb base is zero and if the verb stem is immediately preceded by any subject prefix ending in **sh** or **s** or **h** (Chapter 13.)

Rule Subj-8: If a verb stem begins with a voiced fricative and if the classifier of the verb base is barred-l, then this voiced fricative is devoiced, except if the classifier is preceded by a 1dpl subject prefix ending in **d**, in which case Rule Subj-3 applies normally and there is no change to the voiced fricative at the beginning of the verb stem. If the voiced fricative at the beginning of the verb stem is **z** or **zh**, then when this consonant devoices to **s** or **sh**, the barred-l classifier (that is, the **ł**) is dropped. Incidentally, this prevents Rule Subj-4 from applying (Chapter 13.)

RULES INVOLVING CONJUNCT PREFIXES

Rule Conj-1: If a conjunct prefix (ending in a consonant) is followed directly by a consonant, insert the vowel **i** between the consonant at the end of the conjunct prefix and the consonant that follows it (Chapter 5.) (If the conjunct prefix is just **y**, go to Rule Conj-2 and apply it instead of this rule if it applies. If it doesn't apply, then try to apply this rule. If the conjunct prefix is the unspec object prefix **'**, then go to Rule Conj-5. If the conjunct prefix is the 4 object prefix **hw**, then go to Rule Conj-6.) If the conjunct prefix is the 4 subject prefix **j**, then check to see if Rule Conj-7 applies.

Rule Conj-2: If a conjunct prefix **y** is followed directly by a consonant and preceded by the vowel at the end of a disjunct prefix, then change the **y** to an **i** (Chapter 6.) Note: this **i** acquires a high tone if the following syllable is the verb-stem syllable and the **i** is immediately preceded by a prefix that ends in a high tone (cf. Rule Subj-5.) (Chapter 22) (The sandwiched **y** rule:) if a conjunct prefix **y** is in between two consonants, then change the **y** to **ii** (Chapter 20.) But do not do this if **y** is immediately followed by the 2sg subject prefix **ni**; instead, go to Rule Conj-3 (Chapter 24.)

Rule Conj-3: Let C stand for the consonant at the end of a conjunct prefix. If C is followed immediately by a 2sg subject prefix **ni**, then this **ni** is replaced by **í**, so the combination of the end of the conjunct prefix with the subject prefix looks like this: **Cí**. (Rule Conj-1 doesn't apply in this case.) (Chapter 11) Also: see Rule Conj-6 for the conjunct (object) prefix **hw** (Chapter 12.)

Rule Conj-4: If a conjunct prefix contains a **sh, zh,** or **j**, then this is preferentially changed to an **s, z,** or **dz** if either the verb stem or a prefix between the conjunct prefix in question and the verb stem contains one or more of the consonants **s, z, dz, ts,** or **ts'**. If a conjunct prefix contains an **s, z,** or **dz,** then this is preferentially changed to a **sh, zh,** or **j** if either the verb stem or a prefix between the conjunct prefix in question and the verb stem contains one or more of the consonants: **sh, zh, j, ch,** or **ch'** (Chapter 11.)

Rule Conj-5: If the unspec prefix ' is followed directly by a consonant, insert the vowel **a** between the ' and the consonant following it (Chapter 12.) However, if the unspec prefix ' is preceded by a vowel and the syllable **'a** which we would get by adding the vowel **a** right after ' would not be the pre-stem syllable, then no vowel is inserted after '. (In this case, the ' will end up being followed directly by another consonant.) (Chapter 12) (Exception to last clause: insert **i** after ' if ' is followed directly by **y** and ' was not positioned there by the unspec hopping rule (see below) (Chapter 24.)) If a verb has both the unspec ' and the 4 person **j** as object prefixes, if ' is preceded by a vowel, if **j** is followed by a consonant, and if the syllable which follows **j** is not the verb-stem syllable, then no vowels are inserted either after ' or after **j**, and the ' followed by the **j** together become **zh'** (Chapter 14.) (Unspec hopping rule, a MOVEMENT rule:) if the unspec object prefix ' is preceded by a vowel , is directly in front of a consonant C_1, and if to the right of the C_1 there is a consonant C_2 which is either part of a conjunct prefix (Chapter 15) or the **n** that starts a subject prefix (Chapter 18), and which starts a syllable which is not the verb-stem syllable, then ' hops over to the right and is placed just in front of C_2.

Rule Conj-6:

(a)   If the object prefix **hw** is followed directly by a consonant, then this prefix becomes **ha** if the following syllable is the verb-stem syllable (which means that the syllable **ha** that we get this way is automatically the pre-stem syllable.) But if the following syllable is not the verb-stem syllable, then **hw** becomes **ho** (which is automatically not the pre-stem syllable.) Exception: in the s-P conjugation, if the subject is 3, **hooz** or **hoos** is sometimes used instead of **haz** or **has** (Chapter 12.)

(b)   If **hw** is followed directly by the 2sg subject prefix **ni**, then the **hw** and the **ni** together becomer **hó** (Chapter 12.)

(c)   Normally, if **hw** is followed directly by the vowel **i(i)** or **e(e)**, then no special adjustment is made. If **hw** is followed directly by the vowel **a(a)** or **o(o)**, then the **w** of **hw** disappears and we just get **ha(a)** or **ho(o)** (Chapter 12.)

(d)   (Exceptions to part (c):) however, in the y-P, zero/barred-l conjugation, when **hw** is followed by the 1sg or 3 subject prefix **íí**, this combination of **hw** followed by **íí** regularly becomes **hóó**. (But **hw** followed by the 2sg prefix **ííní** in the y-P conjugation is **hwííní**; that is, part (c) applies normally, in this case.) Also: in the y-P, plain-l/d conjugation, if the subject is 1sg, **hoosh** is sometimes used instead of **hweesh** (Chapter 12.) In the n-I conjugation, and also in the n-P conjugation used with the plain-l/d classifiers, when **hw** is followed by the 3 subject prefix **í**, the combination of these two prefixes comes out as **hó** (Chapter 18.) In the long-vowel-I conjugation, when **hw** is followed by the 1sg subject prefix **iish** or the 2sg/3 prefix **ii**, the combination can become **hoosh** or **hoo** (Chapter 20.) In the long-vowel-P conjugation, when **hw** is followed by the 1sg subject prefix **ii** or **iish** or the 3 prefix **ii**, the combination can become **hoo** or **hoosh** or **hoo** (Chapter 20.)

Rule Conj-7: If the 4 subject prefix **j** is preceded by a vowel and followed by a consonant (other than **j** (Chapter 21)), and the syllable **ji** that we'd get if Rule Conj-1 applied would not be the pre-stem syllable, then no vowel is inserted after the **j**, and, in this case, the **j** is changed to **zh** (Chapter 14.) If a verb has both the unspec ' and the 4 person **j** as object prefixes, if ' is preceded by a vowel, if **j** is followed by a consonant, and if the syllable which follows **j** is not the verb-stem syllable, then no vowels are inserted either after ' or after **j**, and the ' followed by the **j** together become **zh'** (Chapter 14.) (A MOVEMENT rule:) if **j** is followed by both the F mode **d** and the inner **d**, then **j** hops over the F mode **d** and is placed immediately in front of the inner **d** (and the first clause of this rule applies as well) if one of the following situations is also true: (a) there is at least one additional inner prefix in the verb; or (b) at least one of certain prefixes are present in the verb somewhere to the left of the **j**. The prefixes that trigger part (b) include outer **'a** and the seriative prefix **h** (Chapter 21.)

Rule Conj-8:

(a)   Suppose a conjunct high tone is part of a structure like this:

        some conjunct
            prefix

            C   -   high-tone   -   V

(Here "C" is the consonant at the end of the preceding conjunct prefix. This case is where the conjunct high tone is immediately followed by a vowel, represented by "V".) Then:

if V is a short vowel, it acquires a high tone (if it doesn't already have one)

if V is a long vowel or diphthong, then the first vowel letter of V acquires a high tone (if it doesn't already have one)

(b)   Suppose a conjunct high tone is part of a structure like this:

some conjunct
prefix

$$C_1 \quad - \quad \text{high-tone} \quad - \quad C_2$$

(Here "C_1" is the consonant at the end of the preceding conjunct prefix. This case is where the conjunct high tone is immediately followed by a consonant, represented by "C_2".) What happens now depends on what follows C_2. In either case, Rule Conj-1 or Rule Conj-5 or Rule Conj-6 will insert a vowel in between C_1 and C_2, and this vowel acquires a high tone (if it doesn't already have one.) If the syllable following C_2 is the verb-stem syllable, then nothing else happens. But if the syllable following C_2 is not the verb-stem syllable, then the vowel of that syllable acquires a high tone as well, according to the same pattern as described in part (a) (Chapter 21.)

Rule Conj-9: This rule assumes that the basic form of the seriative prefix is **h**, and that the basic position of the seriative prefix is to the left of all other inner prefixes, and also to the left of F mode **d**, but to the right of any object prefixes.

(a)   Form: If the seriative prefix is immediately preceded by a conjunct prefix, then the form of the prefix changes from **h** into **y**. (This applies to the prefix when it is placed at its actual position in the word, that is, after part (d) of this rule moves it around.) Check to see if the sandwiched **y** part of Rule Conj-2 applies to the **y** that has been created by this part of the rule.

(b)   When the seriative (either in the form **h** or in the form **y**) is immediately followed by a subject prefix of the s-P conjugation, the seriative contracts with the subject prefix.

(c)   The seriative in the form **h** undergoes pre-stem vowel harmony.

(d)   Position (a MOVEMENT rule): If the seriative is preceded by an object prefix (not counting 4 person **j**) and followed by one or more conjunct prefixes, then the seriative hops to the right over all the conjunct prefixes and is placed just to the right of the last conjunct prefix. If the only object prefix that precedes the seriative is 4 person **j** and the seriative is followed by a conjunct **d** prefix, then the **j** moves to the right of the seriative. (See also Rule Conj-7, which will apply after this part of Rule Conj-9 has applied.) If the seriative is immediately preceded by the unspec prefix ', check the unspec hopping part of Rule Conj-5 (and apply it) before trying to move the seriative by this rule. If this rule positions the seriative immediately to the right of a conjunct prefix of the form **n**, and if the seriative is followed by a vowel, then the seriative is deleted (Chapter 24.)

RULES INVOLVING DISJUNCT PREFIXES

<u>Rule Disj-1</u>: Whenever the last syllable of a disjunct prefix is the pre-stem syllable and the disjunct prefix is followed by a consonant, make the following changes:

(a)   If the disjunct prefix ends in a short, low-tone **a**, lengthen it to **aa** (Chapter 4.)

(b)   If the disjunct prefix ends in a short, high-tone **í**, change this vowel to short, high-tone **é** (Chapter 7.)

(c)   If the disjunct prefix ends in a short, low-tone **i**, change this vowel to long, low-tone **ee**. Exception: the outer prefix **ni** becomes **nii** (in the rare cases when this outer prefix is in the position for this rule to apply.)

<u>Rule Disj-2</u>: If a disjunct prefix is followed by a vowel, then the following adjustments are made:

(a)   If **a** is followed by **i** or **ii**, then the whole thing becomes **ei** or **eii**, except if the **a** is preceded by **g**, **gh**, **h**, **k**, or **k'**, in which case nothing happens. If the **a** is high tone (that is, **á**), then the new combination is **éi** or **éii** (Chapter 4.)   If high tone **a** (that is **á**) is followed by **í**, then the new combination is **éí**.

(b) If **í** is followed by **ii**, then the whole thing becomes **íi** (Chapter 7.)

(c) If **í** is followed by **o**, then the whole thing becomes **ó** (Chapter 7.)

<u>Rule Disj-3</u>: The syllable **na** becomes **ni**, and the syllable **ná** becomes **ní**, if it is immediately followed by:

(a)   the **j** which indicates 4 person (Chapter 5.)

(b)   the distributive plural prefix **da** (Chapter 5.)

(c)   an s-P subject prefix other than the 3 person prefixes **z** or **s** (Chapter 8.)

(d)   the F mode **d** (Chapter 14) or any inner prefix beginning with **d** (Chapter 21.)

(e)   a cluster of consonants consisting of **zh** or **'** or **zh'** followed directly by the F mode **d** (Chapter 14) or by any inner prefix beginning with **d** (Chapter 21).

(f)   the semeliterative prefix **náá** or **nááná**, or any prefix of the form **ná** (Chapter 22.)

(g)   an s-I subject prefix other than the 3 person zero prefix (Chapter 27.)

Special note: If there is a sequence of prefixes each of the form **na** or **ná**, and if the last one is in a position to change into **ni** or **ní** according to this rule, then the last prefix does not change, but all the other prefixes in this sequence to its left do change. (Incidentally, if there is a sequence like this, the last prefix in the sequence will end up being **ná**. The prefix **na** (with low tone) is never preceded by another **na** or **ná**.)

Convenience note: Rule Disj-3 does not apply:

-- when **na** or **ná** is the pre-stem syllable.

-- when the prefix following **na** or **ná** is an object prefix.

-- when **na** or **ná** is followed by inner **n**, or by a cluster of consonants consisting of **zh** or **'** or **zh'** followed directly by **n**, or by a subject prefix beginning with **n**.

-- when **na** or **ná** is followed by seriative **h** or seriative **y**.

-- when **na** or **ná** is followed by reflexive **'á**.

Rule Disj-4: (Chapter 19)

(a)   Whenever **'a** is followed by a consonant and the **'a** syllable would be the pre-stem syllable, change **'a** into **'ii**.

(b)   If **'a** is followed by **ii** or **o** or **oo**, then **'a** becomes just **'**. Exception: in the O mode, **'a** followed by 1sg **osh** is **'oosh**; **'a** followed by 3 **o** is **'oo**; and **'a** followed by 2sg **óó** is **'oó** (Chapter 23.)

(c)   If **'a** is followed by a conjunct prefix **y** and this **y** is followed directly by a consonant (so that Rule Conj-2 would normally turn the **y** into **i**), the combination of **'a** and **y** becomes **'ii**.

(d)   In the y-P conjugation, the following special changes occur:

If **'a** is followed directly by **v́v́**, the result is **'íí**.

If **'a** is followed directly by **v́ní**, the result is **'ííní**.

If **'a** is followed directly by **vv**, the result is **'ee**.

(e)   If **'a** is followed immediately by the unspec object prefix, then:

(i)   If Rule Conj-5 would insert **a** after the unspec object prefix **'**, the resulting combination **'a'a** changes to **'e'e**. Because of the way Rule Conj-5 works, this will happen just in case the syllable that follows the combination of **'a** with the unspec object prefix is the verb-stem syllable.

(ii)   If the unspec object prefix **'** is followed by a consonant C and Rule Conj-5 would not insert any vowel after **'**, then **'a'**C changes to **'i'**C.

(iii)   If the unspec object prefix **'** is in such a position that Rule Conj-5 would create the combination **zh'**C (where C is a consonant), then **'azh'**C changes to **'izh'**C.

(iv)   If the unspec object prefix **'** is followed directly by a 2sg subject prefix **ni** so that Rule Conj-2 applies, then the resulting combination **'a'í** becomes **'i'í**.

(v)   If the unspec object prefix **'** is followed by a (long or short) vowel (of either high or low tone), then **'a'** becomes **'V'**, where V is the vowel that follows the unspec object prefix; that is, the vowel that follows the unspec **'** substitutes for the **a** of **'a**. However, the syllable **'V** (from **'a**) always has a short vowel and low tone. (More simply: if **'a'** is followed by a vowel, the **a** is changed to match that vowel.)

PART B: SUBJECT PREFIXES

IMPERFECTIVE MODE

Regular I mode conjugation (Chapter 4):

	sg	dpl
1	sh	iid
2	ni	oh
3	zero	

n-I conjugation (Chapter 18):

	sg	dpl
1	nish	niid
2	ní	noh
3	(see (*))	

(*)

If the 3 subject prefix is preceded by:	the 3 subject prefix is:
an outer prefix	zero
distr pl **da**	zero or **í**
an object prefix	**í** (**hw+í --> hó**)
an inner prefix	**ee**
no prefix at all	**yí**

Long-vowel-I mode conjugation (Chapter 20):

not preceded by a disjunct prefix:

	sg	dpl
1	iish	iid
2	ii	ooh
3	ii	

preceded by a disjunct prefix:

	sg	dpl
1	ish	iid
2	i	ooh
3	i (but **yii** after **da**)	

s-I conjugation (Chapter 27):

	sg	dpl
1	shish	siid
2	sí	soh
3	zero	

The regular I, long-vowel I , and s-I subject prefixes are also used for the regular R, long-vowel R, and s-R conjugations, and for the regular U, long-vowel U, and s-U conjugations.

PERFECTIVE MODE

s-P conjugation (Chapter 8):

zero/barred-l classifiers:

	sg	dpl
1	sé	siid
2	síní	soo
3	z or s	

plain-l/d classifiers:

	sg	dpl
1	sis	siid
2	síní	sooh
3	s	

y-P conjugation (Chapters 9 and 10):

zero/barred-l classifiers:

preceded by a disjunct prefix:

	sg	dpl
1	v́v́	iid
2	v́íní	oo
3	v́v́	

preceded by a conjunct prefix:

	sg	dpl
1	íí	iid
2	ííní	oo
3	íí	

preceded by no prefix:

	sg	dpl
1	yí	yiid
2	yíní	woo
3	yí	

plain-ł/d classifiers:

| preceded by a disjunct prefix: | preceded by a conjunct prefix: | preceded by no prefix: |

	sg	dpl
1	vvsh	iid
2	víní	ooh
3	vv	

	sg	dpl
1	eesh	iid
2	ííní	ooh
3	oo	

	sg	dpl
1	yish	yiid
2	yíní	wooh
3	yi	

n-P conjugation (Chapter 18)

zero/barred-l classifiers:

	sg	dpl
1	ní	niid
2	víni/ííní/yíní	noo
3	ní	

plain-ł/d classifiers:

	sg	dpl
1	nish	niid
2	víni/ííní/yíní	nooh
3	(see (*))	

(*)

If the 3 subject prefix is preceded by:	the 3 subject prefix is:
an outer prefix	zero
distr pl **da**	zero or í
an object prefix	í (hw+í --> hó)
an inner prefix	ee
no prefix at all	yí

418

Long-vowel-P conjugation (Chapter 20):

zero/barred-l classifiers:

not preceded by a
disjunct prefix:

	sg	dpl
1	ii	iid
2	(see (**))	oo
3	ii	

preceded by a disjunct prefix:

	sg	dpl
1	i	iid
2	ini	oo
3	i (but **yii** after **da**)	

plain-l/d classifiers:

not preceded by a
disjunct prefix:

	sg	dpl
1	iish	iid
2	(see (**))	ooh
3	ii	

preceded by a disjunct prefix:

	sg	dpl
1	ish	iid
2	ini	ooh
3	i (but **yii** after **da**)	

(**) The long-vowel-P, 2sg subject prefix, when not preceded by a disjunct prefix, is:

iini when preceded by an object prefix
ini otherwise.

FUTURE MODE

Regular F mode conjugation (Chapter 14):   Long-vowel-F conjugation (Chapter 20):

	sg	dpl
1	d-eesh	d-iid
2	d-íí	d-ooh
3	d-oo	

> Same as regular F mode conjugation, except that, in addition, **y** is placed immediately in front of F mode **d**.

OPTATIVE MODE

Regular O mode conjugation (Chapter 23):

Long-vowel O mode conjugation (Chapter 23):

not preceded by disjunct prefix:

	sg	dpl
1	ósh	ood
2	óó	ooh
3	ó	

preceded by disjunct prefix:

	sg	dpl
1	osh	ood
2	óó	ooh
3	o	

	sg	dpl
1	oosh	ood
2	oó	ooh
3	oo	

PROGRESSIVE MODE

Subject prefixes used when distributive **da** is not present:

preceded by no
other prefix:

	sg	dpl
1	yish	yiid
2	yí	woh
3	yi	

preceded by a
conjunct prefix:

	sg	dpl
1	eesh	iid
2	íí	ooh
3	oo	

preceded by a
disjunct prefix:

	sg	dpl
1	vvsh	iid
2	v́v́	oh
3	vv	

Subject prefixes used when distributive **da** is present:

With **da**, with no
conjunct prefixes:

1	deíníid
2	deínóh
3	deí

When **da** is used, and
preceded by a
conjunct prefix:

1	ííníid
2	íínóh
3	ée/í

PART C: VOCABULARY PRINCIPLES

Below are all the vocabulary principles that were introduced in the text. Each one is represented with the help of the shorthand notation developed in Chapter 27 (see also the Verb Base Index for a list of the abbreviations for stem-set types.)

Included are all the formally presented and numbered vocabulary principles. In addition, principles described in the text but not given a number are also shown (as "Vocabulary-(unnumbered)".)

<u>Vocabulary-1</u>: creates verb bases denoting random and round-trip motion

      motion verb themes plus: **na**+cont:+S (Chapter 17)

<u>Vocabulary-2</u>: creates verb bases denoting "be going"

      motion verb themes plus: **d**+mom:+S (Chapter 17)

<u>Vocabulary-3</u>: creates completive verb bases

      motion verb themes plus: mom:+simple (Chapter 18)

<u>Vocabulary-4</u>: creates expressions denoting motion into a thing (denoted by P)

      combine **Piih** with a completive verb (Chapter 18)

<u>Vocabulary-5</u>: creates verb bases denoting motion up to a place

      motion verb themes plus: mom:+N (Chapter 18)

<u>Vocabulary-(unnumbered)</u>: creates expressions denoting "give it to him/her"

      combine **Paa** with verb bases created by Vocabulary-5 using classificatory transitive motion verb themes (Chapter 18)

<u>Vocabulary-6</u>: creates verb bases denoting motion off

      motion verb themes plus: **'a**+mom:+simple (Chapter 19)

Vocabulary-7: creates expressions denoting motion into an area

     combine **yah** with verb bases created by Vocabulary-6 (Chapter 19)

Vocabulary-8: creates verb bases denoting motion horizontally out of an area

     motion verb themes plus: **ch'í**+mom:N (Chapter 19)

Vocabulary-9 and Vocabulary-10: create semelfactive verb bases

     certain verb themes plus: O+sem:+SLV (Chapter 20)

Vocabulary-11: creates simple transitional verb bases

     certain verb themes plus: mom:(or trans:)+FLV (Chapter 20)

Vocabulary-12: creates transitional inceptive verb bases

     motion verb themes plus: **d**+mom:+LV (Chapter 20)

Vocabulary-13: creates inchoative transitional verb bases

     certain verb themes plus Pi+'+**n**+mom:+LV (Chapter 21)

Vocabulary-14: creates semeliterative verb bases

     verb bases plus **nááná**+(restricted)classifier-shift (Chapter 22)

Vocabulary-15: creates reversionary verb bases

     motion verb bases plus **ná**+(restricted)classifier-shift (Chapter 22)

Vocabulary-(unnumbered): creates verb bases denoting "pick it up"

     classificatory transitive motion verb themes plus **ná**+O+**d**+mom:+LV (Chapter 22)

Vocabulary-16: creates seriative verb bases

     motion verb bases plus **h/y**(+simple and N become S) (Chapter 24)

<u>Vocabulary-17</u>: creates verb themes denoting "take it down (from a peg or shelf)"

motion verb themes plus **na**+O+'+**d**+mom:+LV (Chapter 24)

<u>Vocabulary-18</u>: creates cursive verb bases

motion verb themes plus curs:+Pg (Chapter 25)

<u>Vocabulary</u>-(unnumbered): creates expressions denoting "set it up on a shelf"

combine **dah** with verb bases created from classificatory transitive motion verb themes plus mom:+DS (Chapter 27)

<u>Vocabulary</u>-(unnumbered): creates verb bases denoting "hit with a single blow"

certain transitive verb themes of physical action plus **ná**+**d**+mom:+YLV (Chapter 27)

<u>Vocabulary</u>-(unnumbered): creates verb bases denoting an action of physical contact consisting of a series of contacts

certain transitive verb themes of physical contact plus **ná**+**n**+rep:+S (Chapter 27)

<u>Vocabulary</u>-(unnumbered): creates verb bases denoting "uncover it"

certain verb themes plus Pą́ą́+'+**d**+mom:+simple (Chapter 27)

<u>Vocabulary</u>-(unnumbered): creates verb bases denoting "close something"

certain verb themes plus **dá**+'+**d**+mom:+N (Chapter 27)

BIBLIOGRAPHY

The materials referred to many times in the text as "YM" are the following two books:

Young, Robert W. and William Morgan Sr. (1987) The Navajo Language: A Grammar and Colloquial Dictionary. (2nd Edition) Albuquerque: University of New Mexico Press.

Young, Robert W., William Morgan Sr., and Sally Midgette (1992) Analytical Lexicon of Navajo. Albuquerque: University of New Mexico Press.

In addition to these two books, the following new book should be thought of as being part of the YM materials:

Young, Robert W. (in press) The Navajo Verb System: An Overview. Fairbanks: Alaskan Native Language Center.

If you are interested in the scholarly study of the Navajo verb, the bibliographies in the above books will start you off. One important older work which I have cited in the text is:

Kari, James (1976) Navajo Verb Prefix Phonology. New York: Garland Publishing, Inc.

For more recent work, you may wish to have a look at the following two books, each of which is a collection of papers. Many of the papers in them are about Navajo, and some deal specifically with the verb.

Fernald, Theodore B. and Paul Platero (eds.) (in press) Athabaskan: Language & Linguistics. Oxford University Press.

Jelinek, Eloise, Sally Midgette, Keren Rice, and Leslie Saxon (eds.) (1996) Athabaskan Language Studies: Essays in Honor of Robert W. Young. Albuquerque: University of New Mexico Press.

The following recent book does not deal with the forms of Navajo verb, but you may find it interesting as a study of the usage of one of the modes:

Midgette, Sally (1995) The Navajo Progressive In Discourse: A Study in Temporal Semantics. New York: Peter Lang.

To cnd off, here is a list of Navajo language textbooks and dictionaries which appear to be available at this time:

de los Santos, Roman (1995) The English-Navajo Children's Picture Dictionary: Selected words and phrases. Tsaile, Arizona: Navajo Communicty College Press.

Goossen, Irvy W. (1995) Diné Bizaad: Speak, Read, Write Navajo. Flagstaff, Arizona: Salina Bookshelf.

Navajo Language Institute (1986) Diné Bizaad Bóhoo'aah. Farmington, New Mexico.

Neundorf, Alice (1983) Áłchíní Bi Naaltsoostsoh: A Navajo/English Bilingual Dictionary. Albuquerque: Native American Materials Development Center.

Parnwell, E.C. (1989) The New Oxford Picture Dictionary, English/Navajo Edition. Translated by Marvin Yellowhair. Oxford University Press.

Wilson, Alan (1969) Breakthrough Navajo. Gallup, New Mexico: University of New Mexico at Gallup.

Wilson, Garth (1989) Conversational Navajo Dictionary. Blanding, Utah: Conversational Navajo Publications.

Young, Robert W. and William Morgan Sr (1994) Colloquial Navajo: A Dictionary. New York: Hippocrene.

VERB BASE INDEX

The entries in this index are given using the shorthand developed in Chapter 27. Prefixes are listed in the order in which they appear in the verb. The symbols "P" and "O" are used for object prefixes the way these were defined in the text. The classifier is indicated immediately in front of the stem-set type. The conjugation pattern is shown following the root, using the notations found in Chapter 27(4), except for neuters where the (only) mode is shown.

The following abbreviations are used for stem-set types:

concl (conclusive)
cont (continuative)
curs (cursive)
dur (durative)
mom (momentaneous)
neut (neuter)
neut(abs) (absolute neuter)
neut(comp) (comparative neuter)
rep (repetitive)
rev (reversative)
sem (semelfactive)
trans (transitional)

The stem-set type terminology, as well as the choice of which type to assign to the stem-set of each verb base, follows the practice of YMM 92, to facilitate the reader's use of that work as a reference.

The entries are alphabetized according to the following order: **a, b, ch, ch', d, dl, dz, e, g, gh, h, hw, i, j, k, k', kw, ', l, ł, m, n, o, s, sh, t, t', tł, tł', ts, ts', w, y, z, zh**. Double (i.e. long) vowels are alphabetized as written (i.e. assuming two characters for the vowel.) High-tone marks and nasal hooks are ignored. The glottal stop symbol ' is ignored at the beginning of verb stems and in the prefixes **'a** and **'á**, but otherwise is alphabetized as indicated above, after **kw** and before **l**. The symbol **h/y** (for the seriative) is alphabetized as **h** followed by **y**.

Only the boldface characters in an entry (that is, the ones that represent real sounds) count for alphabetization! The remaining characters in the entry are ignored. For example, the first entry in the index is alphabetized as though it were spelled **aaazh**, the second as though it were spelled **aa'dgeed**, etc.

A subentry labelled "stem-set" references a comment concerning the forms of some of the stems in the stem-set for that verb base.

'a+zero+mom:**'áázh**+simple "go off (dual)" 236, 239, 240, 246
      I, P, and F mode chart 240
      verb base 239

P**ą́ą́**+'+**d**+barred-l+mom:**geed**+simple "uncover it (outer object) by digging" 176-180, 335, 403
      F mode chart 178
      I mode chart 177
      O mode chart 335
      P mode chart 178
      verb base 176

O+zero+dur:**'aal**+simple "chew it" 93-95
      P mode chart 93
      stem-set 93
      verb base 93

zero+mom:**'áázh**+simple "go (dual)" 217, 218
      I, P, and F mode chart 218
      verb base 217

zero+mom:**'áázh**+N "get to (a place) (dual)" 228, 229
      I, P, and F mode chart 229
      reversionary added 324
      verb base 228

zero+curs:**'áázh**+Pg "be on the way (dual)" 365
      Pg mode chart 365

'a+**dz**+zero+mom:**táál**+simple "let fly a kick" 388, 389

'ah+**d**+mom:**ghą́ą́'**+simple "fight" 376

'a+O+**h/y**+barred-l+mom:**mááz**+S "roll them away one after another" 352

'a+**d**+mom:**kai**+simple "go off (plural)" 240, 241, 246
      I, P, and F mode chart 240
      verb base 240

'a+**nááná**+**d**+mom:**yá**+simple (irreg.) "go off again (singular)" 317, 318

'a+'+barred-l+mom:**na'**+simple "have a bite to eat" 242-245
      F mode chart 245
      I mode chart 242
      P mode chart 244
      verb base 242

'a+O+zero+mom:**lá**+simple "carry it (a ropelike thing) off" 237, 246-249
      F mode chart 248
      I mode chart 246
      P mode chart 247

'á+barred-l+neut(comp):**nééz**+neuter-n-I(almost) "be this much tall" 297, 298

'á+zero+neut:**t'e'**+neuter-n-I "be" 300
      I mode chart 300

'a+zero+mom:**yá**+simple (irreg.) "go off (singular)" 236, 238, 239, 246, 317
    I, P, and F mode chart 239
    semeliterative added 318
    verb base 238
O+barred-l+concl:**béézh**+S "boil it" 55-58, 79, 92, 155, 335, 379, 395
    classifier 66
    F mode chart 155
    I mode chart 55
    P mode chart 73
    semeliterative added 316, 317
    stem-set 65
    telic activity 67
    verb base 55, 64
zero+concl:**béézh**+S "be boiling" 380, 381
zero+dur:**cha**+simple "cry" 52-57, 82-85, 91, 92, 149-151, 155, 334, 335, 395
    atelic activity 67
    classifier 66
    F mode chart 149
    I mode chart 55
    O mode chart 334
    P mode chart 91
    stem-set 65
    verb base 52, 64
O+zero+rep:**ch'id**+simple "scratch it" 371
ch'í+O+h/y+barred-l+mom:**mááz**+S "roll them out one after another" 351
ch'í+zero+mom:**mááz**+N "roll out" 381
ch'í+d+mom:**na'**+N "crawl out" 253, 254
    P mode chart 254
ch'í+**ná**+d+mom:**zid**+N "wake up" 319, 323, 340
    semeliterative added 324
ch'í+**ná**+O+barred-l+mom:**zid**+N "wake him/her up" 319, 322, 323, 335
    verb base 322
ch'í+**ná**+**nááná**+d+mom:**zid**+N "wake up again" 324
ch'í+O+barred-l+mom:**tį**+N "carry him/her (an animate thing) out" 251-253, 330
    F mode chart 253
    I mode chart 251
    P mode chart 252
    R mode chart 330
    verb base 251
d+zero+mom:**'áázh**+S "be going (dual)" 209-211
    I, P, and F mode chart 210
    verb base 209

d+zero+mom:**'áázh**+LV "start to go (dual)" 278
      I, P, and F mode chart 278
dá+**'**+**d**+barred-l+mom:**kaal**+N "close (a door or house)" 405
d+plain-l+mom:**'eez**+simple "step" 162, 163
      F mode chart 163
      I mode chart 162
      P mode chart 162
      verb base 162
d+zero+mom:**go'**+S "fall" 164, 165
      F mode chart 165
      I mode chart 165
      P mode chart 165
      stem-set 164
      verb base 164
di+O+**d**+barred-l+mom:**jéé'**+simple "make it (a fire)" 170-172
      F mode chart 171
      I mode chart 170
      P mode chart 171
      verb base 170
d+d+mom:**kai**+S "be going (plural)" 210, 211
      I, P, and F mode chart 211
      verb base 210
d+d+mom:**kai**+LV "start to go (plural)" 278
      I, P, and F mode chart 278
O+**d**+barred-l+mom:**mááz**+LV "start to roll it" 279
d+d+mom:**na'**+S "be crawling" 212-214
      verb base 214
d+d+mom:**na'**+LV "start to crawl" 279
(**d**)+zero+neut:**niid**+I-only (irreg.) "say" 188-191
      I mode chart 189
      verb base 188
d+zero+mom:**niid**+simple "say" 191
      verb base 191
P+(**d**)+zero(barred-l)+neut:**niid**+I-only (irreg.) "say to him/her (object)" 189-191
      I mode chart 190
      verb base 190
P+**d**+zero+mom:**niid**+simple "say to him/her (object)" 191
      verb base 191
d+plain-l+mom:**nish**+S "start to work" 166
      P mode chart 166
      verb base 166

O+d+high-tone+n+barred-l+mom:**kaad**+S "start to herd them (animals)" 291-293
    F mode chart 292
    I mode chart 291
    P mode chart 292
    verb base 291
O+d+barred-l+mom:**tí**+S "be carrying him/her" 212
    verb base 212
O+d+barred-l+mom:**tí**+LV "start to carry him/her" 279
d+zero+mom:**yá**+S (irreg.) "be going (singular)" 209-211
    I, P, and F mode chart 110
    verb base 209
d+zero+mom:**yá**+LV (irreg.) "start to go (singular)" 276-278
    I, P, and F mode chart 277
O+d+barred-l+mom:**yíí'**+simple "melt it" 158-161
    F mode chart 161
    I mode chart 159
    P mode chart 160
    verb base 158
O+d+dur:**dlą́ą́'**+simple "drink it" 102-106, 127, 329, 330, 331, 395
    P mode chart 103
    P mode chart with unspec prefix 127
    R mode chart 329
    stem-set 103
    U mode chart 333
    verb base 103
d+mom:**dzíí'**+simple "remain" 105, 106
    P mode chart 105
    stem-set 105
    verb base 105
dz+zero+mom:**táál**+simple "give a kick" 389
dz+yn+d+mom:**li'**+S "become confident" 389
O+zero+sem:**gizh**+SLV "make one cut in it (object)" 257-259, 261
    I mode chart 257
    verb base 257
O+zero+mom:**gháád**+simple "shake it" 393
O+zero+sem:**gháád**+SLV "give it a shake" 393
ha+O+zero+mom:**'á**+simple "take/pull it up and out (a compact rigid object)" 374
ha+O+d+barred-l+mom:**bįįd**+simple (irreg. P mode) "fill with it (object)" 192, 193
    P mode chart 192
    verb base 192

ha+O+zero+mom:**geed**+simple "dig it out" 87-89, 93, 176
      P mode chart 88
      verb base 88

ha+O+barred-l+mom:**gizh**+simple "cut it out" 45-50, 58, 84, 85, 90, 91, 93, 259
      classifier 66
      I mode chart 45
      P mode chart 91
      stem-set 65
      telic activity 67
      verb base 50, 64

ha+**ná**+O+barred-l+mom:**tį**+simple "carry him/her back up out" 320-322
      I mode chart 321

ha+O+n+barred-l+mom:**chaad**+simple "card it (wool)" 283-285, 287
      F mode chart 284
      I mode chart 283
      P mode chart 284
      verb base 283

ha+plain-l+mom:**táál**+simple "dash up out" 98-101
      P mode chart 99
      stem-set 98
      verb base 98

ha+O+barred-l+mom:**tį**+simple "carry him/her up out of something" 109-116, 147, 155, 156, 377, 378
      F mode chart 156
      reversionary added 320-322
          chart 321
      stem-set 109
      verb base 109

h/y+d+curs:**cha'**+Pg "be hobbling along" 368
      Pg mode chart 368

O+**h/y**+barred-l+mom:**mááz**+S "roll them one after another" 342-351
      F mode chart 346
      I mode chart 344
      P mode chart 345
      pre-stem vowel harmony in R mode 348-351
      verb base 342

hw+plain-l+dur:**ne'**+simple "talk about" 130-132, 135, 147, 156
      F mode chart 156
      I mode chart 130
      P mode chart 132
      verb base 130

hw+zero+dur:**táál**+simple "sing" 132-135
       P mode chart 133
       stem-set 132, 133
       verb base 132
Pighá+O+barred-l+mom:**geed**+N "pierce him/her (outer object) with it (object)" 373
Pí+hw+barred-l+trans:**'áá'**+FLV "learn it (outer object)" 273-275
       F mode chart 274
       I mode chart 273
       P mode chart 274
       verb base 273
O+zero+curs/neut?:**'íí'**+I-only (irreg.) "see it" 187-188, 310
       I mode chart 187
       I mode chart with unspec prefix 188
       verb base 187
Pik'í+O+d+zero+rev:**diz**+S "wrap it (object) around it (outer object)" 174-176
       F mode chart 175
       I mode chart 175
       P mode chart 175
       verb base 174
Pi+'+n+barred-l+mom:**yíí'**+LV "start to melt it" 290
Pi+na+plain-l+cont:**nish**+S "work on it (outer object)" 172-174
       I mode chart 172
       verb base 173
Piza+O+h/y+zero+mom:**lá**+S "put them (ropelike things, object) one after another into his/her (outer object) mouth" 399
j+yn+zero+mom:**ba'**+S "behave kindly" 304, 305, 307, 308, 403
       I mode chart 304
       P mode chart 307
       verb base 304
d+mom:**kai**+simple "go (plural)" 217, 218
       I, P, and F mode chart 218
       verb base 217
d+mom:**kai**+N "get to (a place) (plural)" 228-231
       I, P, and F mode chart 230
       reversionary added 324
       verb base 228
d+curs:**kai**+Pg "be on the way (plural)" 365
       Pg mode chart 365
'+zero+curs/neut?:**'íí'**+I-only (irreg.) "see" 188, 266
       I mode chart 188

'+zero+concl:**tł'ǫ́**+S "weave" 127, 128, 147, 151-153
      F mode chart 151
      I mode chart 123
      P mode chart 126
      stem-set 122
      verb base 128
'+zero+dur:**yą́ą́'**+simple (irreg.) "eat" 186, 249
      P mode chart 186
'+**yn**+high-tone+barred-l+rep:**ta'**+simple "go to school" 304, 308, 336
'+plain-l+rep:**zhiizh**+simple "dance" 138, 139, 141
      I mode chart 138
      P mode chart 139
      stem-set 138
      verb base 138
O+zero+mom:**lá**+simple "move it (a ropelike thing)" 220, 224
O+zero+mom:**lá**+N "take it (a ropelike thing) to (a place)" 232, 233
O+zero+mom:**lá**+DS "set it (a ropelike thing)" 384
zero+neut:**líí'**+neuter-n-I "be" 300, 301
      I mode chart 301
      verb base 300
łe+'+zero+mom:**geed**+simple "dig (a cellar or pit, in the ground)" 399
O+barred-l+mom:**mááz**+simple "roll it" 223
      verb base 223
O+barred-l+mom:**mááz**+N "roll it to (a place)" 233
O+barred-l+curs:**mááz**+Pg "be rolling it along" 367
      Pg mode chart 367
na+zero+cont:**'áázh**+S "go (dual) around" 198, 202, 205
      I, P, and F mode chart 202
      verb base 198
ná+d+curs:**'áázh**+Pg "be on the way back (dual)" 366
      Pg mode chart 366
nááná+O+barred-l+concl:**béézh**+S "boil more stuff" 316, 317
ná+O+d+barred-l+mom:**ghaal**+YLV "hit him/her once with a club" 385
ná+O+d+zero+mom:**kaad**+YLV "give him/her one slap" 385
ná+O+d+zero+mom:**lá**+LV "pick it up (a ropelike object)" 324, 325
      reversionary added 324, 325
ná+O+barred-l+mom:**ne'**+YLV "hit it once with a solid roundish object" 385
na+zero+cont:**'éél**+S "float around" 382
na+O+h/y+barred-l+cont:**nii'**+S "buy it" 340, 341
ná+O+h/y+n+zero+rev:**'izh**+S "sew it (a moccasin)" 360

na+hw+zero+**lin**+neuter-n-I "look like" 298
      I mode chart 298
      verb base 298
na+O+barred-l+cont:**káá'**+S "investigate it" 72, 73
      P mode chart 72
      verb base 72
na+d+cont:**kai**+S "go (plural) around" 198, 202, 205
      I, P, and F mode chart 202
      verb base 198
ná+d+curs:**kai**+Pg "be on the way back (plural)" 366
      Pg mode chart 366
d+mom:**na'**+simple "crawl" 219
      verb base 219
d+mom:**na'**+N "crawl to (a place) 231
na+'+zero+cont:**'éél**+S "float around (unspec conveyance)" 382
na+O+'+h/y+d+zero+mom:**lá**+LV "take them down one after another (ropelike things)" 358-
      360
      I mode chart 358
      P mode chart 360
na+O+zero+cont:**lá**+S "carry it (a ropelike thing) around" 140-142, 156, 157, 204, 205, 234
      F mode chart 157
      I mode chart 140
      P mode chart 142
      stem-set irregularity 140, 141
      verb base 140
na+**nááná**+zero+cont:**ne'**+S "play some more" 315, 316
na+d+cont:**na'**+S "crawl around" 41-43, 79, 80, 204, 205, 213, 234
      atelic activity 67
      classifier 66
      I mode chart 43
      P mode chart 76
      verb base 76
na+zero+cont:**ne'**+S "play" 7, 8, 13, 17, 18, 20, 22, 24-28, 31, 33-38, 70, 71, 79, 80, 233, 234,
      330, 331, 381
      atelic activity 67
      classifier 66
      I mode chart 22, 37
      P mode chart 70
      R mode chart 330
      semeliterative added 315, 316
      stem-set 18, 65
      verb base 50, 64

na+plain-l+cont:**nish**+S "work" 47-49, 79, 154, 166, 167, 172, 174, 335
    atelic activity 67
    classifier 66
    F mode chart 154
    I mode chart 47
    O mode chart 335
    P mode chart 75
    verb base 75
na+'+zero+cont:**nish**+S "work goes on" 382
na+O+n+barred-l+cont:**kaad**+S "herd them (animals)" 288, 289, 291
    P mode chart 289
    verb base 288
ná+O+n+zero+rep:**táál**+S "give him/her a kicking" 371, 372
ná+O+n+zero+rep:**ts'ǫ́ǫz**+S "give him/her a series of kisses" 1, 394, 404
na+O+barred-l+cont:**tį**+S "carry him/her around" 116-120, 204, 205
    verb base 116
na+zero+cont:**yá**+S (irreg.) "go (singular) around" 197-203, 205, 230
    I, P, and F mode chart 201
    verb base 197
ná+d+curs:**yá**+Pg (irreg.) "be on the way back (singular)" 366
    Pg mode chart 366
zero+neut(abs):**neez**+neuter-n-I "be tall" 296-298
    I mode chart 296
    verb base 296
barred-l+neut(comp):**nééz**+neuter-n-I(almost) "be how tall" 297, 298
    I mode chart 297
    verb base 297
ni+dz+barred-l+mom:**ts'in**+N "strike with the fist" 389
O+n+high-tone+barred-l+dur:**'įį'**+simple (irreg.) "look at it" 310, 311, 375, 376
    I mode chart 310
    P mode chart 311
    verb base 310
ni+'+h/y+zero+mom:**la'**+S "make a series of payments" 353-357
    F mode chart 356
    I mode chart 354
    P mode chart 355
    verb base 353
ni+tsí+zero+concl:**kééz**+S "think" 61, 62, 402
    classifier 66
    I mode chart 62
    stem-set 65
    verb base 61, 64

n+plain-l+mom:**jį́įd**+S "squat down" 289
    P mode chart 289
    verb base 289
(O)+**n**+zero+neut:**zį́į'**+neuter-I (irreg.) "want it/think" 183-185
    I mode chart 184
    verb base 183
so+**d**+plain-l+dur:**yįįd**+simple "pray" 168-170, 181, 182
    F mode chart 170
    I mode chart 169
    P mode chart 169
    verb base 168
shó+(O)+(**yn**?)+barred-l+mom:**t'e'**+S? "get it" 391
O+barred-l+mom:**tį́**+simple "move it (an animate thing)" 220, 221
O+barred-l+mom:**tį́**+N "take it (an animate thing) to (a place)" 232
zero+neut:**t'e'**+neuter-n-I "be in a condition" 299, 300
    I mode chart 299
    verb base 299
O+zero+concl:**tł'ǫ́**+S "weave it" 122-126, 147, 151-153, 395
    F mode chart with unspec prefix 151
    I mode chart 125
    I mode chart with unspec prefix 123
    P mode chart with unspec prefix 126
    stem-set 122
    verb base 122
O+barred-l+trans:**tsą́**+FLV "see it" 266, 267, 270-272, 395
    P mode chart 267
    verb base 266
O+zero+sem:**ts'ǫ́ǫz**+SLV "kiss him/her (once)" 262, 263, 331, 337, 404
    F mode chart 263
    I mode chart 263
    O mode chart 337
    P mode chart 263
    R mode chart 331
    verb base 262
zero+mom:**yá**+simple (irreg.) "go (singular)" 216-219, 338
    I, P, and F mode chart 217
    verb base 216
zero+mom:**yá**+N (irreg.) "get to (a place) (singular)" 228-231
    I, P, and F mode chart 228
    reversionary added 324
    reversionary and semeliterative added 323, 324
    verb base 228

zero+curs:**yá**+Pg (irreg.) "be on the way (singular)" 365
       Pg mode chart 365
O+zero+dur:**yą́ą́'**+simple (irreg.) "eat it" 185-186, 314, 338, 395
       F mode chart 186
       I mode chart 185
       P mode chart 186
       P mode chart with unspec prefix 186
       verb base 185
yá+**ná**+**dz**+barred-l+mom:**don**+FLV "shoot into the air" 389
yá+barred-l+dur:**ti'**+simple "speak" 59, 60, 82, 83, 87, 95, 96, 317
       classifier 66
       I mode chart 59
       P mode chart 96
       stem-set 65
       verb base 59, 64
O+**y**+barred-l+mom:**bá**+S "earn it" 390
O+barred-l+mom:**yíí'**+simple "melt it (snow)" 142-144
       I mode chart 143
       P mode chart 144
       stem-set 142
       verb base 142
O+**yn**+high-tone+d+mom:**dzíí'**+simple "curse him/her out" 306, 307
       P mode chart 307
       verb base 306
O+**yn**+high-tone+barred-l+rep:**ta'**+simple "read it" 303, 304, 306, 308, 332, 336
       I mode chart 304
       O mode chart 336
       P mode chart 306
       semeliterative added 317
       verb base 303
y+(**y?**)+zero+concl:**nah**+S? "forget" 390, 391
zero+neut:**zį'**+s-P "stand" 78
       P mode chart 78
       verb base 78
d+trans:**zhį́į́'**+FLV "become black" 267, 268, 272, 395
       I mode chart 268
       P mode chart 268
       verb base 267
O+barred-l+dur:**zhóó'**+simple "brush it" 144, 145
       I mode chart 144
       P mode chart 145
       verb base 144

ENGLISH VERB INDEX

Below is an alphabetic list of English verbs corresponding to the Navajo verb bases that are discussed in the text. Each English verb is translated into one (or occasionally two) Navajo verb bases, which are represented using the shorthand developed in Chapter 27 - see also the Verb Base Index for more information on this notation and for the abbreviations used for stem-set types. The singular, dual, and plural forms of go-verbs are given separate entries, in the order mentioned.

be: **'á**+zero+neut:**t'e'**+neuter-n-I; zero+neut:**líí'**+neuter-n-I
be boiling: zero+concl:**béézh**+S
be carrying him/her: O+**d**+barred-l+mom:**tį**+S
be crawling: **d**+d+mom:**na'**+S
be going (singular): **d**+zero+mom:**yá**+S
be going (dual): **d**+zero+mom:**'áázh**+S
be going (plural): **d**+d+mom:**kai**+S
be hobbling along: **h/y**+d+curs:**cha'**+Pg
be how tall: barred-l+neut(comp):**nééz**+neuter-n-I(almost)
be in a condition: zero+neut:**t'e'**+neuter-n-I
be on the way (singular): zero+curs:**yá**+Pg
be on the way (dual): zero+curs:**'áázh**+Pg
be on the way (plural): d+curs:**kai**+Pg
be on the way back (singular): **ná**+d+curs:**yá**+Pg
be on the way back (dual): **ná**+d+curs:**'áázh**+Pg
be on the way back (plural): **ná**+d+curs:**kai**+Pg
be rolling it along: O+barred-l+curs:**mááz**+Pg
be tall: zero+neut(abs):**neez**+neuter-n-I
be this much tall: **'á**+barred-l+neut(comp):**nééz**+neuter-n-I(almost)
become black: d+trans:**zhįį'**+FLV
become confident: **dz**+yn+d+mom:**li'**+S
behave kindly: **j**+yn+zero+mom:**ba'**+S
bite: see "have a bite to eat"
black: see "become black"
boil it: O+barred-l+concl:**béézh**+S
boil more stuff: **nááná**+O+barred-l+concl:**béézh**+S
boiling: see "be boiling"
brush it: O+barred-l+dur:**zhóó'**+simple
buy it: **na**+O+h/y+barred-l+cont:**nii'**+S
card it (wool): **ha**+O+n+barred-l+mom:**chaad**+simple
carry: see also "be carrying", "start to carry"
carry him/her around: **na**+O+barred-l+cont:**tį**+S

carry him/her back up out: **ha**+**ná**+O+barred-l+mom:**tį́**+simple

carry him/her out: **ch'í**+O+barred-l+mom:**tį́**+N

carry him/her up out: **ha**+O+barred-l:mom:**tį́**+simple

carry it (ropelike thing) around: **na**+O+zero+cont:**lá**+S

carry it (ropelike thing) off: **'a**+O+zero+mom:**lá**+simple

chew it: O+zero+dur:**'aal**+simple

close: **dá**+**'**+**d**+barred-l+mom:**kaal**+N

confident: see "become confident"

crawl: see also "be crawling", "start to crawl"

crawl: d+mom:**na'**+simple

crawl around: **na**+d+cont:**na'**+S

crawl to (a place): d+mom:**na'**+N

crawl out: **ch'í**+d+mom:**na'**+N

cry: zero+dur:**cha**+simple

curse him/her out: O+**yn**+high-tone+d+mom:**dzíí'**+simple

cut: see also "make one cut"

cut it out: **ha**+O+barred-l+mom:**gizh**+simple

dance: **'**+plain-l+rep+**zhiizh**+simple

dash up out: **ha**+plain-l+mom:**táál**+simple

dig (celler, in the ground): **łe**+**'**+zero+mom:**geed**+simple

dig it out: **ha**+O+zero+mom:**geed**+simple

drink it: O+d+dur:**dlą́ą́'**+simple

earn it: O+y+barred-l+mom:**bą́**+S

eat: **'**+zero+dur:**yą́ą́'**+simple

eat it: O+zero+dur:**yą́ą́'**+simple

fight: **'ah**+d+mom:**ghą́ą́'**+simple

fall: **d**+zero+mom:**go'**+S

fill with it: **ha**+O+d+barred-l+mom:**bįįd**+simple

float around: **na**+zero+cont:**'éél**+S; **na**+**'**+zero+cont:**'éél**+S

forget: **y**+(**y**?)+zero+concl:**nah**+S?

get it: **shó**+(O)+(**yn**?)+barred-l+mom:**t'e'**+S?

get to (a place) (singular): zero+mom:**yá**+N

get to (a place) (dual): zero+mom:**'áázh**+N

get to (a place) (plural): d+mom:**kai**+N

give a kick: **dz**+zero+mom:**táál**+simple

give him/her a kicking: **ná**+O+**n**+zero+rep:**táál**+S

give him/her a series of kisses: **ná**+O+**n**+zero+rep:**ts'ǫ́ǫ́z**+S

give him/her one slap: **ná**+O+**d**+zero+mom:**kaad**+YLV

give it a shake: O+zero+sem:**gháád**+SLV

go: see also "be going", "get", "start to go", "be on the way"

go (singular): zero+mom:**yá**+simple

go (dual): zero+mom:**'áázh**+simple
go (plural): d+mom:**kai**+simple
go (singular) around: **na**+zero+cont:**yá**+S
go (dual) around: **na**+zero+cont:**'áázh**+S
go (plural) around: **na**+d+cont:**kai**+S
go off (singular): **'a**+zero+mom:**yá**+simple
go off (dual): **'a**+zero+mom:**'áázh**+simple
go off (plural): **'a**+d+mom:**kai**+simple
go off again (singular): **'a**+**nááná**+d+mom:**yá**+simple
go to school: **'**+**yn**+high-tone+barred-l+rep:**ta'**+simple
have a bite to eat: **'a**+**'**+barred-l+mom:**na'**+simple
herd: see also "start to herd"
herd them: **na**+O+**n**+barred-l+cont:**kaad**+S
hit him/her once with a club: **ná**+O+**d**+barred-l+mom:**ghaal**+YLV
hit it once with a solid roundish object: **ná**+O+**d**+barred-l+mom:**ne'**+YLV
hobble: see "be hobbling"
investigate it: **na**+O+barred-l+cont:**káá'**+S
kick: see "give a kick", "give him/her a kicking", "let fly a kick"
kiss: see also "give him/her a series of kisses"
kiss him/her (once): O+zero+sem:**ts'óóz**+SLV
learn it: **Pí**+**hw**+barred-l+trans:**'áá'**+FLV
let fly a kick: **'a**+**dz**+zero+mom:**táál**+simple
look at it: O+**n**+high-tone+barred-l+dur:**'íí'**:simple
look like: **na**+**hw**+zero+**lin**+neuter-n-I
make a series of payments: **ni**+**'**+**h/y**+zero+mom:**la'**+S
make it (fire): **di**+O+**d**+barred-l+mom:**jéé'**+simple
make one cut in it: O+zero+sem:**gish**+SLV
melt: see also "start to melt"
melt it: O+**d**+barred-l+mom:**yíí'**+simple
melt it (snow): O+barred-l+mom:**yíí'**+simple
move it (animate thing): O+barred-l+mom:**tí**+simple
move it (ropelike thing): O+zero+mom:**lá**+simple
pierce him/her with it: **Pighá**+O+barred-l+mom:**geed**+N
pick it up (ropelike object): **ná**+O ǀ **d**+zero+mom:**lá**+LV
play: **na**+zero+cont:**ne'**+S
play some more: **na**+**nááná**+zero+cont:**ne'**+S
pray: **so**+**d**+plain-l+dur:**yįįd**+simple
pull: see "take"
put them (ropelike things) one after another into his/her mouth: **Piza**+O+**h/y**+zero+mom:**lá**+S
read it: O+**yn**+high-tone+barred-l+rep:**ta'**+simple
remain: d+mom:**dzíí'**+simple

roll: see also "start to roll", "be rolling"

roll it: O+barred-l+mom:**mááz**+simple

roll it to (a place): O+barred-l+mom:**mááz**+N

roll out: **ch'í**+zero+mom:**mááz**+N

roll them away one after another: **'a**+O+**h/y**+barred-l+mom:**mááz**+S

roll them one after another: O+**h/y**+barred-l+mom:**mááz**+S

roll them out one after another: **ch'í**+O+**h/y**+barred-l+mom:**mááz**+S

say: (**d**)+zero+neut:**niid**+I-only; **d**+zero+mom:**niid**+simple

say to him/her: P+(**d**)+zero(barred-l)+neut:**niid**+I-only; P+**d**+zero+mom:**niid**+simple

scratch it: O+zero+rep:**ch'id** simple

see: '+zero+curs/neut?:**'íí'**+I-only

see it: O+zero+curs/neut?:**'íí'**+I-only; O+barred-l+trans:**tsą́**+FLV

set it (ropelike thing): O+zero+mom:**lá**+DS

sew it (moccasin): **ná**+O+**h/y**+zero+rev:**'izh**+S

shake: see also "give it a shake"

shake it: O+zero+mom:**gháád**+simple

shoot into the air: **yá**+**ná**+**dz**+barred-l+mom:**don**+FLV

sing: **hw**+zero+dur:**táál**+simple

slap: see "give him/her one slap"

speak: **yá**+barred-l+dur:**ti'**+simple

squat down: **n**+plain-l+mom:**jííd**+S

stand: zero+neut:**zį'**+s-P

start to carry him/her: O+**d**+barred-l+mom:**tį́**+LV

start to crawl: **d**+d+mom:**na'**+LV

start to go (singular): **d**+zero+mom:**yá**+LV

start to go (dual): **d**+zero+mom:**'áázh**+LV

start to go (plural): **d**+d+mom:**kai**+LV

start to herd them: O+**d**+high-tone+**n**+barred-l+mom:**kaad**+S

start to melt it: Pi+'+**n**+barred-l+mom:**yíí'**+LV

start to roll it: O+**d**+barred-l+mom:**mááz**+LV

start to work: **d**+plain-l+mom:**nish**+S

step: **d**+plain-l+mom:**'eez**+simple

strike with the fist: **ni**+**dz**+barred-l+mom:**ts'in**+N

take it (animate thing) to (a place): O+barred-l+mom:**tį́**+N

take it (ropelike thing) to (a place): O+zero+mom:**lá**+N

take it (compact rigid object) up and out: **ha**+O+zero+mom:**'ą́**+simple

take them down one after another (ropelike things): **na**+O+'+**h/y**+**d**+zero+mom:**lá**+LV

talk about: **hw**+plain-l+dur:**ne'**+simple

tall: see "be how tall", "be tall", "be this much tall"

think: see also "want it"

think: **ni**+**tsí**+zero+concl+ **kééz**+S

uncover it by digging: Páá̧+'+**d**+barred-l+mom:**geed**+simple

wake him/her up: **ch'í**+**ná**+O+barred-l+mom:**zid**+N

wake up: **ch'í**+**ná**+d+mom:**zid**+N

wake up again: **ch'í**+**ná**+**nááná**+d+mom:**zid**+N

want it: O+**n**+zero+neut:**zį́į́'**+neuter-I

weave: '+zero+concl+**tł'ó̧**+S

weave it: O+zero+concl+**tł'ó̧**+S

work: see also "start to work"

work: **na**+plain-l+cont:**nish**+S

work goes on: **na**+'+zero+cont:**nish**+S

work on it: Pi+**na**+plain-l+cont:**nish**+S

wrap it around it: Pik'í+O+**d**+zero+rev:**diz**+S

Verb Theme Index

This short list contains only those verb themes that were formally presented as such in the text, either using a chart or else by means of a description giving the salient structure of the theme. For each theme, only the page containing the presentation of the theme is given.

transitive+zero+'ą́ "carry it (a compact rigid object)" 374
intransitive+zero+'áázh "go (dual)" 208
intransitive+d+plain-l+kééz "cough" 402
intransitive+zero+'éél "float" 382
transitive+zero+gháád "shake it" 392
transitive+zero+gháą́' "kill them" 376
transitive+barred-l+kaal "execute a chopping motion with a rigid object" 405
intransitive+d+kai "go (plural)" 209
transitive+zero+lá "carry it (a ropelike thing)" 220
transitive+barred-l+mááz "roll it" 222
intransitive+zero+mááz "roll" 381
intransitive+d+na' "crawl" 213
transitive+barred-l+tį́ "carry him/her (an animate thing)" 206
tsí+intransitive+zero+kééz "think" 402
transitive+zero+ts'ǫ́ǫz "suck at it" 262
intransitive+zero+yá "go (singular)" 208

INDEX

A

active verb 294
ambiguous verb forms
    ádích'id 371
    bíhooł'ą́ą́' 274
    hanííltį́ 115
    haniłteeh 113
    hóótáál 133
    i'íílna' 244
    náádááł 366
    naashnish 76, 79
    naniłté 118
    yáálti' 82, 96
    yishbéézh 79, 380
    yishóóh 145
    yiigish 258
    yiijį́į́h 268
    yíyá 218
aspect 404
    continuative aspect 167
    cursive aspect 362
    momentaneous aspect 167
assimilation 60, 119
atelic activity 67, 75, 167, 363
atelic prefix 67, 75, 117, 197, 203, 234, 382, 400
    as part of Vocabulary-1 215, 230, 232
    distinguished from "down" na 357, 400
    not thematic 402
    requires continuative stem-set 167, 176
    requires s-P conjugation 68, 400

B

barred-l classifier 43, 44
    exceptionally with intransitive verb base 61
"be in a location" 203

C

classifier 11, 22, 40
    choice of related to transitivity 51, 66, 103,
        380, 381
    recognizing it 43, 48, 49, 141, 143, 145, 169
    part of verb base 50
    part of verb theme 205
classifier shift 312-314, 316-318
    in iterative mode 328, 329
    irregularities 313, 314
"come" not distinguished from "go" in Navajo 231
completive verb base 215, 216, 219, 220, 222
conjugation 16
    combinations 384-386, 391

part of verb base 227
conjunct high tone
    always preceded by conjunct prefix 285, 286
    as lexical prefix 291, 297, 310, 311
    in F mode caused by inner **n** 284, 285
    in neuter verb 296
    with **yn** inner prefix 301-308
conjunct prefix 12, 33
    ends in consonant 34, 38
    followed by long-vowel subject prefix 255,
        264, 265, 277, 280, 281, 293, 294
    followed by n-I or n-P subject prefix 224-226,
        405
    followed by O mode subject prefix 333
    followed by Pg mode subject prefix 364
    followed by y-P subject prefix 83-86, 89, 98-
        100, 280, 281, 294
consonants
    glottalized 5
    pronunciation 4, 5
continuative: see aspect; stem-set
contraction
    inner **d** with s-P subject prefixes 163-166,
        175, 210, 212
    inner **n** with s-P subject prefixes 284, 287-
        289, 292, 294
    ná with outer prefixes 319-325
        forms 320
        recognizing them 323, 324
        same contexts as short form of
            semeliterative 320
    seriative **h** with s-P subject prefixes 345, 349,
        350
    seriative **y** with s-P subject prefixes 352, 353,
        355
cursive: see aspect, stem-set

D

d classifier
    causes d-effect 41, 42, 76, 103, 137, 267
    exceptionally with transitive verb base 103
    P mode subject prefixes 43
    recognizing 43
d-effect 29-31
    caused by 1dpl subject prefix 29, 31; see also
        Rule Subj-1
    caused by d classifier 41, 42, 76, 103, 137,
        267
    chart 30

irregularity 140, 141, 157, 185, 200, 201
devoicing 139, 143, 144
diphthong 3, 60, 317, 330, 331, 334
direct form 109-111, 115, 173, 178, 179
disjunct prefix 12, 22-28, 37
    ends in vowel 27, 38
    followed by long-vowel subject prefix 255, 264, 265
    followed by n-I or n-P subject prefix 224-226
    followed by O mode subject prefix 334, 400
    followed by Pg mode subject prefix 364
    followed by y-P subject prefixes 81-83, 87-89, 97, 98, 100, 101, 106
distributive plural 11, 12, 22, 23, 36-38, 135
    causes na/ná reduction 36
    in Pg mode 363, 366-368
    optionally allows yy 94, 95
    recognizing it 38, 181
    same for all modes 36
    with go-verbs 198, 199
"do it" 203
doubling of y 92-95, 161, 305, 344, 346; see als Rule Str-1
duoplural subjects 20, 36

F
first person 20
F mode d 147, 326
    as conjunct prefix 148, 161
    causes na/ná reduction 154
    position 148
    recognizing it 181, 182
form
    determined after movement 180, 181
fourth person 32-35, 38, 39
    object prefix 129-135
        as lexical prefix 129, 130, 132, 135
        distinguished from seriative h 360, 361
        forms: see Rule Conj-6
        recognizing it 134, 135, 338
        referring to area/space 129
            in neuter verb 296, 300
            refers to subject 296
    subject prefix 32, 35
        as object prefix 32, 33, 46, 74, 83, 84, 88, 98, 100, 104, 106, 229
        as conjunct prefix 33, 87, 98
        becomes zh: see Rule Conj-7
        causes na/ná reduction 34-35

    preceded by other object prefixes 114
    recognizing it 39
    same for all modes 32
    switch with unspec prefix 152, 153, 177
    takes third person prefix in subject position 32, 33, 42, 100, 106, 134
fricative 136, 137, 141, 143, 146
future marker **dooleeł** 15
future mode 14
    long-vowel-F y 269-272
    subject prefixes 147, 148, 268
    usage 15
    verb stem 17, 18
        form 65, 66, 76, 88, 93, 103, 105, 109, 122, 142;
    see also F mode **d**

G
"get into" 218, 219
"give" 232, 233
glottal stop 3-5; see also Rule Conj-5, Rule Disj-4
"go to see" 231
go-verbs
    irregularities 199-201, 208, 210, 216, 217, 229, 277, 323, 338
    singular, dual, plural 196, 197, 216
    subject prefixes with 198, 199
    verb themes 207-209

I
imperative 232
imperfective mode 14
    long-vowel conjugation 255
        subject prefixes 255
            compared with regular I mode 255, 256
            with inner **n** 293
    n-I conjugation 224
        subject prefixes 224, 226
            compared with **na** 233, 234
            recognizing them 233, 234, 293, 294
        seriative 360
        used only together with n-P 224
regular imperfective mode 21
    subject prefixes 21
s-I conjugation
    requires s-P, s-R, and s-U

conjugations 383, 384
subject prefixes 383
usage 15
verb stem 17, 18
inceptive 404
inflectional prefix 8, 11, 399
inflectional suffix 6
inner **d**
always precedes inner **n** 291
as part of agentive passive 377, 378
as part of reflexive 369, 370
as part of Vocabulary-2 215
causes **na/ná** reduction 289
contracts with s-P subject prefixes 163-166, 175
in neuter verb 299
irregularities 191-193
no specific meaning 393
occasionally thematic 402
recognizing forms with 164, 181, 182, 192, 193, 280-282
usually not thematic 402
inner **dz** 388, 389
inner **j** 304, 305, 308
always thematic 403
inner **n**
alwys follows inner **d** 291
causes conjunct high tone in F mode 284, 285
contracts with s-P subject prefixes 284, 287-289, 292, 294
in irregular neuter verb 183-185
in neuter verb 297, 299
irregularities 297, 299, 310, 311
no **na/ná** reduction in front of 289
no specific meaning 398
present in all modes 293, 294
usually not thematic 402
with seriative 360
inner **y**
analyzed as part of long-vowel I mode subject prefixcs 389, 390
as part of **yn** prefix 301, 308, 309, 389, 390
becomes **oo** in pre-stem syllable 309, 390, 391
in "forget" 390, 391
in "get" 391
precedes F mode **d** 390
inner prefix 10-12, 37, 38
recognizing by position 38
intransitive verb 9

related pair with different classifier 381, 382
related to transitive verb 380, 381
inverse forms 108-111, 115, 172, 173, 178
iterative mode 14, 326-332
classifier shift 328, 329
no n-R conjugation 328, 330
recognizing forms 332
rule for forms 326, 327
s-R conjugation 384
usage 15
verb stem 18
form 327, 328, 392-394, 396
rule for form 327
L
lexical object 127-130, 132, 135, 138, 176, 177, 273
lexical prefix 8, 10, 11, 17, 135
M
"make it" 193, 250, 374, 375
mode 14
signals of 15, 19
usages 15, 16
momentaneous: see aspect; stem-set
motion verb 194-196
classificatory motion verb theme 221-224, 232, 233, 279, 325, 384
manner-of-motion verb theme 221, 223, 233, 279
transitivity 195, 196, 204, 381
with unspecified conveyance 382
movement 180, 181, 293
N
neuter n-I conjugation 295, 296
neuter verb 16, 183, 294-301
classifier in 298, 299
common I mode subject prefixes 295
denoting adjective of size 296-298, 310
denoting color 299
grouped into classes 294, 298, 299
of being 299-301
of position, using s-P 77
null postposition 399
O
object 10
object prefix 10-12, 18, 22
cannot be used reflexively 108, 116
chart 107
no **na/ná** reduction in front of 118, 154
outer object 172-178, 273, 290
plurality 108, 340
same as possessive prefixes 108
same for all modes 19, 107

one-way motion 230
optative mode 14, 333-339
    outer prefixes with 337, 338, 400
    recognizing forms 338
    subject prefixes
        long-vowel 337
        regular 333, 334
        with **yn** inner prefix 336
    usage 16, 339
    verb stem 18, 333, 396
outer prefix 10-12, 22-25, 37, 38
    derived from nouns 399
    forms of 400
    have specific meanings 398
    recognizing by position 37, 38
    requires particular conjugation pattern 68, 90,
        99, 101, 283, 309, 400
    with O mode 337, 338, 400

P
P as object pronoun 173, 386
    in ordinary object position 189-191
    in agentive passive 377
passive 376-382
    agentive passitve 377-379
        recognizing it 378, 379
        rule 377
    Passive A: see simple passive
    Passive B: see agentive passive
    simple passive 379, 380
        compared with intransitive verb 380,
          381
        possibly applied to intransitive verb
          381, 382
        rule 379
past marker **nít'éé'** 15
peg element 53, 56, 58, 77, 159, 380
    in y-P conjugation 86
    si as peg 77, 381
peg rule: see Rule Str-2
perfective **da**-shift 90-92, 99, 101, 171, 247, 253, 284
    common with n-P conjugation 226
perfective mode 14
    conjugation determined by lexical prefix 68,
        90, 99, 101, 283, 309, 400
    conjugation part of verb base 64
    more than one regular conjugation 63
    subject prefixes
        1sg and 2dpl compared with I mode
          70, 74, 75, 85, 87, 101,
          102, 266

2sg and 1spl do not depend on
    classifier 74, 97, 101, 102,
    266
dependence on classifier 63, 76, 77,
    103
long-vowel conjugation 264-266
    compared with other
        conjugations 265,
        267
    with inner **n** 294
n-P conjugation 225, 226
    causes unspec hopping
        233, 234
    compared with **na** 233,
        234
    compared with y-P prefixes
        225
    no **na/ná** reduction in front
        of 324
    recognizing them 234, 293,
        294
    seriative 360
s-P conjugation
    cause **na/ná** reduction 70
    compared with I mode 79
    contract with inner **d** 163-
        166, 175, 210,
        212
    contract with inner **n** 284,
        287-289, 292,
        294
    contract with seriative **h**
        345, 349, 350
    contract with seriative **y**
        352, 353, 355
    plain-l/d 74
    zero/barred-l 68
y-P conjugation
    compared with I mode 85,
        87
    compared with s-P prefixes
        85, 101, 102
    plain-l/d 97, 99, 101
    zero/barred-l 81, 84, 86
usage 15
verb stem 17, 18
    form 93, 98, 105, 109, 122, 132,
        133, 142, 146, 162, 164
    same for related stem-sets 166, 177,
        213

person 20
    first 20
    second 21
    third 21
    fourth 32
phonological rule 18, 23
plain-l classifier 47, 48
plural 10, 22
    of objects 108, 340
prefix 7
pre-stem syllable 27, 35, 132, 297, 298
    'a becomes **'ii** 236
    'a'a becomes **'e'e** 242
    acquires high tone 58
    hw becomes **ha** 129-131, 135
    last syllable to be affected by conjunct high
        tone 286, 287
    inner **y** becomes **oo** 309
    missing in **ní** 189
    nááná in 315
    ná doesn't contract 320, 321
    no **na/ná** reduction 70, 71
    o vowel 338, 339
    protects vowel after **j** 150, 169
    supplied by peg element 53, 159
    triggers Rule Disj-1, 27, 28, 254
    vowel harmony 349, 386, 387
pre-stem vowel harmony 341, 343, 348-352, 360, 399
    effects 350
    general rule 349
    prevented by Rule Conj-3 350
    seriative compared with unspec 386, 387
    syllables affected 349, 350
progressive mode 14
    can be used with semeliterative, reversionary,
        and seriative 362, 364
    incompatible with many outer prefixes 362,
        363
    only mode of cursive verb bases 362
    recognizing forms 368
    subject prefixes 364-366, 367
        compared with other modes 365,
            366
    usage 16, 362
    verb stem 18
        rule 363
pronunciation
    of consonants 4,5
    of vowels 3, 4;
    see also variation

"put into" 220-224
R
reciprocal 375, 376
    recognizing it 376
        compared with seriative 376
    rule 375
recognizing forms
    1sg I mode versus 3 s-P 79, 80
    agentive passive 378, 379
    classifier 43, 48, 49, 141, 143, 145, 169
    contractions of **ná** 323, 324
    distributive plural 38, 181
    F mode **d** 181, 182
    fourth person object 134, 135, 338
    fourth person subject 139
    inner **d** 164, 181, 182, 192, 193, 280-282
    inner **n** 293, 294
    long-vowel conjugation 344, 346, 361
    O mode 338
    Pg mode 368
    reciprocal 376
    reflexive 375
    R mode 332
    semeliterative prefix 318
    seriative 344, 346, 360, 361
    U mode 332
reference time 15
reflexive 108, 116, 369-375
    classifier shift 369-375
    inner **d** added 369, 370, 372
    outer object 373, 374
    possessive 374
    postpositional object 374
    prefix **'á** 369, 399
        'ád as outer object 373
        'ád as postpositional object 374
        no **na/ná** reduction in front of 370
        position 369-372
        possessive 374
    recognizing it 375
    rule 369
reversionary prefix 318-325, 399, 404
    contractions 319-325
    term 319
R mode **ná** 327, 399
    causes **na/ná** reduction 329
    form 329
    discourages contraction of reversionary 320,
        331
    reversionary 329, 331

position 327
root 396, 397, 401
round-trip motion 119, 203-206, 230
Rule Conj-1 33-35, 58, 71, 74, 85, 86, 94, 112-114,
     122, 124, 150, 155, 159-161, 176, 179, 201,
     243, 258, 269-272, 286, 287, 308, 323, 343,
     347-351, 354, 357, 359, 360, 372, 375, 376,
     386, 389, 390, 399
Rule Conj-2 44, 57, 58, 73, 85, 86, 89, 94, 95, 118,
     125, 126, 171, 236, 237, 252, 269, 272, 317,
     330, 331, 359, 372, 373, 389, 390
     sandwiched **y** rule 269-271, 274, 275, 308,
          322, 343, 344, 347, 354, 356-358,
          360
          weaker than Rule Conj-3 354
Rule Conj-3 112, 113, 118, 131, 159, 184, 189, 210,
     241, 243, 343, 350, 353, 383
     not applying 297, 310
     potential extension 301
     prevents vowel harmony 340
     stronger than sandwiched **y** rule 354
Rule Conj-4 119, 120, 169, 184, 383, 388
Rule Conj-5 122-127, 150-153, 177, 179-181, 235,
     241, 243, 245, 248, 277, 286, 290, 354, 355,
     356, 377, 386
     conflict with Rule Conj-9 358, 359
Rule Conj-6 129-134, 156, 226, 256, 265, 266, 273,
     274, 286, 296, 298, 338
Rule Conj-7 150-153, 160, 271, 297, 305, 308, 342,
     348, 357
     j-hopping 292, 293
Rule Conj-8 286, 287, 291, 296, 303, 308, 310
     compared with Rule Subj-5 287
Rule Conj-9 341-344, 346-349, 351, 353, 354, 356,
     359, 360, 368, 388
Rule Disj-1 23-28, 34, 35, 57, 58, 60-62, 70, 71, 98,
     113, 115, 126, 149, 168, 199, 200, 236-238,
     254, 316, 360, 397, 400
     clause (a) 23, 27
     clause (b) 61
     clause (c) 309
Rule Disj-2 26-28, 34, 37, 57, 60-62, 70, 73, 83, 89,
     94, 96, 118, 126, 168, 236, 238, 256, 271,
     308, 316, 317, 322, 331, 359, 399, 400
     clause (a) 26, 83
     clause (b) 61
     clause (c) 61
Rule Disj-3 34-37, 70, 71, 73, 118, 201, 316, 318,
     323, 329-331
     clause (a) 34
     clause (b) 36

clause (c) 70
clause (d) 154, 289
clause (e) 154
clause (f) 315, 329
doesn't apply in front of inner **n** 289
doesn't apply in front of n-P subject prefix
     324
doesn't apply in front of object prefix 118
doesn't apply in front of reflexive **'á** 370
doesn't apply in front of seriative 352
doesn't apply in pre-stem syllable 70, 71
special note 329
Rule Disj-4 235-248, 250, 337, 352, 387
Rule Str-1 44, 56, 57, 73, 74, 85, 88, 89, 93, 104, 105,
     108, 111, 122, 155, 159, 171-174, 184, 212,
     247, 270
     doubling of **y** 92-95, 256, 258, 265, 271, 305,
          344, 346
     b in inverse forms 108
Rule Str-2 53, 56, 57, 74, 78, 103, 104, 123, 217, 218,
     229, 381, 397
     si peg 77
     y-P conjugation 86
Rule Str-3 54, 86, 87, 104, 126, 218, 256, 258, 303,
     304, 334, 390
Rule Str-4 114, 124, 152, 274, 358
Rule Str-5 270-272, 274
Rule Str-6 285, 292, 318
Rule Str-7 314, 315, 317, 318, 320, 322, 324, 329
Rule Subj-1 29-31, 71, 78, 95, 104, 140, 149
Rule Subj-2 (sandwich rule) 48, 49, 56, 59, 69, 72, 76,
     91, 98, 101, 112, 139, 140, 161, 212, 243,
     270, 321, 343, 346, 352
Rule Subj-3 49, 56, 59, 72, 76, 91, 96, 114, 139, 140,
     149, 244, 316
Rule Subj-4 49, 56, 59, 73, 76, 91, 101, 114, 131, 139,
     140, 144
Rule Subj-5 58-62, 96, 176, 178, 251, 254, 317, 321,
     331, 334, 349-351, 360, 371
     applies to 3 object **i** created from **y** 317, 330
     compared with Rule Conj-8 287
Rule Subj-6 60-62, 73, 74, 76, 79, 91, 106, 162, 166,
     168, 202, 263, 270, 289, 343, 349, 351, 381,
     383
Rule Subj-7 139-142, 145, 354, 357
Rule Subj-8 143-145, 159, 161
S
sandwich rule: see Rule Subj-2
second person 21
semeliterative prefix 312-318, 399, 404

form: see Rule Str-7
term 315
    recognizing it 318
seriative prefix
    as lexical prefix 340
    basic form 341
    basic position 341, 346
    changes conjugation pattern 341
    contracts with s-P subject prefixes 345, 349,
        350, 352, 353, 355
    distinguished from **hw** 360, 361
    distinguished from outer **ha** 360
    forms resemble long-vowel forms 344, 346,
        361
    in n-I and n-P conjugations 360
    no **na/ná** reduction in front of 352
    recognizing it 360, 361
            compared with reciprocal 376
    triggers **j**-hopping 292
    usage 340, 404
    vowel harmony compared with unspec prefix
        386, 387
    with inner **n** 360
sibilant 60, 119
singular subjects 20
spelling
        ' omitted at beginning of word 3, 4, 54, 123,
            125, 126, 151, 215
        single for double consonant 78, 145, 184
        x for **h** 5, 143, 159
        y sometimes dropped between **a** and **i** 373
        y sometimes dropped between **i**'s 252, 355;
        see also variation
stem-set 18, 65, 66
    conclusive stem-set 395, 396
    continuative stem-set 167, 176, 197, 203-
        206, 208, 213, 230, 232, 259, 261,
        363, 391, 394-396
    cursive stem-set 392, 401
    durative stem-set 395, 396
    momentaneous stem-set 167, 176, 197, 204,
        207, 208, 213, 230, 232, 259, 276,
        277, 290, 363, 391-396
    neuter stem-set 396, 401
    related 117, 166-168, 176, 177, 391-397
            share P mode stem 166, 177, 213
    repetitive stem-set 393, 394, 401
    root 396, 397, 401
    semelfactive stem-set 259, 260, 392, 393,
        401

transitional stem-set 395
subaspect 404
subject 10
    duoplural 20
    singular 20
subject prefix 10, 18
    chart of arrangement of 20
    possibilities with go-verbs 198, 199
    some end in consonants 47
    various forms of 398
suffix 6
    -go 15
syllable 24
T
telic activity 67, 259
terminative 233, 404
thematic prefix 402, 403
third person 21
third person objects 44-47
    tone of 176;
    see also Rule Str-1, Rle Conj-1
tone 3, 4
    determines form 92, 133, 149, 162, 229, 230
transitional aspect 275, 276, 290, 357
    inchoative transitional 291
    simple 275
    transitional inceptive 279
transitive verb 9
    related to intransitive verb 189-191, 380
transitivity
    part of verb base 50, 64, 66, 67
    related to classifier 51, 66, 380
U
unspec prefix 111
    alters meaning of "drink" 126
    as lexical prefix 127, 128, 138, 176, 177
    compared with **'a** 244, 248, 249
    preceded by **'a** 239, 241-245
    pre-stem vowel harmony 352
            compared with seriative 386, 387
    protects vowel of **da** 126
    referring to subject 377, 381, 382
    signalled by initial written vowel 123, 125,
        126, 151
    switch with **j** 152, 153, 177
    unspec hopping 179-181, 233, 234, 290, 355,
        358, 359, 405
    usage 121-123, 381, 382
unvoiced fricative 137, 141-143, 145, 146
usitative mode 14, 332, 333

rule for forms 332
s-U conjugation 384
usage 15
verb stem 18

V

variation

3 n-I/n-P subject prefix after **da**: zero versus **í** 226

áo versus **á** 60

ao versus **aa** 7, 26, 49, 60

bíhoo versus **bóhoo** 275

biih yíyá versus **biihíyá** 218, 219

contractions 163, 164

dah jid- versus **dashd-** 277, 278

doohsį́į́ł versus **doohshį́į́ł** 186

é versus **á** 69

ei versus **ayi** 58, 94, 257

hizhdoo versus **jidiyoo** 348

j versus **dz** 62

'd versus **t'** 153

naa yinílá versus **neinílá** 232, 233

ni versus **n** 35, 172

Pg mode stem 363

Pg mode subject prefixes 367

Rule Str-5(b) 272

yy versus **y** 94;

see also perfective **da**-shift, Rule Conj-4, spelling

verb, general structure of 10

verb base 8, 11, 18, 50, 64-68, 227, 401

related 117, 194

shorthand notation 385, 386, 393, 396, 397, 401

verb stem 6, 7, 16

verb theme 206, 207, 401

thematic prefix 402, 403

semelfactive 259-261

transitive/intransitive pair 381

Vocabulary-1 206, 213-215, 230, 232

Vocabulary-2 207, 209-215, 279, 404

Vocabulary-3 215, 216, 219, 220, 222, 227, 233

Vocabulary-4 216, 218-220, 222, 233, 246, 342

Vocabulary-5 226, 227, 230-233, 324

Vocabulary-6 238-240, 246, 247, 249, 254, 318, 403

Vocabulary-7 246, 248, 249, 254, 317, 403

Vocabulary-8 250, 251, 254, 351, 381, 403, 405

Vocabulary-9 259-262, 404

Vocabulary-10 261-263, 404

Vocabulary-11 275, 279

Vocabulary-12 276-280, 404

Vocabulary-13 290

Vocabulary-14 312-319, 364, 404

Vocabulary-15 319, 320, 323, 364, 365, 404

Vocabulary-16 340-342, 351, 360, 364, 404

Vocabulary-17 357, 358

Vocabulary-18 363, 367

vocabulary principle 194, 207, 403-406

shorthand notation for 405

voiced fricative 136, 137, 141-143, 159, 168, 184, 185

voiceless fricative 137, 141-143, 145, 146

voicing 5, 136, 137

vowels

cannot begin word 3, 54, 235

length 3

nasal 3, 4

pronunciation 3, 4

tone 3, 4

vowel harmony 386, 387; see also pre-stem vowel harmony

Y

yn inner prefix 301-309

choice of conjugation 302

I mode subject prefixes 302, 303

O mode subject prefixes 336

P mode subject prefixes 305-308

transitivity 302

y element in 301, 308, 309, 389, 390

Z

zero classifier 40